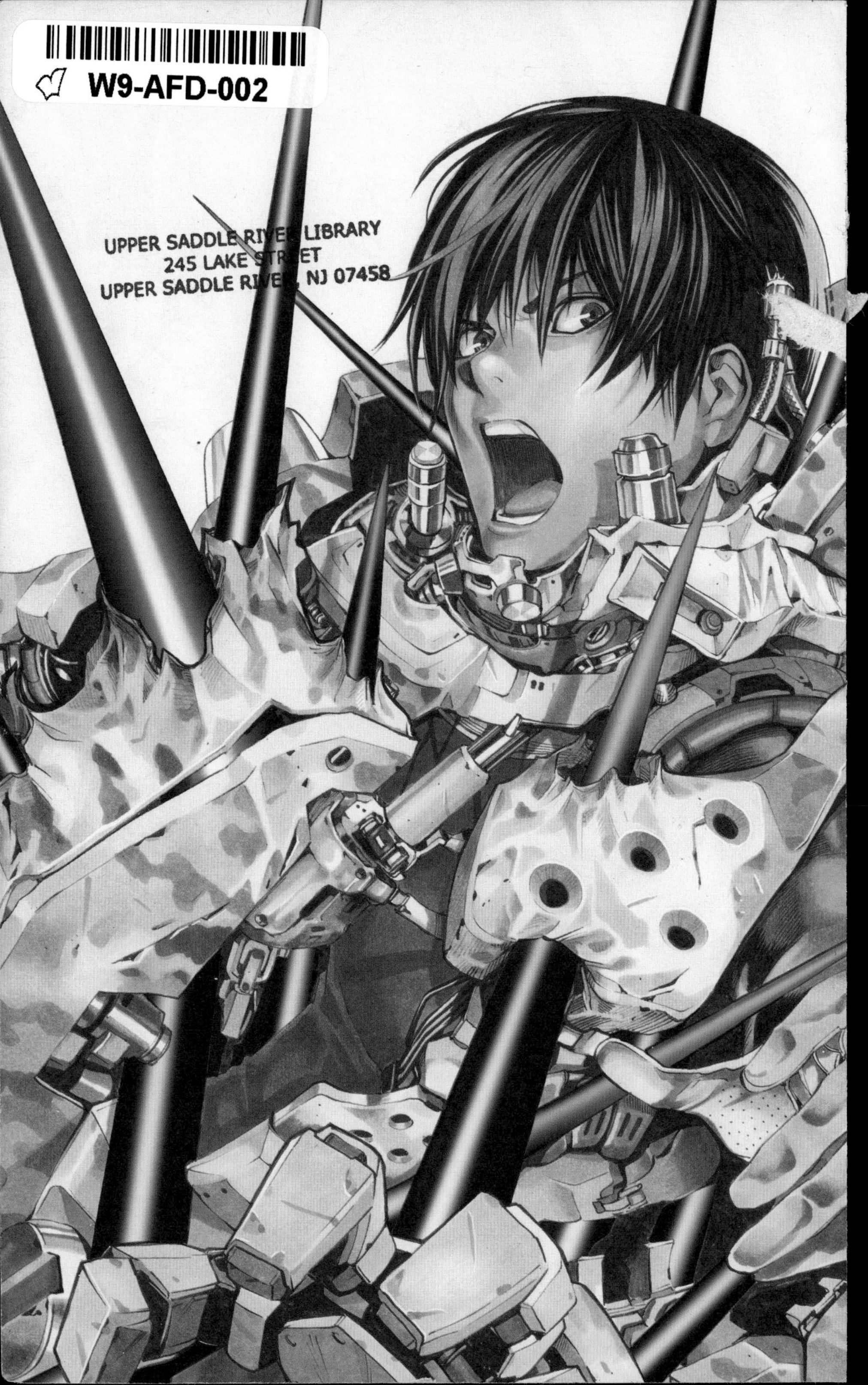

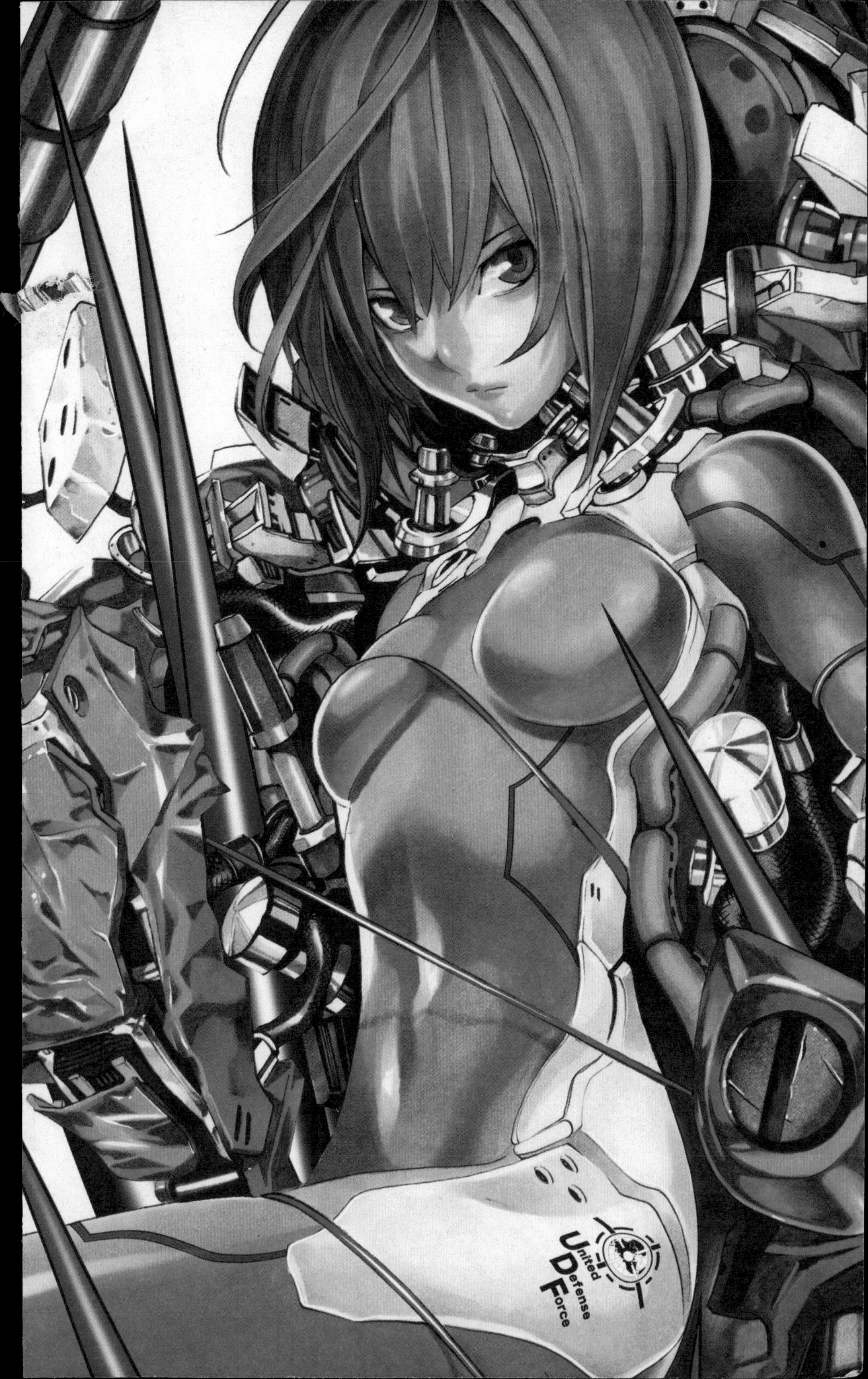
United
Defense
Force

All You Need Is Kill

Original Story by Hiroshi Sakurazaka
Storyboards by Ryosuke Takeuchi
Original Illustrations by yoshitoshi ABe

Art by Takeshi Obata

Based on the novel *All You Need Is Kill*

C o n t e n t s

#1 Keiji Kiriya

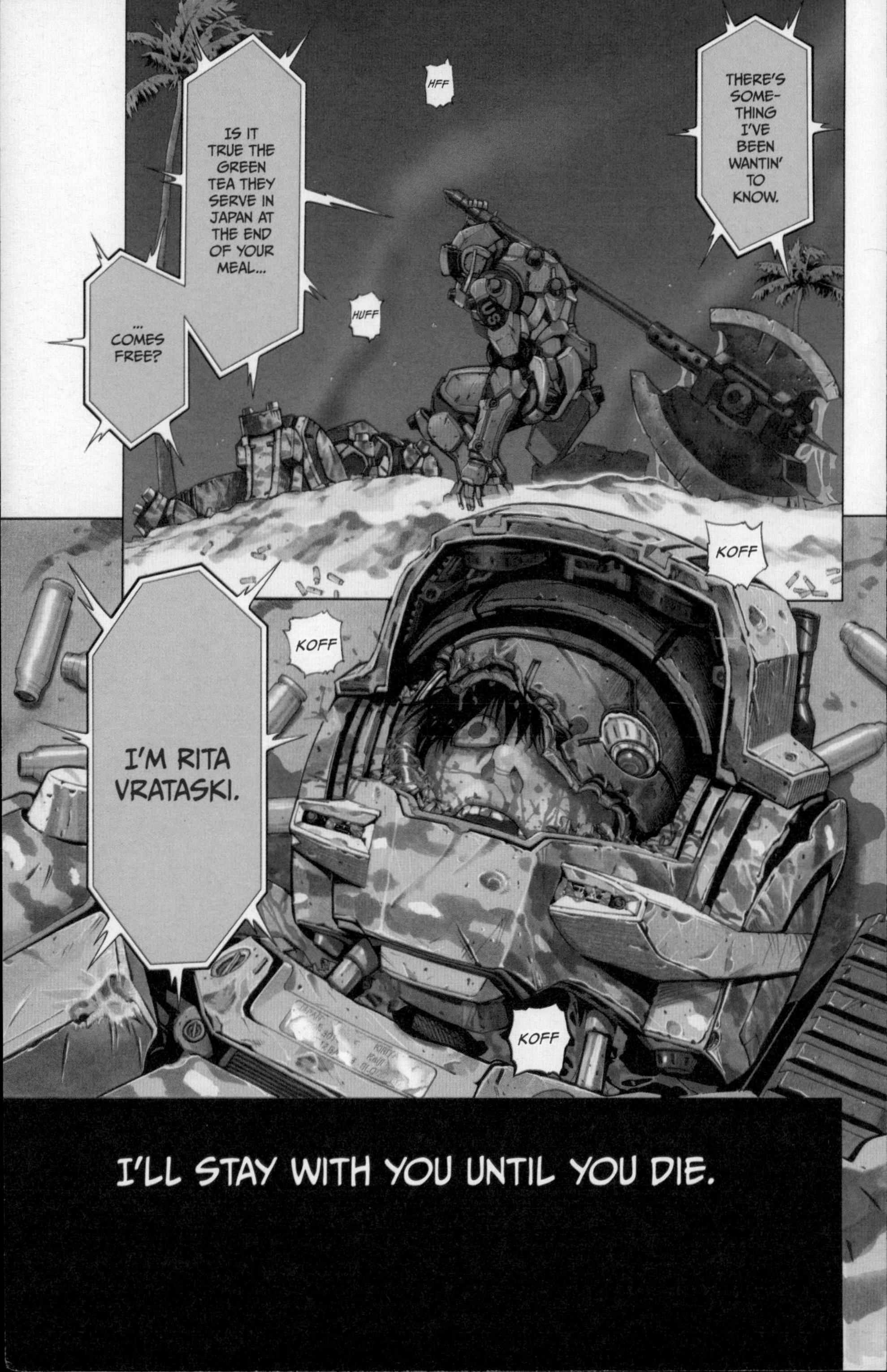
THERE'S SOME-THING I'VE BEEN WANTIN' TO KNOW.
HFF
IS IT TRUE THE GREEN TEA THEY SERVE IN JAPAN AT THE END OF YOUR MEAL...
HUFF
... COMES FREE?
KOFF
KOFF
I'M RITA VRATASKI.
KOFF
I'LL STAY WITH YOU UNTIL YOU DIE.

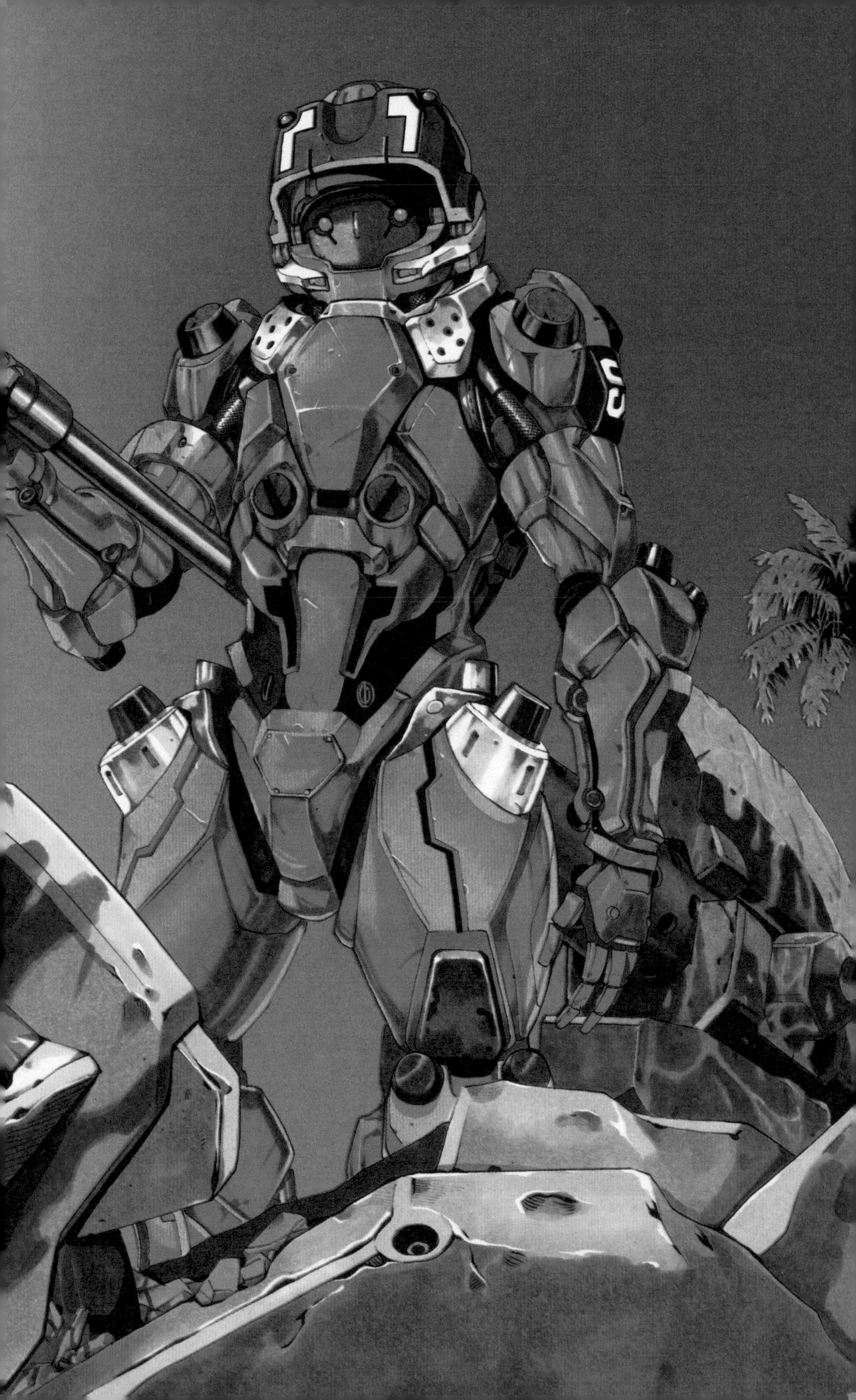

#1 Keiji Kiriya

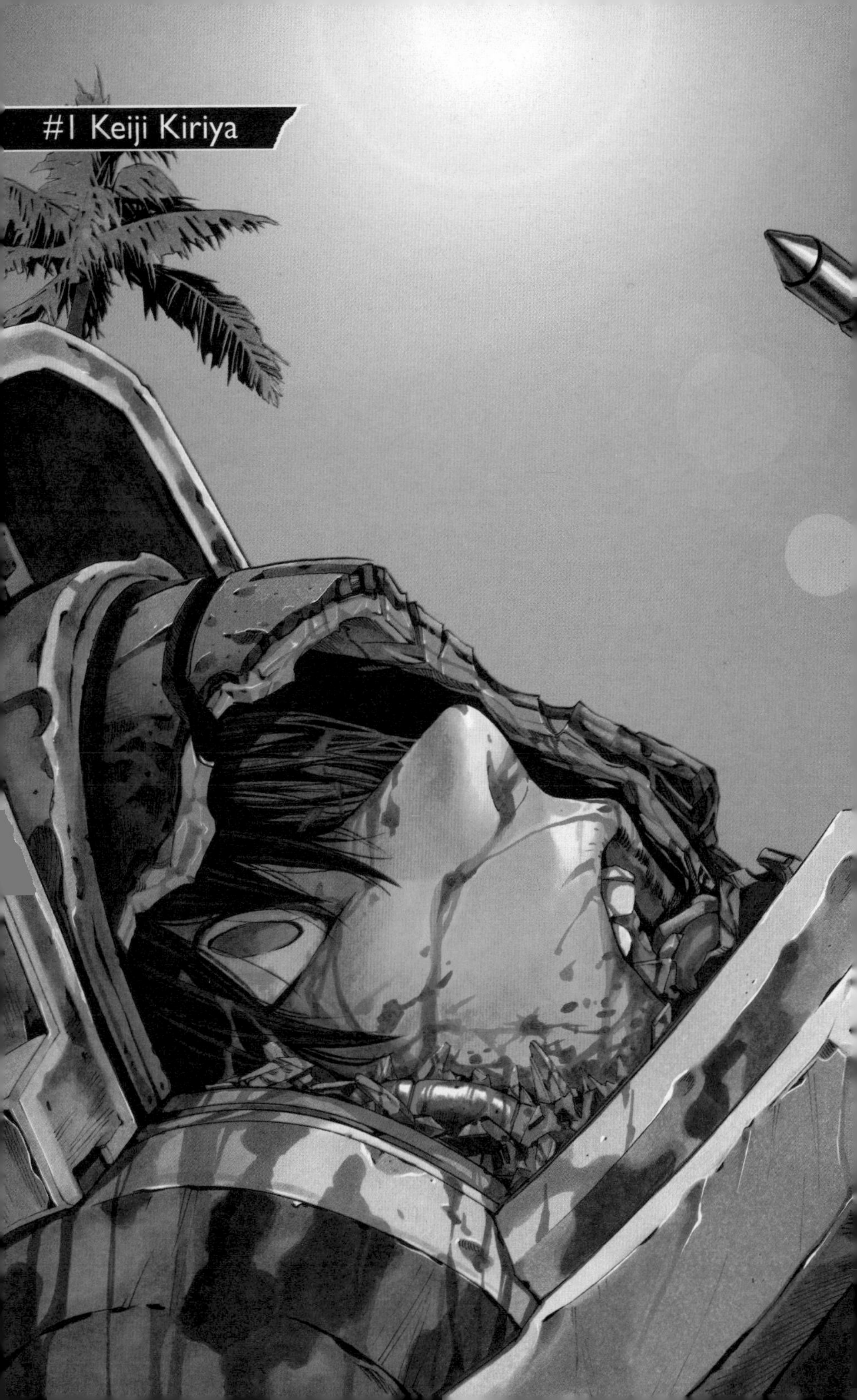

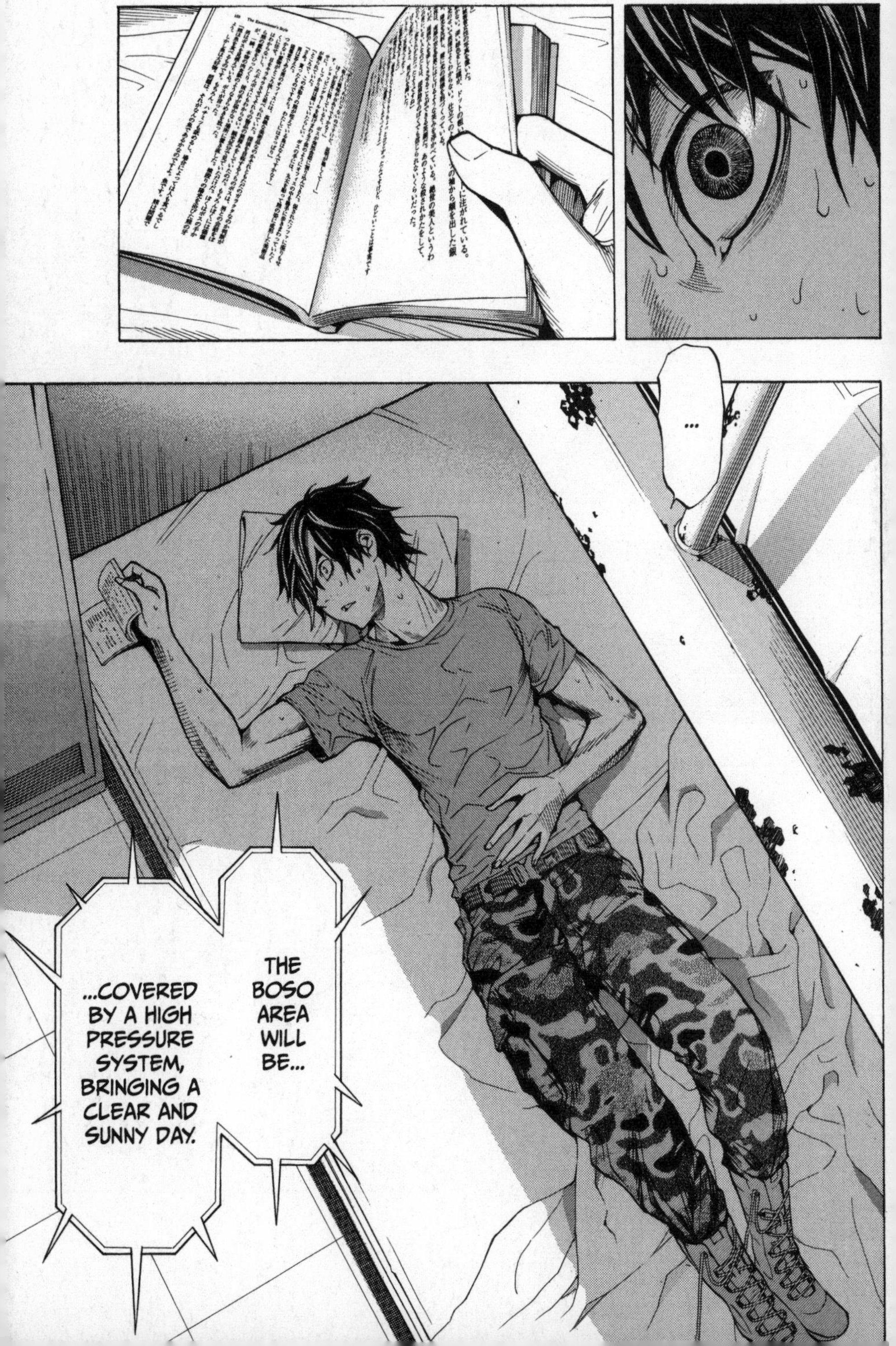
...
THE BOSO AREA WILL BE...
...COVERED BY A HIGH PRESSURE SYSTEM, BRINGING A CLEAR AND SUNNY DAY.

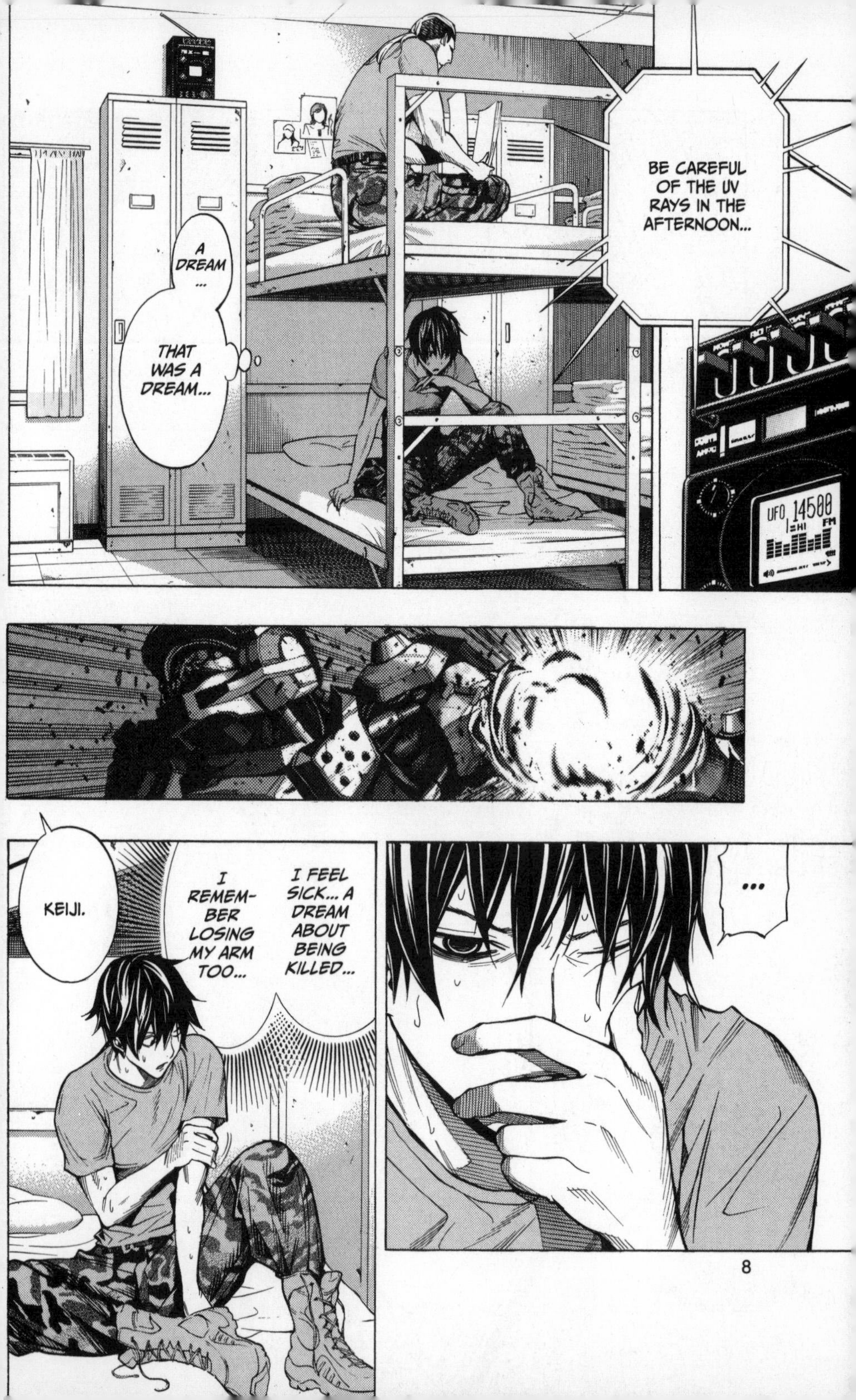
BE CAREFUL OF THE UV RAYS IN THE AFTERNOON...
A DREAM ...
THAT WAS A DREAM...
...
I FEEL SICK... A DREAM ABOUT BEING KILLED...
I REMEMBER LOSING MY ARM TOO...
KEIJI.

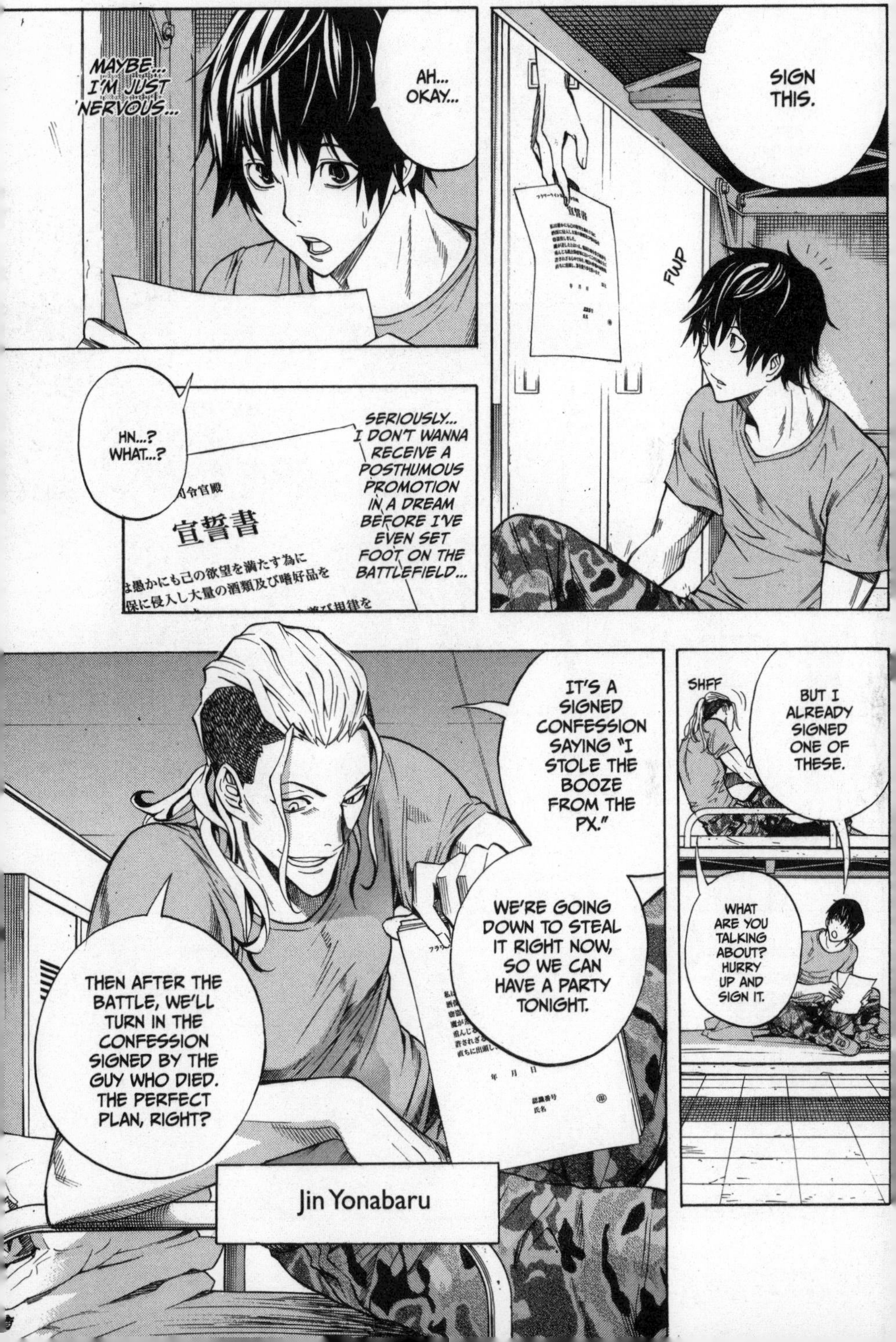

SIGN THIS.
FWP
AH... OKAY...
MAYBE... I'M JUST NERVOUS...
SERIOUSLY... I DON'T WANNA RECEIVE A POSTHUMOUS PROMOTION IN A DREAM BEFORE I'VE EVEN SET FOOT ON THE BATTLEFIELD...
HN...? WHAT...?
司令官殿
宣誓書
は愚かにも己の欲望を満たす為に
保に侵入し大量の酒類及び嗜好品を
SHFF
BUT I ALREADY SIGNED ONE OF THESE.
WHAT ARE YOU TALKING ABOUT? HURRY UP AND SIGN IT.
IT'S A SIGNED CONFESSION SAYING "I STOLE THE BOOZE FROM THE PX."
WE'RE GOING DOWN TO STEAL IT RIGHT NOW, SO WE CAN HAVE A PARTY TONIGHT.
THEN AFTER THE BATTLE, WE'LL TURN IN THE CONFESSION SIGNED BY THE GUY WHO DIED. THE PERFECT PLAN, RIGHT?
Jin Yonabaru

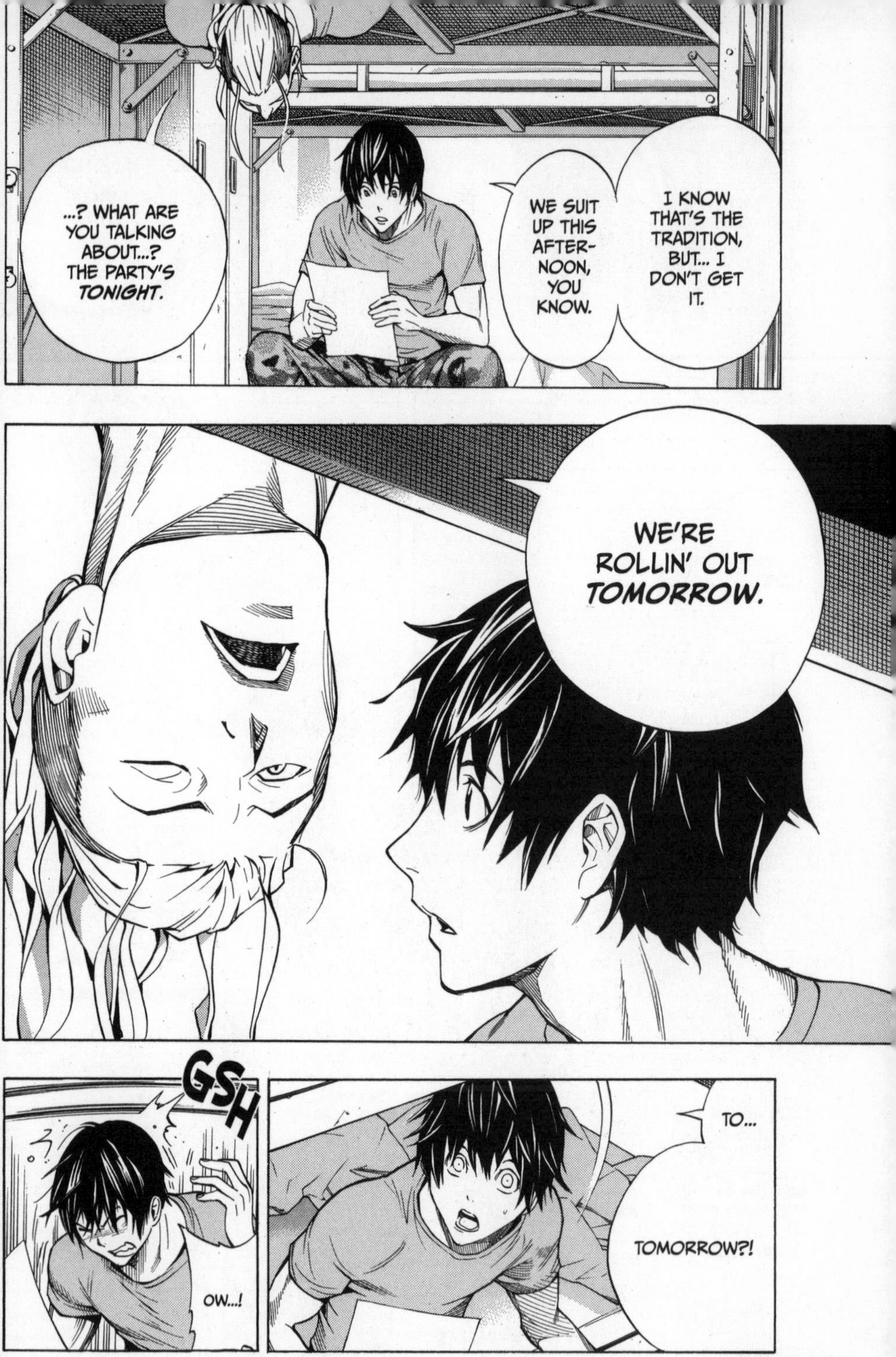
I KNOW THAT'S THE TRADITION, BUT... I DON'T GET IT.
WE SUIT UP THIS AFTER-NOON, YOU KNOW.
...? WHAT ARE YOU TALKING ABOUT...? THE PARTY'S *TONIGHT*.
WE'RE ROLLIN' OUT *TOMORROW*.
TO...
TOMORROW?!
GSH
OW...!

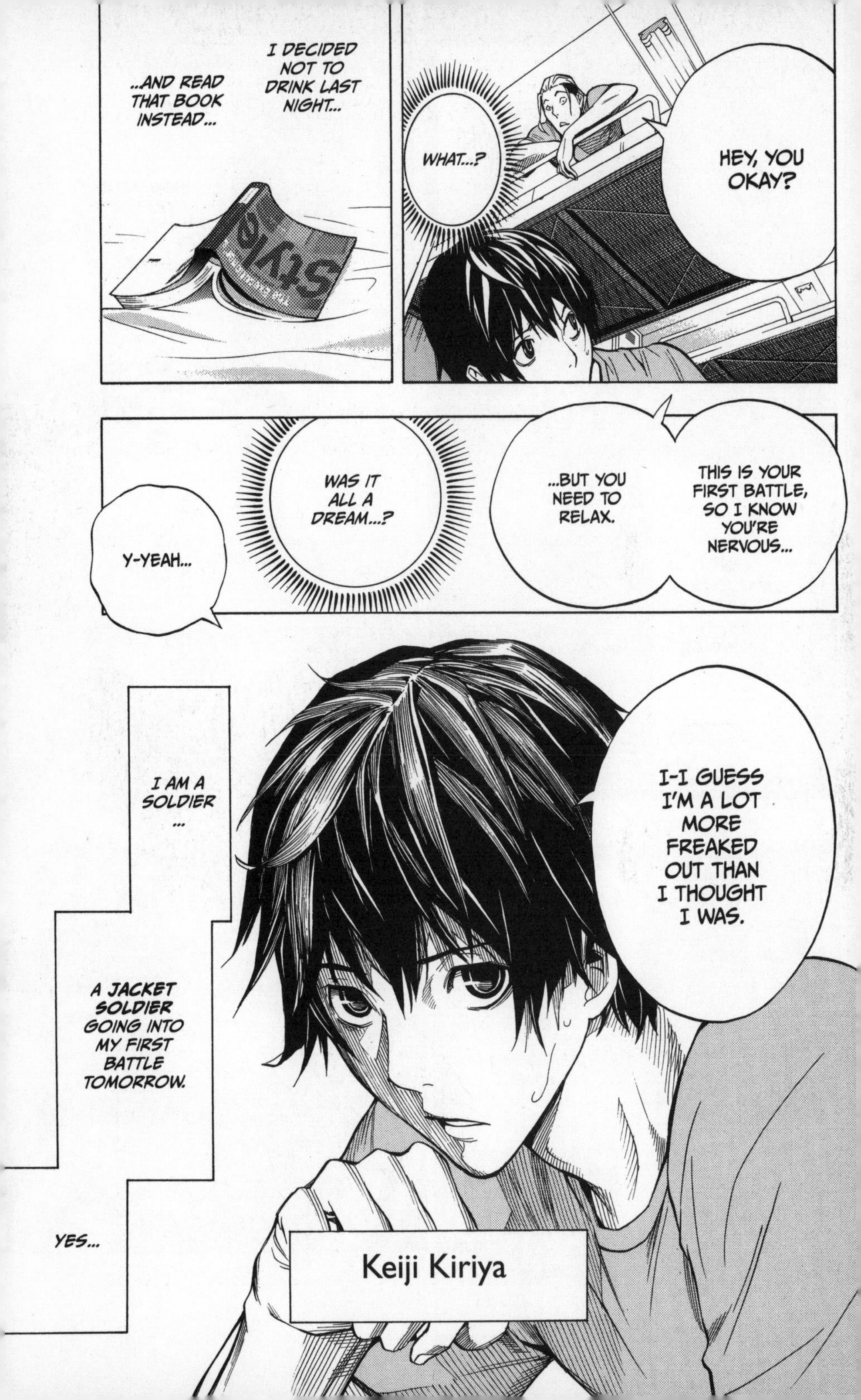
HEY, YOU OKAY?
WHAT...?
I DECIDED NOT TO DRINK LAST NIGHT...
...AND READ THAT BOOK INSTEAD...
THIS IS YOUR FIRST BATTLE, SO I KNOW YOU'RE NERVOUS...
...BUT YOU NEED TO RELAX.
WAS IT ALL A DREAM...?
Y-YEAH...
I-I GUESS I'M A LOT MORE FREAKED OUT THAN I THOUGHT I WAS.
I AM A SOLDIER...
A JACKET SOLDIER GOING INTO MY FIRST BATTLE TOMORROW.
YES...
Keiji Kiriya

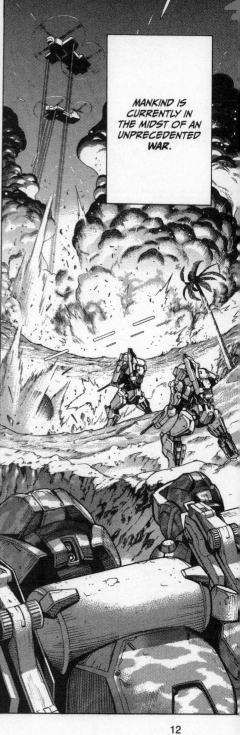

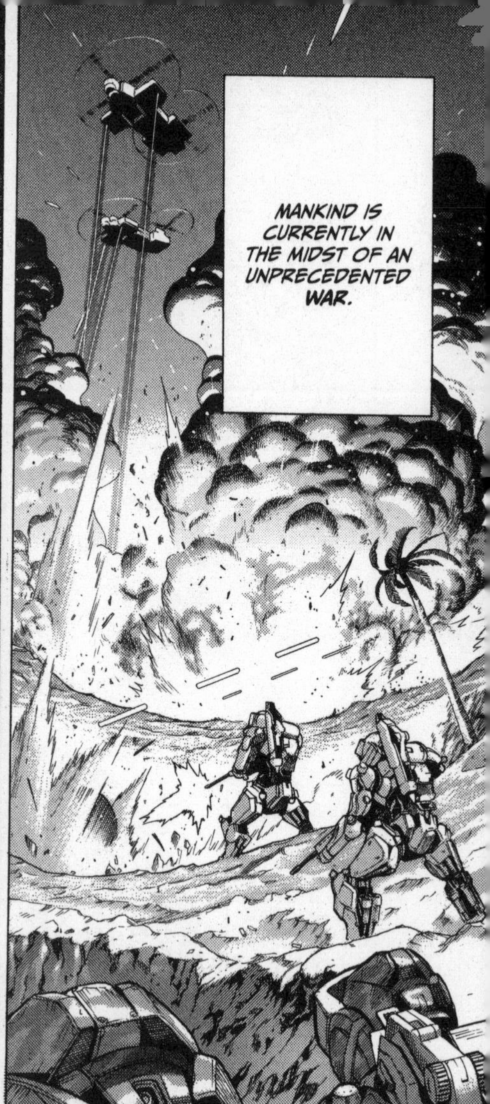
MANKIND IS CURRENTLY IN THE MIDST OF AN UNPRECEDENTED WAR.
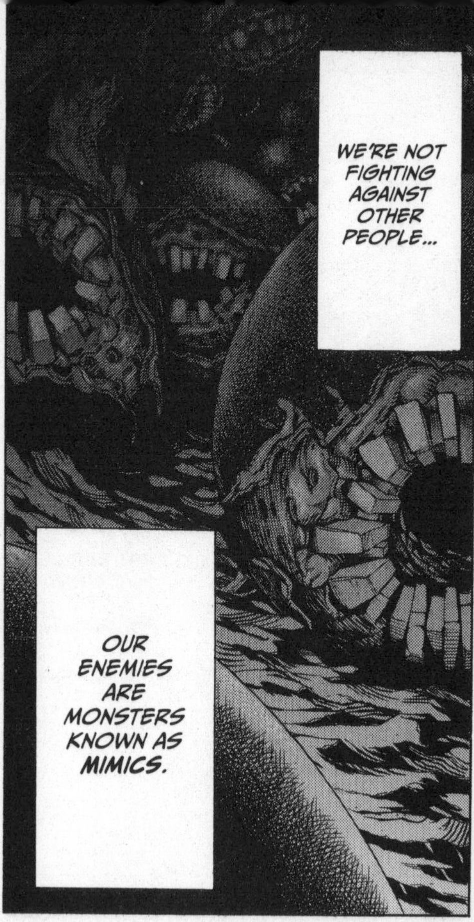
WE'RE NOT FIGHTING AGAINST OTHER PEOPLE...
OUR ENEMIES ARE MONSTERS KNOWN AS MIMICS.
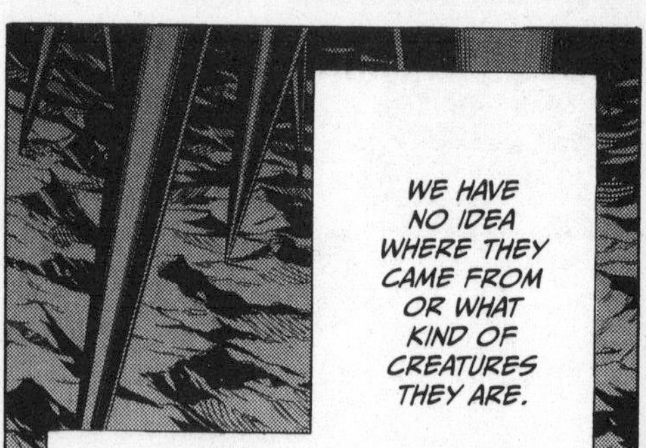
WE HAVE NO IDEA WHERE THEY CAME FROM OR WHAT KIND OF CREATURES THEY ARE.
THE ONLY THING WE KNOW IS THAT...

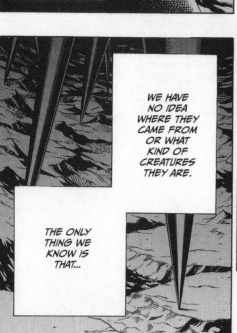

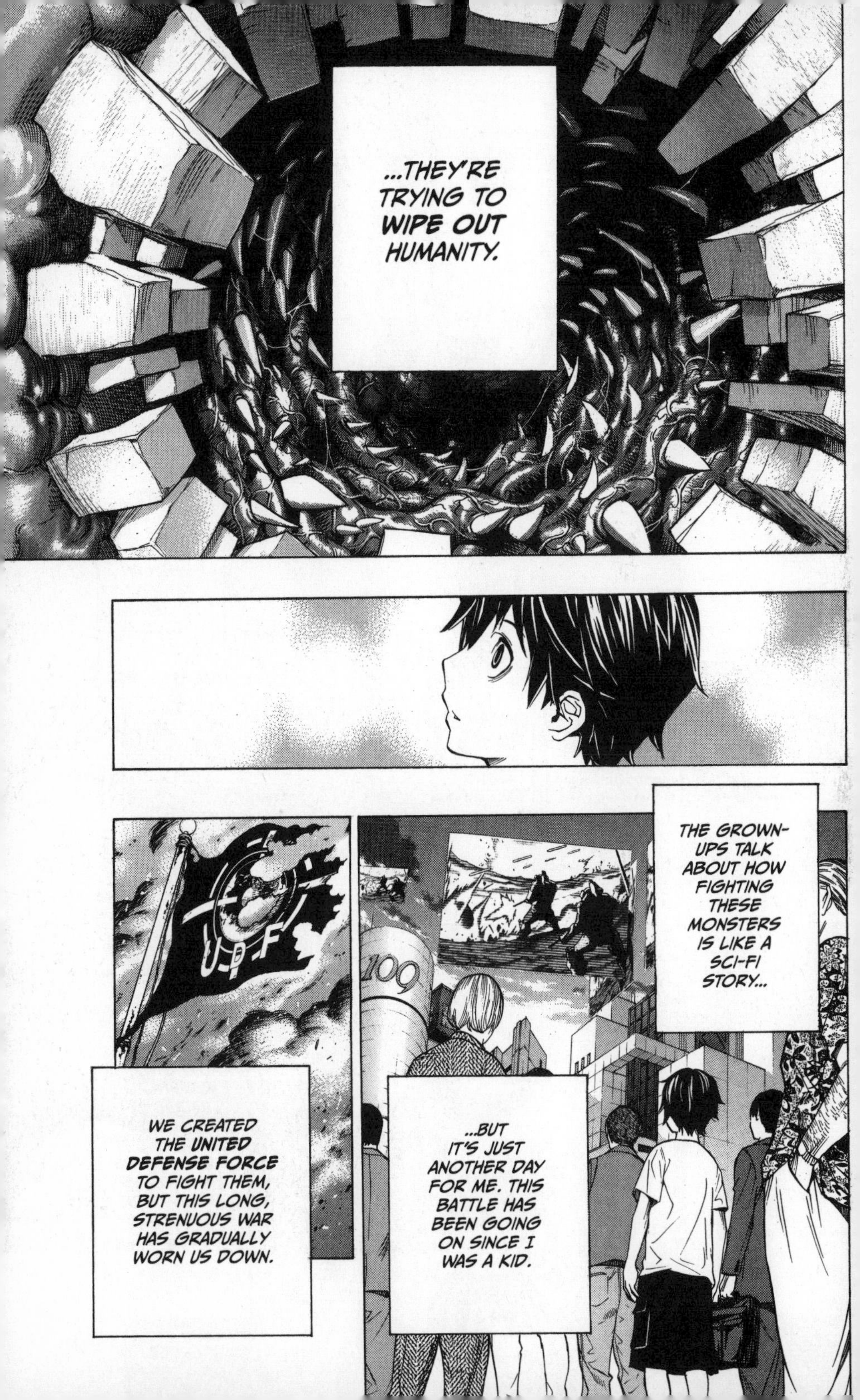
...THEY'RE TRYING TO WIPE OUT HUMANITY.
THE GROWN-UPS TALK ABOUT HOW FIGHTING THESE MONSTERS IS LIKE A SCI-FI STORY...
...BUT IT'S JUST ANOTHER DAY FOR ME. THIS BATTLE HAS BEEN GOING ON SINCE I WAS A KID.
U.D.F
109
WE CREATED THE UNITED DEFENSE FORCE TO FIGHT THEM, BUT THIS LONG, STRENUOUS WAR HAS GRADUALLY WORN US DOWN.

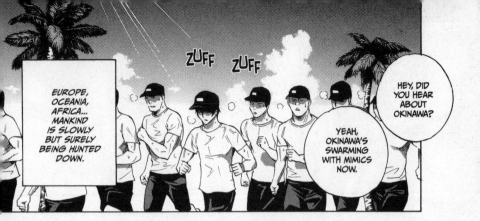

ZUFF ZUFF
HEY, DID YOU HEAR ABOUT OKINAWA?
YEAH, OKINAWA'S SWARMING WITH MIMICS NOW.
EUROPE, OCEANIA, AFRICA... MANKIND IS SLOWLY BUT SURELY BEING HUNTED DOWN.
AND A HORDE OF MIMICS HAVE FINALLY BEGUN AN ATTACK ON JAPAN TOO.
BASE FLOWER LINE, LOCATED ON THE BOSO PENINSULA, IS THE FRONT LINE OF THAT BATTLE.
JAPAN IS THE ONLY INDUSTRIAL NATION IN THE WORLD CAPABLE OF CREATING THE COMPOSITE ARMOR FOR THE BATTLE JACKETS...
AND IN ORDER TO PROTECT IT, THE ARMY HAS SENT A SPECIAL MILITARY UNIT TO OUR BASE.

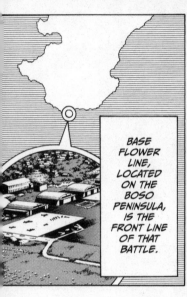

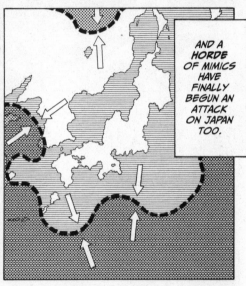

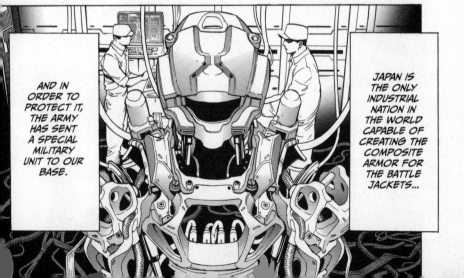

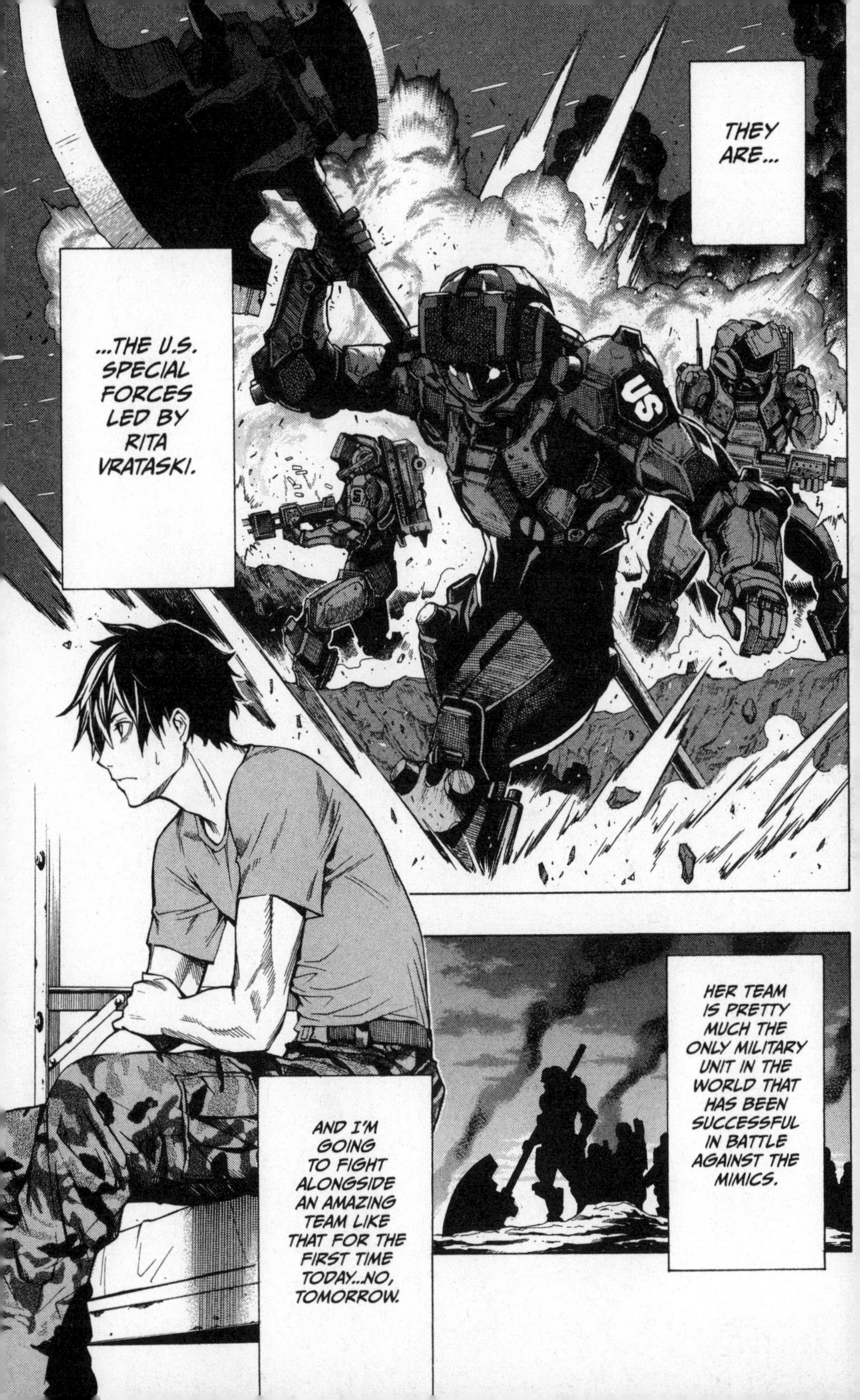
THEY ARE...
...THE U.S. SPECIAL FORCES LED BY RITA VRATASKI.
US
HER TEAM IS PRETTY MUCH THE ONLY MILITARY UNIT IN THE WORLD THAT HAS BEEN SUCCESSFUL IN BATTLE AGAINST THE MIMICS.
AND I'M GOING TO FIGHT ALONGSIDE AN AMAZING TEAM LIKE THAT FOR THE FIRST TIME TODAY...NO, TOMORROW.

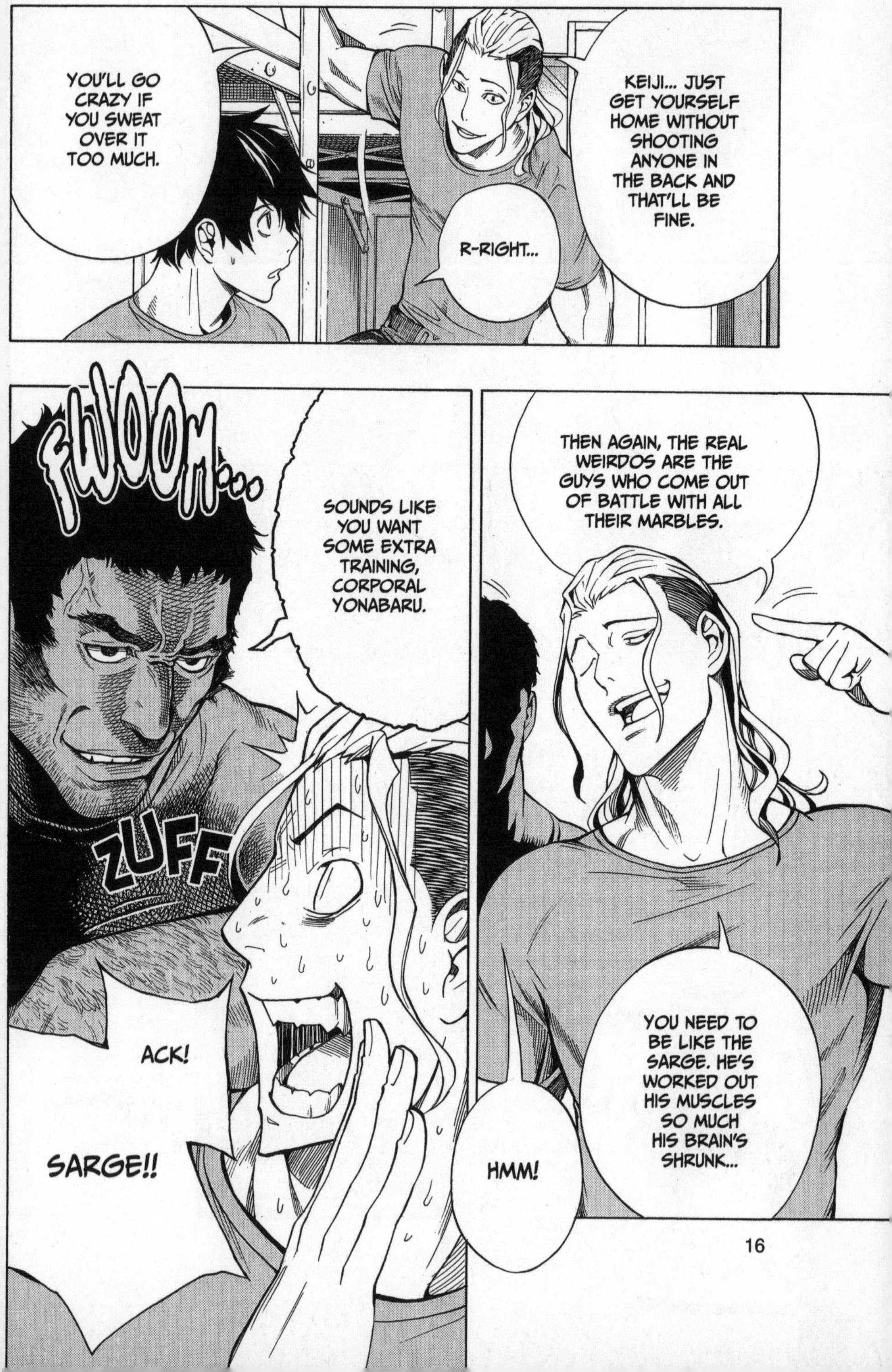
KEIJI... JUST GET YOURSELF HOME WITHOUT SHOOTING ANYONE IN THE BACK AND THAT'LL BE FINE.
YOU'LL GO CRAZY IF YOU SWEAT OVER IT TOO MUCH.
R-RIGHT...
THEN AGAIN, THE REAL WEIRDOS ARE THE GUYS WHO COME OUT OF BATTLE WITH ALL THEIR MARBLES.
YOU NEED TO BE LIKE THE SARGE. HE'S WORKED OUT HIS MUSCLES SO MUCH HIS BRAIN'S SHRUNK...
HMM!
FWOOM...
SOUNDS LIKE YOU WANT SOME EXTRA TRAINING, CORPORAL YONABARU.
ZUFF
ACK!
SARGE!!

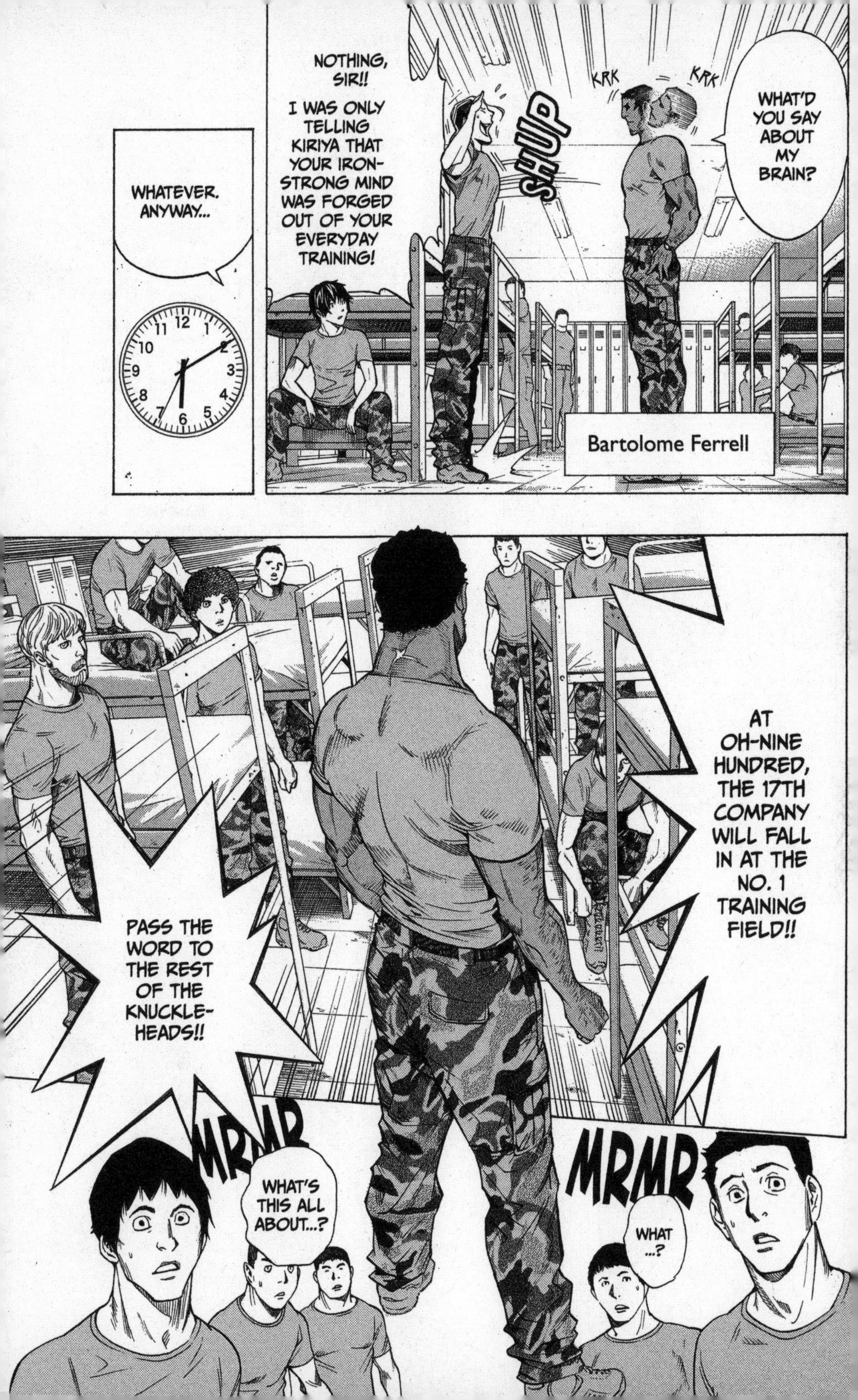
KRK
KRK
WHAT'D YOU SAY ABOUT MY BRAIN?
SHUP
NOTHING, SIR!!
I WAS ONLY TELLING KIRIYA THAT YOUR IRON-STRONG MIND WAS FORGED OUT OF YOUR EVERYDAY TRAINING!
Bartolome Ferrell
WHATEVER. ANYWAY...
AT OH-NINE HUNDRED, THE 17TH COMPANY WILL FALL IN AT THE NO. 1 TRAINING FIELD!!
PASS THE WORD TO THE REST OF THE KNUCKLE-HEADS!!
MRMR
WHAT ...?
MRMR
WHAT'S THIS ALL ABOUT...?

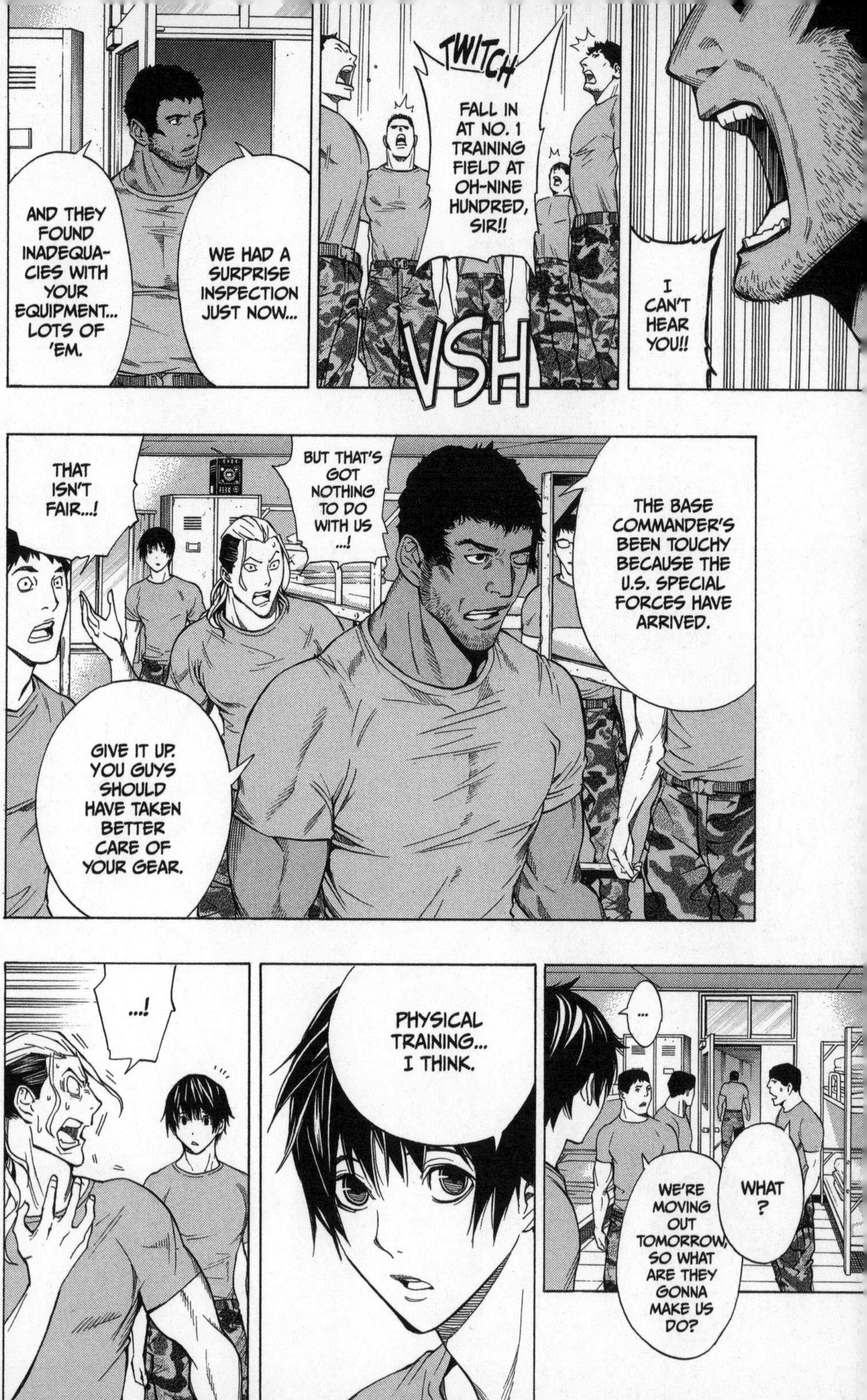
I CAN'T HEAR YOU!!
TWITCH
FALL IN AT NO. 1 TRAINING FIELD AT OH-NINE HUNDRED, SIR!!
VSH
WE HAD A SURPRISE INSPECTION JUST NOW...
AND THEY FOUND INADEQUACIES WITH YOUR EQUIPMENT... LOTS OF 'EM.
THE BASE COMMANDER'S BEEN TOUCHY BECAUSE THE U.S. SPECIAL FORCES HAVE ARRIVED.
BUT THAT'S GOT NOTHING TO DO WITH US ...!
THAT ISN'T FAIR...!
GIVE IT UP. YOU GUYS SHOULD HAVE TAKEN BETTER CARE OF YOUR GEAR.
...
WHAT ?
WE'RE MOVING OUT TOMORROW, SO WHAT ARE THEY GONNA MAKE US DO?
PHYSICAL TRAINING... I THINK.
...!

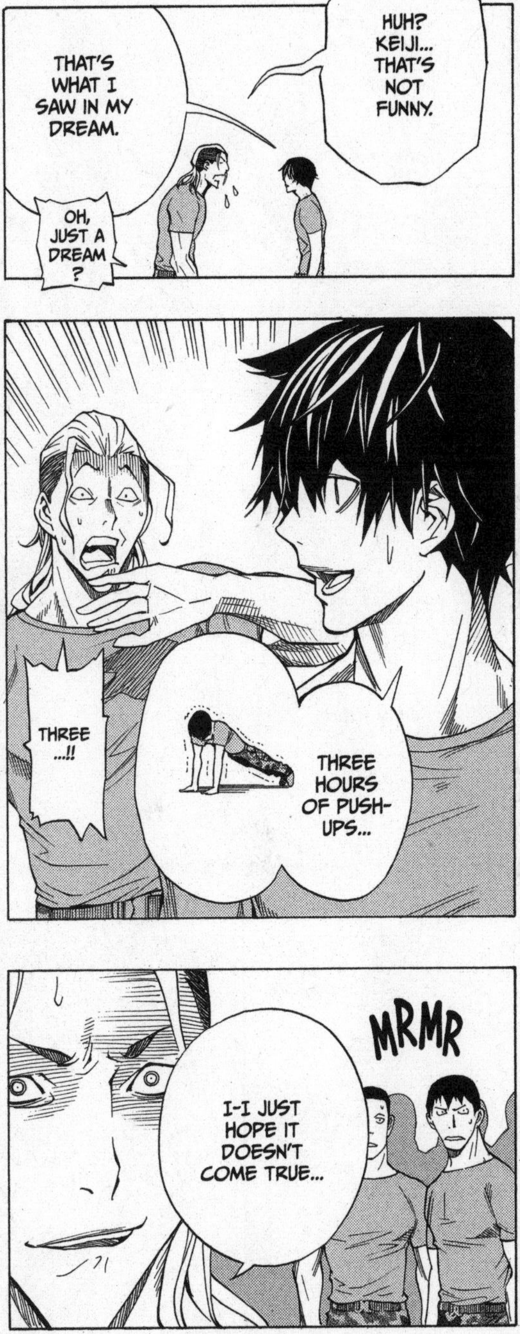
HUH? KEIJI... THAT'S NOT FUNNY.
THAT'S WHAT I SAW IN MY DREAM.
OH, JUST A DREAM?
THREE HOURS OF PUSH-UPS...
THREE ...!!
MRMR
I-I JUST HOPE IT DOESN'T COME TRUE...

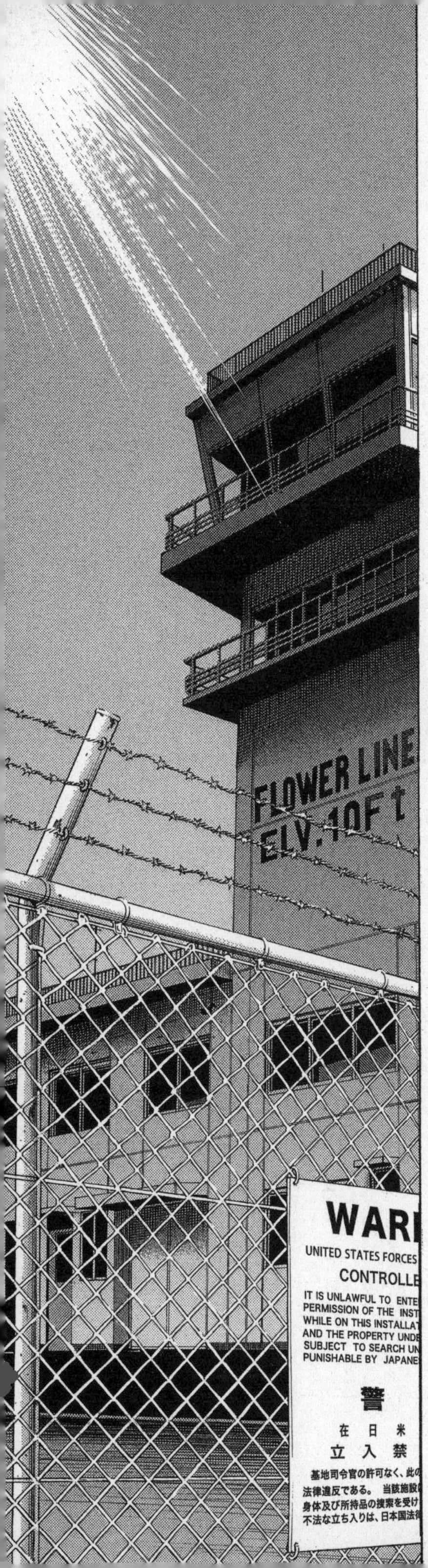
FLOWER LINE
ELV. 10Ft
WAR
UNITED STATES FORCES
CONTROLLE
IT IS UNLAWFUL TO ENTE
PERMISSION OF THE INST
WHILE ON THIS INSTALLAT
AND THE PROPERTY UNDE
SUBJECT TO SEARCH UN
PUNISHABLE BY JAPANE
警
在 日 米
立 入 禁
基地司令官の許可なく、此の
法律違反である。 当該施設
身体及び所持品の捜索を受け
不法な立ち入りは、日本国法

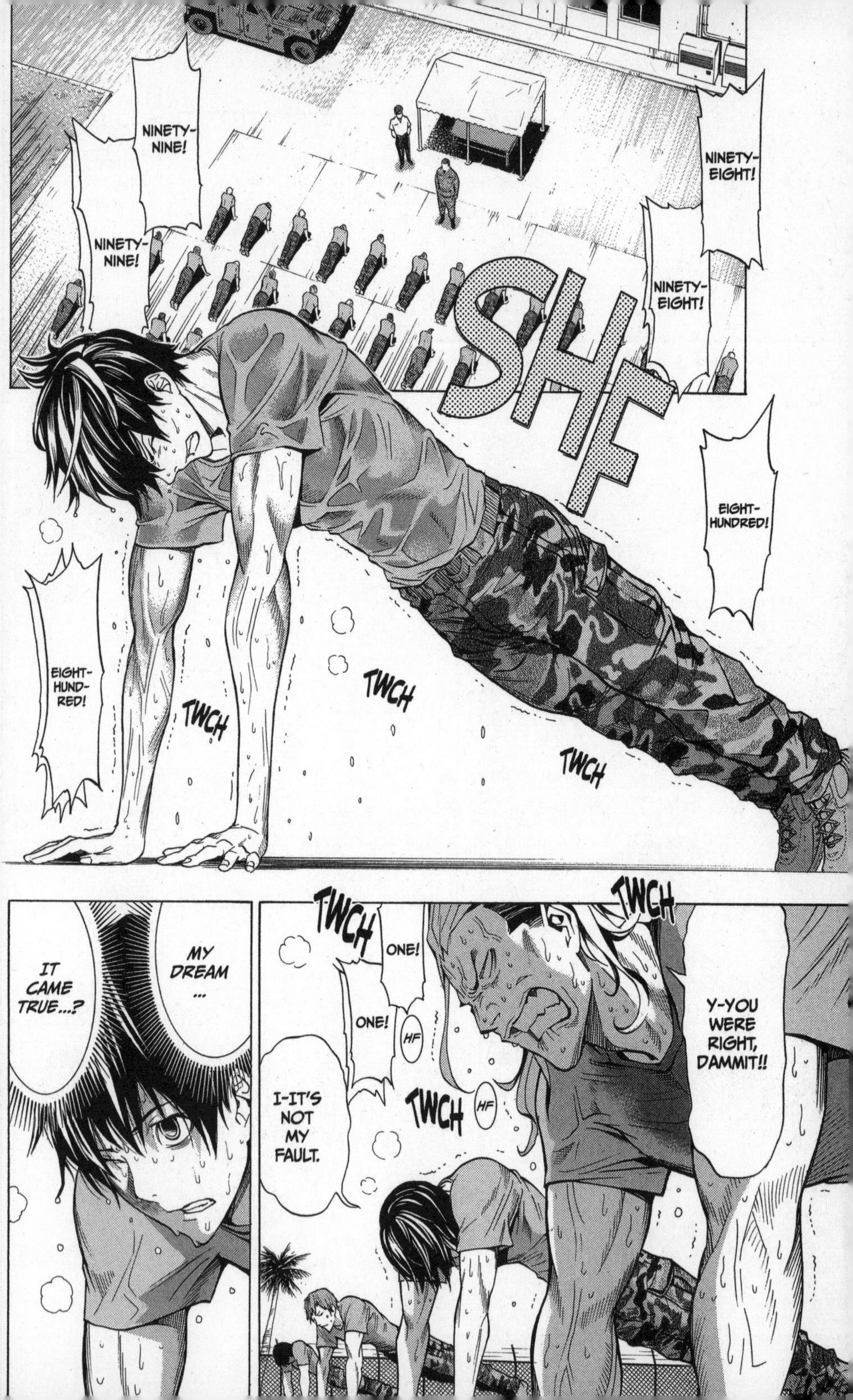
NINETY-EIGHT!
NINETY-EIGHT!
NINETY-NINE!
NINETY-NINE!
SHF
EIGHT-HUNDRED!
TWCH
TWCH
EIGHT-HUNDRED!
TWCH
TWCH
Y-YOU WERE RIGHT, DAMMIT!!
TWCH
ONE!
ONE!
HF
HF
TWCH
I-IT'S NOT MY FAULT.
MY DREAM ...
IT CAME TRUE...?

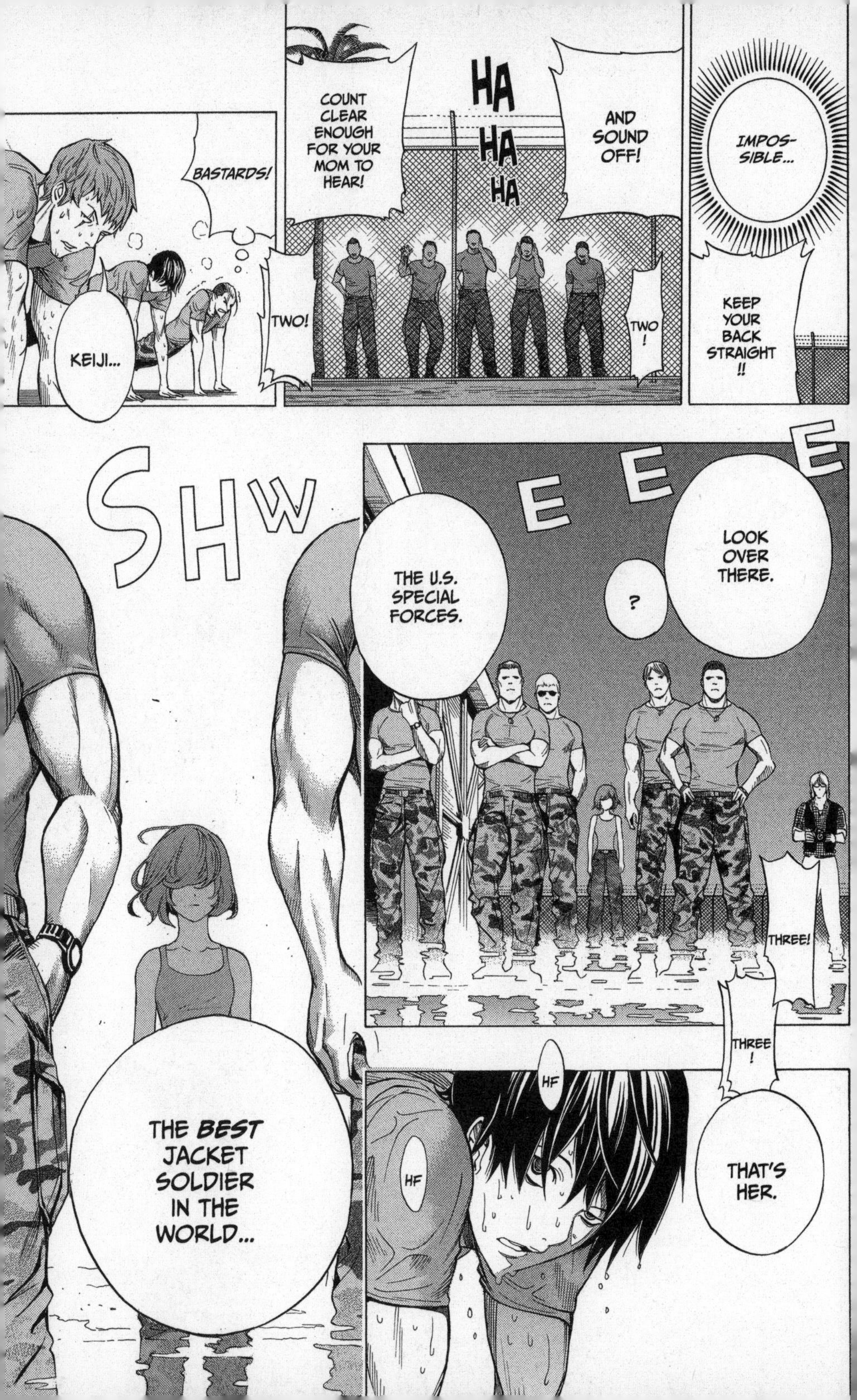
IMPOS-SIBLE...
KEEP YOUR BACK STRAIGHT!!
AND SOUND OFF!
HA HA HA
COUNT CLEAR ENOUGH FOR YOUR MOM TO HEAR!
TWO!
TWO!
BASTARDS!
KEIJI...
SHWEEE
LOOK OVER THERE.
?
THE U.S. SPECIAL FORCES.
THREE!
THREE!
HF
HF
THAT'S HER.
THE *BEST* JACKET SOLDIER IN THE WORLD...

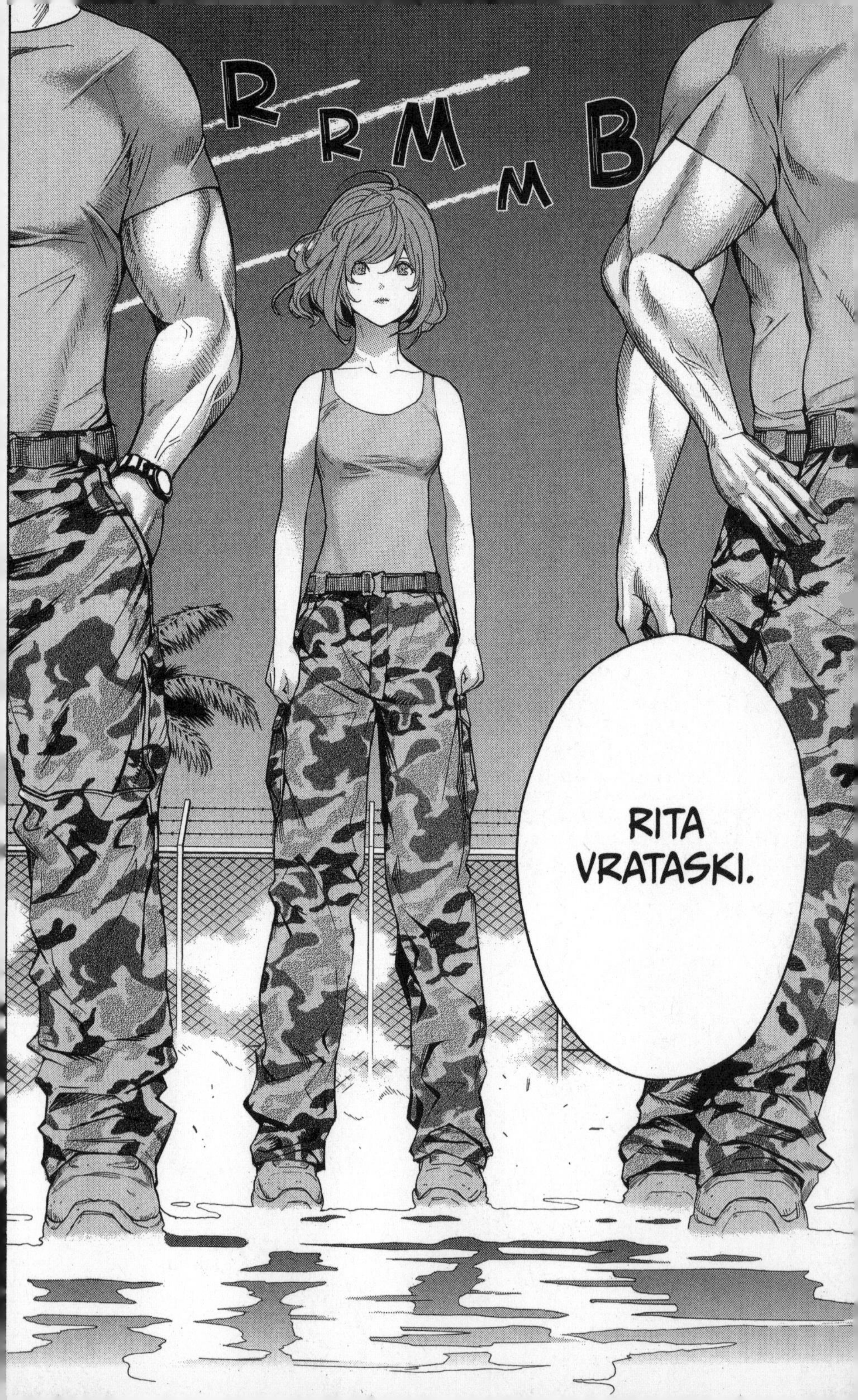
RRRMMMB
RITA VRATASKI.

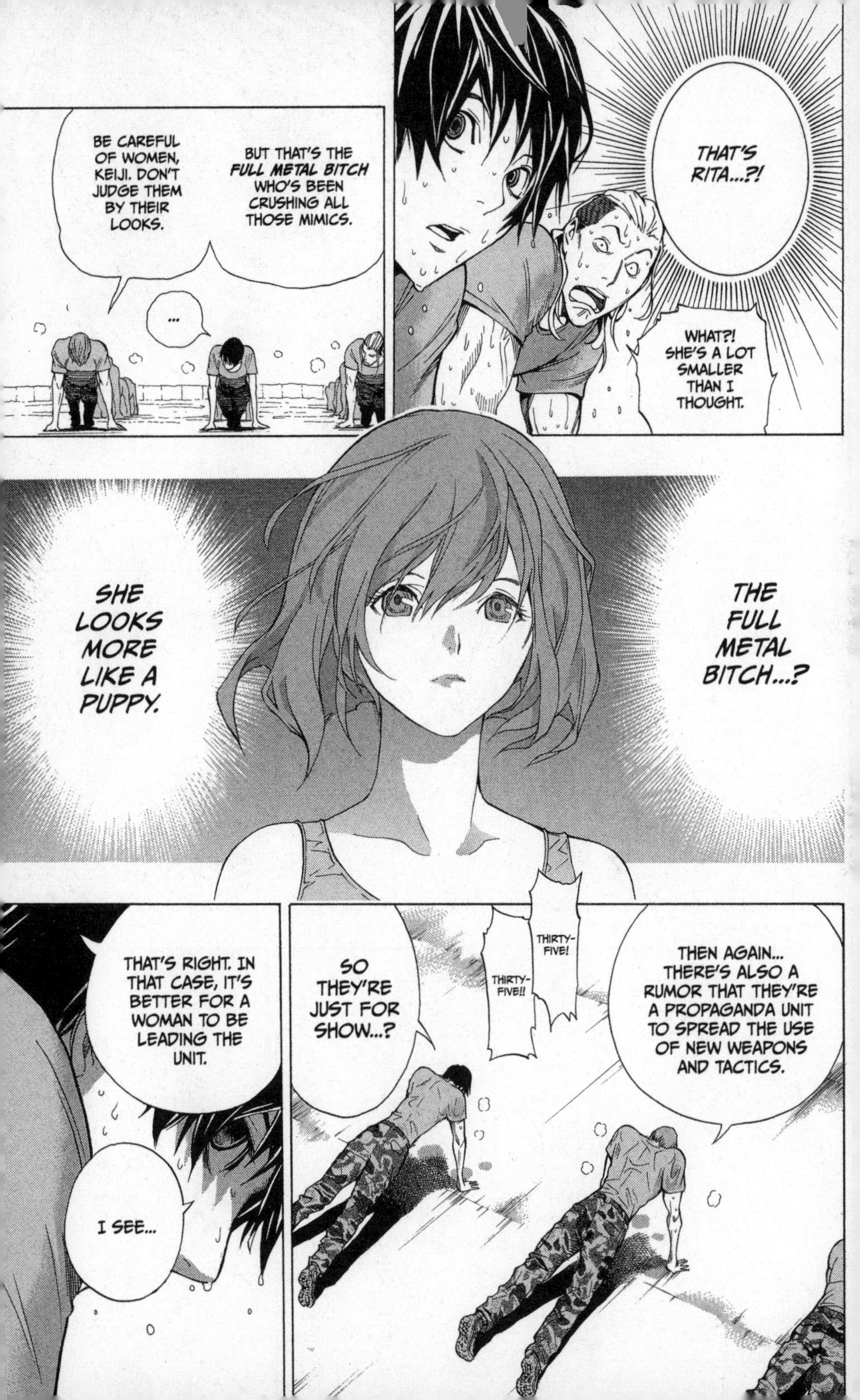
THAT'S RITA...?!
WHAT?! SHE'S A LOT SMALLER THAN I THOUGHT.
BUT THAT'S THE *FULL METAL BITCH* WHO'S BEEN CRUSHING ALL THOSE MIMICS.
BE CAREFUL OF WOMEN, KEIJI. DON'T JUDGE THEM BY THEIR LOOKS.
...
THE FULL METAL BITCH...?
SHE LOOKS MORE LIKE A PUPPY.
THEN AGAIN... THERE'S ALSO A RUMOR THAT THEY'RE A PROPAGANDA UNIT TO SPREAD THE USE OF NEW WEAPONS AND TACTICS.
THIRTY-FIVE!
THIRTY-FIVE!!
SO THEY'RE JUST FOR SHOW...?
THAT'S RIGHT. IN THAT CASE, IT'S BETTER FOR A WOMAN TO BE LEADING THE UNIT.
I SEE...

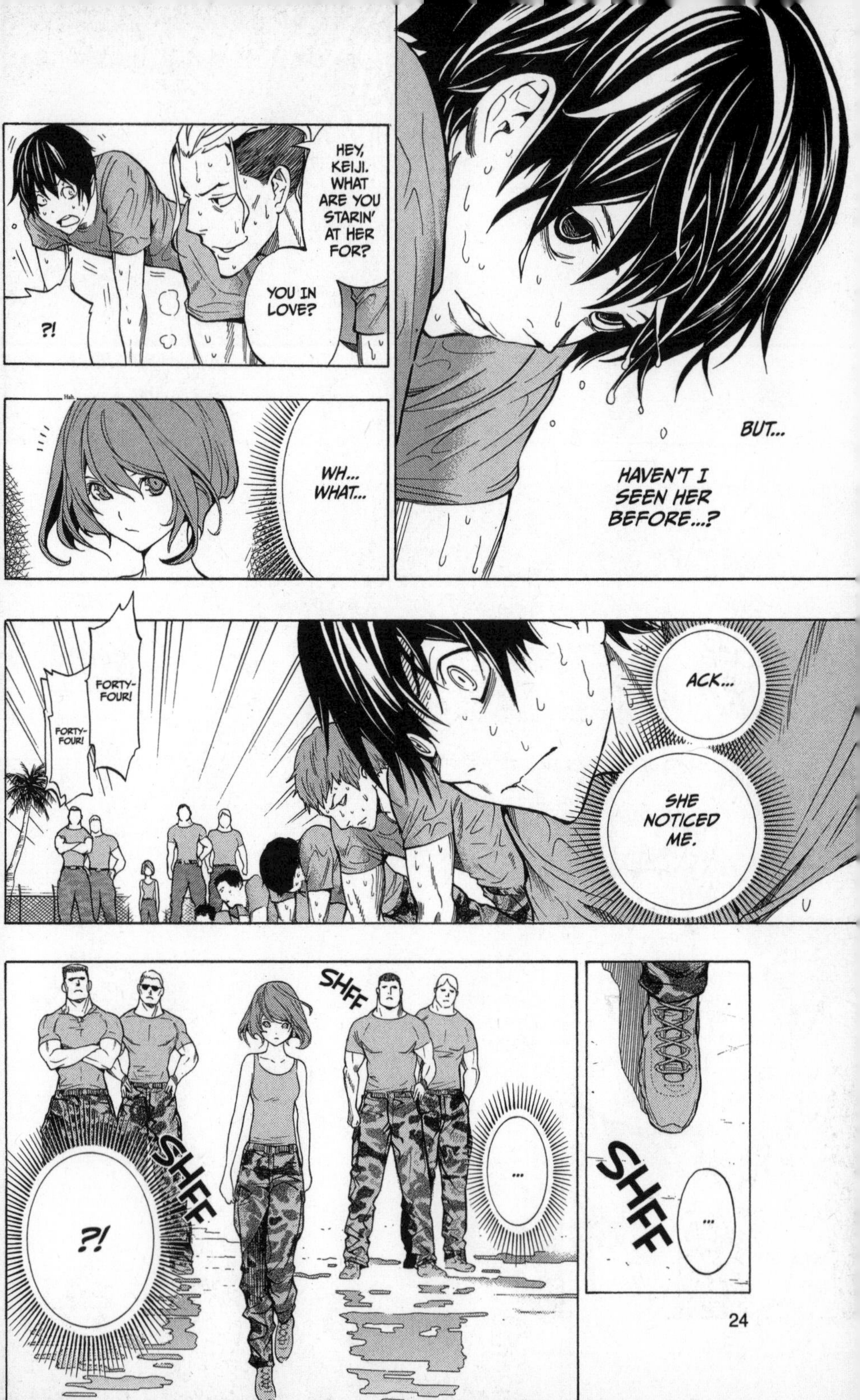
BUT...
HAVEN'T I SEEN HER BEFORE...?
HEY, KEIJI. WHAT ARE YOU STARIN' AT HER FOR?
YOU IN LOVE?
?!
WH... WHAT...
ACK...
SHE NOTICED ME.
FORTY-FOUR!
FORTY-FOUR!
SHFF
...
SHFF
...
SHFF
?!

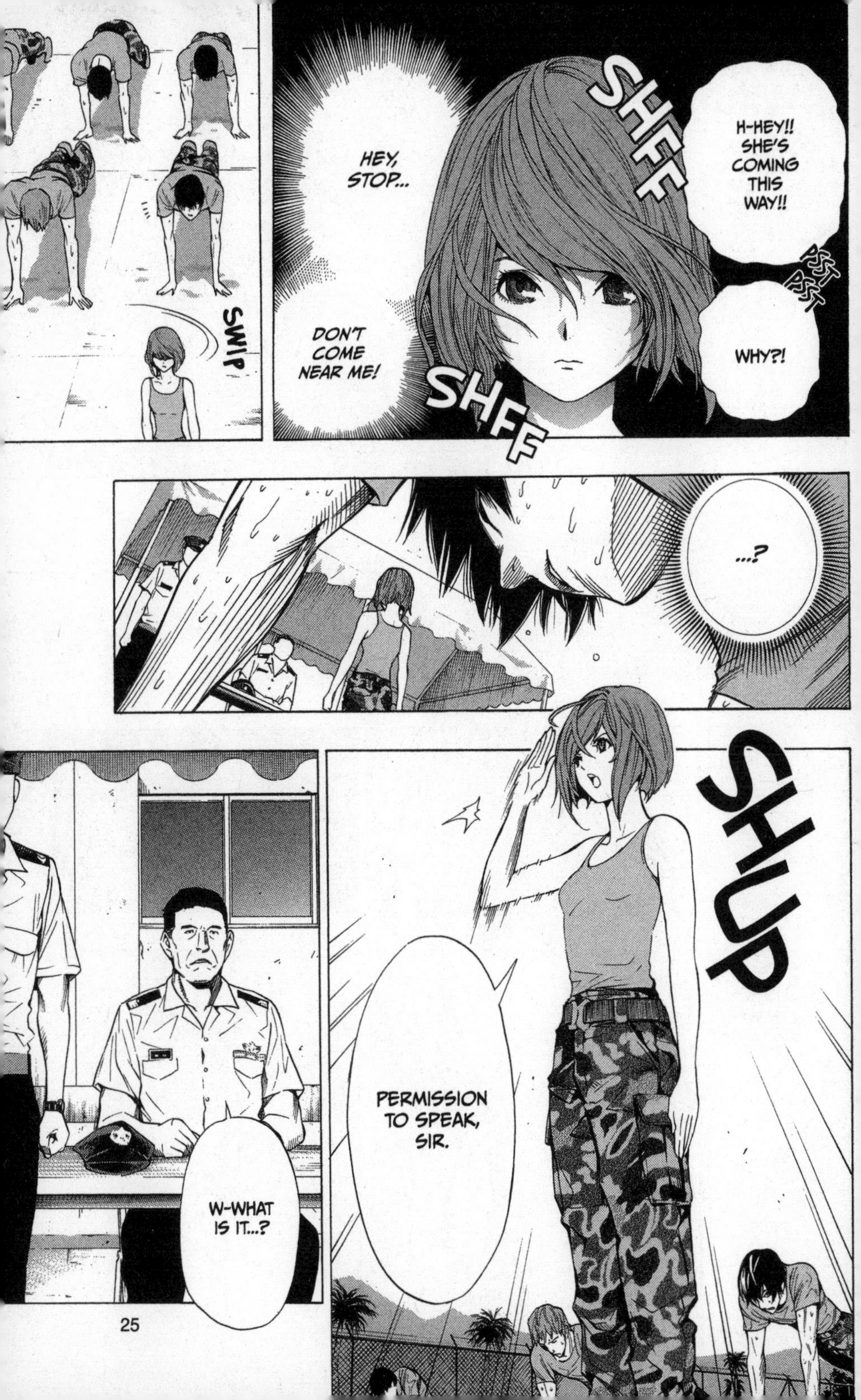
H-HEY!! SHE'S COMING THIS WAY!!
SHFF
PSST PSST
HEY, STOP...
WHY?!
DON'T COME NEAR ME!
SHFF
SWIP
...?
SHUP
PERMISSION TO SPEAK, SIR.
W-WHAT IS IT...?

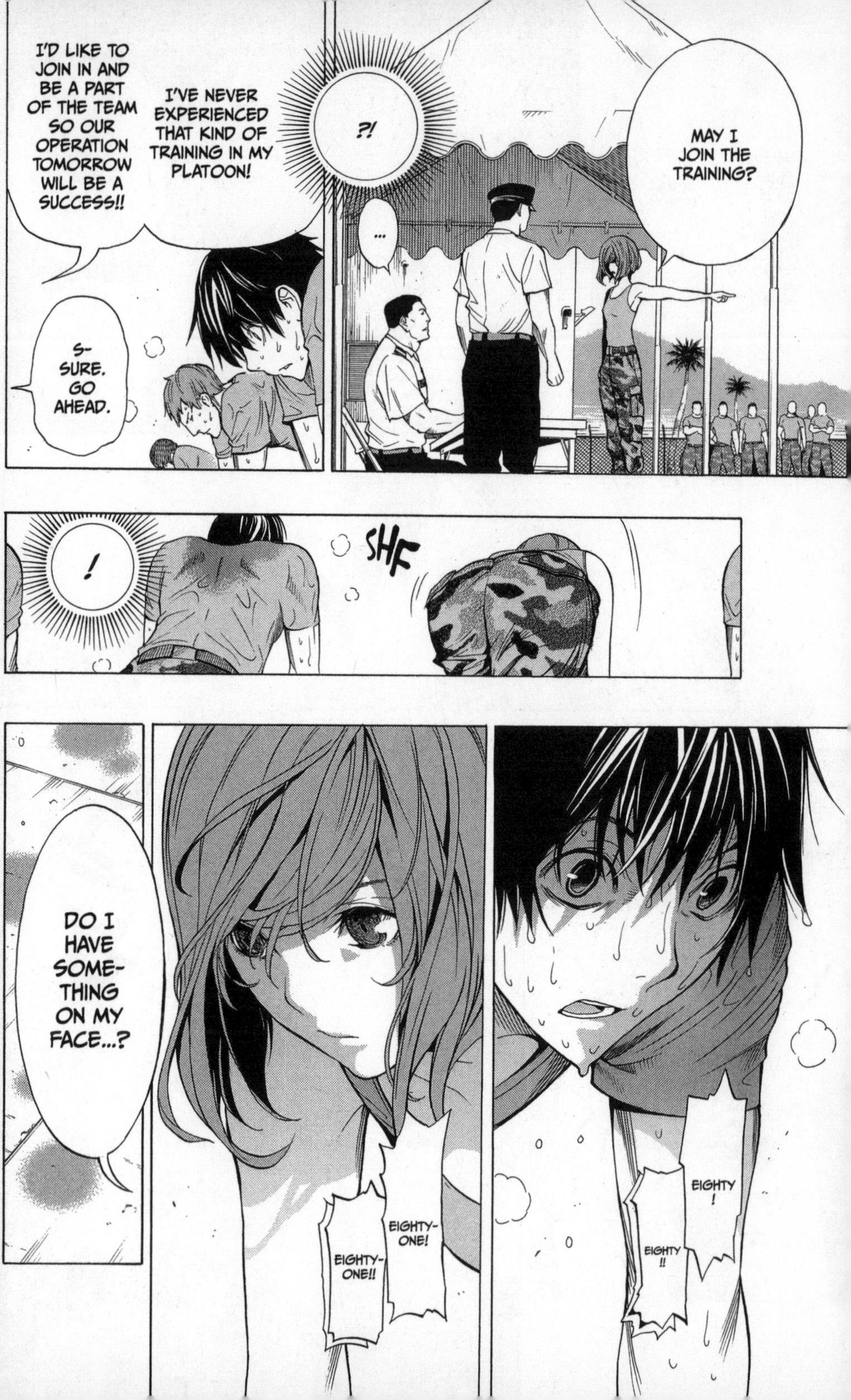
MAY I JOIN THE TRAINING?
...
?!
I'VE NEVER EXPERIENCED THAT KIND OF TRAINING IN MY PLATOON!
I'D LIKE TO JOIN IN AND BE A PART OF THE TEAM SO OUR OPERATION TOMORROW WILL BE A SUCCESS!!
S-SURE. GO AHEAD.
SHF
!
EIGHTY!
EIGHTY!!
EIGHTY-ONE!
EIGHTY-ONE!!
DO I HAVE SOMETHING ON MY FACE...?

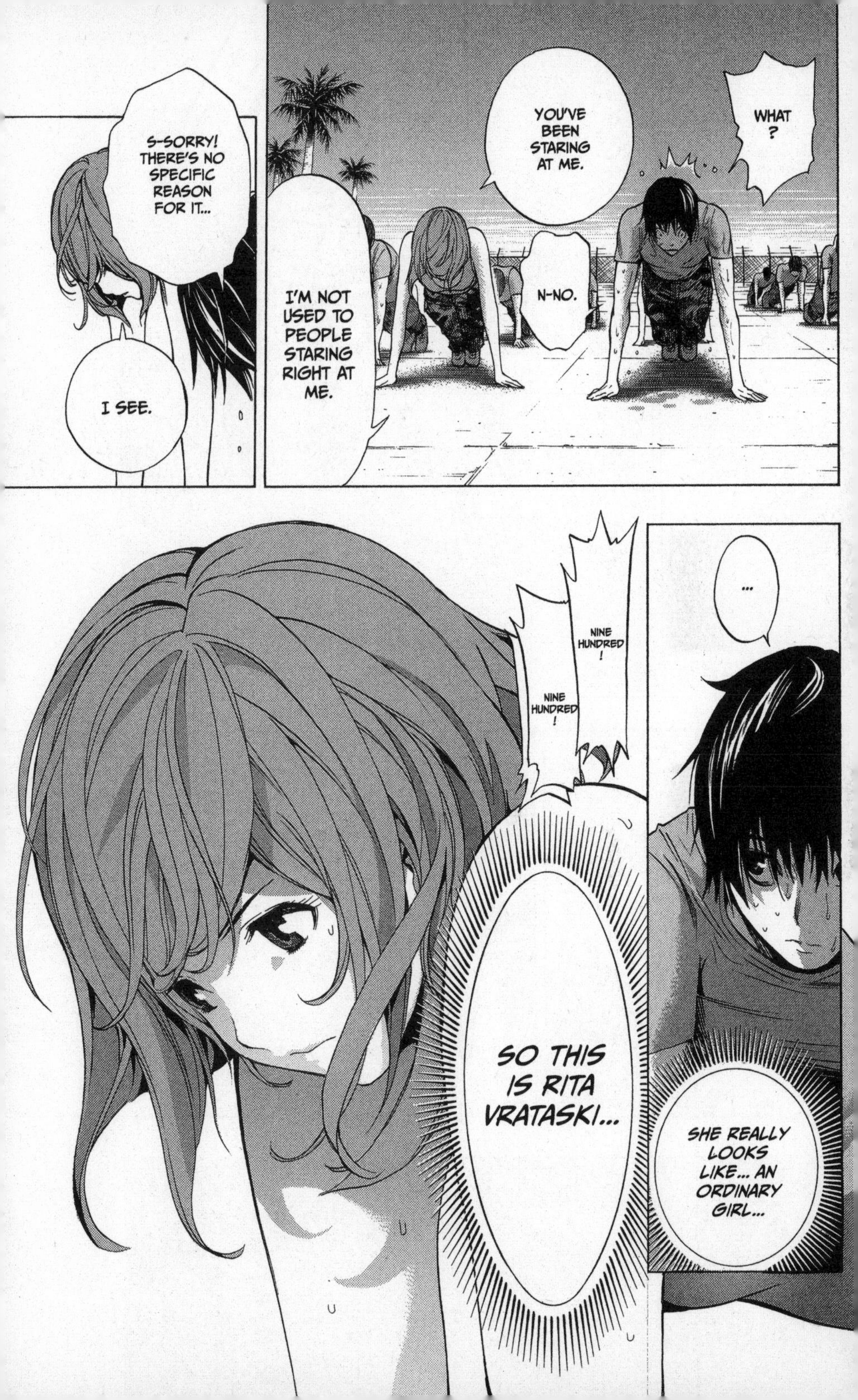
WHAT?
YOU'VE BEEN STARING AT ME.
N-NO.
I'M NOT USED TO PEOPLE STARING RIGHT AT ME.
S-SORRY! THERE'S NO SPECIFIC REASON FOR IT...
I SEE.
...
NINE HUNDRED!
NINE HUNDRED!
SO THIS IS RITA VRATASKI...
SHE REALLY LOOKS LIKE... AN ORDINARY GIRL...

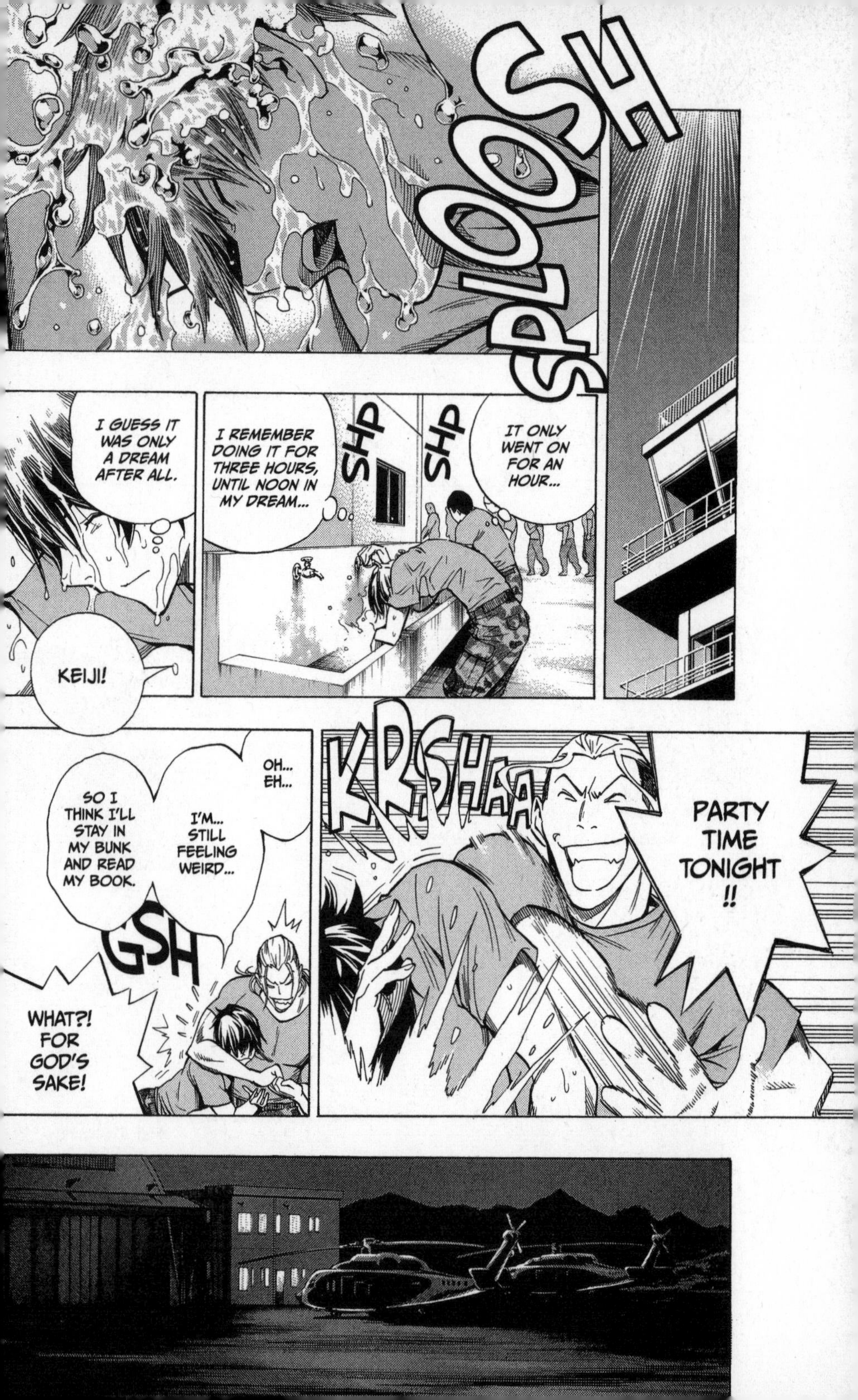
SPLOOSH
IT ONLY WENT ON FOR AN HOUR...
SHP
SHP
I REMEMBER DOING IT FOR THREE HOURS, UNTIL NOON IN MY DREAM...
I GUESS IT WAS ONLY A DREAM AFTER ALL.
KEIJI!
KRSHAAA
PARTY TIME TONIGHT!!
OH... EH...
I'M... STILL FEELING WEIRD...
SO I THINK I'LL STAY IN MY BUNK AND READ MY BOOK.
GSH
WHAT?! FOR GOD'S SAKE!

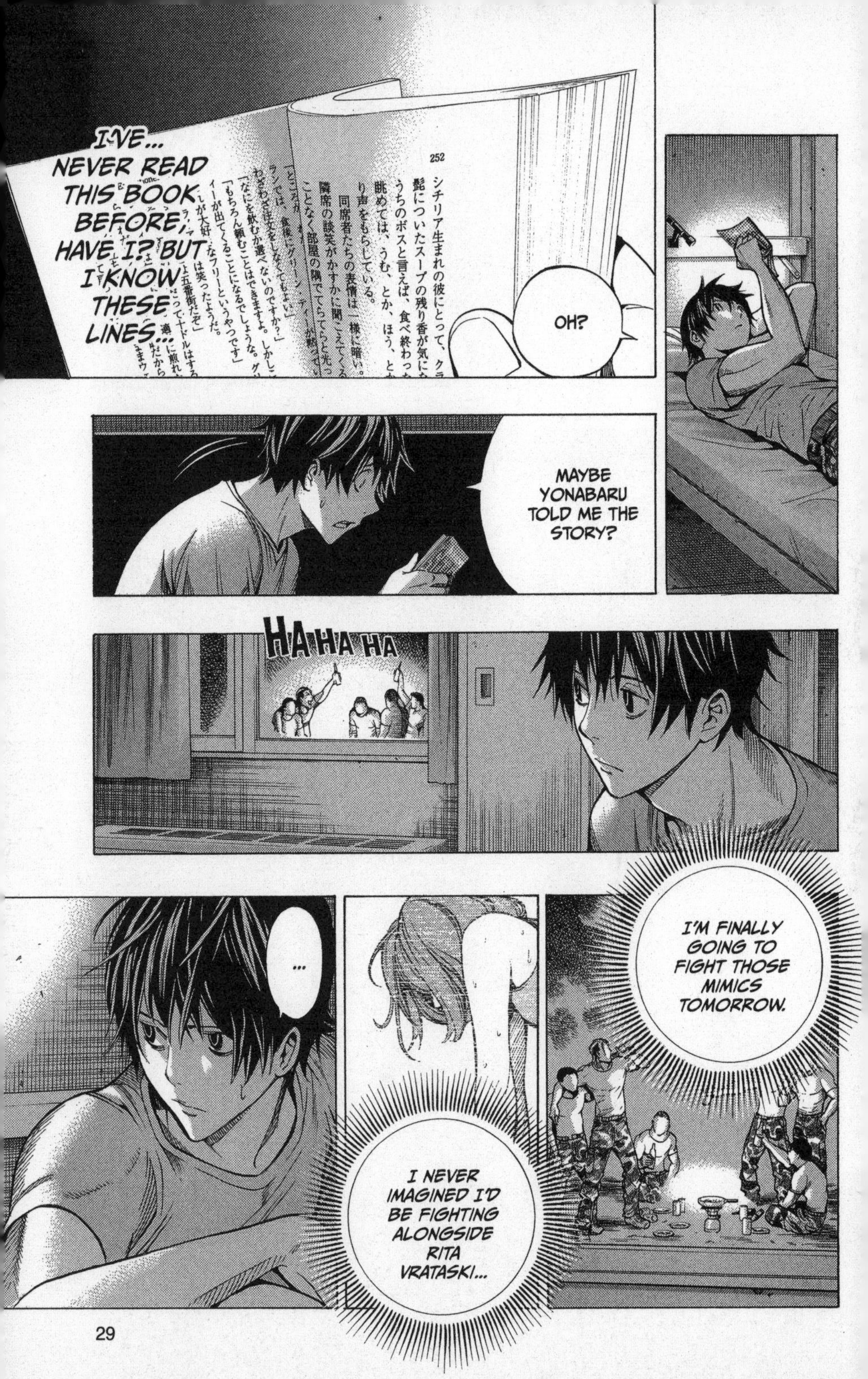
OH?
I'VE... NEVER READ THIS BOOK BEFORE, HAVE I? BUT I KNOW THESE LINES...
MAYBE YONABARU TOLD ME THE STORY?
HA HA HA
I'M FINALLY GOING TO FIGHT THOSE MIMICS TOMORROW.
I NEVER IMAGINED I'D BE FIGHTING ALONGSIDE RITA VRATASKI...
...

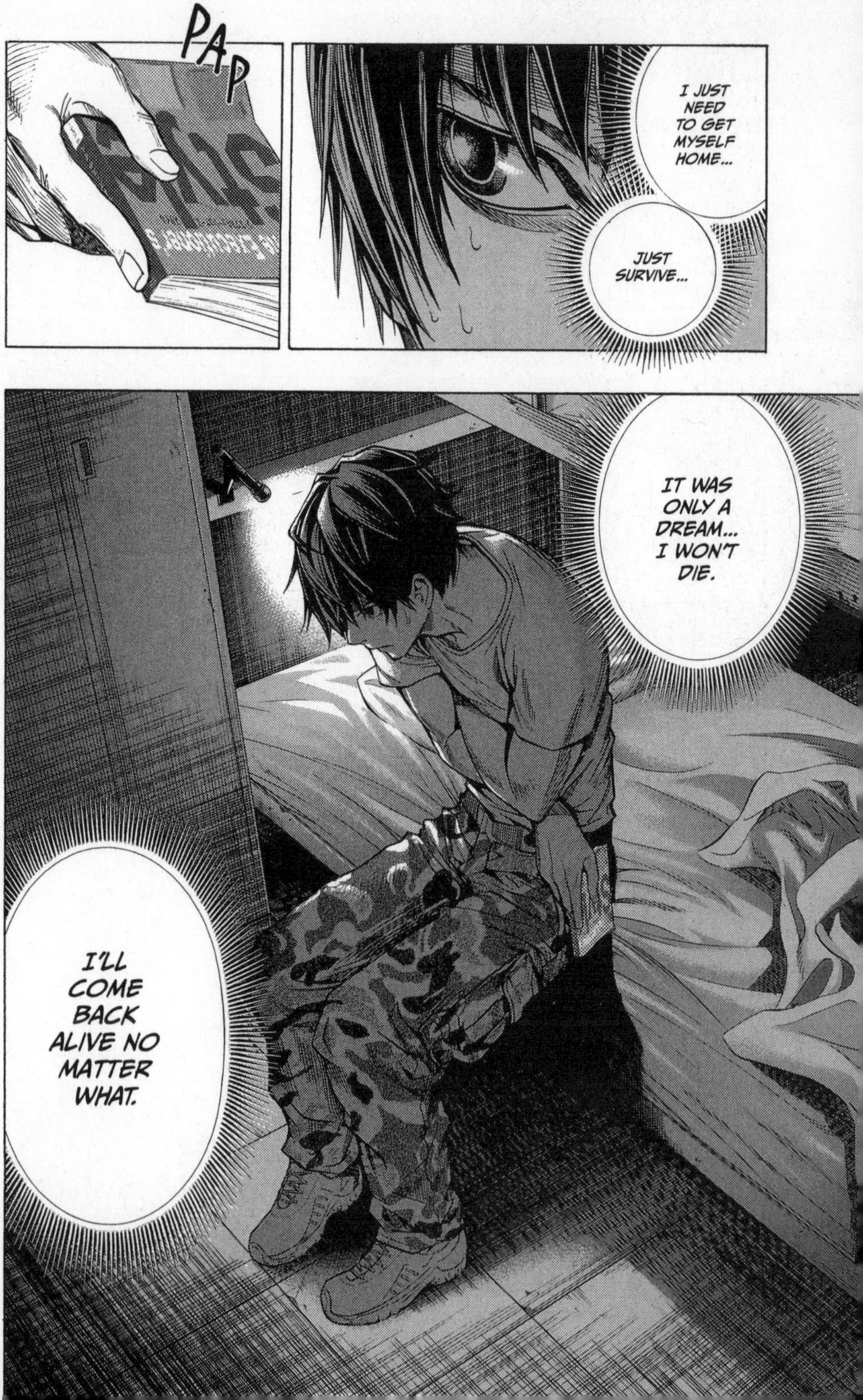
I JUST NEED TO GET MYSELF HOME...
JUST SURVIVE...
PAP
IT WAS ONLY A DREAM... I WON'T DIE.
I'LL COME BACK ALIVE NO MATTER WHAT.

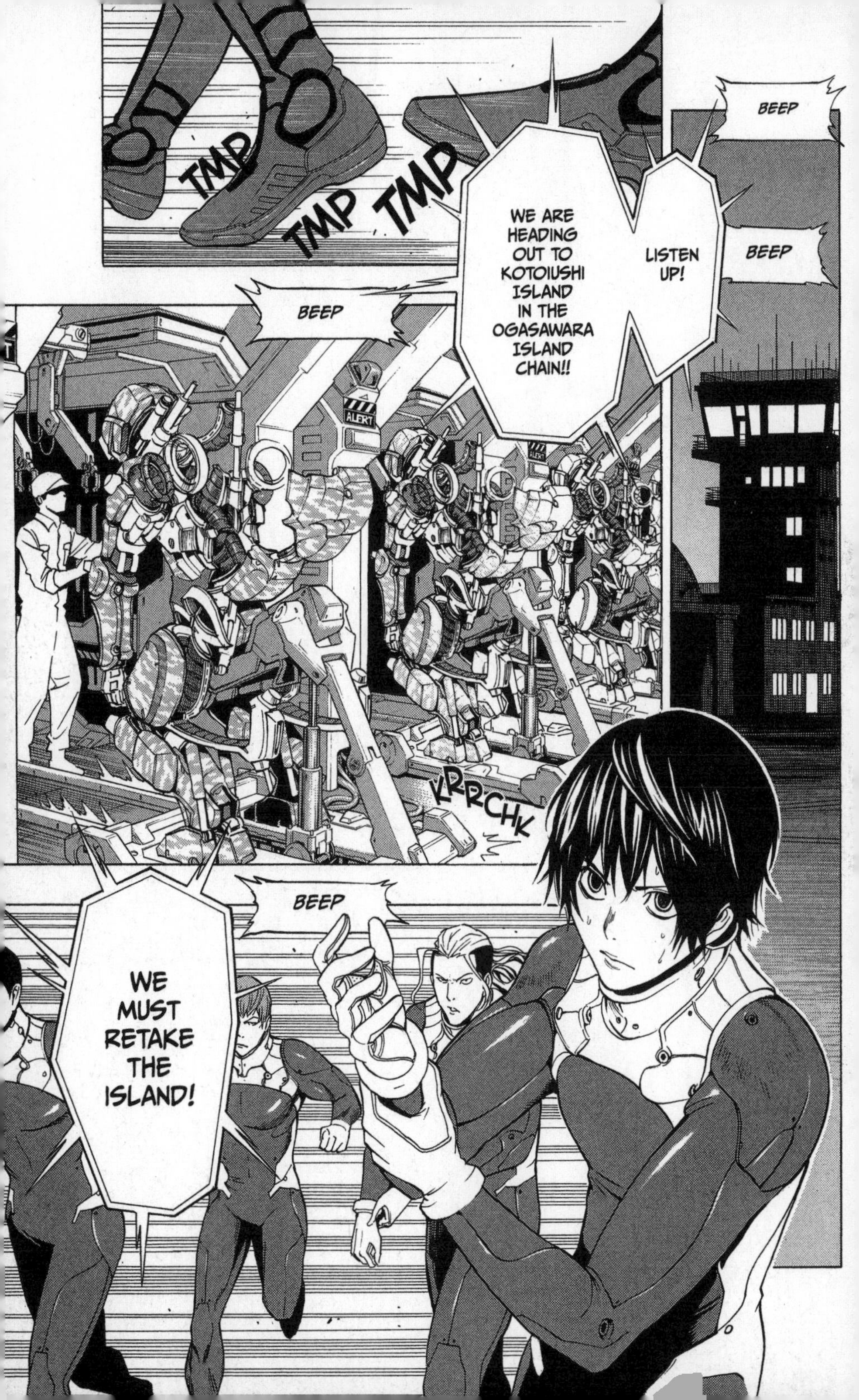
BEEP
BEEP
LISTEN UP!
WE ARE HEADING OUT TO KOTOIUSHI ISLAND IN THE OGASAWARA ISLAND CHAIN!!
TMP TMP TMP
BEEP
KRRRCHK
BEEP
WE MUST RETAKE THE ISLAND!

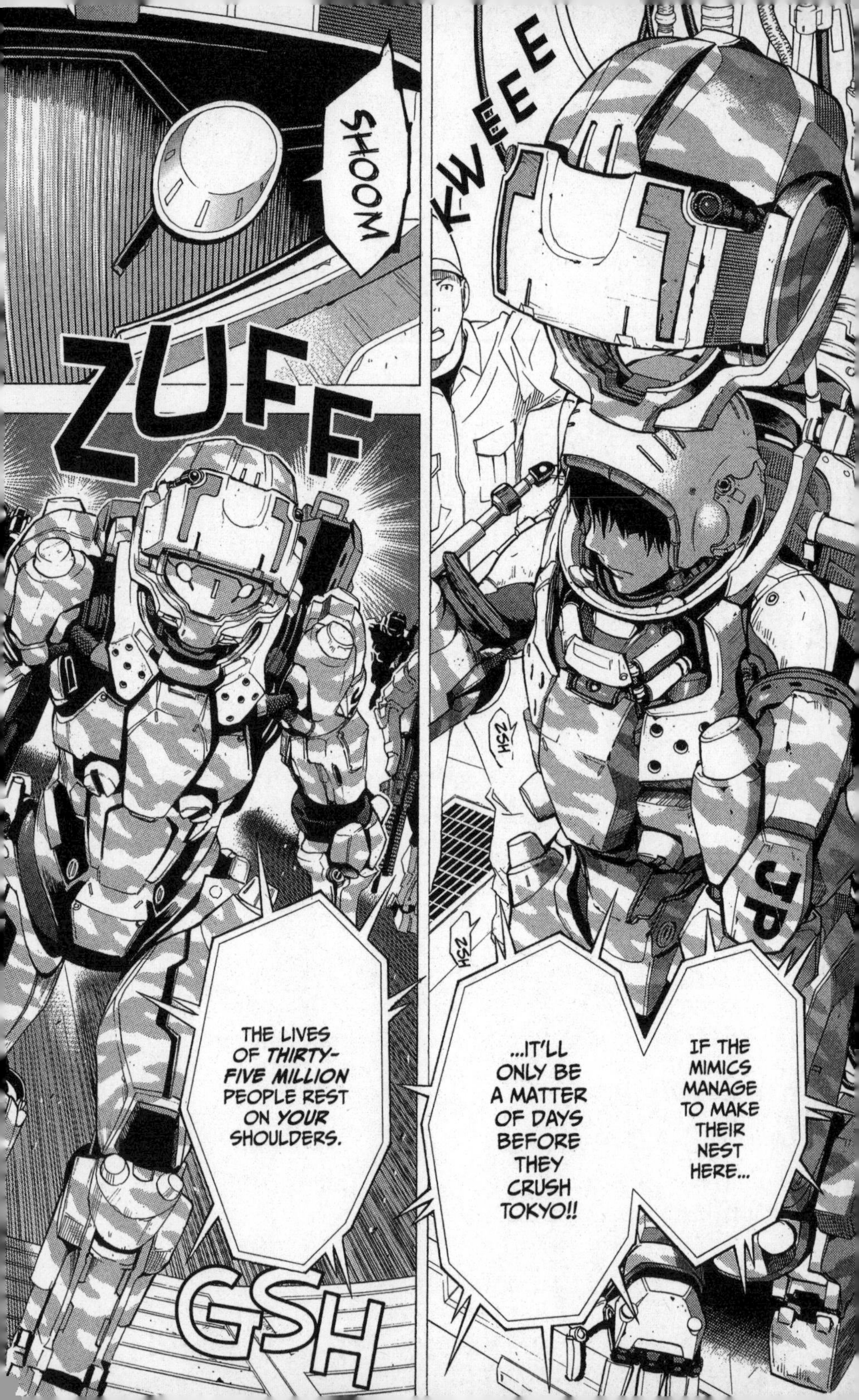
KWEEE
ZSH
ZSH
IF THE MIMICS MANAGE TO MAKE THEIR NEST HERE...
...IT'LL ONLY BE A MATTER OF DAYS BEFORE THEY CRUSH TOKYO!!
SHOOM
ZUFF
THE LIVES OF *THIRTY-FIVE MILLION* PEOPLE REST ON *YOUR* SHOULDERS.
GSH

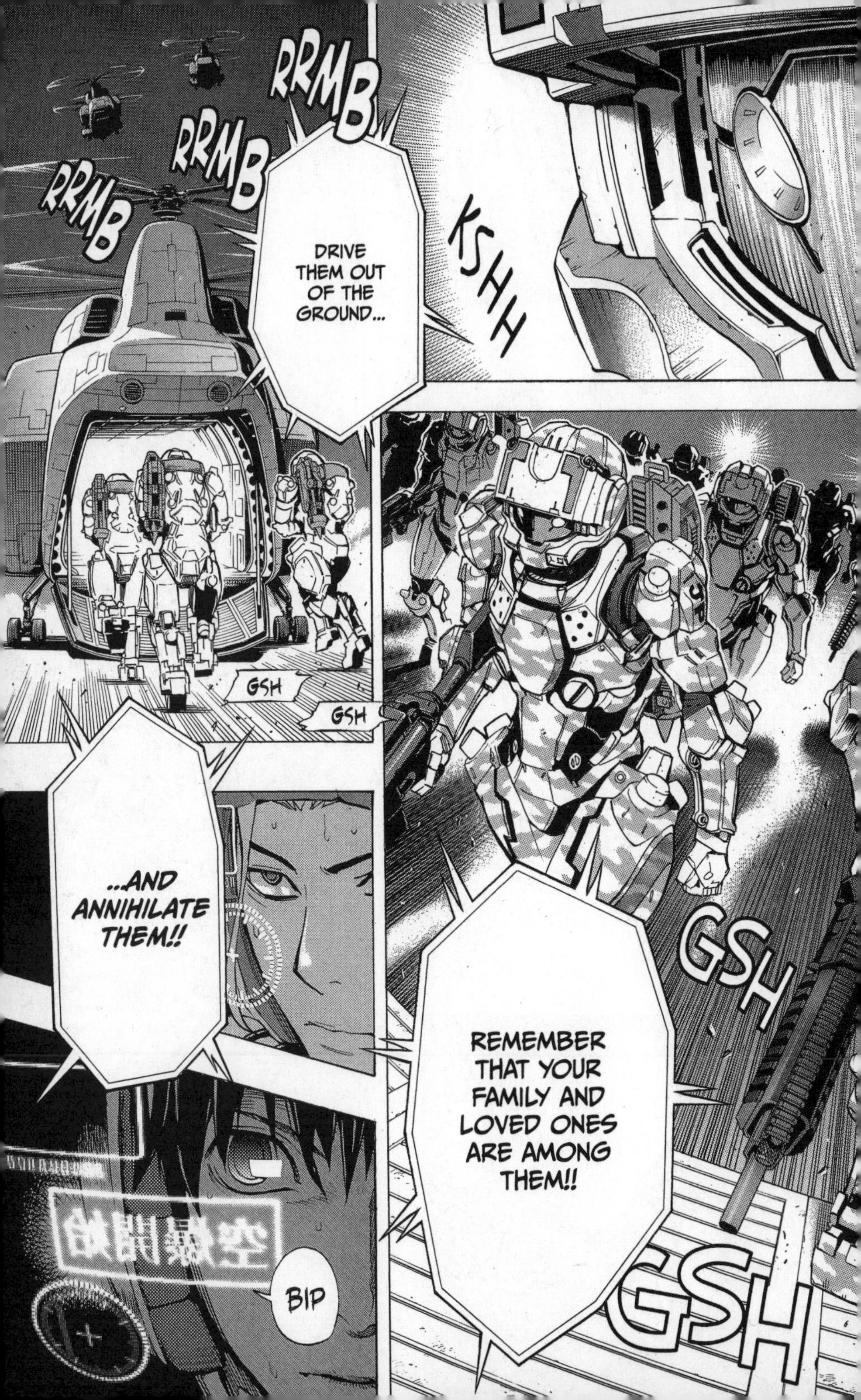
KSHH
RRMB
RRMB
RRMB
DRIVE THEM OUT OF THE GROUND...
GSH
GSH
...AND ANNIHILATE THEM!!
BIP
REMEMBER THAT YOUR FAMILY AND LOVED ONES ARE AMONG THEM!!
GSH
GSH

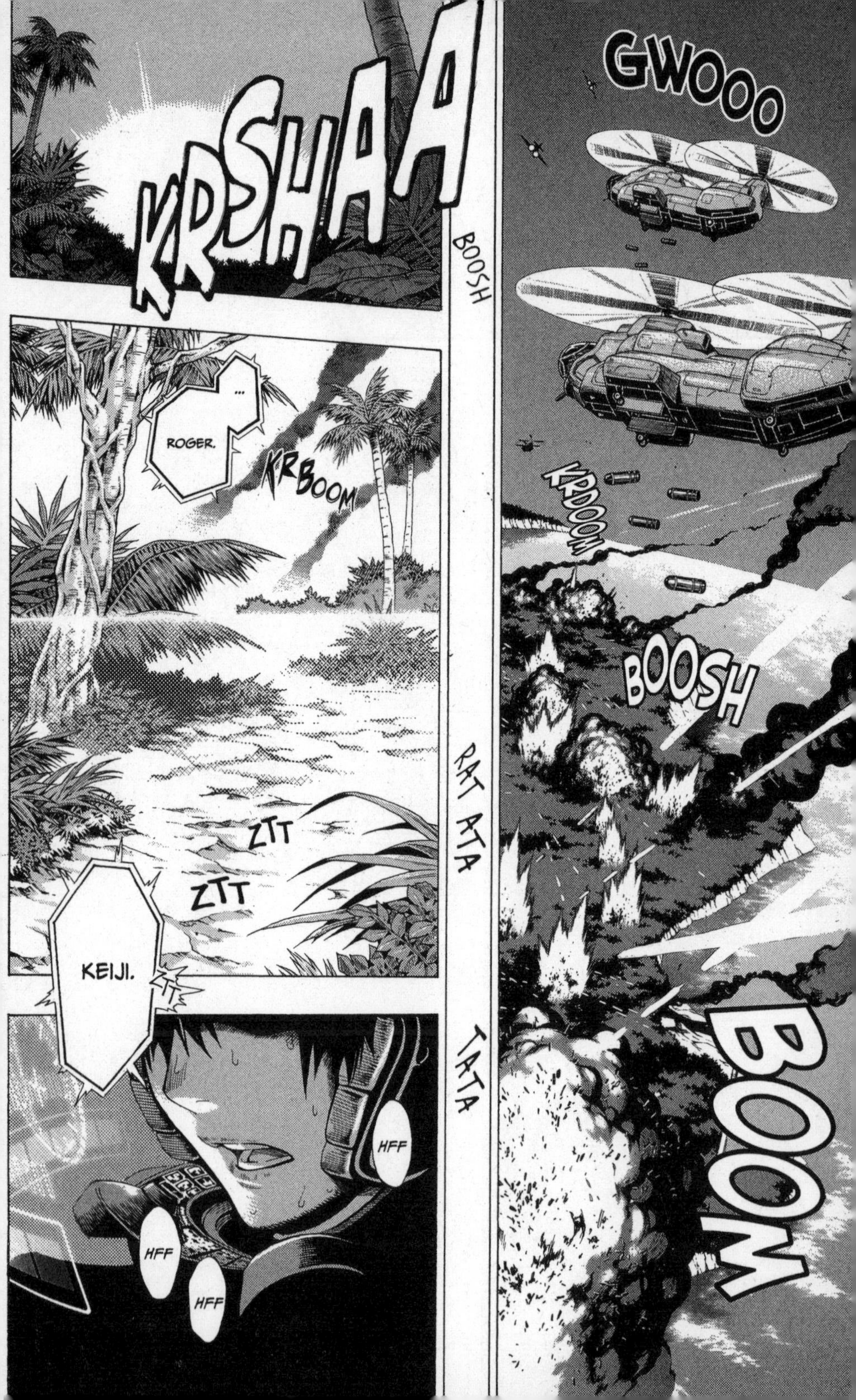
GWOOO
KRDOOM
BOOSH
BOOM
BOOSH
RAT ATA
TATA
KRSHAA
...
ROGER.
KRBOOM
ZTT
ZTT
KEIJI.
TT
HFF
HFF
HFF

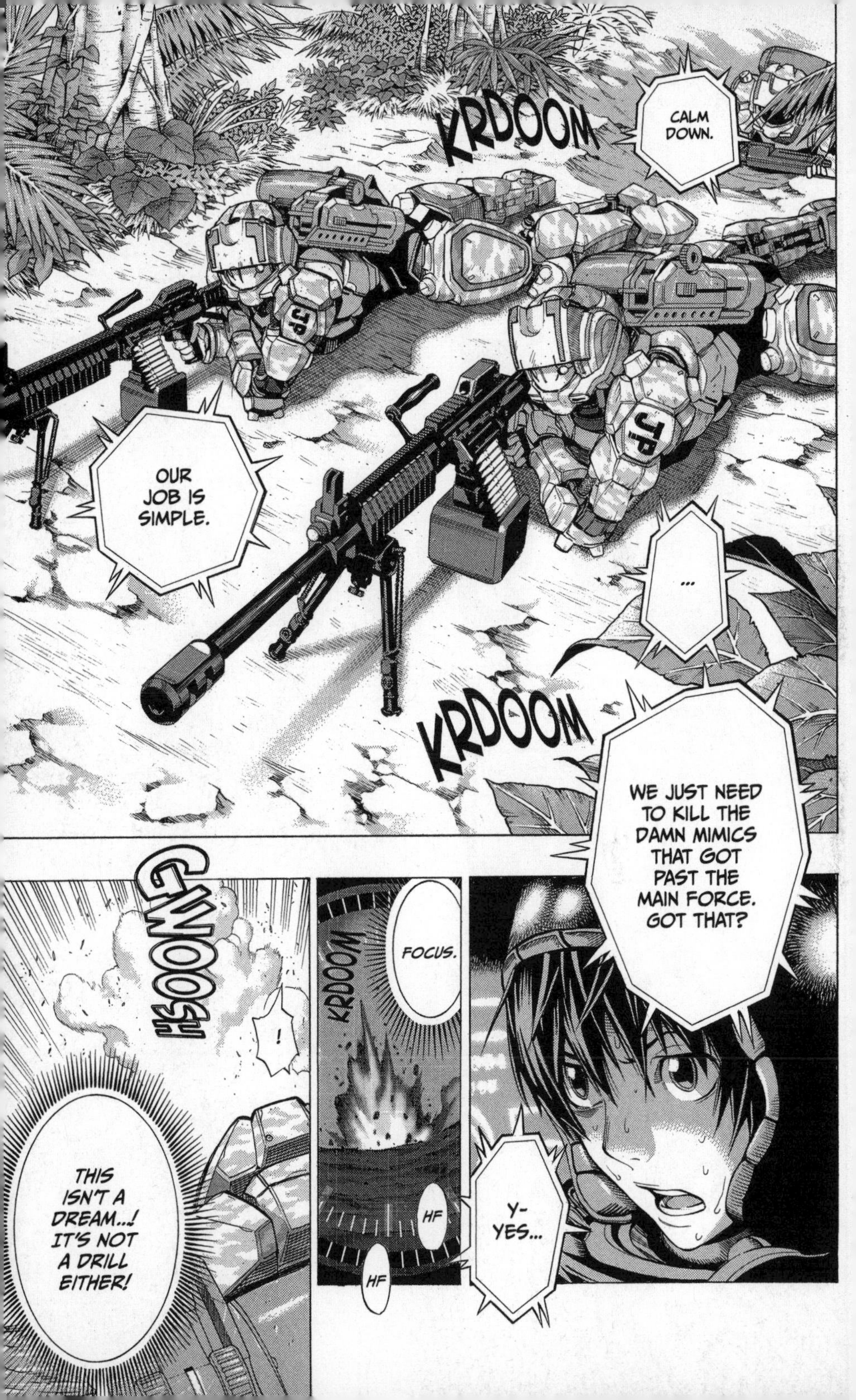
CALM DOWN.
KRDOOM
OUR JOB IS SIMPLE.
...
KRDOOM
WE JUST NEED TO KILL THE DAMN MIMICS THAT GOT PAST THE MAIN FORCE. GOT THAT?
Y- YES...
FOCUS.
KRDOOM
HF
HF
GWOOSH
!
THIS ISN'T A DREAM...! IT'S NOT A DRILL EITHER!

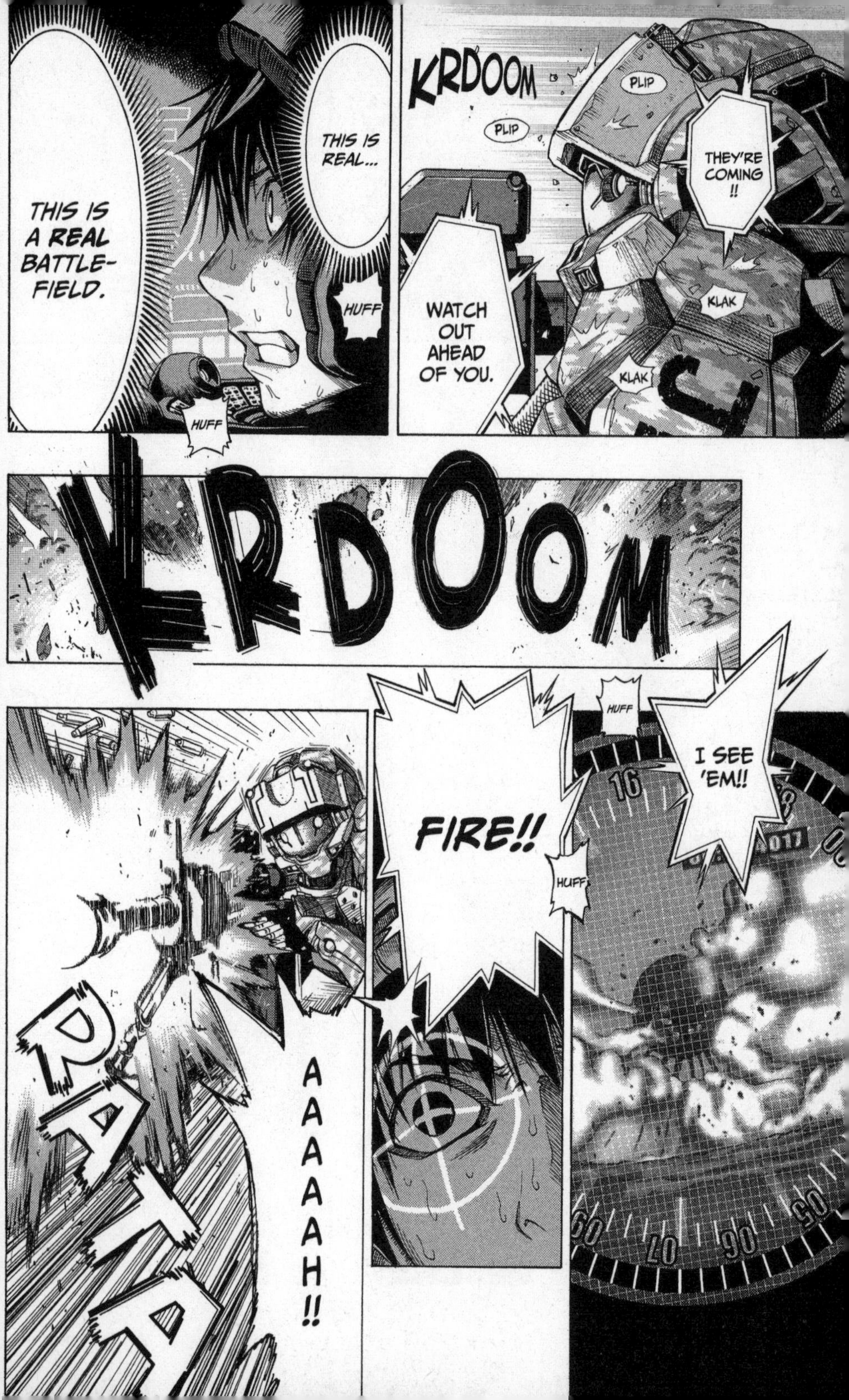
PLIP
THEY'RE COMING!!
KRDOOM
PLIP
KLAK
WATCH OUT AHEAD OF YOU.
KLAK
THIS IS REAL...
THIS IS A REAL BATTLE-FIELD.
HUFF
HUFF
KRDOOM
HUFF
I SEE 'EM!!
HUFF
FIRE!!
AAAAAAH!!
PATA

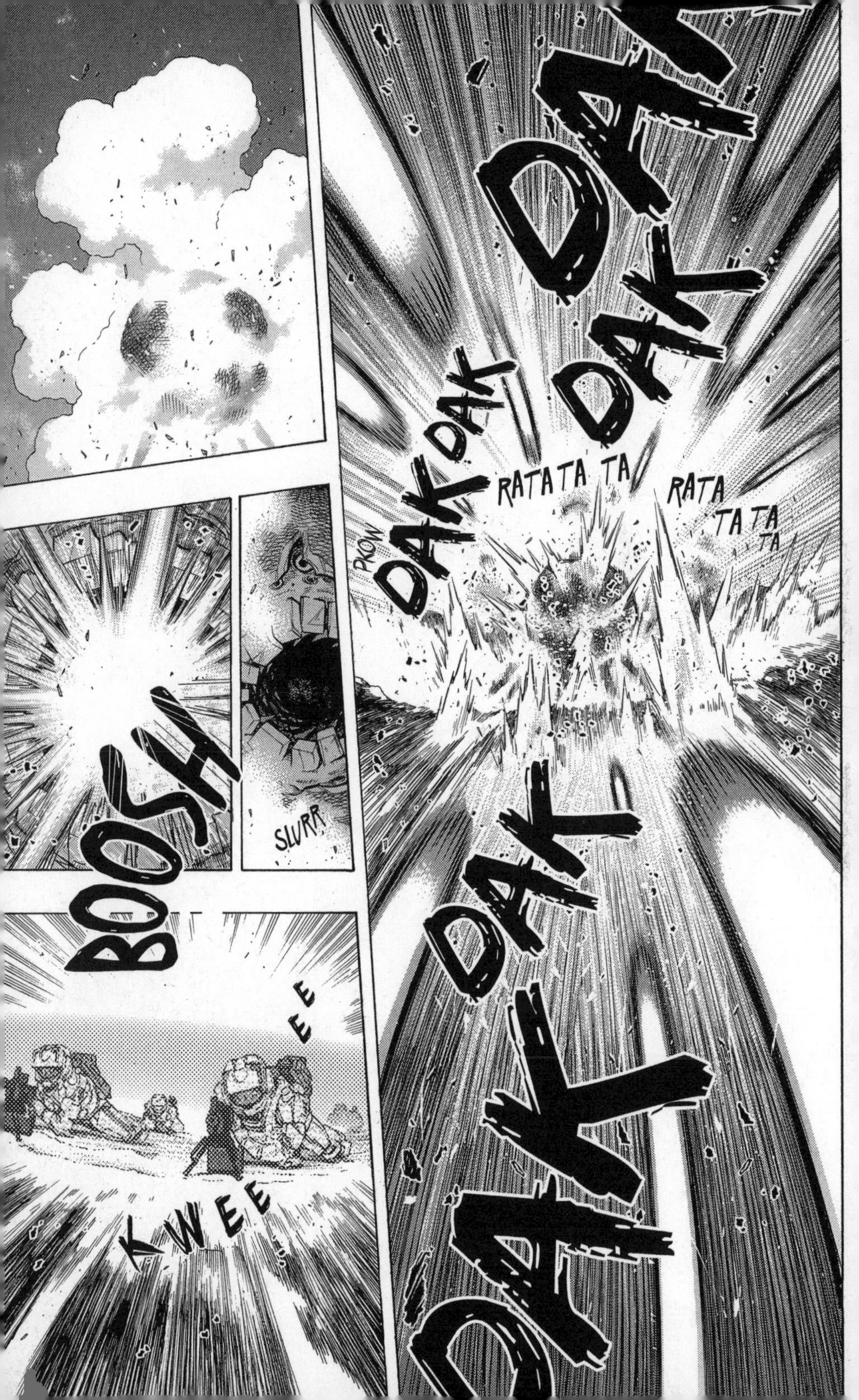
DAK DAK
DAK DAK
RATATA TA
RATA TA TA TA
PKOW
DAK DAK
DAK
SLURR
BOOSH!!
KWEEEE

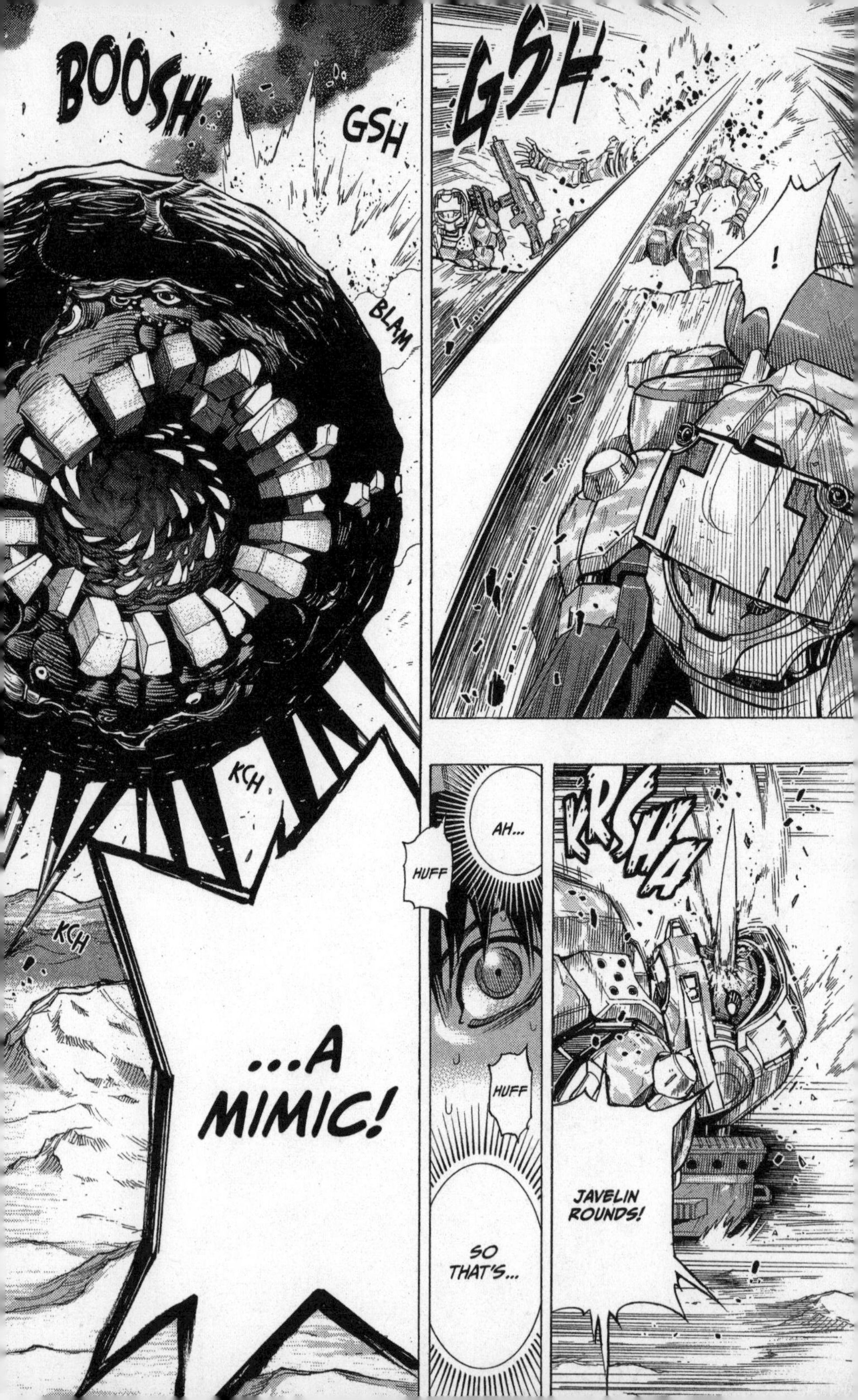
GSH
!
KRSHA
JAVELIN ROUNDS!
AH...
HUFF
HUFF
SO THAT'S...
BOOSH
GSH
BLAM
KCH
KCH
...A MIMIC!

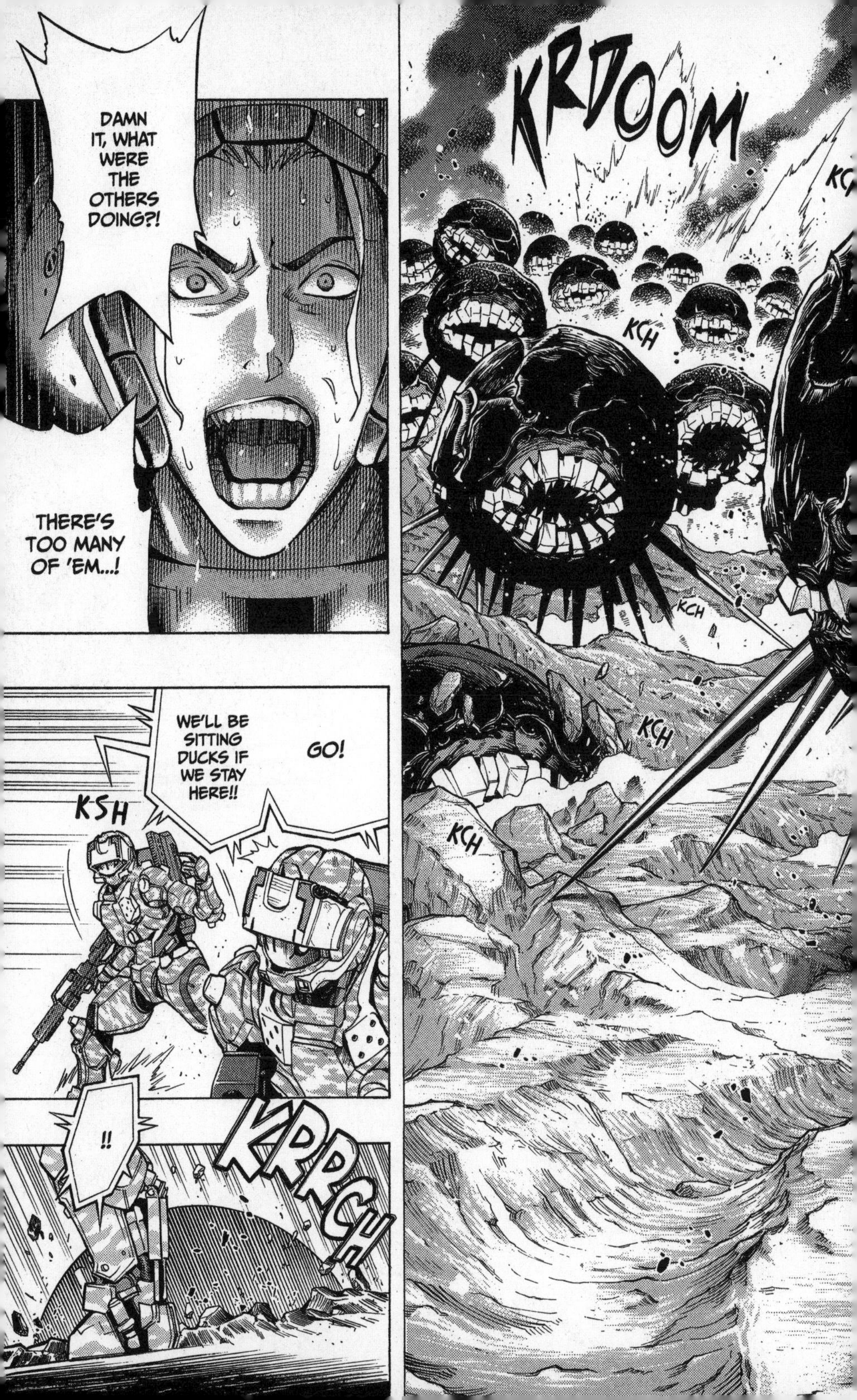
KRDOOM
KCH
KCH
KCH
KCH
DAMN IT, WHAT WERE THE OTHERS DOING?!
THERE'S TOO MANY OF 'EM...!
GO!
WE'LL BE SITTING DUCKS IF WE STAY HERE!!
KSH
!!
KRRCH

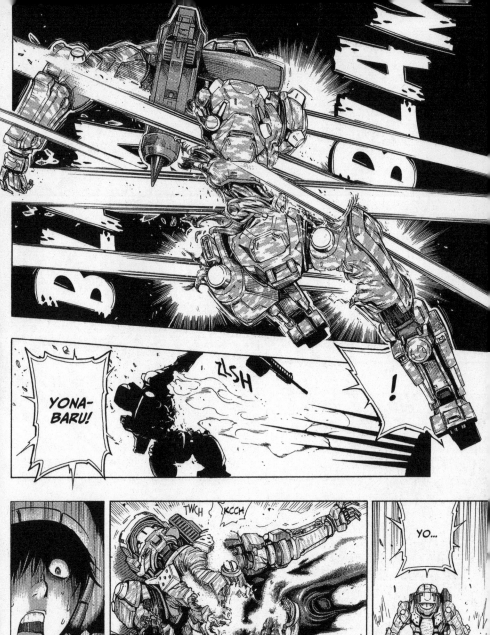

YONA-
BARU!

ZLSH

!

...

TWCH   KCCH

TWCH

KCCH

YO...

!!

KRSHAA

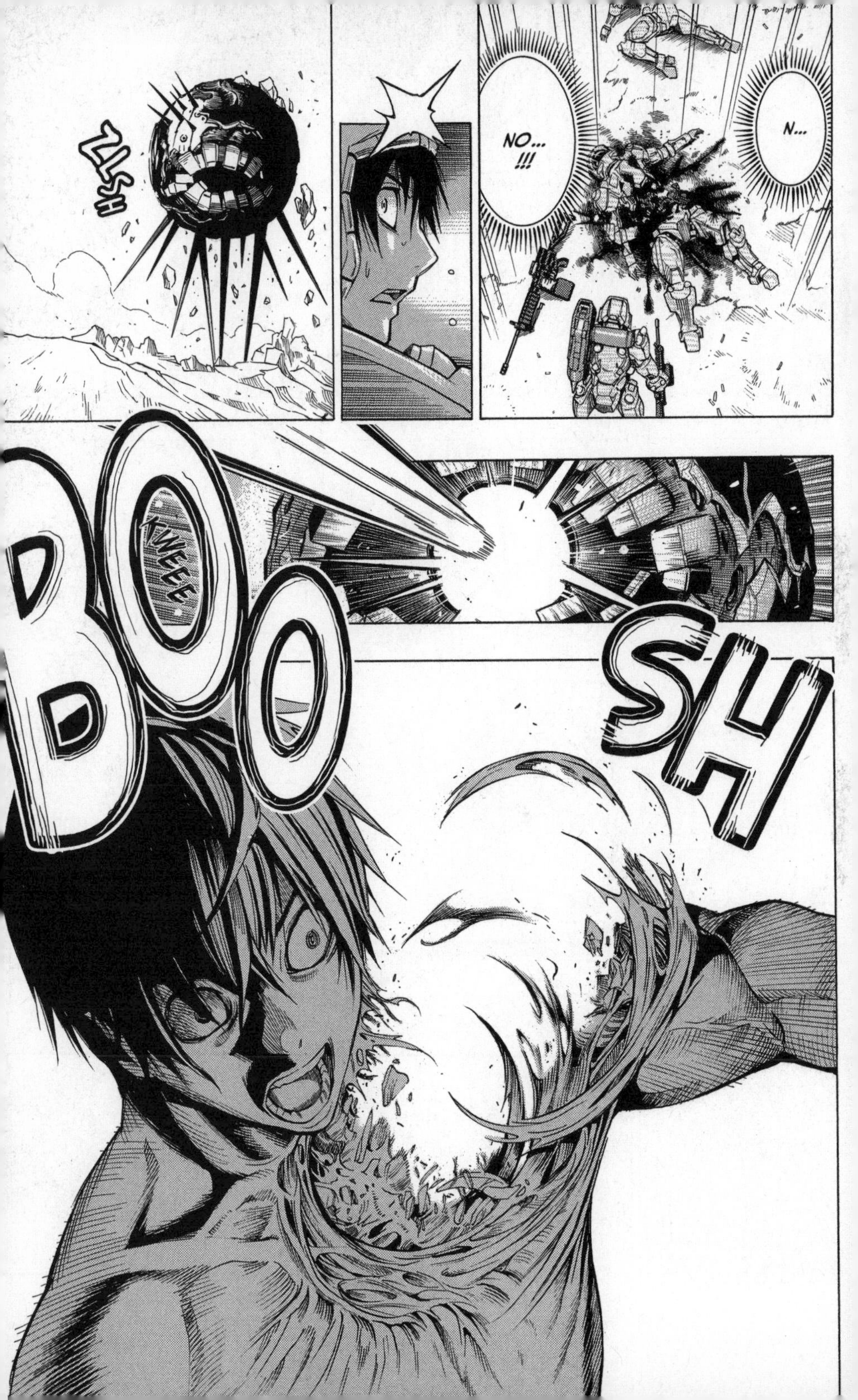
N...
NO... !!!
ZLSH
KWEEEE
BOOOSH

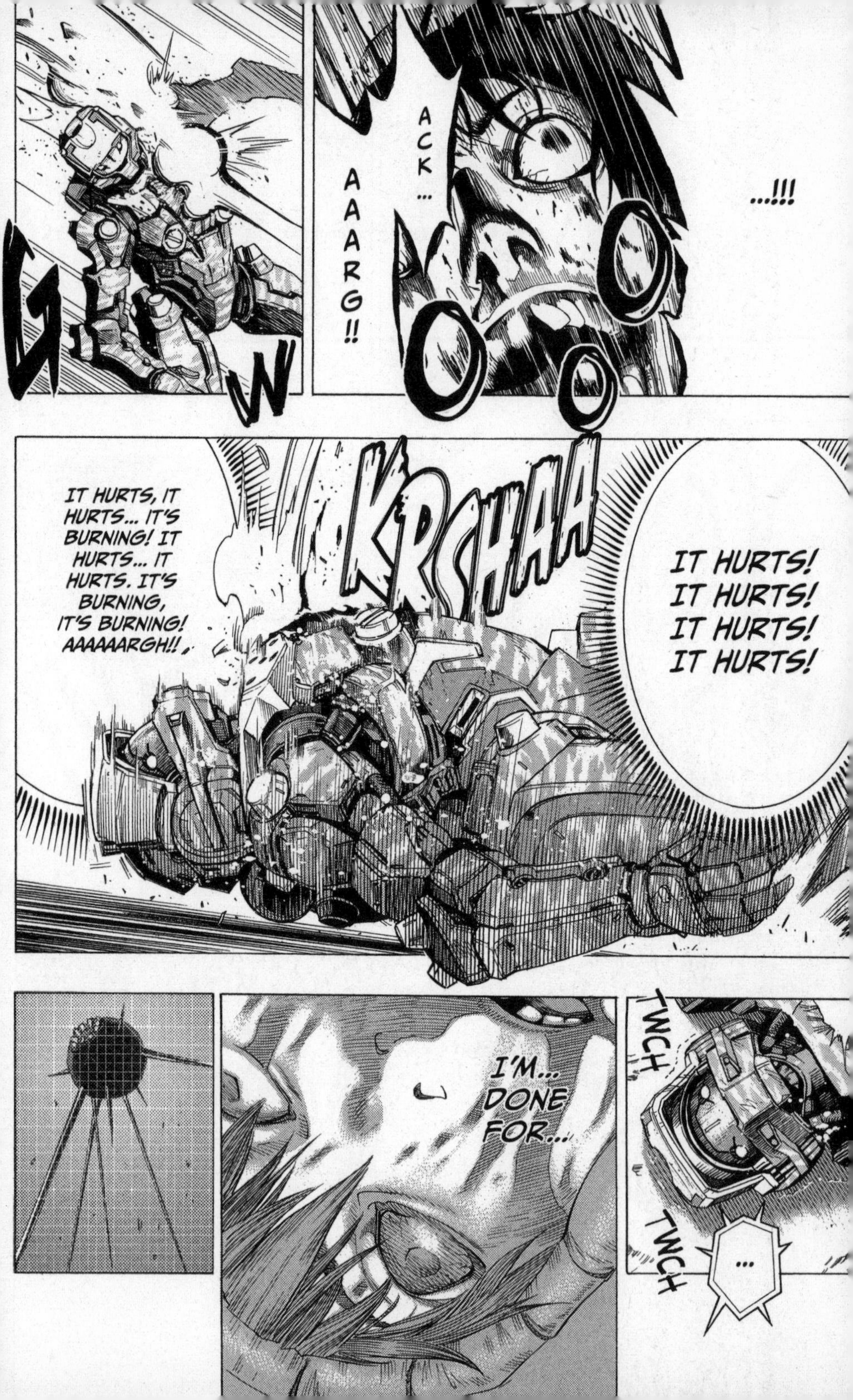
...!!!
ACK...
AAAARG!!
GW
IT HURTS! IT HURTS! IT HURTS! IT HURTS!
KRSHAA
IT HURTS, IT HURTS... IT'S BURNING! IT HURTS... IT HURTS. IT'S BURNING, IT'S BURNING! AAAAAARGH!!
TWCH
...
TWCH
I'M... DONE FOR...

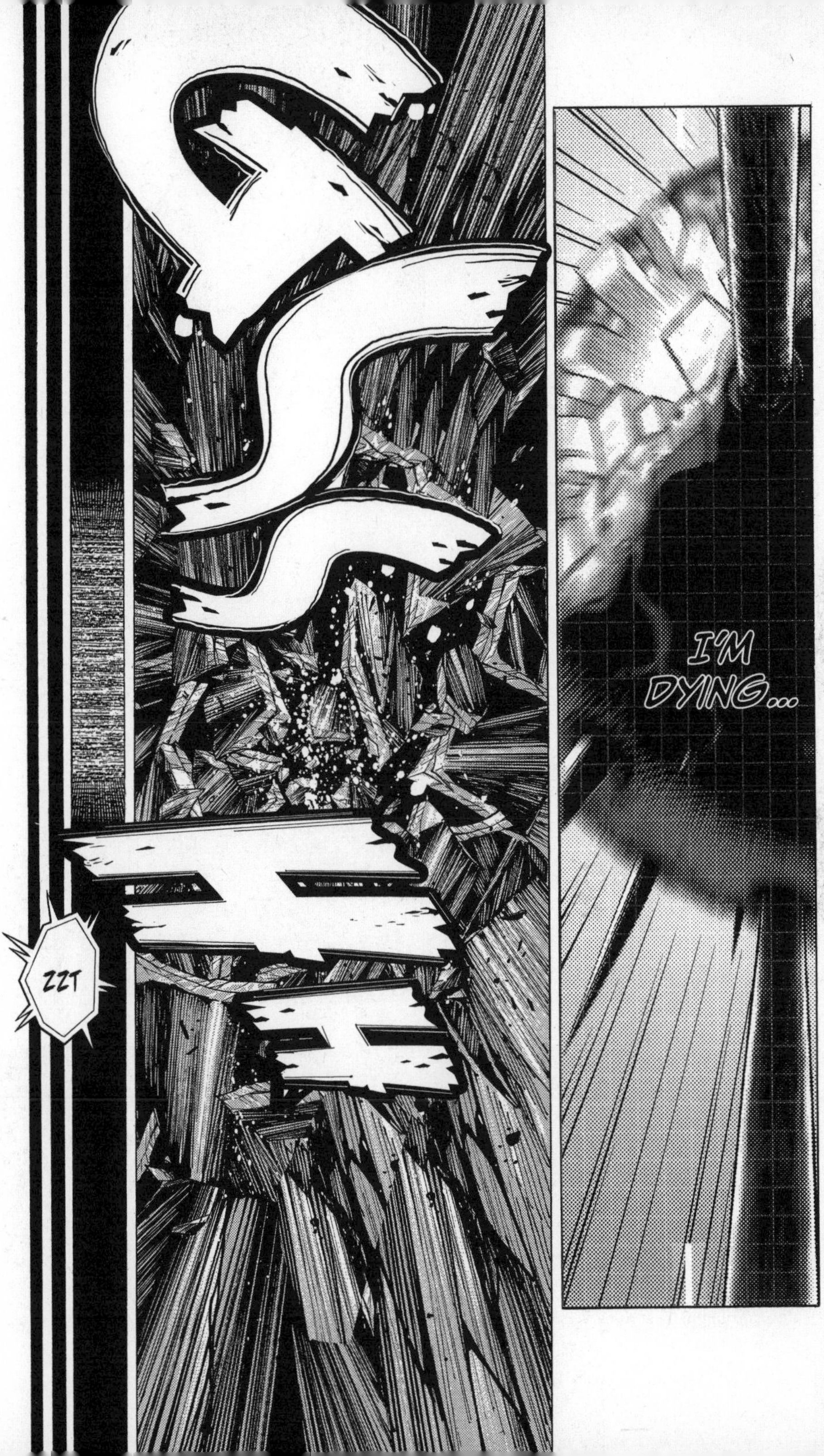
I'M DYING...
ZZT

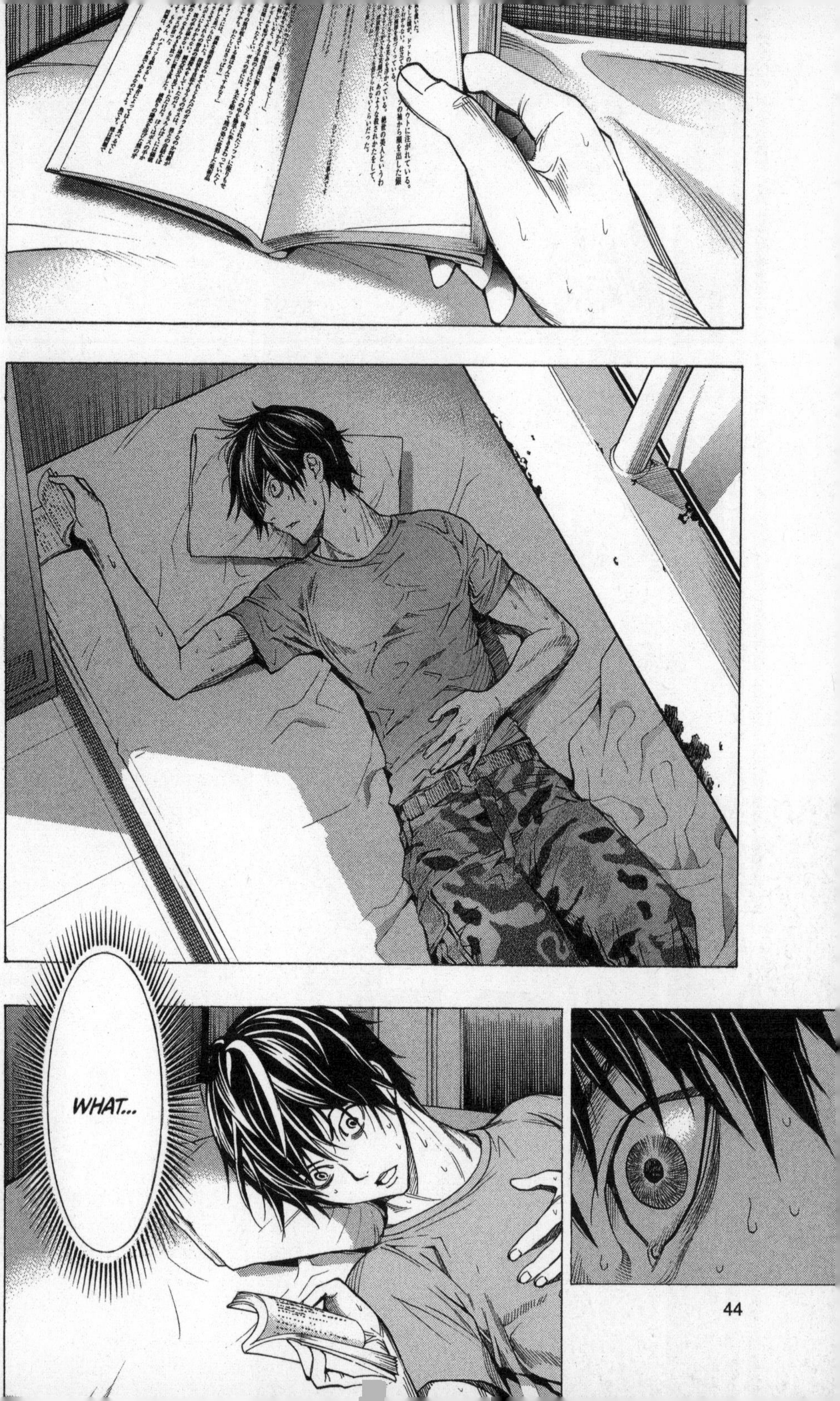
WHAT...

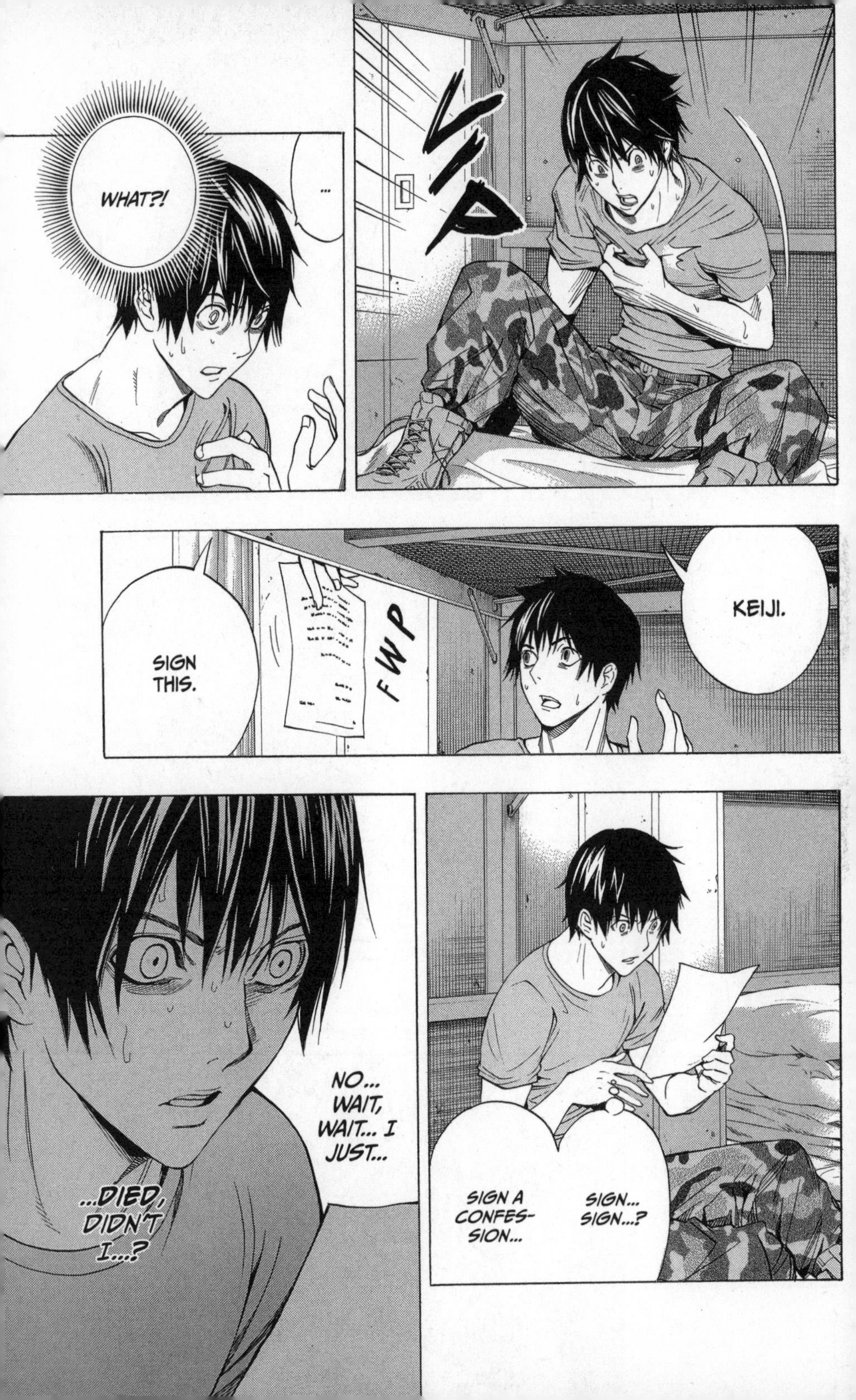
VIP
...
WHAT?!
KEIJI.
FWP
SIGN THIS.
SIGN... SIGN...?
SIGN A CONFES-SION...
NO... WAIT, WAIT... I JUST...
...DIED, DIDN'T I...?

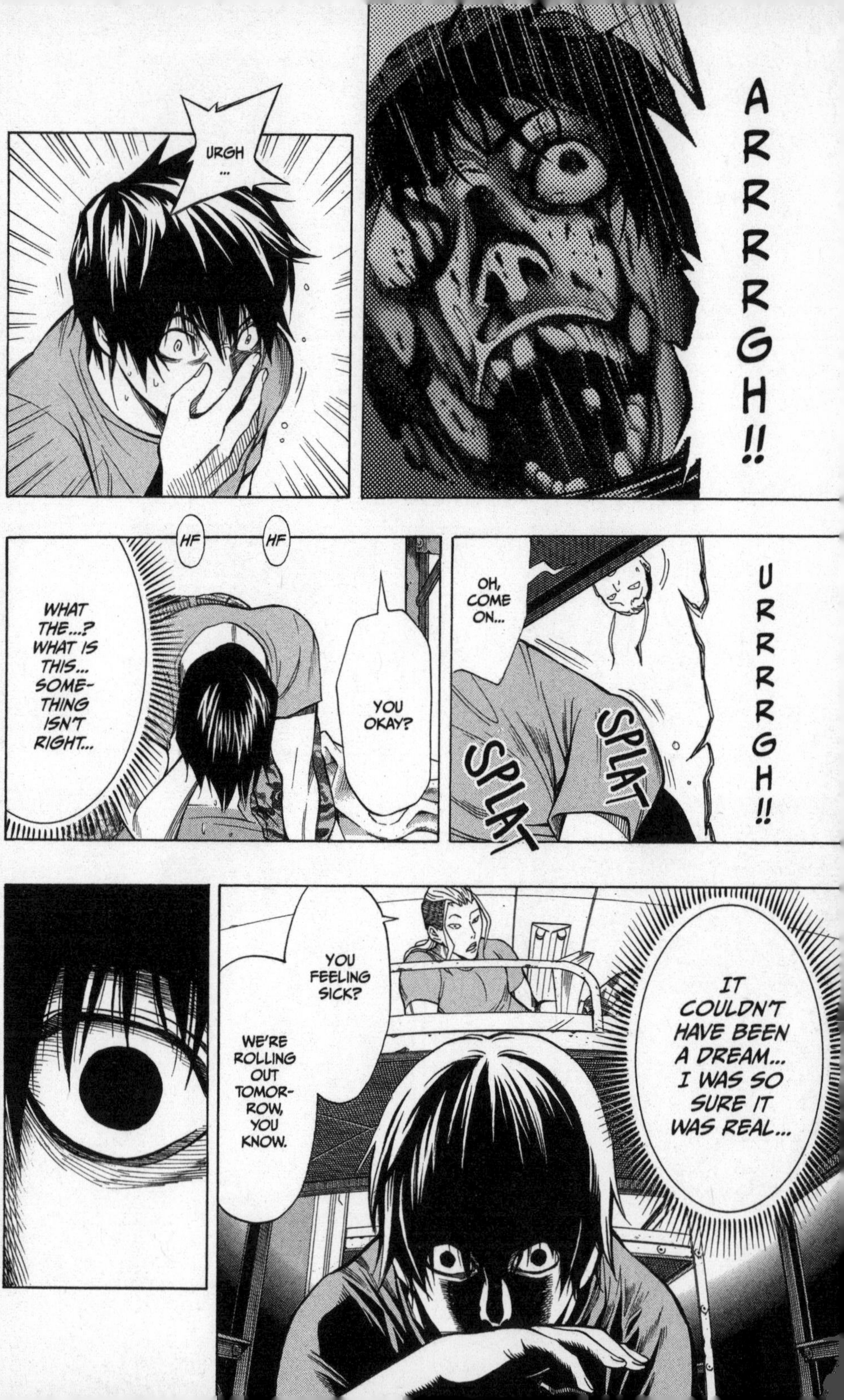
ARRRRGH!!
URGH...
URRRRGH!!
OH, COME ON...
SPLAT
SPLAT
HF
HF
YOU OKAY?
WHAT THE...? WHAT IS THIS... SOMETHING ISN'T RIGHT...
YOU FEELING SICK?
WE'RE ROLLING OUT TOMORROW, YOU KNOW.
IT COULDN'T HAVE BEEN A DREAM... I WAS SO SURE IT WAS REAL...

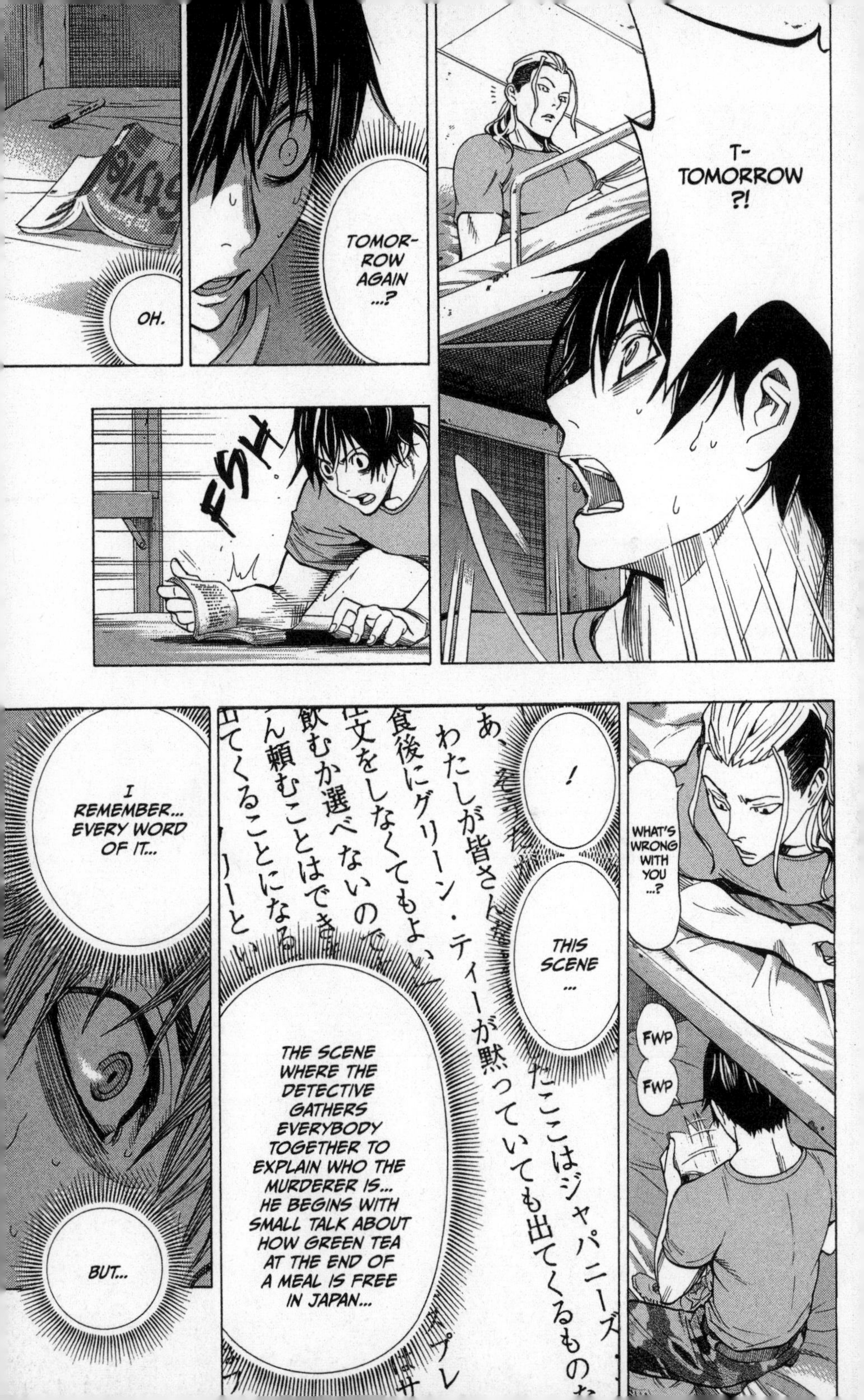
T- TOMORROW ?!
TOMORROW AGAIN ...?
OH.
WHAT'S WRONG WITH YOU ...?
FWP
FWP
!
THIS SCENE ...
THE SCENE WHERE THE DETECTIVE GATHERS EVERYBODY TOGETHER TO EXPLAIN WHO THE MURDERER IS... HE BEGINS WITH SMALL TALK ABOUT HOW GREEN TEA AT THE END OF A MEAL IS FREE IN JAPAN...
I REMEMBER... EVERY WORD OF IT...
BUT...

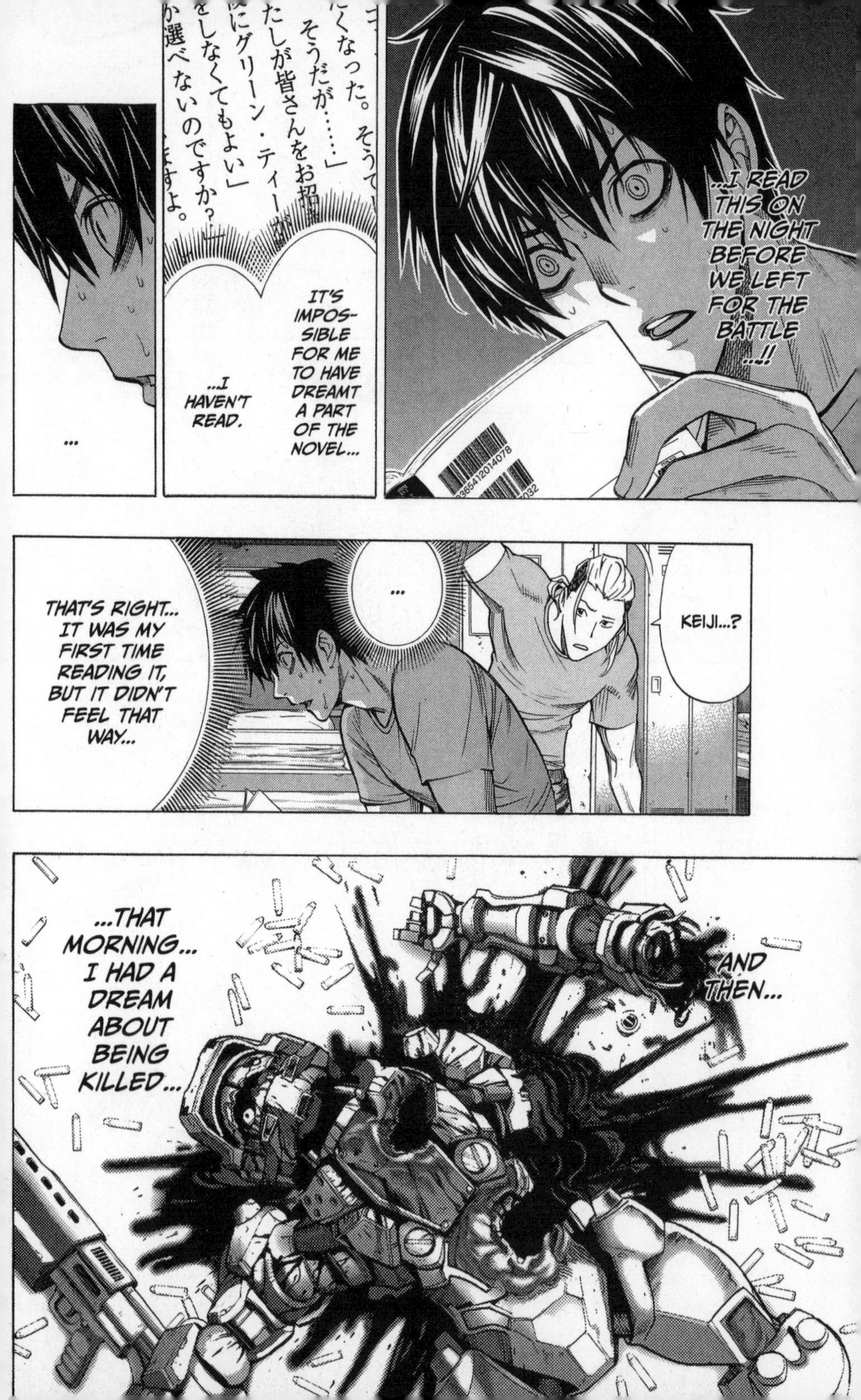
...I READ THIS ON THE NIGHT BEFORE WE LEFT FOR THE BATTLE...!!
くなった。そうで
そうだが……」
たしが皆さんをお招
にグリーン・ティーが
をしなくてもよい」
か選べないのですか？」
ますよ。
IT'S IMPOSSIBLE FOR ME TO HAVE DREAMT A PART OF THE NOVEL...
...I HAVEN'T READ.
...
KEIJI...?
...
THAT'S RIGHT... IT WAS MY FIRST TIME READING IT, BUT IT DIDN'T FEEL THAT WAY...
AND THEN...
...THAT MORNING... I HAD A DREAM ABOUT BEING KILLED...

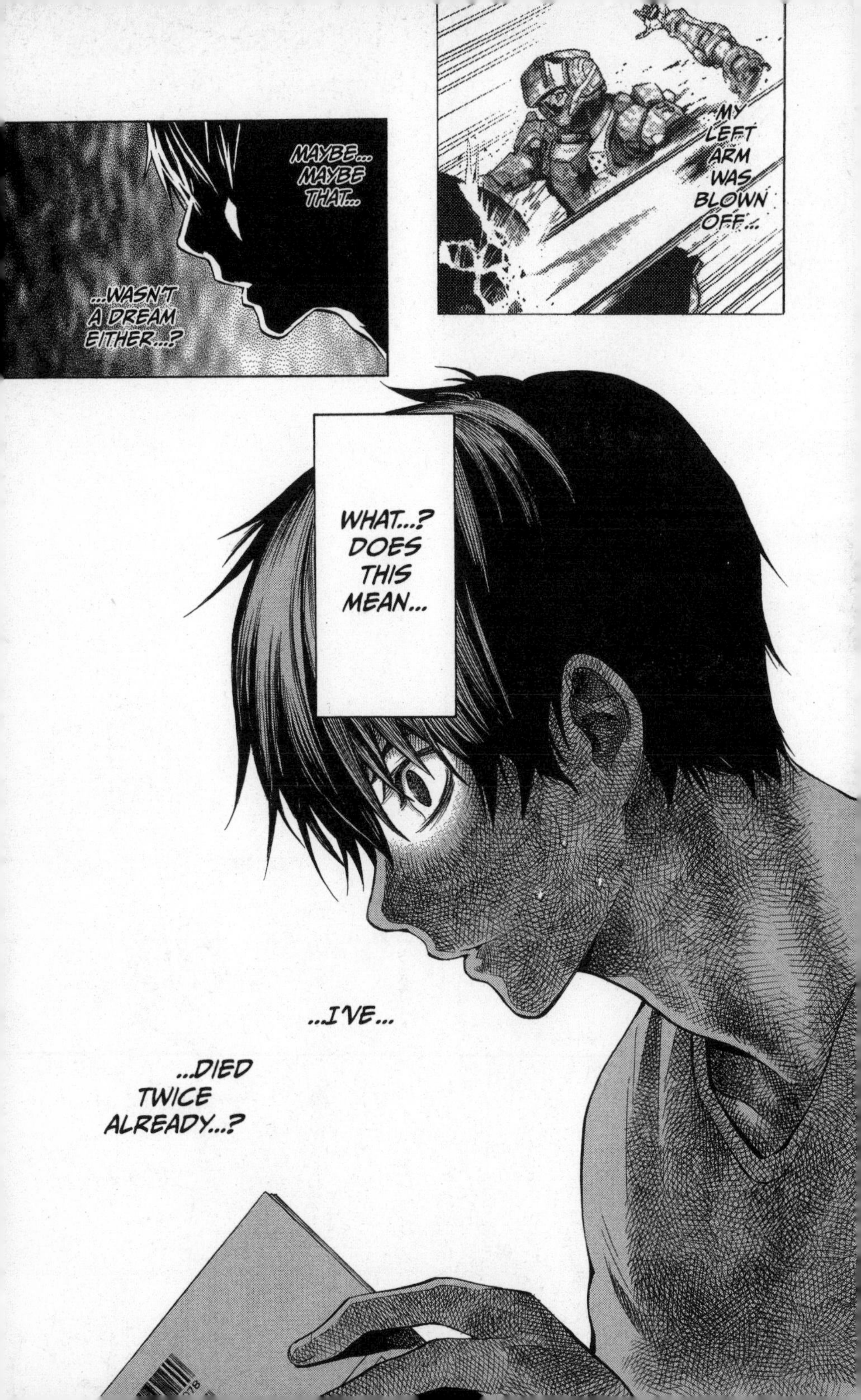
MY LEFT ARM WAS BLOWN OFF...
MAYBE... MAYBE THAT...
...WASN'T A DREAM EITHER...?
WHAT...? DOES THIS MEAN...
...I'VE...
...DIED TWICE ALREADY...?

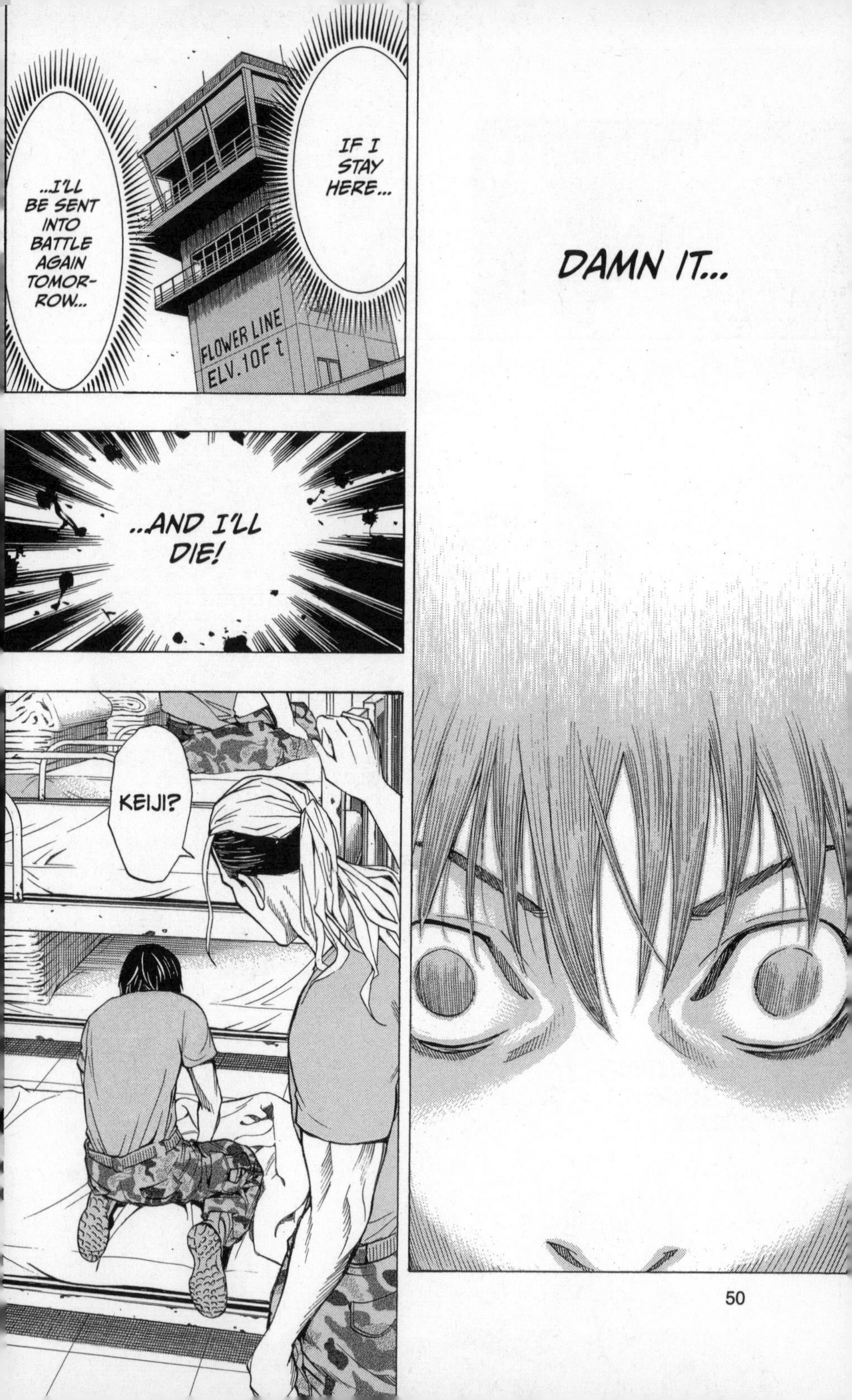
DAMN IT...
IF I STAY HERE...
...I'LL BE SENT INTO BATTLE AGAIN TOMOR-ROW...
FLOWER LINE ELV.10F t
...AND I'LL DIE!
KEIJI?

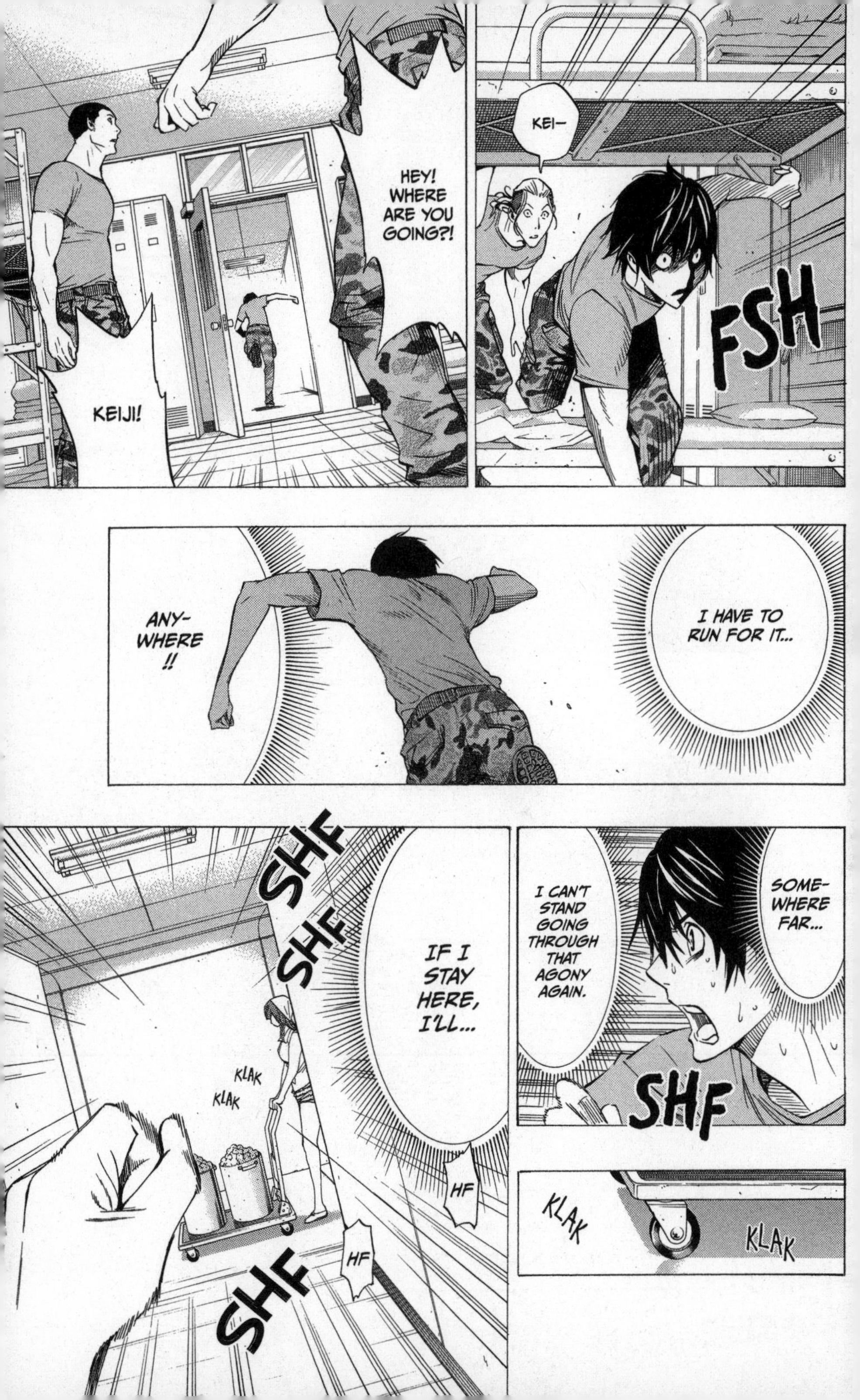
KEI—
FSH
HEY! WHERE ARE YOU GOING?!
KEIJI!
I HAVE TO RUN FOR IT...
ANY-WHERE !!
SOME-WHERE FAR...
I CAN'T STAND GOING THROUGH THAT AGONY AGAIN.
SHF
KLAK
KLAK
SHF
SHF
IF I STAY HERE, I'LL...
KLAK
KLAK
HF
HF
SHF

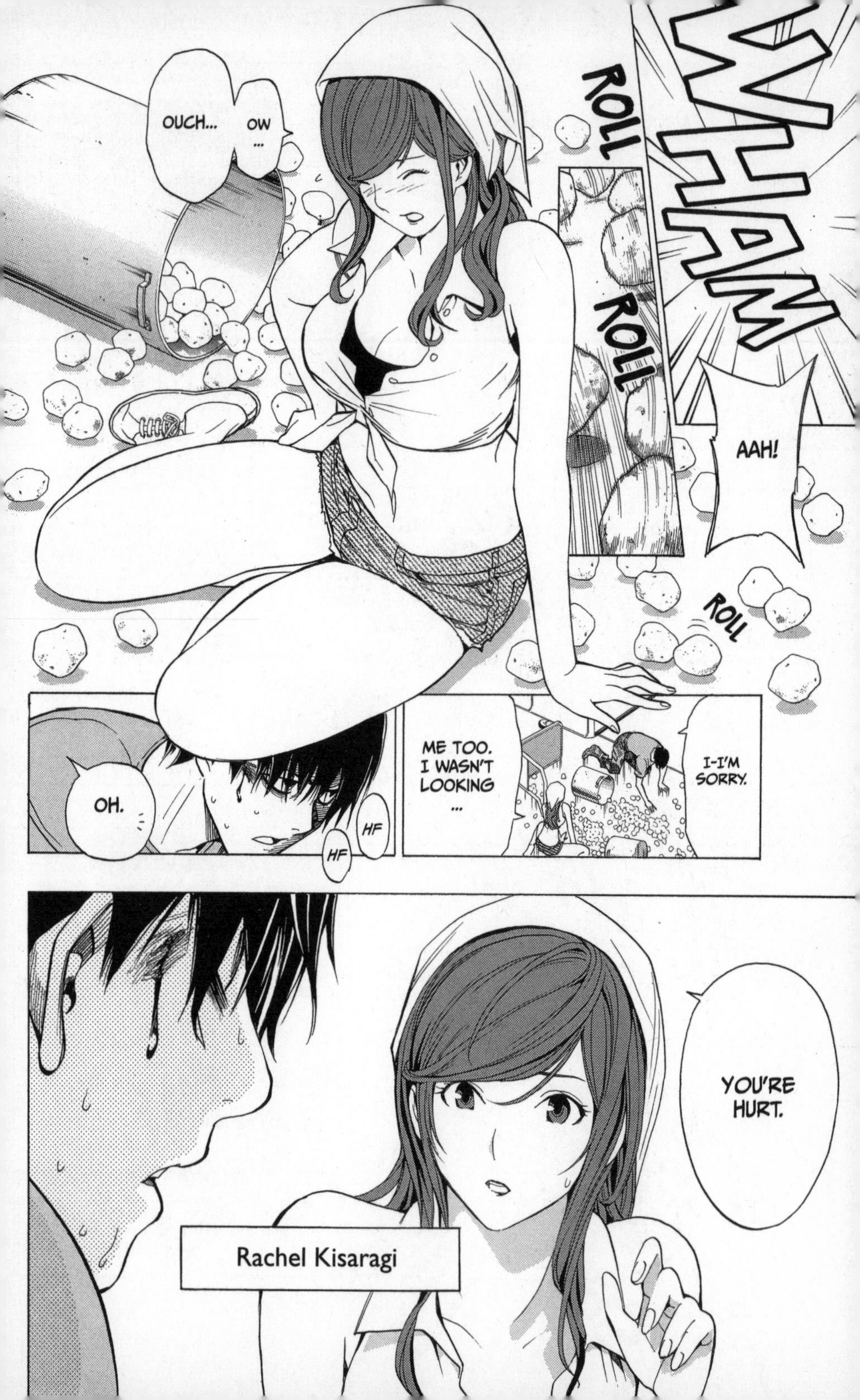
WHAM
ROLL
ROLL
AAH!
OUCH...
OW ...
ROLL
I-I'M SORRY.
ME TOO. I WASN'T LOOKING ...
OH.
HF
HF
YOU'RE HURT.
Rachel Kisaragi

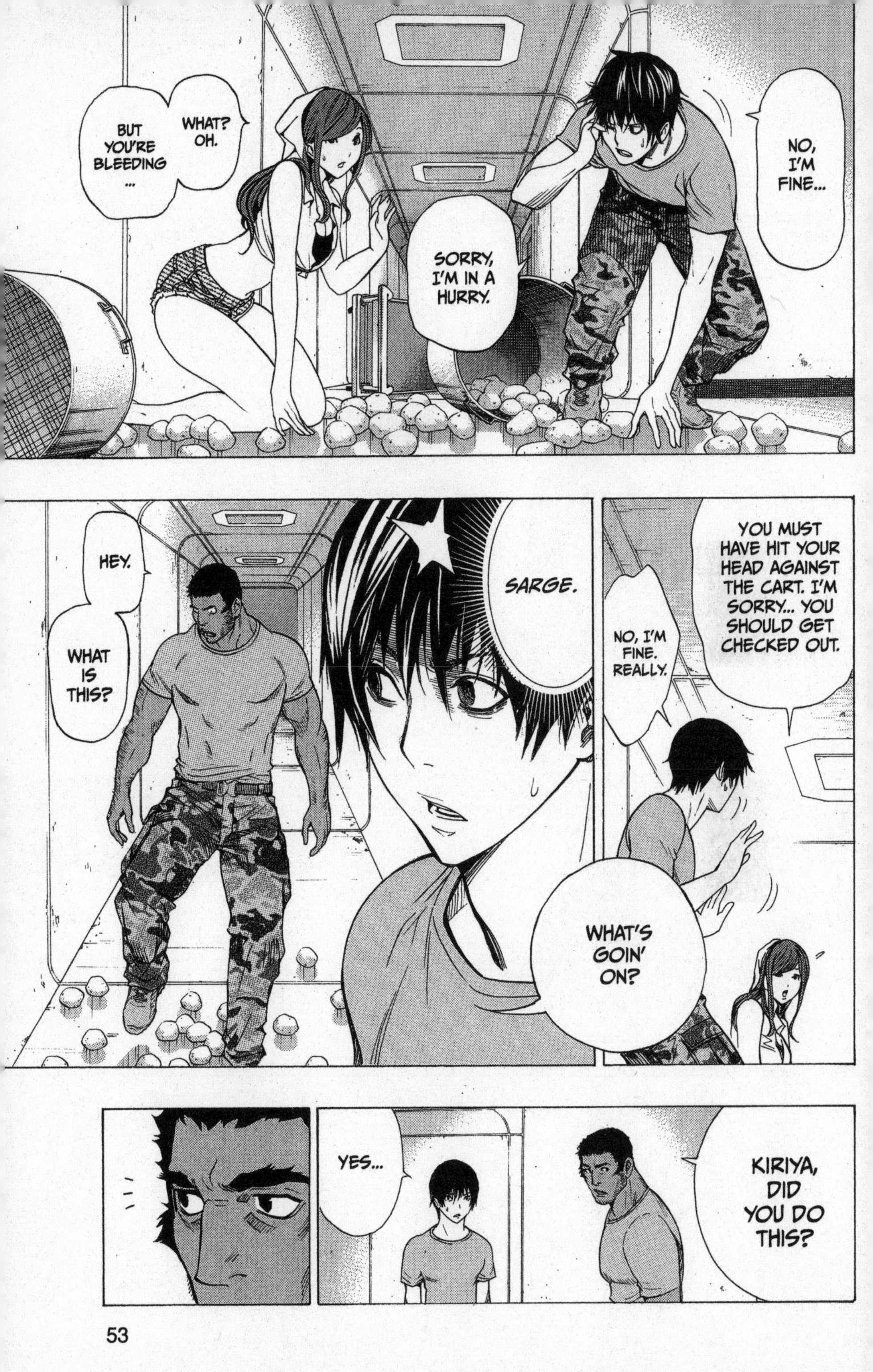
SORRY, I'M IN A HURRY.
WHAT? OH.
BUT YOU'RE BLEEDING ...
NO, I'M FINE...
YOU MUST HAVE HIT YOUR HEAD AGAINST THE CART. I'M SORRY... YOU SHOULD GET CHECKED OUT.
NO, I'M FINE. REALLY.
WHAT'S GOIN' ON?
SARGE.
HEY.
WHAT IS THIS?
KIRIYA, DID YOU DO THIS?
YES...

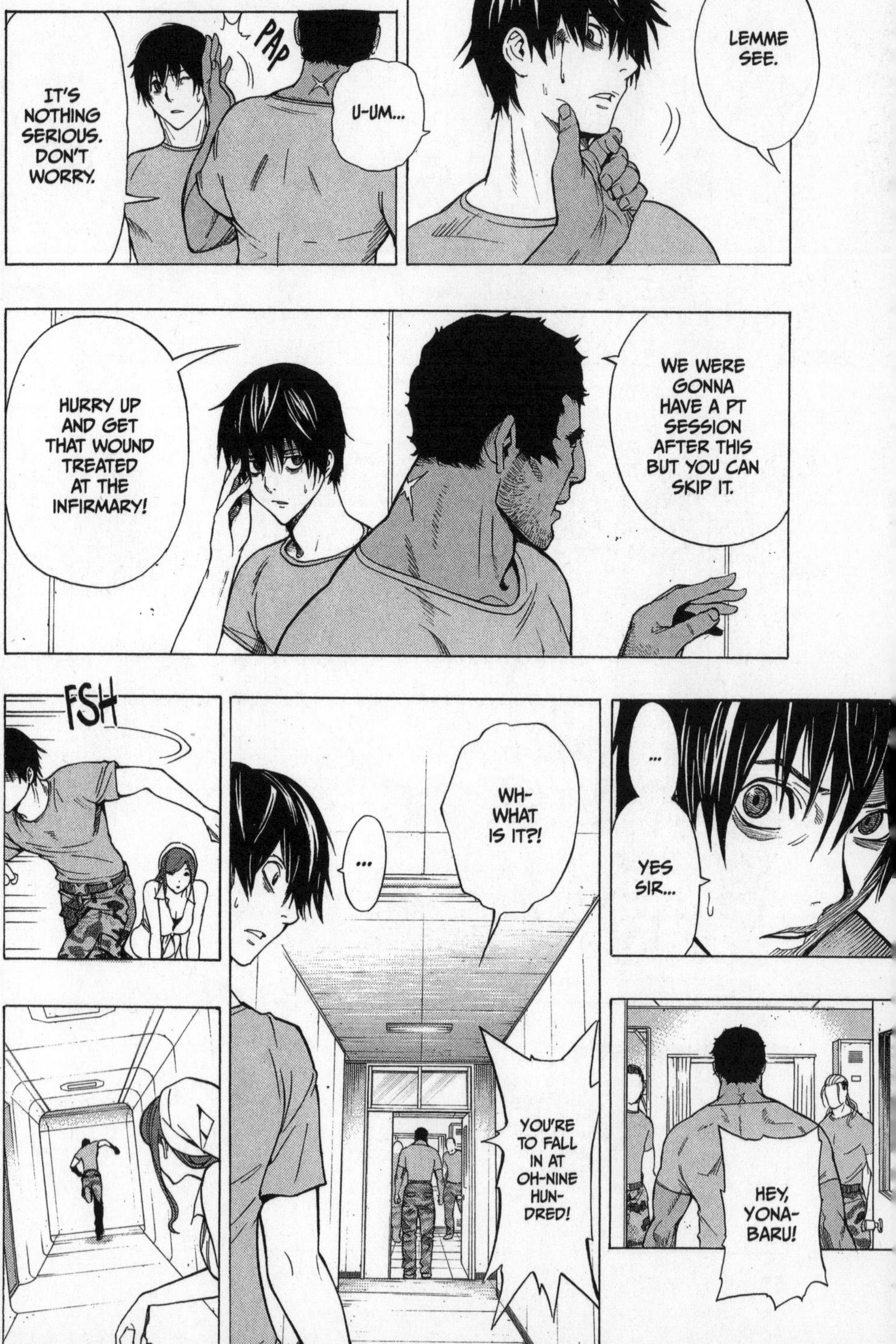
LEMME SEE.
PAP
U-UM...
IT'S NOTHING SERIOUS. DON'T WORRY.
WE WERE GONNA HAVE A PT SESSION AFTER THIS BUT YOU CAN SKIP IT.
HURRY UP AND GET THAT WOUND TREATED AT THE INFIRMARY!
...
YES SIR...
HEY, YONA-BARU!
WH- WHAT IS IT?!
...
YOU'RE TO FALL IN AT OH-NINE HUN-DRED!
FSH

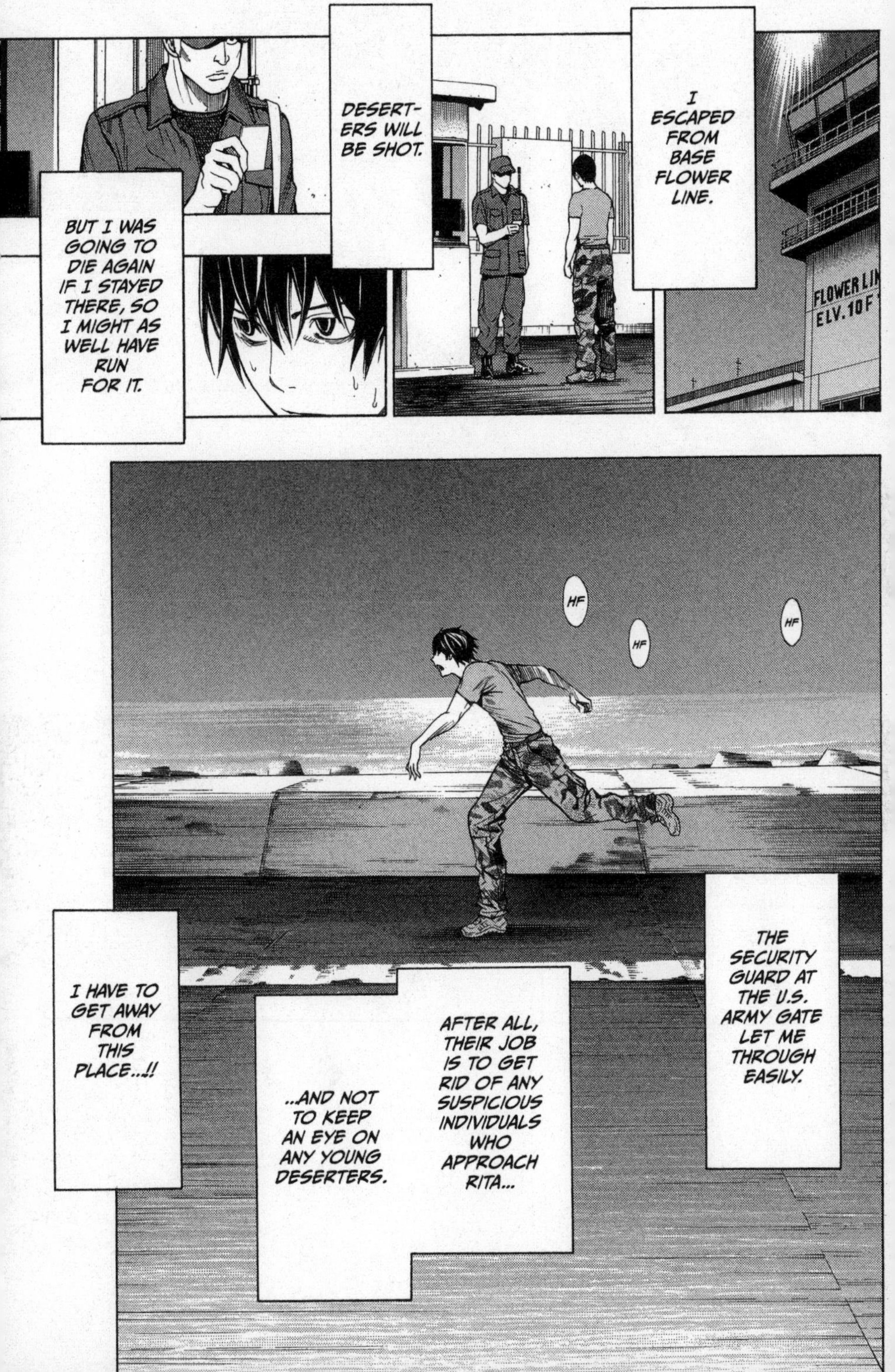
I ESCAPED FROM BASE FLOWER LINE.
FLOWER LIN
ELV. 10 F
DESERTERS WILL BE SHOT.
BUT I WAS GOING TO DIE AGAIN IF I STAYED THERE, SO I MIGHT AS WELL HAVE RUN FOR IT.
HF
HF
HF
THE SECURITY GUARD AT THE U.S. ARMY GATE LET ME THROUGH EASILY.
AFTER ALL, THEIR JOB IS TO GET RID OF ANY SUSPICIOUS INDIVIDUALS WHO APPROACH RITA...
...AND NOT TO KEEP AN EYE ON ANY YOUNG DESERTERS.
I HAVE TO GET AWAY FROM THIS PLACE...!!

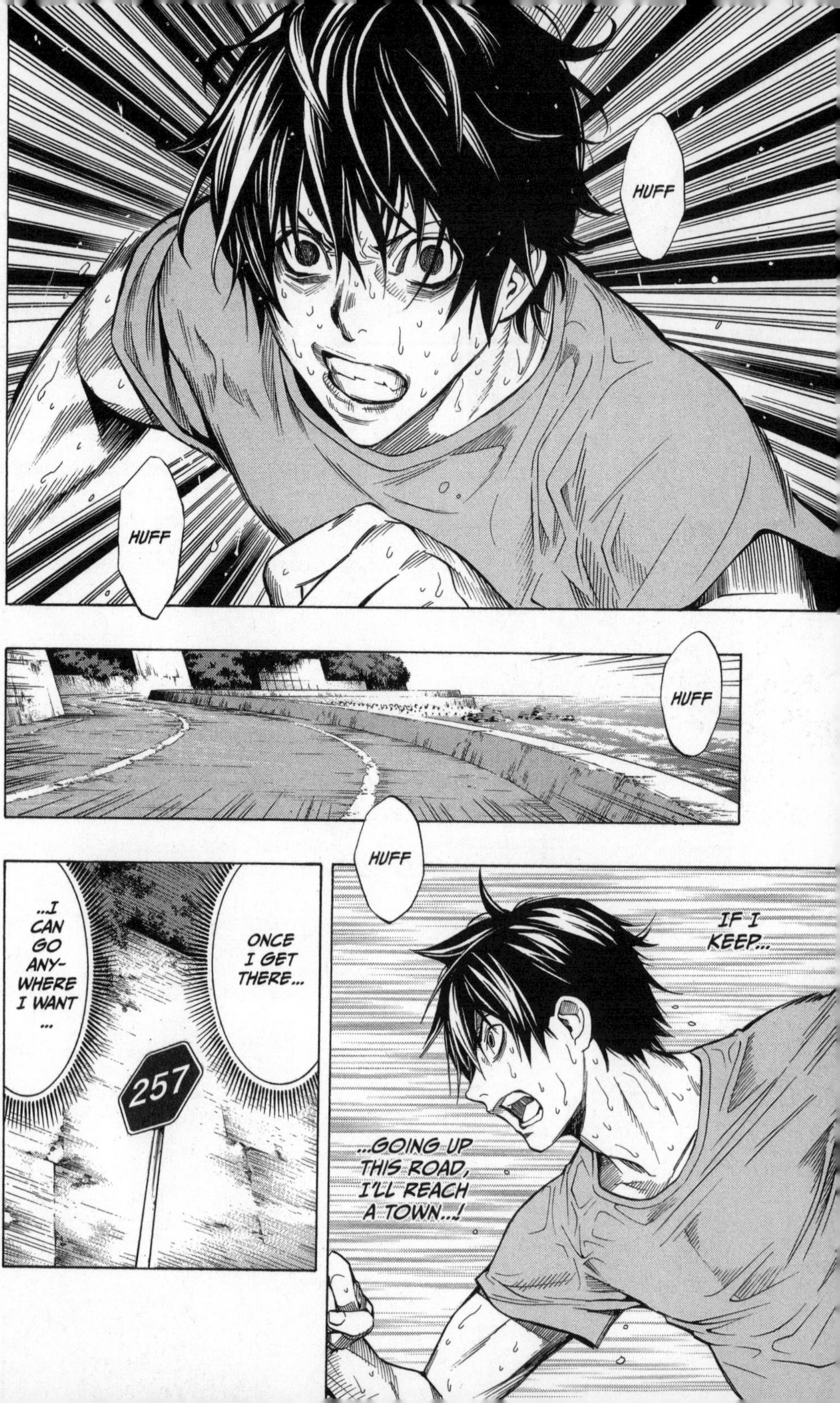
HUFF
HUFF
HUFF
HUFF
IF I KEEP...
...GOING UP THIS ROAD, I'LL REACH A TOWN...!
ONCE I GET THERE...
...I CAN GO ANYWHERE I WANT...
257

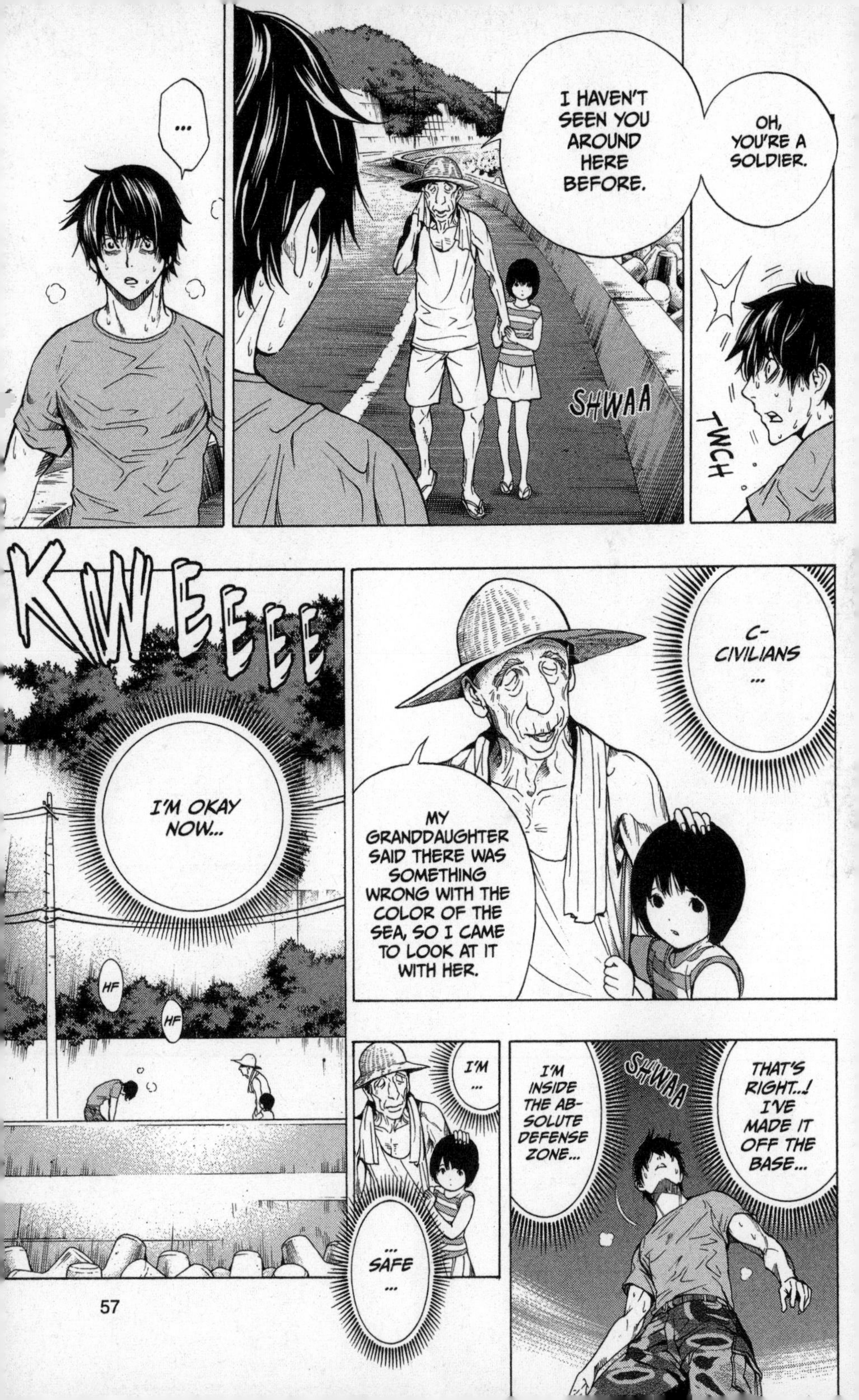
OH, YOU'RE A SOLDIER.
TWCH
I HAVEN'T SEEN YOU AROUND HERE BEFORE.
SHWAA
...
C-CIVILIANS...
MY GRANDDAUGHTER SAID THERE WAS SOMETHING WRONG WITH THE COLOR OF THE SEA, SO I CAME TO LOOK AT IT WITH HER.
THAT'S RIGHT...! I'VE MADE IT OFF THE BASE...
SHWAA
I'M INSIDE THE AB-SOLUTE DEFENSE ZONE...
I'M...
...SAFE...
KWEEEE
I'M OKAY NOW...
HF
HF

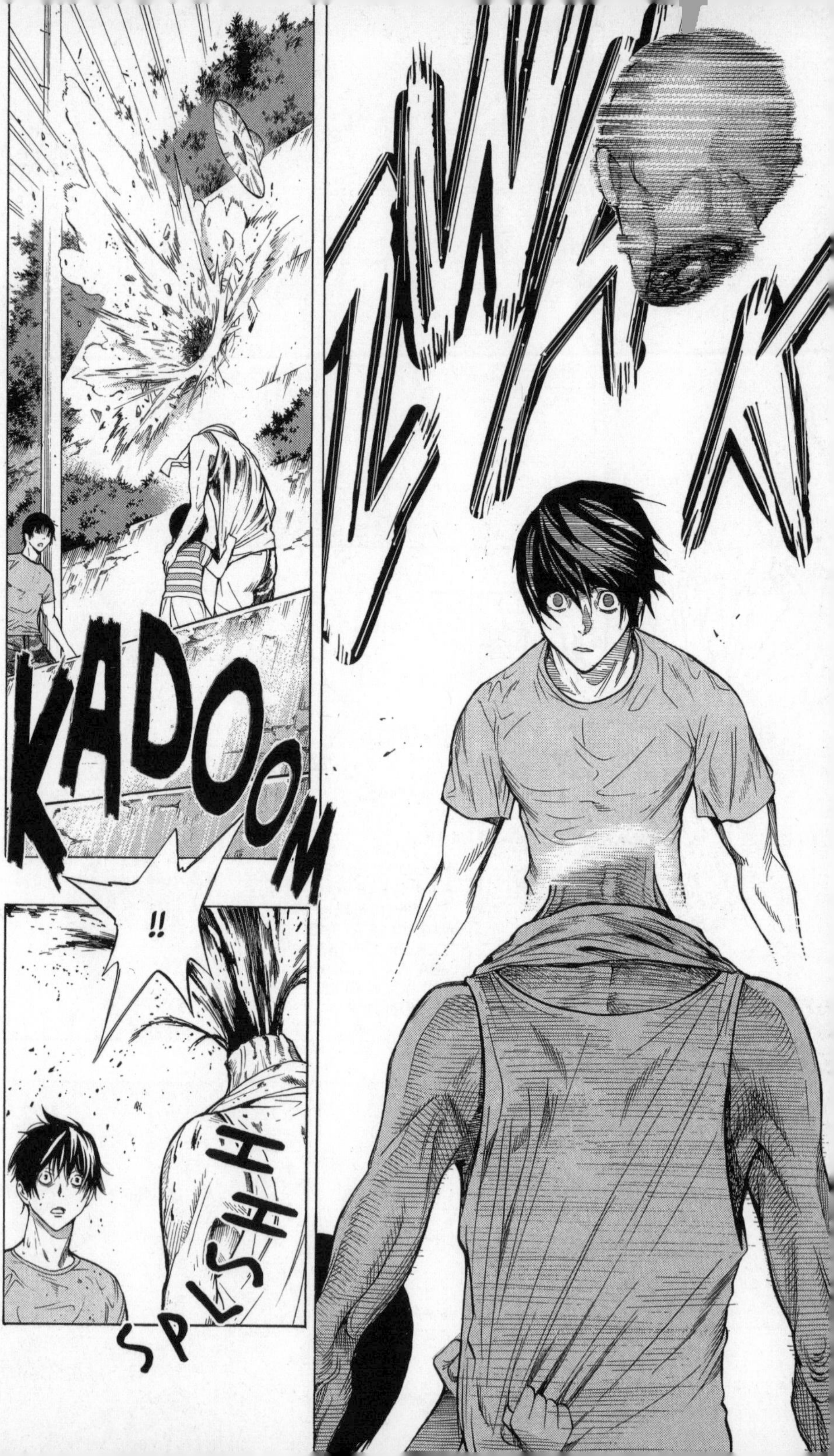
KADOOM
!!
SPLSHHH

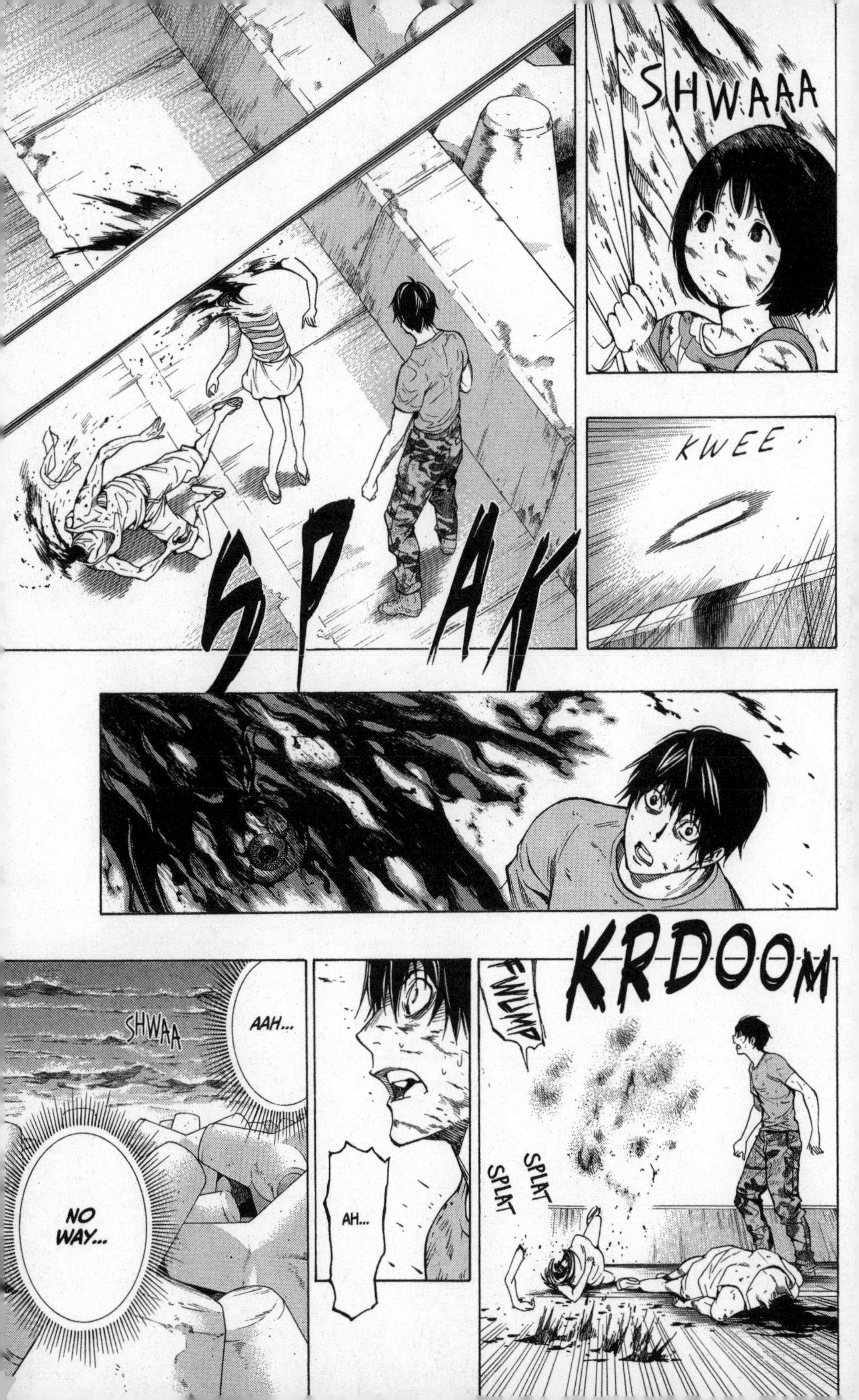
SHWAAA
KWEE
SPAK
KRDOOM
FWUMP
SPLAT
SPLAT
AH...
SHWAA
AAH...
NO WAY...

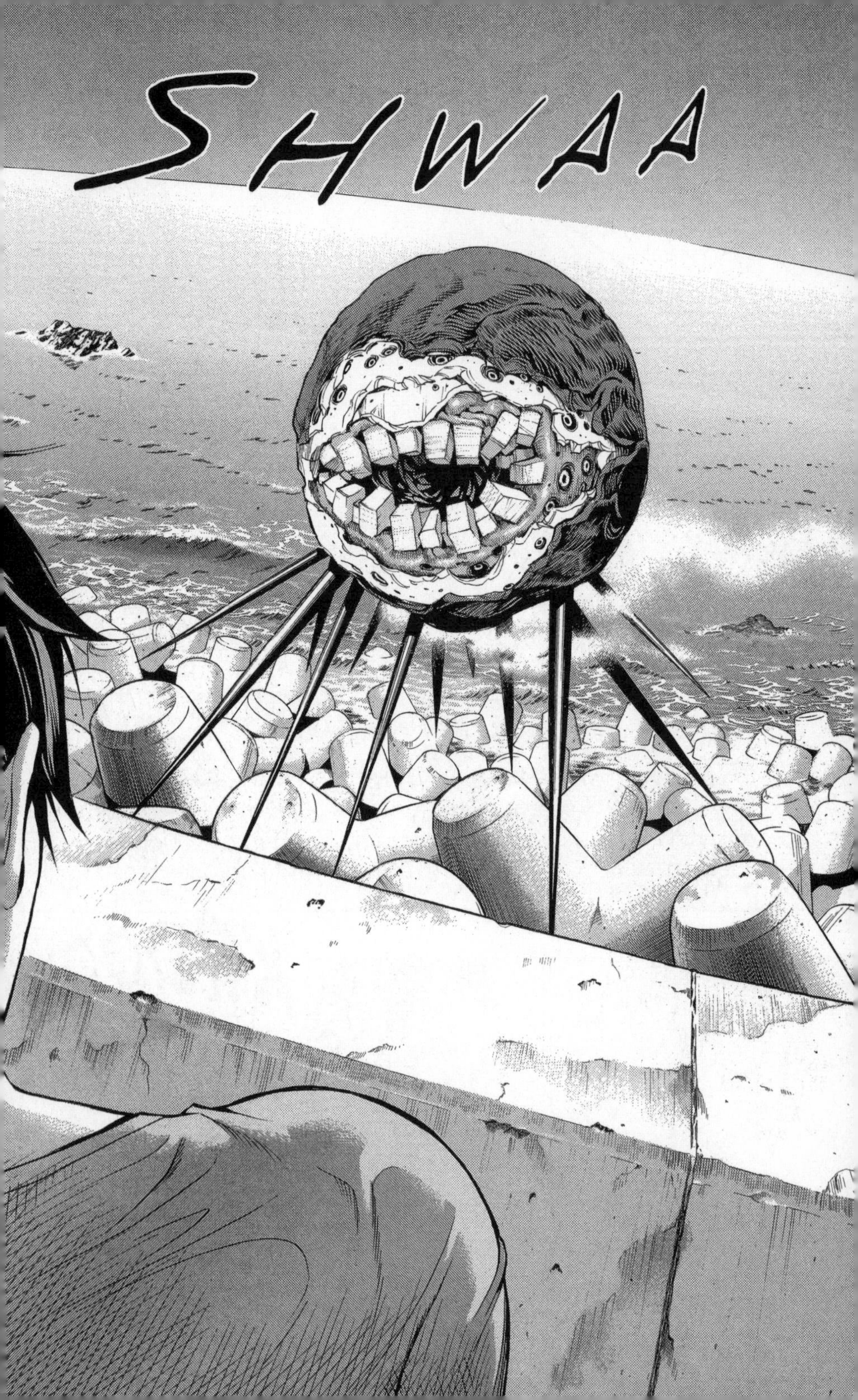
SHWAA

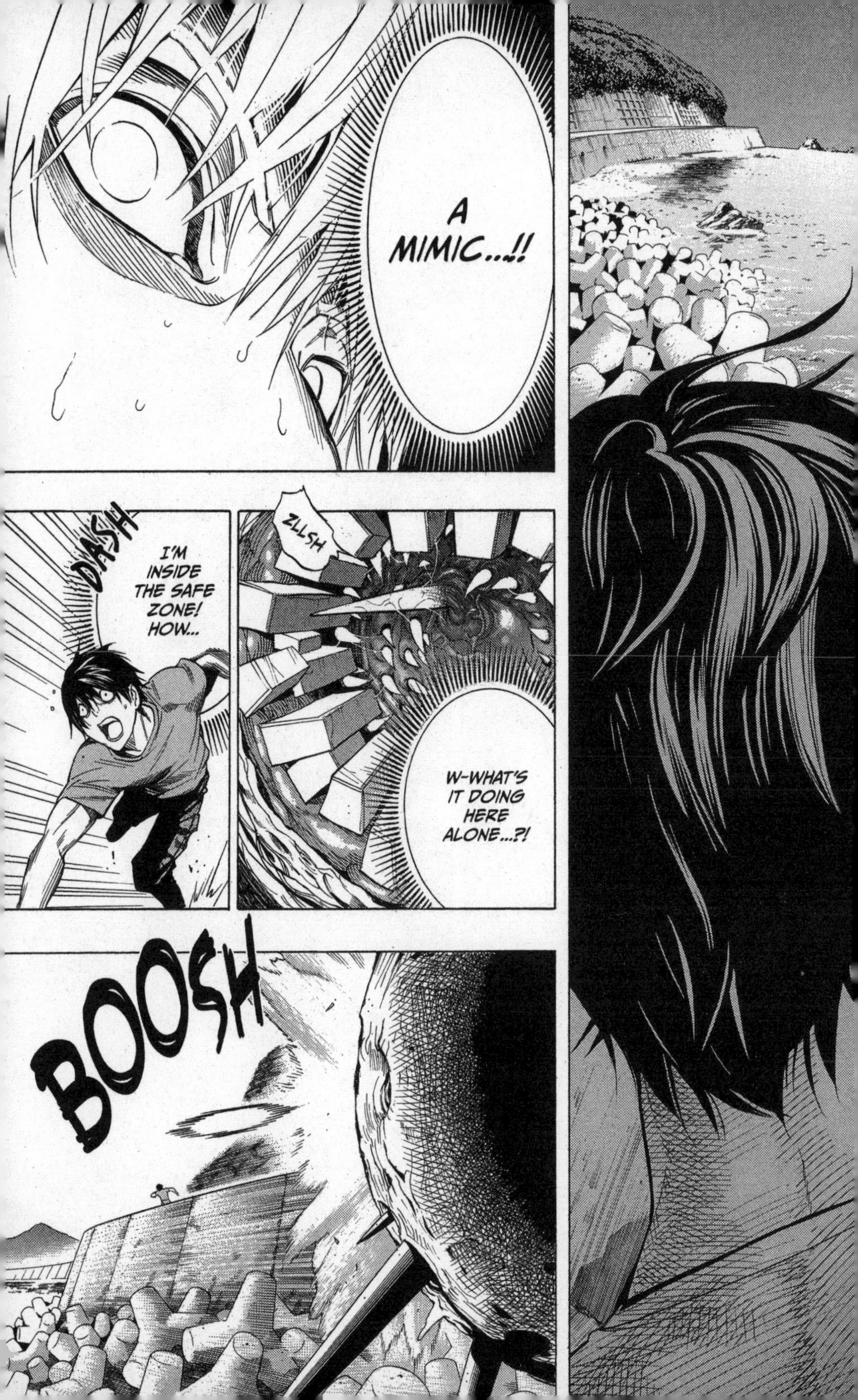
A MIMIC...!!
ZLLSH
W-WHAT'S IT DOING HERE ALONE...?!
DASH
I'M INSIDE THE SAFE ZONE! HOW...
BOOSH

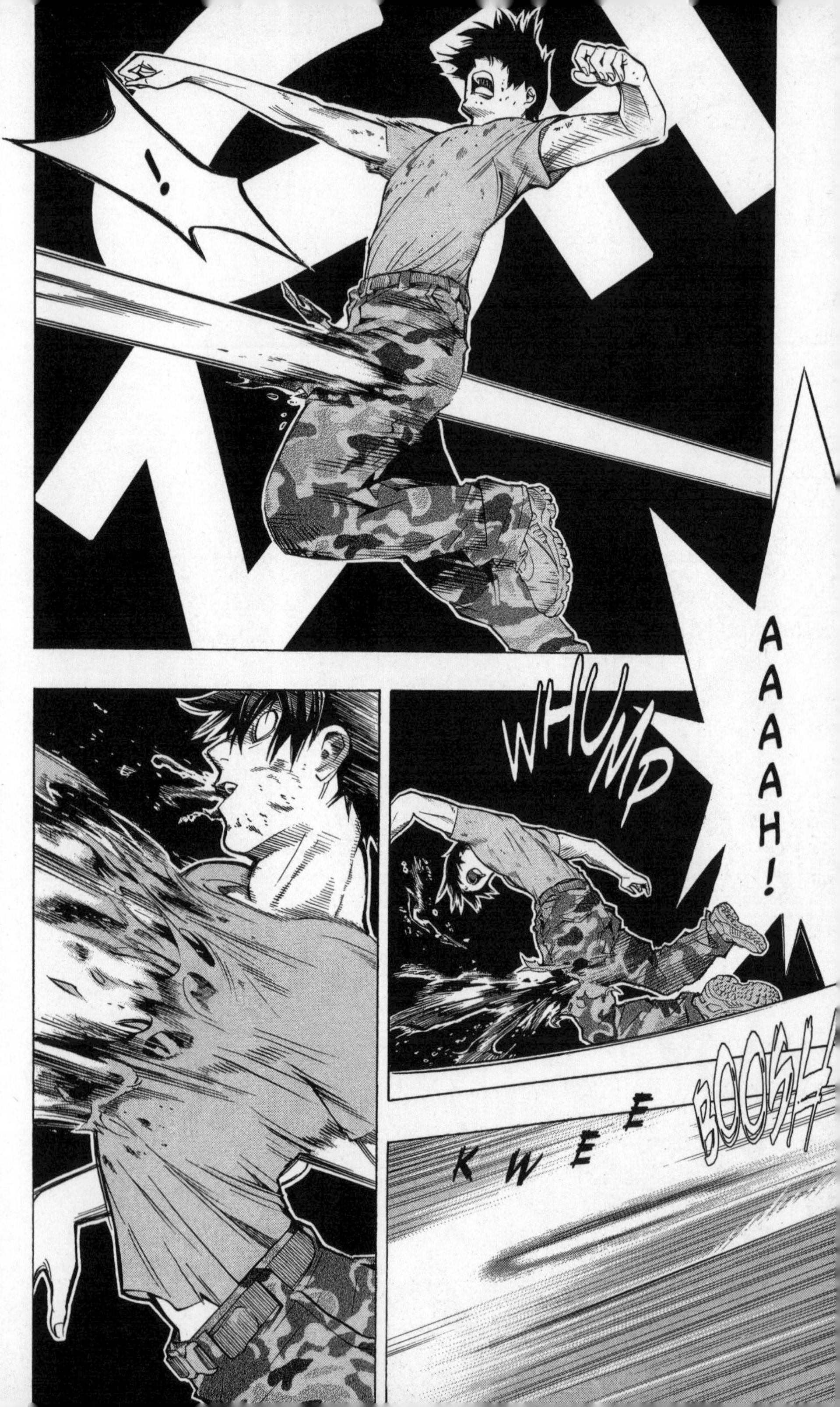
!
AAAAH!
WHUMP
KWEE
BOOSH

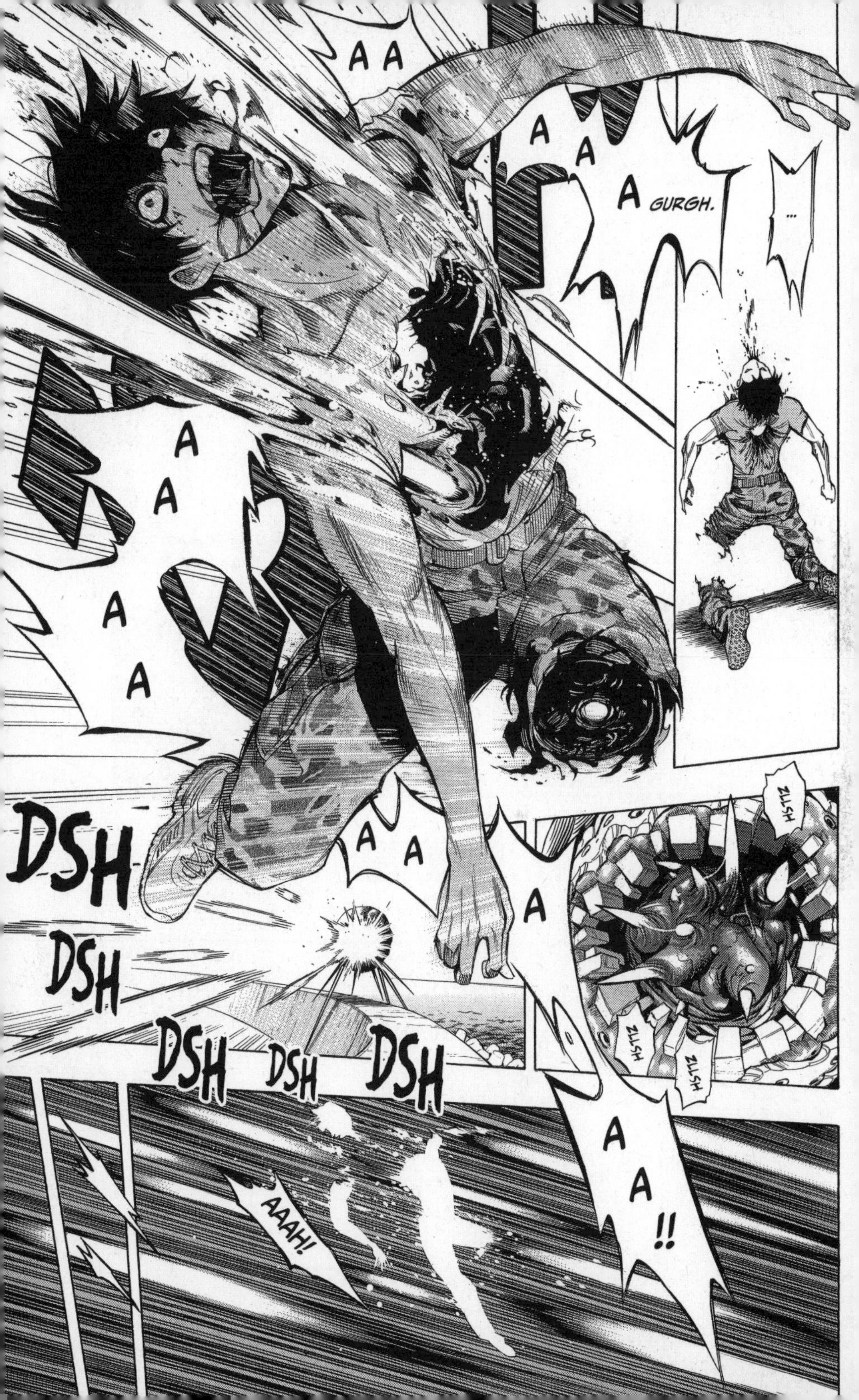
...
AAAAAAAAAAAAAAAA
GURGH.
ZLLSH
ZLLSH
ZLLSH
DSH
DSH
DSH
DSH
DSH
AAAH!
!!

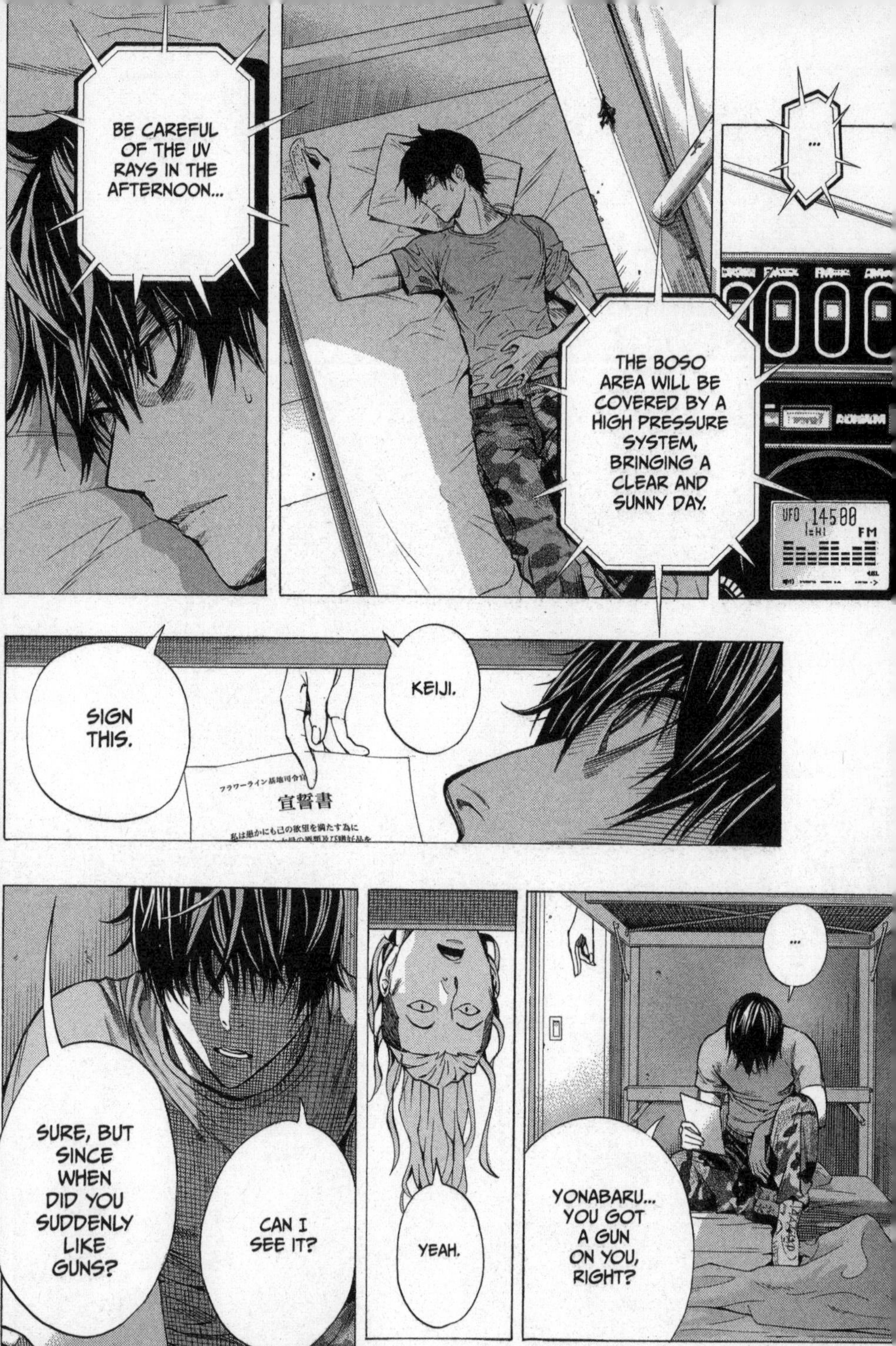
...
THE BOSO AREA WILL BE COVERED BY A HIGH PRESSURE SYSTEM, BRINGING A CLEAR AND SUNNY DAY.
BE CAREFUL OF THE UV RAYS IN THE AFTERNOON...
UFO 145.00 FM
KEIJI.
SIGN THIS.
フラワーライン基地司令官
宣誓書
...
YONABARU... YOU GOT A GUN ON YOU, RIGHT?
YEAH.
CAN I SEE IT?
SURE, BUT SINCE WHEN DID YOU SUDDENLY LIKE GUNS?

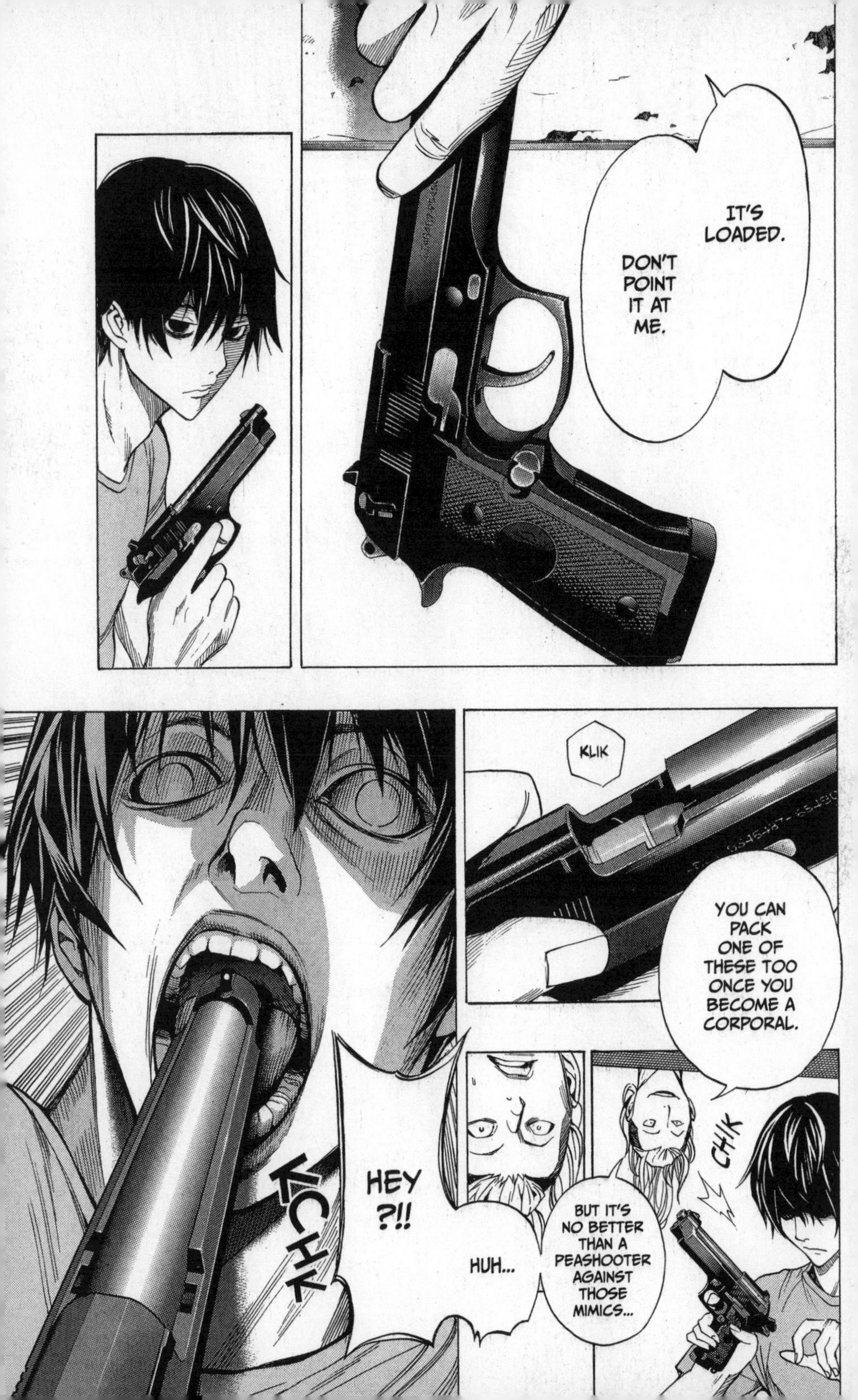
IT'S LOADED.
DON'T POINT IT AT ME.
KLIK
YOU CAN PACK ONE OF THESE TOO ONCE YOU BECOME A CORPORAL.
CHIK
BUT IT'S NO BETTER THAN A PEASHOOTER AGAINST THOSE MIMICS...
HUH...
HEY ?!!
KCHK

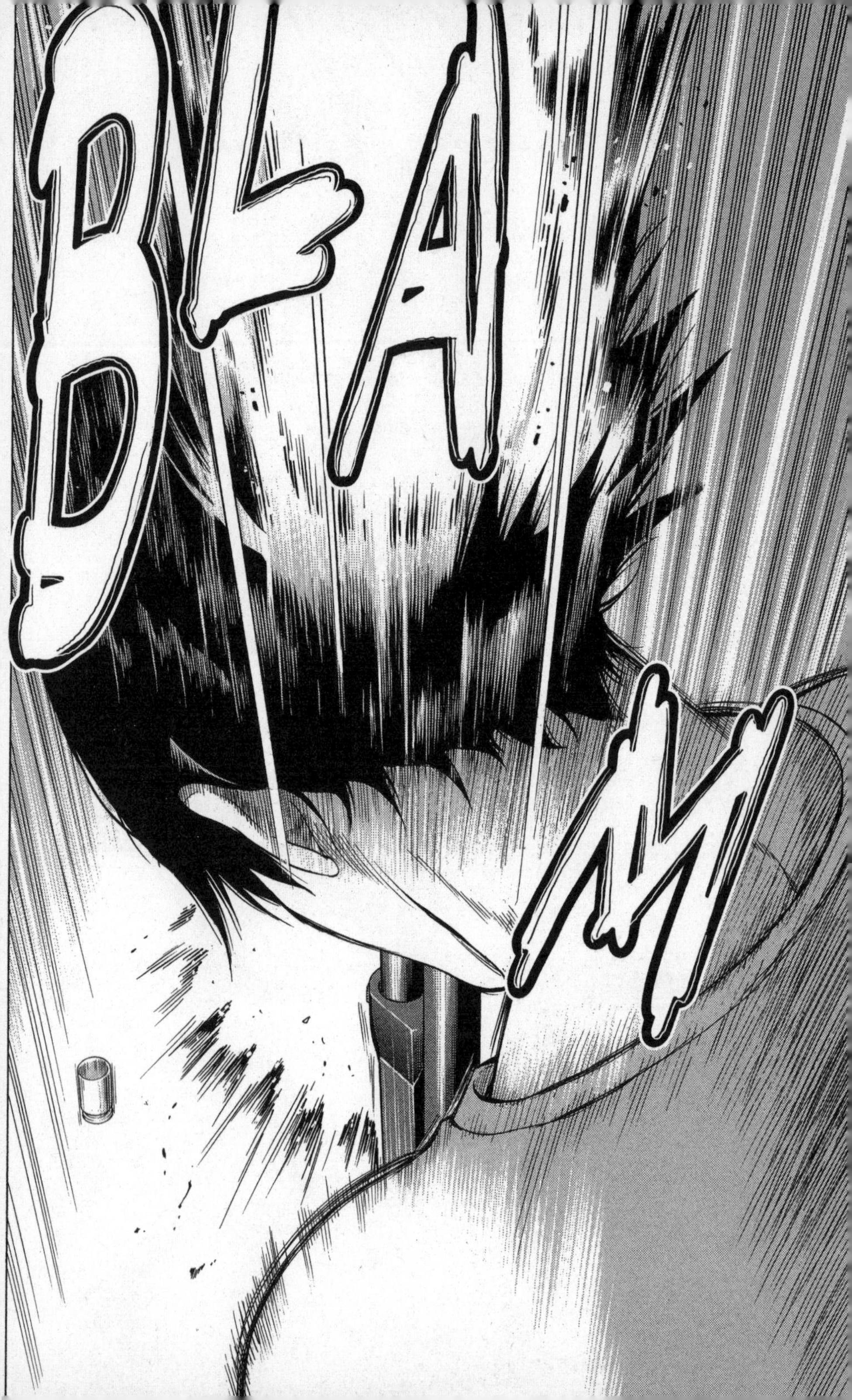
BLAM

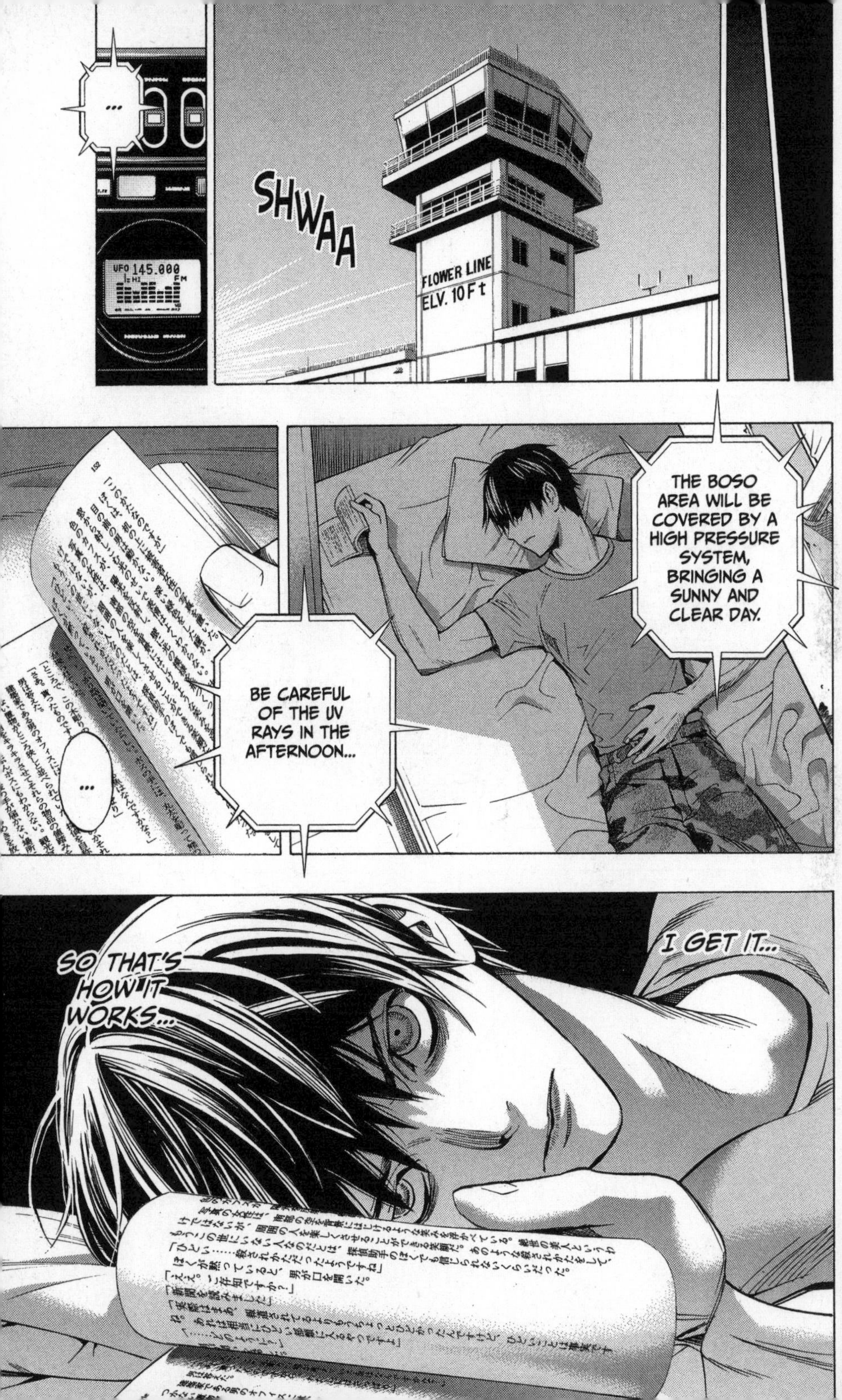
SHWAA
FLOWER LINE
ELV. 10 Ft
VFO 145.000
...
THE BOSO AREA WILL BE COVERED BY A HIGH PRESSURE SYSTEM, BRINGING A SUNNY AND CLEAR DAY.
BE CAREFUL OF THE UV RAYS IN THE AFTERNOON...
...
I GET IT...
SO THAT'S HOW IT WORKS...

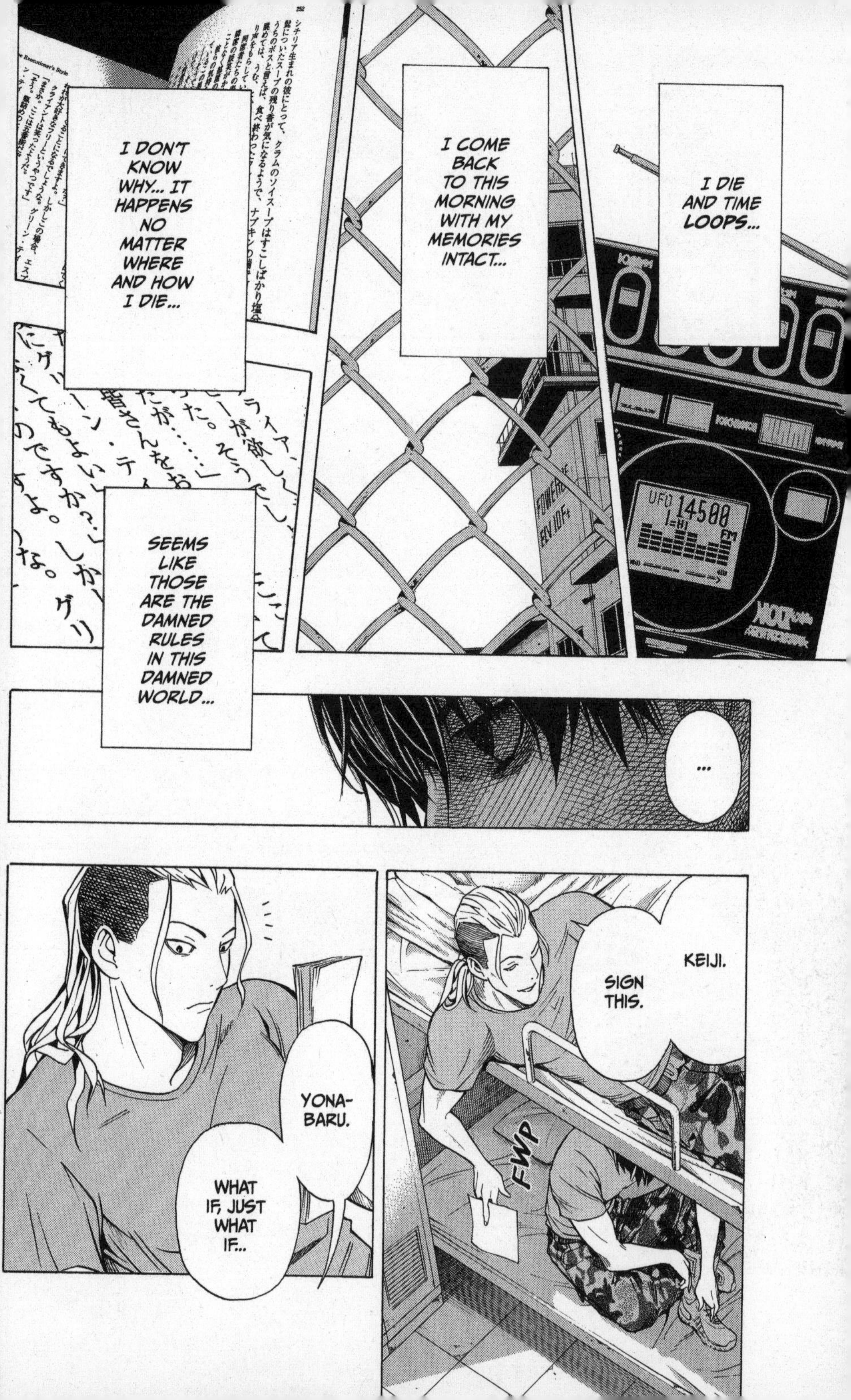

I DIE AND TIME LOOPS...
I COME BACK TO THIS MORNING WITH MY MEMORIES INTACT...
I DON'T KNOW WHY... IT HAPPENS NO MATTER WHERE AND HOW I DIE...
SEEMS LIKE THOSE ARE THE DAMNED RULES IN THIS DAMNED WORLD...
...
KEIJI.
SIGN THIS.
FWP
YONA-BARU.
WHAT IF, JUST WHAT IF...

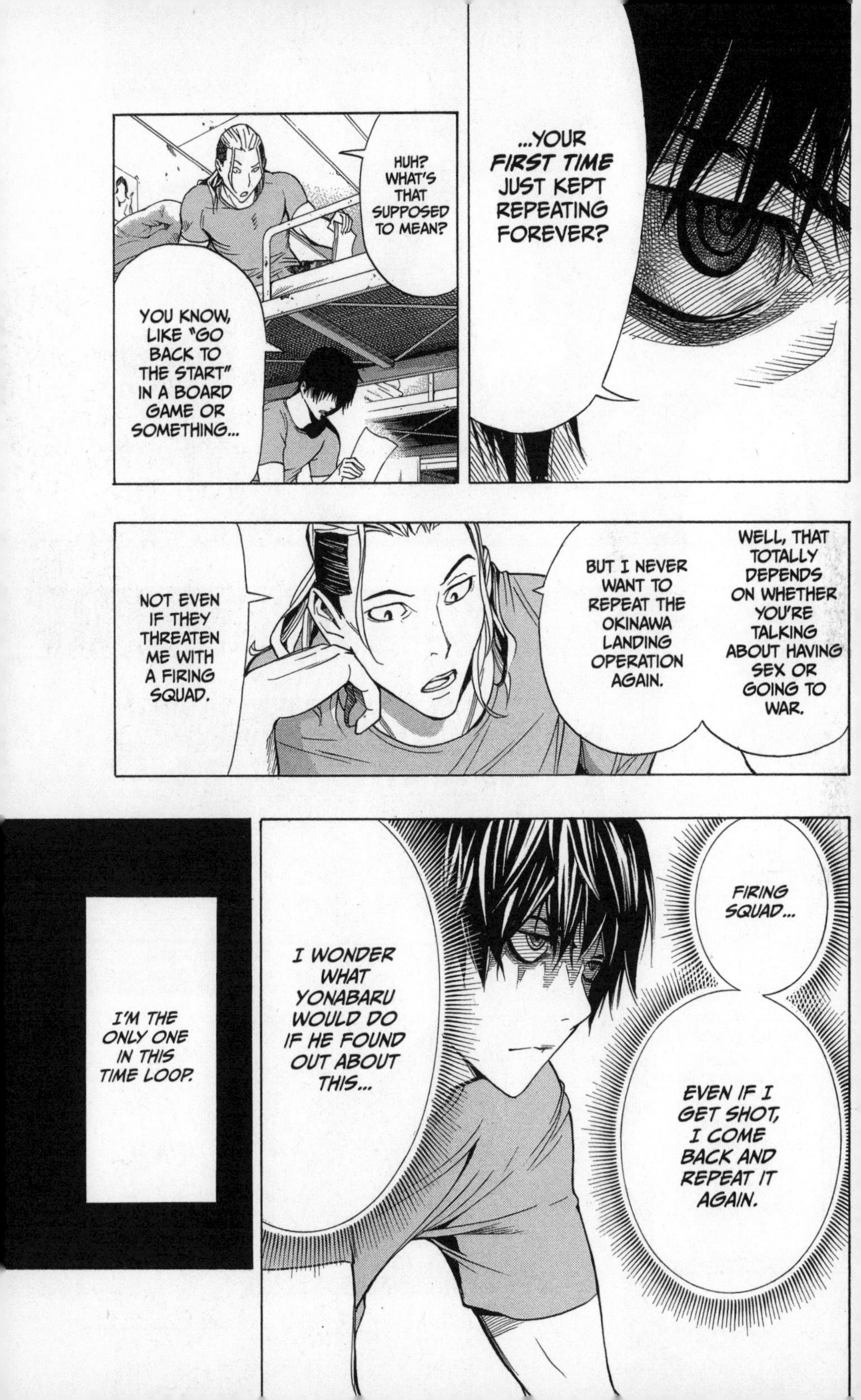
...YOUR *FIRST TIME* JUST KEPT REPEATING FOREVER?
HUH? WHAT'S THAT SUPPOSED TO MEAN?
YOU KNOW, LIKE "GO BACK TO THE START" IN A BOARD GAME OR SOMETHING...
WELL, THAT TOTALLY DEPENDS ON WHETHER YOU'RE TALKING ABOUT HAVING SEX OR GOING TO WAR.
BUT I NEVER WANT TO REPEAT THE OKINAWA LANDING OPERATION AGAIN.
NOT EVEN IF THEY THREATEN ME WITH A FIRING SQUAD.
FIRING SQUAD...
EVEN IF I GET SHOT, I COME BACK AND REPEAT IT AGAIN.
I WONDER WHAT YONABARU WOULD DO IF HE FOUND OUT ABOUT THIS...
I'M THE ONLY ONE IN THIS TIME LOOP.

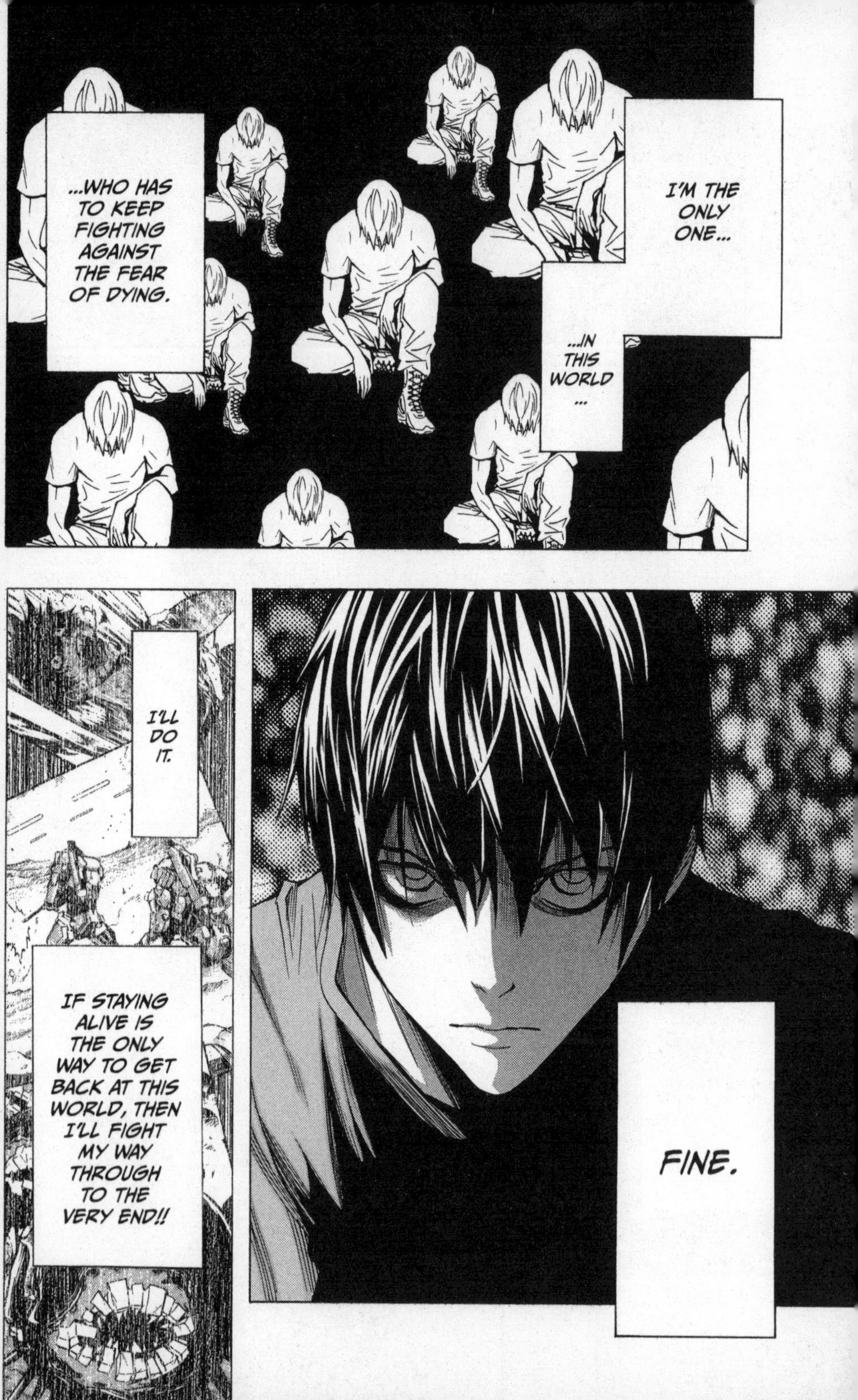
I'M THE ONLY ONE...
...IN THIS WORLD ...
...WHO HAS TO KEEP FIGHTING AGAINST THE FEAR OF DYING.
FINE.
I'LL DO IT.
IF STAYING ALIVE IS THE ONLY WAY TO GET BACK AT THIS WORLD, THEN I'LL FIGHT MY WAY THROUGH TO THE VERY END!!

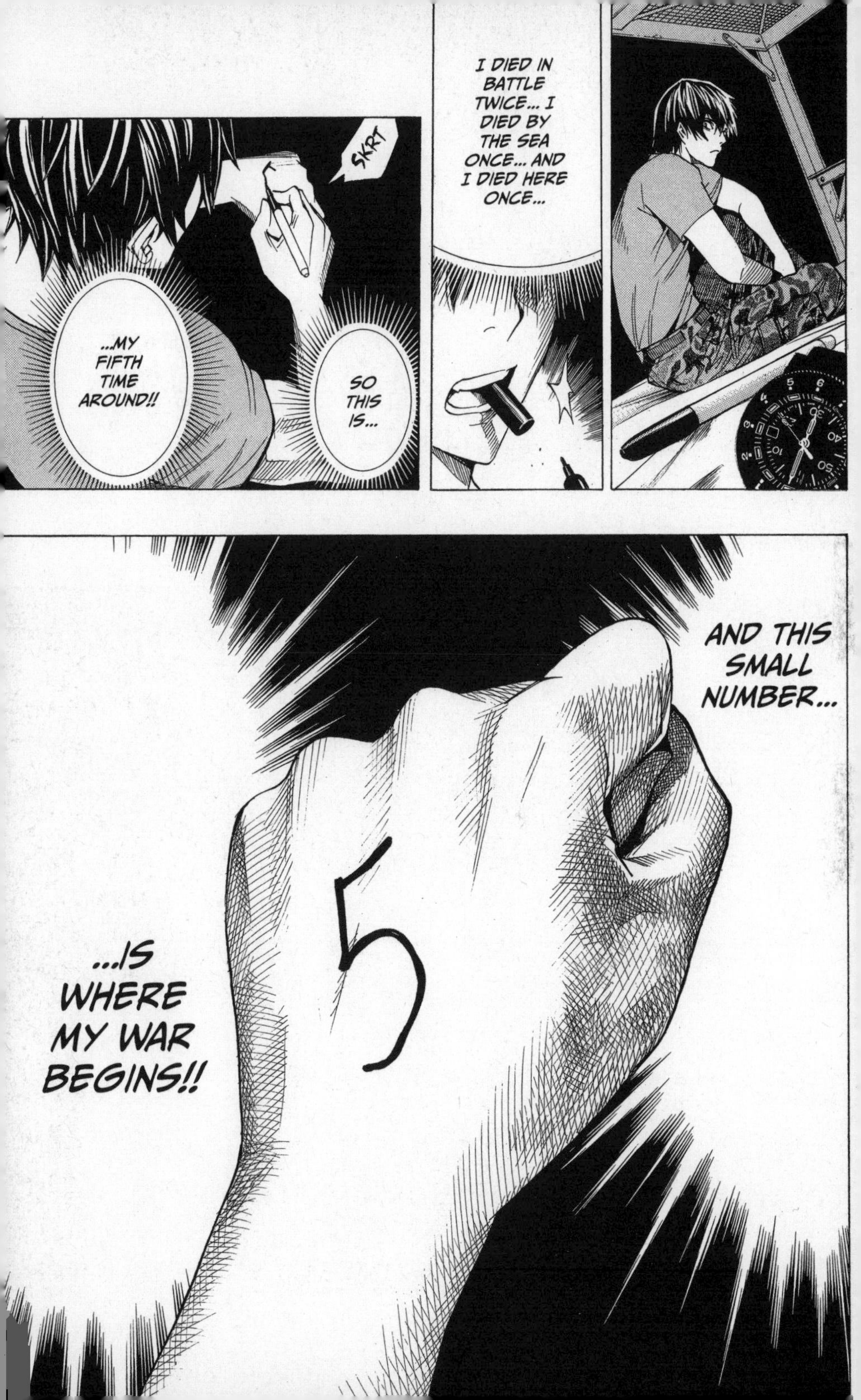

I DIED IN BATTLE TWICE... I DIED BY THE SEA ONCE... AND I DIED HERE ONCE...
SKRT
SO THIS IS...
...MY FIFTH TIME AROUND!!
AND THIS SMALL NUMBER...
5
...IS WHERE MY WAR BEGINS!!

Death comes quick,
in the beat of a heart.
And he ain't picky about
who he takes.

#2 Rita Vrataski

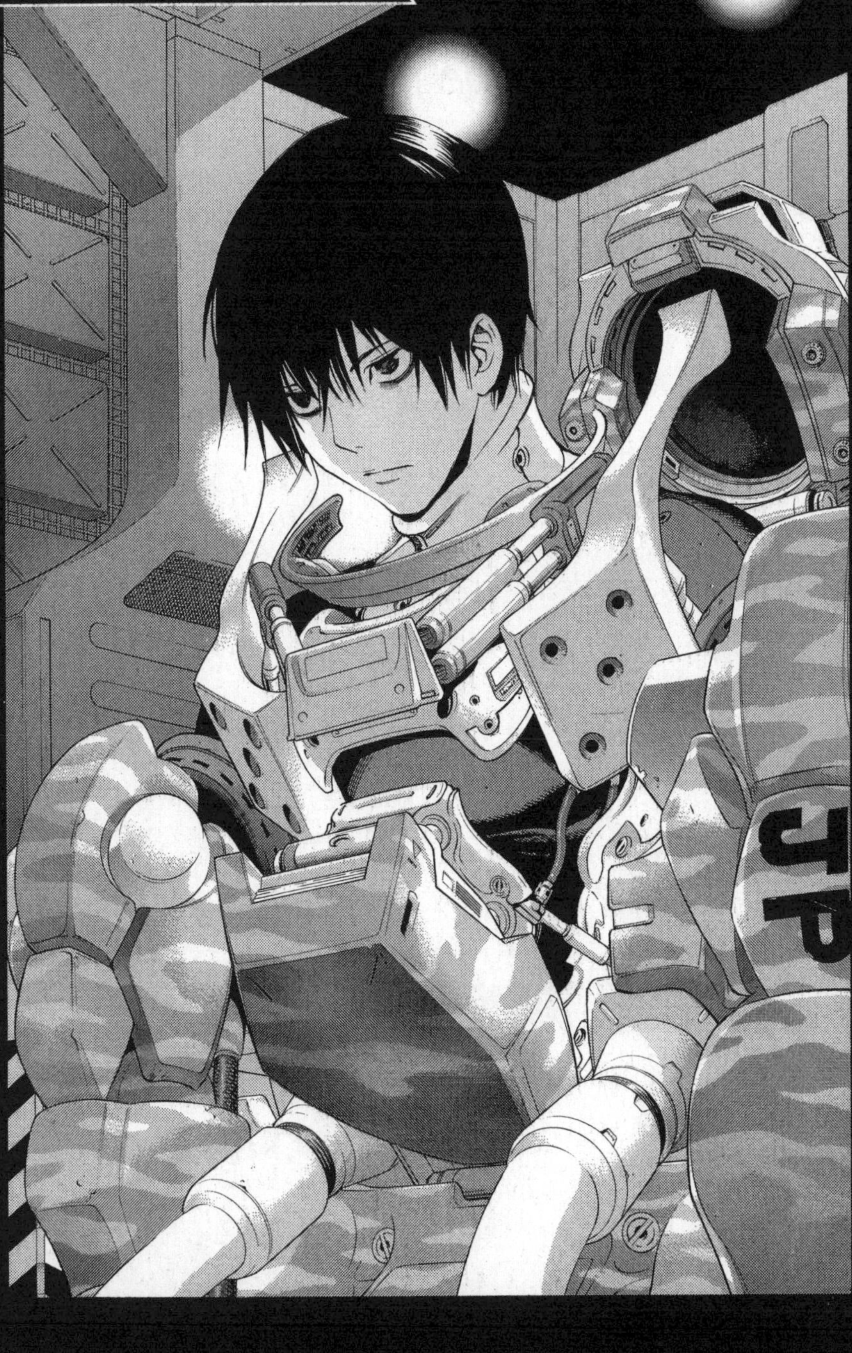

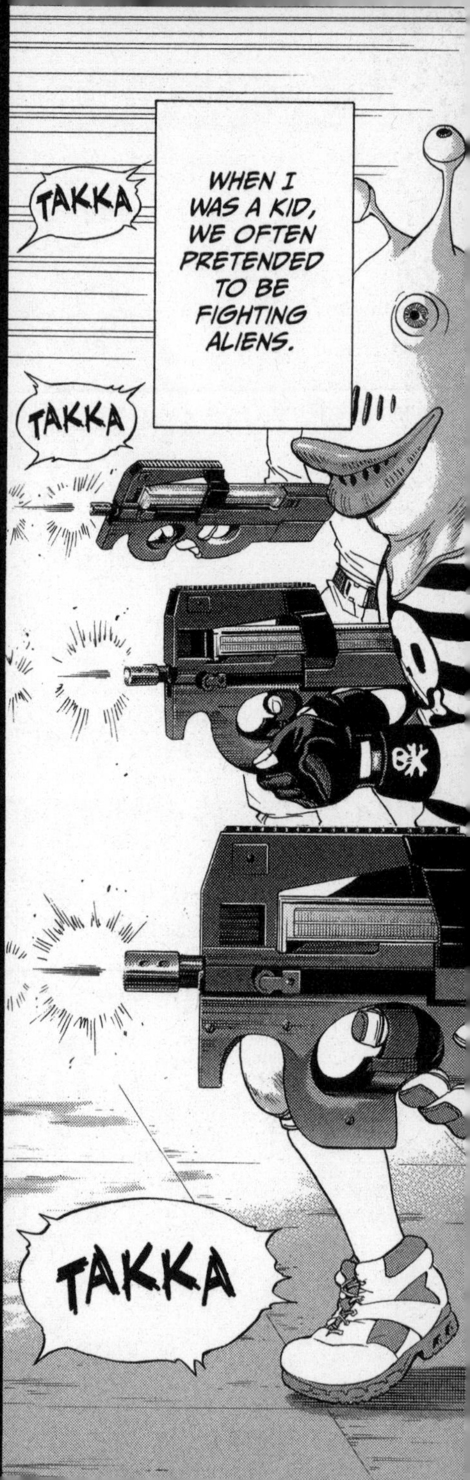
WHEN I WAS A KID, WE OFTEN PRETENDED TO BE FIGHTING ALIENS.
TAKKA
TAKKA
TAKKA
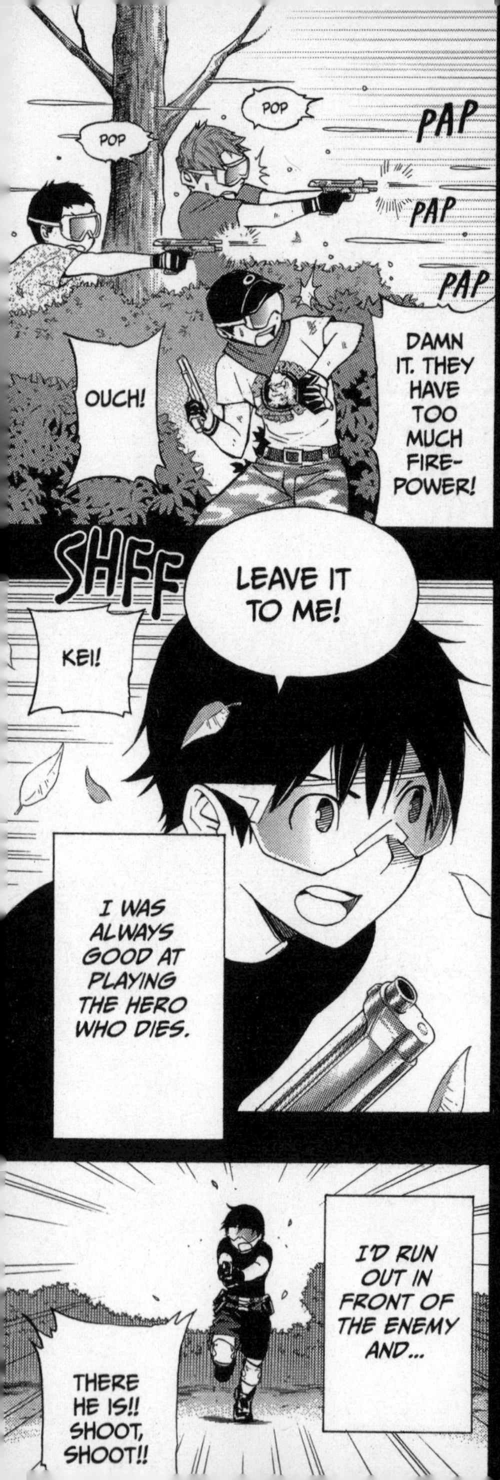
PAP
PAP
PAP
DAMN IT. THEY HAVE TOO MUCH FIRE-POWER!
POP
POP
OUCH!
LEAVE IT TO ME!
SHFF
KEI!
I WAS ALWAYS GOOD AT PLAYING THE HERO WHO DIES.
I'D RUN OUT IN FRONT OF THE ENEMY AND...
THERE HE IS!! SHOOT, SHOOT!!

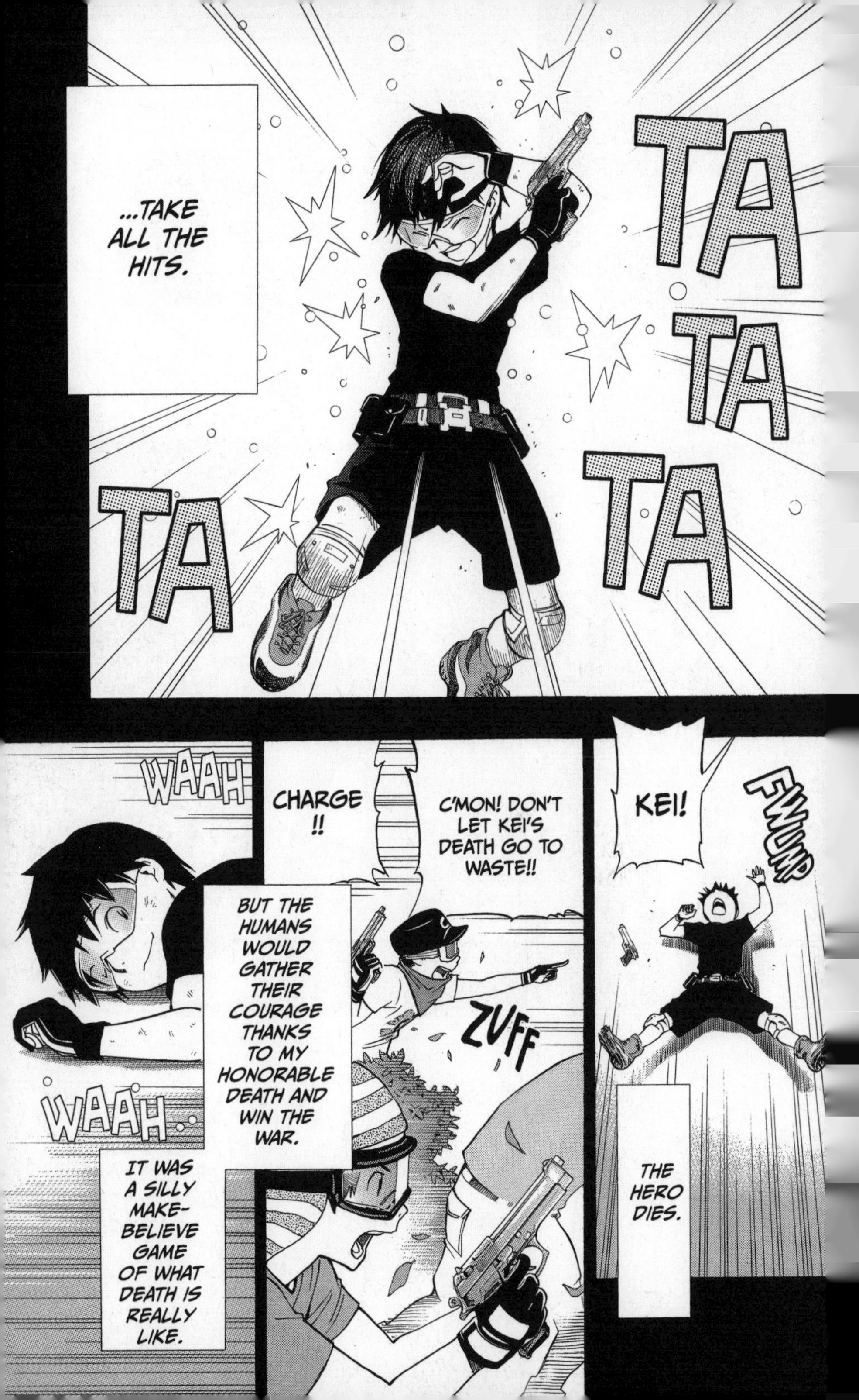
TA
TA
TA
...TAKE ALL THE HITS.
TA
KEI!
FWUMP
THE HERO DIES.
C'MON! DON'T LET KEI'S DEATH GO TO WASTE!!
CHARGE !!
ZUFF
BUT THE HUMANS WOULD GATHER THEIR COURAGE THANKS TO MY HONORABLE DEATH AND WIN THE WAR.
WAAH
WAAH
IT WAS A SILLY MAKE-BELIEVE GAME OF WHAT DEATH IS REALLY LIKE.

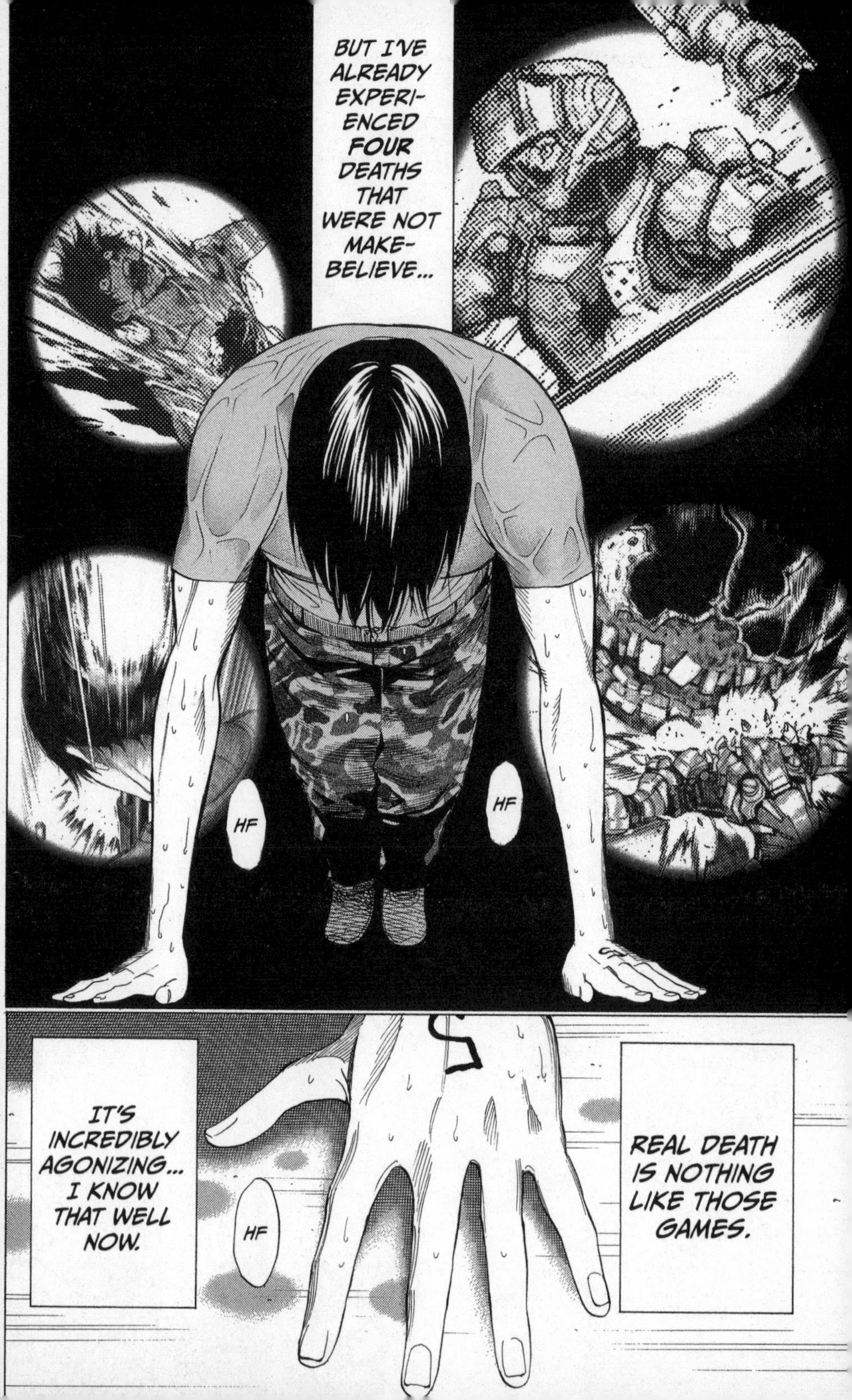
BUT I'VE ALREADY EXPERI- ENCED FOUR DEATHS THAT WERE NOT MAKE- BELIEVE...
HF
HF
REAL DEATH IS NOTHING LIKE THOSE GAMES.
IT'S INCREDIBLY AGONIZING... I KNOW THAT WELL NOW.
HF

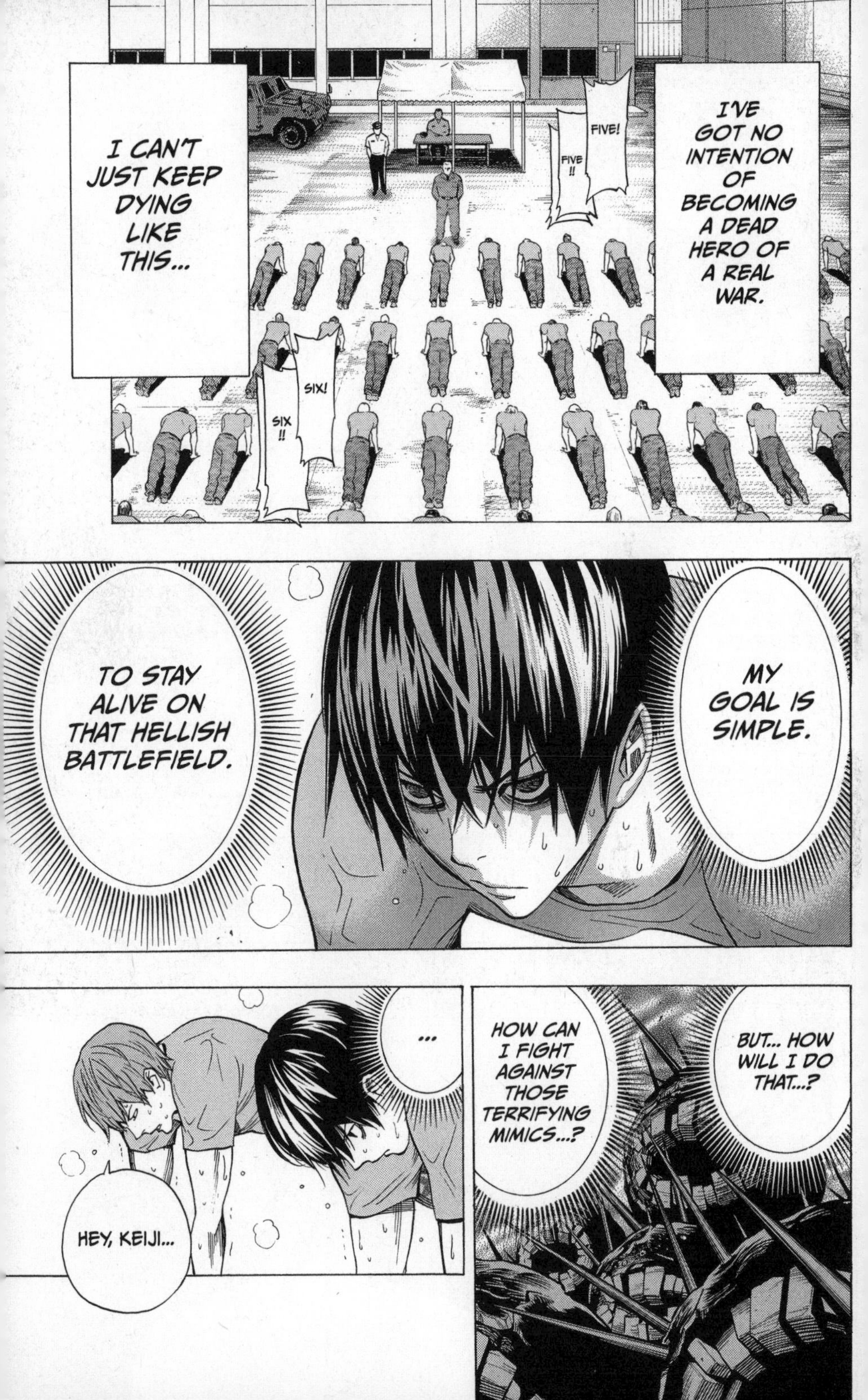
I'VE GOT NO INTENTION OF BECOMING A DEAD HERO OF A REAL WAR.
FIVE!
FIVE !!
I CAN'T JUST KEEP DYING LIKE THIS...
SIX!
SIX !!
MY GOAL IS SIMPLE.
TO STAY ALIVE ON THAT HELLISH BATTLEFIELD.
BUT... HOW WILL I DO THAT...?
HOW CAN I FIGHT AGAINST THOSE TERRIFYING MIMICS...?
...
HEY, KEIJI...

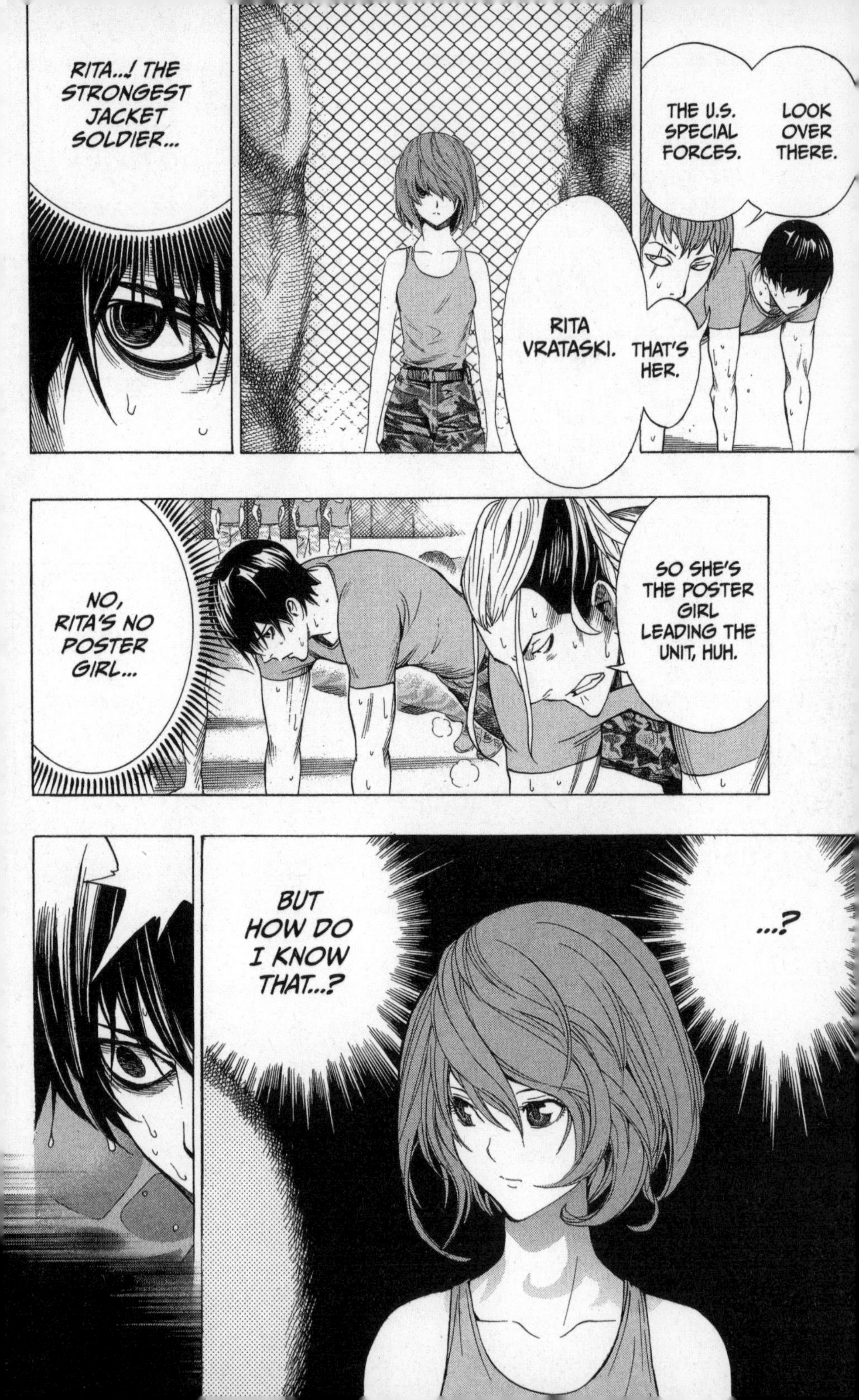
LOOK OVER THERE.
THE U.S. SPECIAL FORCES.
THAT'S HER.
RITA VRATASKI.
RITA...! THE STRONGEST JACKET SOLDIER...
SO SHE'S THE POSTER GIRL LEADING THE UNIT, HUH.
NO, RITA'S NO POSTER GIRL...
...?
BUT HOW DO I KNOW THAT...?

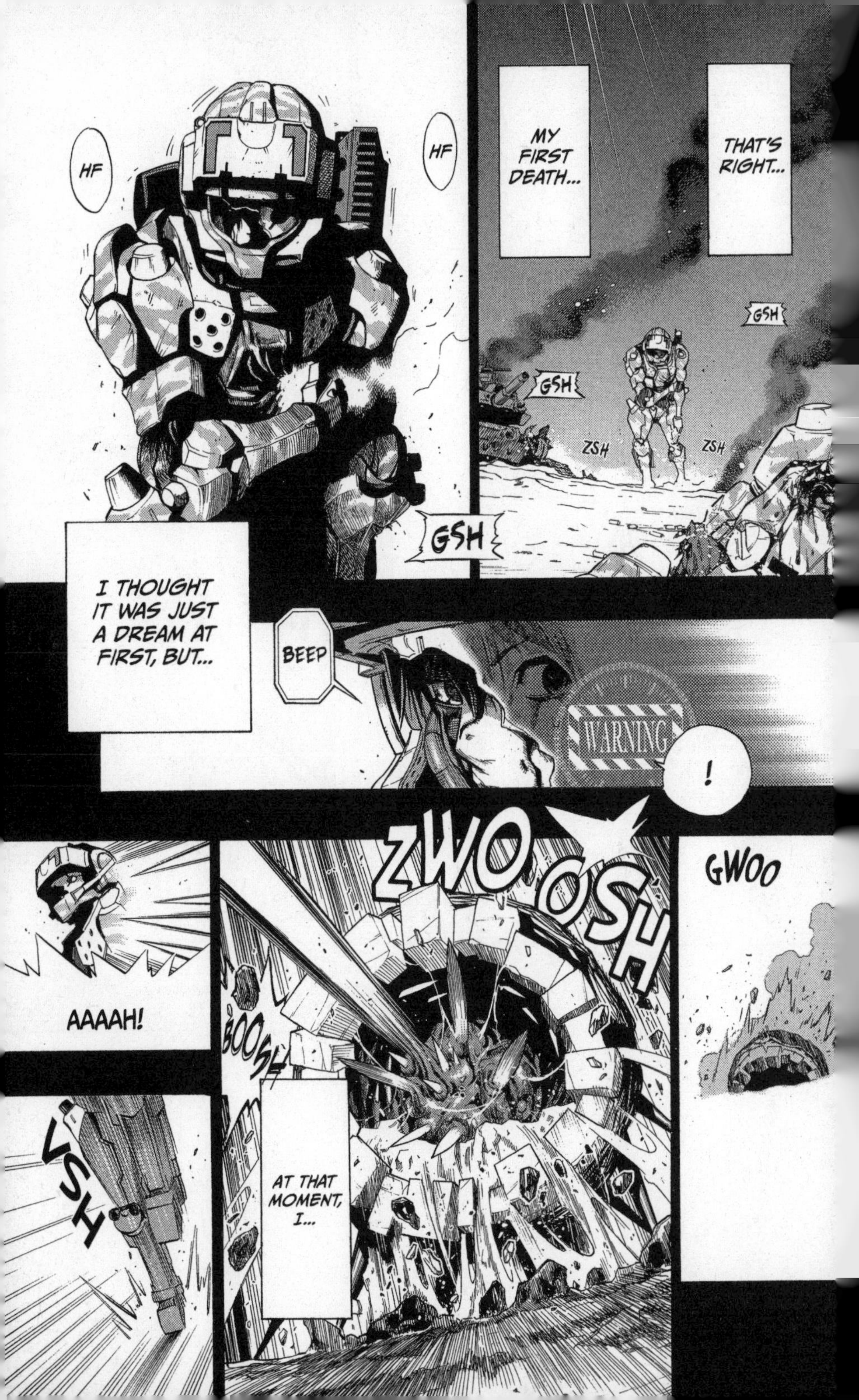
THAT'S RIGHT...
MY FIRST DEATH...
GSH
GSH
ZSH
ZSH
HF
HF
GSH
I THOUGHT IT WAS JUST A DREAM AT FIRST, BUT...
BEEP
WARNING
!
GWOO
ZWOOSH
BOOSH
AT THAT MOMENT, I...
AAAAH!
VSH

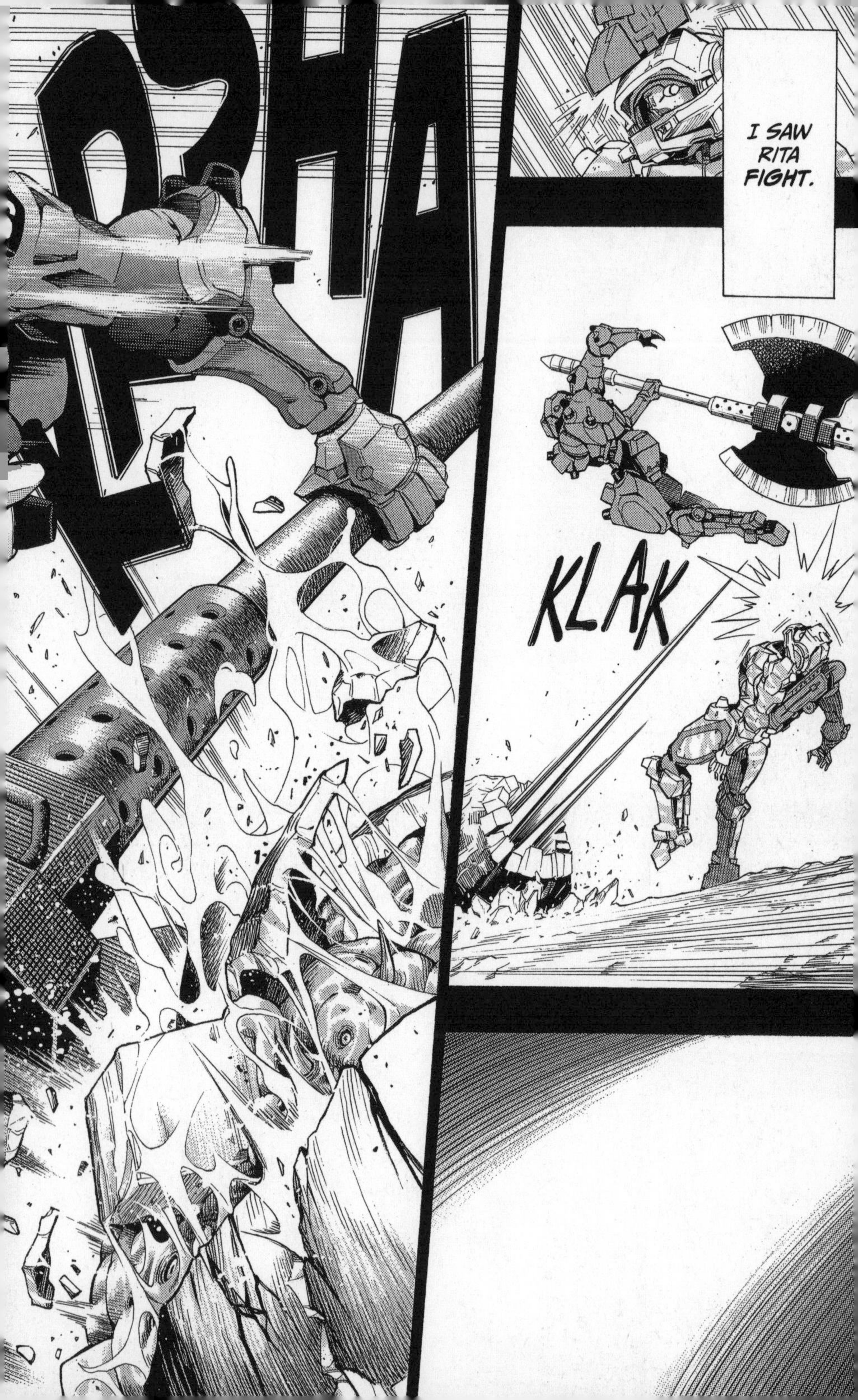
I SAW RITA FIGHT.
KLAK

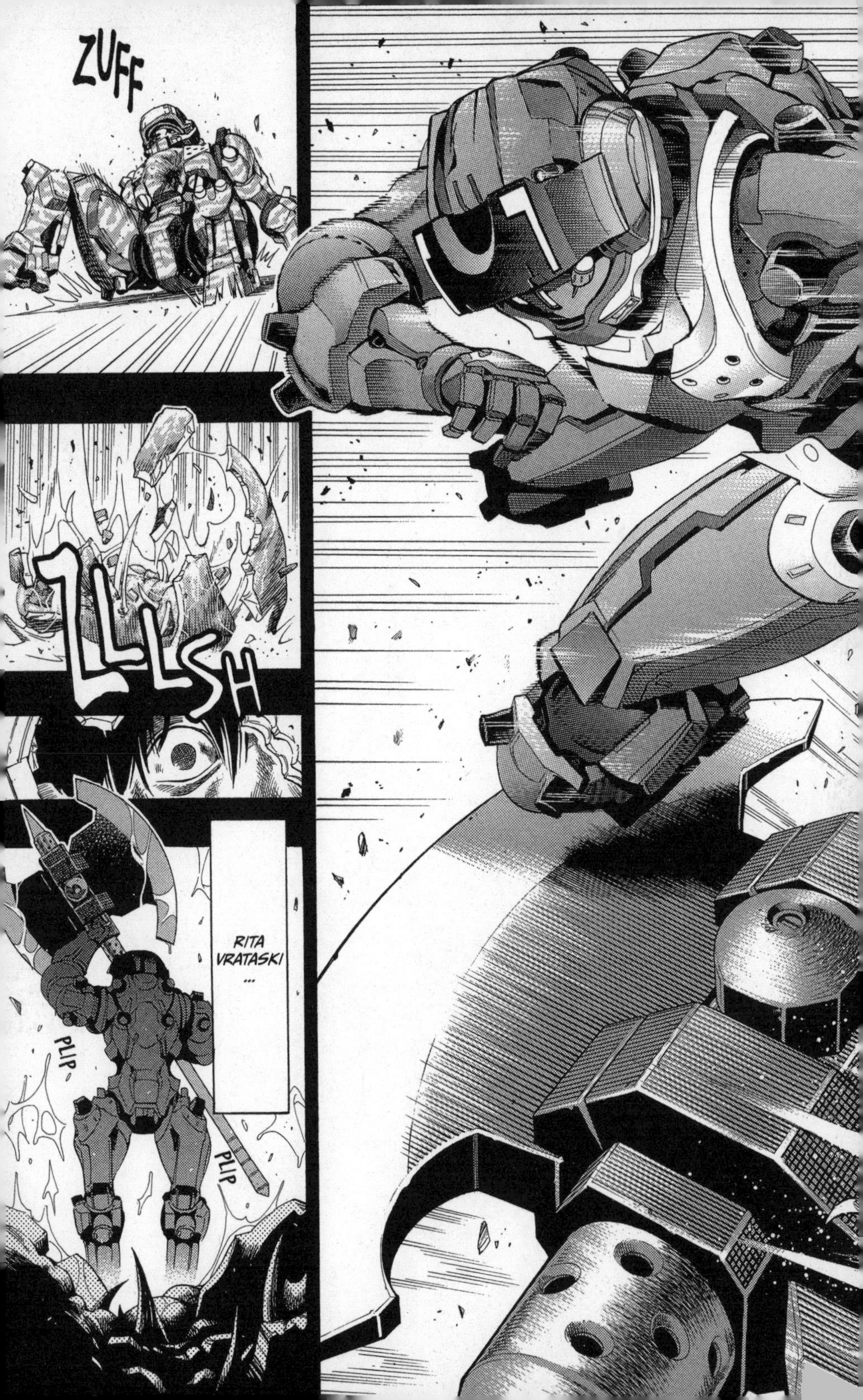
ZUFF
LLSH
RITA VRATASKI ...
PLIP
PLIP

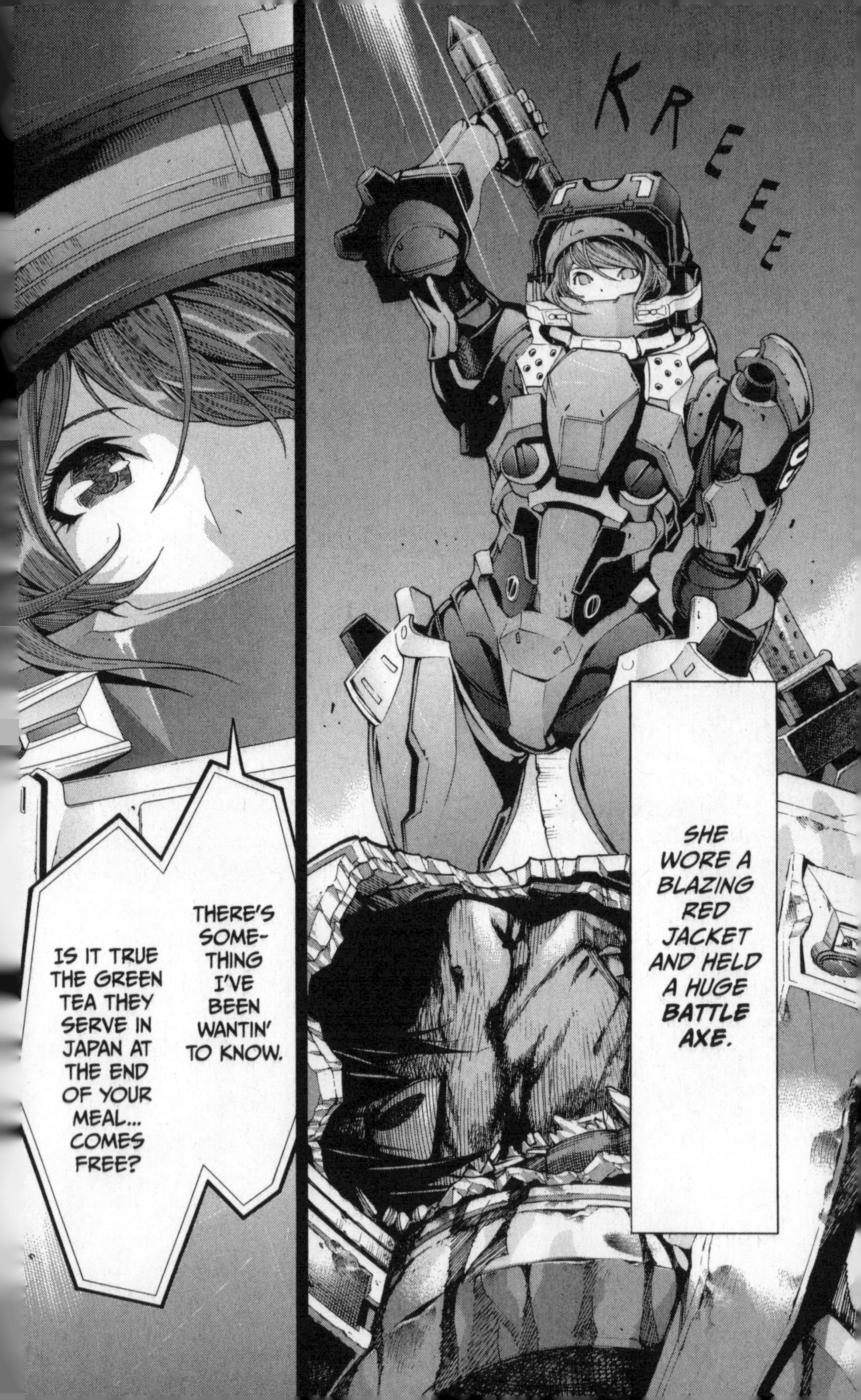
KREEE
SHE WORE A BLAZING RED JACKET AND HELD A HUGE BATTLE AXE.
THERE'S SOMETHING I'VE BEEN WANTIN' TO KNOW.
IS IT TRUE THE GREEN TEA THEY SERVE IN JAPAN AT THE END OF YOUR MEAL... COMES FREE?

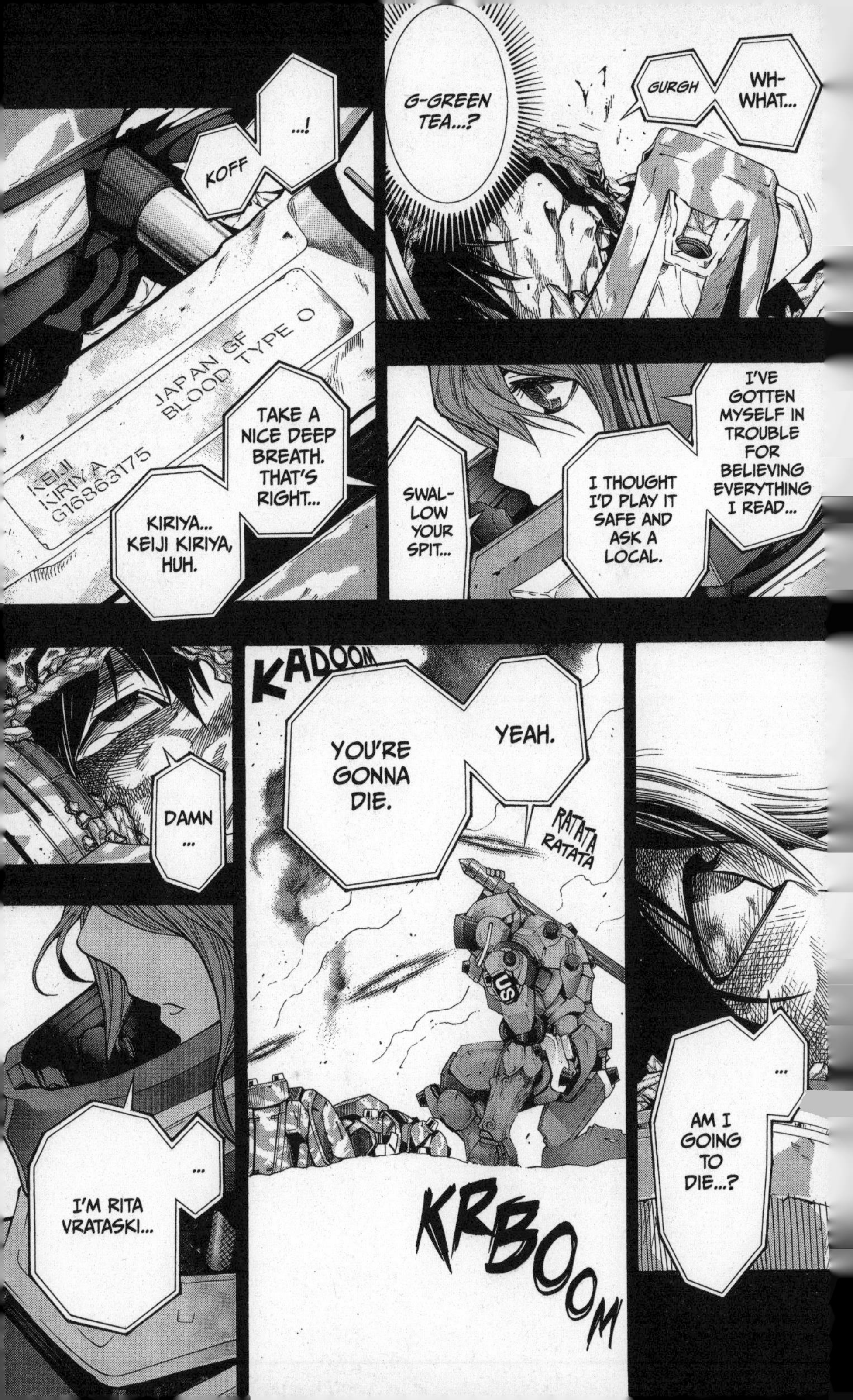
WH- WHAT...
GURGH
G-GREEN TEA...?
I'VE GOTTEN MYSELF IN TROUBLE FOR BELIEVING EVERYTHING I READ...
I THOUGHT I'D PLAY IT SAFE AND ASK A LOCAL.
SWAL- LOW YOUR SPIT...
...!
KOFF
JAPAN GF
BLOOD TYPE O
KEIJI
KIRIYA A
G16863175
TAKE A NICE DEEP BREATH. THAT'S RIGHT...
KIRIYA... KEIJI KIRIYA, HUH.
...
AM I GOING TO DIE...?
KADOOM
YEAH.
YOU'RE GONNA DIE.
RATATA RATATA
US
KRBOOM
DAMN ...
...
I'M RITA VRATASKI...

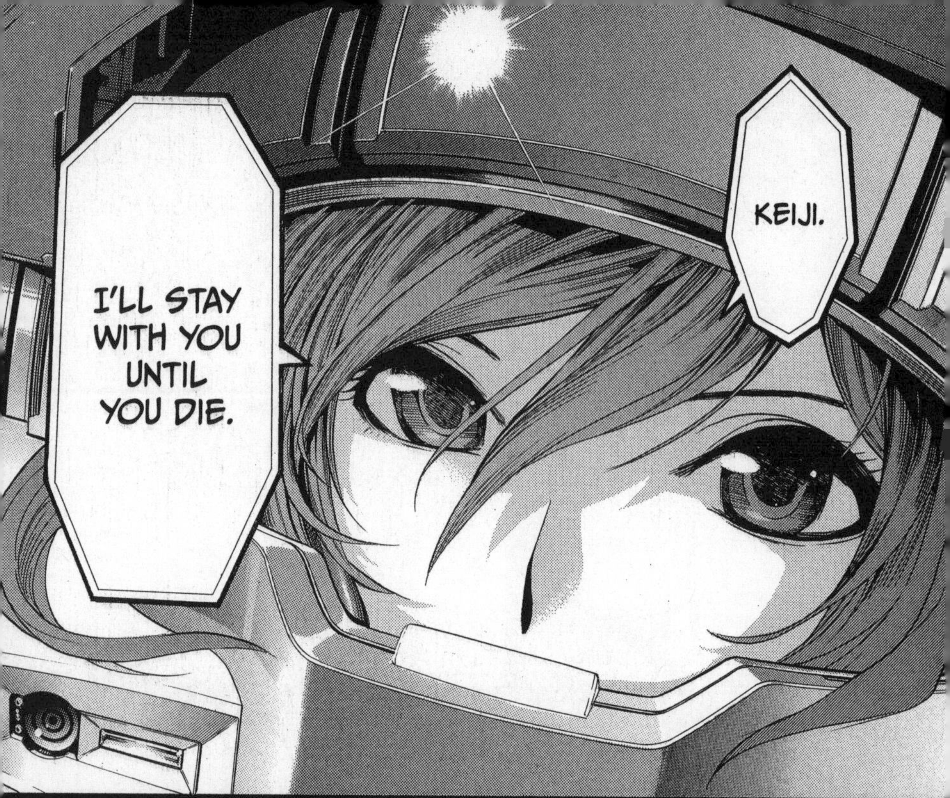
KEIJI.
I'LL STAY WITH YOU UNTIL YOU DIE.
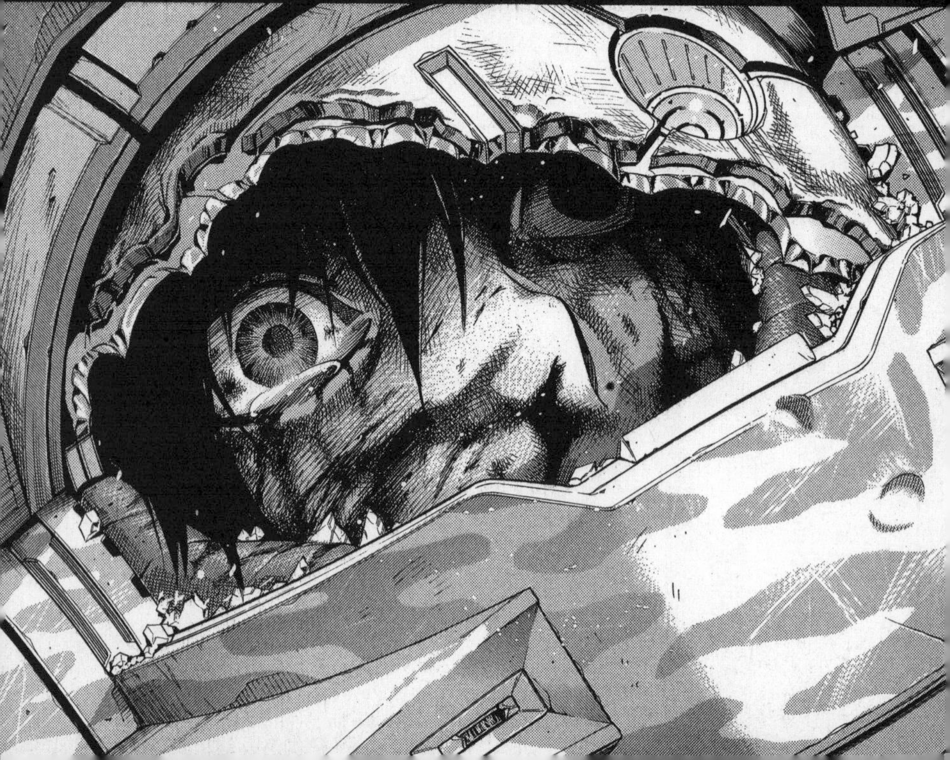

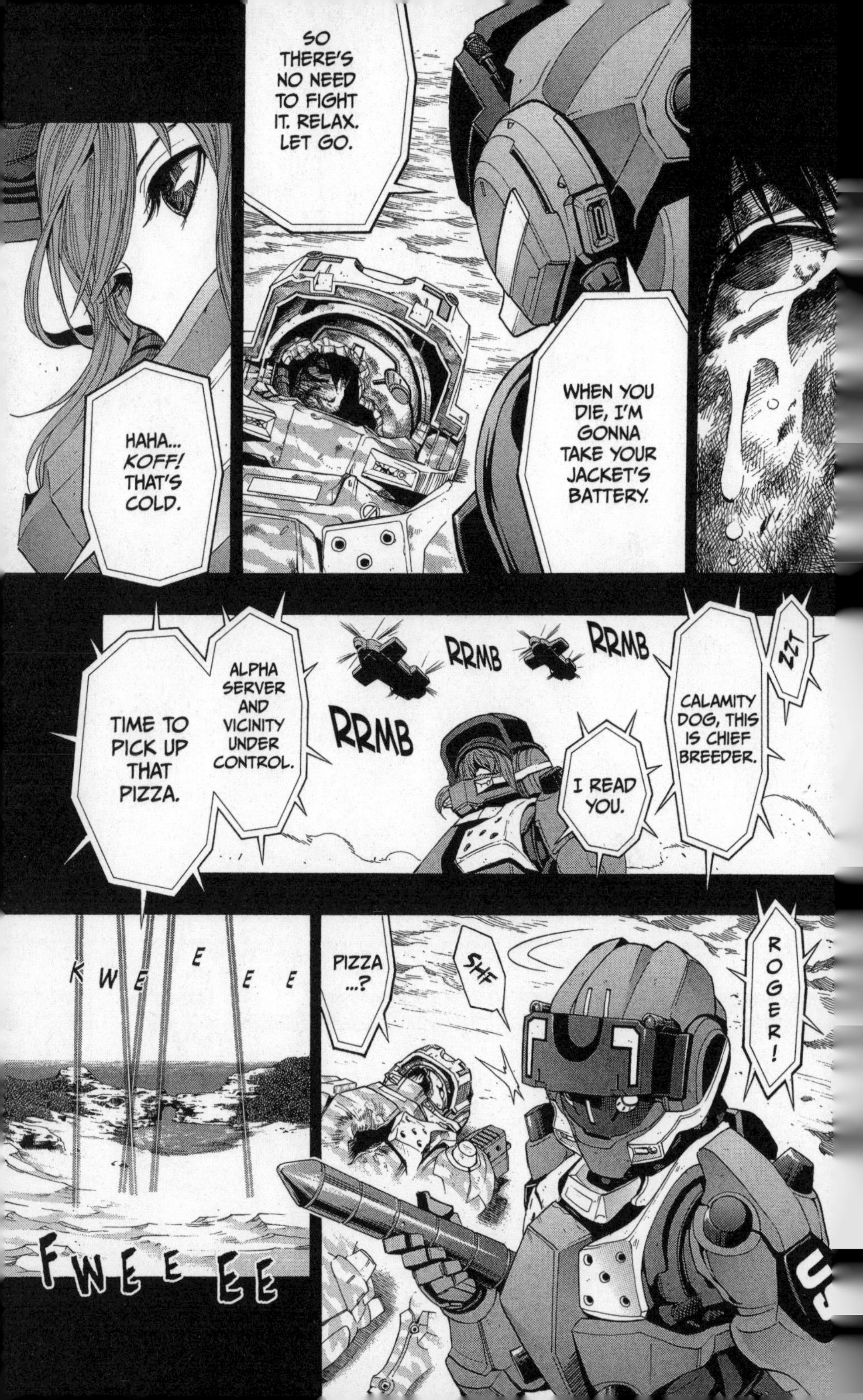
SO THERE'S NO NEED TO FIGHT IT. RELAX. LET GO.
WHEN YOU DIE, I'M GONNA TAKE YOUR JACKET'S BATTERY.
HAHA... KOFF! THAT'S COLD.
ZZT
CALAMITY DOG, THIS IS CHIEF BREEDER.
I READ YOU.
RRMB
RRMB
RRMB
ALPHA SERVER AND VICINITY UNDER CONTROL.
TIME TO PICK UP THAT PIZZA.
ROGER!
SHF
PIZZA ...?
KWEEEE
FWEEEE

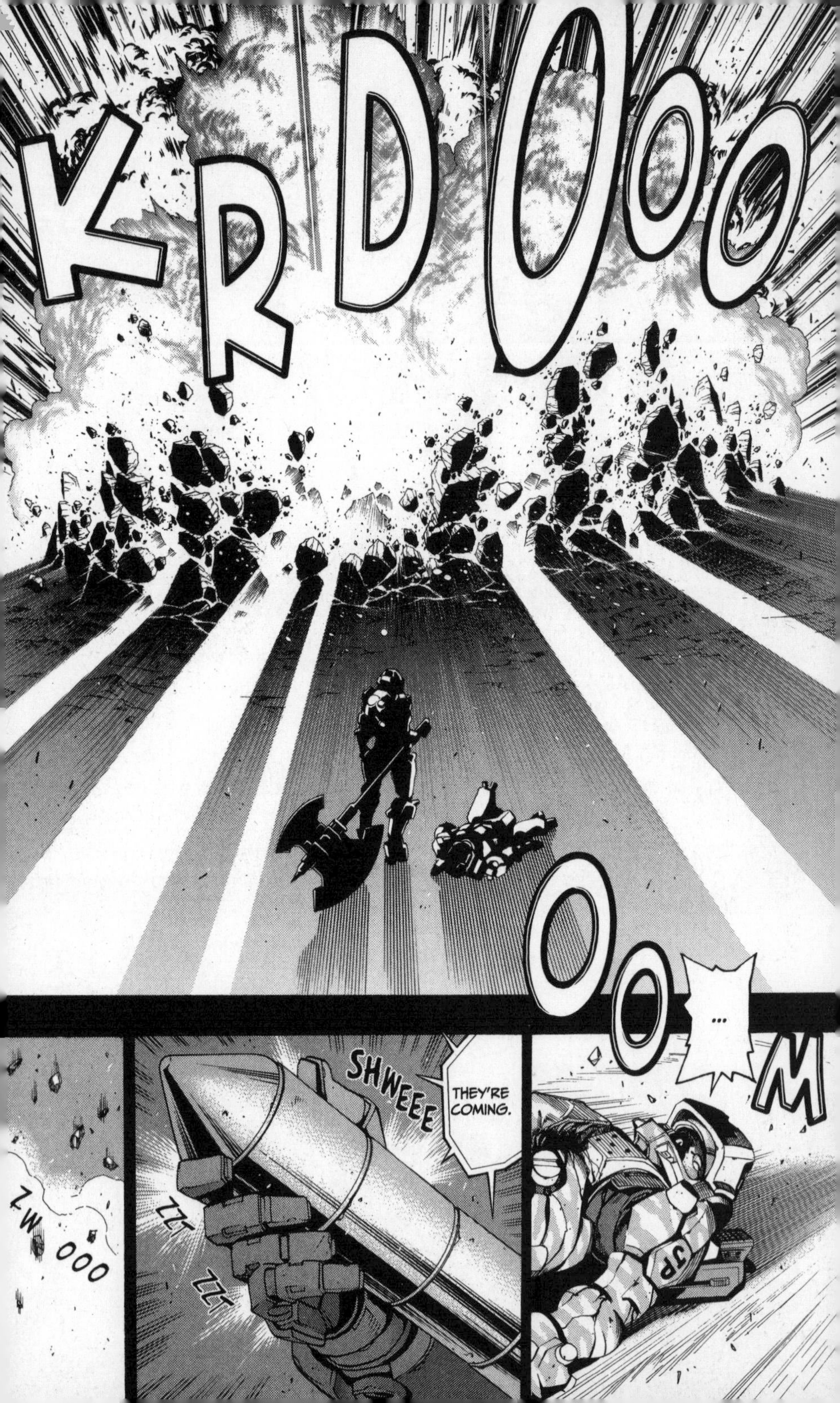
KRDOOOOOOM
...
SHWEEE
THEY'RE COMING.
ZZT
ZZT
ZWOOO

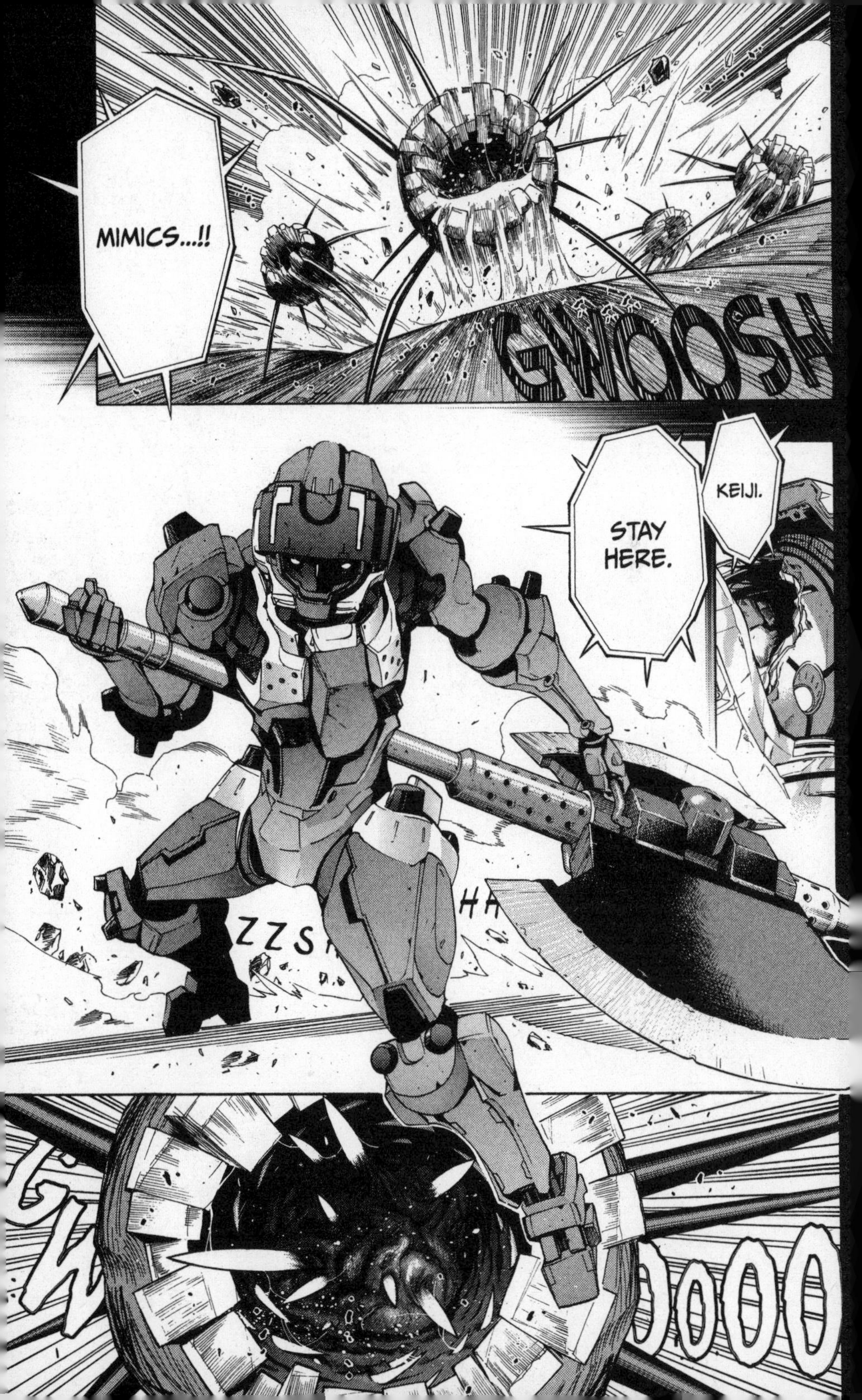
MIMICS...!!
GWOOSH
KEIJI.
STAY HERE.
ZZS
HH
GW
OOOOO

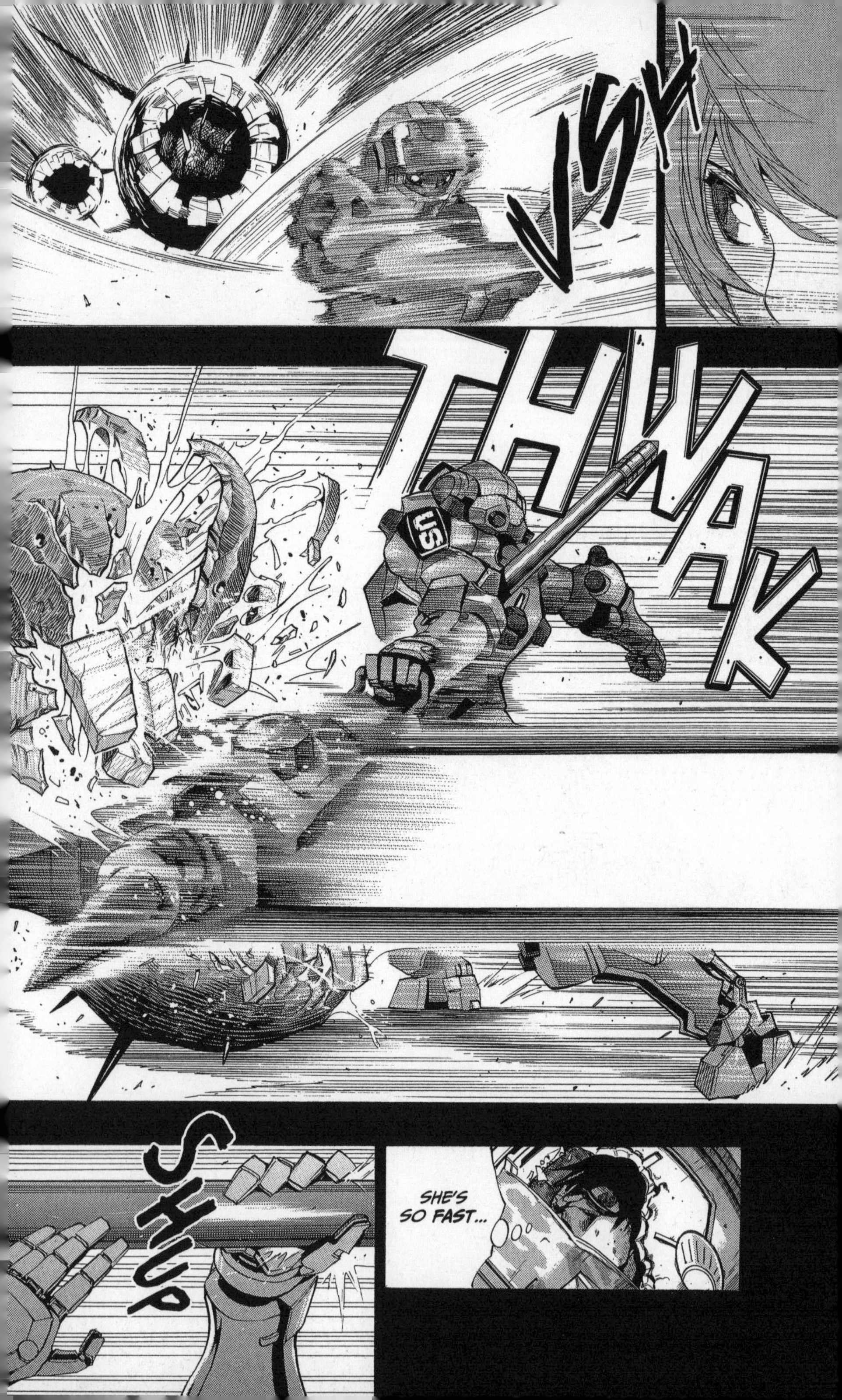
VSH
THWAK
SHE'S SO FAST...
SHUP

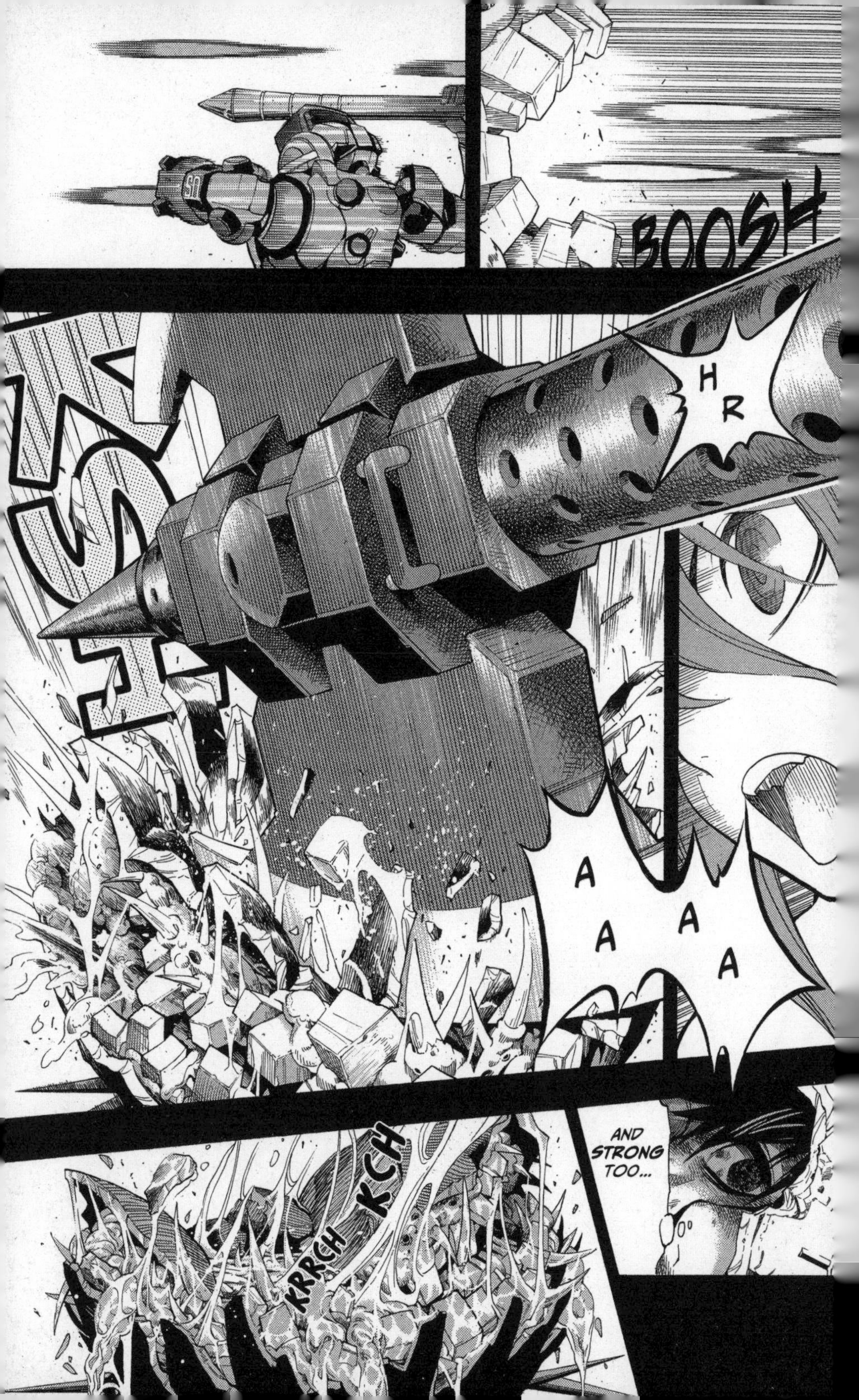
BOOSH
HR
AAAA
AND STRONG TOO...
KRRCH KCH

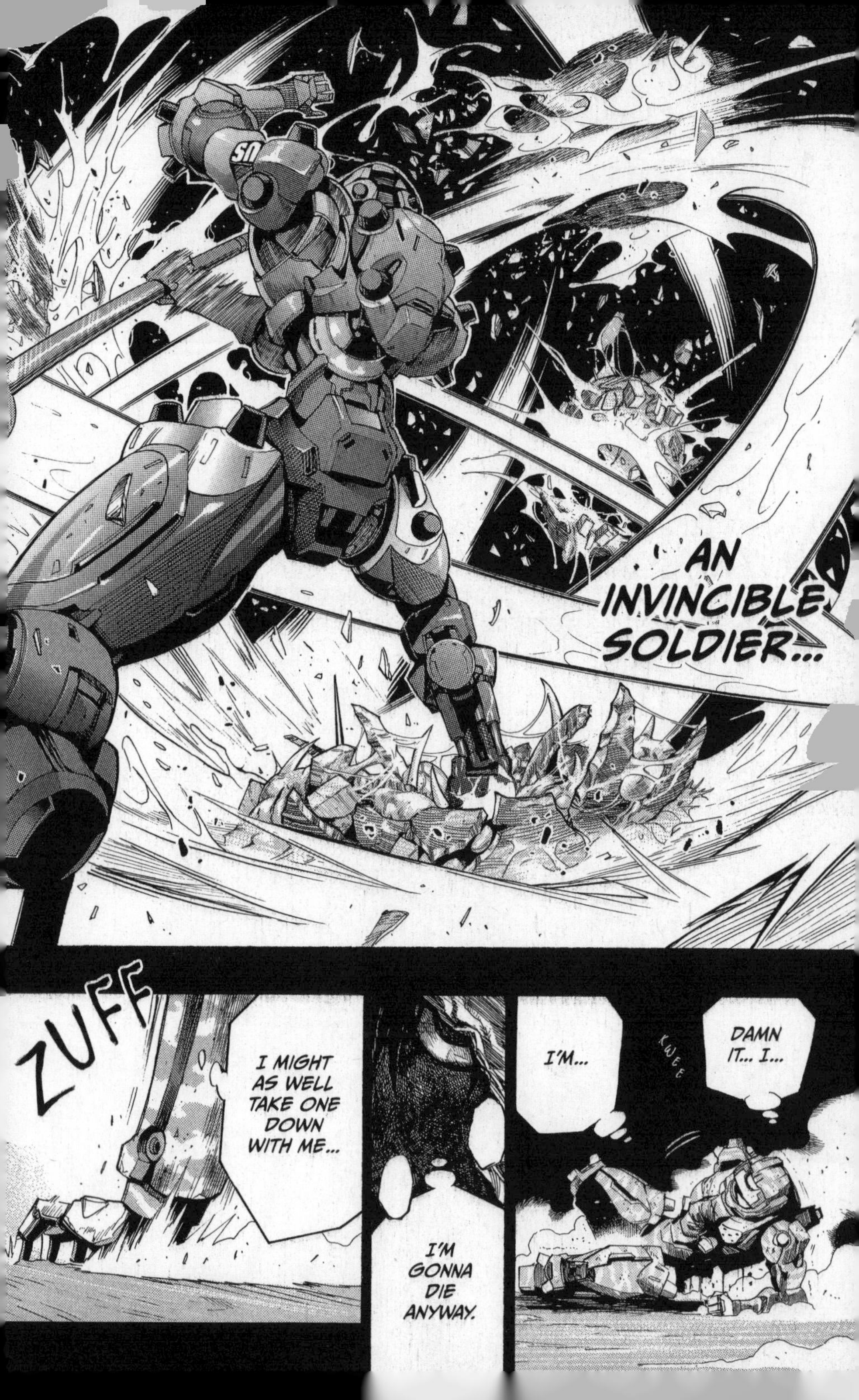
AN INVINCIBLE SOLDIER...
DAMN IT... I...
KWEE
I'M...
I'M GONNA DIE ANYWAY.
ZUFF
I MIGHT AS WELL TAKE ONE DOWN WITH ME...

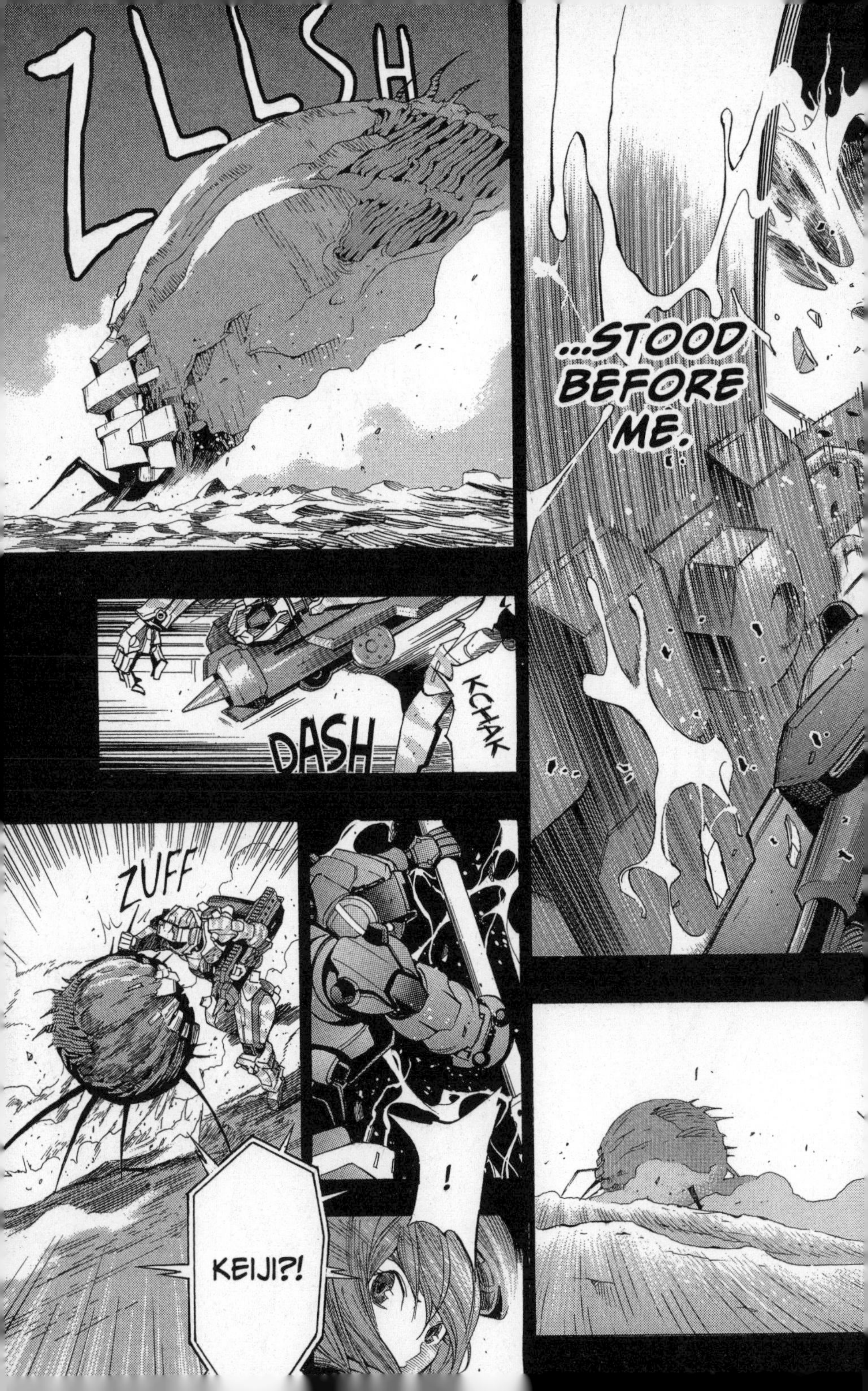
...STOOD BEFORE ME.
ZLLSH
KCHAK
DASH
!
ZUFF
KEIJI?!

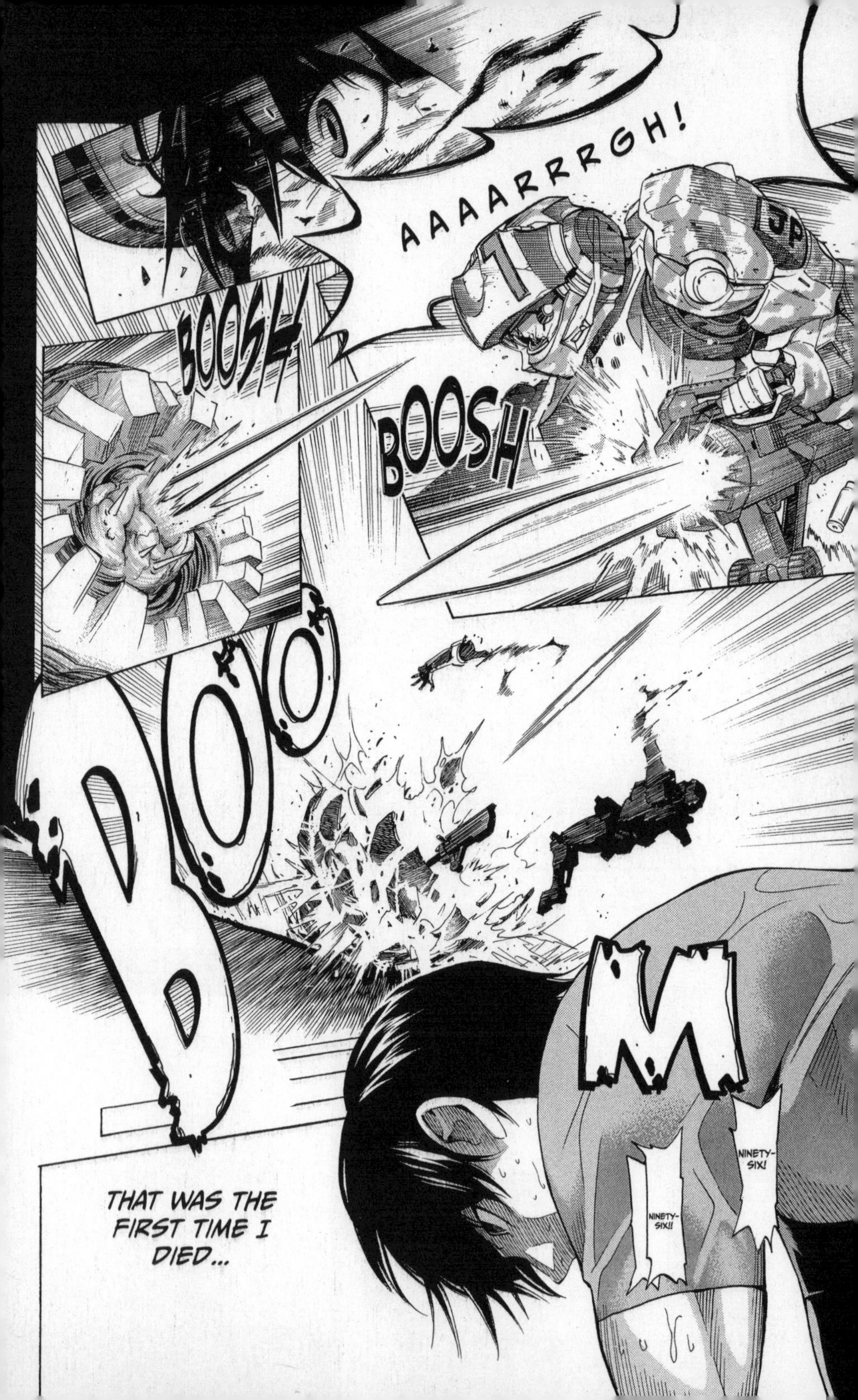
AAAARRRGH!
BOOSH
BOOSH
BOOOM
NINETY-SIX!
NINETY-SIX!!
THAT WAS THE FIRST TIME I DIED...

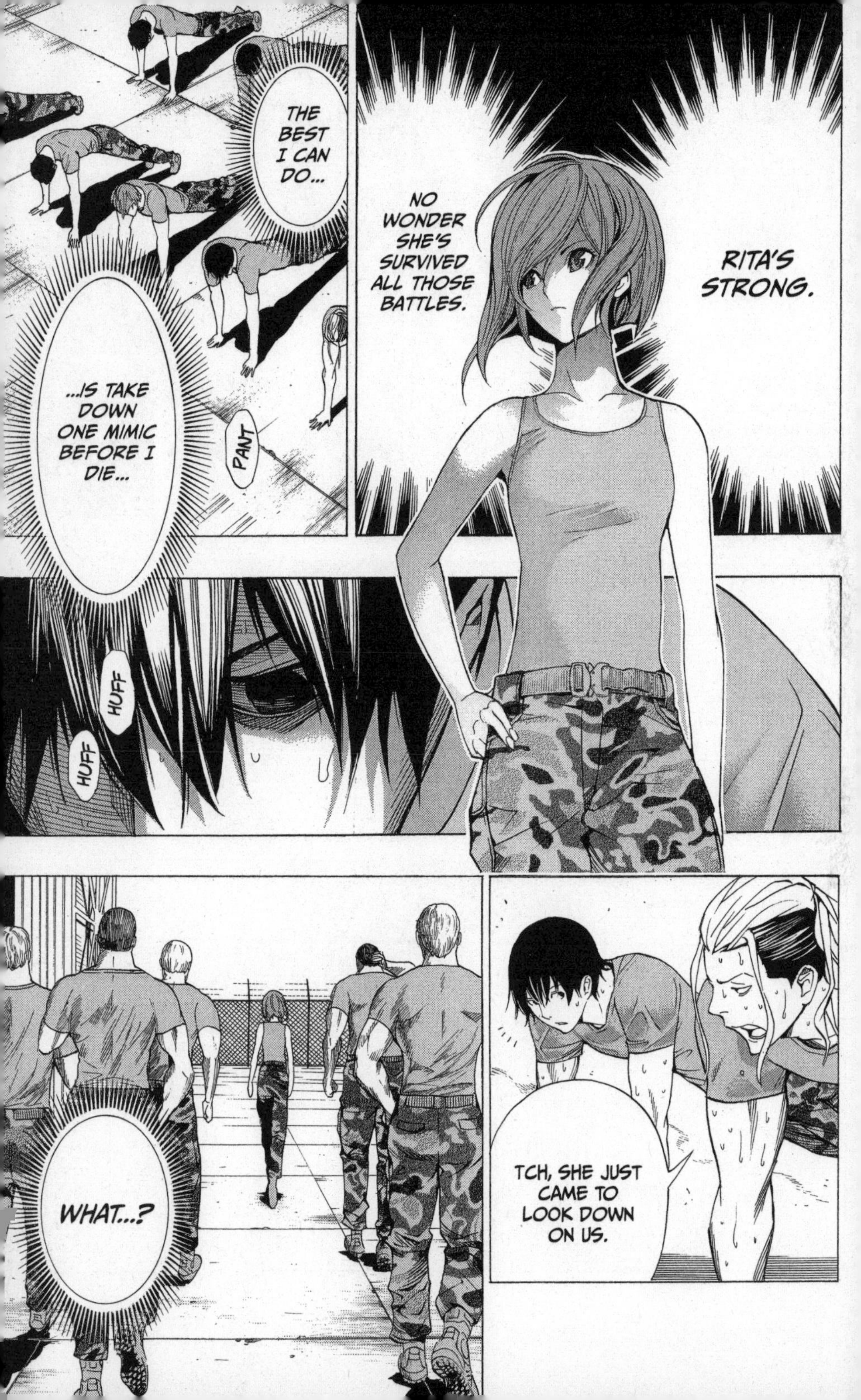
RITA'S STRONG.
NO WONDER SHE'S SURVIVED ALL THOSE BATTLES.
THE BEST I CAN DO...
...IS TAKE DOWN ONE MIMIC BEFORE I DIE...
PANT
HUFF
HUFF
TCH, SHE JUST CAME TO LOOK DOWN ON US.
WHAT...?

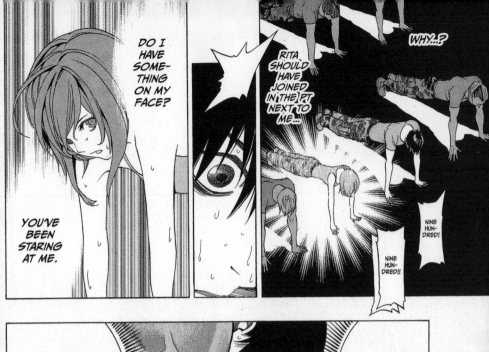

WHY...?
RITA SHOULD HAVE JOINED IN THE PT NEXT TO ME...
NINE HUNDRED!
NINE HUNDRED!!
DO I HAVE SOME-THING ON MY FACE?
YOU'VE BEEN STARING AT ME.
IS IT BECAUSE I WASN'T STARING AT RITA...?
IF I HAD BEEN STARING AT HER, RITA WOULD HAVE COME HERE... THAT MEANS...
I CAN CHANGE WHAT WILL HAPPEN IN THE FUTURE... !!
THEN...

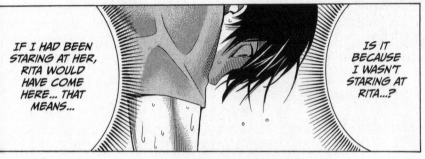

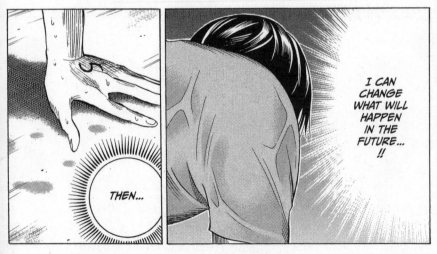

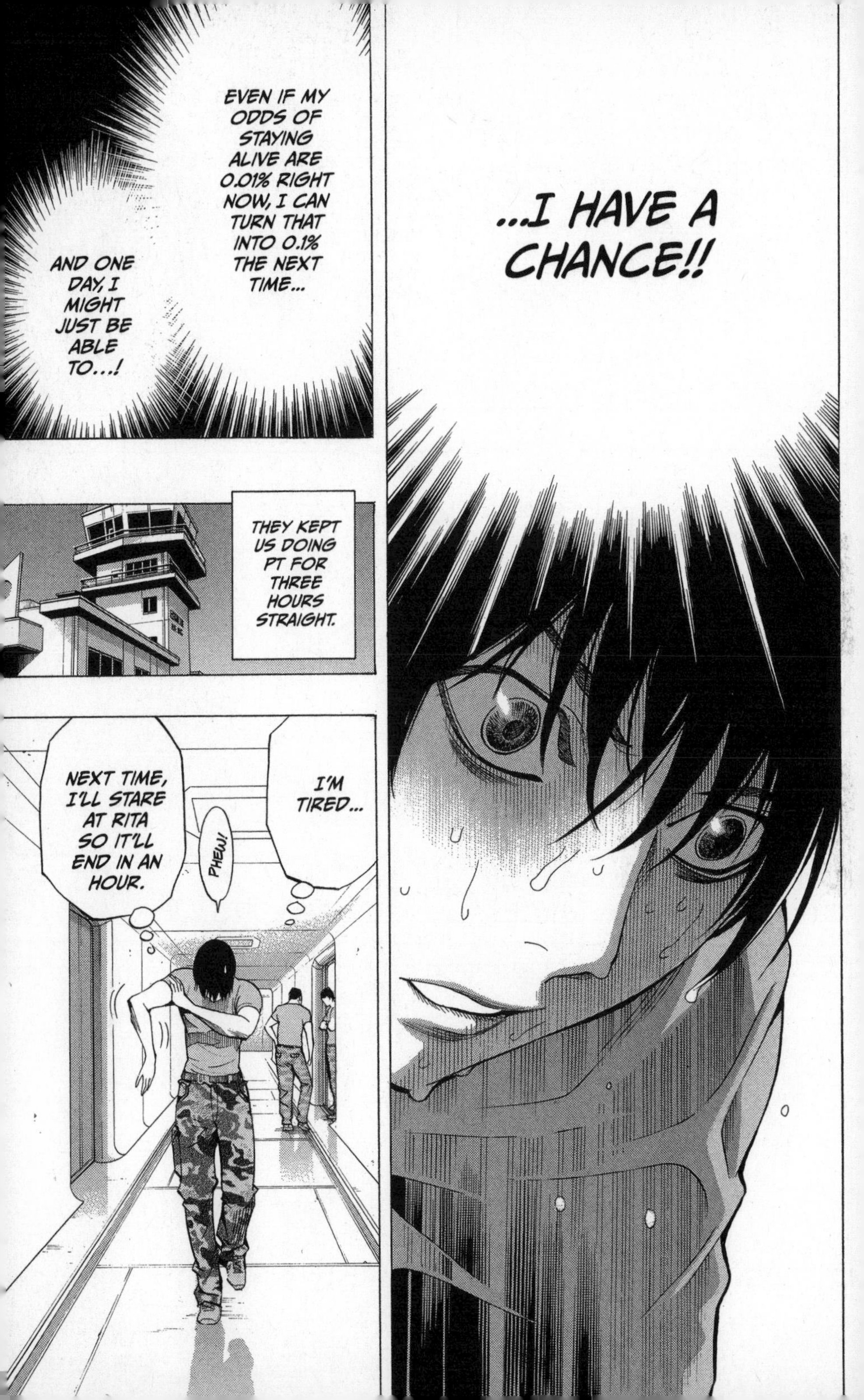
...I HAVE A CHANCE!!
EVEN IF MY ODDS OF STAYING ALIVE ARE 0.01% RIGHT NOW, I CAN TURN THAT INTO 0.1% THE NEXT TIME...
AND ONE DAY, I MIGHT JUST BE ABLE TO...!
THEY KEPT US DOING PT FOR THREE HOURS STRAIGHT.
I'M TIRED...
PHEW!
NEXT TIME, I'LL STARE AT RITA SO IT'LL END IN AN HOUR.

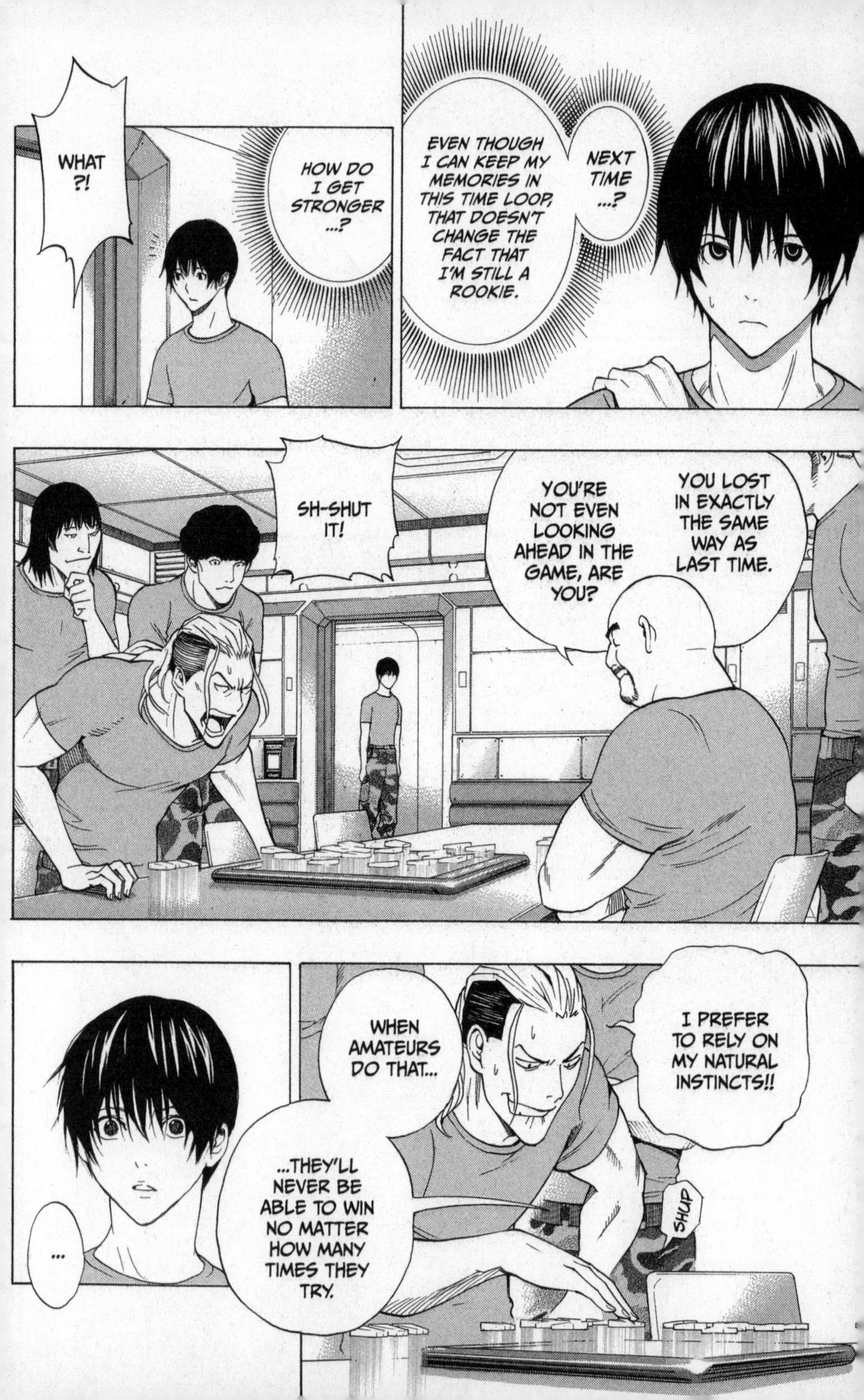
NEXT TIME ...?
EVEN THOUGH I CAN KEEP MY MEMORIES IN THIS TIME LOOP, THAT DOESN'T CHANGE THE FACT THAT I'M STILL A ROOKIE.
HOW DO I GET STRONGER ...?
WHAT ?!
YOU LOST IN EXACTLY THE SAME WAY AS LAST TIME.
YOU'RE NOT EVEN LOOKING AHEAD IN THE GAME, ARE YOU?
SH-SHUT IT!
I PREFER TO RELY ON MY NATURAL INSTINCTS!!
WHEN AMATEURS DO THAT...
SHUP
...THEY'LL NEVER BE ABLE TO WIN NO MATTER HOW MANY TIMES THEY TRY.
...

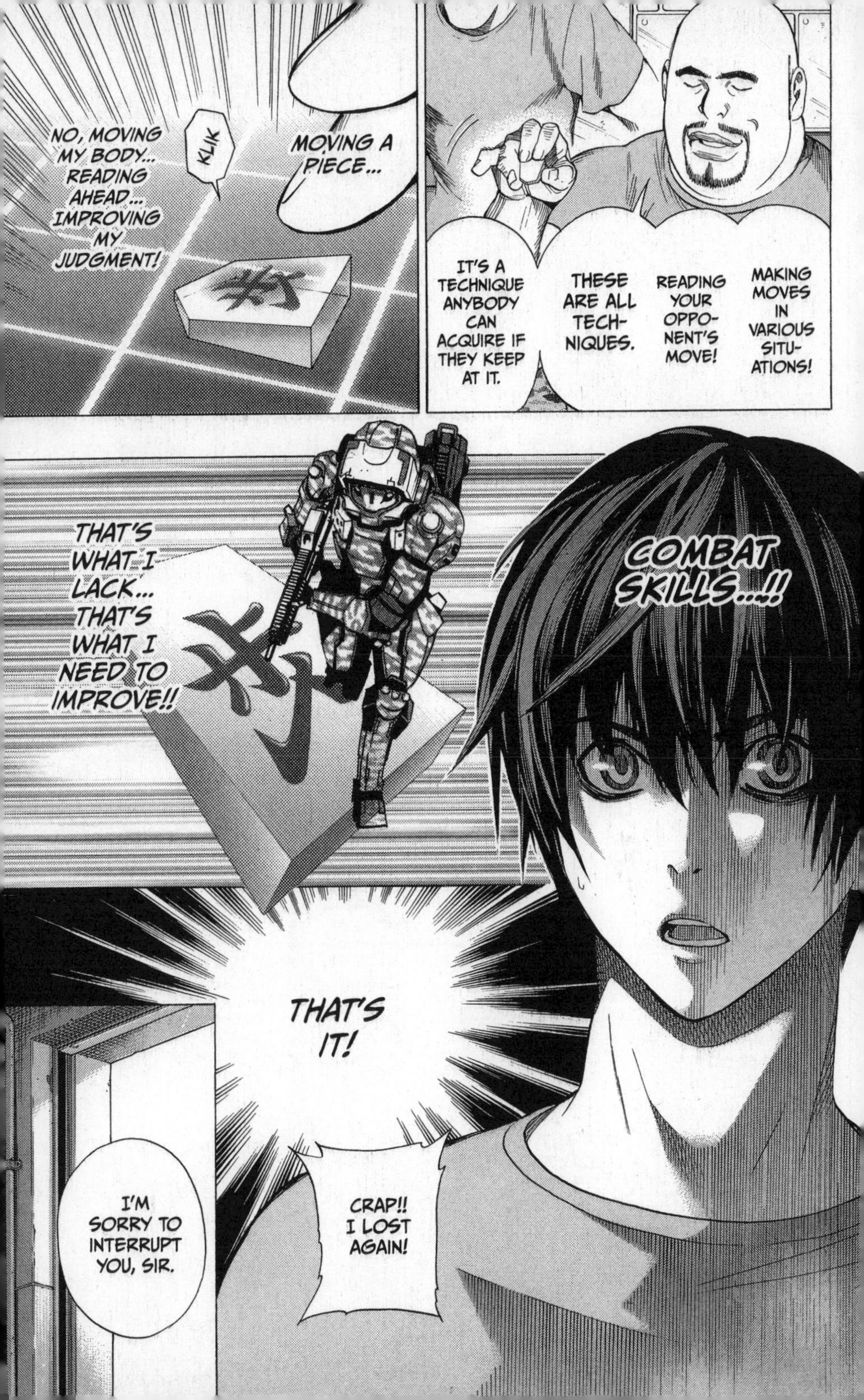
MAKING MOVES IN VARIOUS SITUATIONS!
READING YOUR OPPONENT'S MOVE!
THESE ARE ALL TECHNIQUES.
IT'S A TECHNIQUE ANYBODY CAN ACQUIRE IF THEY KEEP AT IT.
MOVING A PIECE...
KLIK
NO, MOVING MY BODY... READING AHEAD... IMPROVING MY JUDGMENT!
COMBAT SKILLS...!!
THAT'S WHAT I LACK... THAT'S WHAT I NEED TO IMPROVE!!
THAT'S IT!
CRAP!! I LOST AGAIN!
I'M SORRY TO INTERRUPT YOU, SIR.

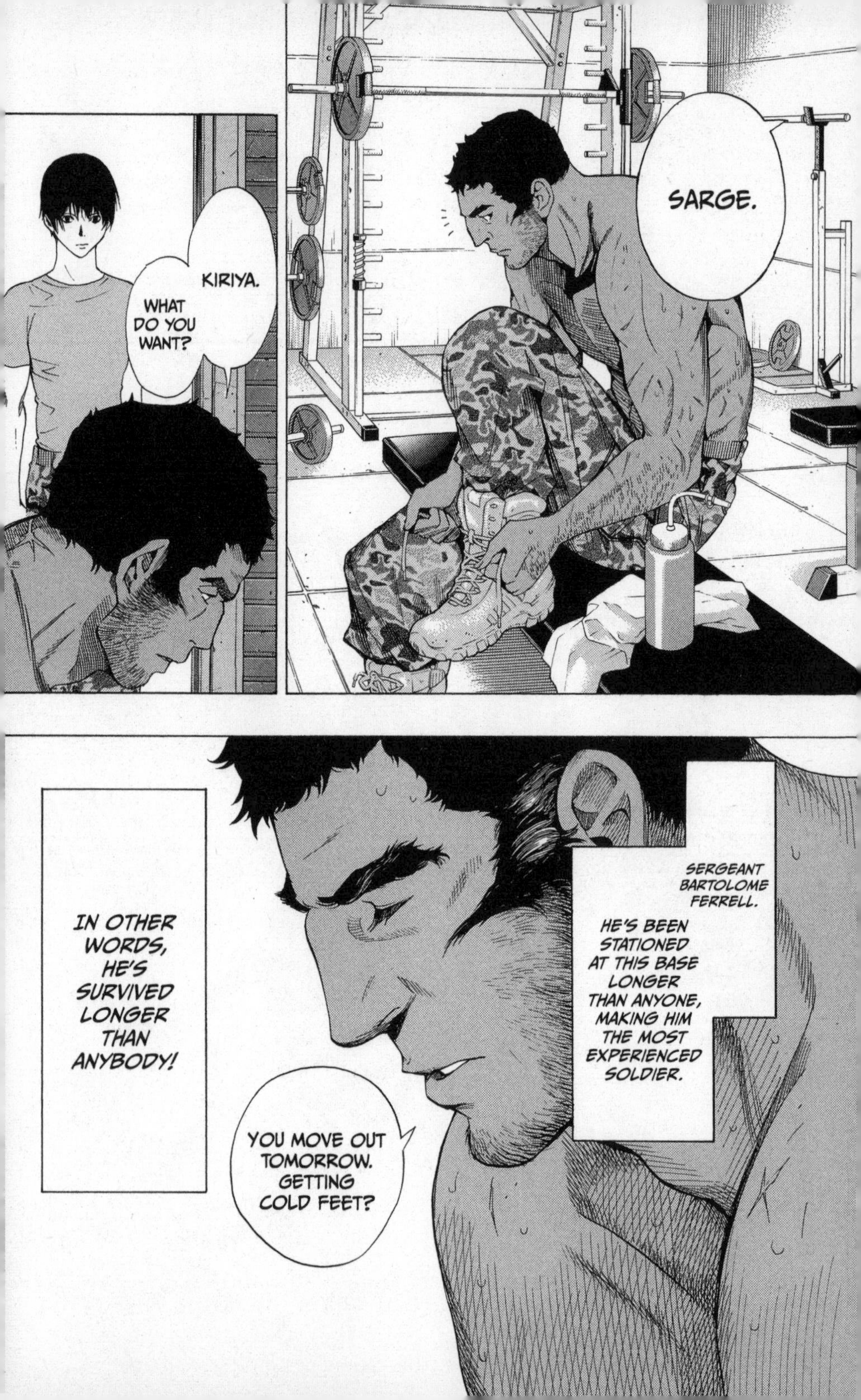
SARGE.
KIRIYA.
WHAT DO YOU WANT?
SERGEANT BARTOLOME FERRELL.
HE'S BEEN STATIONED AT THIS BASE LONGER THAN ANYONE, MAKING HIM THE MOST EXPERIENCED SOLDIER.
IN OTHER WORDS, HE'S SURVIVED LONGER THAN ANYBODY!
YOU MOVE OUT TOMORROW. GETTING COLD FEET?

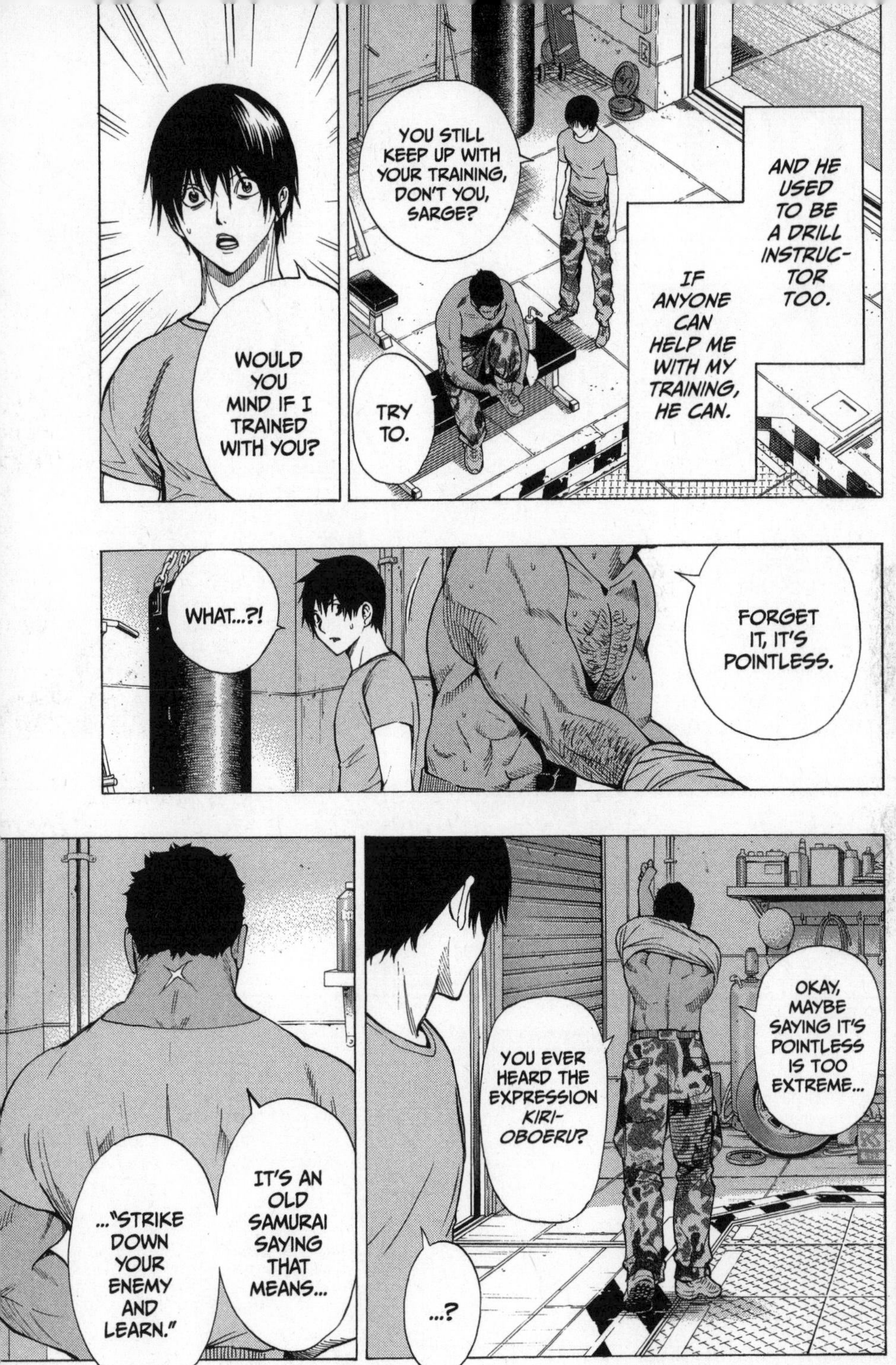
AND HE USED TO BE A DRILL INSTRUCTOR TOO.
IF ANYONE CAN HELP ME WITH MY TRAINING, HE CAN.
YOU STILL KEEP UP WITH YOUR TRAINING, DON'T YOU, SARGE?
TRY TO.
WOULD YOU MIND IF I TRAINED WITH YOU?
FORGET IT, IT'S POINTLESS.
WHAT...?!
OKAY, MAYBE SAYING IT'S POINTLESS IS TOO EXTREME...
YOU EVER HEARD THE EXPRESSION *KIRI-OBOERU*?
...?
IT'S AN OLD SAMURAI SAYING THAT MEANS...
..."STRIKE DOWN YOUR ENEMY AND LEARN."

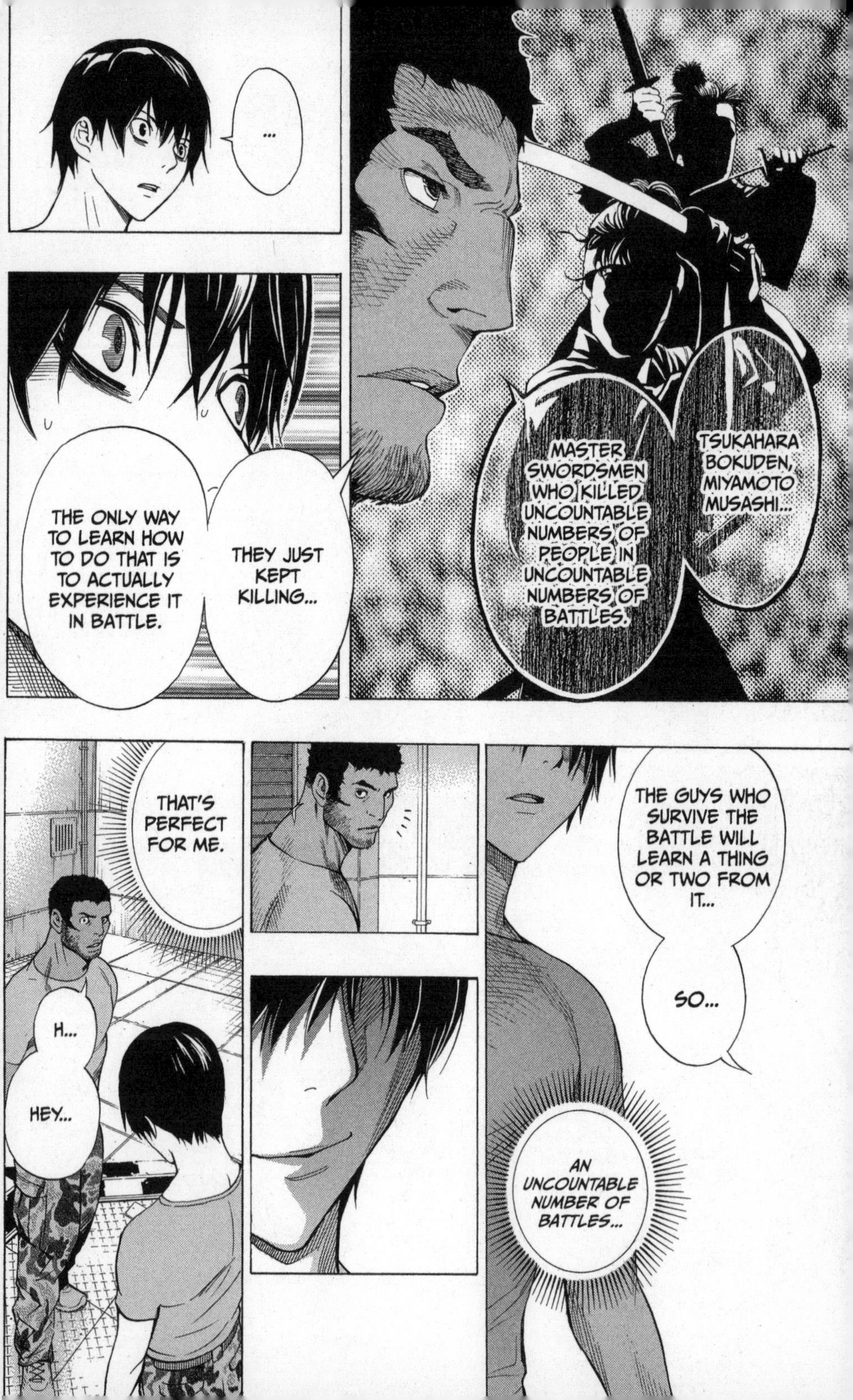
TSUKAHARA BOKUDEN, MIYAMOTO MUSASHI...
MASTER SWORDSMEN WHO KILLED UNCOUNTABLE NUMBERS OF PEOPLE IN UNCOUNTABLE NUMBERS OF BATTLES.
...
THEY JUST KEPT KILLING...
THE ONLY WAY TO LEARN HOW TO DO THAT IS TO ACTUALLY EXPERIENCE IT IN BATTLE.
THE GUYS WHO SURVIVE THE BATTLE WILL LEARN A THING OR TWO FROM IT...
SO...
AN UNCOUNTABLE NUMBER OF BATTLES...
THAT'S PERFECT FOR ME.
H...
HEY...

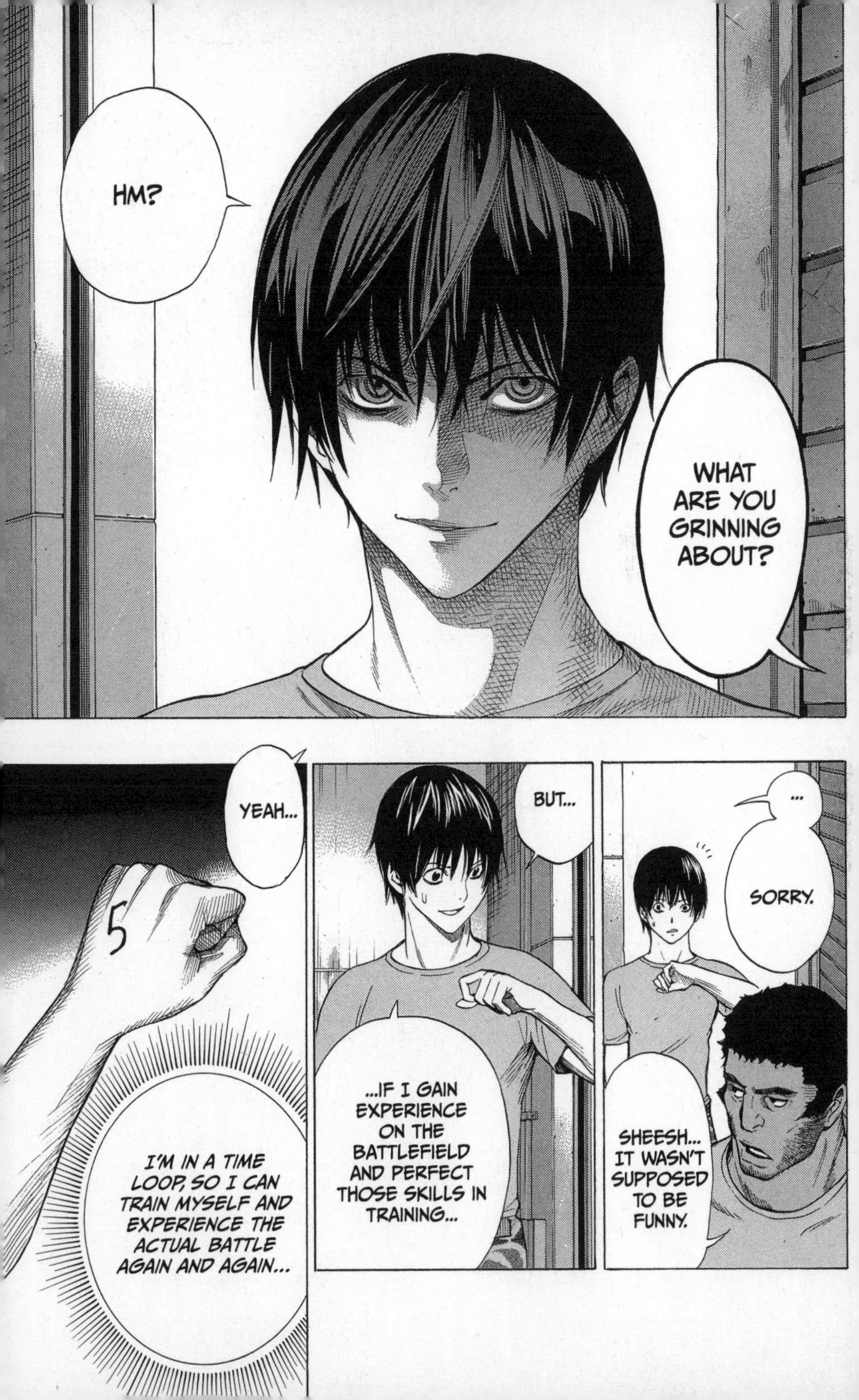
HM?
WHAT ARE YOU GRINNING ABOUT?
YEAH...
I'M IN A TIME LOOP, SO I CAN TRAIN MYSELF AND EXPERIENCE THE ACTUAL BATTLE AGAIN AND AGAIN...
BUT...
...IF I GAIN EXPERIENCE ON THE BATTLEFIELD AND PERFECT THOSE SKILLS IN TRAINING...
SHEESH... IT WASN'T SUPPOSED TO BE FUNNY.
...
SORRY.
5

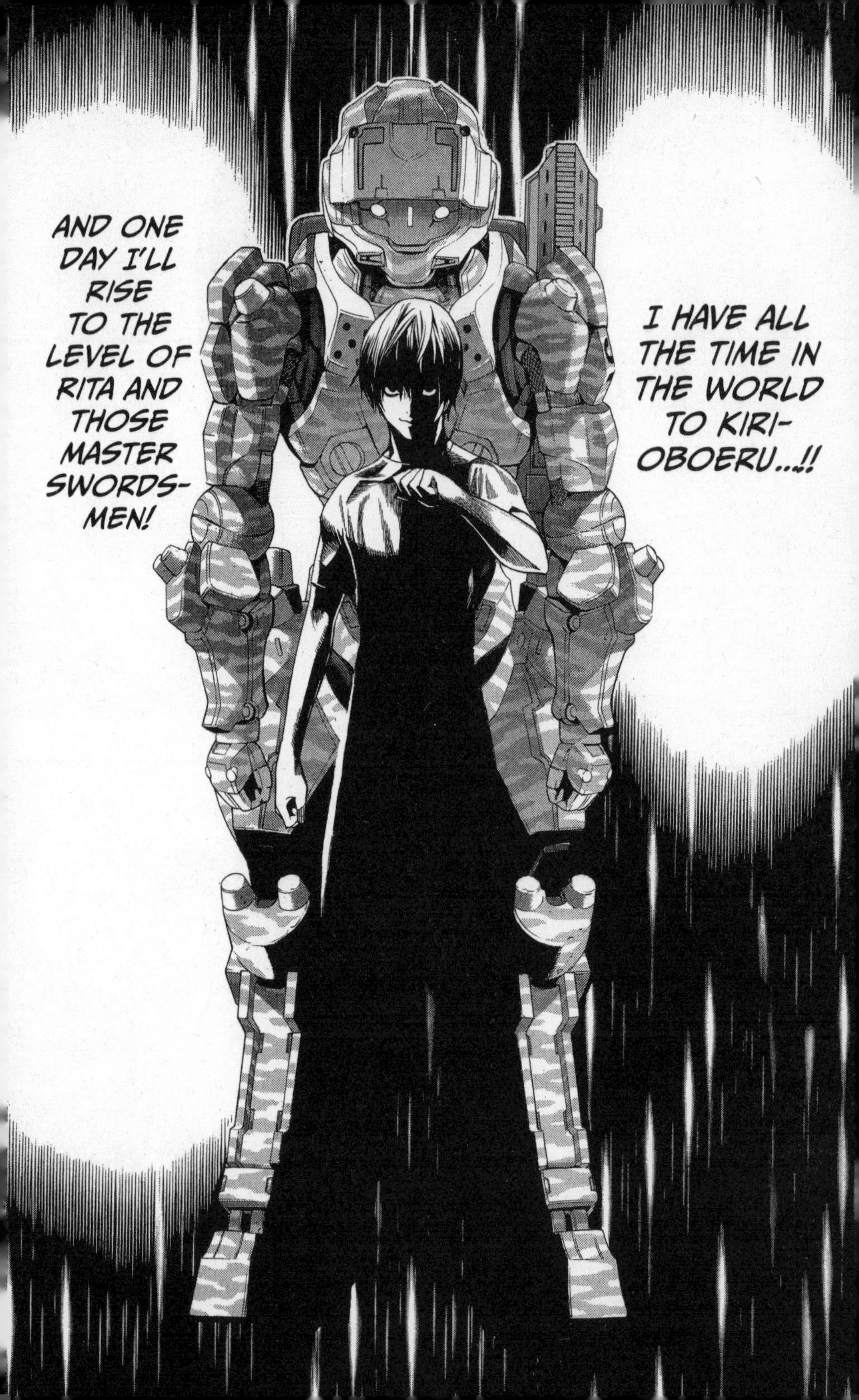
I HAVE ALL THE TIME IN THE WORLD TO KIRI-OBOERU...!!
AND ONE DAY I'LL RISE TO THE LEVEL OF RITA AND THOSE MASTER SWORDS-MEN!

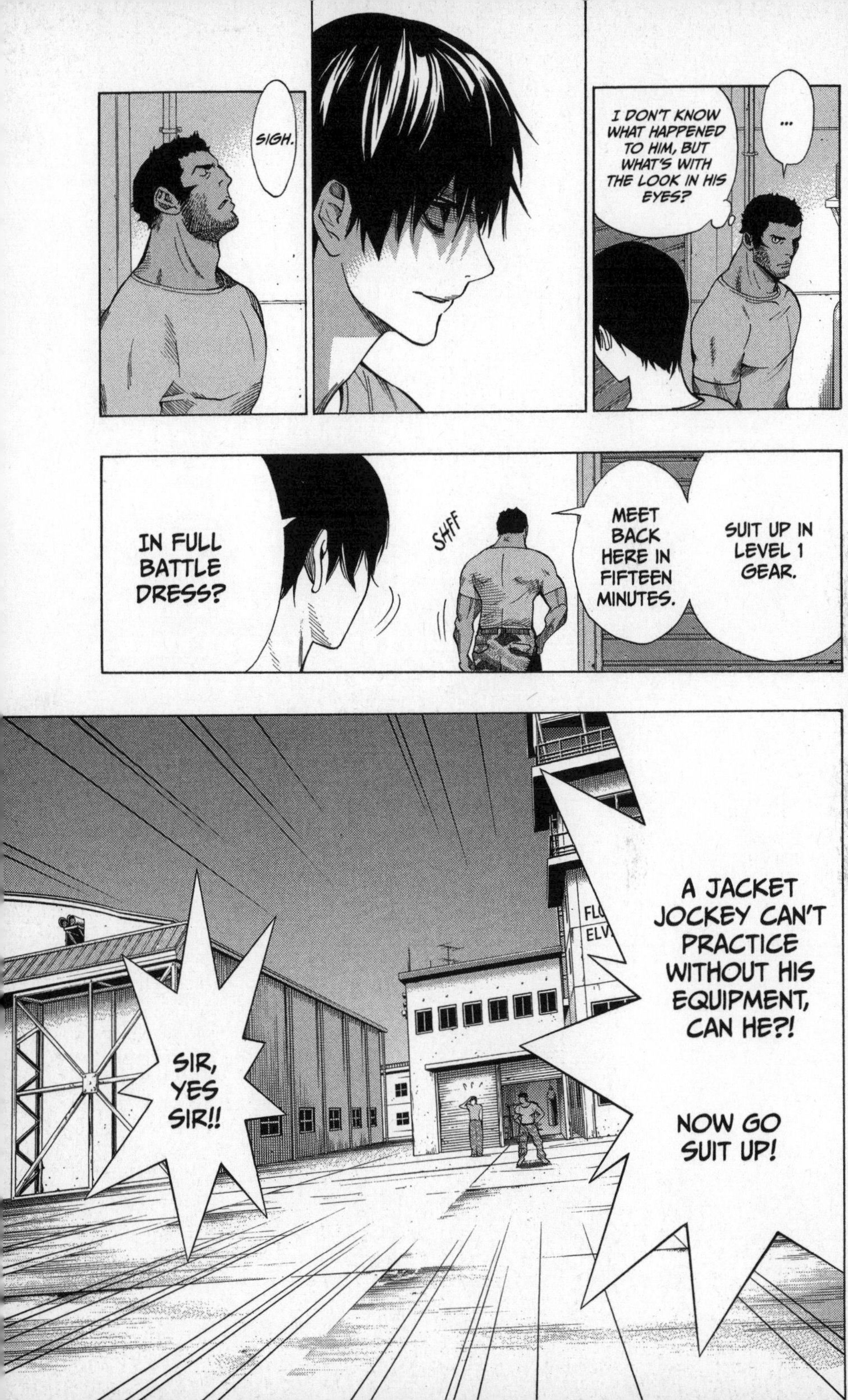
...
I DON'T KNOW WHAT HAPPENED TO HIM, BUT WHAT'S WITH THE LOOK IN HIS EYES?
SIGH.
SUIT UP IN LEVEL 1 GEAR.
MEET BACK HERE IN FIFTEEN MINUTES.
SHFF
IN FULL BATTLE DRESS?
A JACKET JOCKEY CAN'T PRACTICE WITHOUT HIS EQUIPMENT, CAN HE?!
NOW GO SUIT UP!
SIR, YES SIR!!

A window of opportunity
might present itself in
tomorrow's battle.
The odds of that happening
might be 0.1 percent, or even
0.01 percent, but if I could
improve my combat skills
even the slightest bit—if
that window were to open
even a crack—I'd find a way
to force it open wide.
If I could train to jump every
hurdle this little track meet
of death threw at me, maybe
someday I'd wake up in a
world with a tomorrow.

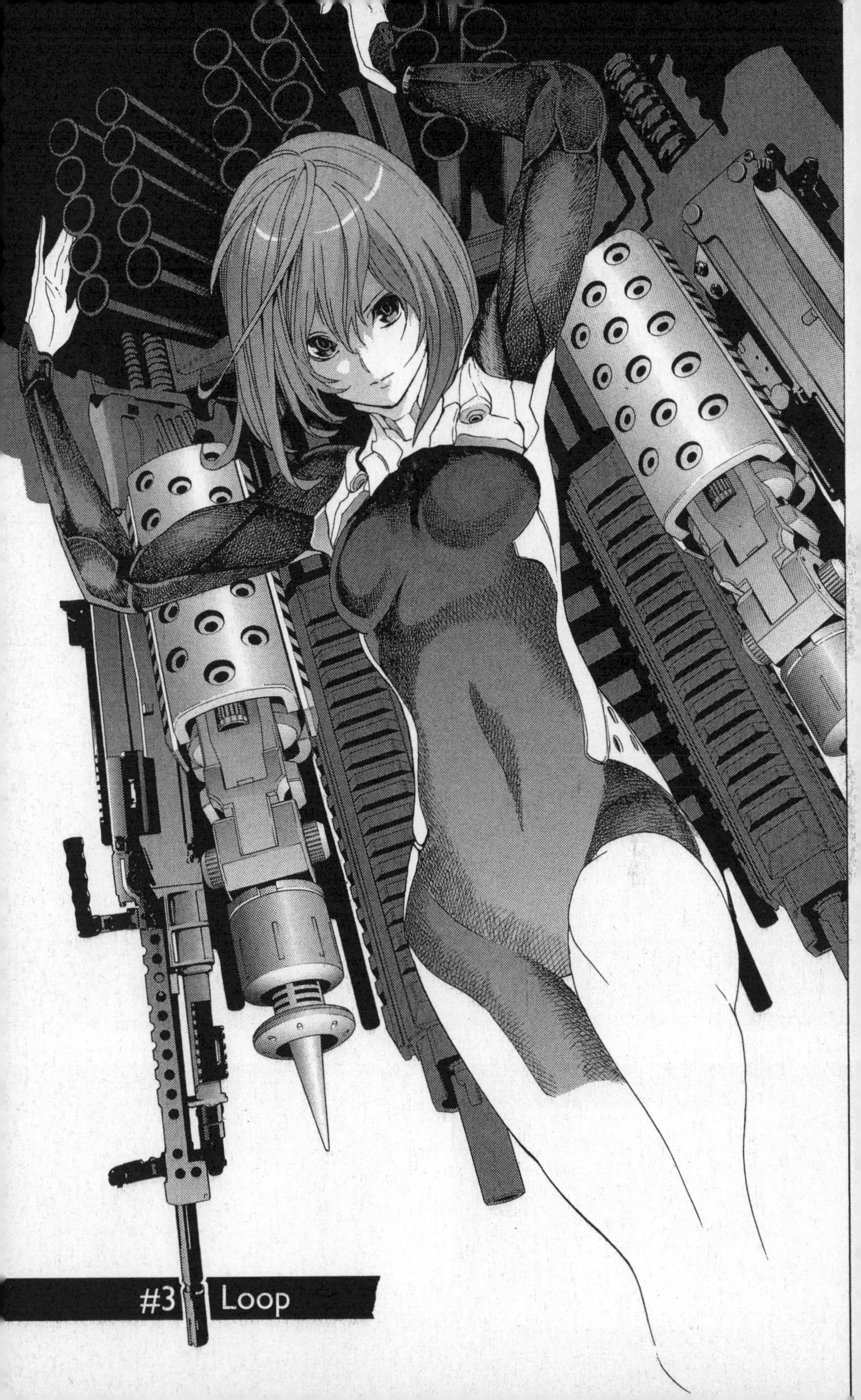
#3 Loop

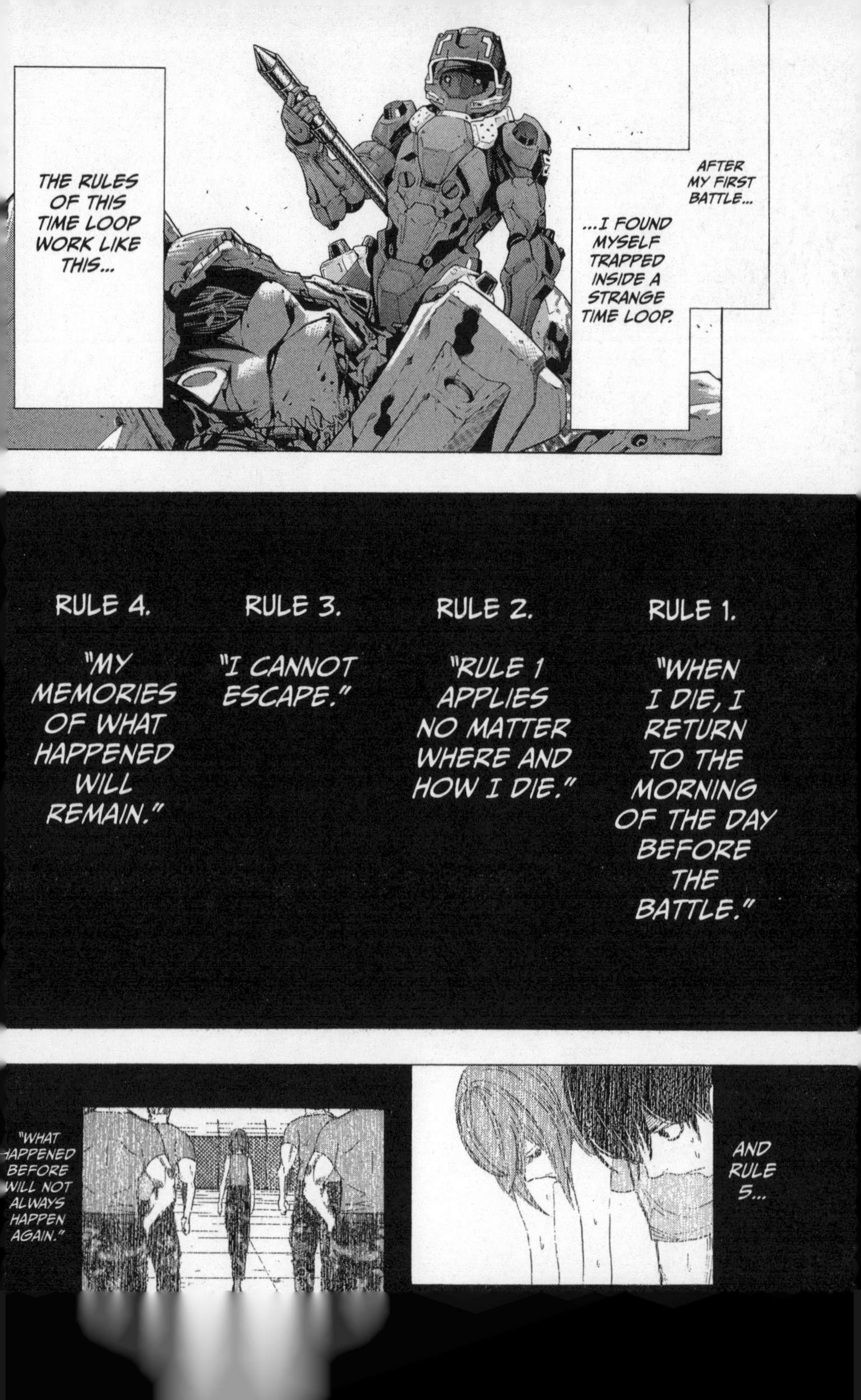
AFTER MY FIRST BATTLE...
...I FOUND MYSELF TRAPPED INSIDE A STRANGE TIME LOOP.
THE RULES OF THIS TIME LOOP WORK LIKE THIS...
RULE 1.
"WHEN I DIE, I RETURN TO THE MORNING OF THE DAY BEFORE THE BATTLE."
RULE 2.
"RULE 1 APPLIES NO MATTER WHERE AND HOW I DIE."
RULE 3.
"I CANNOT ESCAPE."
RULE 4.
"MY MEMORIES OF WHAT HAPPENED WILL REMAIN."
AND RULE 5...
"WHAT HAPPENED BEFORE WILL NOT ALWAYS HAPPEN AGAIN."

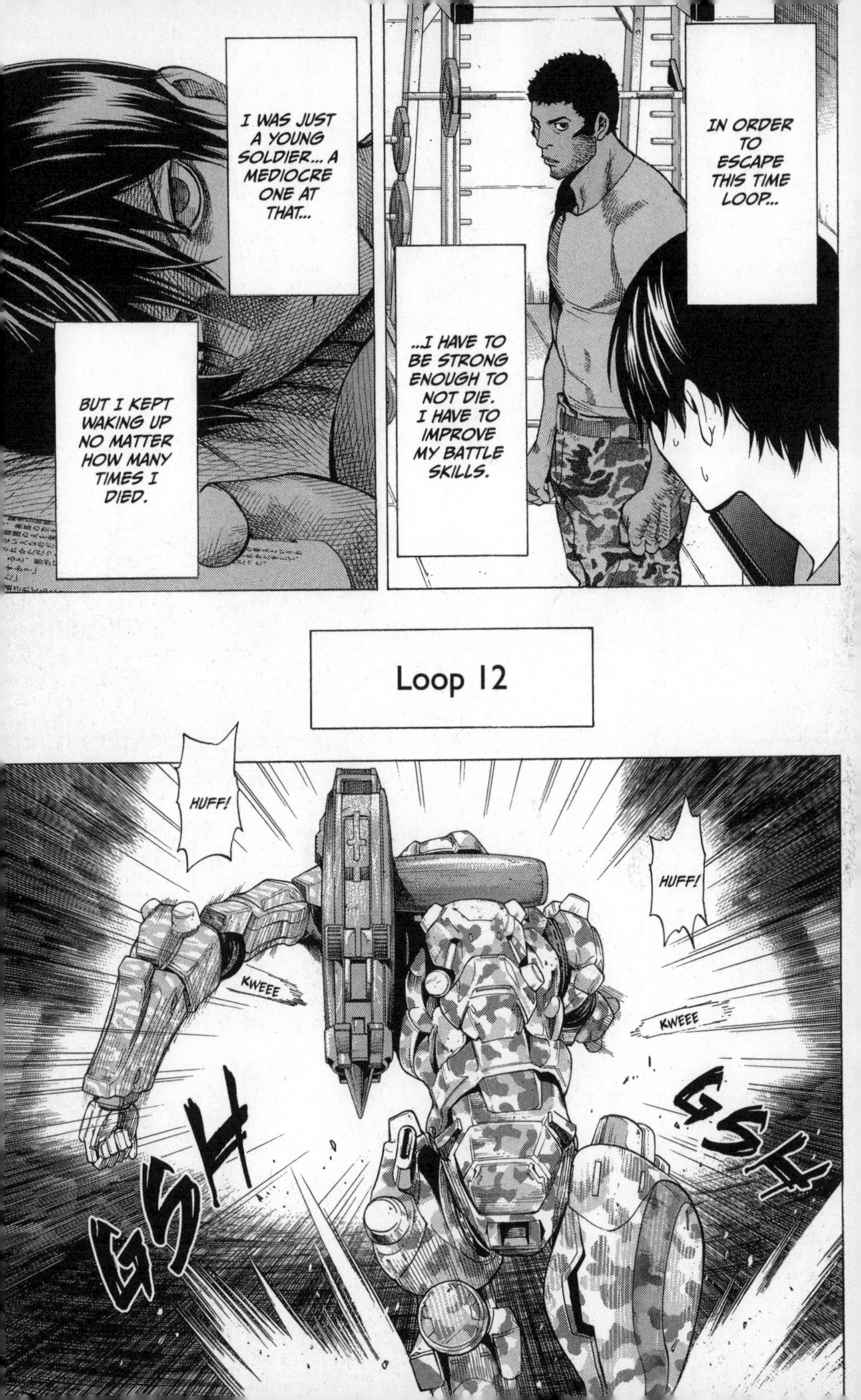
IN ORDER TO ESCAPE THIS TIME LOOP...
...I HAVE TO BE STRONG ENOUGH TO NOT DIE. I HAVE TO IMPROVE MY BATTLE SKILLS.
I WAS JUST A YOUNG SOLDIER... A MEDIOCRE ONE AT THAT...
BUT I KEPT WAKING UP NO MATTER HOW MANY TIMES I DIED.
Loop 12
HUFF!
HUFF!
KWEEE
KWEEE
GSH
GSH

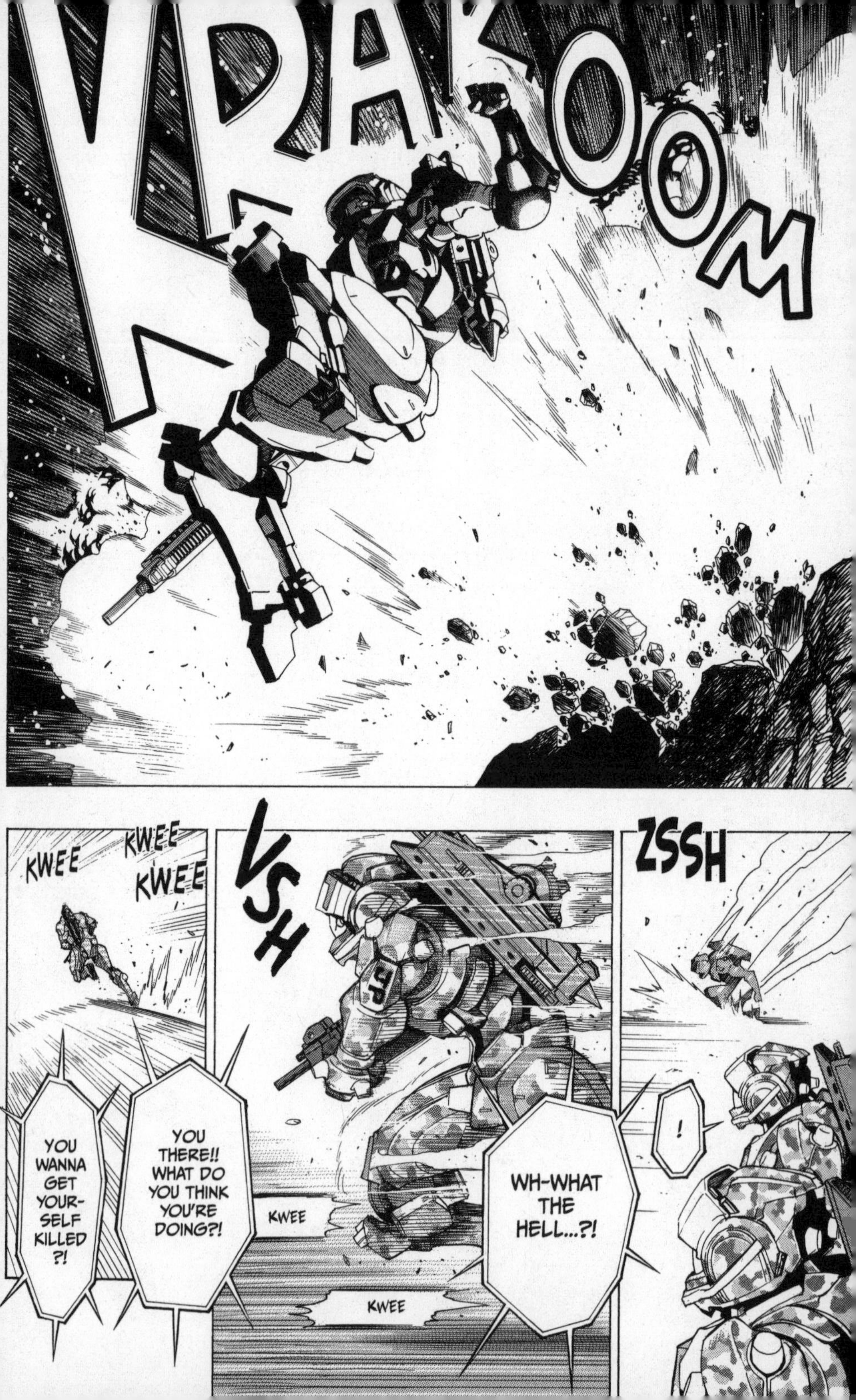
VRAKOOM
ZSSH
!
WH-WHAT THE HELL...?!
VSH
KWEE
KWEE
KWEE
KWEE
KWEE
YOU THERE!! WHAT DO YOU THINK YOU'RE DOING?!
YOU WANNA GET YOURSELF KILLED?!

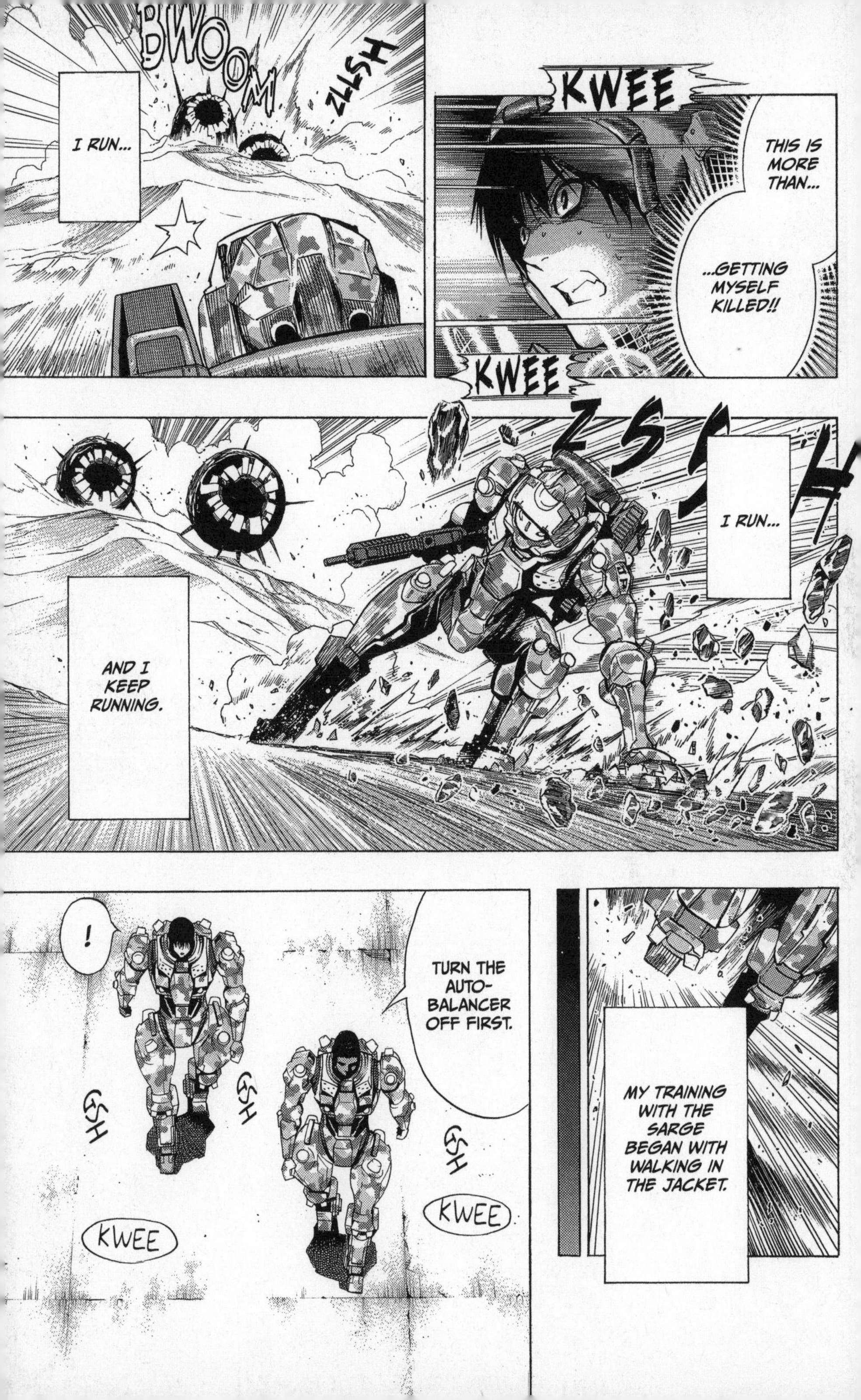
KWEE
THIS IS MORE THAN...
...GETTING MYSELF KILLED!!
KWEE
BWOOM
ZLLSH
I RUN...
ZSSH
I RUN...
AND I KEEP RUNNING.
MY TRAINING WITH THE SARGE BEGAN WITH WALKING IN THE JACKET.
TURN THE AUTO-BALANCER OFF FIRST.
GSH
KWEE
!
GSH
GSH
KWEE

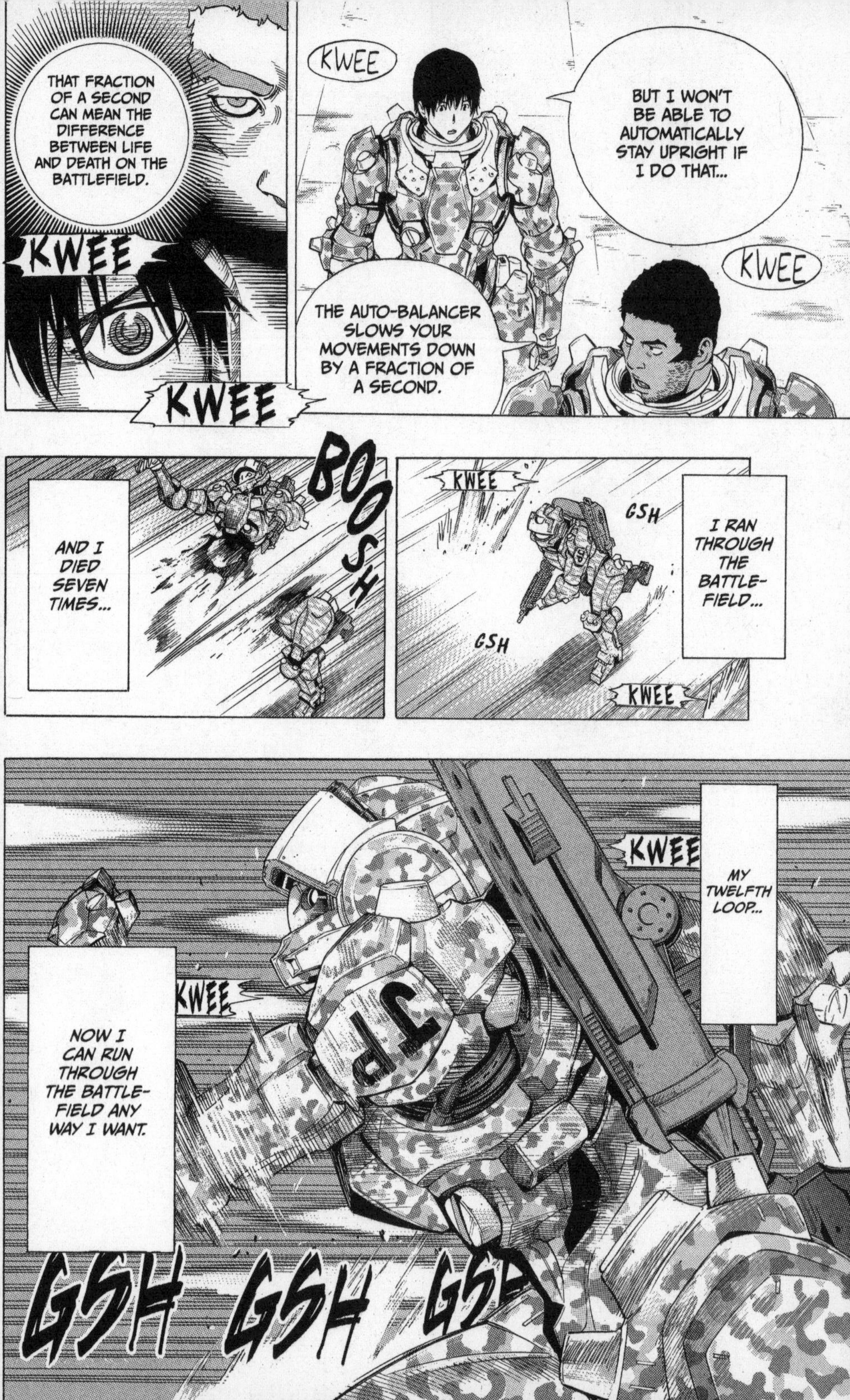
BUT I WON'T BE ABLE TO AUTOMATICALLY STAY UPRIGHT IF I DO THAT...
KWEE
KWEE
THE AUTO-BALANCER SLOWS YOUR MOVEMENTS DOWN BY A FRACTION OF A SECOND.
THAT FRACTION OF A SECOND CAN MEAN THE DIFFERENCE BETWEEN LIFE AND DEATH ON THE BATTLEFIELD.
KWEE
KWEE
I RAN THROUGH THE BATTLE-FIELD...
KWEE
GSH
GSH
KWEE
BOOSH
AND I DIED SEVEN TIMES...
MY TWELFTH LOOP...
KWEE
KWEE
NOW I CAN RUN THROUGH THE BATTLE-FIELD ANY WAY I WANT.
GSH GSH GS

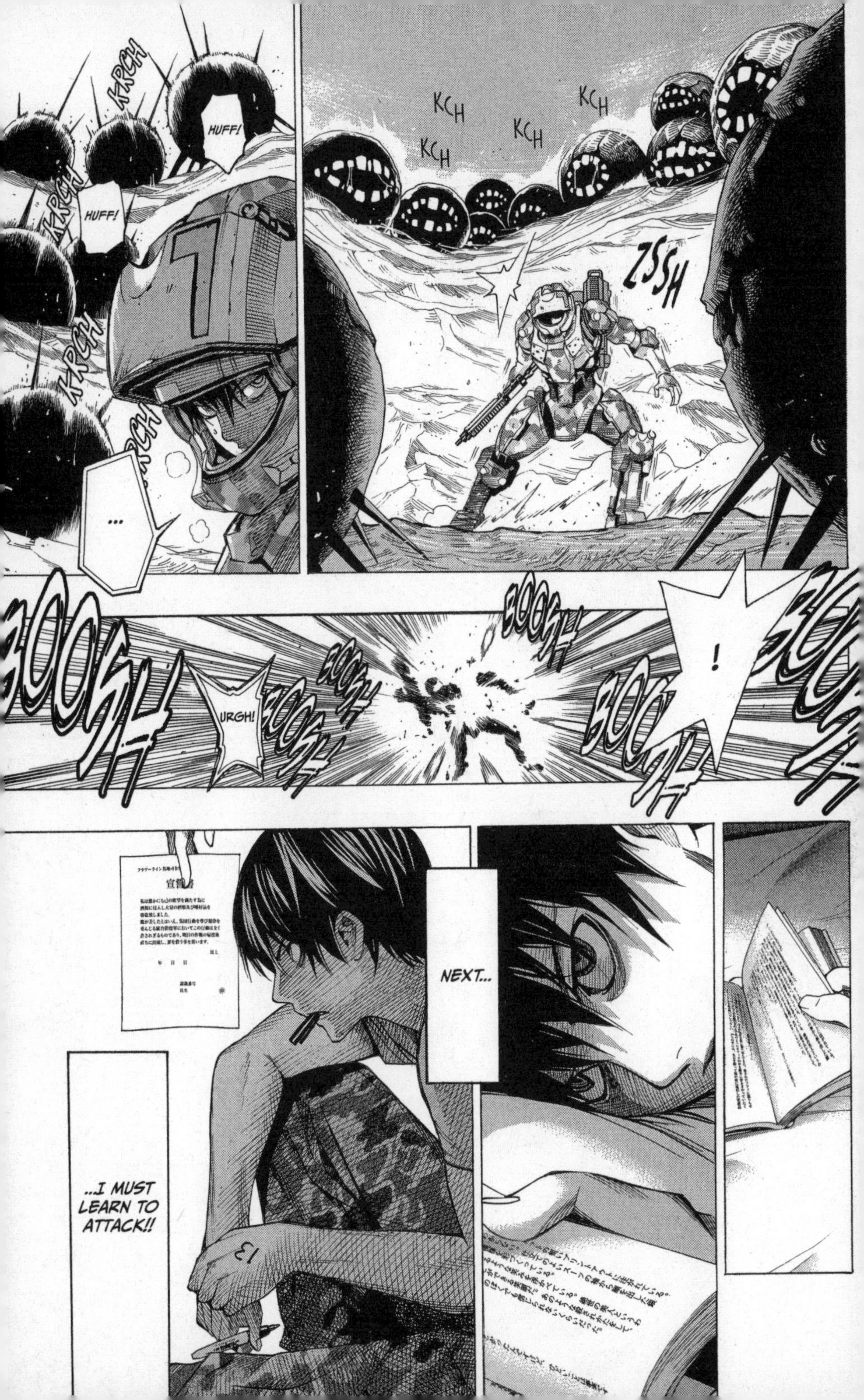
KCH
KCH
KCH
KCH
ZSSH
KRCH
HUFF!
KRCH
HUFF!
KRCH
KRCH
...
BOOOSH
!
BOOOSH
BOOSH!
BOOSH!
BOOOSH!
URGH!
BOOOSH
NEXT...
宣誓書
...I MUST LEARN TO ATTACK!!
13

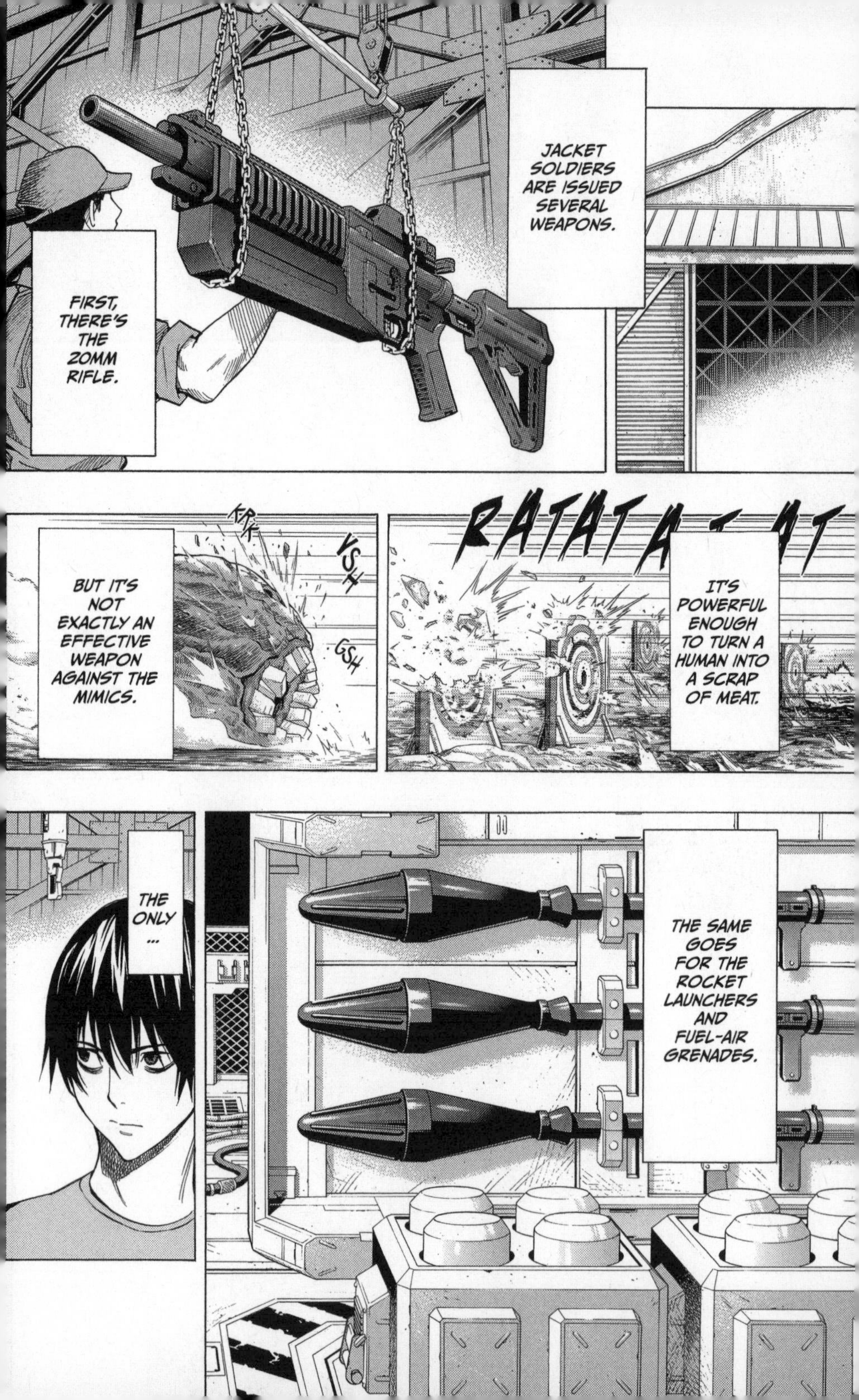
JACKET SOLDIERS ARE ISSUED SEVERAL WEAPONS.
FIRST, THERE'S THE ZOMM RIFLE.
RATATAT
IT'S POWERFUL ENOUGH TO TURN A HUMAN INTO A SCRAP OF MEAT.
KRK
VSH
GSH
BUT IT'S NOT EXACTLY AN EFFECTIVE WEAPON AGAINST THE MIMICS.
THE SAME GOES FOR THE ROCKET LAUNCHERS AND FUEL-AIR GRENADES.
THE ONLY ...

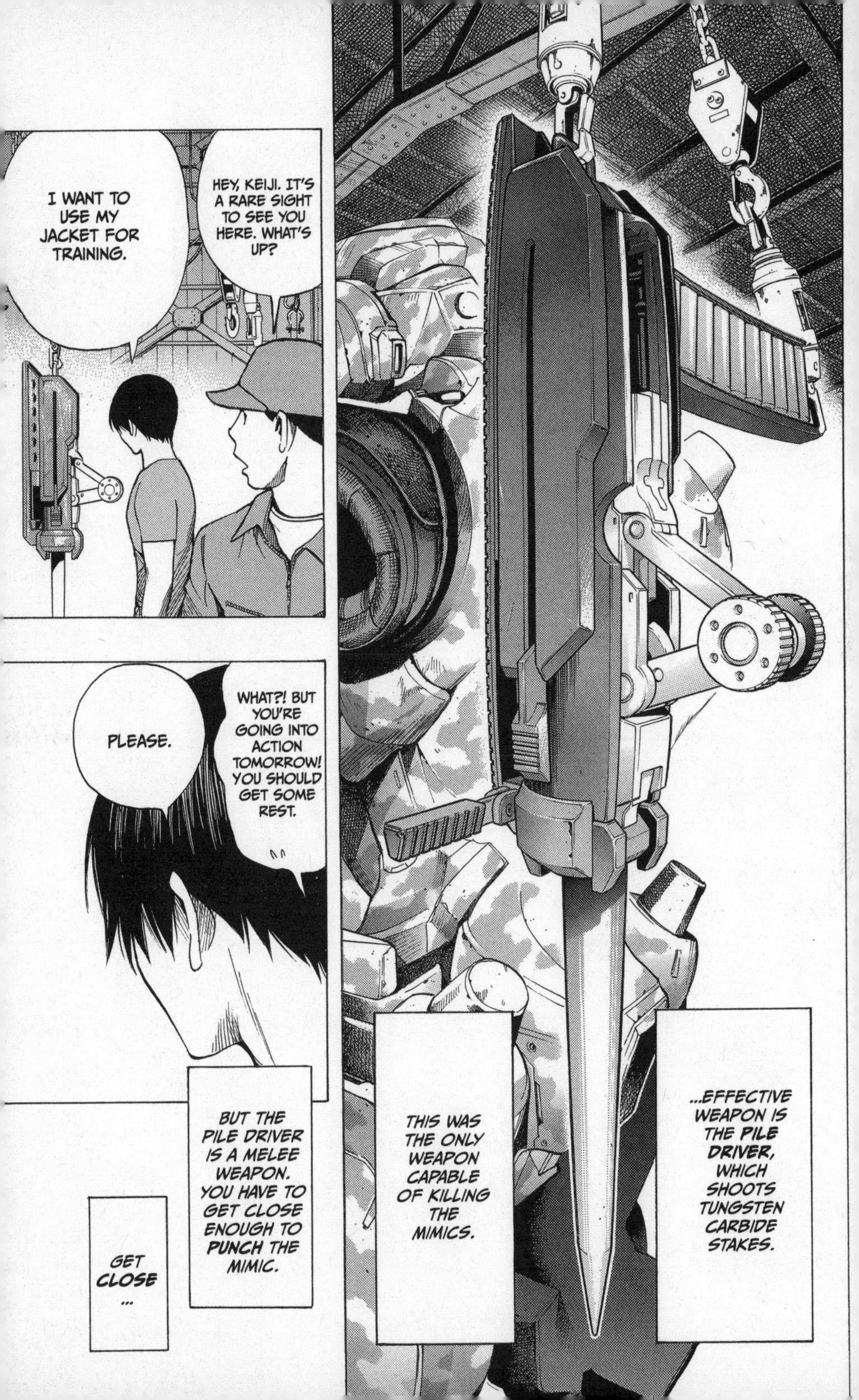
...EFFECTIVE WEAPON IS THE PILE DRIVER, WHICH SHOOTS TUNGSTEN CARBIDE STAKES.
THIS WAS THE ONLY WEAPON CAPABLE OF KILLING THE MIMICS.
HEY, KEIJI. IT'S A RARE SIGHT TO SEE YOU HERE. WHAT'S UP?
I WANT TO USE MY JACKET FOR TRAINING.
WHAT?! BUT YOU'RE GOING INTO ACTION TOMORROW! YOU SHOULD GET SOME REST.
PLEASE.
BUT THE PILE DRIVER IS A MELEE WEAPON. YOU HAVE TO GET CLOSE ENOUGH TO PUNCH THE MIMIC.
GET CLOSE ...

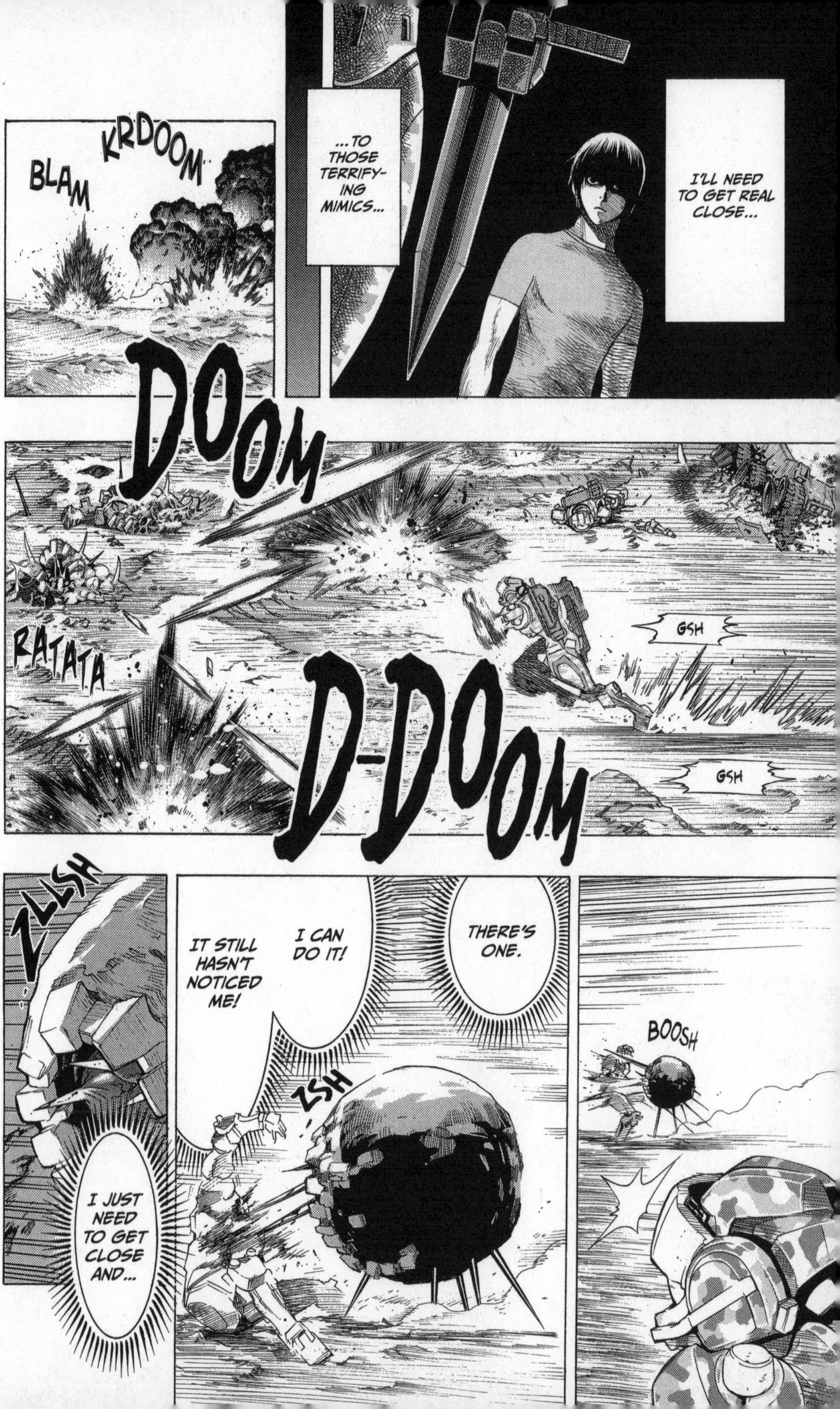
I'LL NEED TO GET REAL CLOSE...
...TO THOSE TERRIFYING MIMICS...
KRDOOM
BLAM
DOOM
GSH
GSH
D-DOOM
RATATA
BOOSH
THERE'S ONE.
I CAN DO IT!
IT STILL HASN'T NOTICED ME!
ZSH
ZLLSH
I JUST NEED TO GET CLOSE AND...

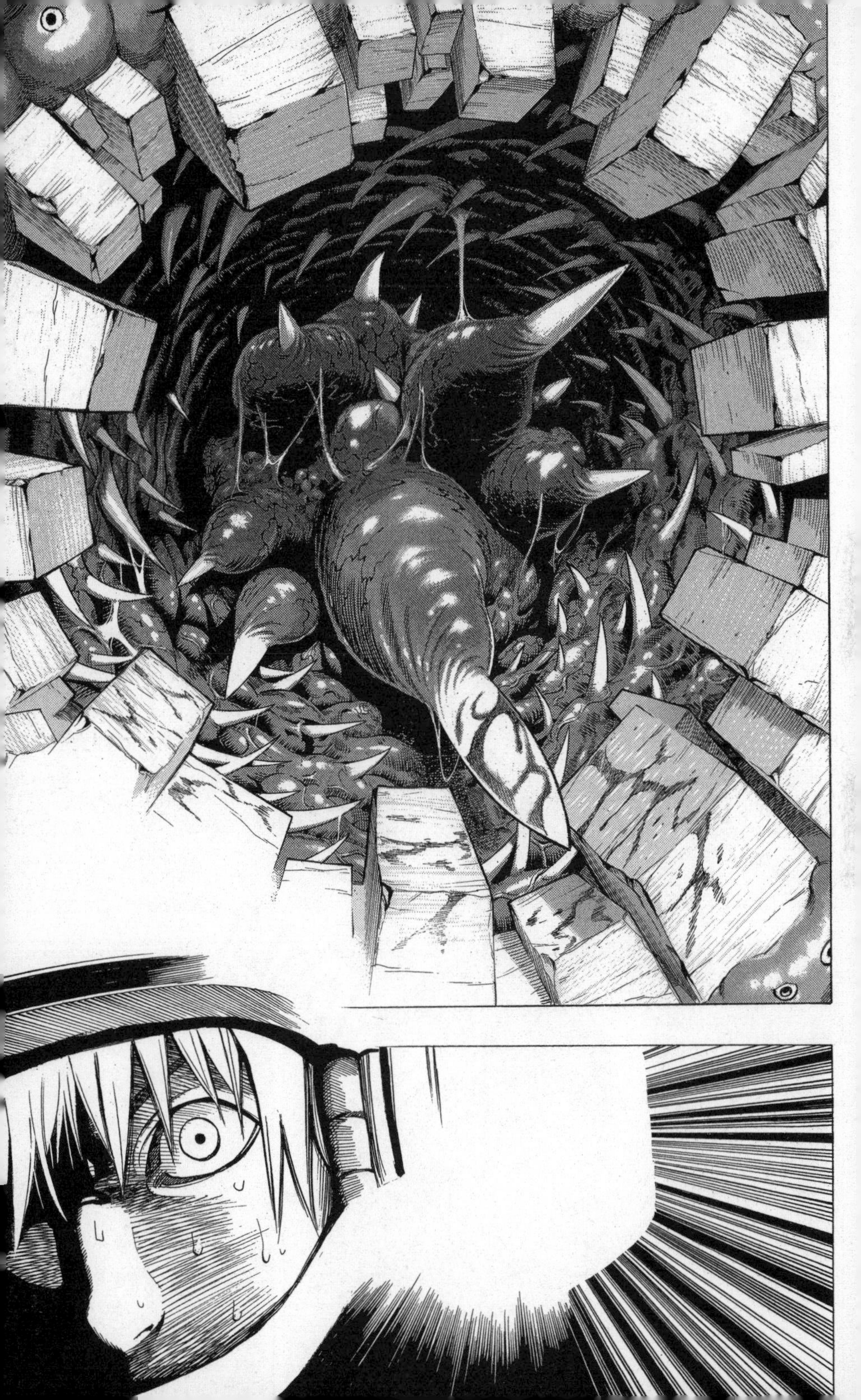

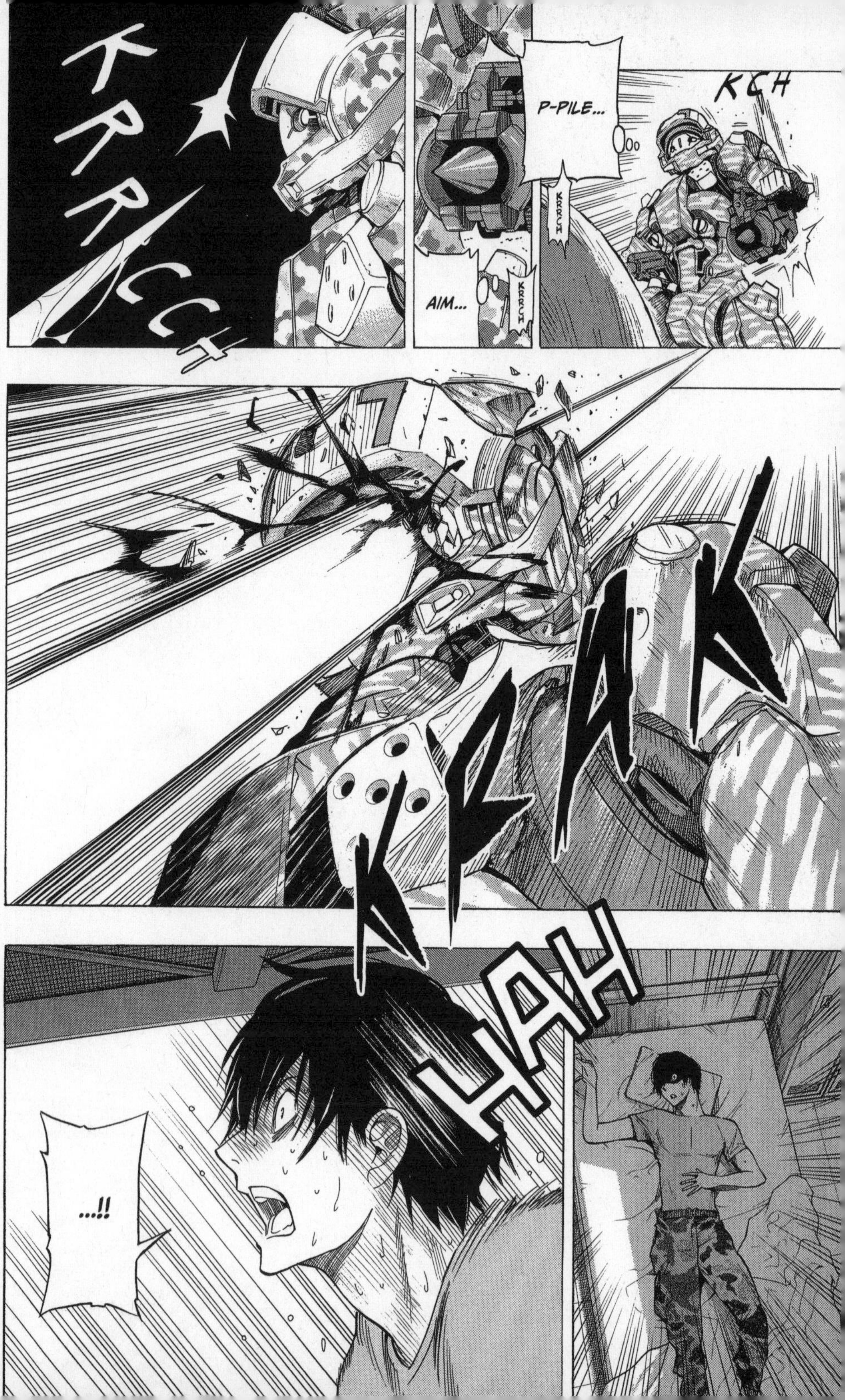
KCH
P-PILE...
KRRCH
AIM...
KRRCH
KRRRCCH
KRAK
HAH
...!!

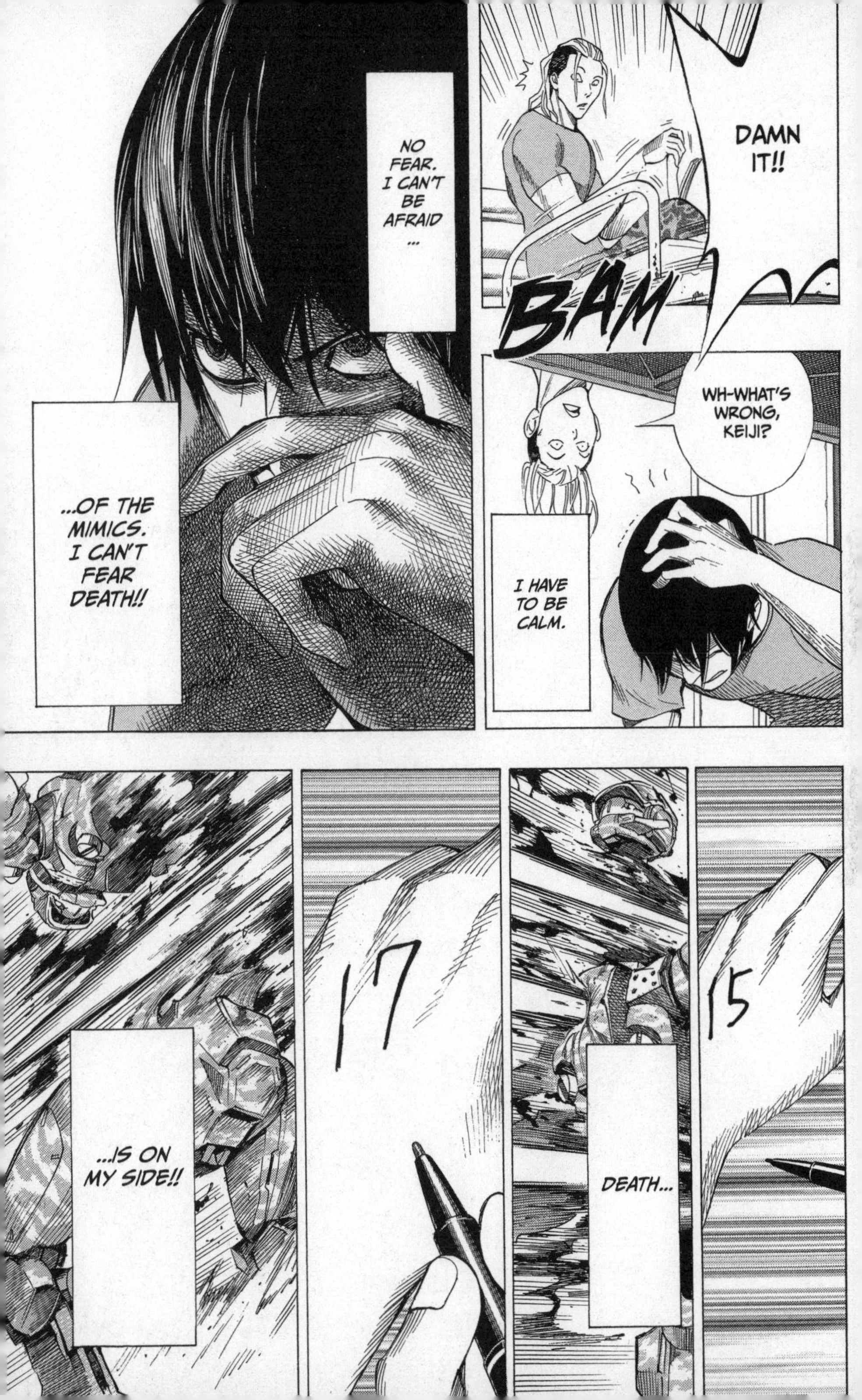
DAMN IT!!
BAM
WH-WHAT'S WRONG, KEIJI?
I HAVE TO BE CALM.
NO FEAR. I CAN'T BE AFRAID ...
...OF THE MIMICS. I CAN'T FEAR DEATH!!
15
DEATH...
17
...IS ON MY SIDE!!

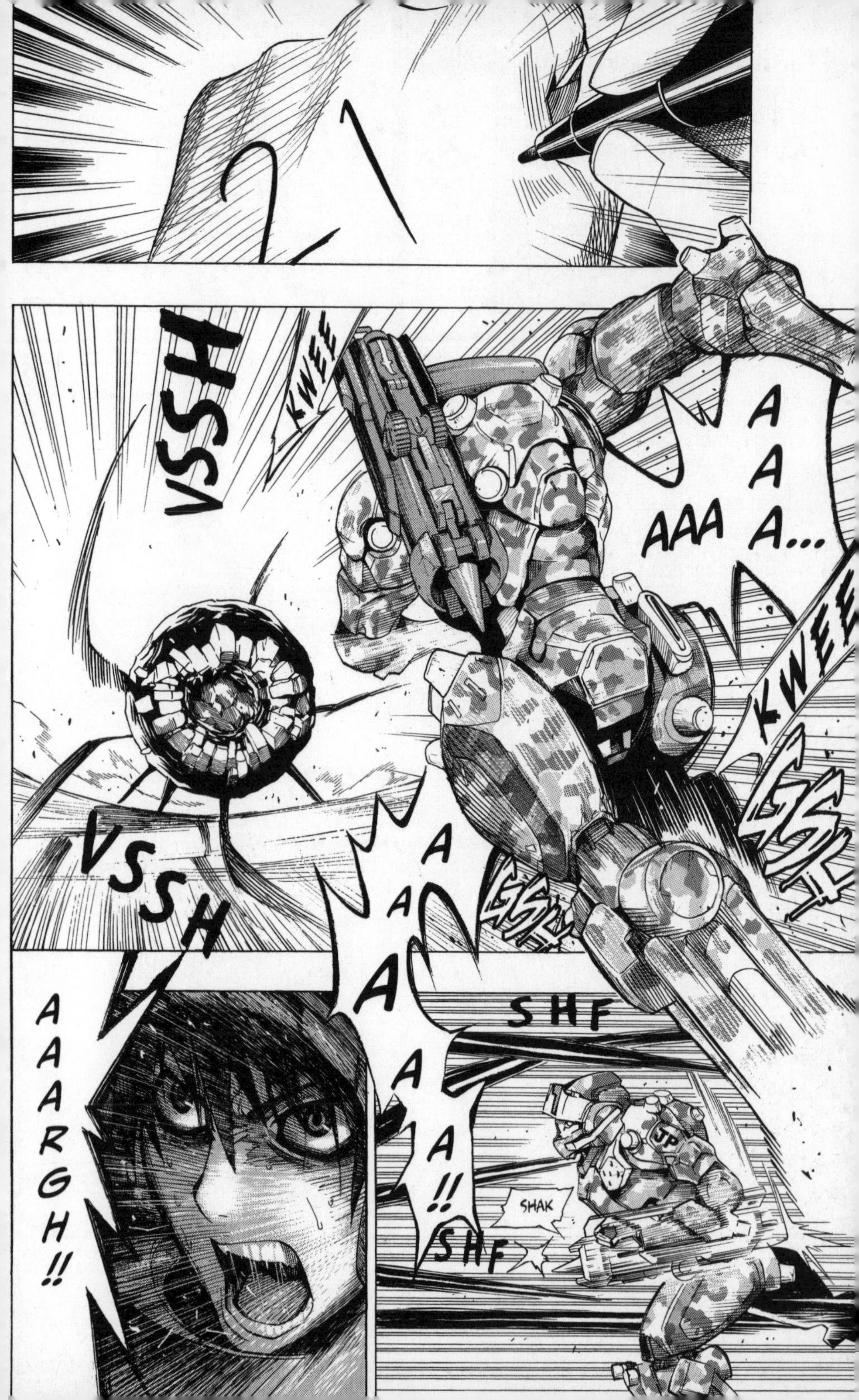
KWEE
VSSH
AAAA...
AAA
KWEE
VSSH
AAAAAA!!
SHF
SHAK
SHF
AAAARGH!!

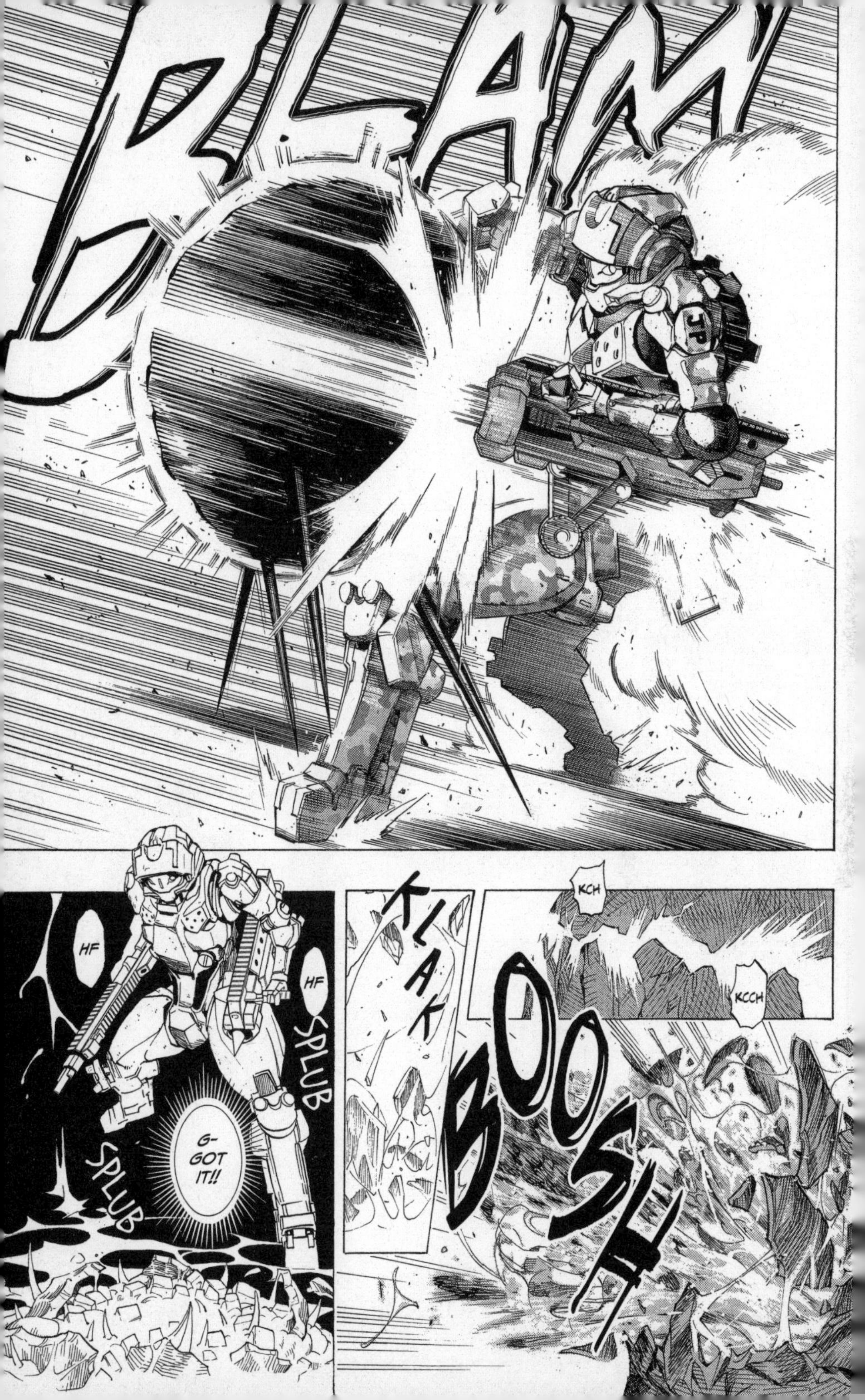
BLAM!
KCH
KCCH
KLAK
BOOSH
HF
HF
SPLUB
SPLUB
G-GOT IT!!

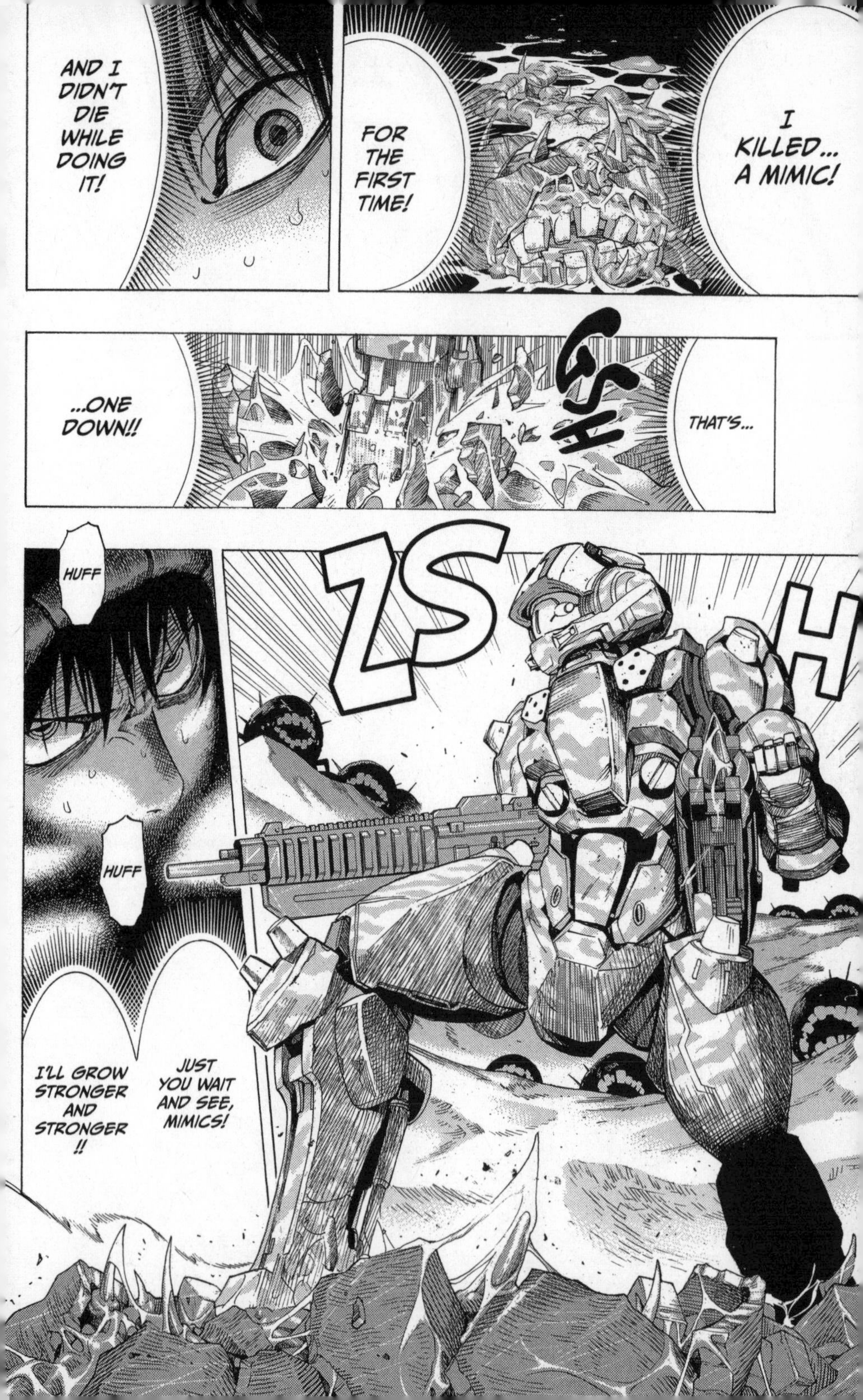
I KILLED... A MIMIC!
FOR THE FIRST TIME!
AND I DIDN'T DIE WHILE DOING IT!
THAT'S...
GSH
...ONE DOWN!!
ZSH
HUFF
HUFF
JUST YOU WAIT AND SEE, MIMICS!
I'LL GROW STRONGER AND STRONGER!!

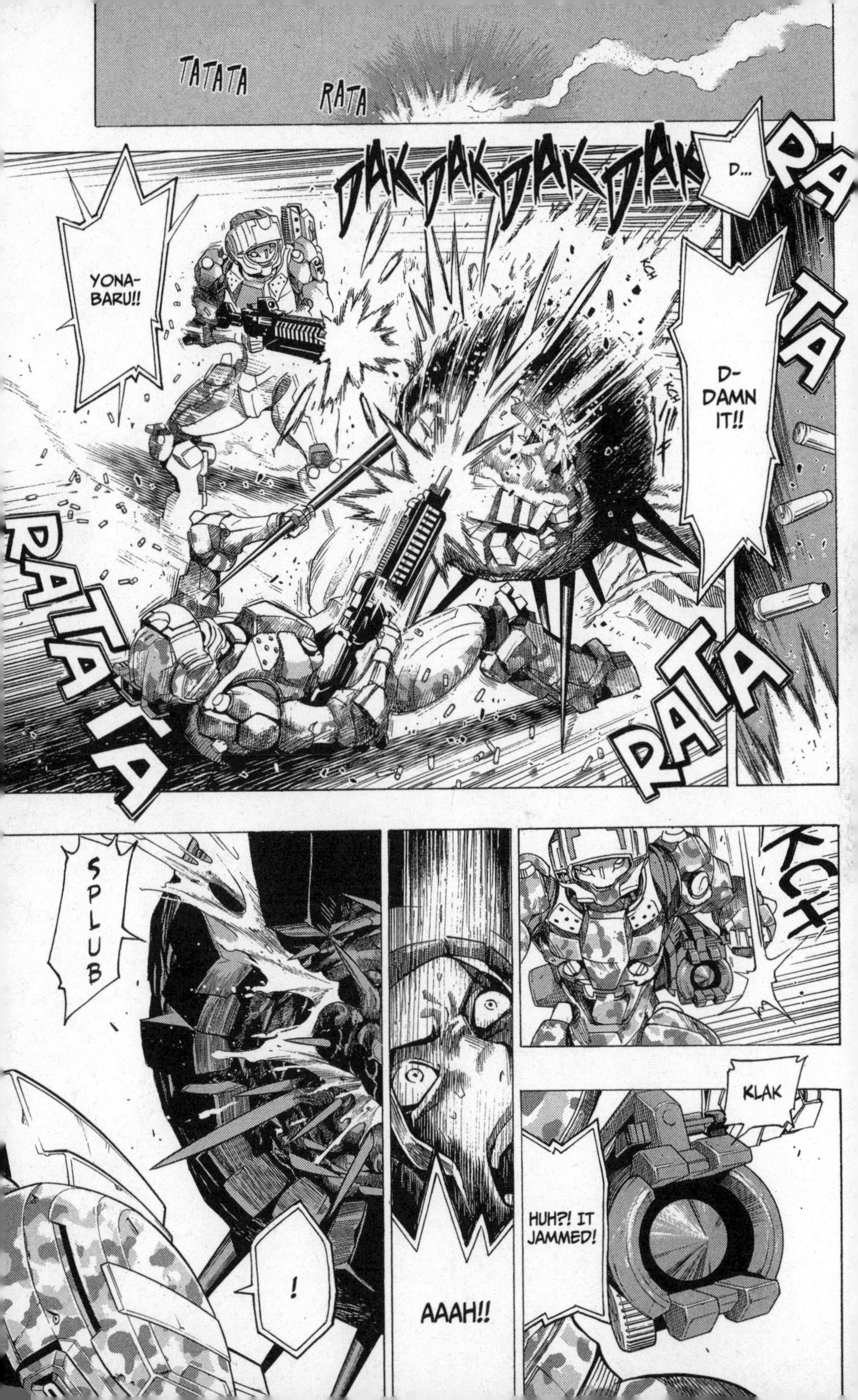
TATATA
RATA
D...
RATATA
KCH
KCH
D-DAMN IT!!
DAK DAK DAK DAK
YONA-BARU!!
RATA
RATATA
KCH
KLAK
HUH?! IT JAMMED!
AAAH!!
SPLUB
!

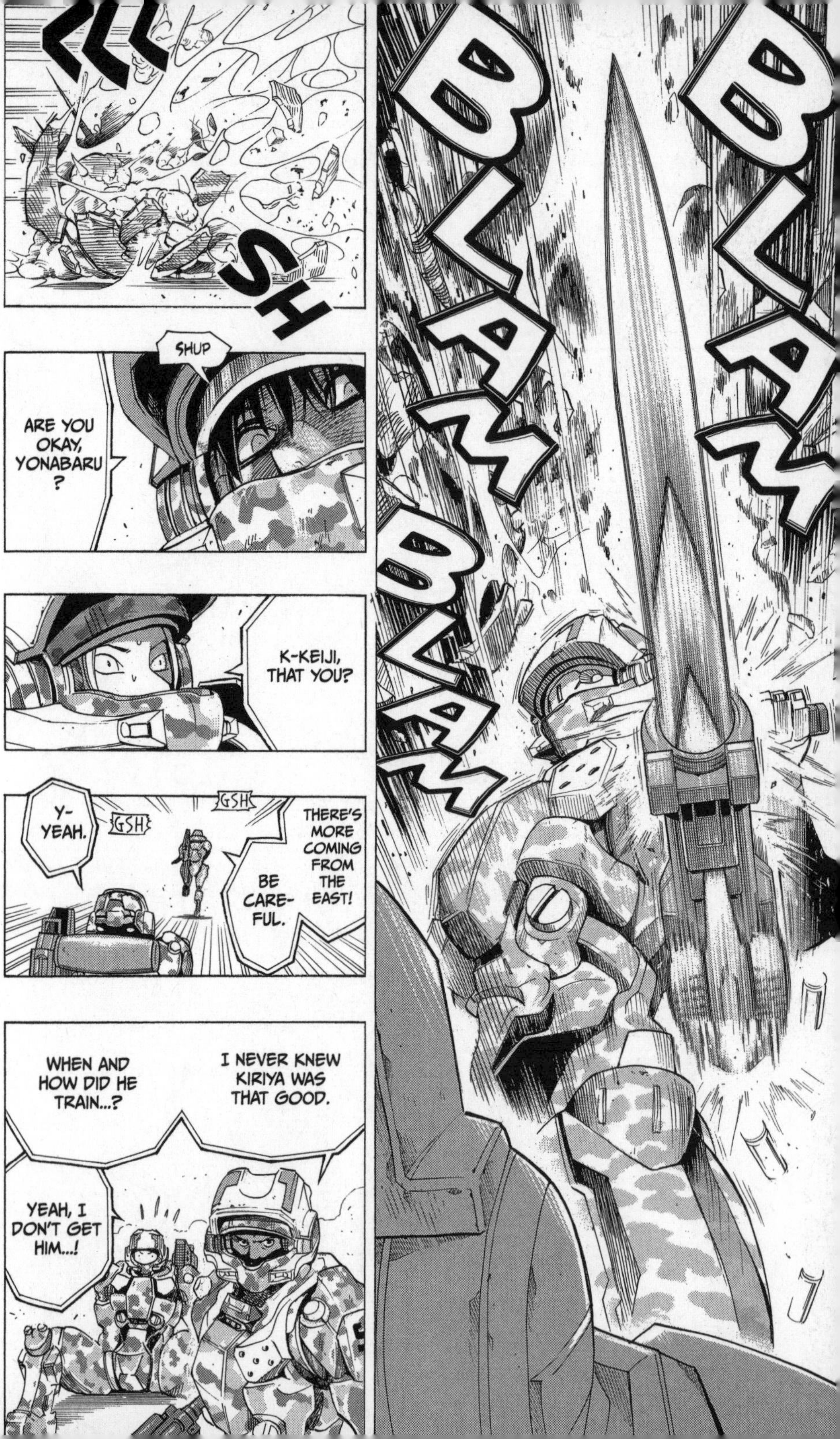
BLAM
BLAM
BLAM
SH
SHUP
ARE YOU OKAY, YONABARU?
K-KEIJI, THAT YOU?
THERE'S MORE COMING FROM THE EAST!
BE CAREFUL.
GSH
GSH
Y-YEAH.
I NEVER KNEW KIRIYA WAS THAT GOOD.
WHEN AND HOW DID HE TRAIN...?
YEAH, I DON'T GET HIM...!

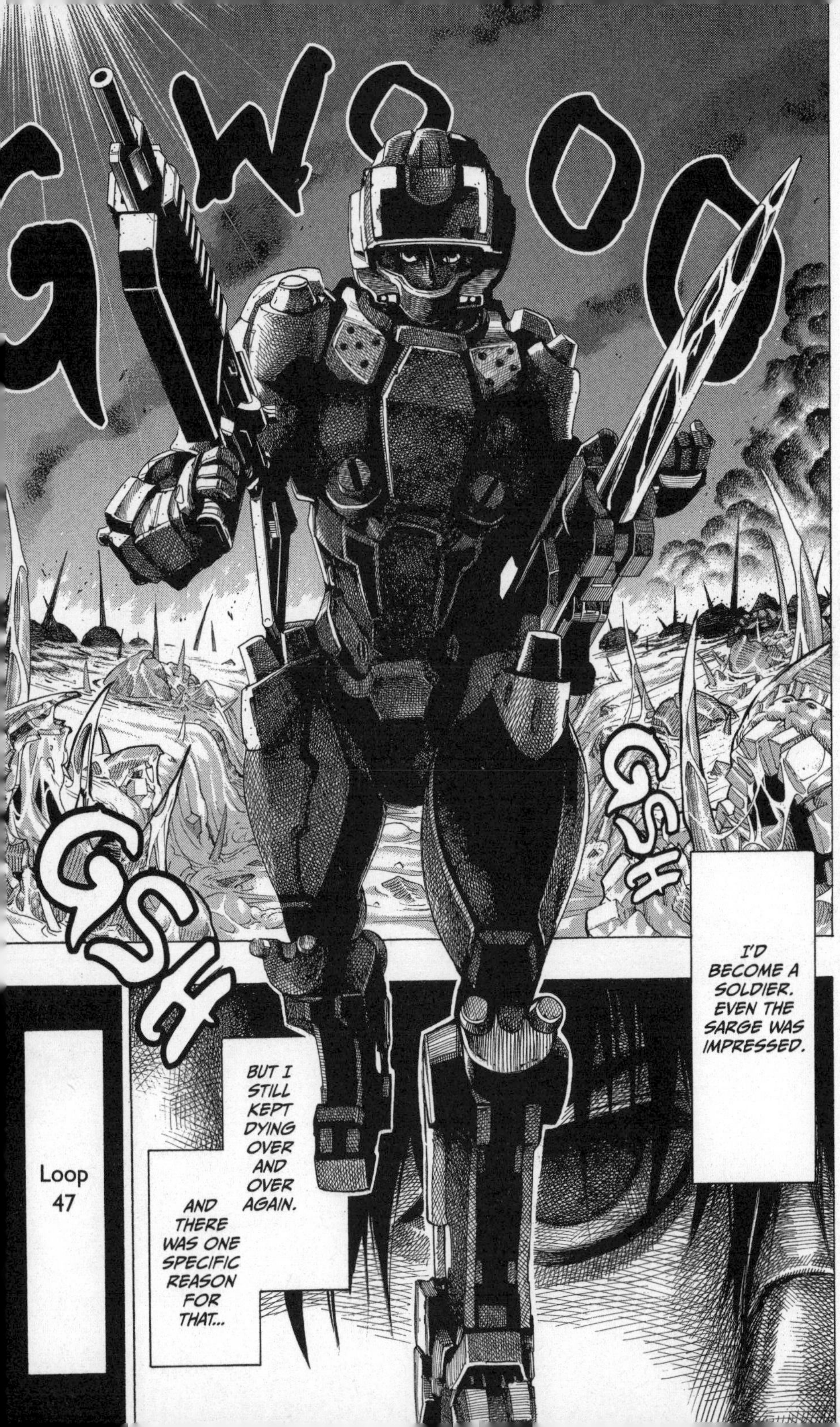
GWOOO
GSH
GSH
I'D BECOME A SOLDIER. EVEN THE SARGE WAS IMPRESSED.
BUT I STILL KEPT DYING OVER AND OVER AGAIN.
AND THERE WAS ONE SPECIFIC REASON FOR THAT...
Loop 47

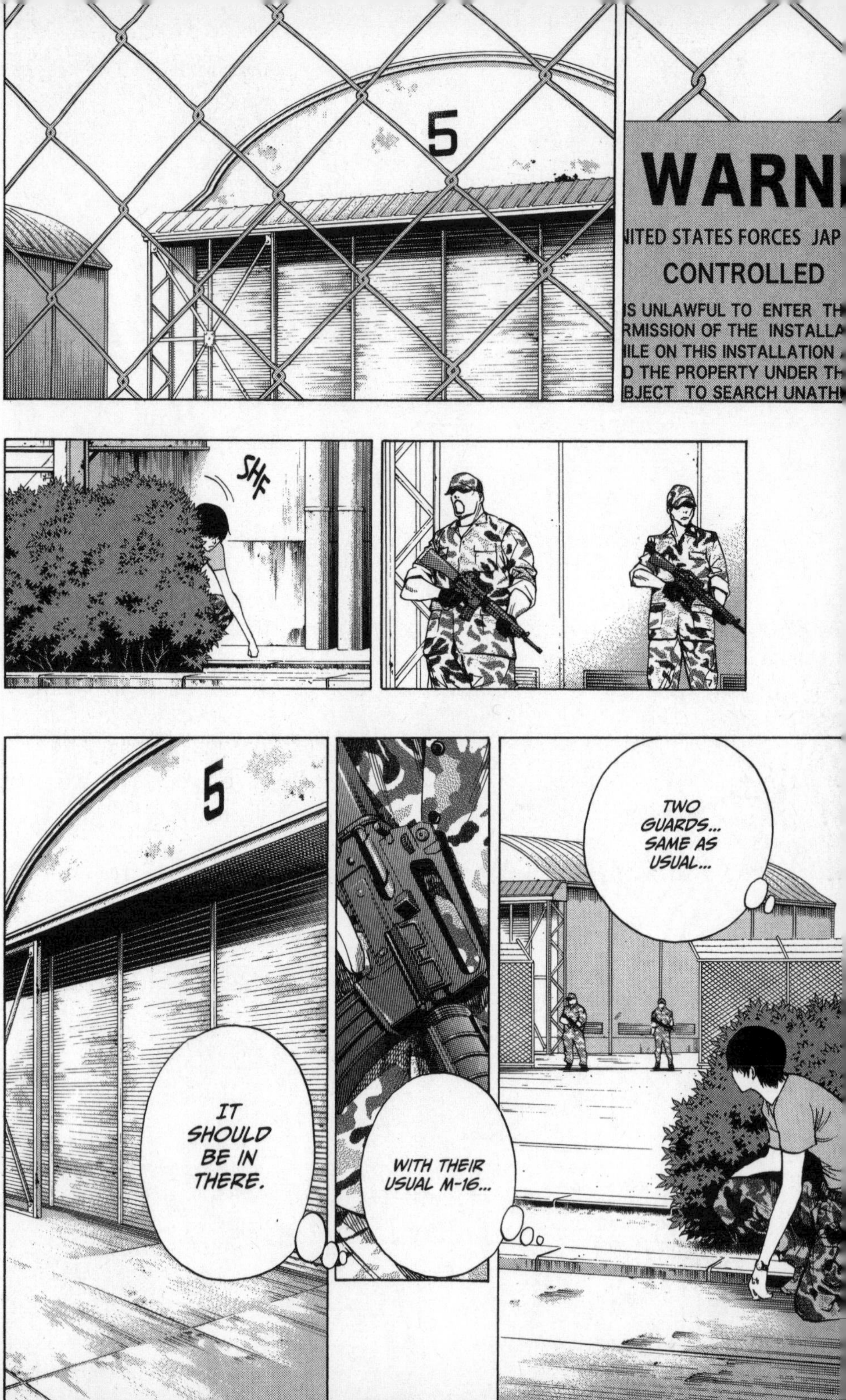
WARN
NITED STATES FORCES JAP
CONTROLLED
IS UNLAWFUL TO ENTER TH
RMISSION OF THE INSTALLA
HILE ON THIS INSTALLATION
D THE PROPERTY UNDER TH
BJECT TO SEARCH UNATH
5
SHF
TWO GUARDS... SAME AS USUAL...
WITH THEIR USUAL M-16...
5
IT SHOULD BE IN THERE.

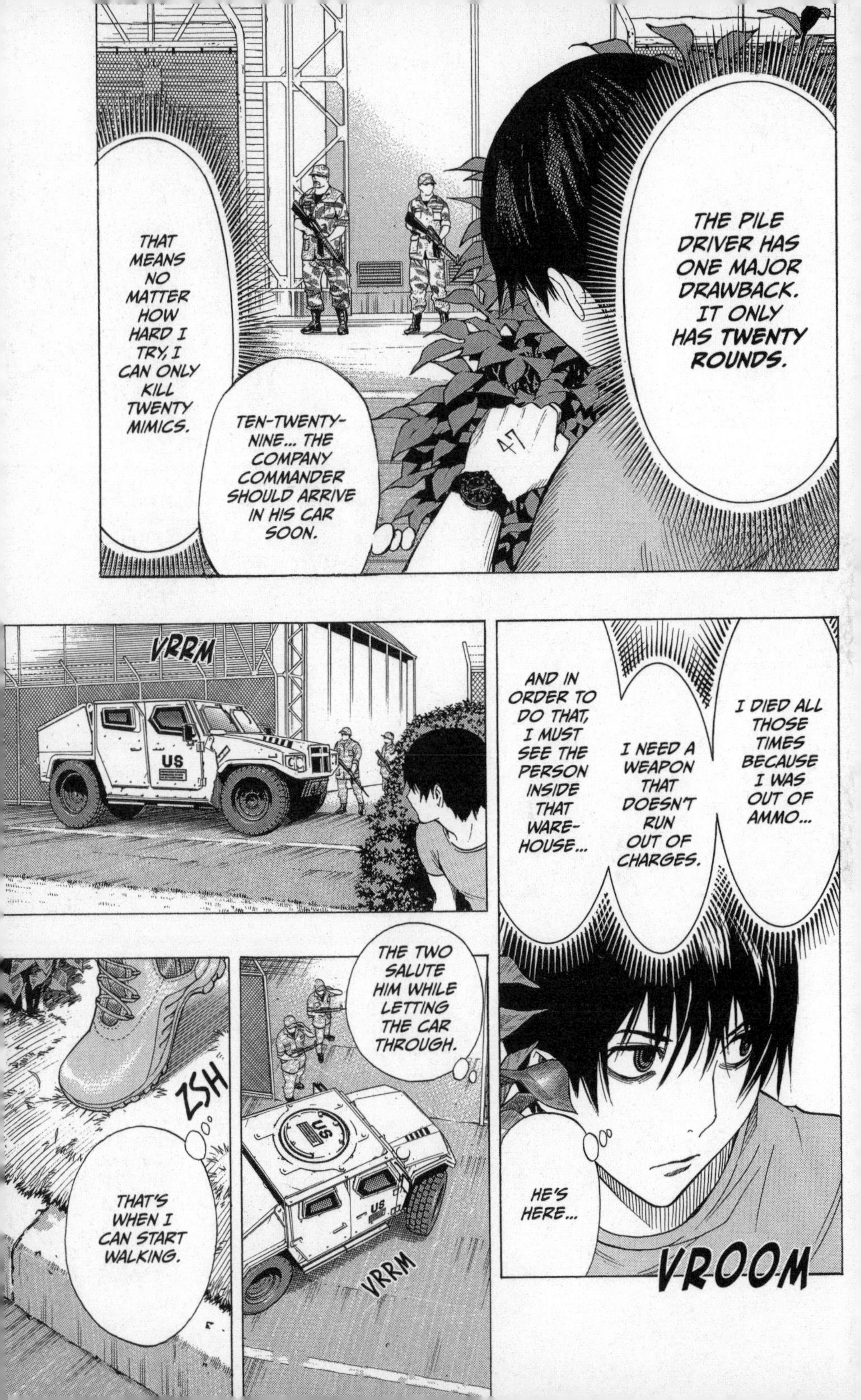
THE PILE DRIVER HAS ONE MAJOR DRAWBACK. IT ONLY HAS TWENTY ROUNDS.
THAT MEANS NO MATTER HOW HARD I TRY, I CAN ONLY KILL TWENTY MIMICS.
TEN-TWENTY-NINE... THE COMPANY COMMANDER SHOULD ARRIVE IN HIS CAR SOON.
I DIED ALL THOSE TIMES BECAUSE I WAS OUT OF AMMO...
I NEED A WEAPON THAT DOESN'T RUN OUT OF CHARGES.
AND IN ORDER TO DO THAT, I MUST SEE THE PERSON INSIDE THAT WAREHOUSE...
HE'S HERE...
V-R-O-O-M
VRRM
US
THE TWO SALUTE HIM WHILE LETTING THE CAR THROUGH.
US
VRRM
ZSH
THAT'S WHEN I CAN START WALKING.

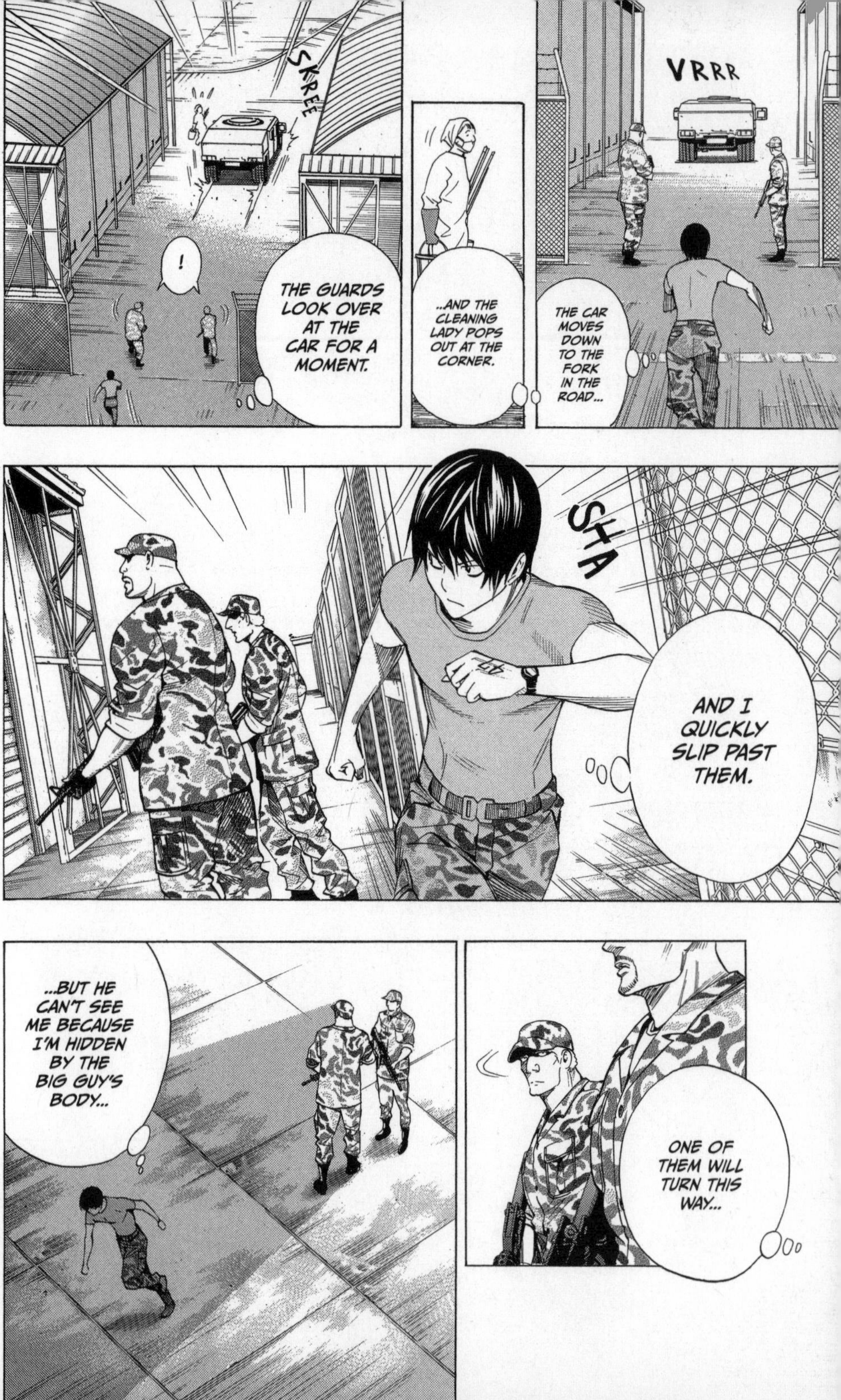
VRRR
THE CAR MOVES DOWN TO THE FORK IN THE ROAD...
...AND THE CLEANING LADY POPS OUT AT THE CORNER.
SKREE
!
THE GUARDS LOOK OVER AT THE CAR FOR A MOMENT.
SHA
AND I QUICKLY SLIP PAST THEM.
ONE OF THEM WILL TURN THIS WAY...
...BUT HE CAN'T SEE ME BECAUSE I'M HIDDEN BY THE BIG GUY'S BODY...

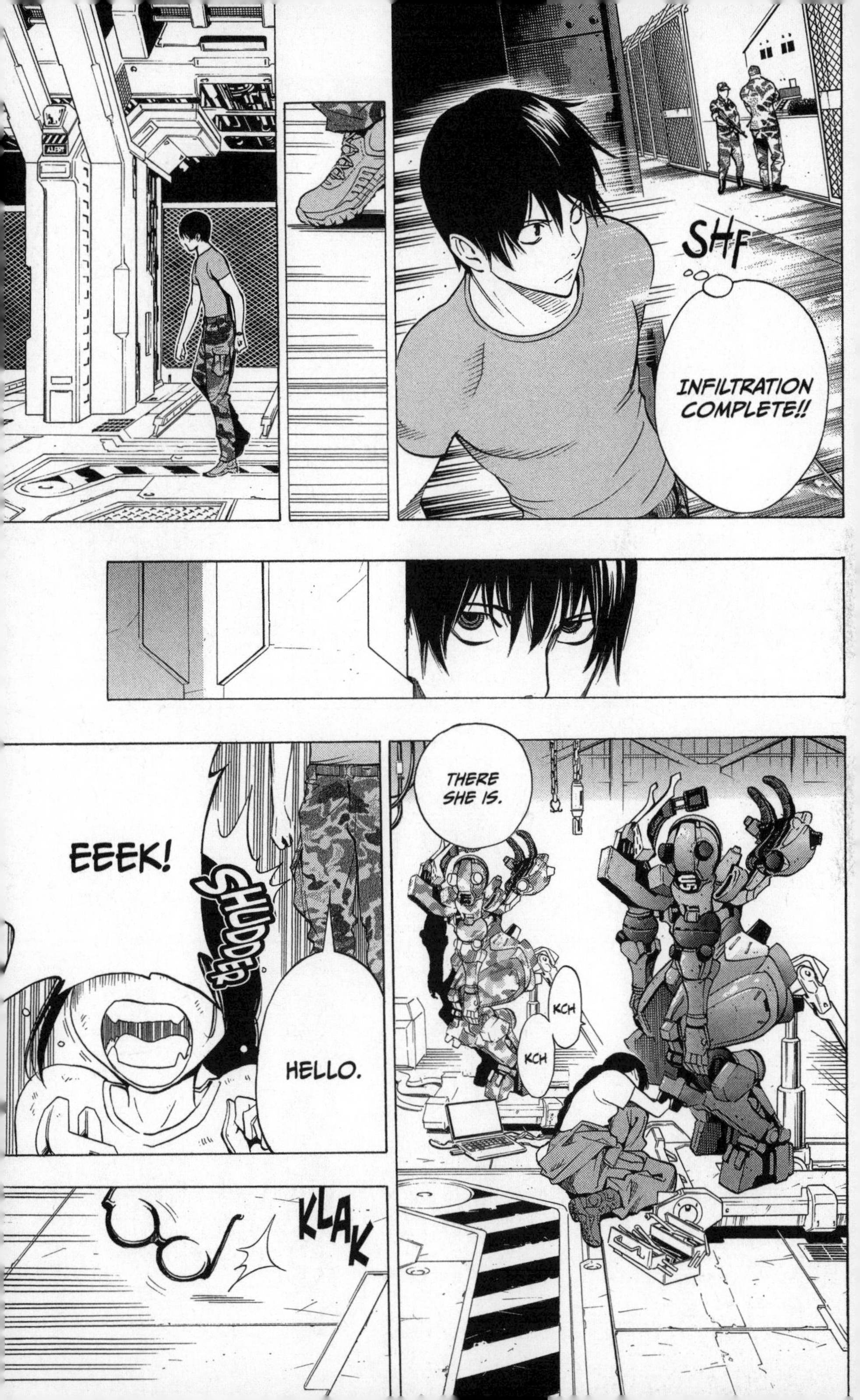
SHF
INFILTRATION COMPLETE!!
THERE SHE IS.
KCH
KCH
HELLO.
SHUDDER
EEEK!
KLAK

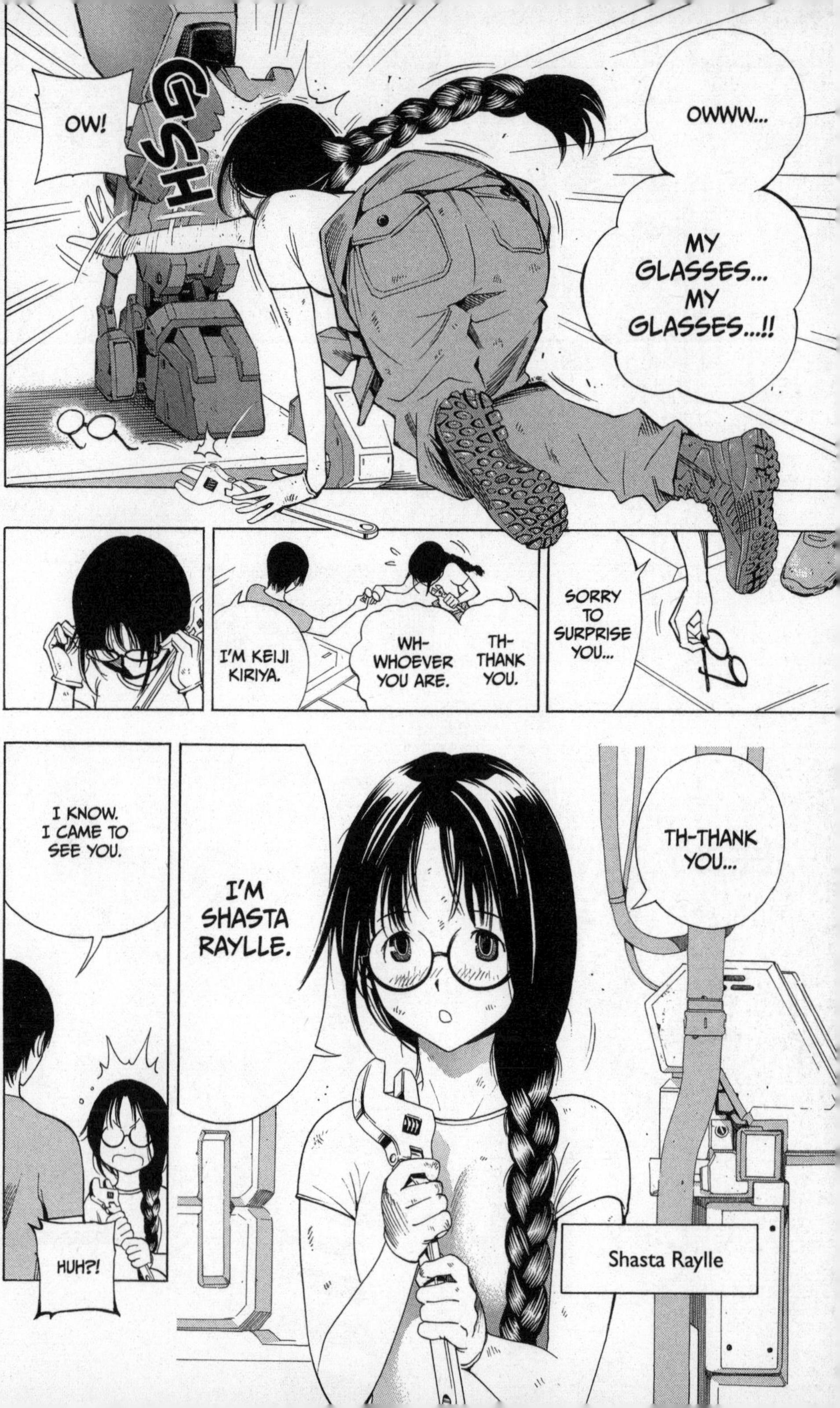
OWWW...
MY GLASSES... MY GLASSES...!!
GSH
OW!
SORRY TO SURPRISE YOU...
TH- THANK YOU.
WH- WHOEVER YOU ARE.
I'M KEIJI KIRIYA.
TH-THANK YOU...
I'M SHASTA RAYLLE.
Shasta Raylle
I KNOW. I CAME TO SEE YOU.
HUH?!

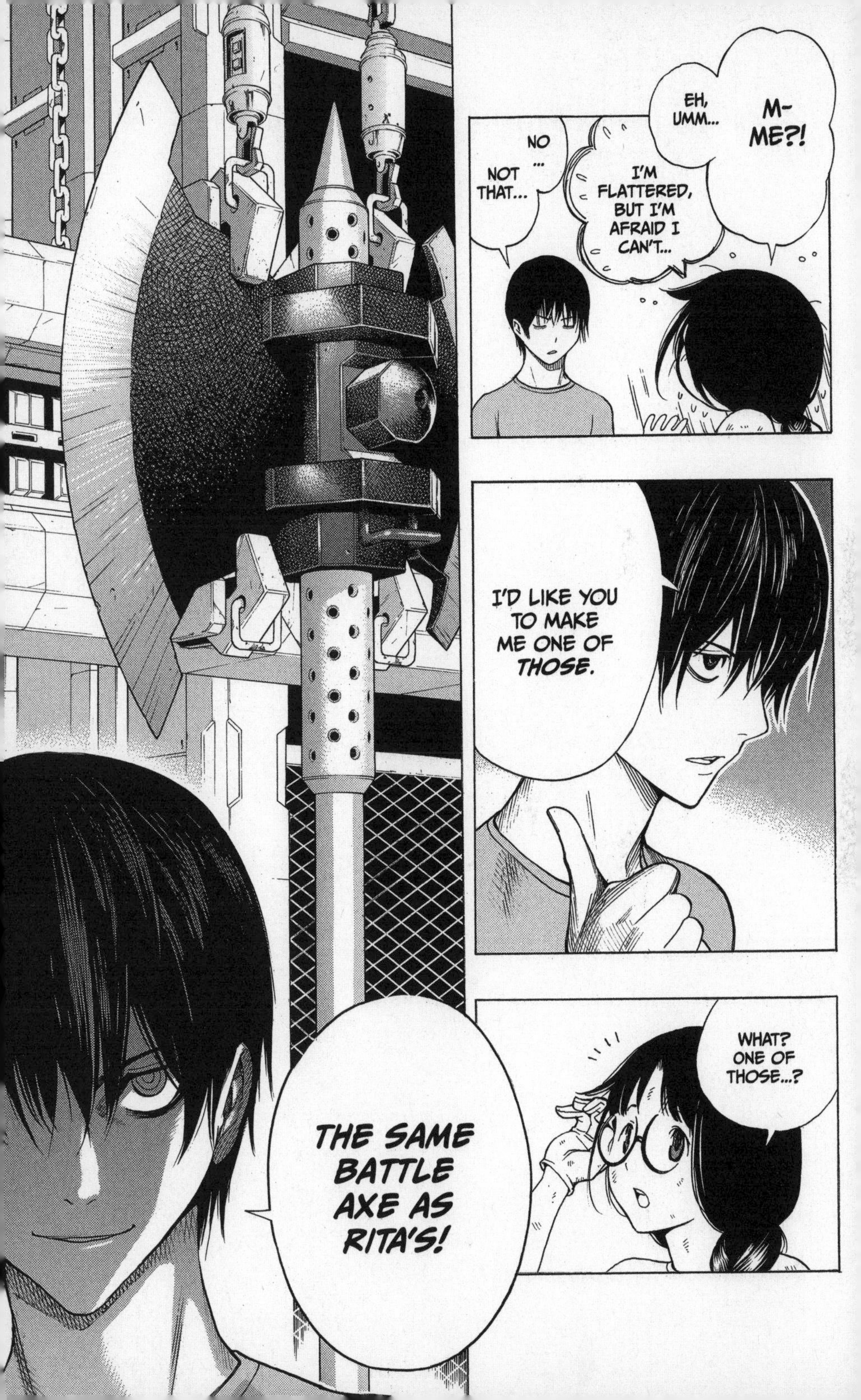
M-ME?!
EH, UMM...
I'M FLATTERED, BUT I'M AFRAID I CAN'T...
NO... NOT THAT...
I'D LIKE YOU TO MAKE ME ONE OF *THOSE*.
WHAT? ONE OF THOSE...?
THE SAME BATTLE AXE AS RITA'S!

Fuck that. Running out
of charges had killed me
plenty of times.
Another dead end.
The only way to avoid it
was to find a weapon that
didn't run out of ammo.

#4 Battle Axe

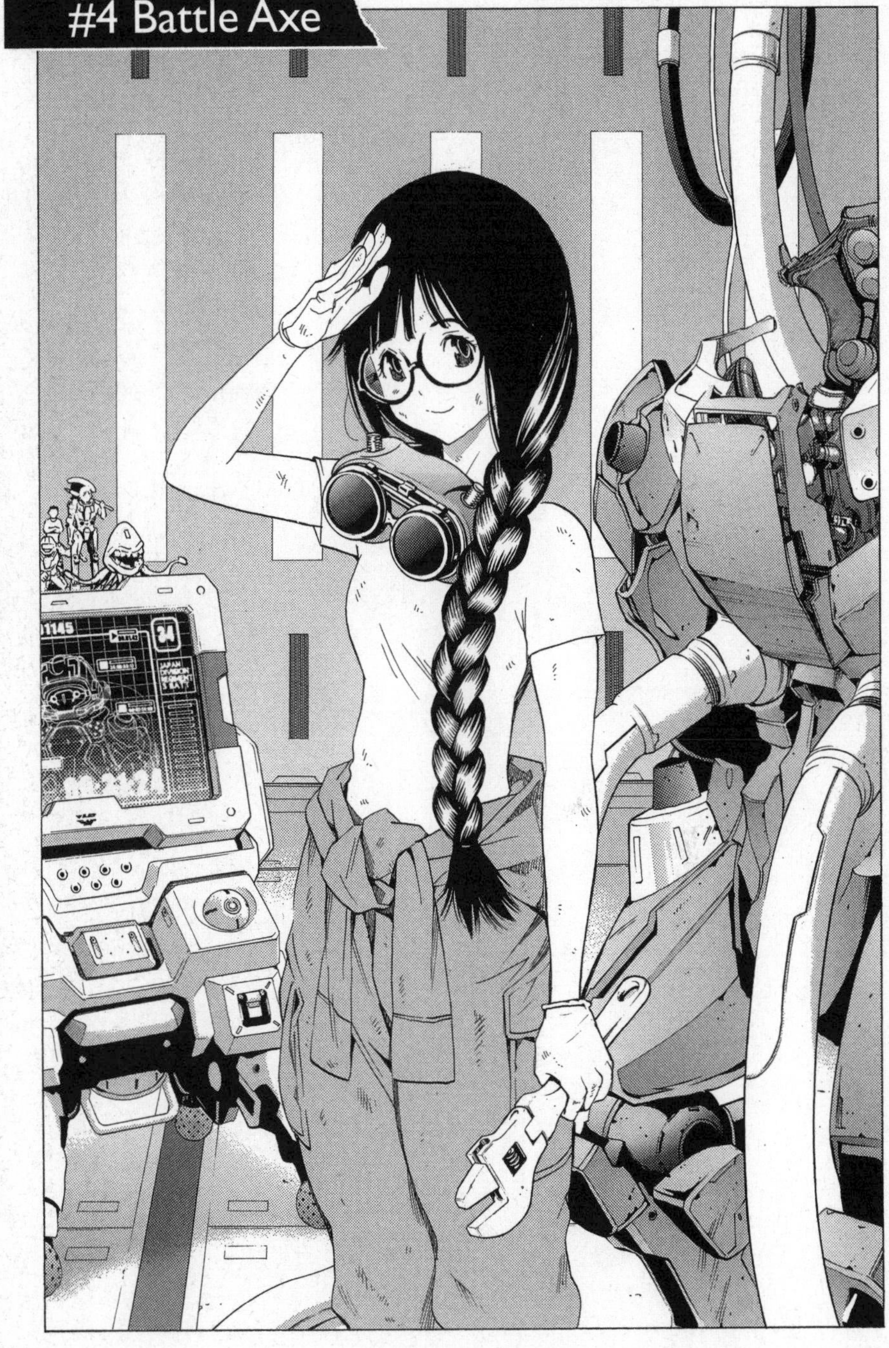

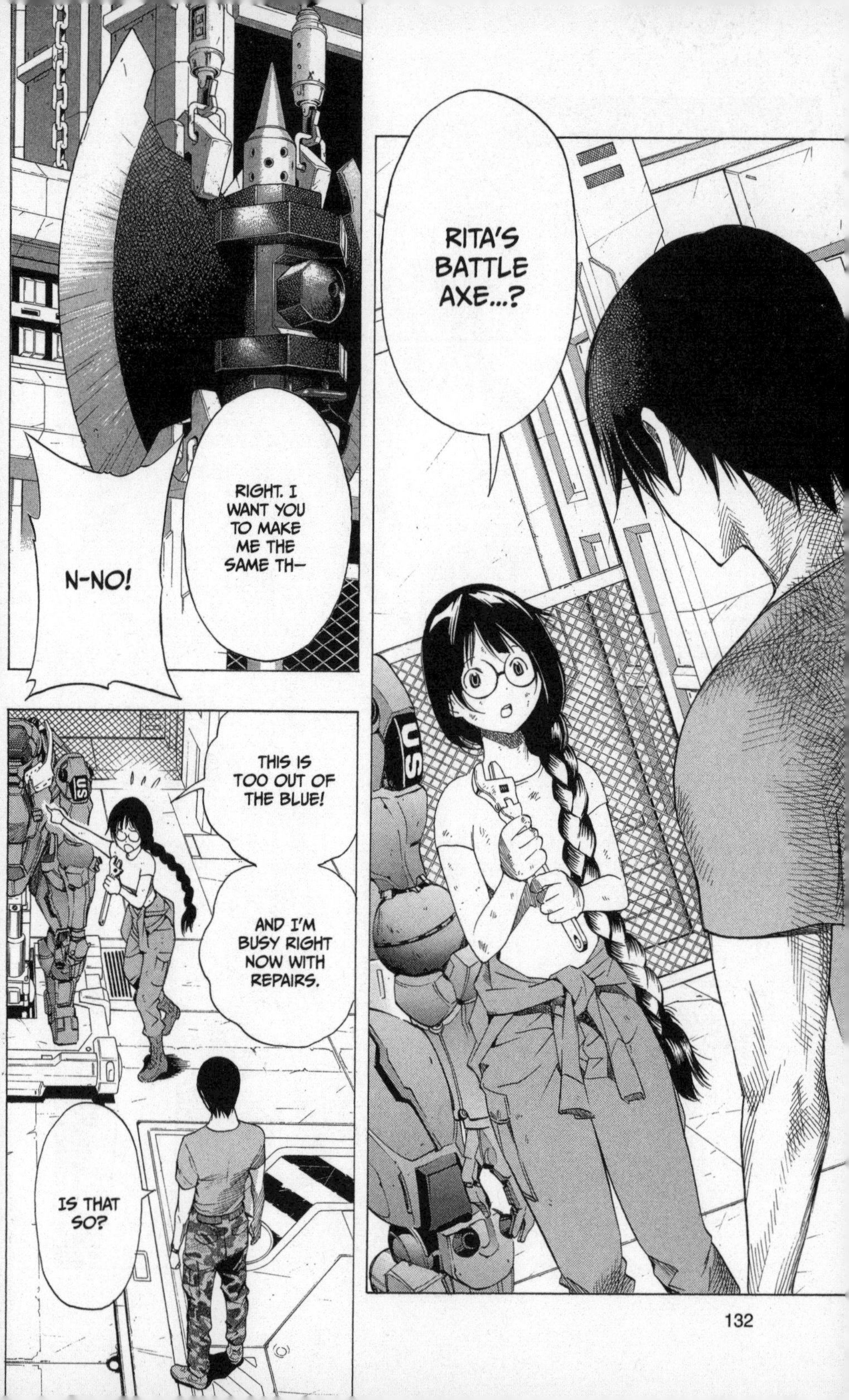
RITA'S BATTLE AXE...?
RIGHT. I WANT YOU TO MAKE ME THE SAME TH—
N-NO!
THIS IS TOO OUT OF THE BLUE!
AND I'M BUSY RIGHT NOW WITH REPAIRS.
IS THAT SO?

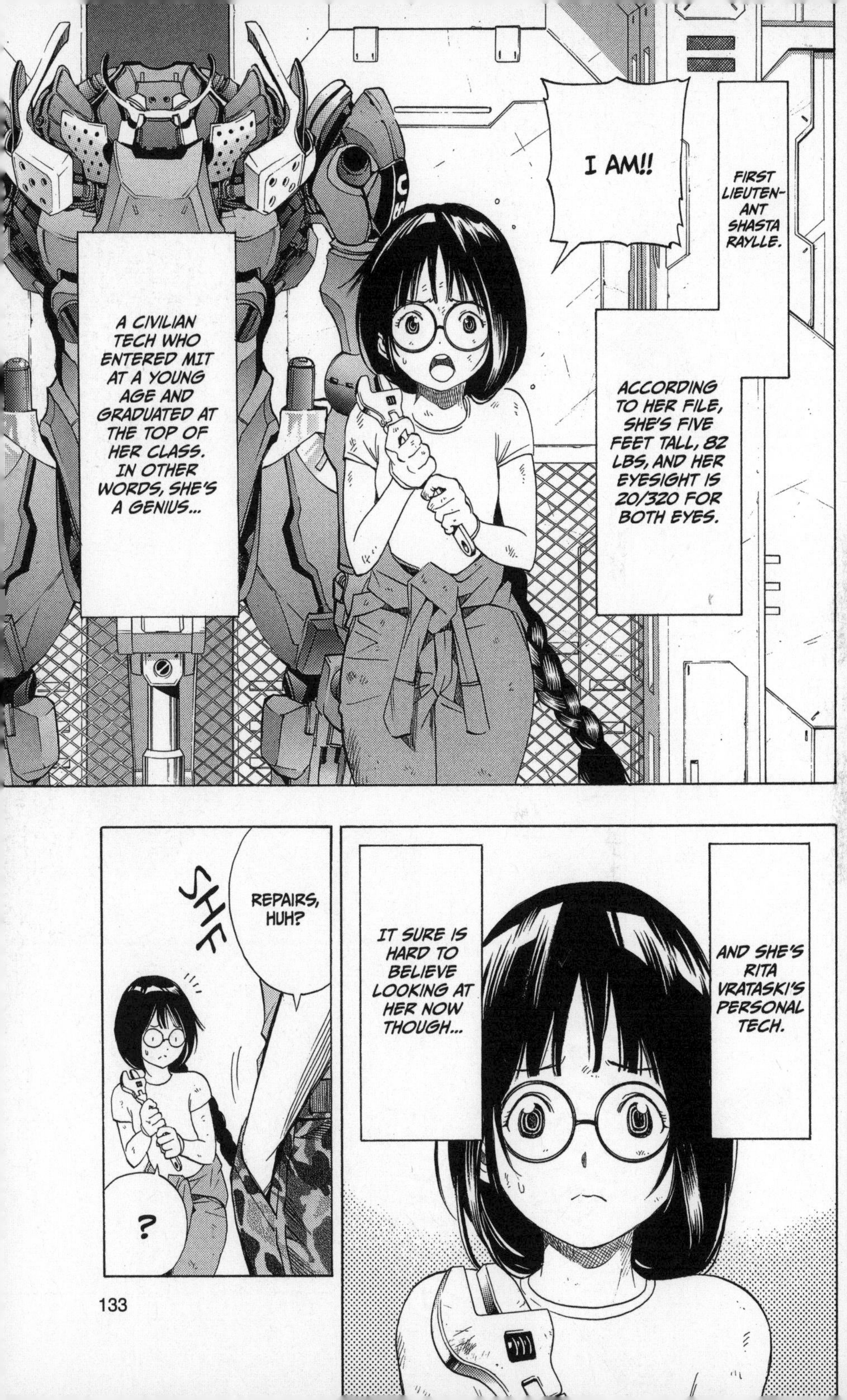
FIRST LIEUTENANT SHASTA RAYLLE.
I AM!!
ACCORDING TO HER FILE, SHE'S FIVE FEET TALL, 82 LBS, AND HER EYESIGHT IS 20/320 FOR BOTH EYES.
A CIVILIAN TECH WHO ENTERED MIT AT A YOUNG AGE AND GRADUATED AT THE TOP OF HER CLASS. IN OTHER WORDS, SHE'S A GENIUS...
AND SHE'S RITA VRATASKI'S PERSONAL TECH.
IT SURE IS HARD TO BELIEVE LOOKING AT HER NOW THOUGH...
SHF
REPAIRS, HUH?
?

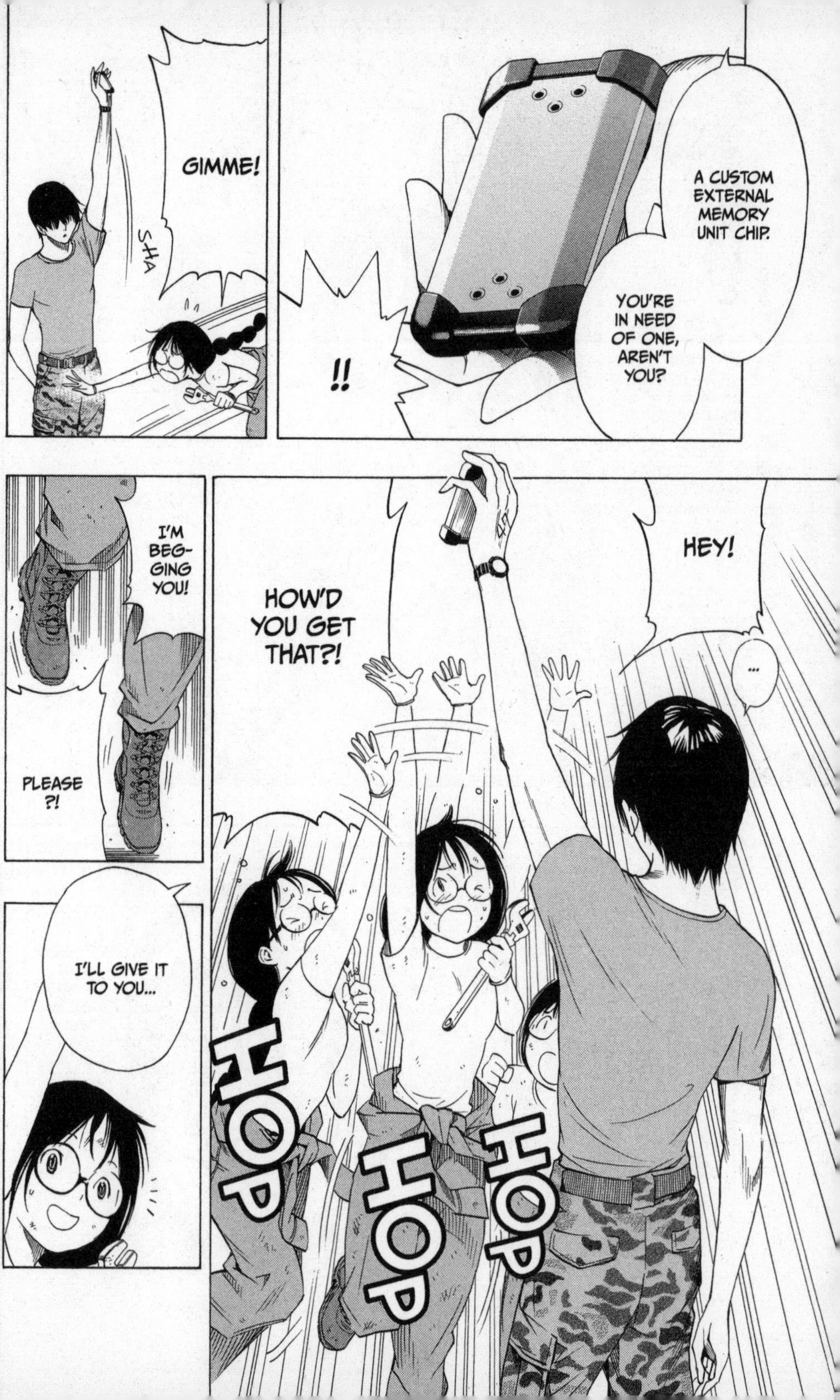
A CUSTOM EXTERNAL MEMORY UNIT CHIP.
YOU'RE IN NEED OF ONE, AREN'T YOU?
!!
GIMME!
SHA
HEY!
HOW'D YOU GET THAT?!
...
HOP
HOP
HOP
I'M BEG-GING YOU!
PLEASE ?!
I'LL GIVE IT TO YOU...

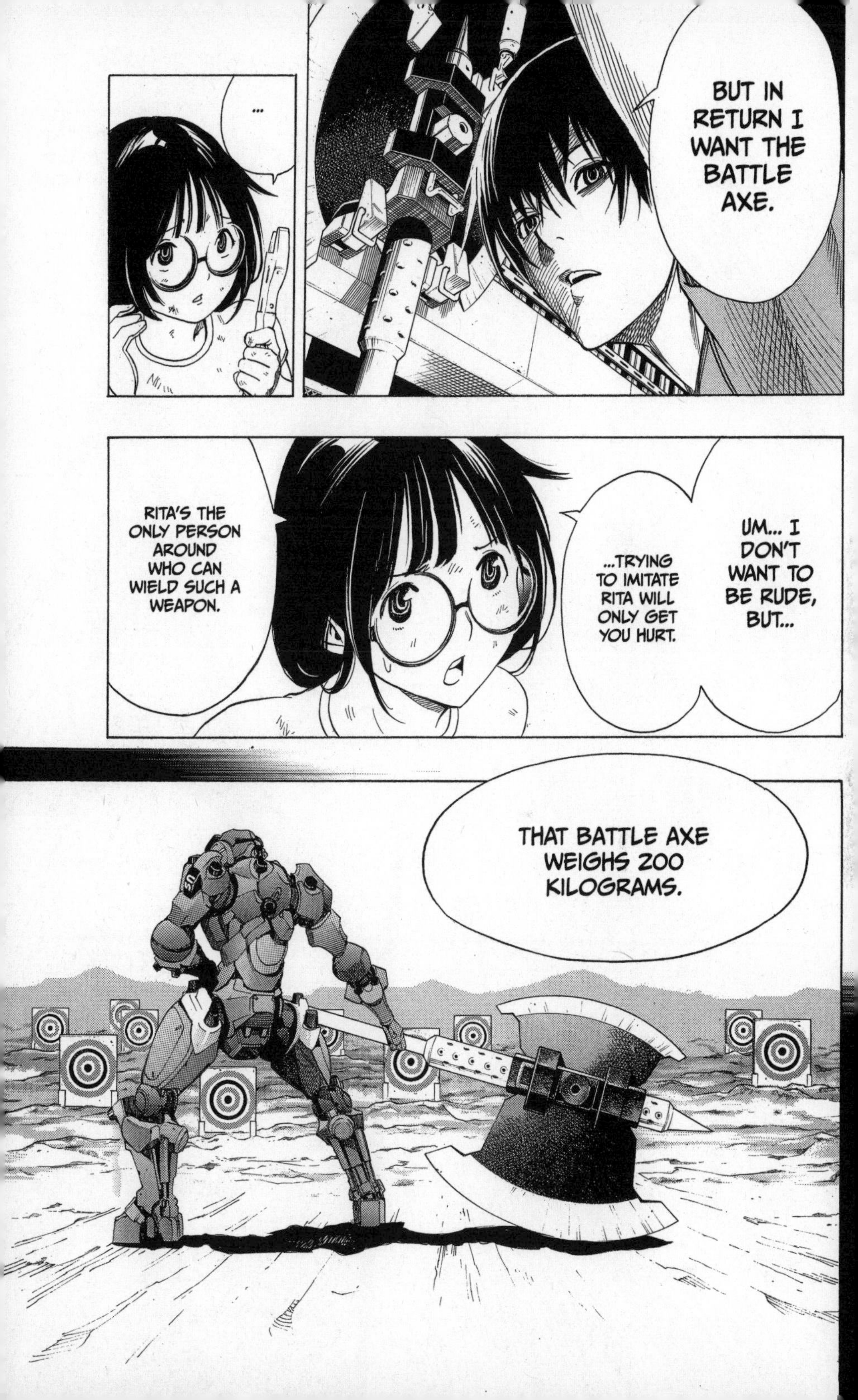
BUT IN RETURN I WANT THE BATTLE AXE.
...
UM... I DON'T WANT TO BE RUDE, BUT...
...TRYING TO IMITATE RITA WILL ONLY GET YOU HURT.
RITA'S THE ONLY PERSON AROUND WHO CAN WIELD SUCH A WEAPON.
THAT BATTLE AXE WEIGHS 200 KILOGRAMS.

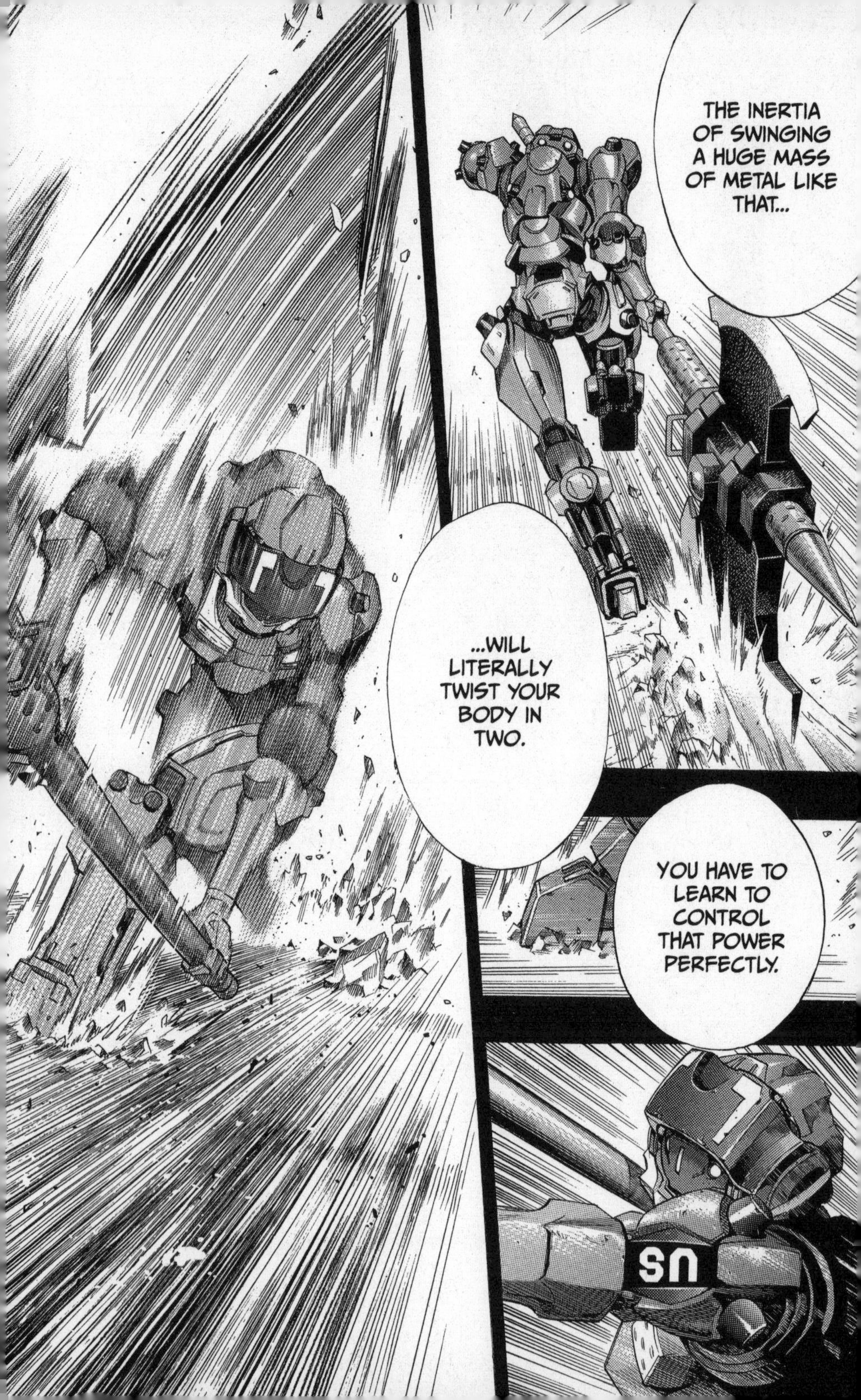
THE INERTIA OF SWINGING A HUGE MASS OF METAL LIKE THAT...
...WILL LITERALLY TWIST YOUR BODY IN TWO.
YOU HAVE TO LEARN TO CONTROL THAT POWER PERFECTLY.
US

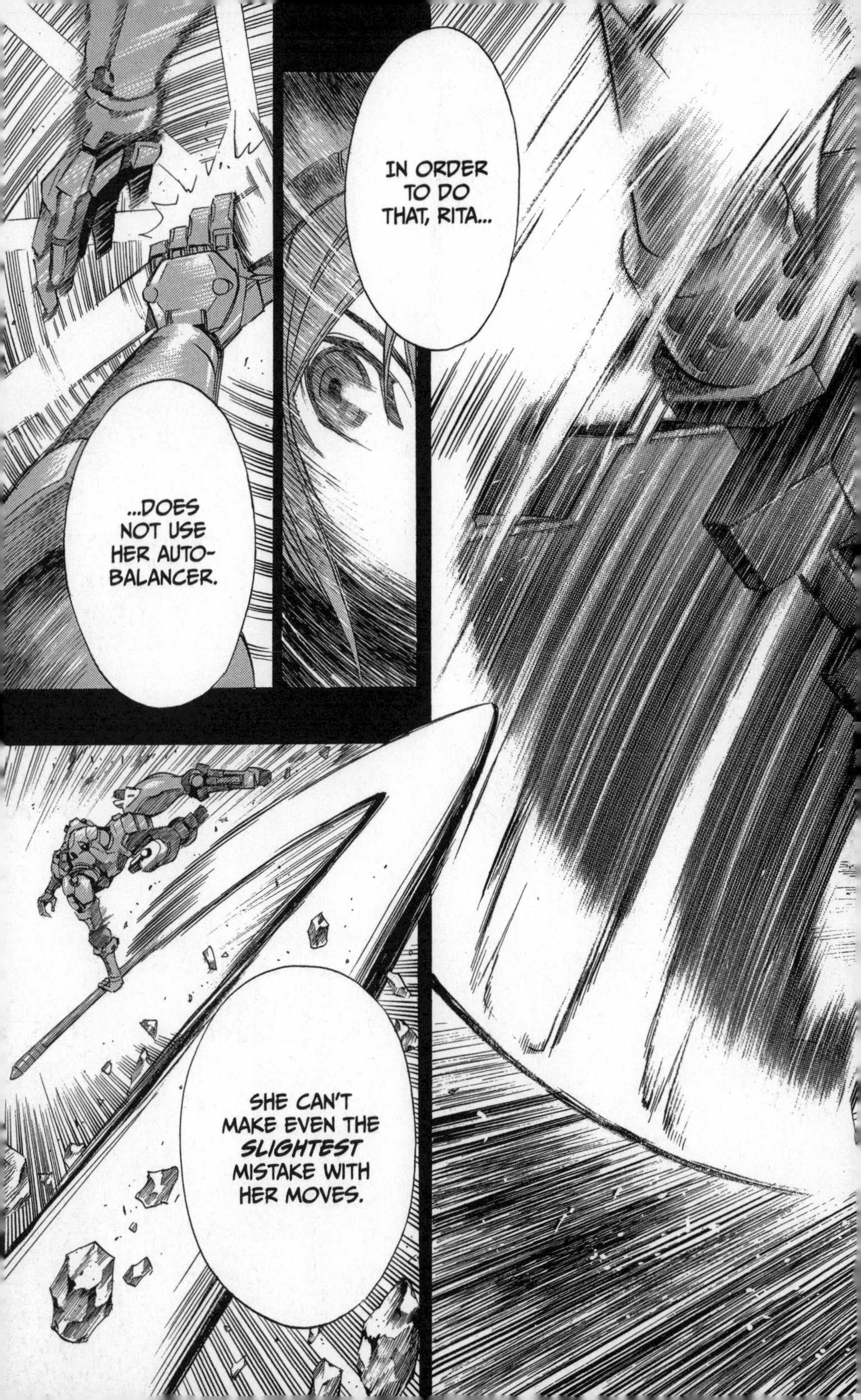
IN ORDER TO DO THAT, RITA...
...DOES NOT USE HER AUTO-BALANCER.
SHE CAN'T MAKE EVEN THE *SLIGHTEST* MISTAKE WITH HER MOVES.

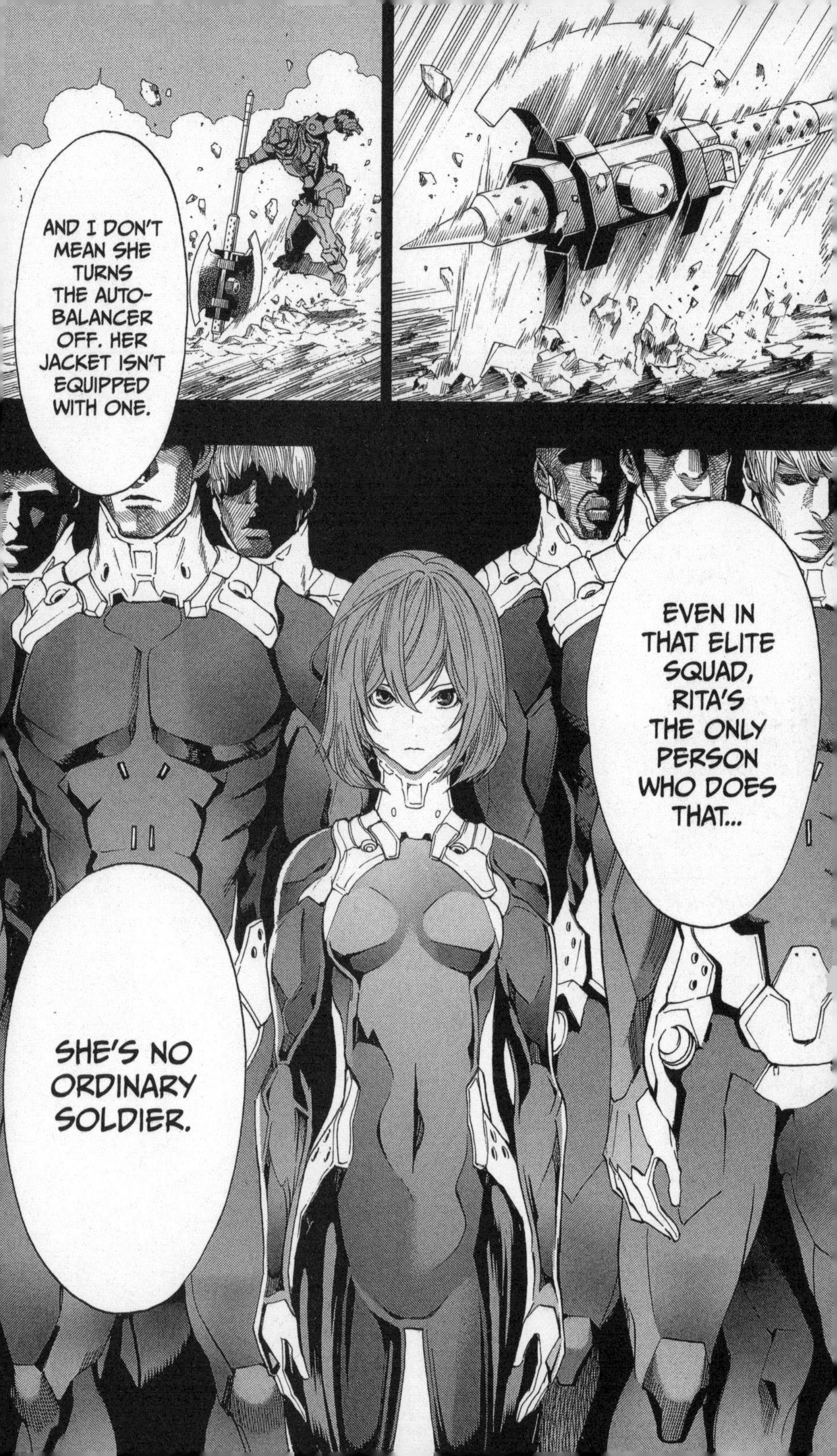
AND I DON'T MEAN SHE TURNS THE AUTO-BALANCER OFF. HER JACKET ISN'T EQUIPPED WITH ONE.
EVEN IN THAT ELITE SQUAD, RITA'S THE ONLY PERSON WHO DOES THAT...
SHE'S NO ORDINARY SOLDIER.

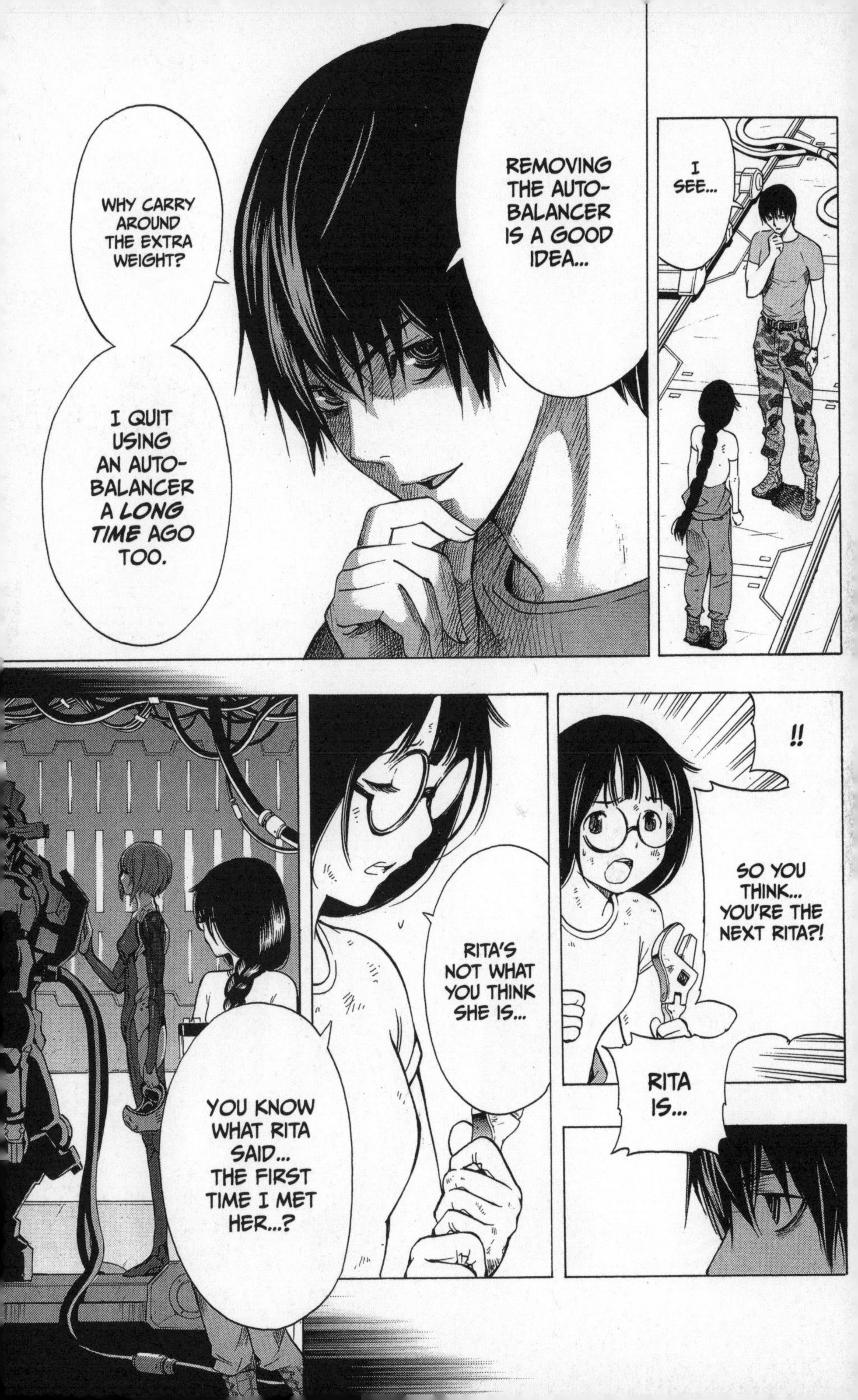
I SEE...
REMOVING THE AUTO-BALANCER IS A GOOD IDEA...
WHY CARRY AROUND THE EXTRA WEIGHT?
I QUIT USING AN AUTO-BALANCER A *LONG TIME* AGO TOO.
!!
SO YOU THINK... YOU'RE THE NEXT RITA?!
RITA IS...
RITA'S NOT WHAT YOU THINK SHE IS...
YOU KNOW WHAT RITA SAID... THE FIRST TIME I MET HER...?

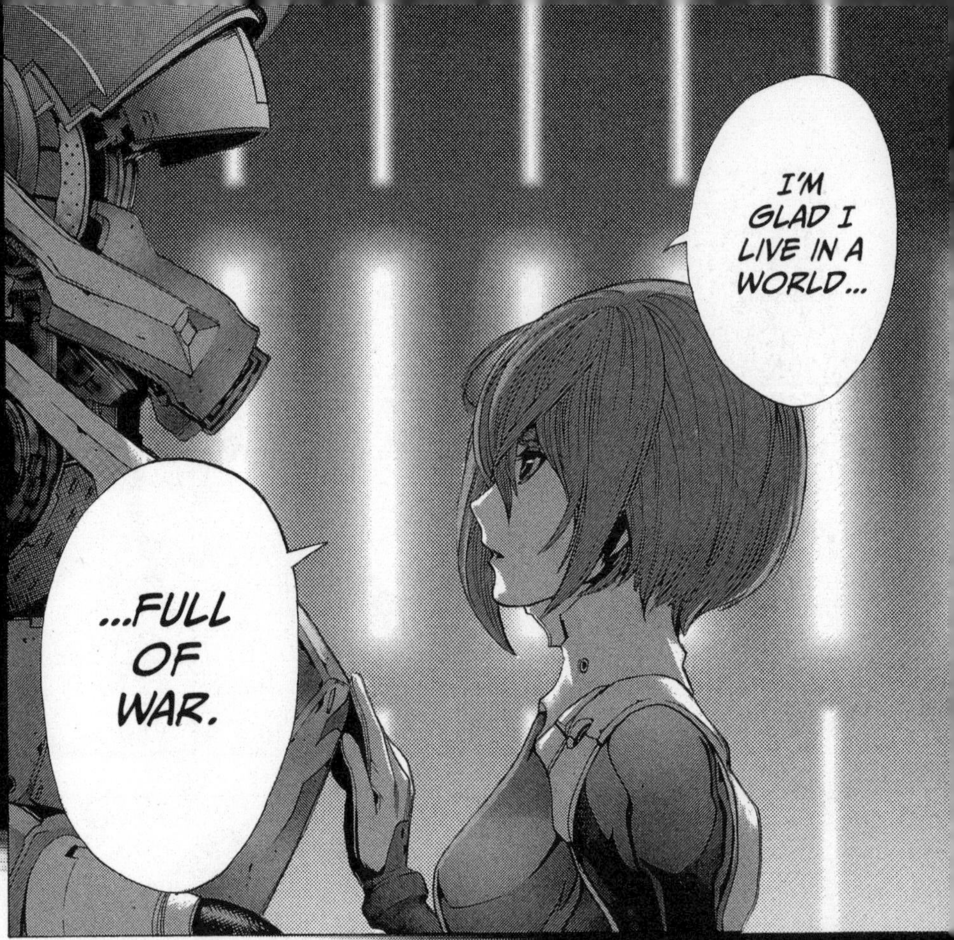
I'M GLAD I LIVE IN A WORLD...
...FULL OF WAR.

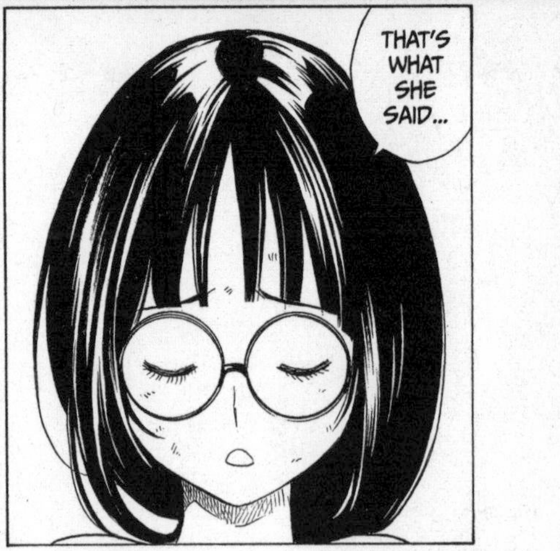
THAT'S WHAT SHE SAID...

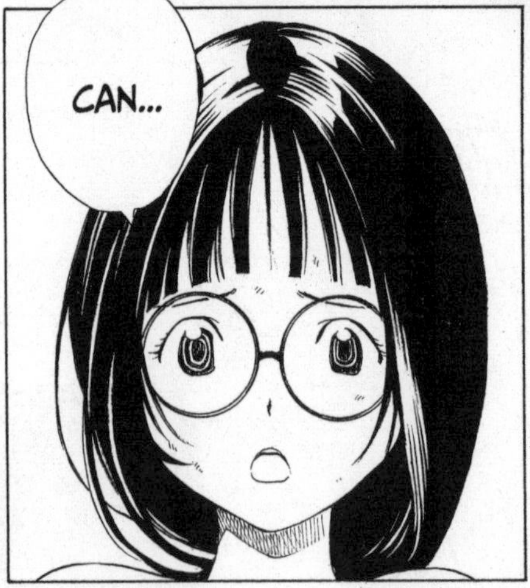
CAN...

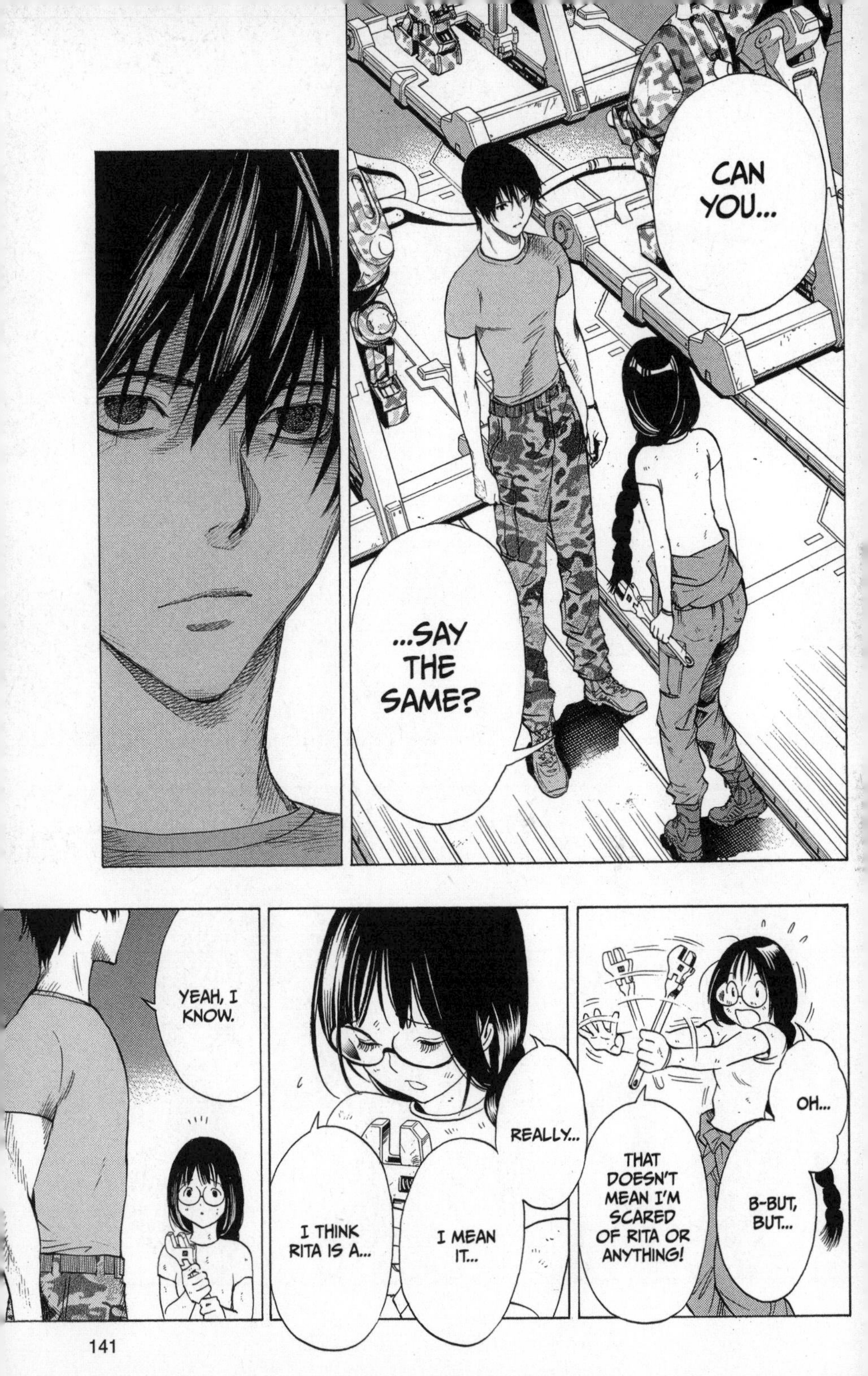
CAN YOU...
...SAY THE SAME?
OH...
B-BUT, BUT...
THAT DOESN'T MEAN I'M SCARED OF RITA OR ANYTHING!
REALLY...
I MEAN IT...
I THINK RITA IS A...
YEAH, I KNOW.

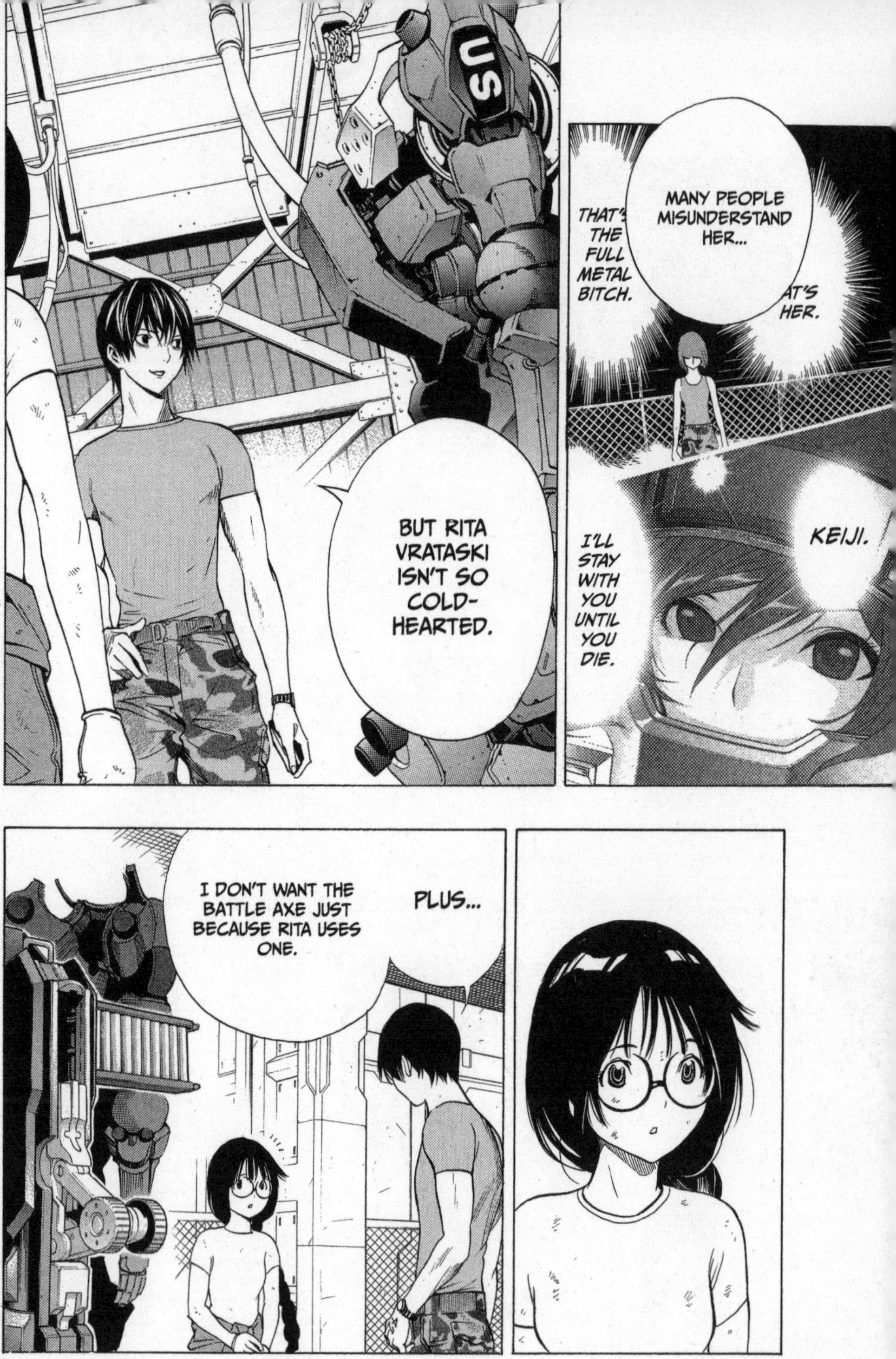

MANY PEOPLE MISUNDERSTAND HER...
AT'S HER.
THAT'S THE FULL METAL BITCH.
KEIJI.
I'LL STAY WITH YOU UNTIL YOU DIE.
BUT RITA VRATASKI ISN'T SO COLD-HEARTED.
PLUS...
I DON'T WANT THE BATTLE AXE JUST BECAUSE RITA USES ONE.

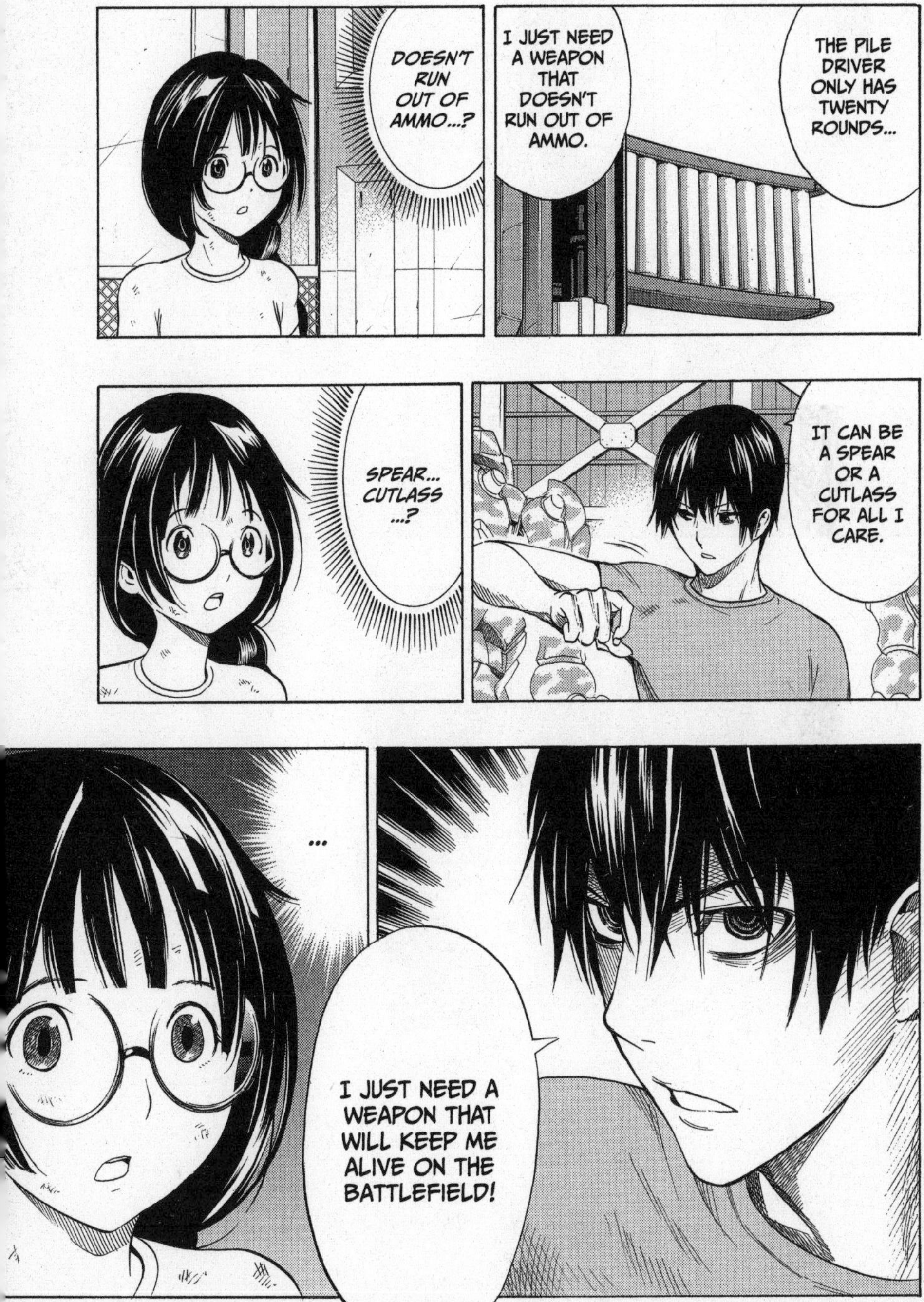
THE PILE DRIVER ONLY HAS TWENTY ROUNDS...
I JUST NEED A WEAPON THAT DOESN'T RUN OUT OF AMMO.
DOESN'T RUN OUT OF AMMO...?
IT CAN BE A SPEAR OR A CUTLASS FOR ALL I CARE.
SPEAR... CUTLASS ...?
I JUST NEED A WEAPON THAT WILL KEEP ME ALIVE ON THE BATTLEFIELD!
...

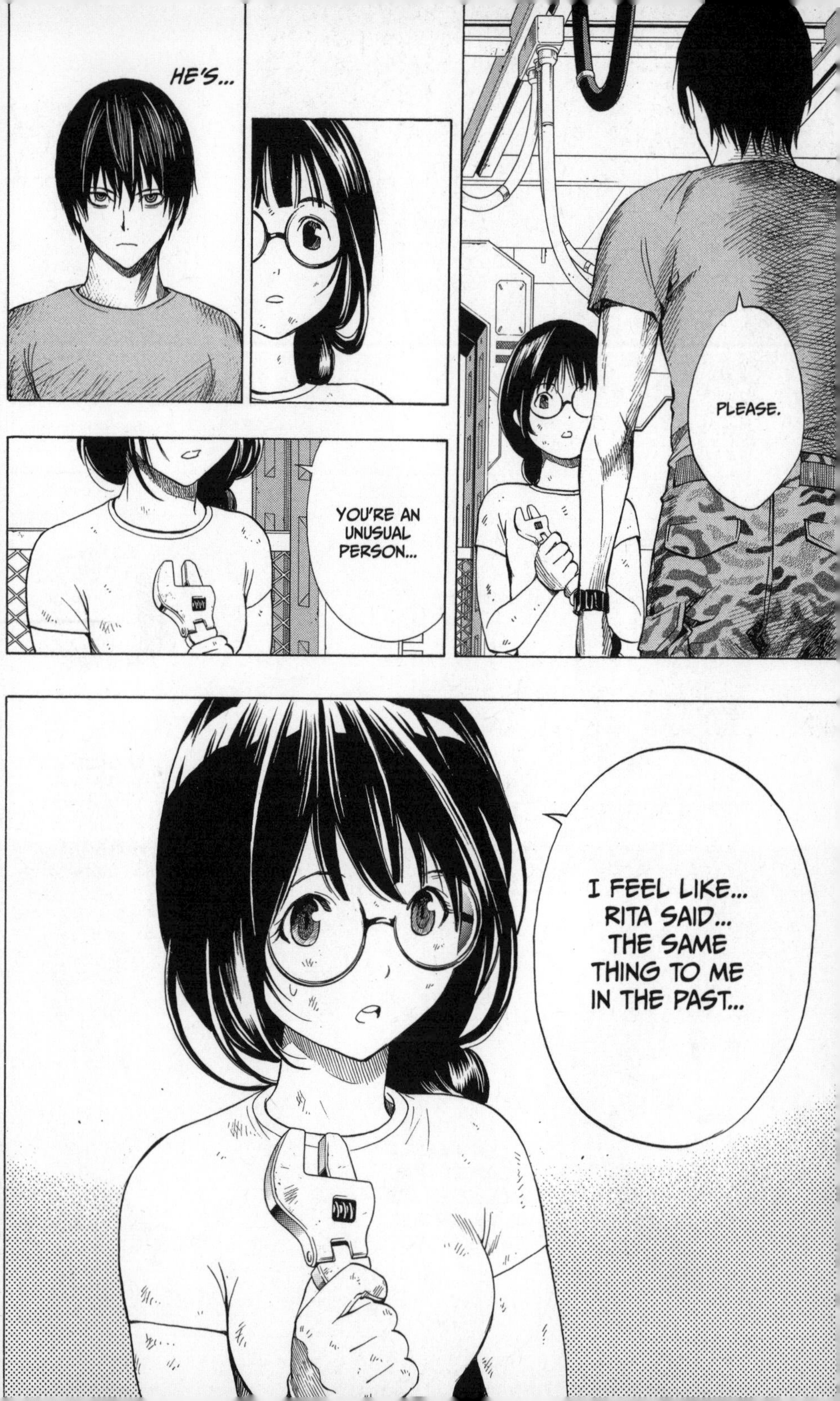
PLEASE.
HE'S...
YOU'RE AN UNUSUAL PERSON...
I FEEL LIKE... RITA SAID... THE SAME THING TO ME IN THE PAST...

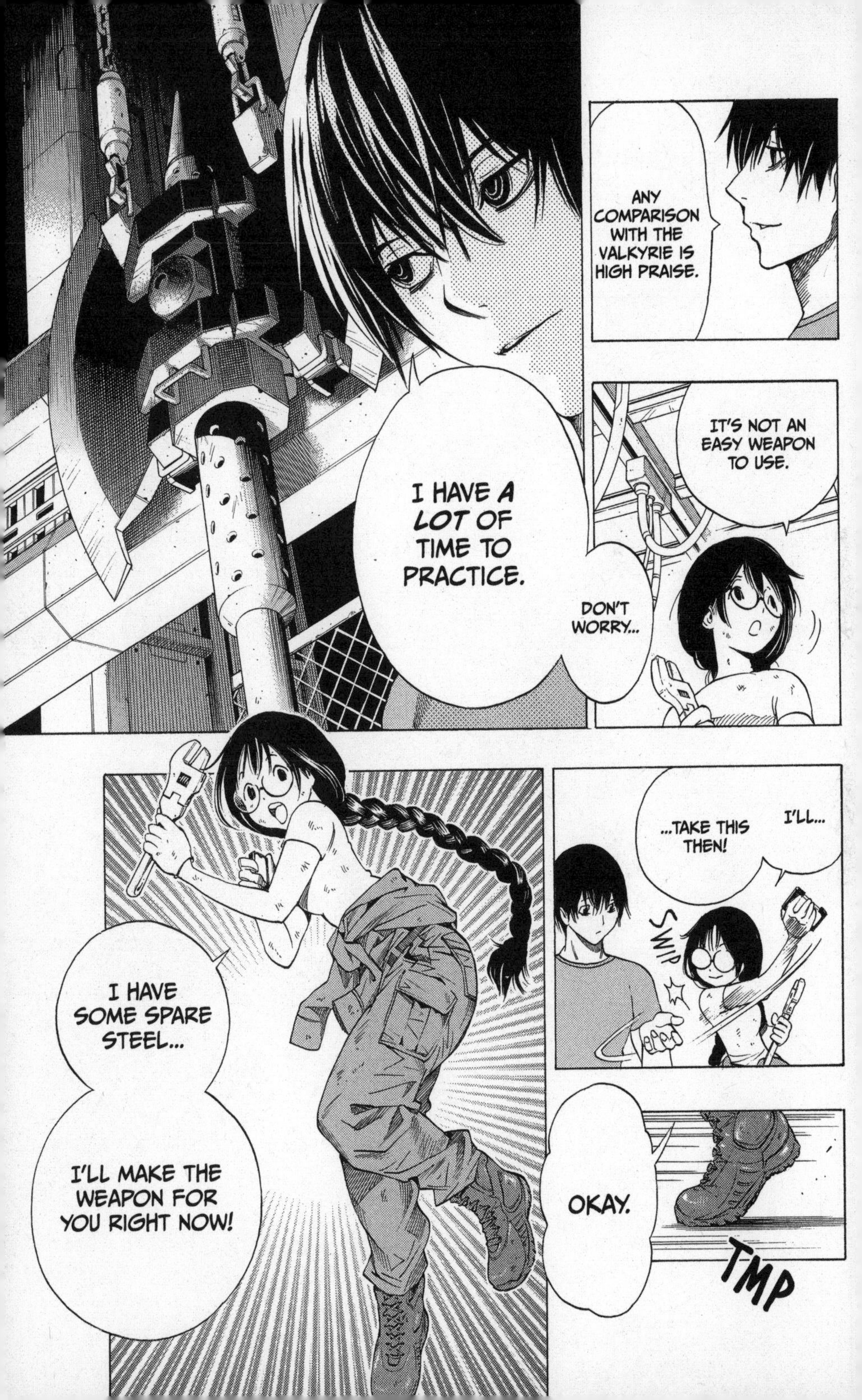
ANY COMPARISON WITH THE VALKYRIE IS HIGH PRAISE.
IT'S NOT AN EASY WEAPON TO USE.
DON'T WORRY...
I HAVE A *LOT* OF TIME TO PRACTICE.
I'LL...
...TAKE THIS THEN!
SWIP
OKAY.
TMP
I HAVE SOME SPARE STEEL...
I'LL MAKE THE WEAPON FOR YOU RIGHT NOW!

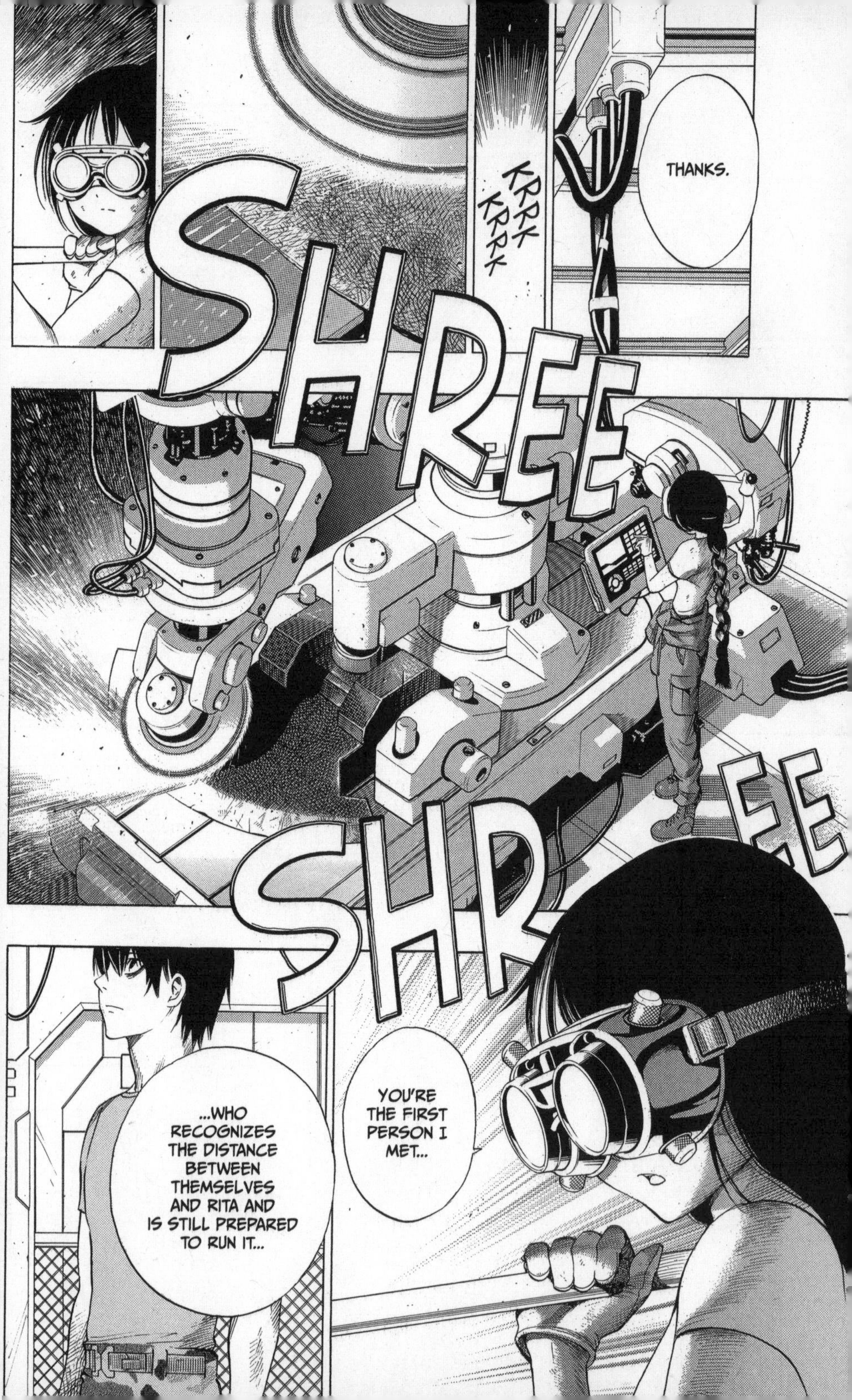

THANKS.
KRRK KRRK
SHREE
SHREE
YOU'RE THE FIRST PERSON I MET...
...WHO RECOGNIZES THE DISTANCE BETWEEN THEMSELVES AND RITA AND IS STILL PREPARED TO RUN IT...

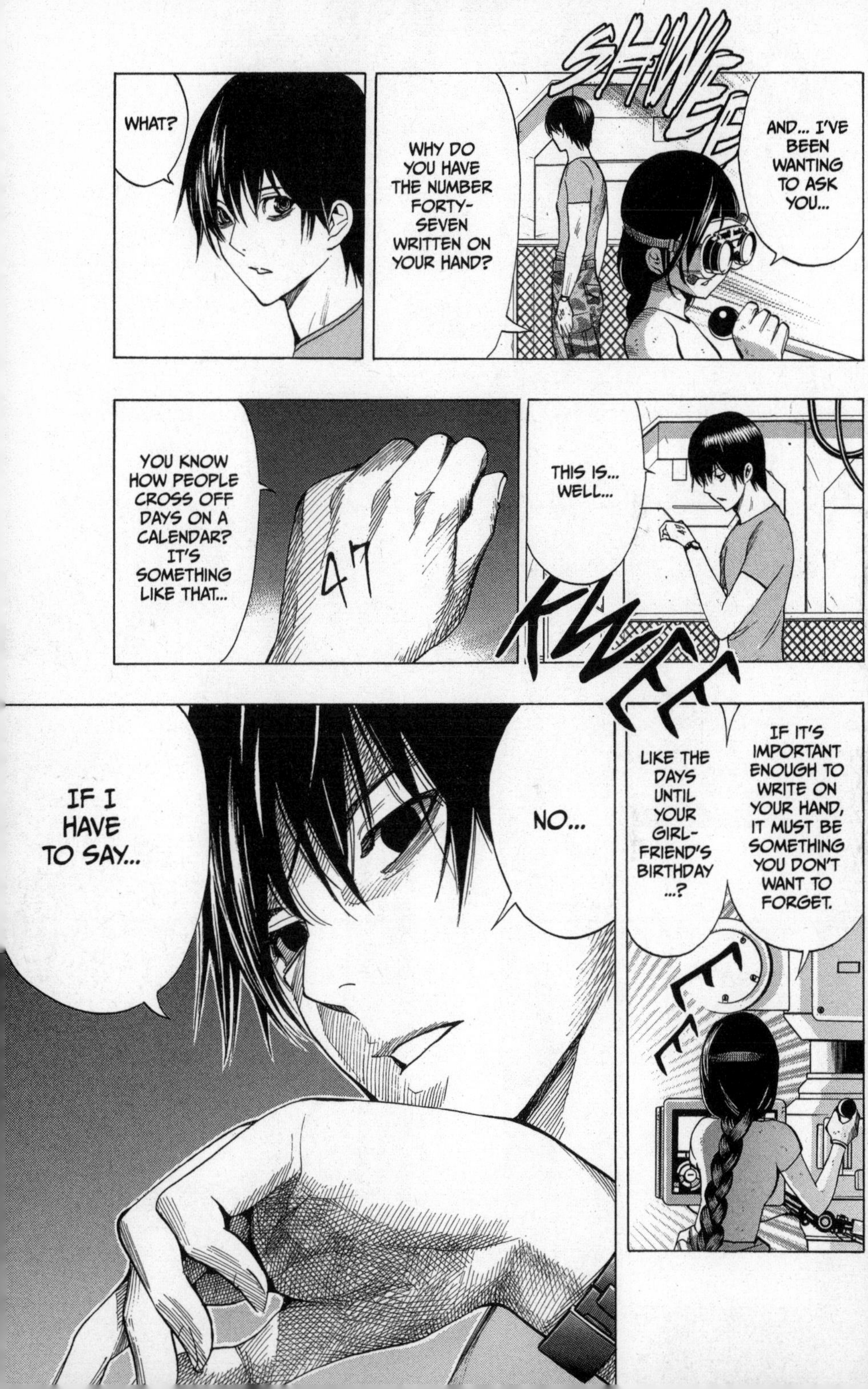
SHWEE
AND... I'VE BEEN WANTING TO ASK YOU...
WHY DO YOU HAVE THE NUMBER FORTY-SEVEN WRITTEN ON YOUR HAND?
WHAT?
THIS IS... WELL...
KWEEEE
YOU KNOW HOW PEOPLE CROSS OFF DAYS ON A CALENDAR? IT'S SOMETHING LIKE THAT...
47
IF IT'S IMPORTANT ENOUGH TO WRITE ON YOUR HAND, IT MUST BE SOMETHING YOU DON'T WANT TO FORGET.
LIKE THE DAYS UNTIL YOUR GIRL-FRIEND'S BIRTHDAY ...?
NO...
IF I HAVE TO SAY...

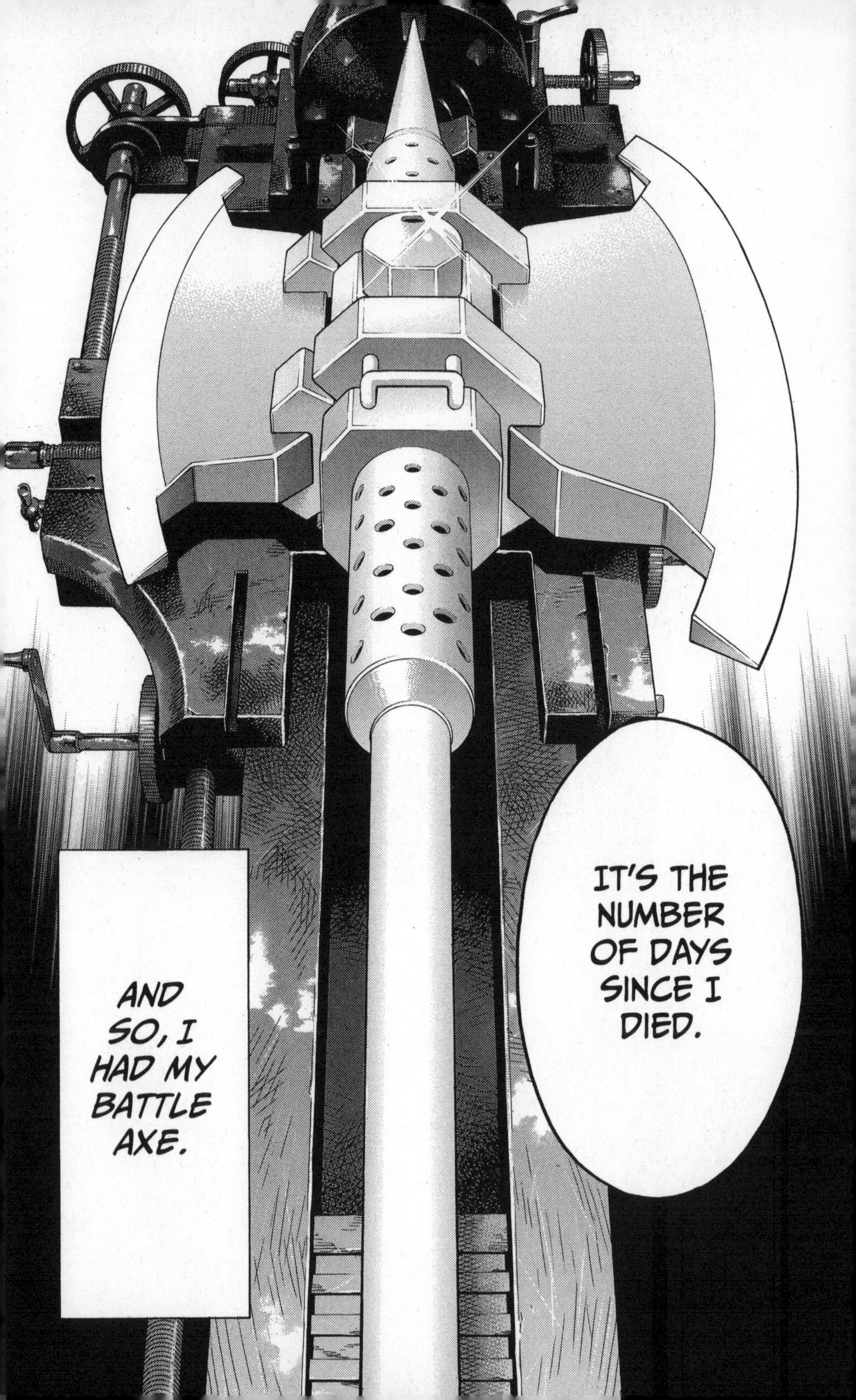
IT'S THE NUMBER OF DAYS SINCE I DIED.
AND SO, I HAD MY BATTLE AXE.

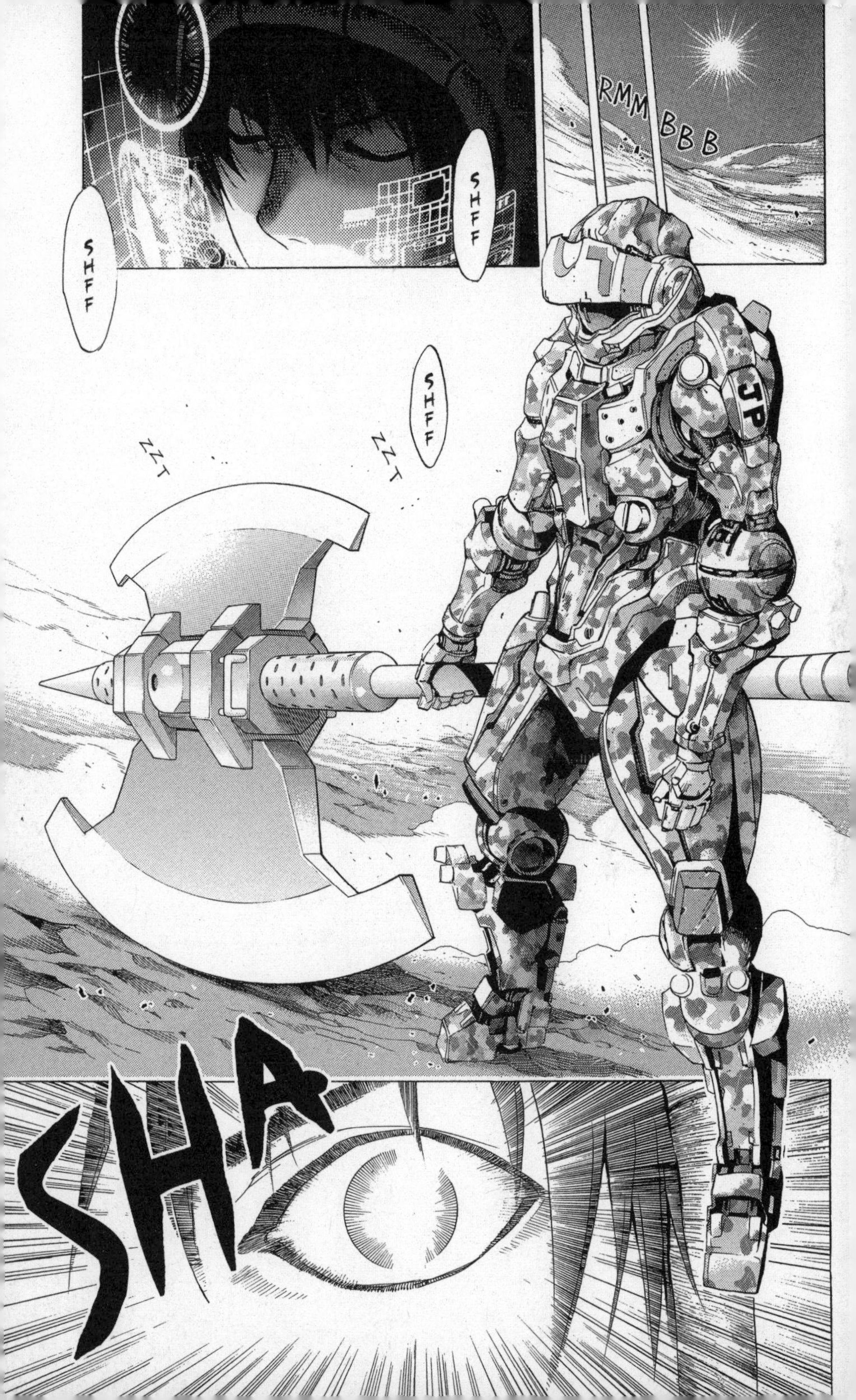
RMM BBB
SHFF
SHFF
SHFF
ZZT
ZZT
SHA

It took something massive
to shatter a Mimic
endoskeleton in one hit.
That it could kill me
in the process was
beside the point.

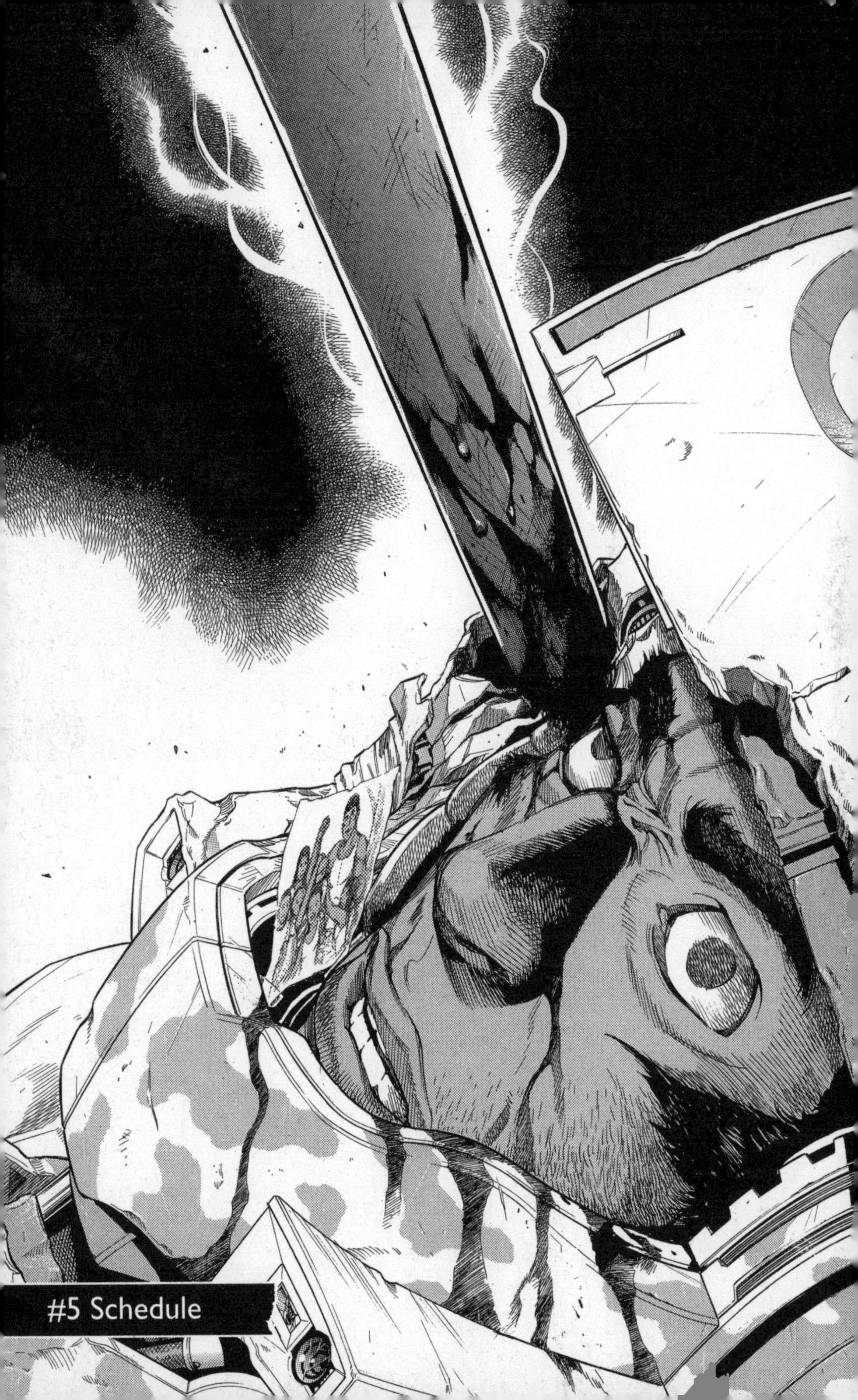

#5 Schedule

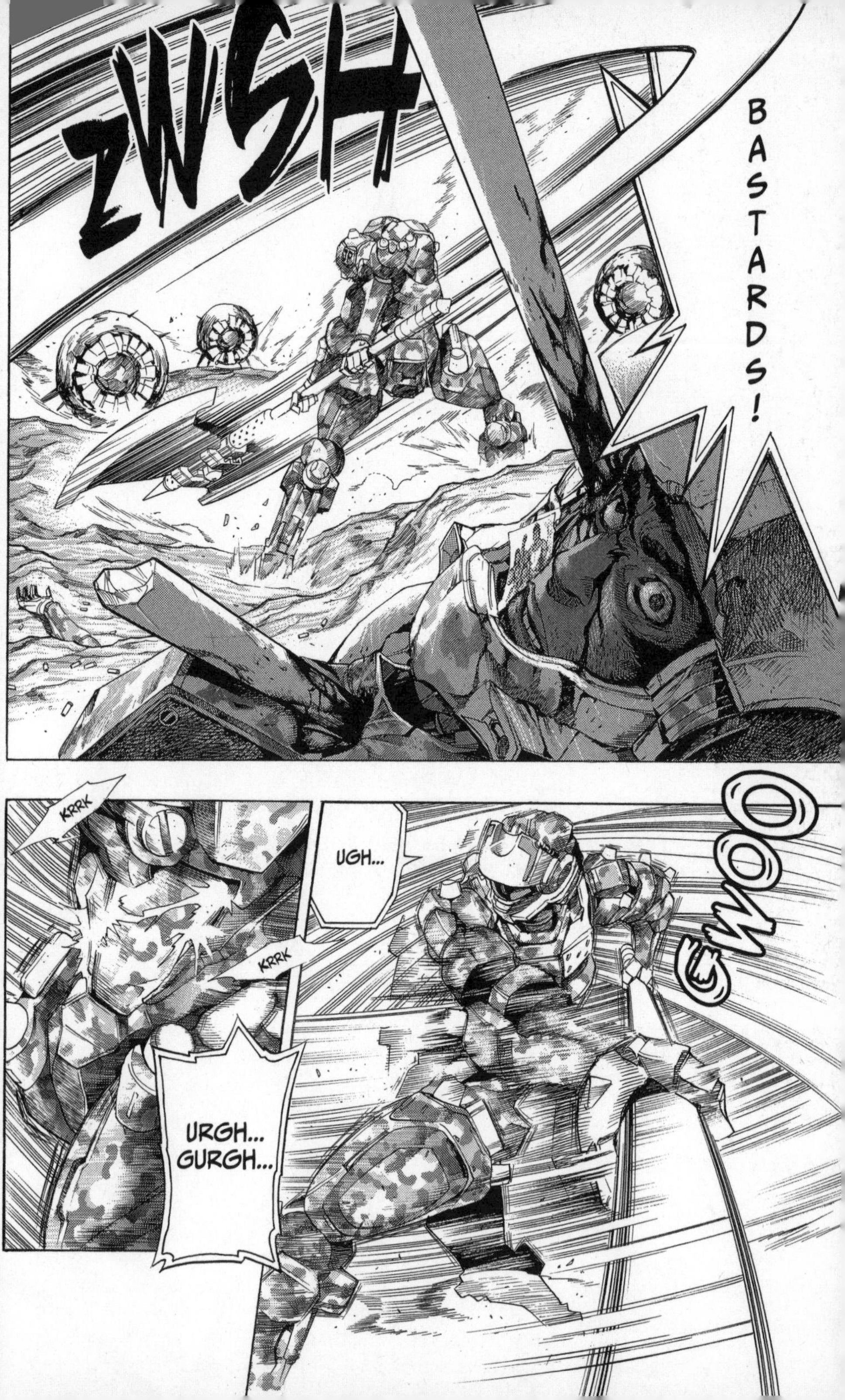
ZWSH
BASTARDS!
GWOO
UGH...
KRRK
KRRK
URGH... GURGH...

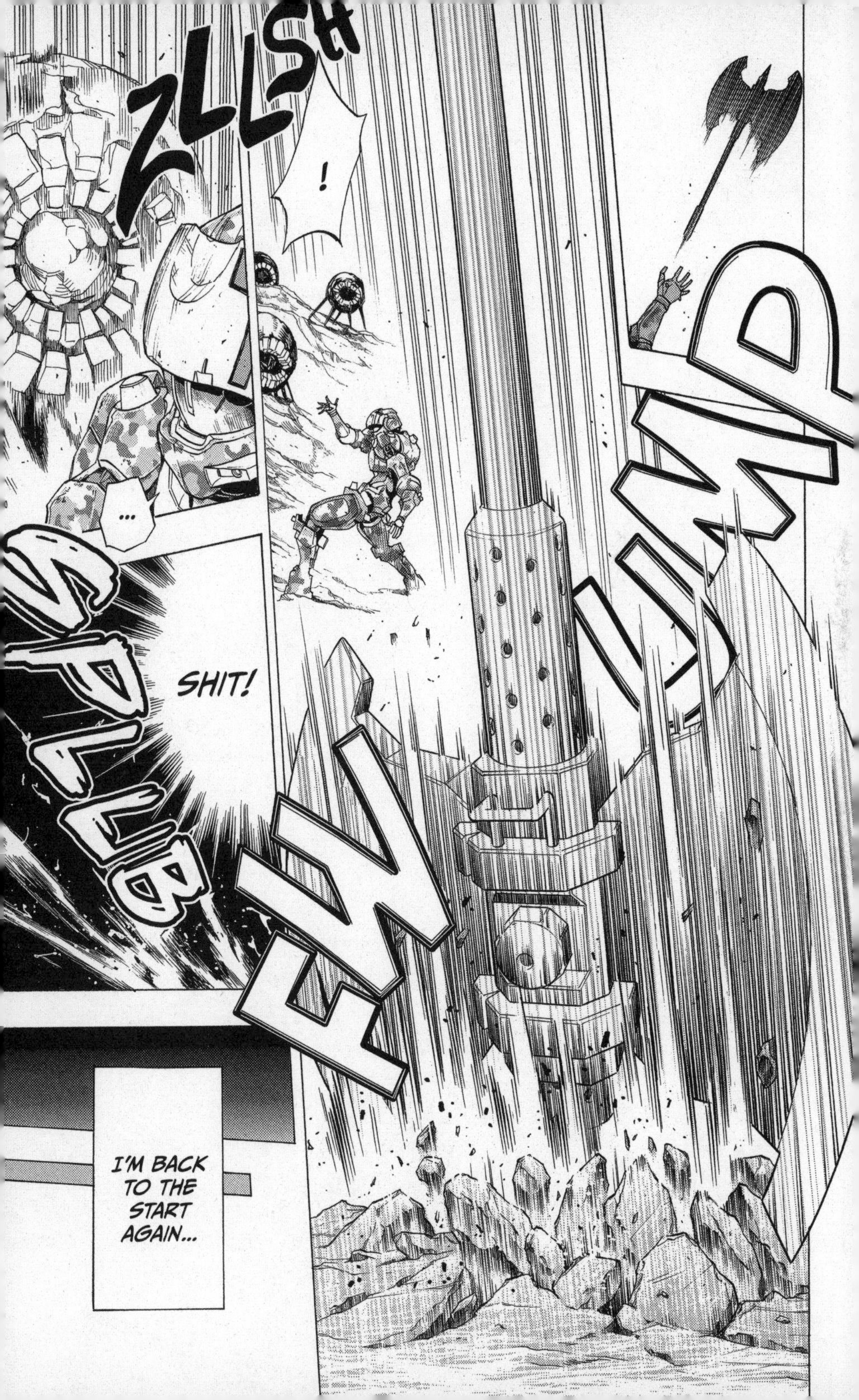
THUMP
FWY
ZLLSH
!
...
SPLUB
SHIT!
I'M BACK TO THE START AGAIN...

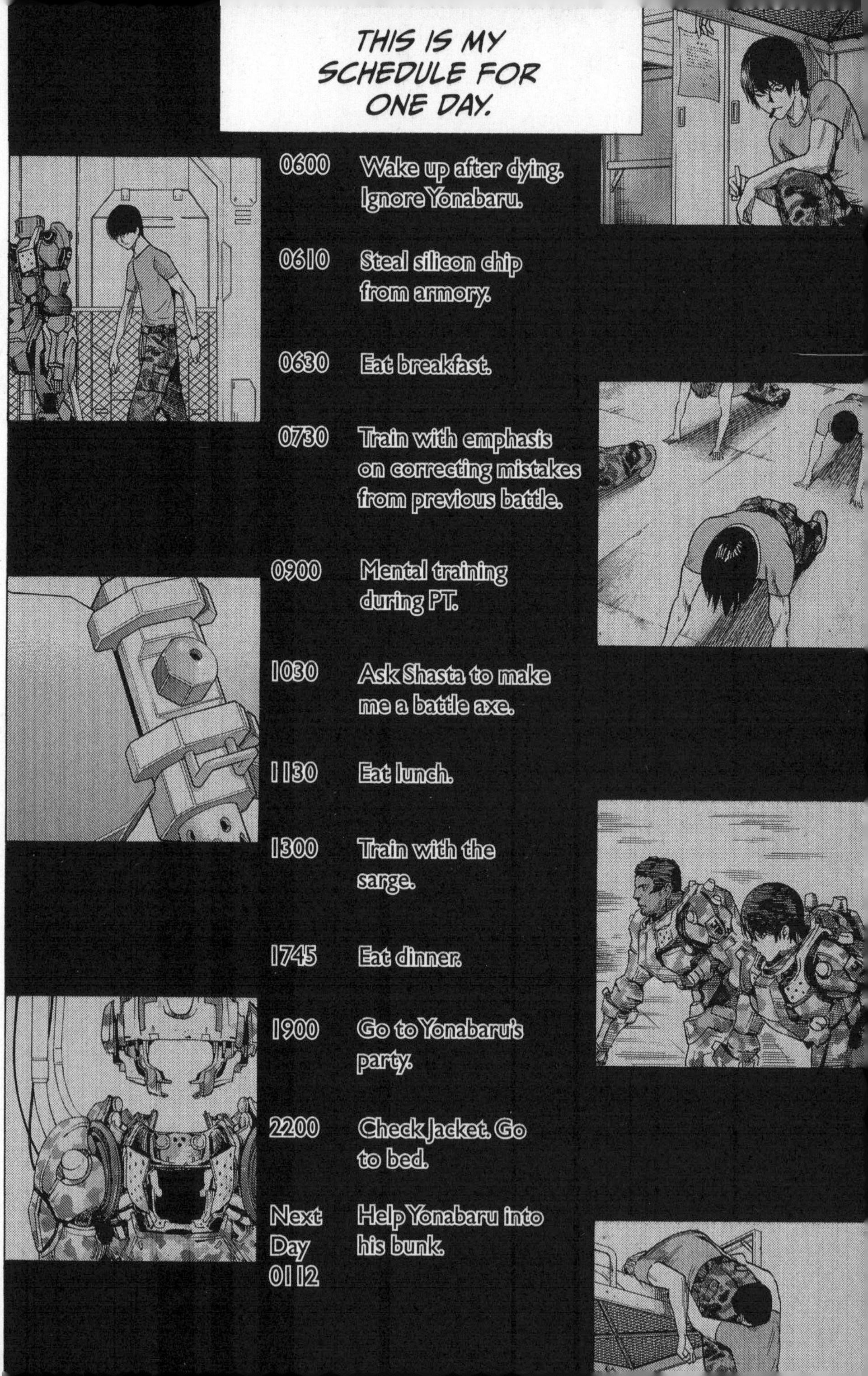

THIS IS MY SCHEDULE FOR ONE DAY.

0600	Wake up after dying. Ignore Yonabaru.
0610	Steal silicon chip from armory.
0630	Eat breakfast.
0730	Train with emphasis on correcting mistakes from previous battle.
0900	Mental training during PT.
1030	Ask Shasta to make me a battle axe.
1130	Eat lunch.
1300	Train with the sarge.
1745	Eat dinner.
1900	Go to Yonabaru's party.
2200	Check Jacket. Go to bed.
Next Day 0112	Help Yonabaru into his bunk.

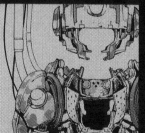

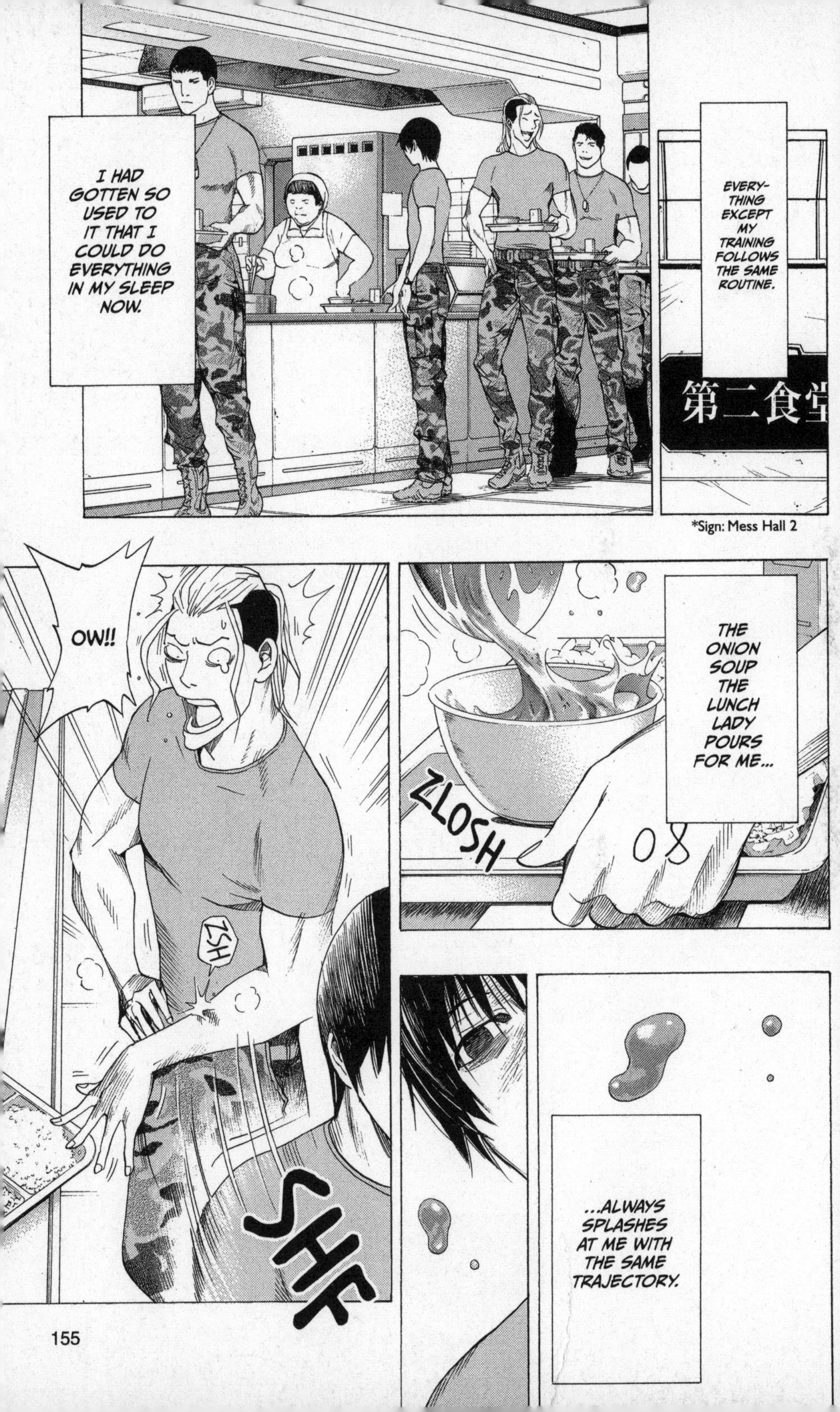
EVERY-THING EXCEPT MY TRAINING FOLLOWS THE SAME ROUTINE.
第二食堂
I HAD GOTTEN SO USED TO IT THAT I COULD DO EVERYTHING IN MY SLEEP NOW.
THE ONION SOUP THE LUNCH LADY POURS FOR ME...
ZLOSH
08
...ALWAYS SPLASHES AT ME WITH THE SAME TRAJECTORY.
OW!!
ZSH
SHF
*Sign: Mess Hall 2

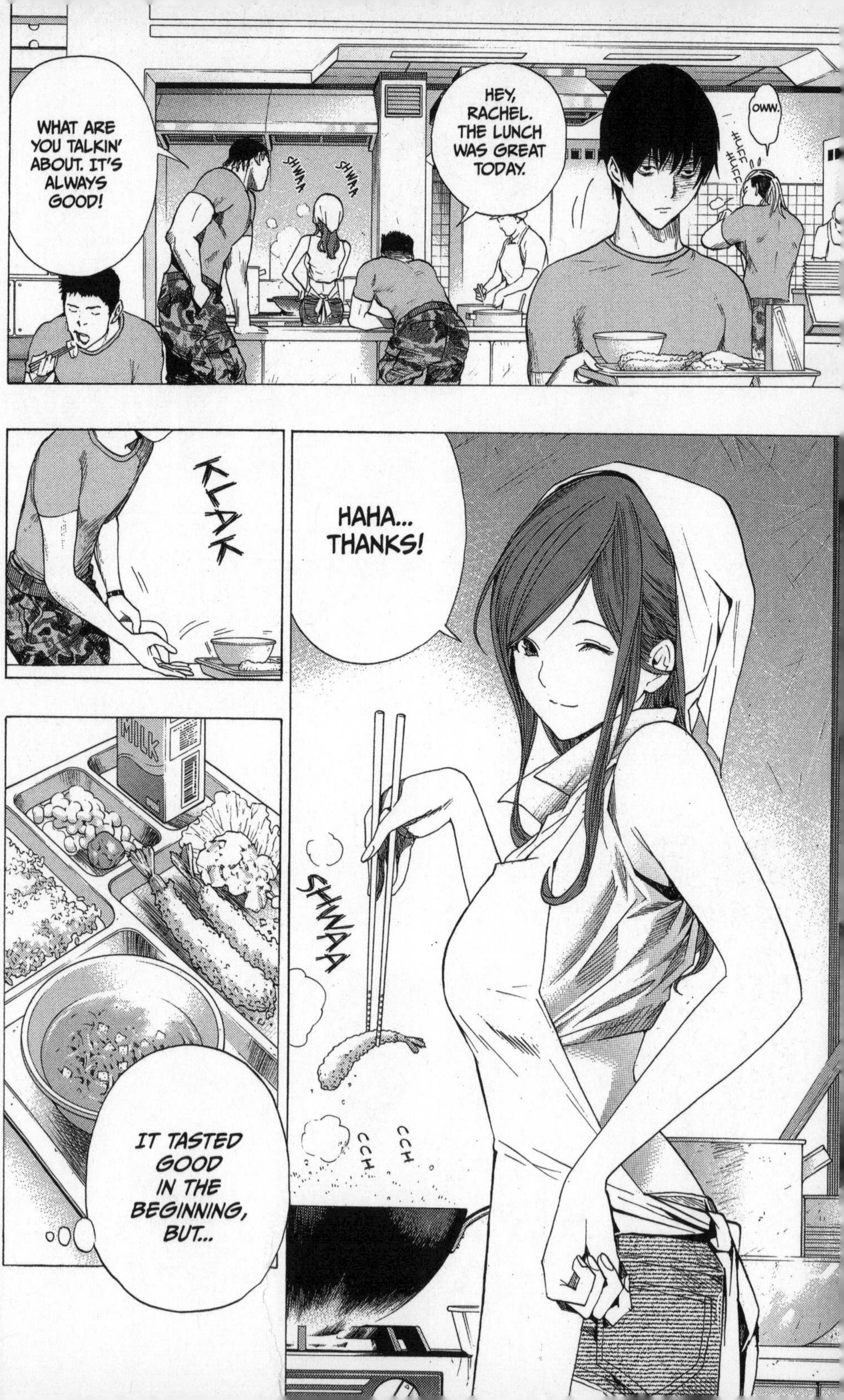
OWW.
HUFF HUFF
HEY, RACHEL. THE LUNCH WAS GREAT TODAY.
SHWAA SHWAA
WHAT ARE YOU TALKIN' ABOUT. IT'S ALWAYS GOOD!
HAHA... THANKS!
SHWAA
CCH CCH
KLAK
IT TASTED GOOD IN THE BEGINNING, BUT...

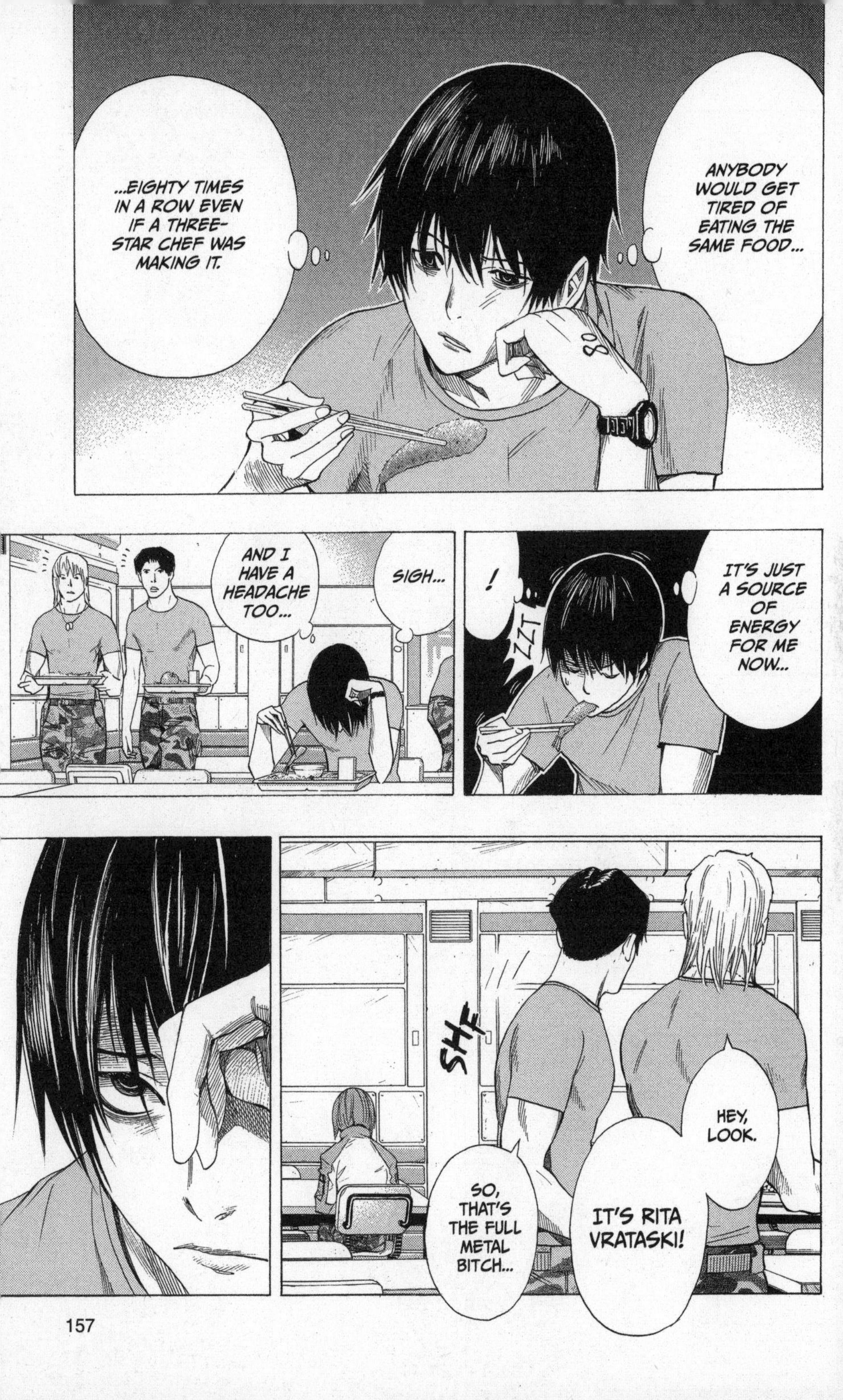
ANYBODY WOULD GET TIRED OF EATING THE SAME FOOD...
...EIGHTY TIMES IN A ROW EVEN IF A THREE-STAR CHEF WAS MAKING IT.
IT'S JUST A SOURCE OF ENERGY FOR ME NOW...
!
ZZT
SIGH...
AND I HAVE A HEADACHE TOO...
HEY, LOOK.
IT'S RITA VRATASKI!
SO, THAT'S THE FULL METAL BITCH...
SHF

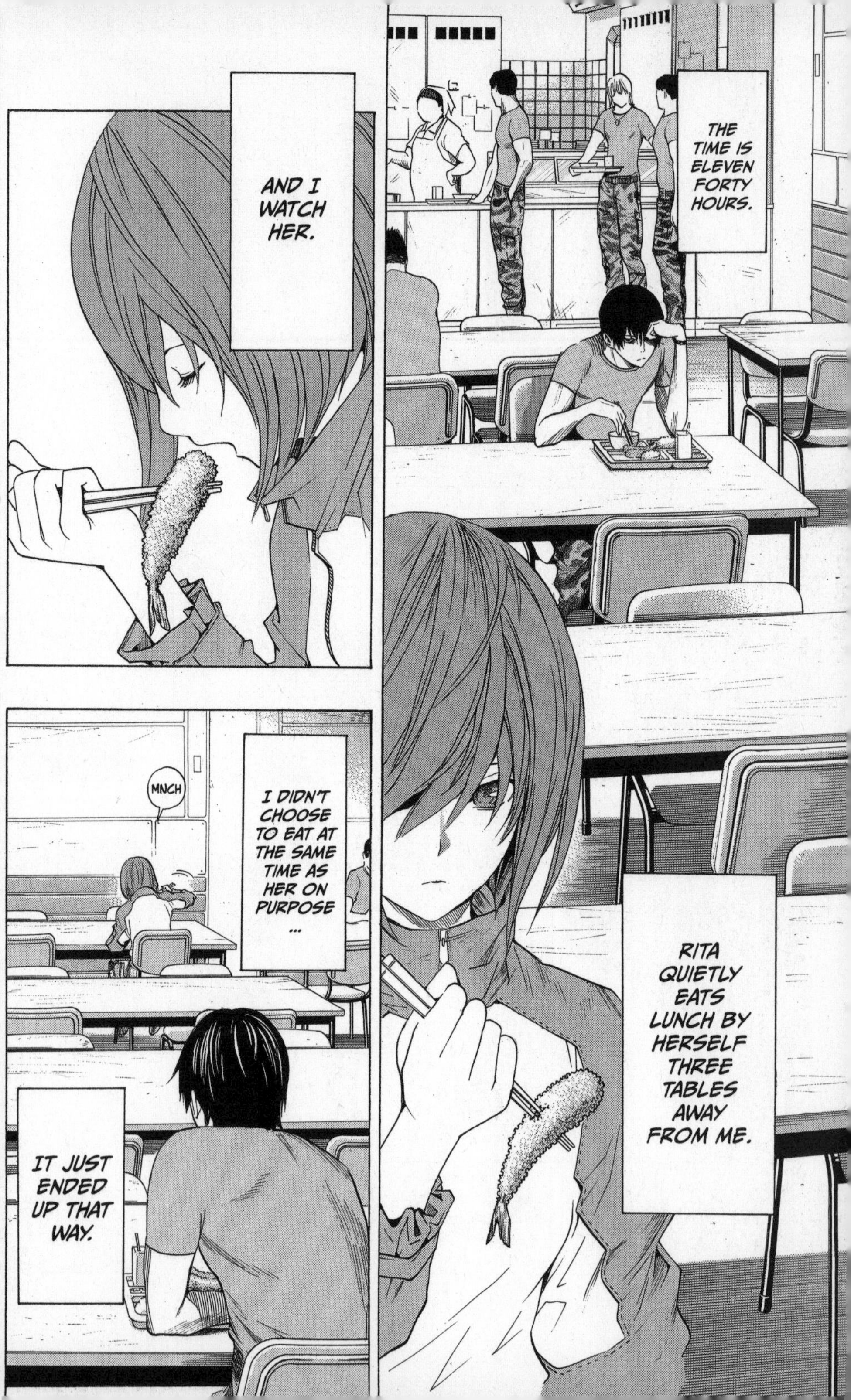
THE TIME IS ELEVEN FORTY HOURS.
RITA QUIETLY EATS LUNCH BY HERSELF THREE TABLES AWAY FROM ME.
AND I WATCH HER.
MNCH
I DIDN'T CHOOSE TO EAT AT THE SAME TIME AS HER ON PURPOSE ...
IT JUST ENDED UP THAT WAY.

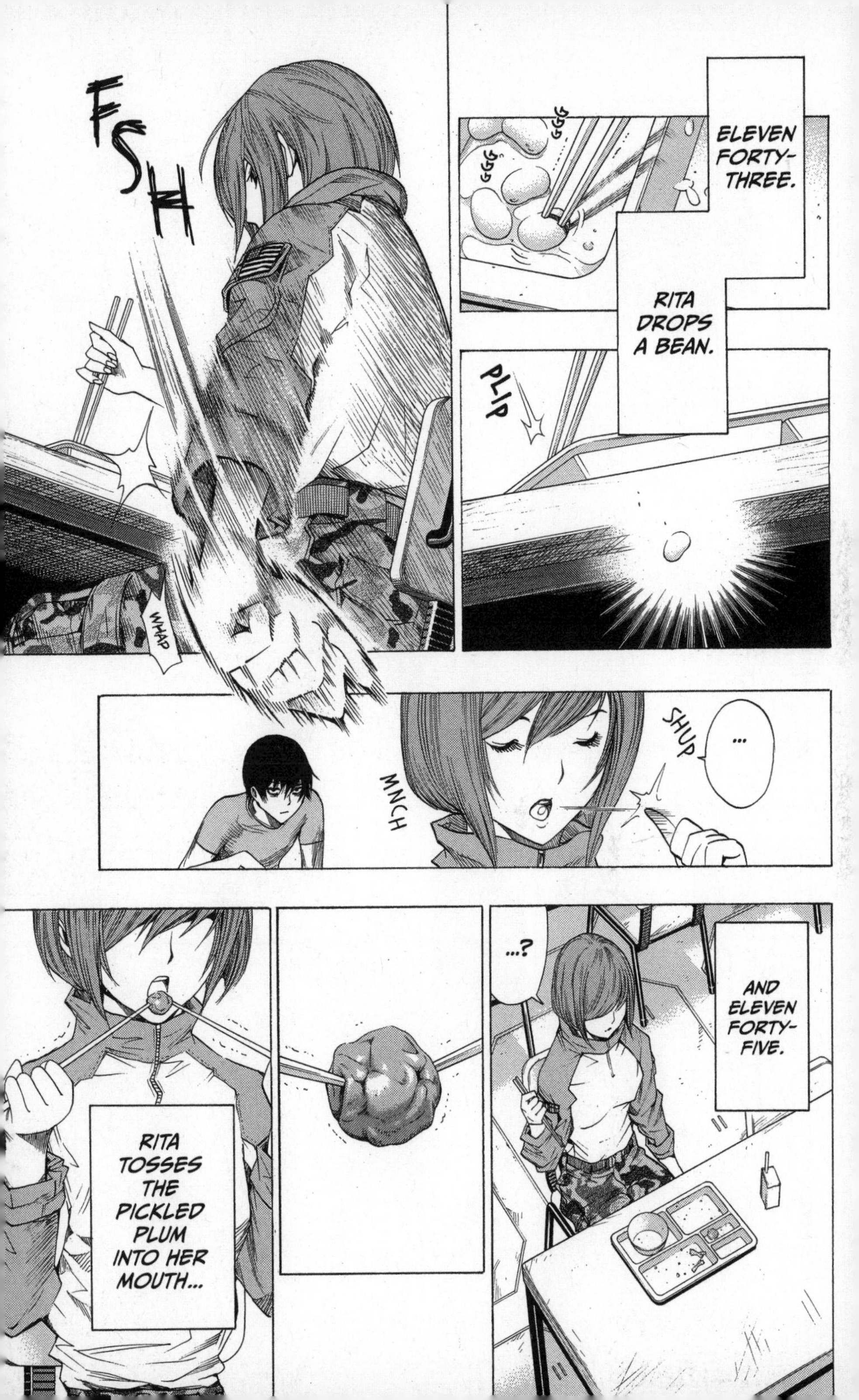
ELEVEN FORTY-THREE.
GGG
GGG
RITA DROPS A BEAN.
PLIP
FSH
WHAP
SHUP
...
MNCH
...?
AND ELEVEN FORTY-FIVE.
RITA TOSSES THE PICKLED PLUM INTO HER MOUTH...

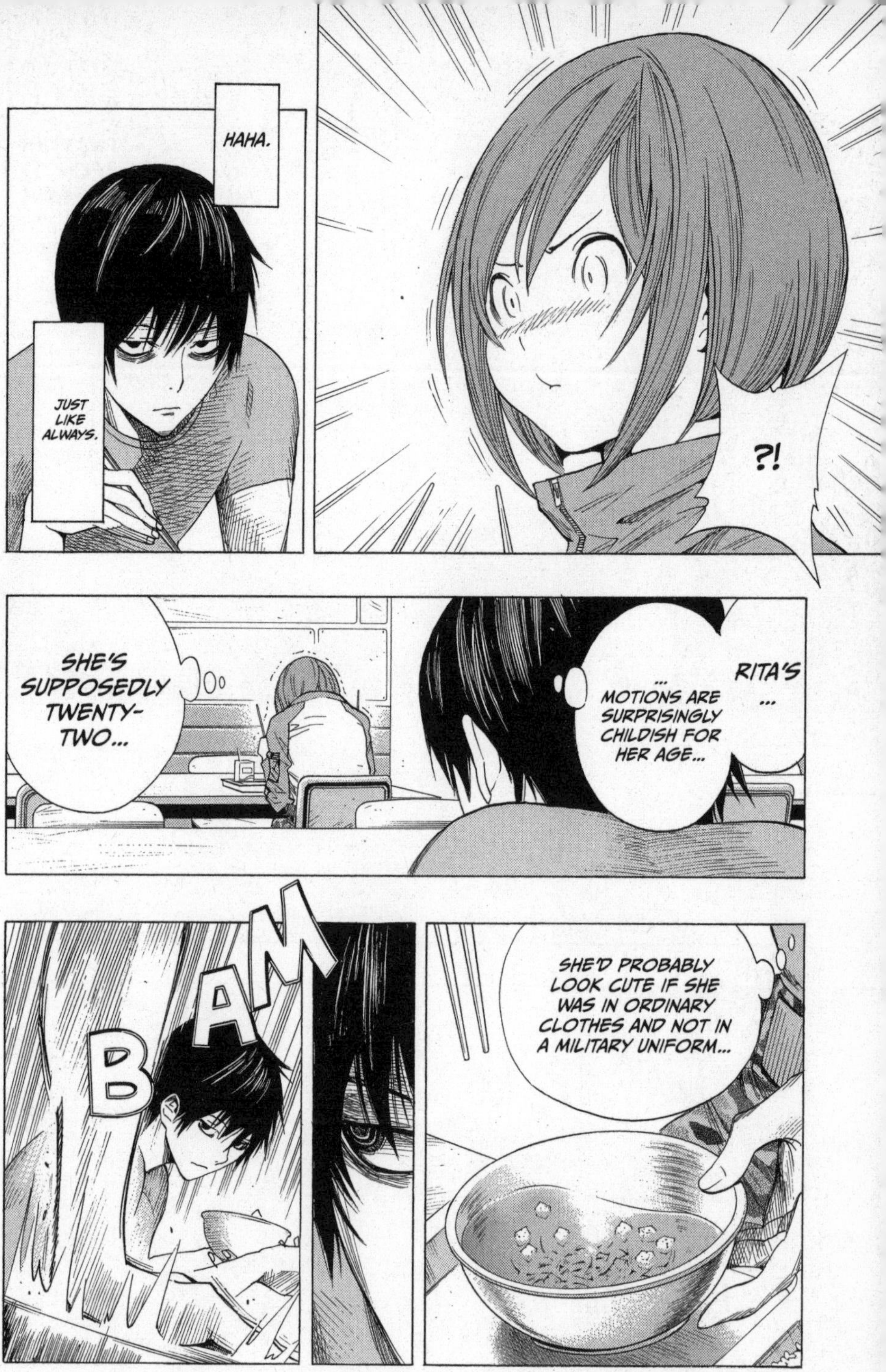
?!
HAHA.
JUST LIKE ALWAYS.
RITA'S ...
... MOTIONS ARE SURPRISINGLY CHILDISH FOR HER AGE...
SHE'S SUPPOSEDLY TWENTY-TWO...
SHE'D PROBABLY LOOK CUTE IF SHE WAS IN ORDINARY CLOTHES AND NOT IN A MILITARY UNIFORM...
BAM

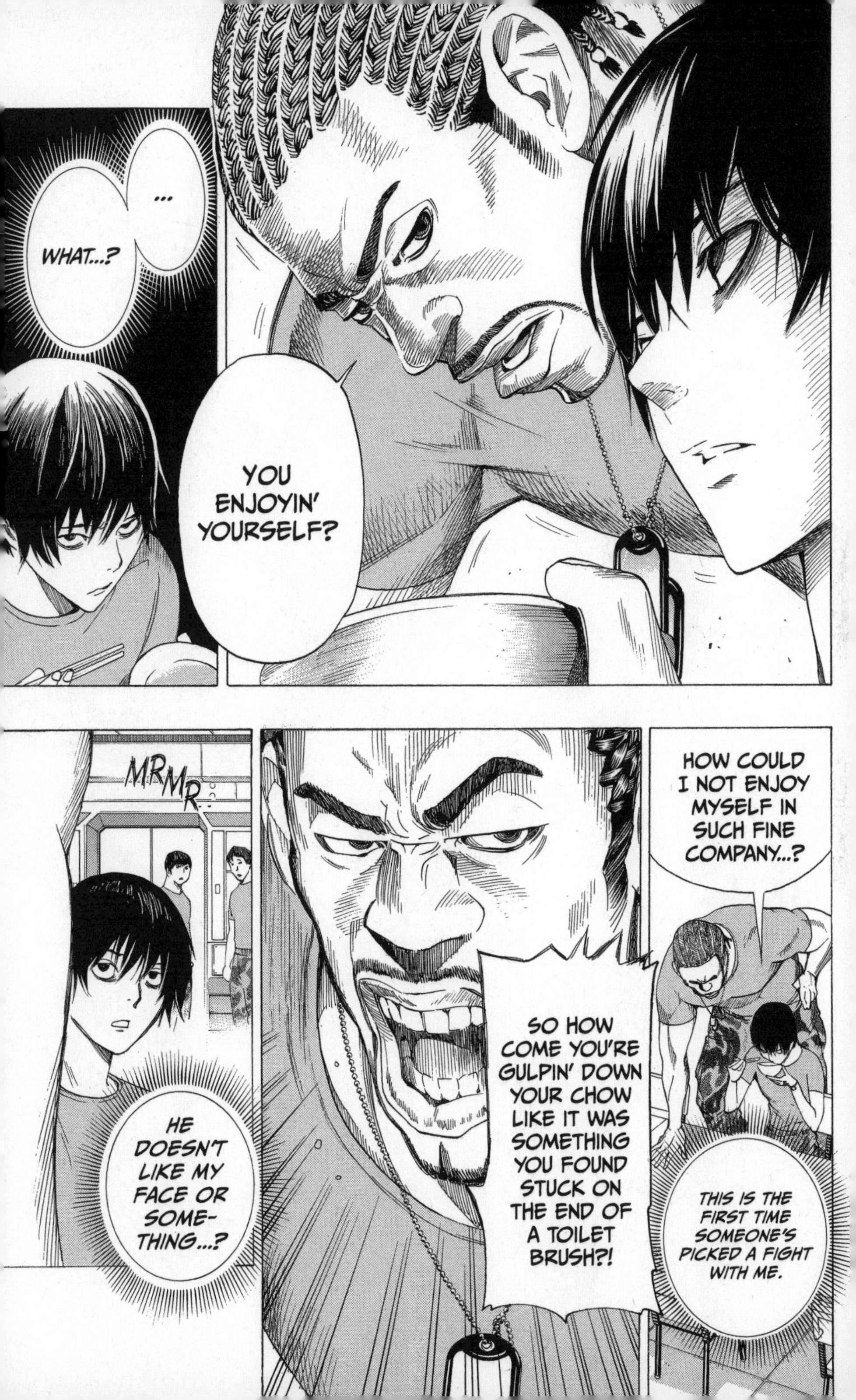
YOU ENJOYIN' YOURSELF?
...
WHAT...?
HOW COULD I NOT ENJOY MYSELF IN SUCH FINE COMPANY...?
THIS IS THE FIRST TIME SOMEONE'S PICKED A FIGHT WITH ME.
SO HOW COME YOU'RE GULPIN' DOWN YOUR CHOW LIKE IT WAS SOMETHING YOU FOUND STUCK ON THE END OF A TOILET BRUSH?!
MRMR
HE DOESN'T LIKE MY FACE OR SOME-THING...?

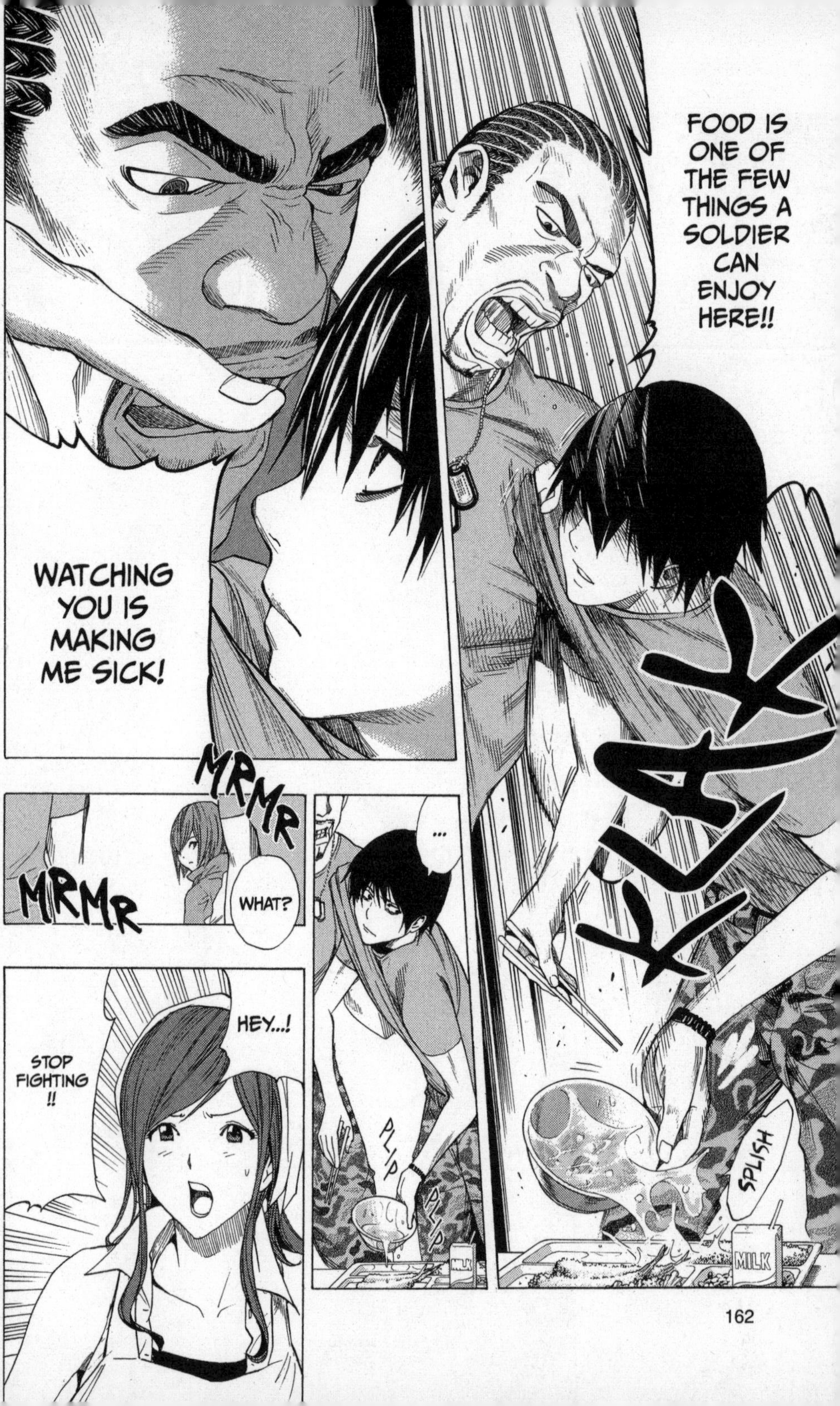
FOOD IS ONE OF THE FEW THINGS A SOLDIER CAN ENJOY HERE!!
KLAK
SPLISH
WATCHING YOU IS MAKING ME SICK!
...
PLIP
PLIP
MRMR
MRMR
WHAT?
HEY...!
STOP FIGHTING !!

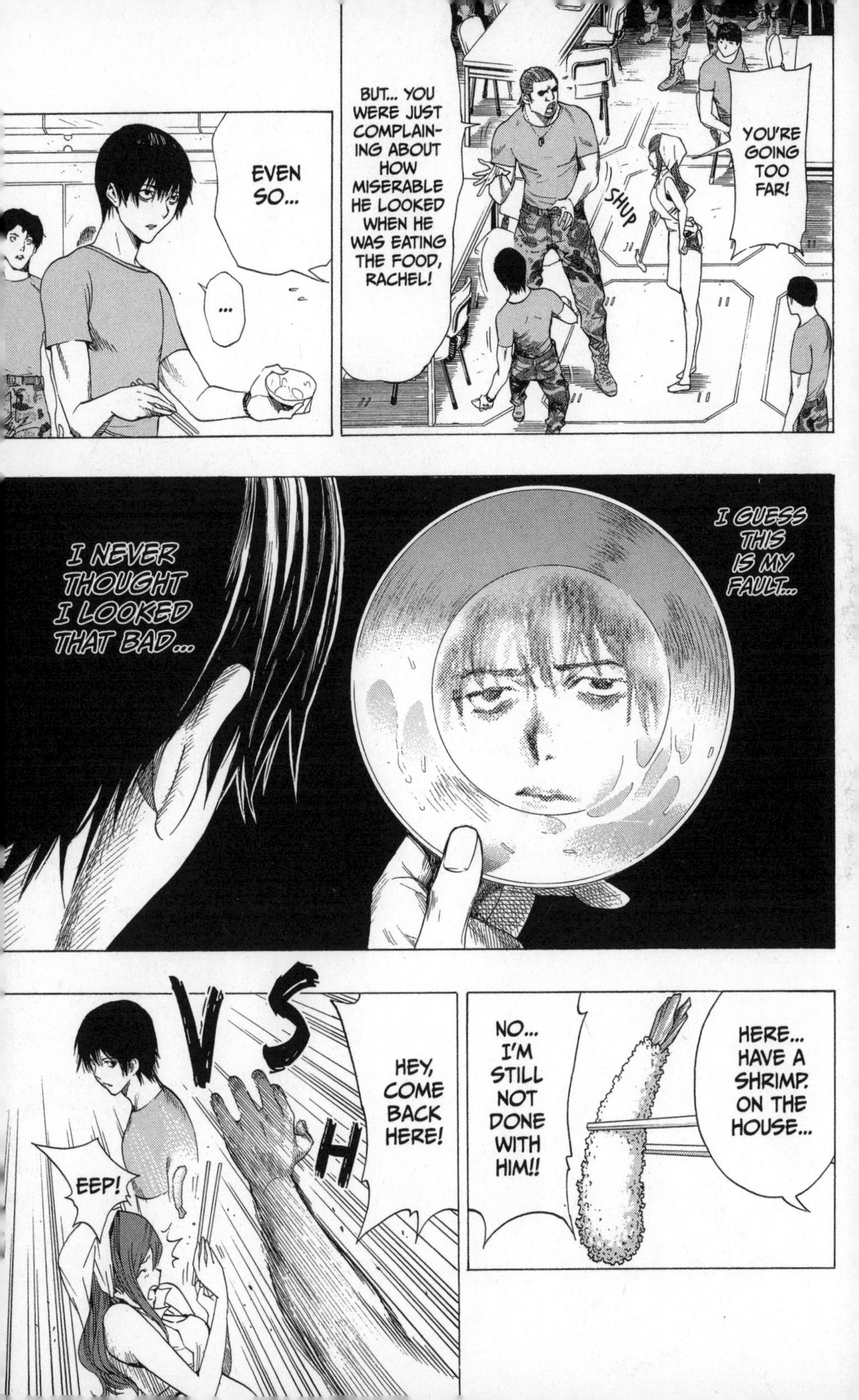
YOU'RE GOING TOO FAR!
BUT... YOU WERE JUST COMPLAINING ABOUT HOW MISERABLE HE LOOKED WHEN HE WAS EATING THE FOOD, RACHEL!
SHUP
EVEN SO...
...
I GUESS THIS IS MY FAULT...
I NEVER THOUGHT I LOOKED THAT BAD...
HERE... HAVE A SHRIMP. ON THE HOUSE...
NO... I'M STILL NOT DONE WITH HIM!!
HEY, COME BACK HERE!
VSH
EEP!

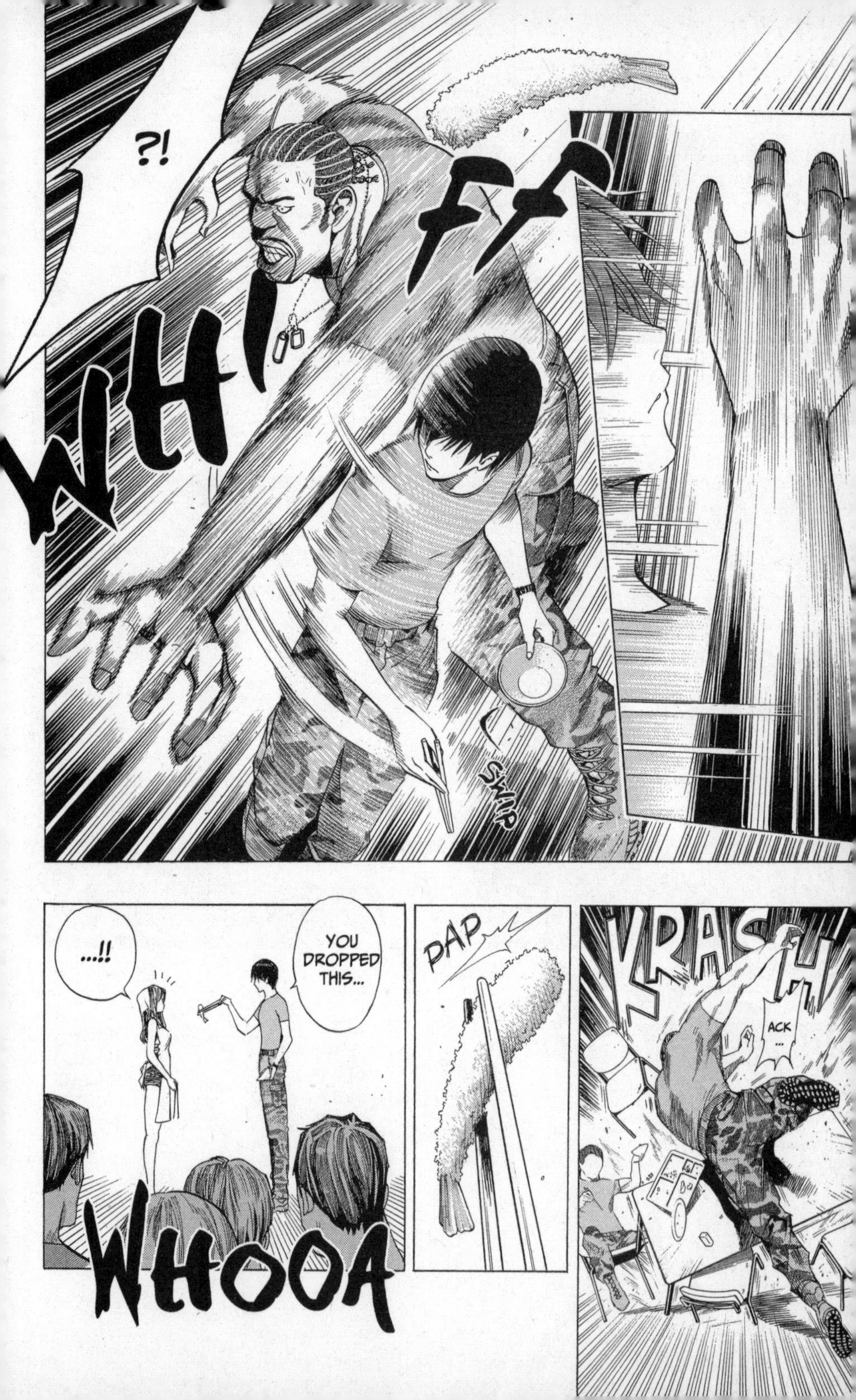
?!
WHIFF
SWIP
KRASH
ACK...
PAP
YOU DROPPED THIS...
...!!
WHOOA

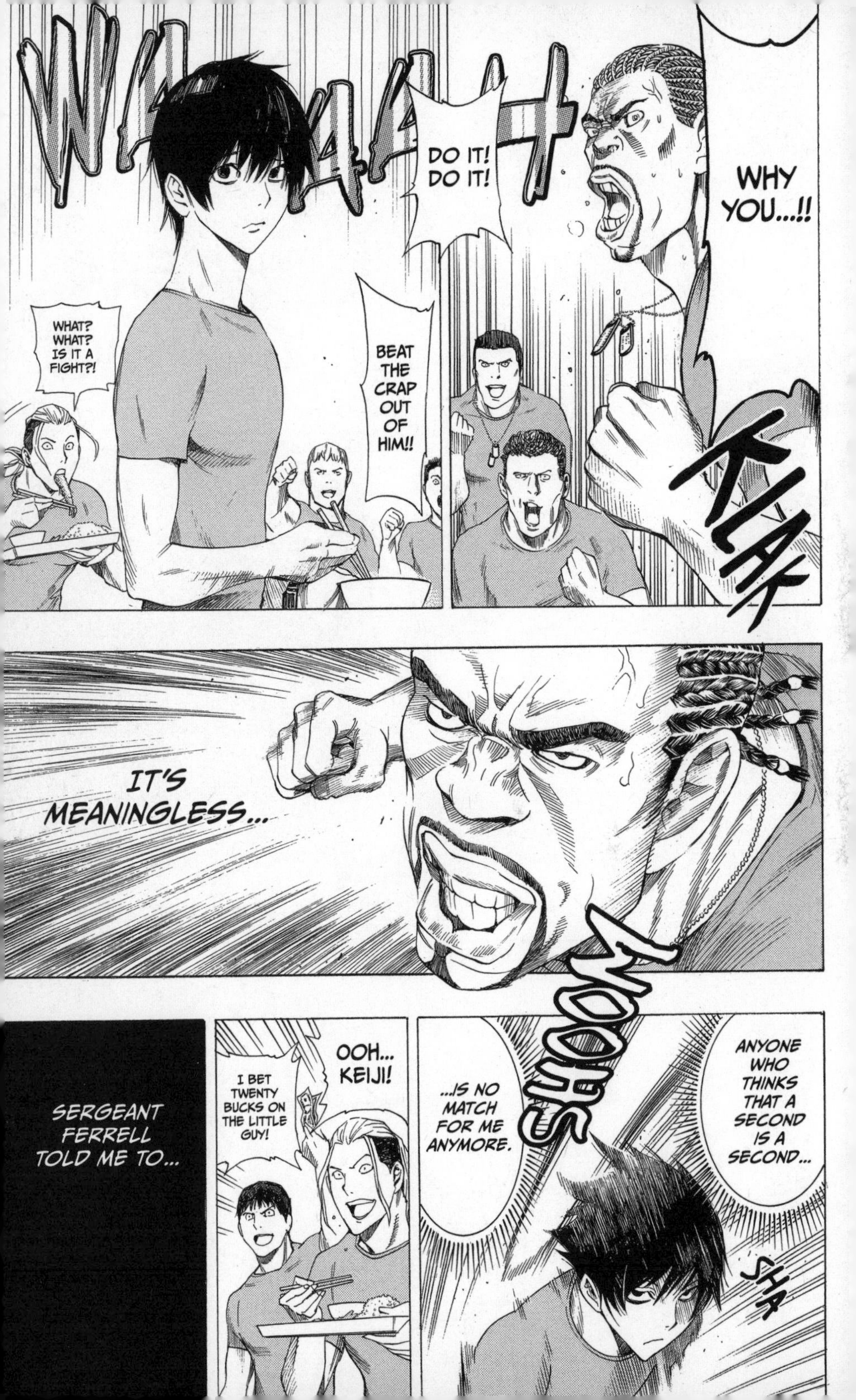
WHY YOU...!!
KLAK
DO IT! DO IT!
BEAT THE CRAP OUT OF HIM!!
WHAT? WHAT? IS IT A FIGHT?!
IT'S MEANINGLESS...
ANYONE WHO THINKS THAT A SECOND IS A SECOND...
...IS NO MATCH FOR ME ANYMORE.
SHOOSH
SHA
OOH... KEIJI!
I BET TWENTY BUCKS ON THE LITTLE GUY!
SERGEANT FERRELL TOLD ME TO...

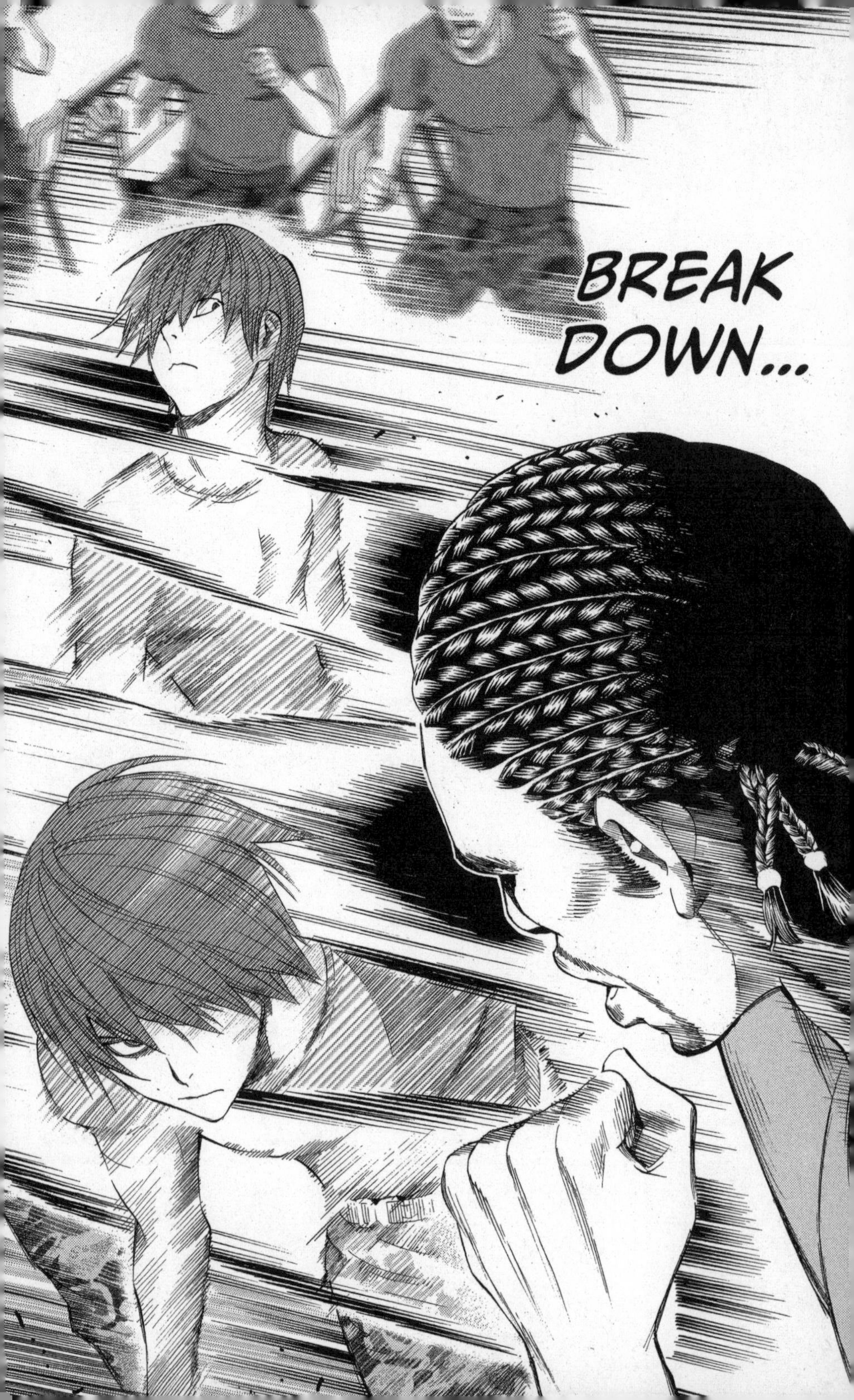
BREAK DOWN...

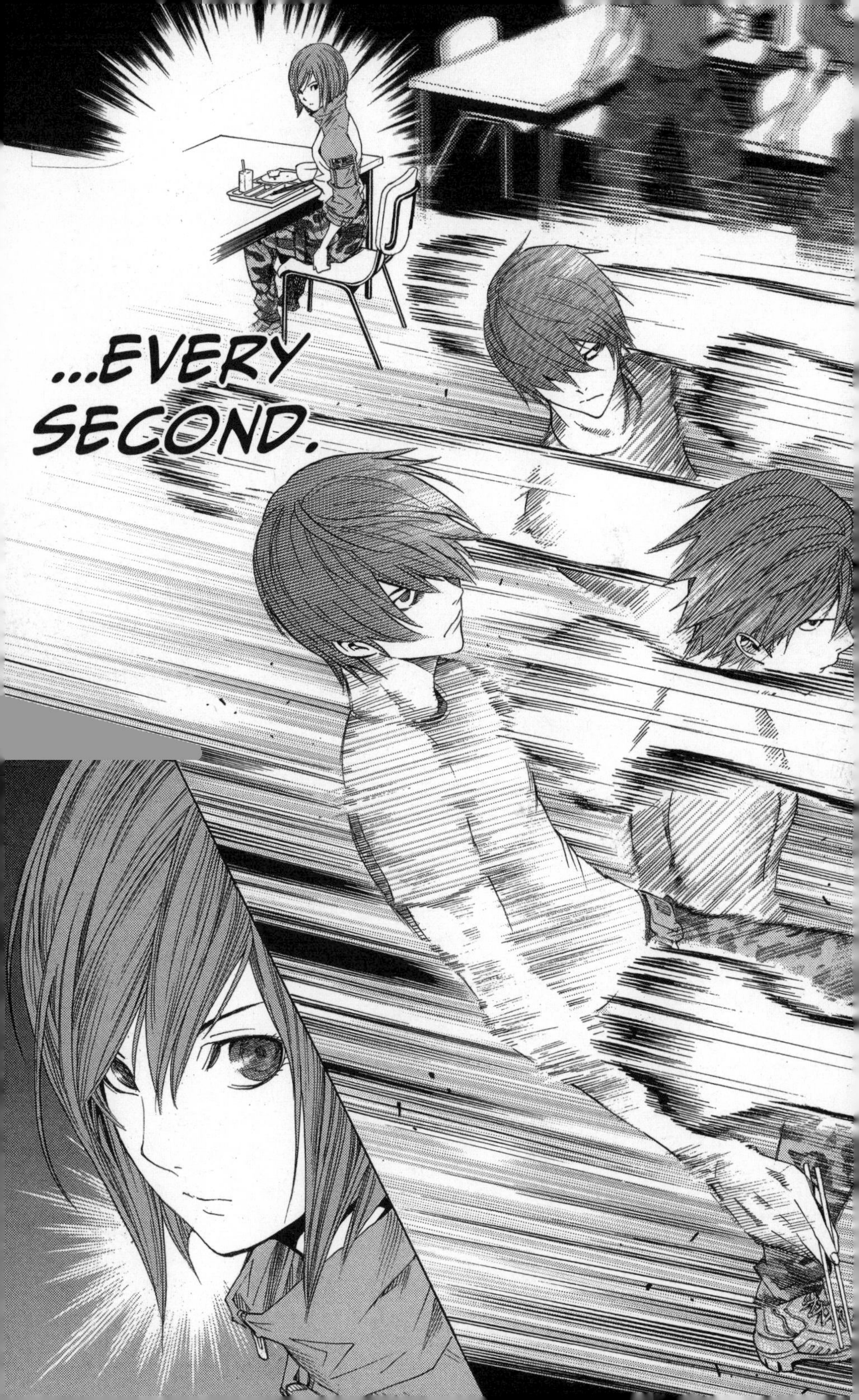
...EVERY SECOND.

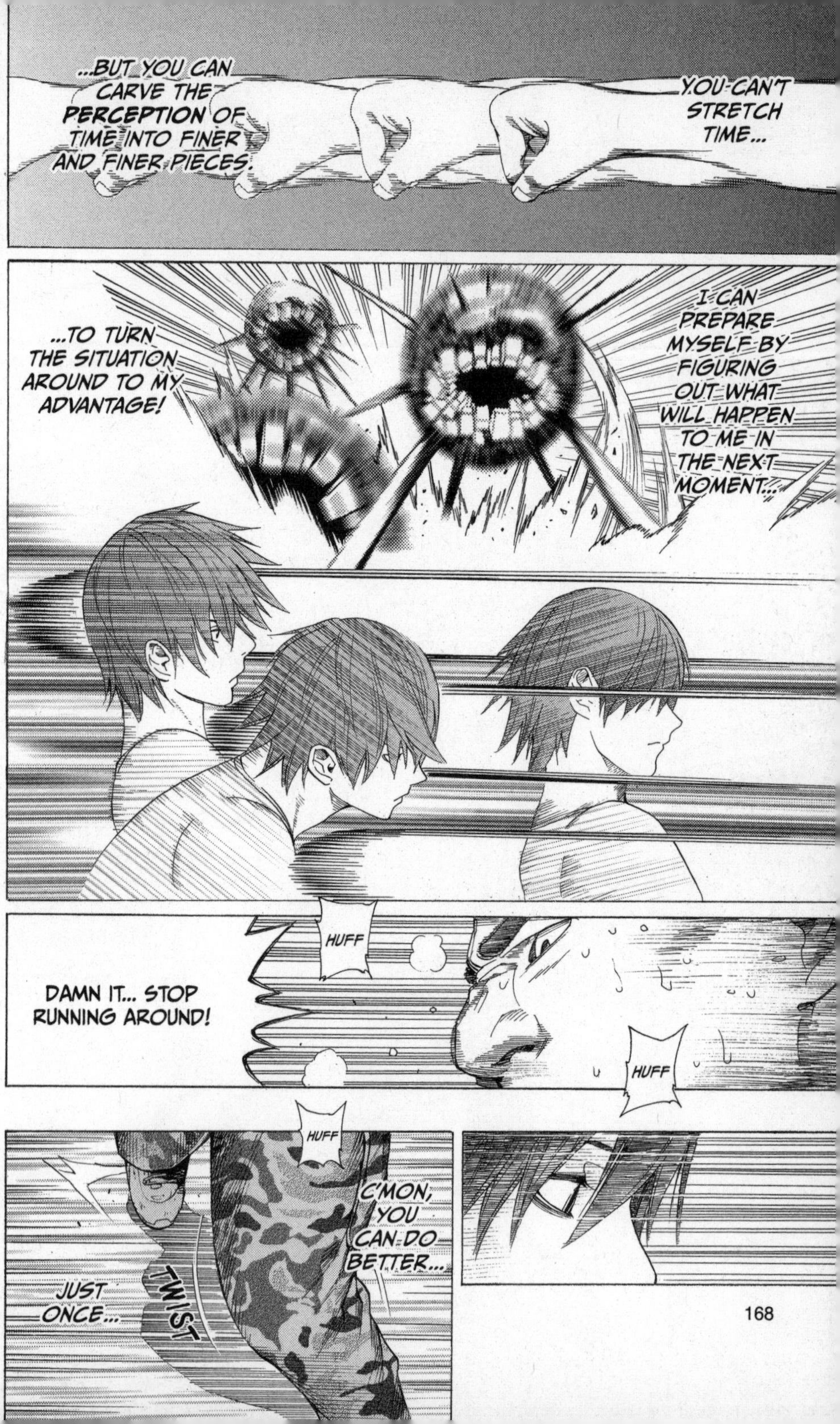
YOU CAN'T STRETCH TIME...
...BUT YOU CAN CARVE THE PERCEPTION OF TIME INTO FINER AND FINER PIECES.
I CAN PREPARE MYSELF BY FIGURING OUT WHAT WILL HAPPEN TO ME IN THE NEXT MOMENT...
...TO TURN THE SITUATION AROUND TO MY ADVANTAGE!
HUFF
HUFF
DAMN IT... STOP RUNNING AROUND!
HUFF
C'MON, YOU CAN DO BETTER...
TWIST
JUST ONCE...

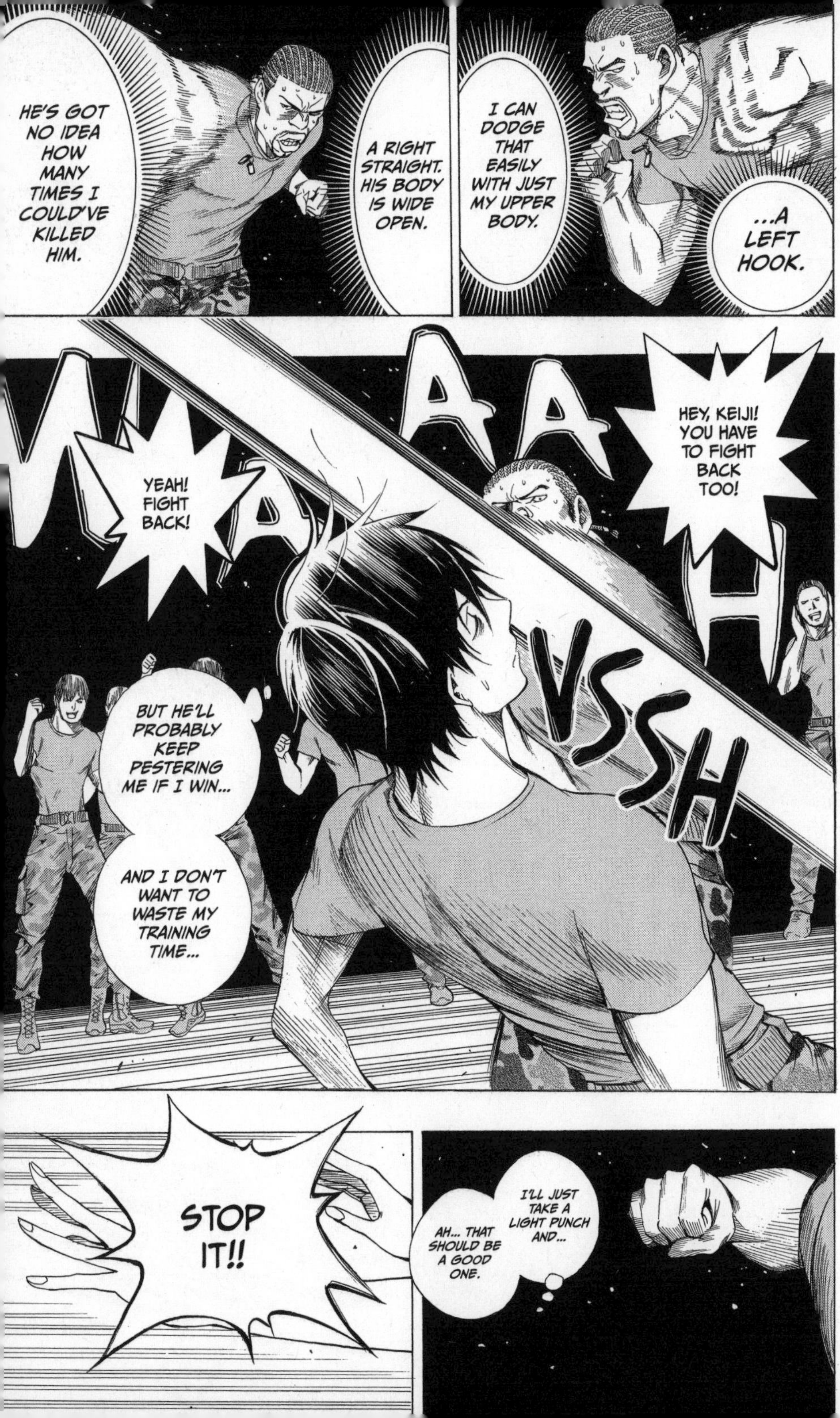
...A LEFT HOOK.
I CAN DODGE THAT EASILY WITH JUST MY UPPER BODY.
A RIGHT STRAIGHT. HIS BODY IS WIDE OPEN.
HE'S GOT NO IDEA HOW MANY TIMES I COULD'VE KILLED HIM.
WAAAH
HEY, KEIJI! YOU HAVE TO FIGHT BACK TOO!
YEAH! FIGHT BACK!
VSSH
BUT HE'LL PROBABLY KEEP PESTERING ME IF I WIN...
AND I DON'T WANT TO WASTE MY TRAINING TIME...
I'LL JUST TAKE A LIGHT PUNCH AND...
AH... THAT SHOULD BE A GOOD ONE.
STOP IT!!

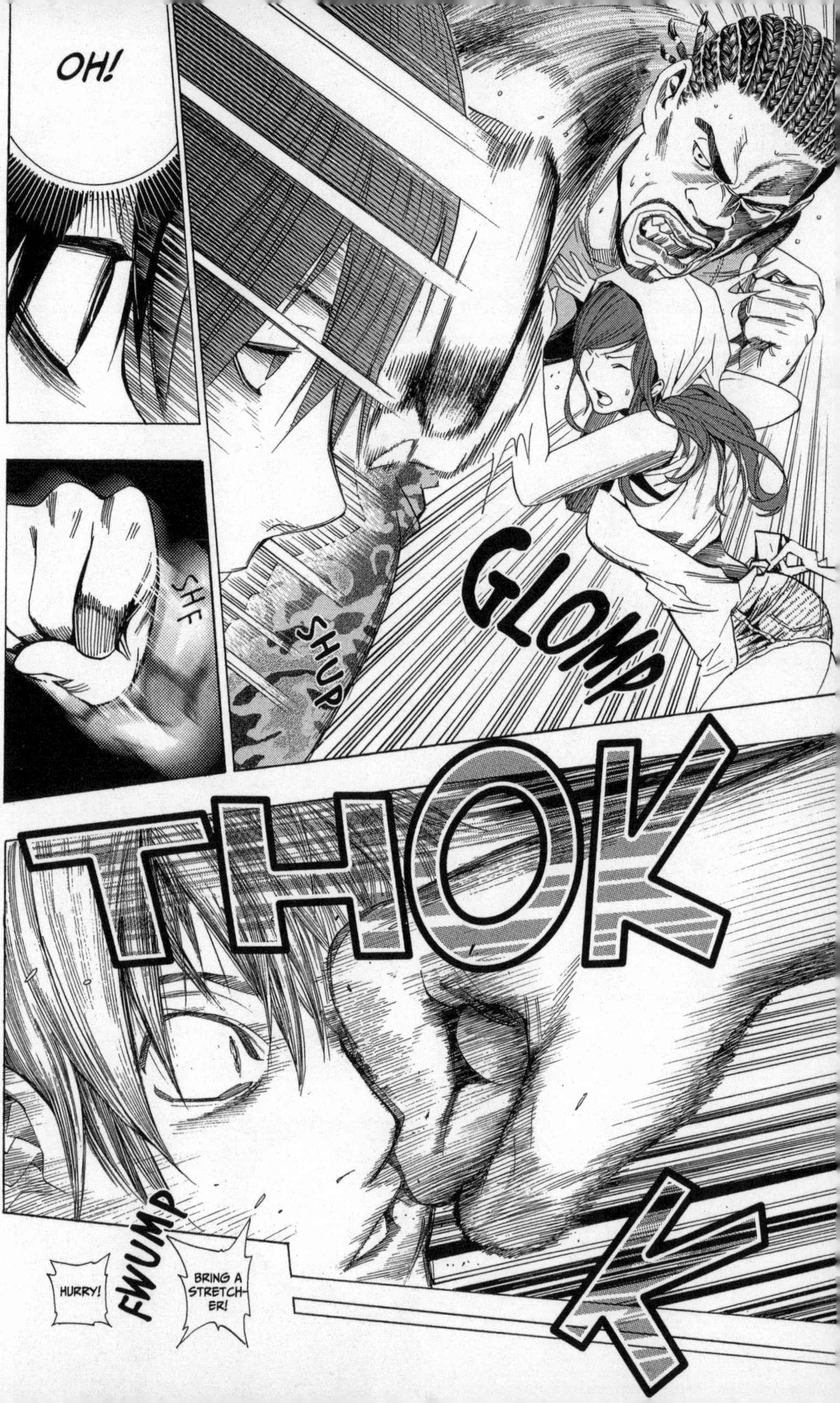
GLOMP
SHUP
OH!
SHF
THOK
FWUMP
BRING A STRETCH-ER!
HURRY!

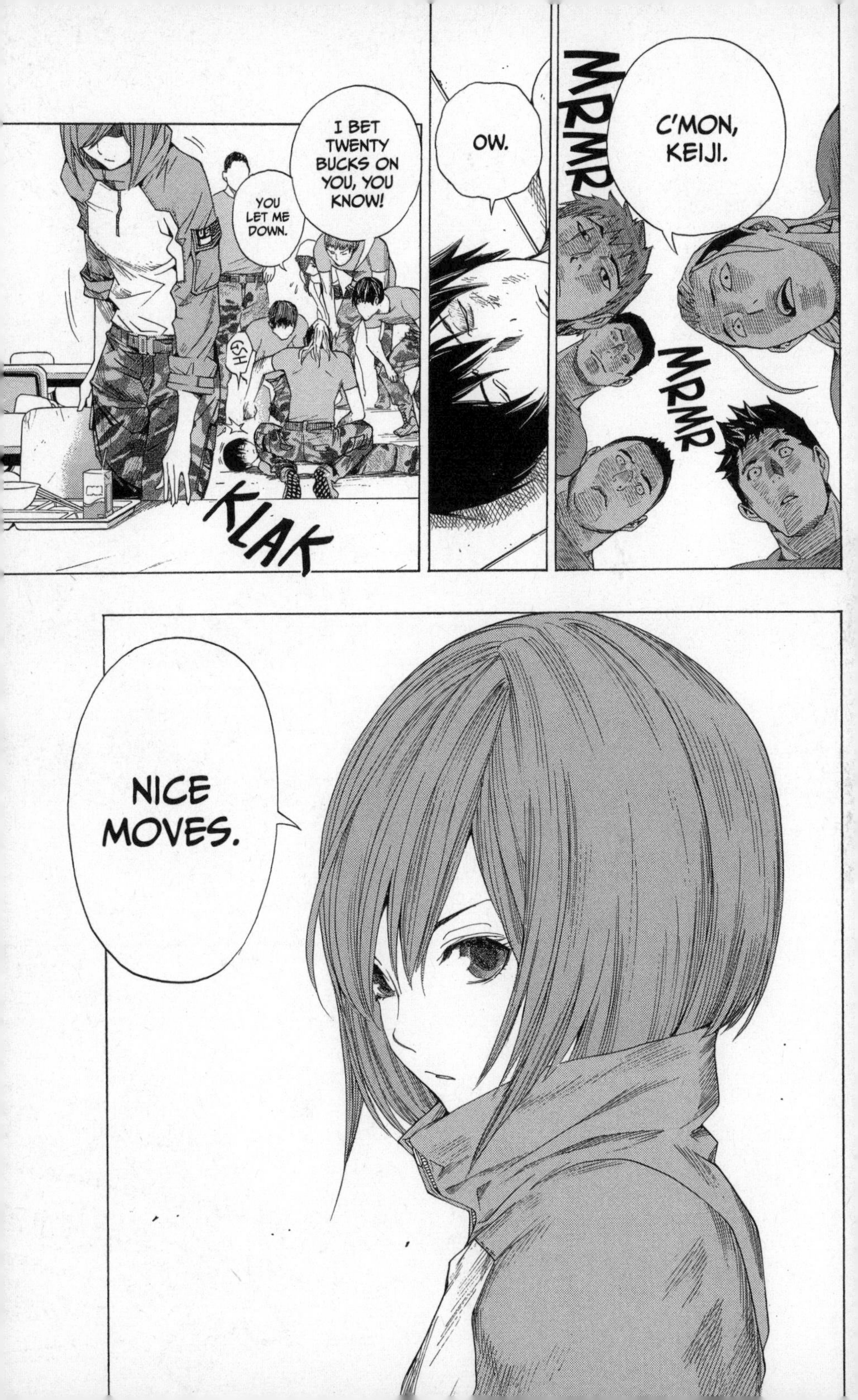
C'MON, KEIJI.
MRMR
MRMR
OW.
I BET TWENTY BUCKS ON YOU, YOU KNOW!
YOU LET ME DOWN.
GSH
KLAK
NICE MOVES.

If you flipped a switch in the
back of your brain, you could
watch a second go by like the
frames of a movie.
Once you figured out what
would be happening ten frames
later, you could take whatever
steps you needed to turn the
situation to your advantage.
All at a subconscious level. In
battle, you couldn't count on
anyone who didn't understand
how to break down time.

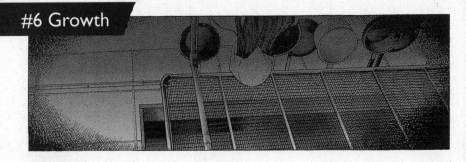

#6 Growth

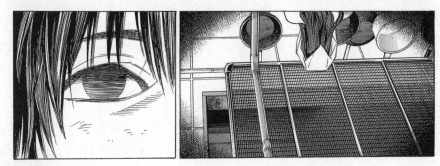

ARE YOU AWAKE?

UM...

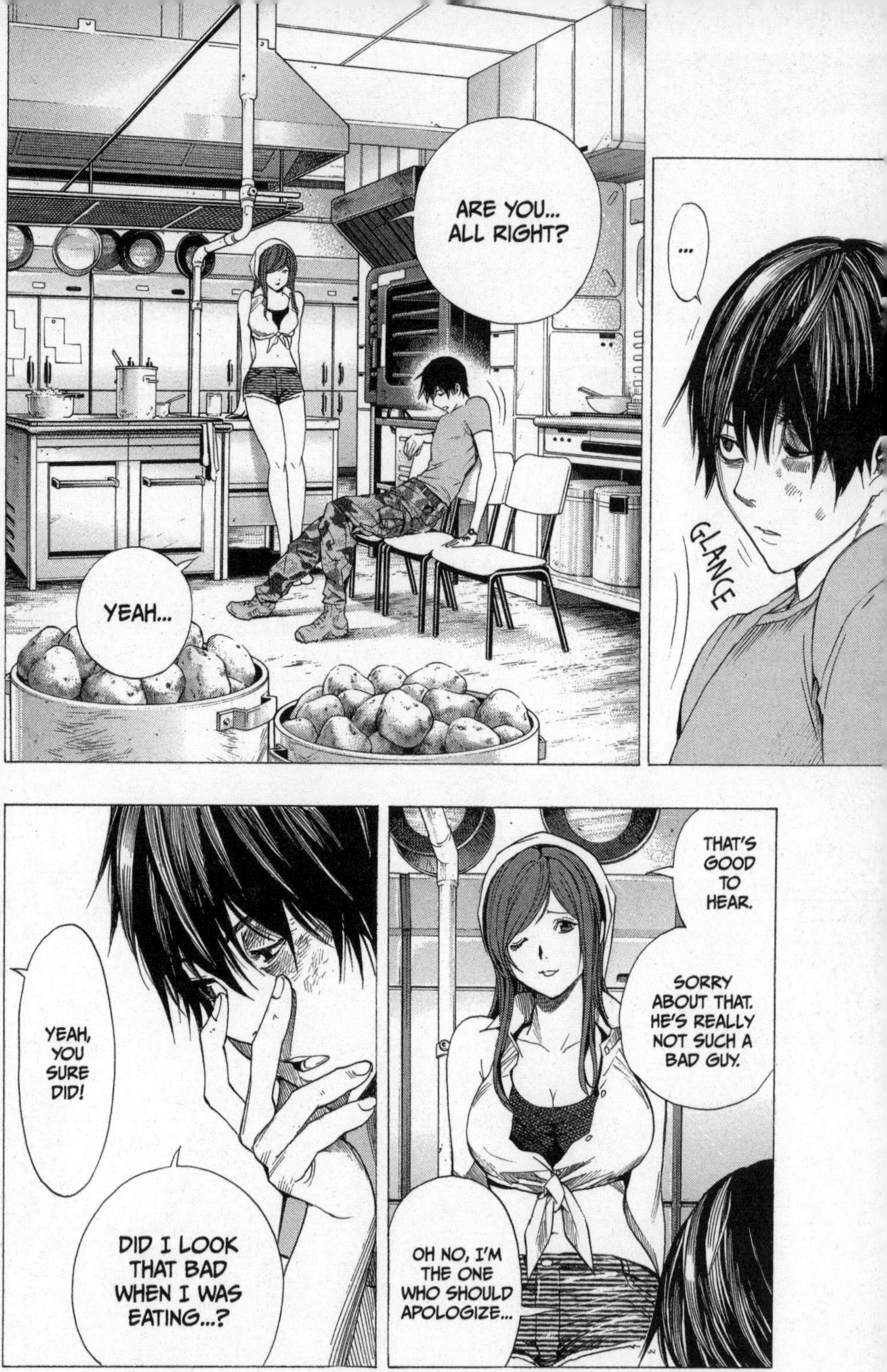
...
GLANCE
ARE YOU... ALL RIGHT?
YEAH...
THAT'S GOOD TO HEAR.
SORRY ABOUT THAT. HE'S REALLY NOT SUCH A BAD GUY.
OH NO, I'M THE ONE WHO SHOULD APOLOGIZE...
DID I LOOK THAT BAD WHEN I WAS EATING...?
YEAH, YOU SURE DID!

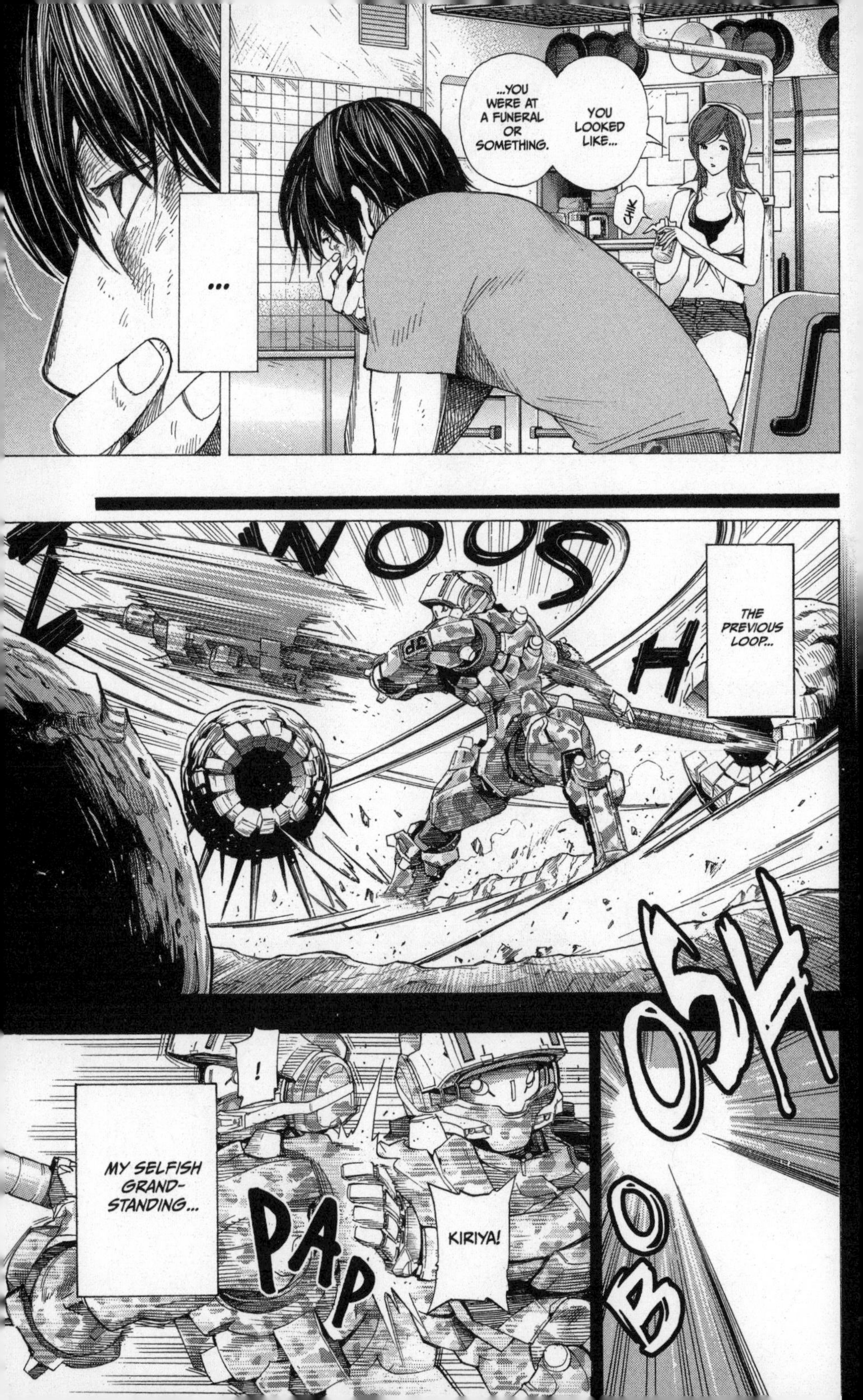
YOU LOOKED LIKE...
...YOU WERE AT A FUNERAL OR SOMETHING.
CHIK
...
WOOSH
THE PREVIOUS LOOP...
BOOSH
!
MY SELFISH GRAND-STANDING...
KIRIYA!
PAP

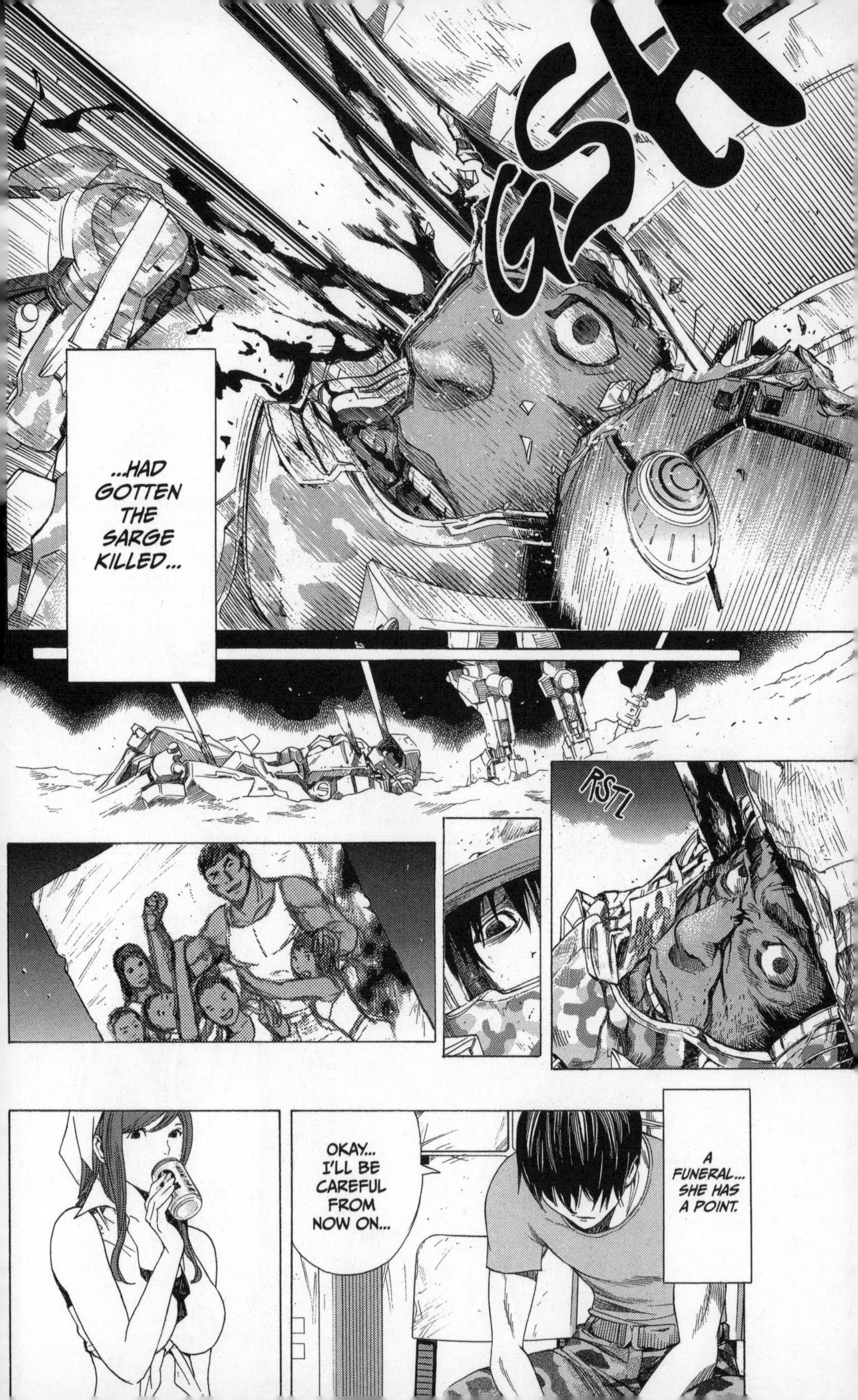
GASH
...HAD GOTTEN THE SARGE KILLED...
RSTL
A FUNERAL... SHE HAS A POINT.
OKAY... I'LL BE CAREFUL FROM NOW ON...

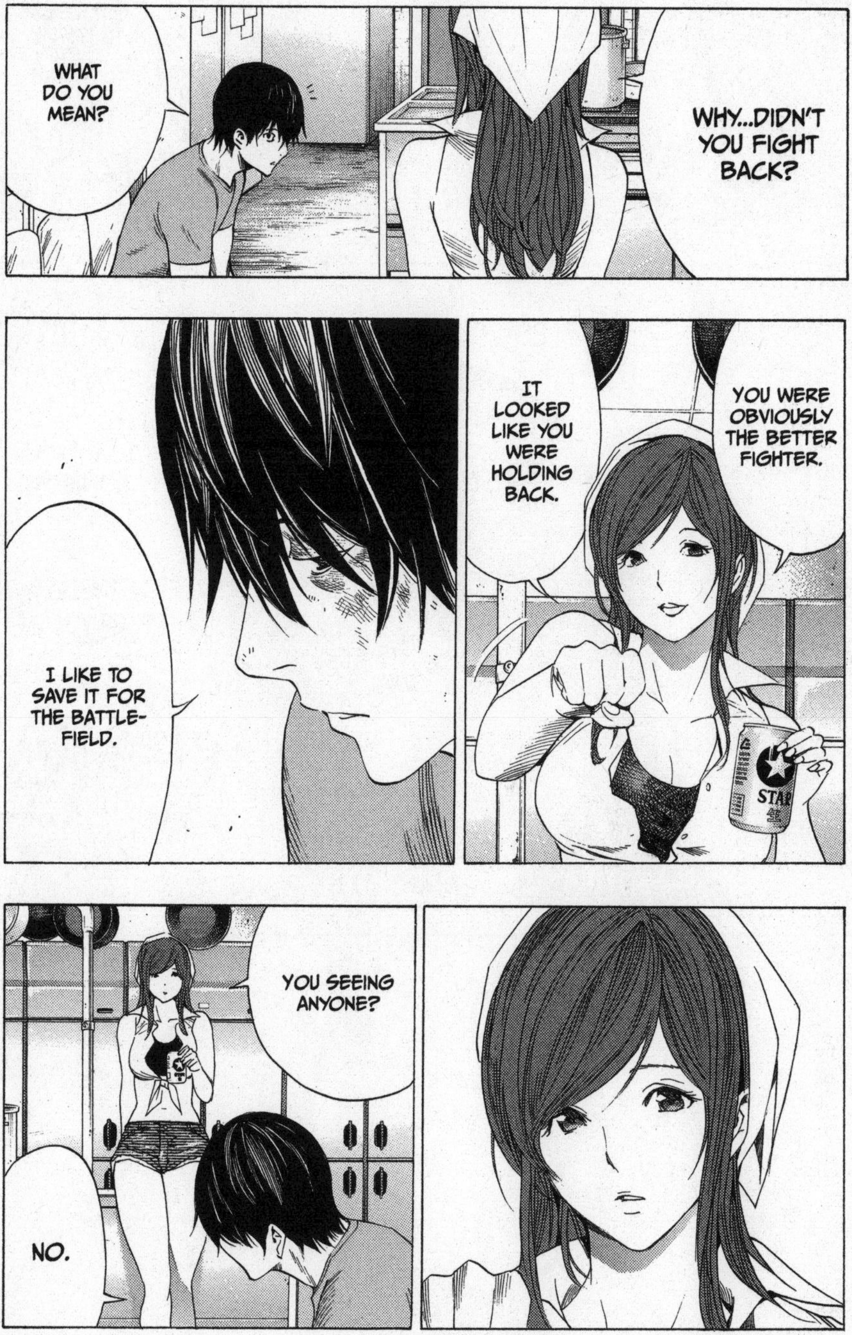
WHY...DIDN'T YOU FIGHT BACK?
WHAT DO YOU MEAN?
YOU WERE OBVIOUSLY THE BETTER FIGHTER.
IT LOOKED LIKE YOU WERE HOLDING BACK.
I LIKE TO SAVE IT FOR THE BATTLE-FIELD.
YOU SEEING ANYONE?
NO.

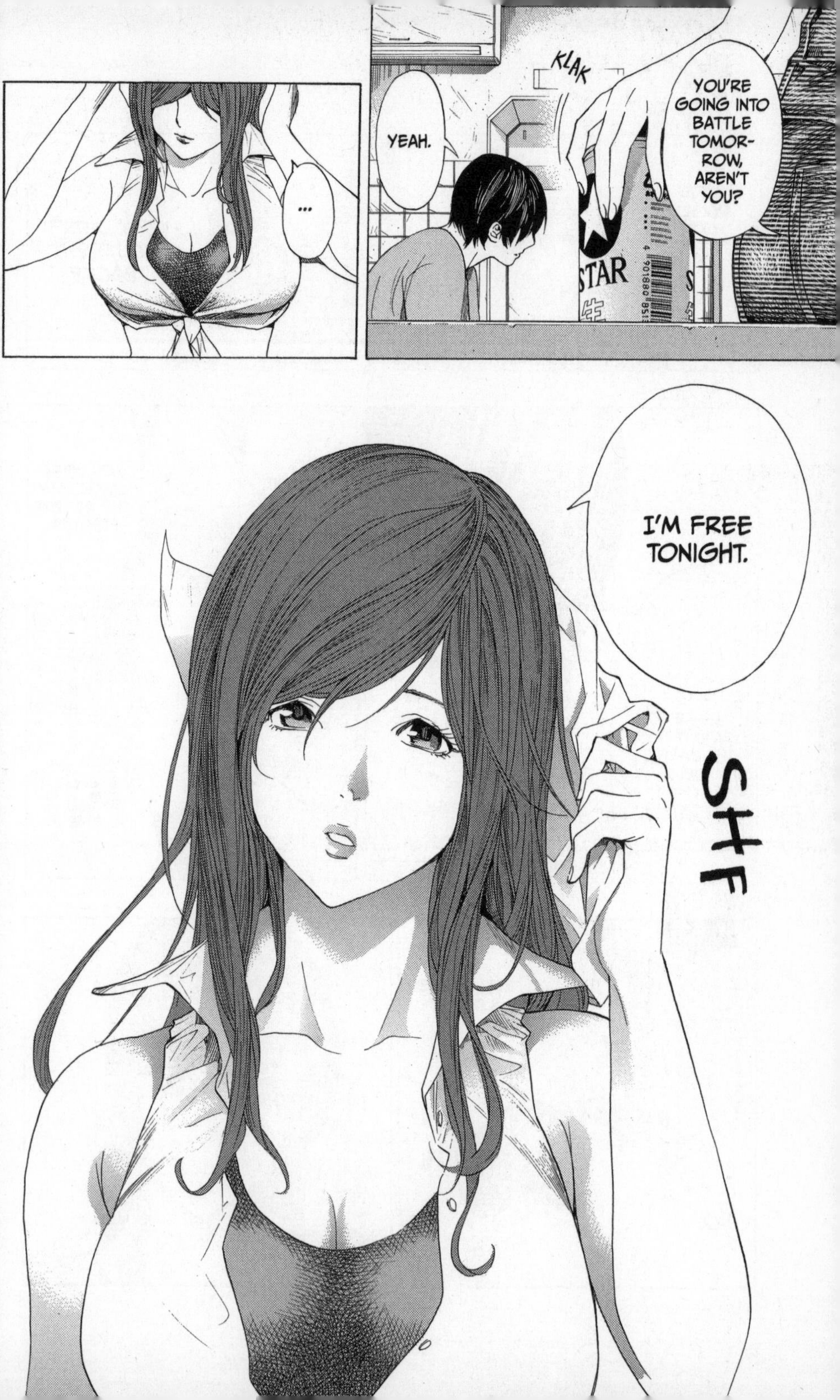
KLAK
YOU'RE GOING INTO BATTLE TOMOR-ROW, AREN'T YOU?
STAR
YEAH.
...
I'M FREE TONIGHT.
SHF

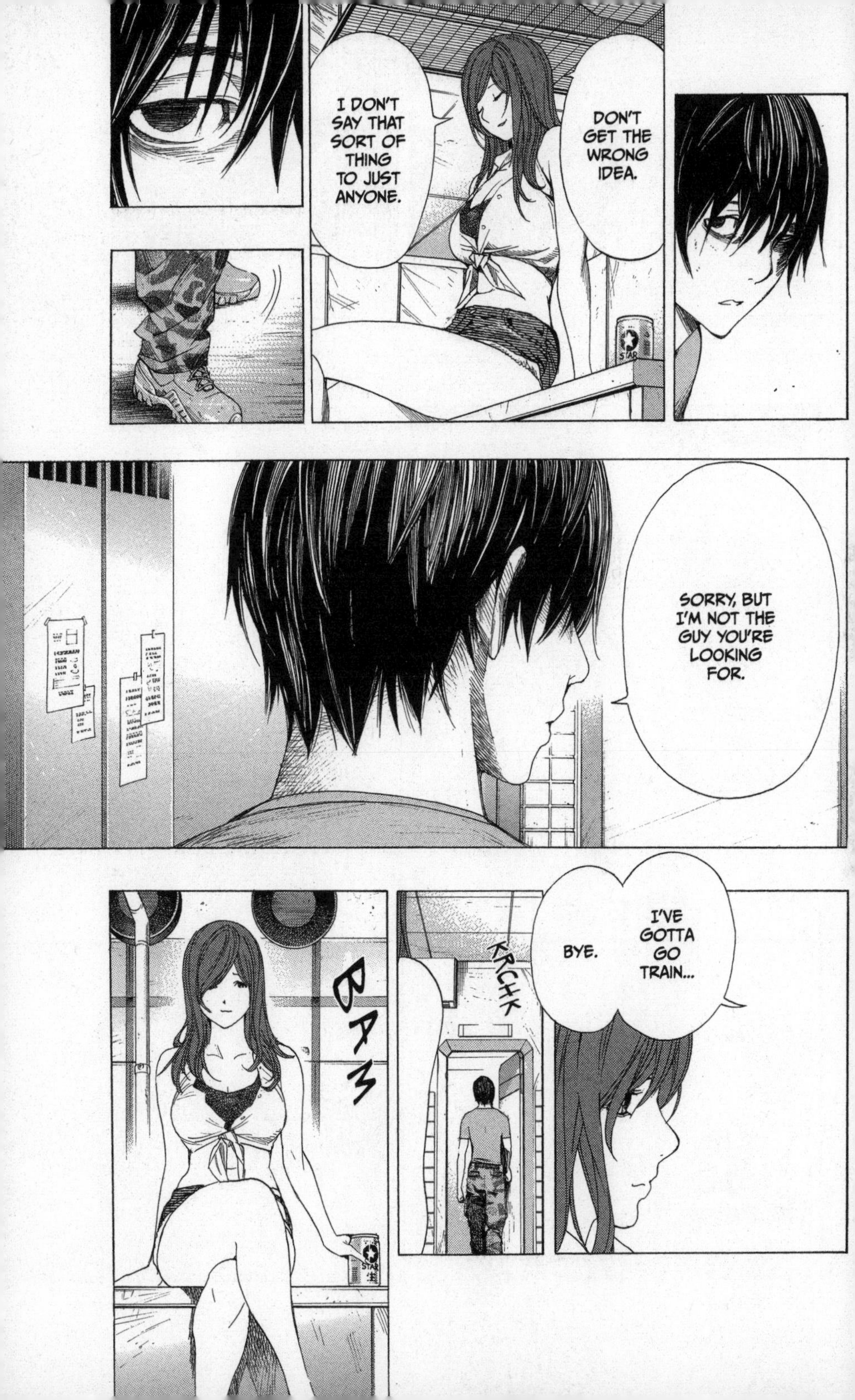
DON'T GET THE WRONG IDEA.
I DON'T SAY THAT SORT OF THING TO JUST ANYONE.
SORRY, BUT I'M NOT THE GUY YOU'RE LOOKING FOR.
I'VE GOTTA GO TRAIN...
BYE.
KRCHK
BAM

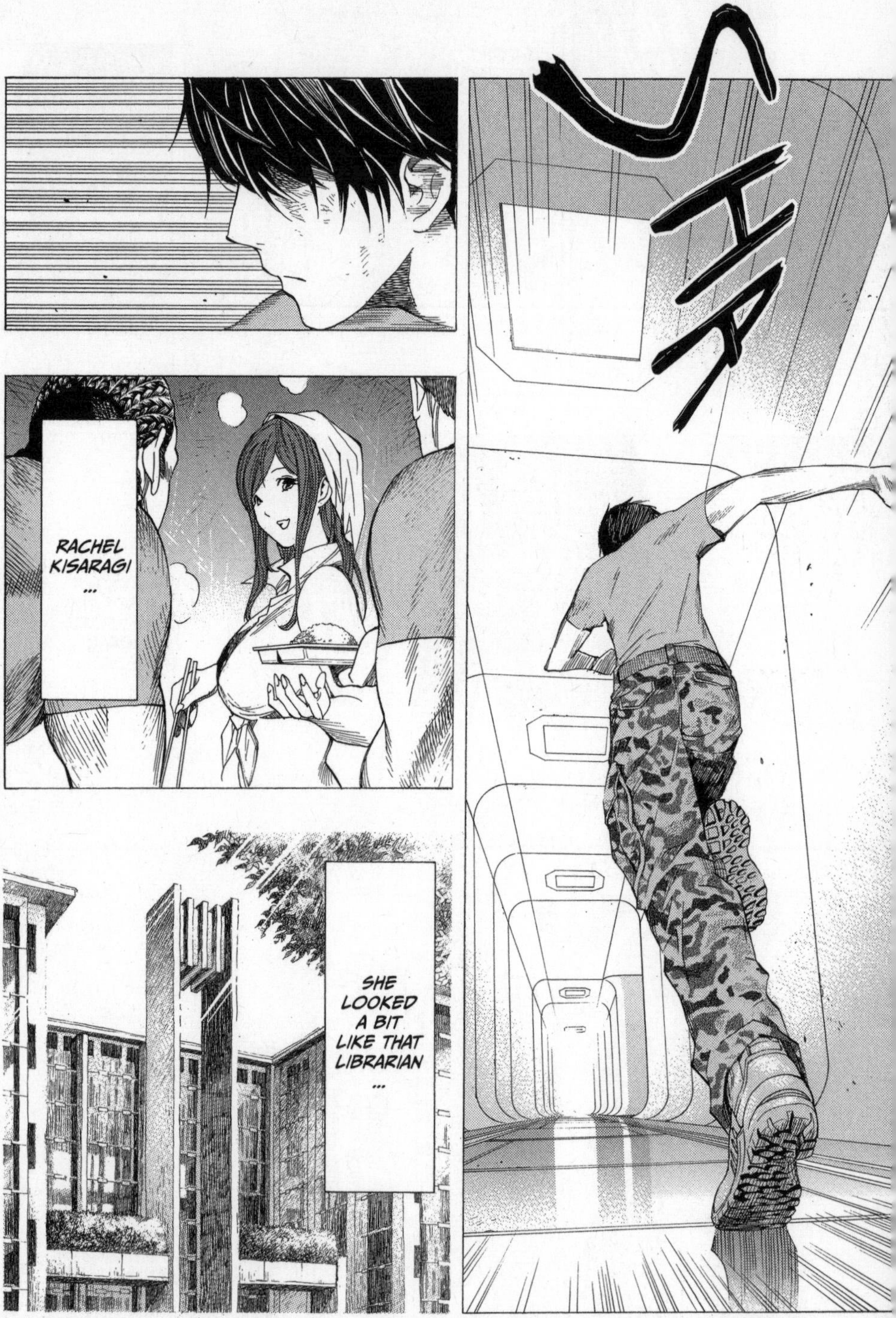
シュァ
RACHEL KISARAGI ...
SHE LOOKED A BIT LIKE THAT LIBRARIAN ...

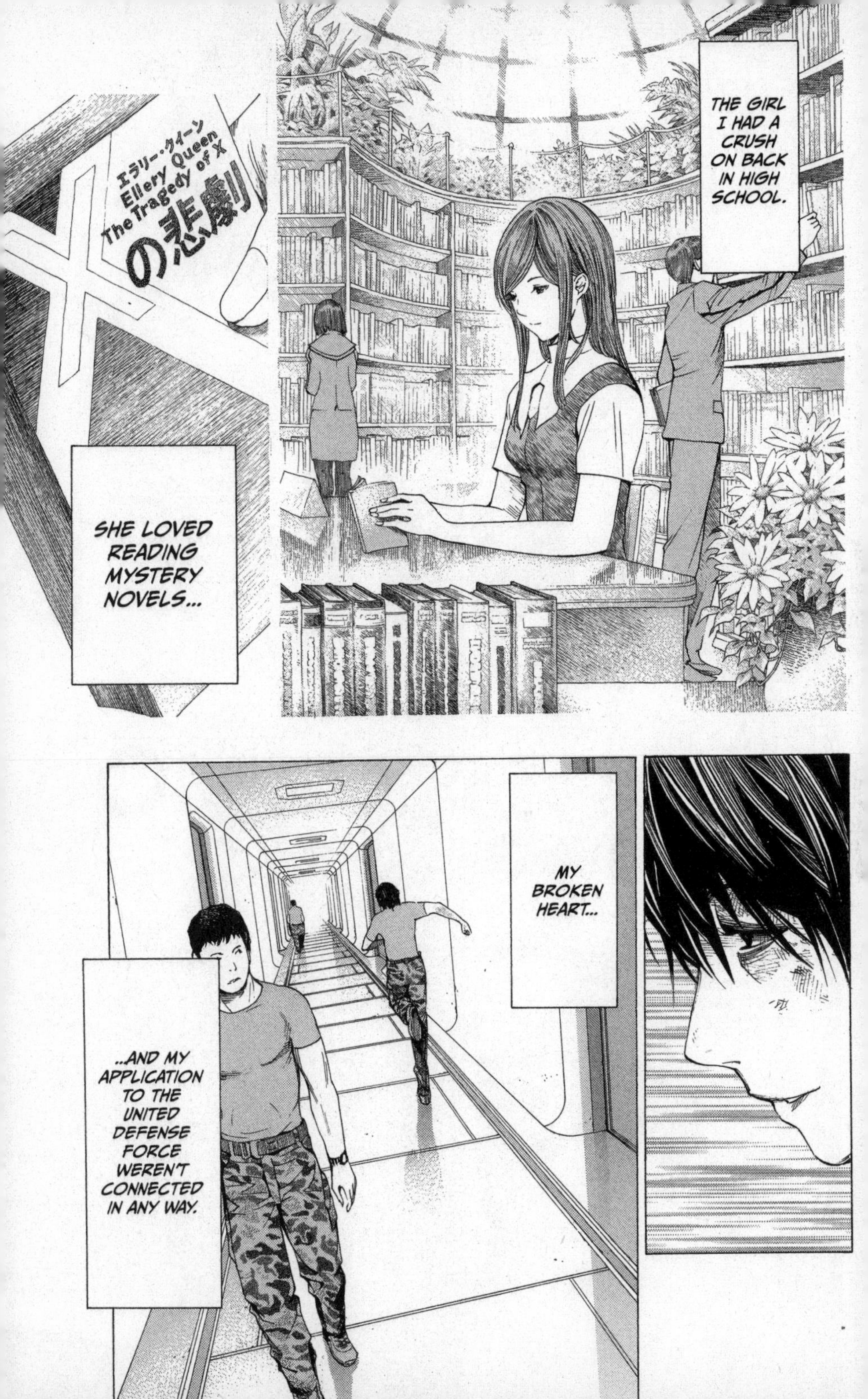
THE GIRL I HAD A CRUSH ON BACK IN HIGH SCHOOL.
エラリー・クイーン
Ellery Queen
The Tragedy of X
Xの悲劇
SHE LOVED READING MYSTERY NOVELS...
MY BROKEN HEART...
...AND MY APPLICATION TO THE UNITED DEFENSE FORCE WEREN'T CONNECTED IN ANY WAY.

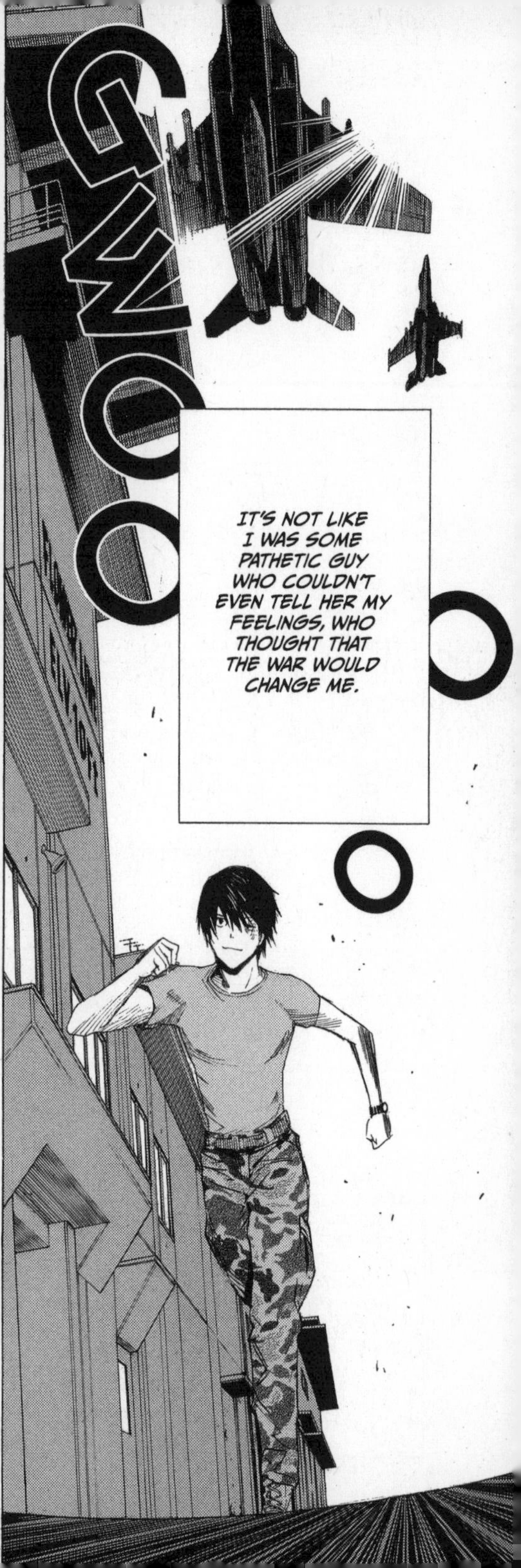
GWOOOO
IT'S NOT LIKE I WAS SOME PATHETIC GUY WHO COULDN'T EVEN TELL HER MY FEELINGS, WHO THOUGHT THAT THE WAR WOULD CHANGE ME.

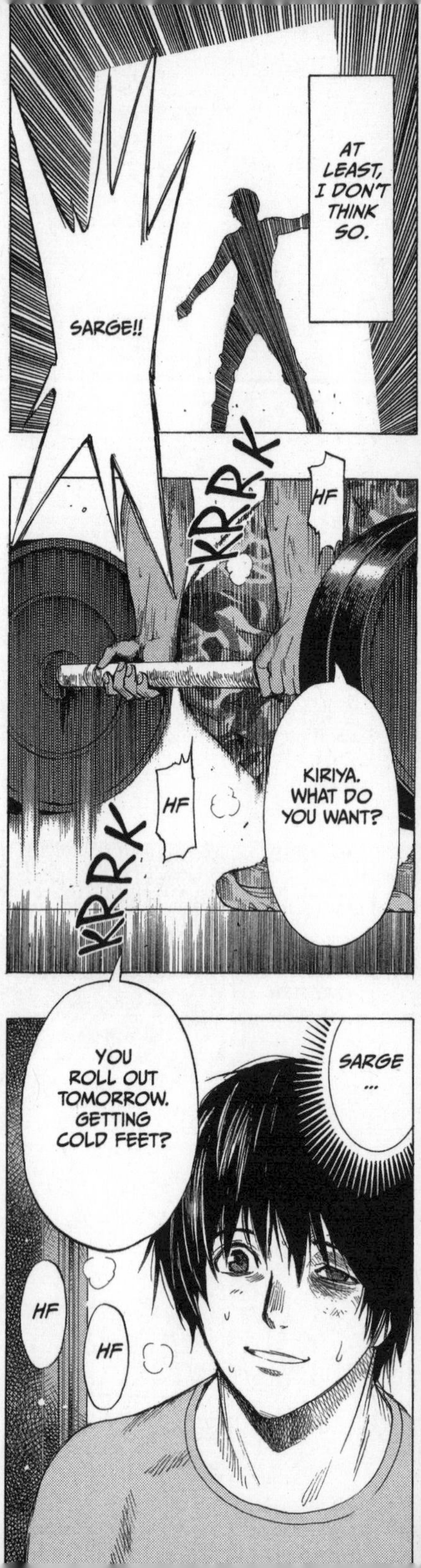
AT LEAST, I DON'T THINK SO.
SARGE!!
HF
KRRK
KIRIYA. WHAT DO YOU WANT?
HF
KRRK
SARGE ...
YOU ROLL OUT TOMORROW. GETTING COLD FEET?
HF
HF

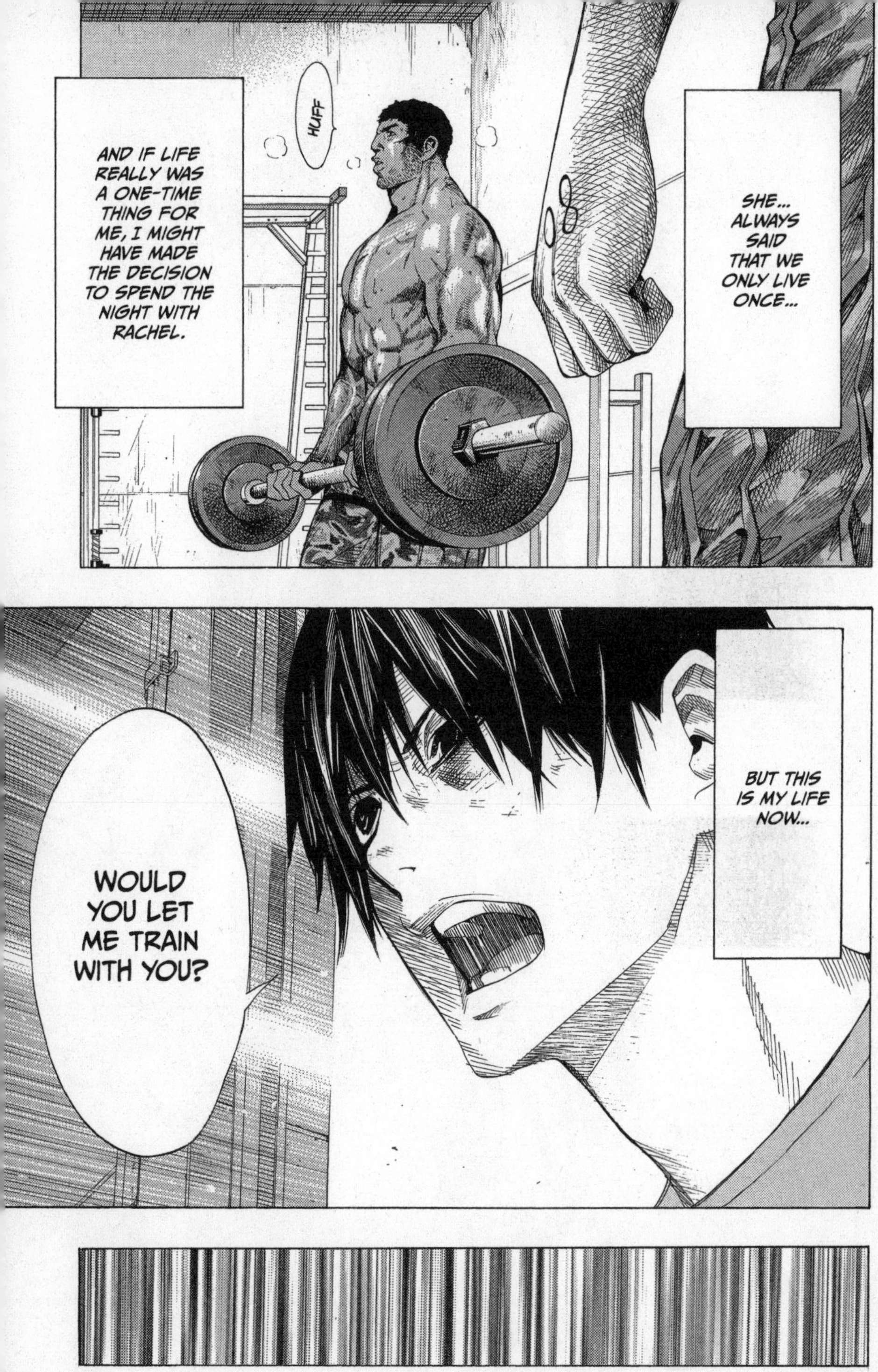
SHE... ALWAYS SAID THAT WE ONLY LIVE ONCE...
HUFF
AND IF LIFE REALLY WAS A ONE-TIME THING FOR ME, I MIGHT HAVE MADE THE DECISION TO SPEND THE NIGHT WITH RACHEL.
BUT THIS IS MY LIFE NOW...
WOULD YOU LET ME TRAIN WITH YOU?

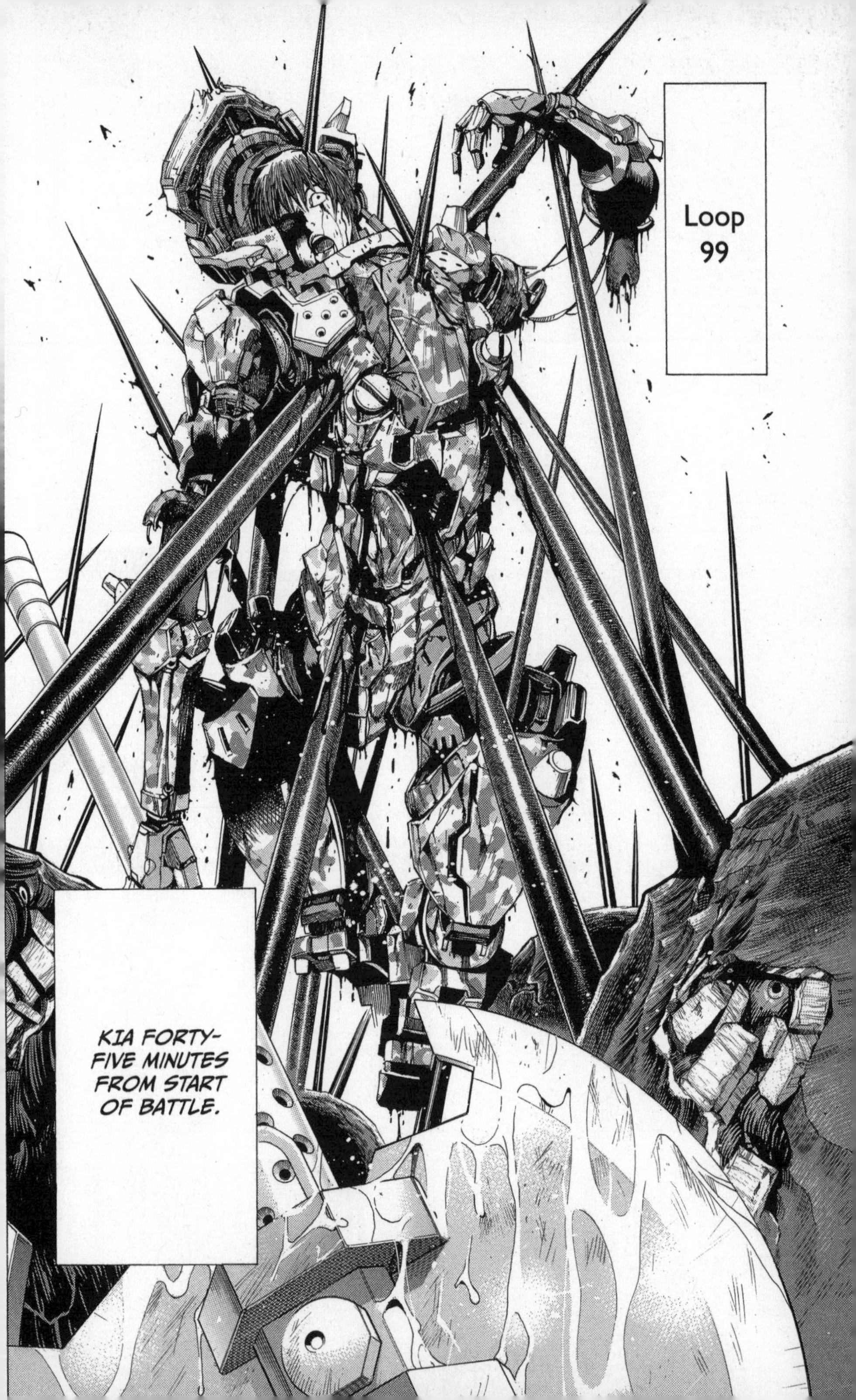
Loop 99
KIA FORTY-FIVE MINUTES FROM START OF BATTLE.

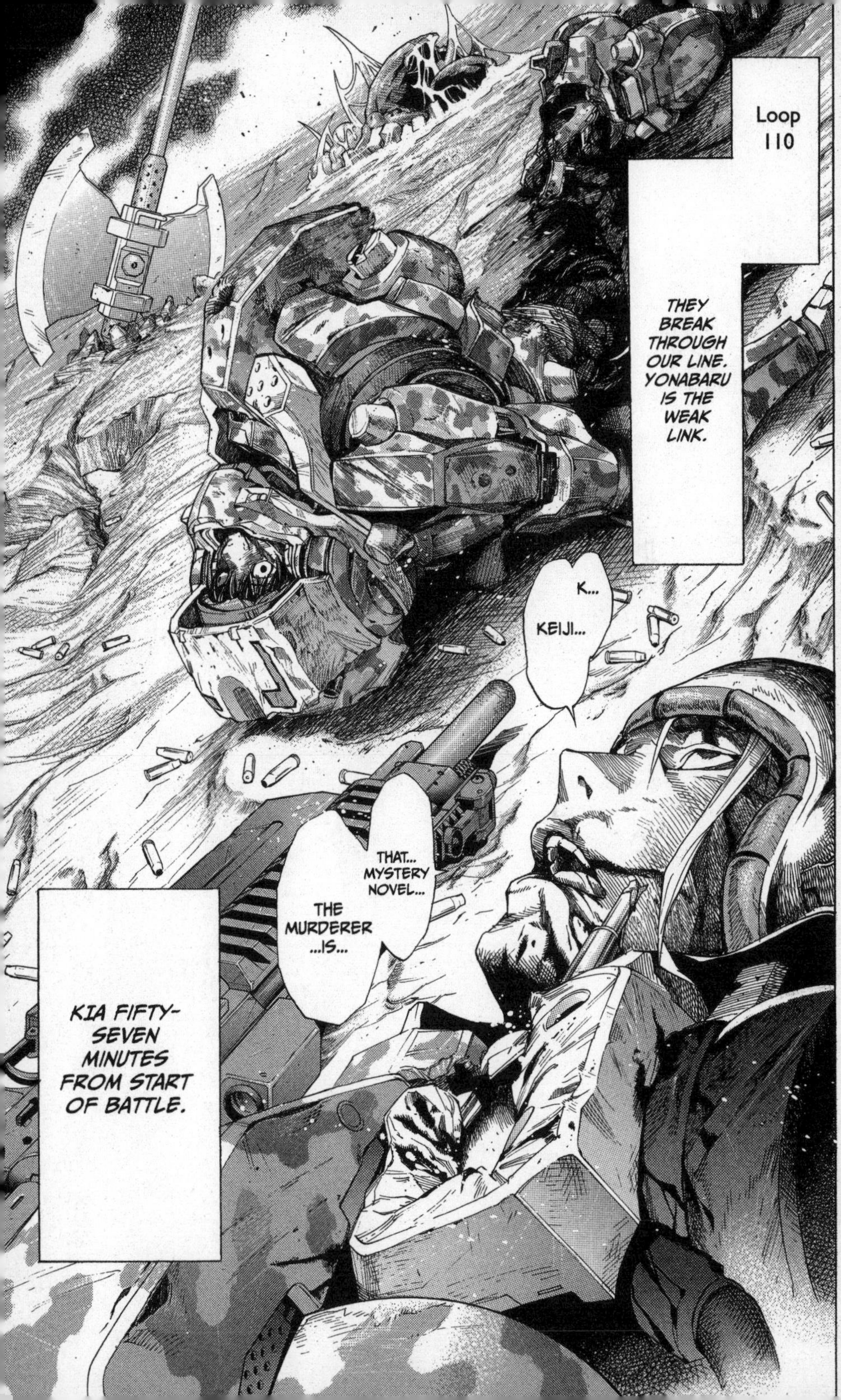
Loop 110
THEY BREAK THROUGH OUR LINE. YONABARU IS THE WEAK LINK.
K...
KEIJI...
THAT... MYSTERY NOVEL...
THE MURDERER ...IS...
KIA FIFTY-SEVEN MINUTES FROM START OF BATTLE.

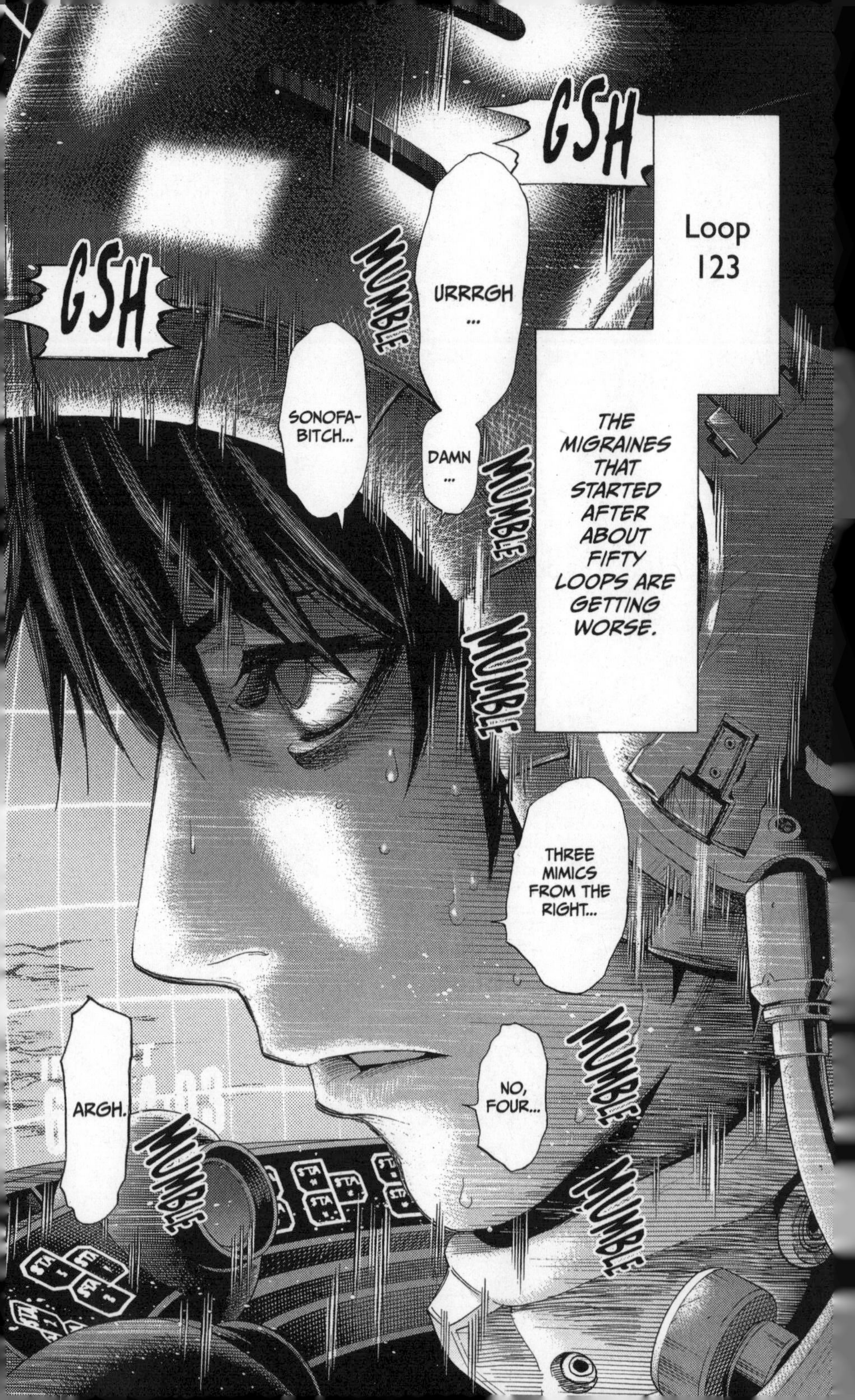
GSH
Loop 123
THE MIGRAINES THAT STARTED AFTER ABOUT FIFTY LOOPS ARE GETTING WORSE.
MUMBLE
URRRGH...
GSH
DAMN...
MUMBLE
SONOFA-BITCH...
MUMBLE
THREE MIMICS FROM THE RIGHT...
MUMBLE
NO, FOUR...
MUMBLE
ARGH.
MUMBLE

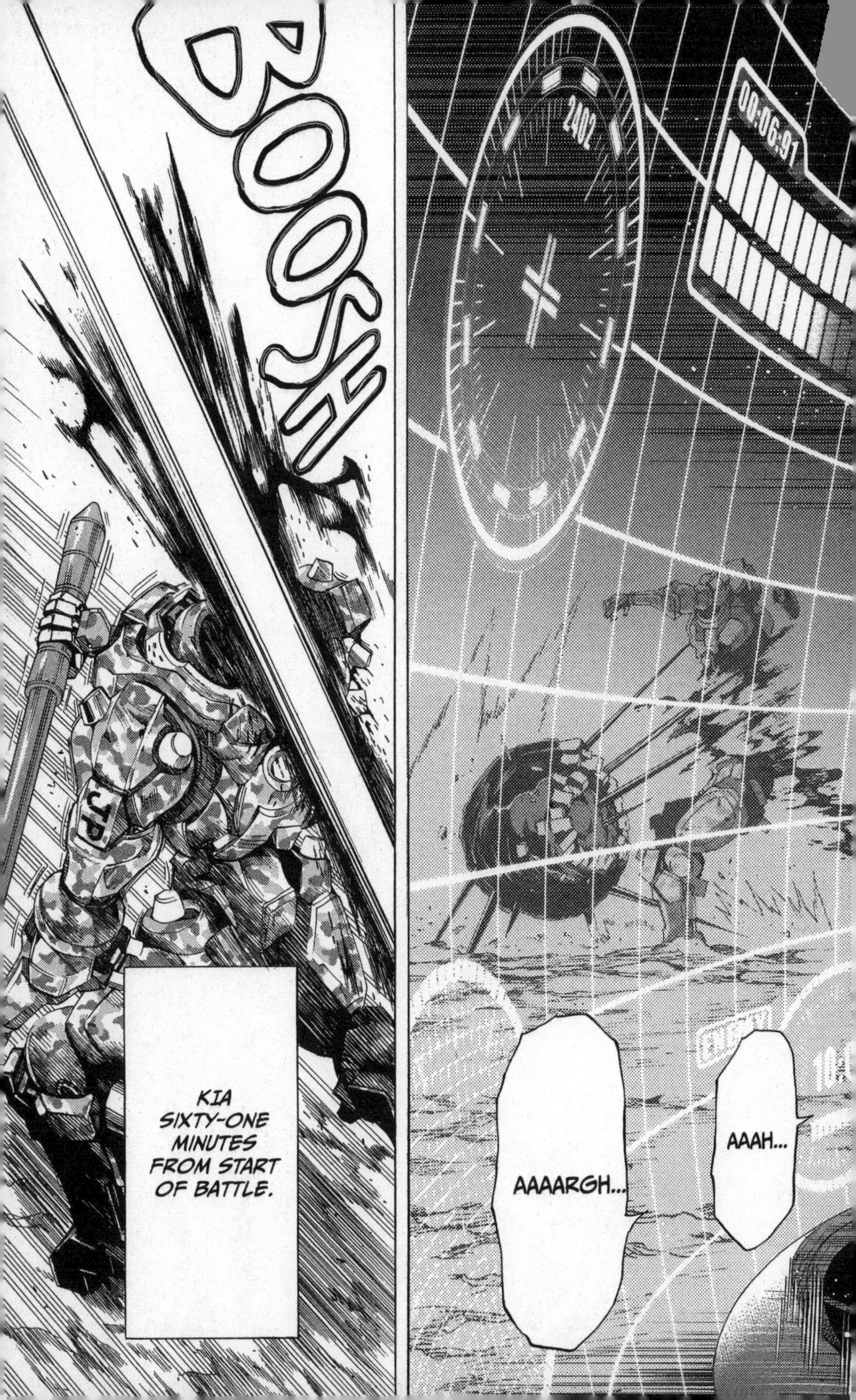
00:06:91
2402
AAAH...
AAAARGH...
BOOSH
KIA SIXTY-ONE MINUTES FROM START OF BATTLE.

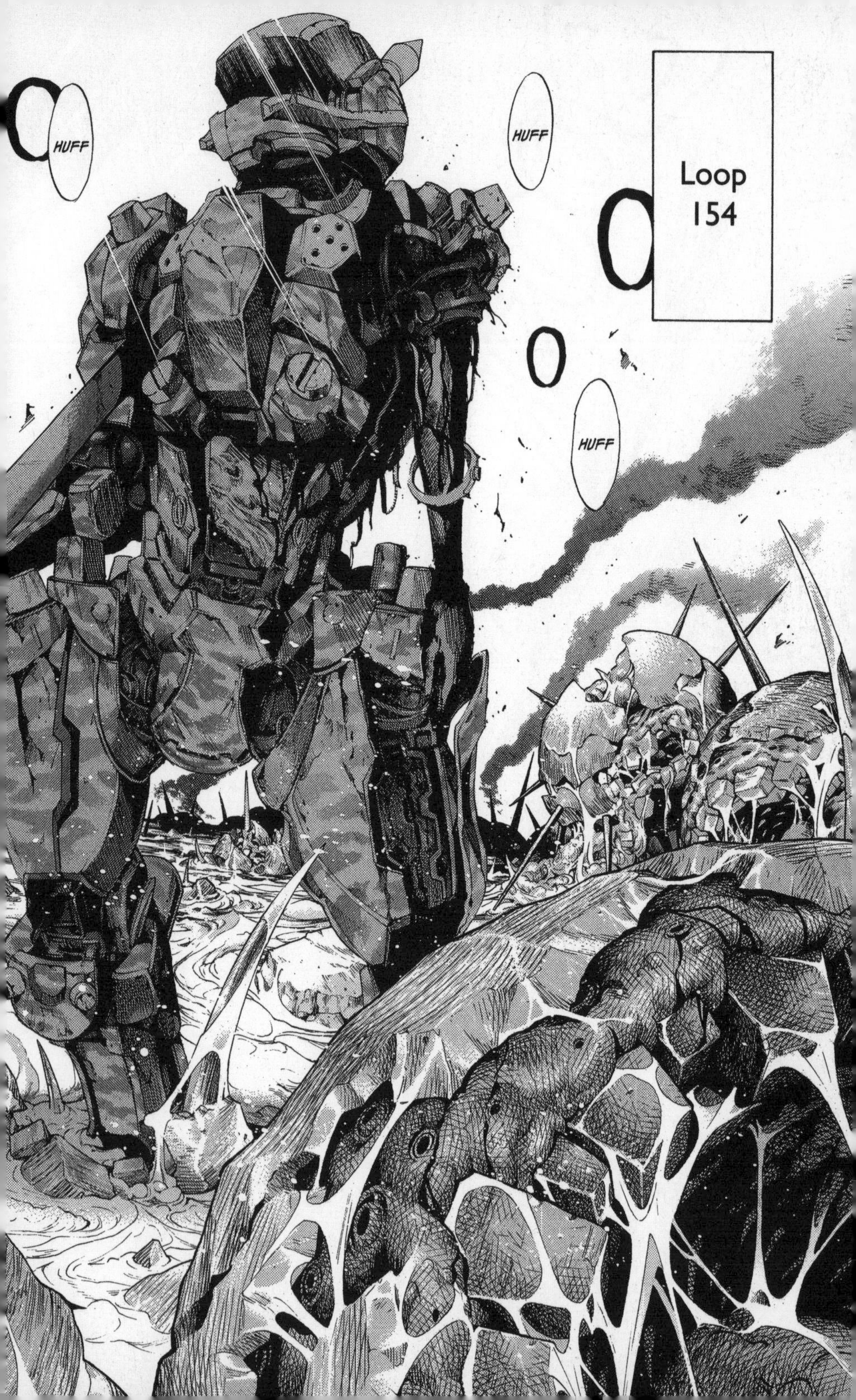
Loop 154
HUFF
HUFF
HUFF

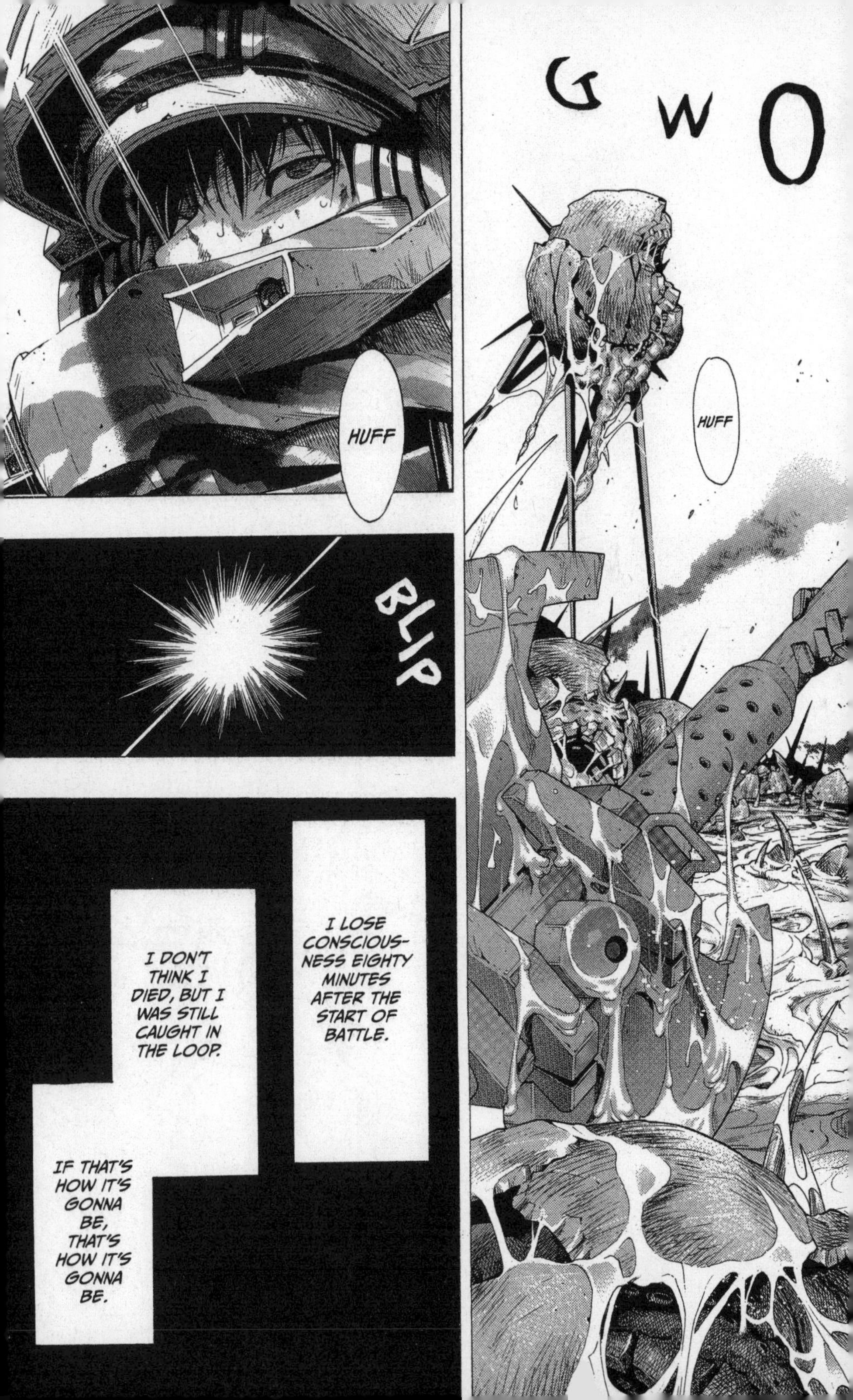
GWO
HUFF
HUFF
BLIP
I LOSE CONSCIOUSNESS EIGHTY MINUTES AFTER THE START OF BATTLE.
I DON'T THINK I DIED, BUT I WAS STILL CAUGHT IN THE LOOP.
IF THAT'S HOW IT'S GONNA BE, THAT'S HOW IT'S GONNA BE.

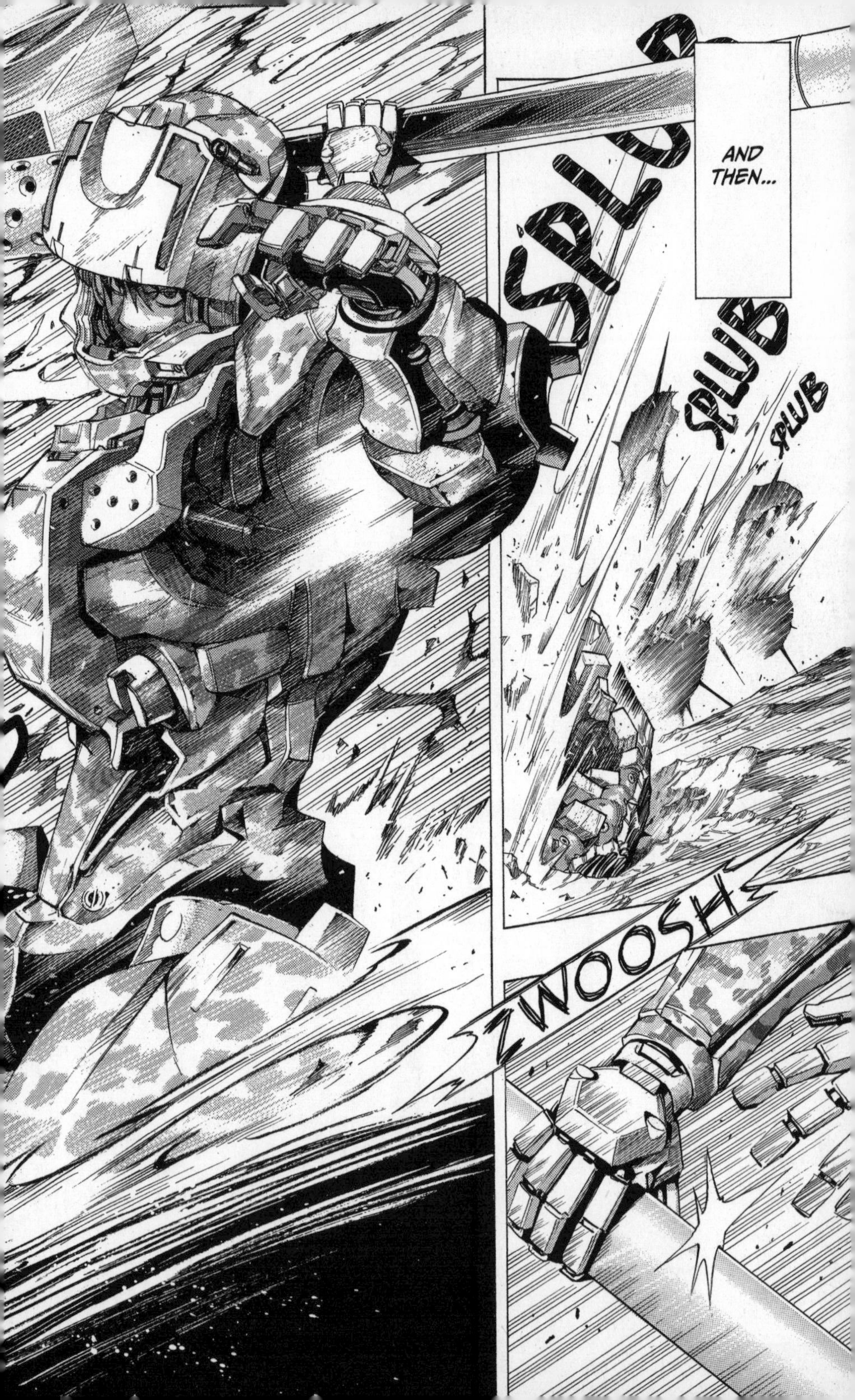
AND THEN...
SPLUB
SPLUB
SPLUB
ZWOOSH

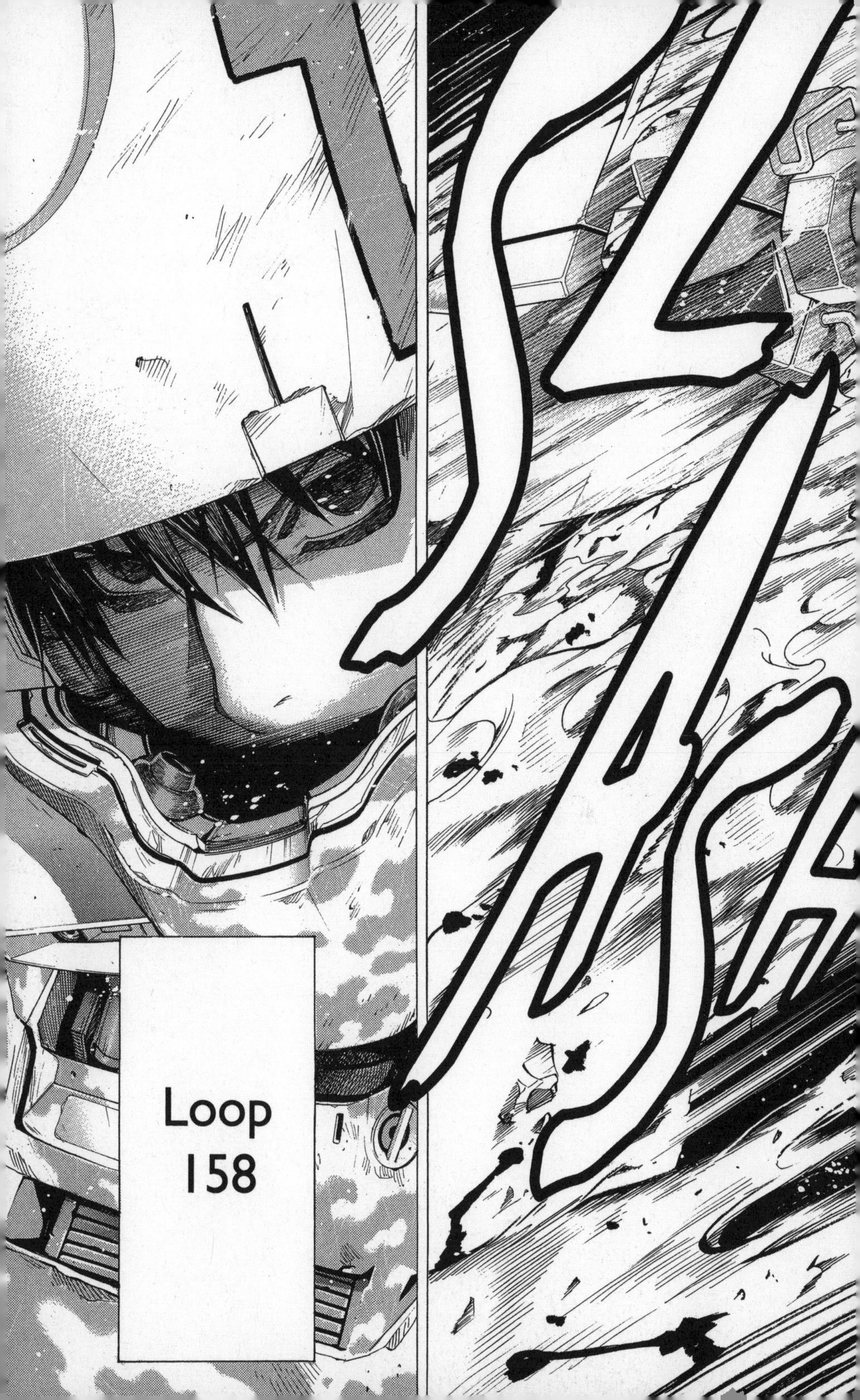
Loop
158

"Our lives should be
written in stone.
Paper is too temporary—
too easy to rewrite."

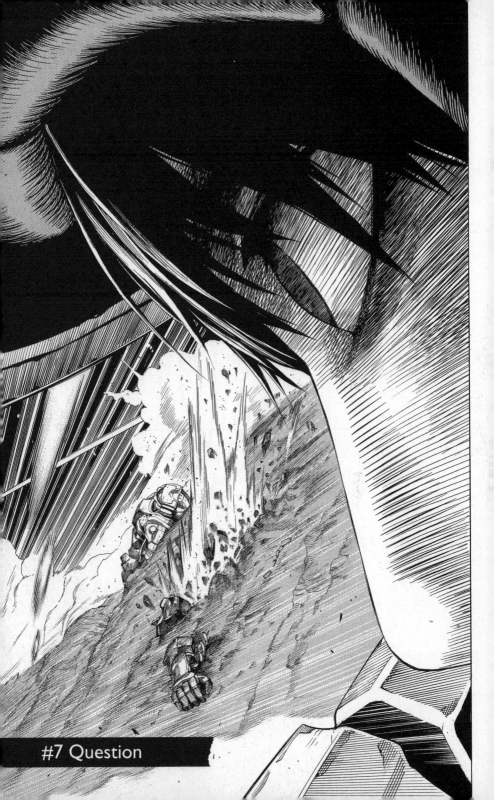

#7 Question

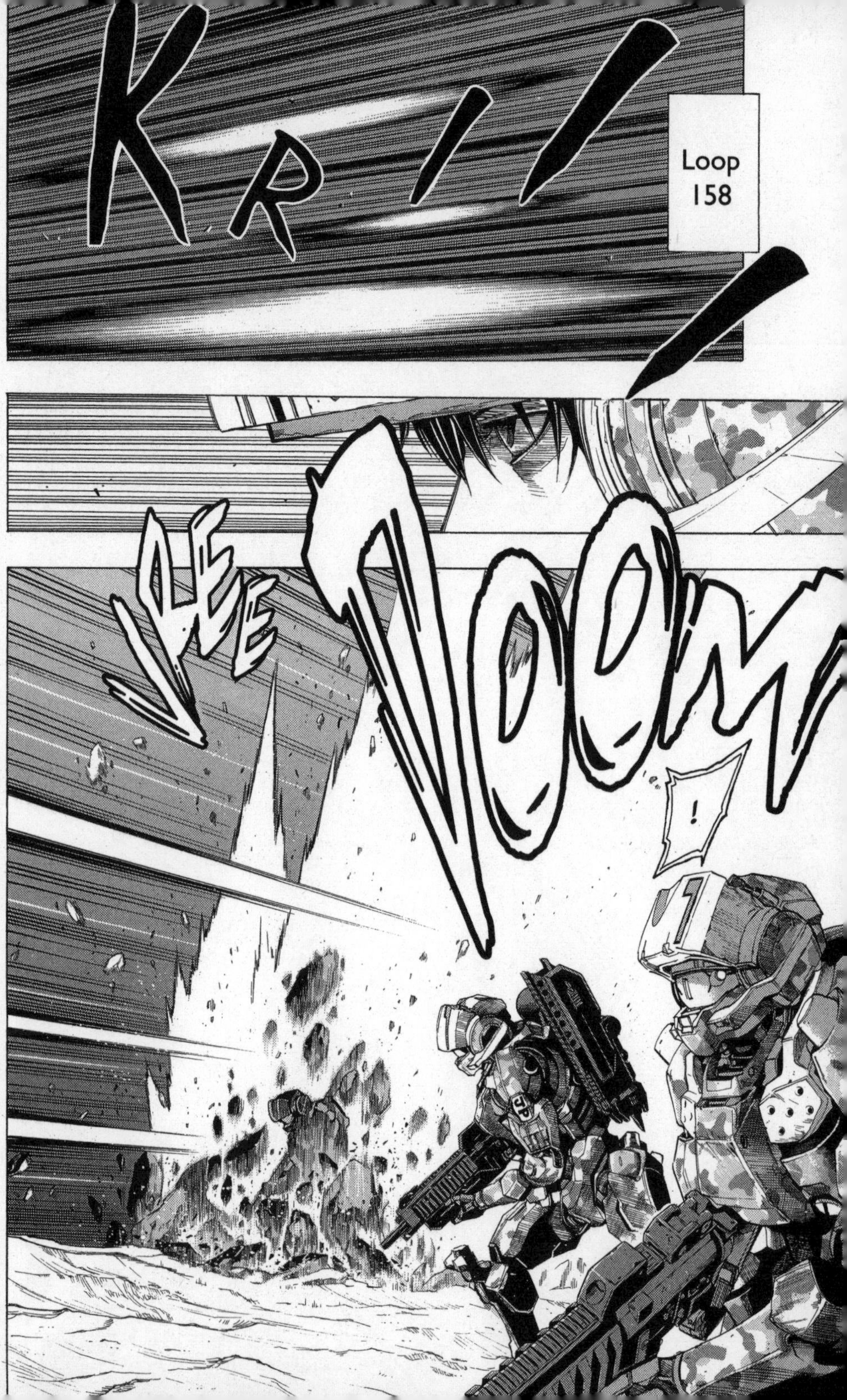
Loop 158
KRIII
VEE
VOOM
!

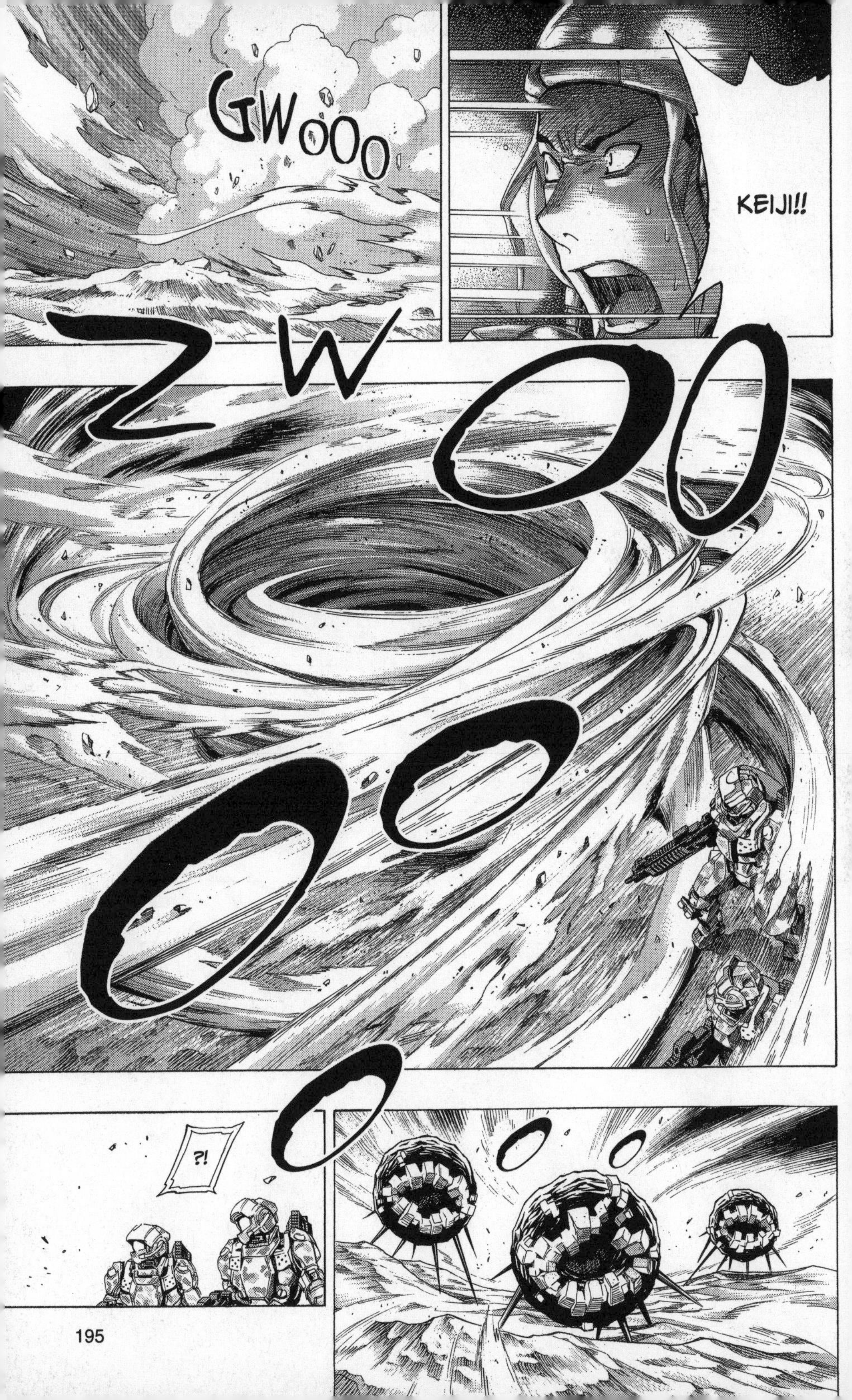
KEIJI!!
GWOOO
ZWOOOOOO
?!

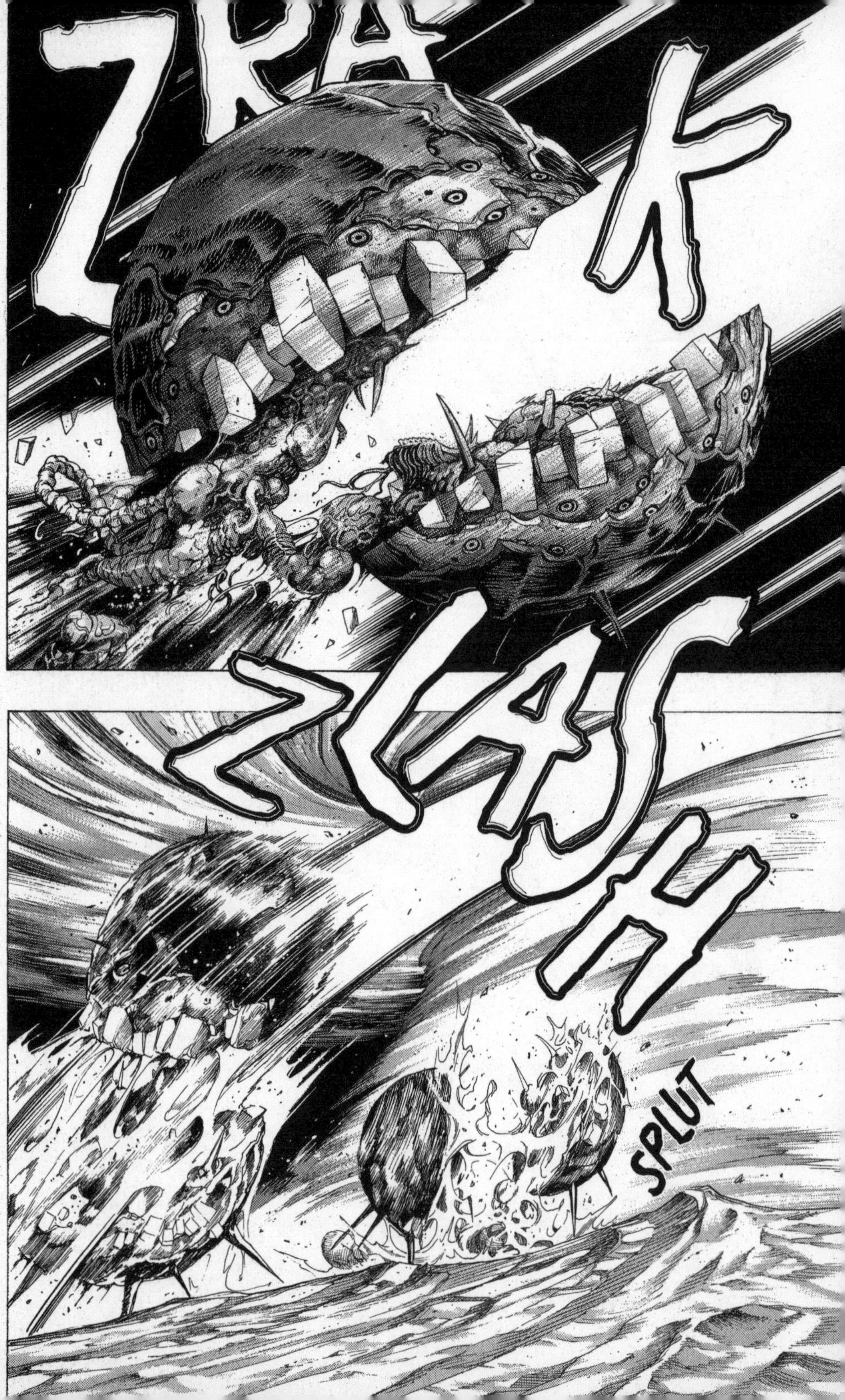
ZRAK
ZLASH
SPLUT

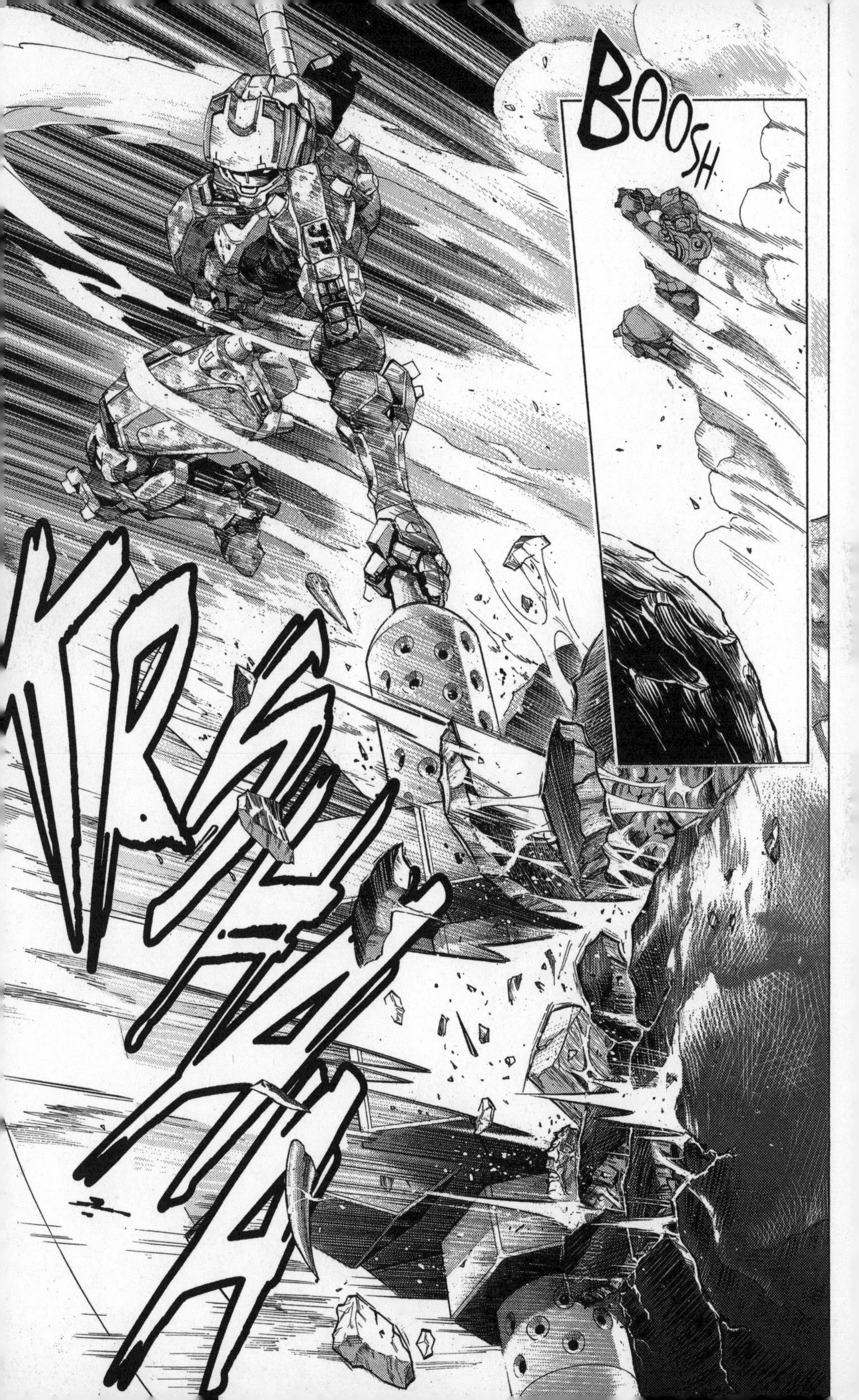
BOOSH

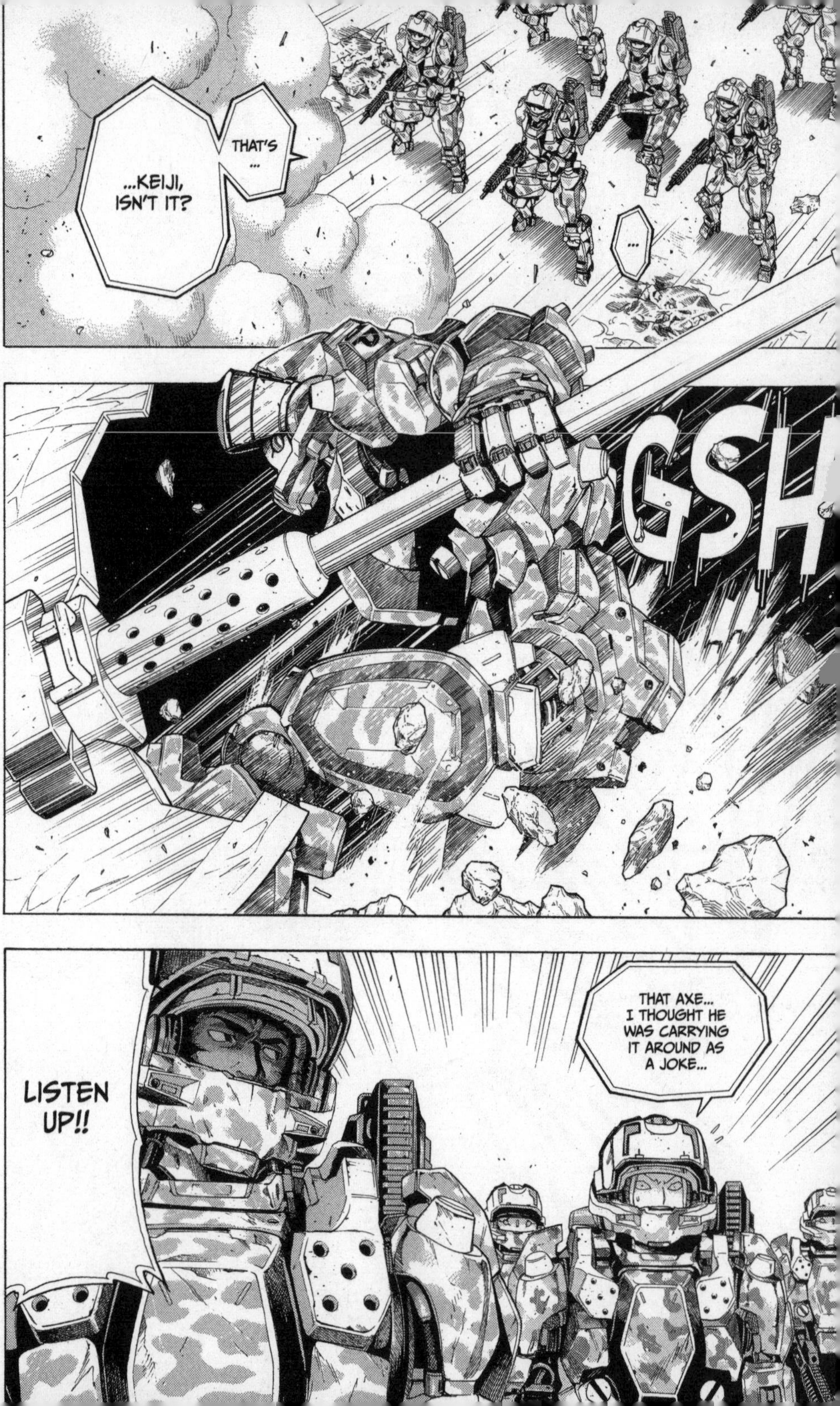
...
THAT'S ...
...KEIJI, ISN'T IT?
GSH
THAT AXE... I THOUGHT HE WAS CARRYING IT AROUND AS A JOKE...
LISTEN UP!!

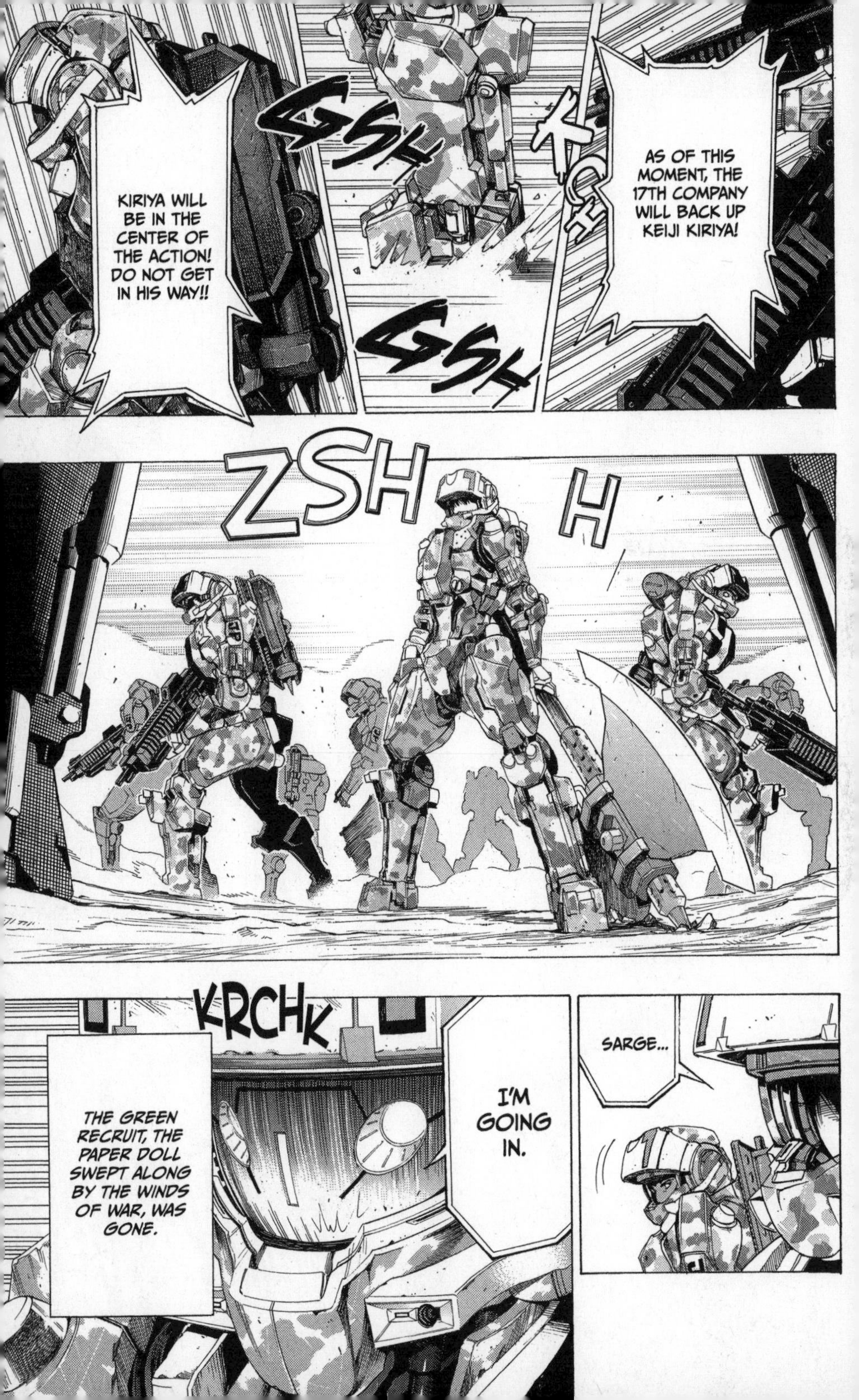
AS OF THIS MOMENT, THE 17TH COMPANY WILL BACK UP KEIJI KIRIYA!
KCH
GSH
GSH
KIRIYA WILL BE IN THE CENTER OF THE ACTION! DO NOT GET IN HIS WAY!!
ZSHH
SARGE...
I'M GOING IN.
KRCHK
THE GREEN RECRUIT, THE PAPER DOLL SWEPT ALONG BY THE WINDS OF WAR, WAS GONE.

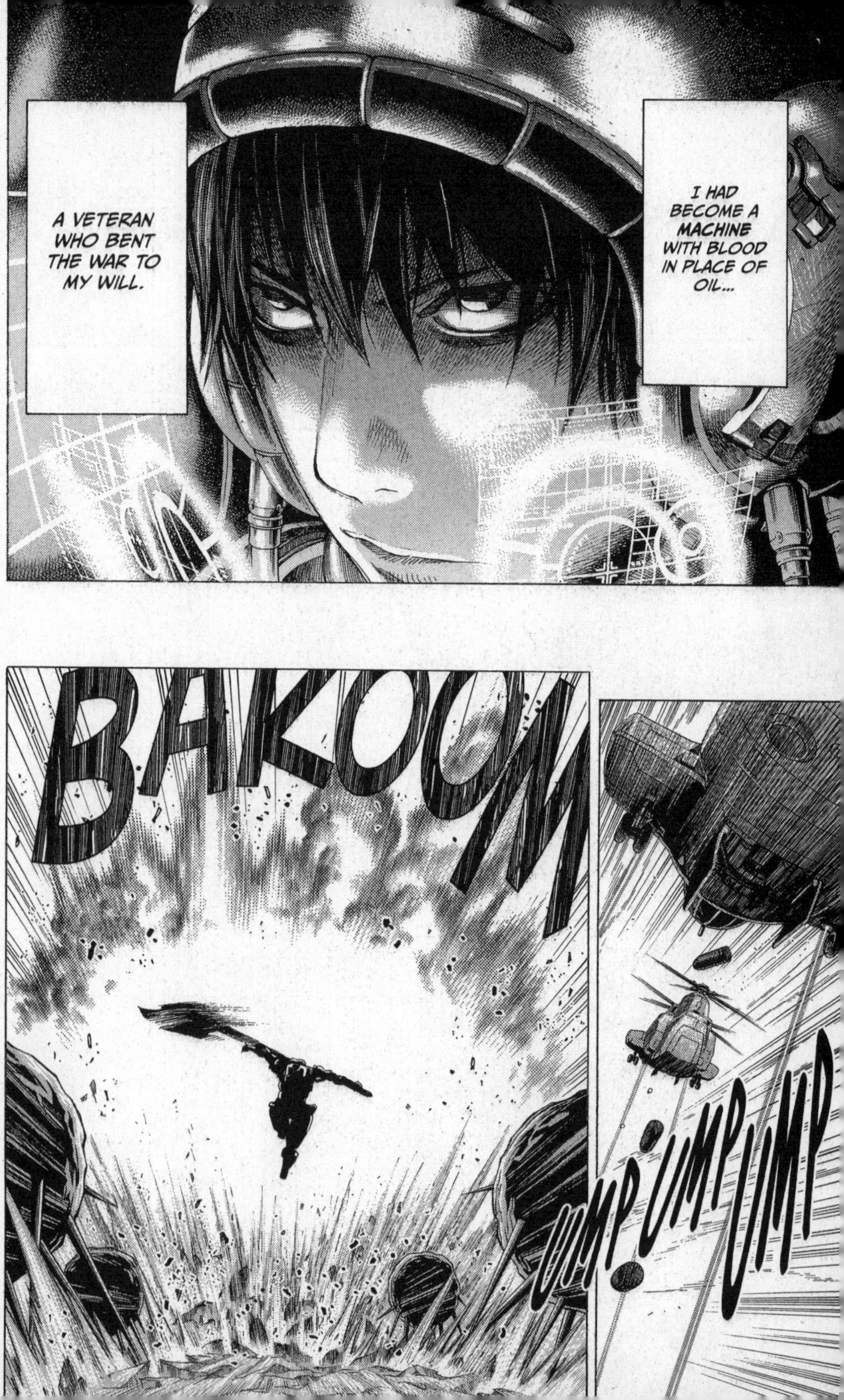
I HAD BECOME A MACHINE WITH BLOOD IN PLACE OF OIL...
A VETERAN WHO BENT THE WAR TO MY WILL.
UMP UMP UMP
BAKOOM

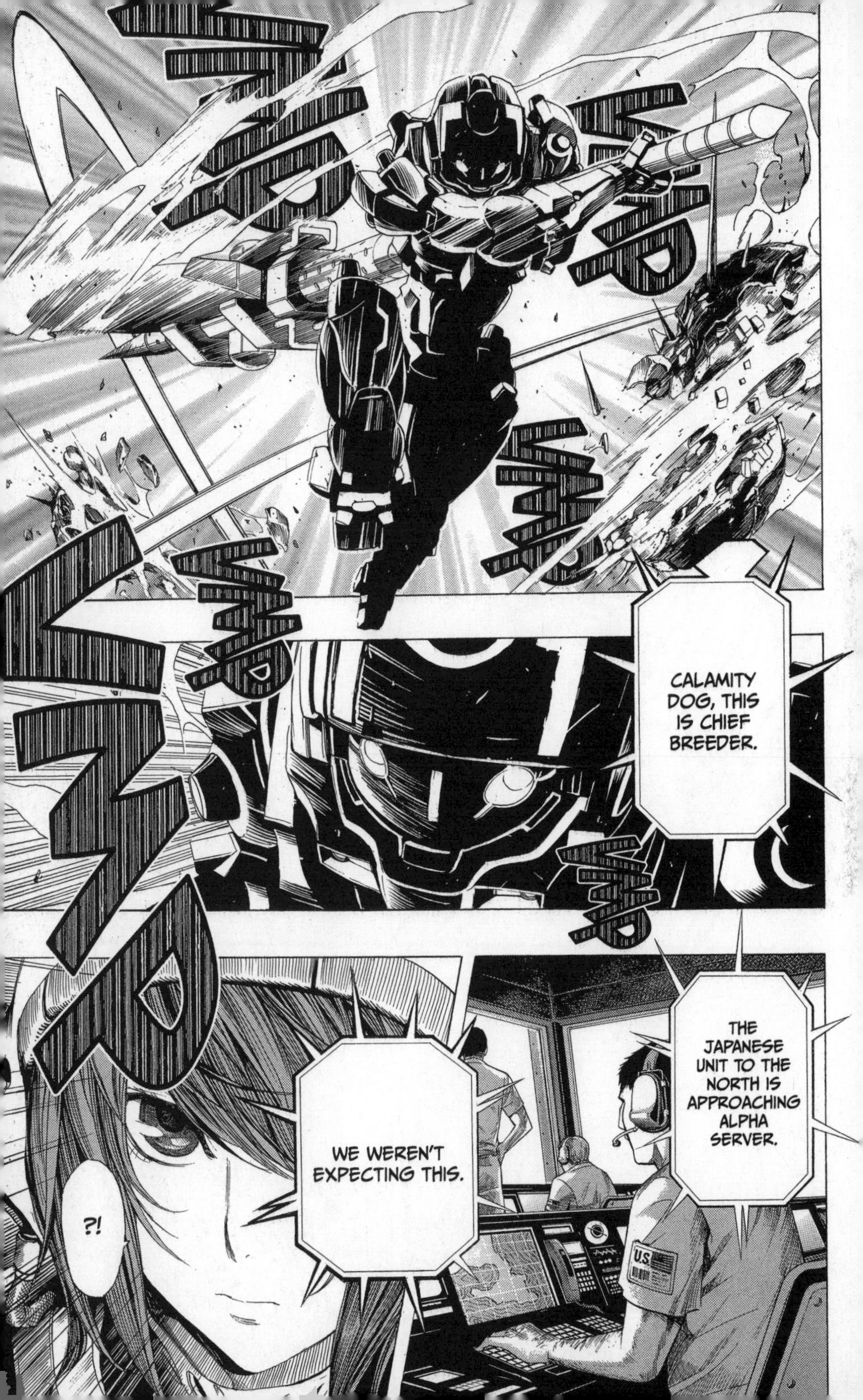
VWMP
VWMP
CALAMITY DOG, THIS IS CHIEF BREEDER.
VWMP
THE JAPANESE UNIT TO THE NORTH IS APPROACHING ALPHA SERVER.
WE WEREN'T EXPECTING THIS.
?!

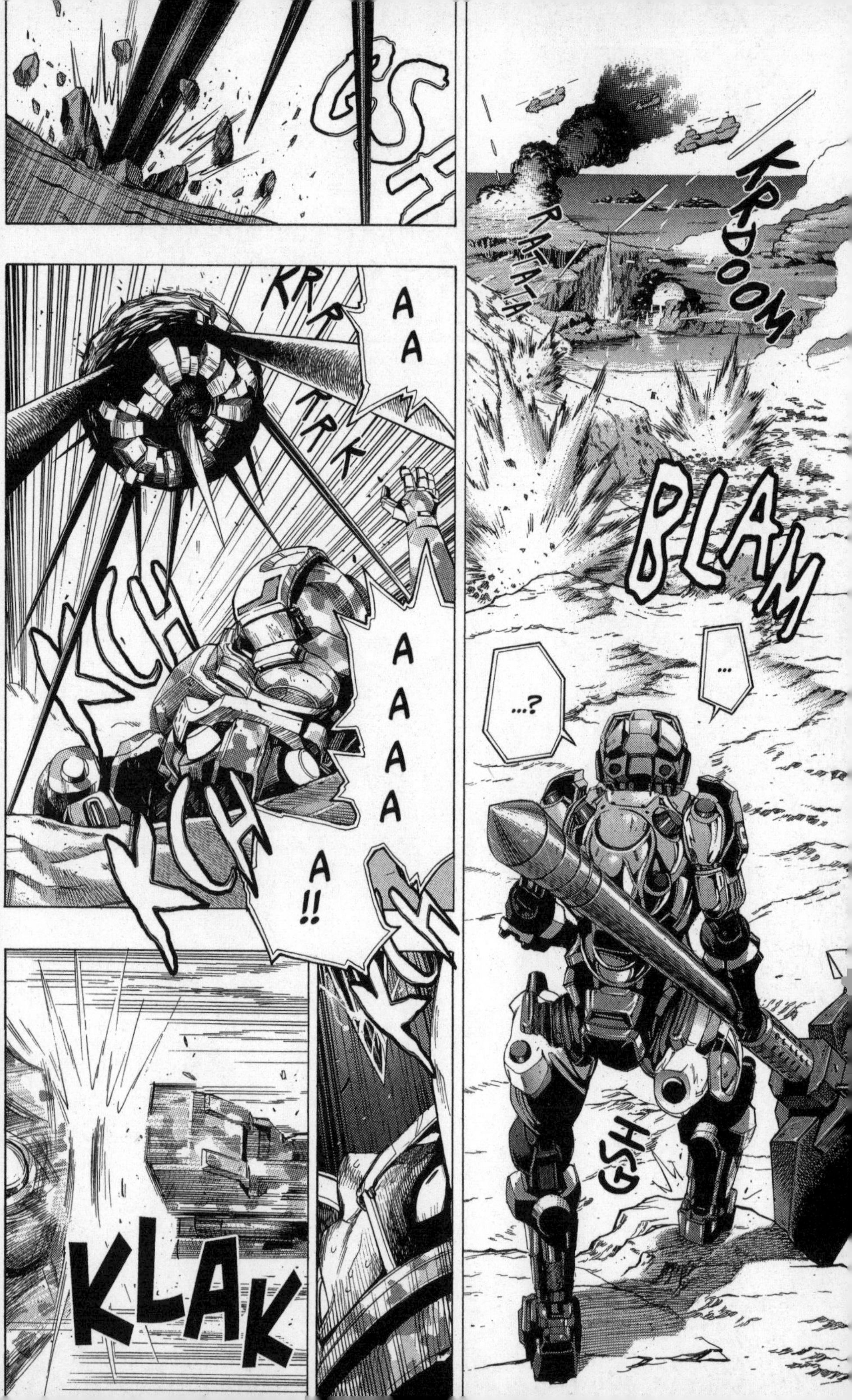
KRDOOM
RATATATA
BLAM
...
...?
GSH
GSH
KRR TRK
AAAAAAAAA!!
KCHK
KLAK

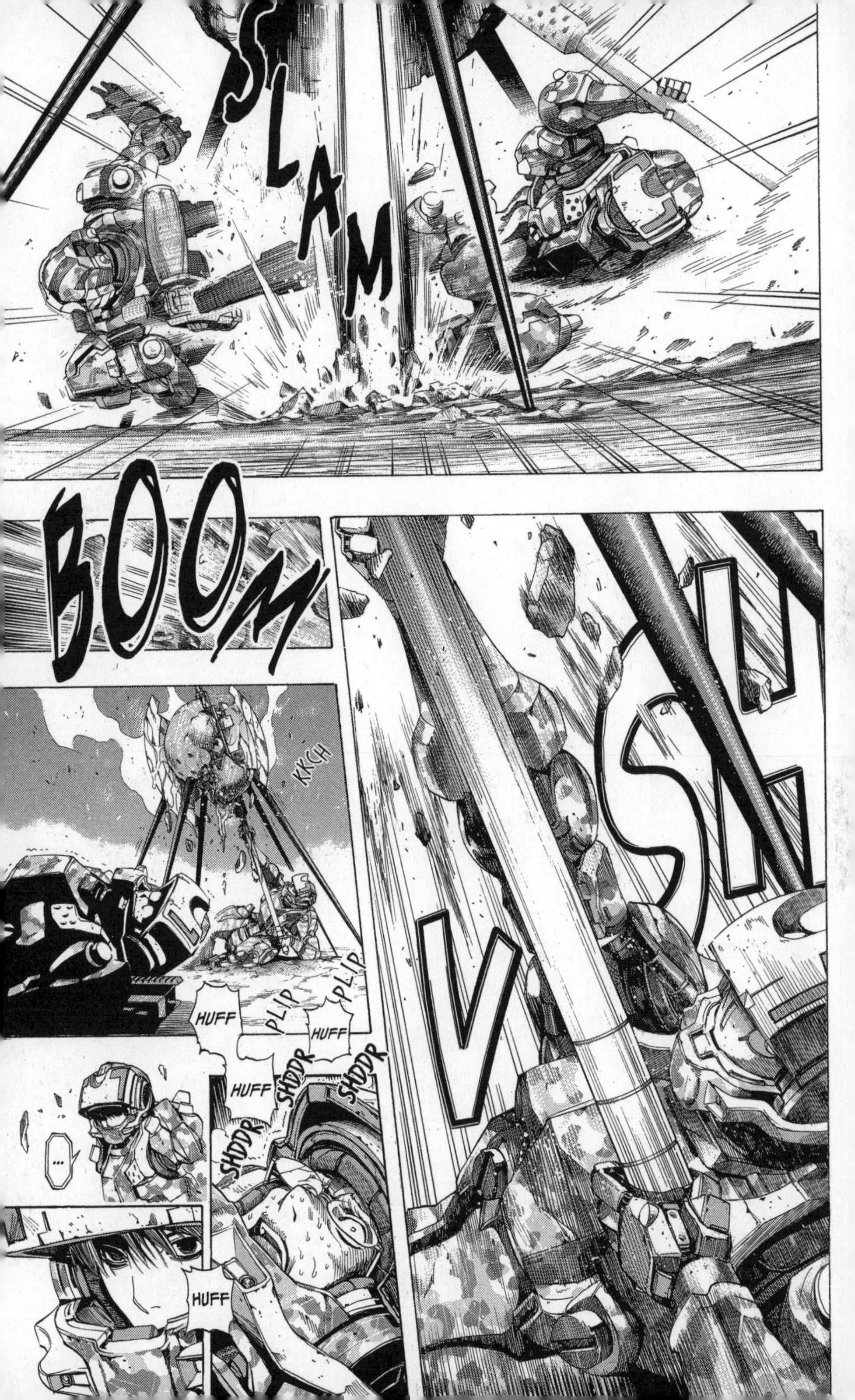
SLAM
BOOM
KKCH
PLIP
PLIP
HUFF
HUFF
HUFF
SHDDR
SHDDR
SHDDR
...
HUFF

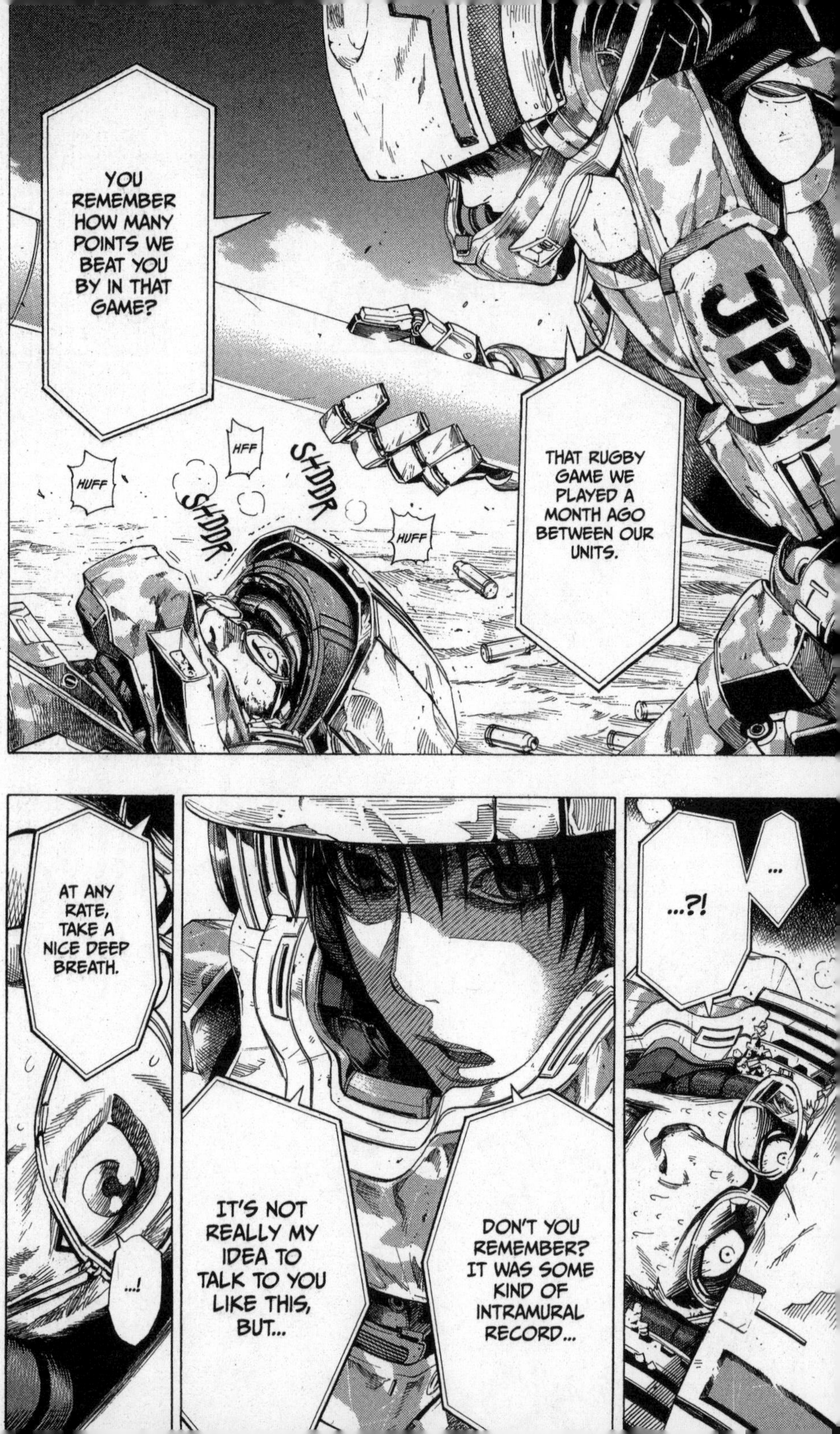
THAT RUGBY GAME WE PLAYED A MONTH AGO BETWEEN OUR UNITS.
SHDDR
HUFF
HFF
SHDDR
HUFF
YOU REMEMBER HOW MANY POINTS WE BEAT YOU BY IN THAT GAME?
...
...?!
DON'T YOU REMEMBER? IT WAS SOME KIND OF INTRAMURAL RECORD...
IT'S NOT REALLY MY IDEA TO TALK TO YOU LIKE THIS, BUT...
AT ANY RATE, TAKE A NICE DEEP BREATH.
...!

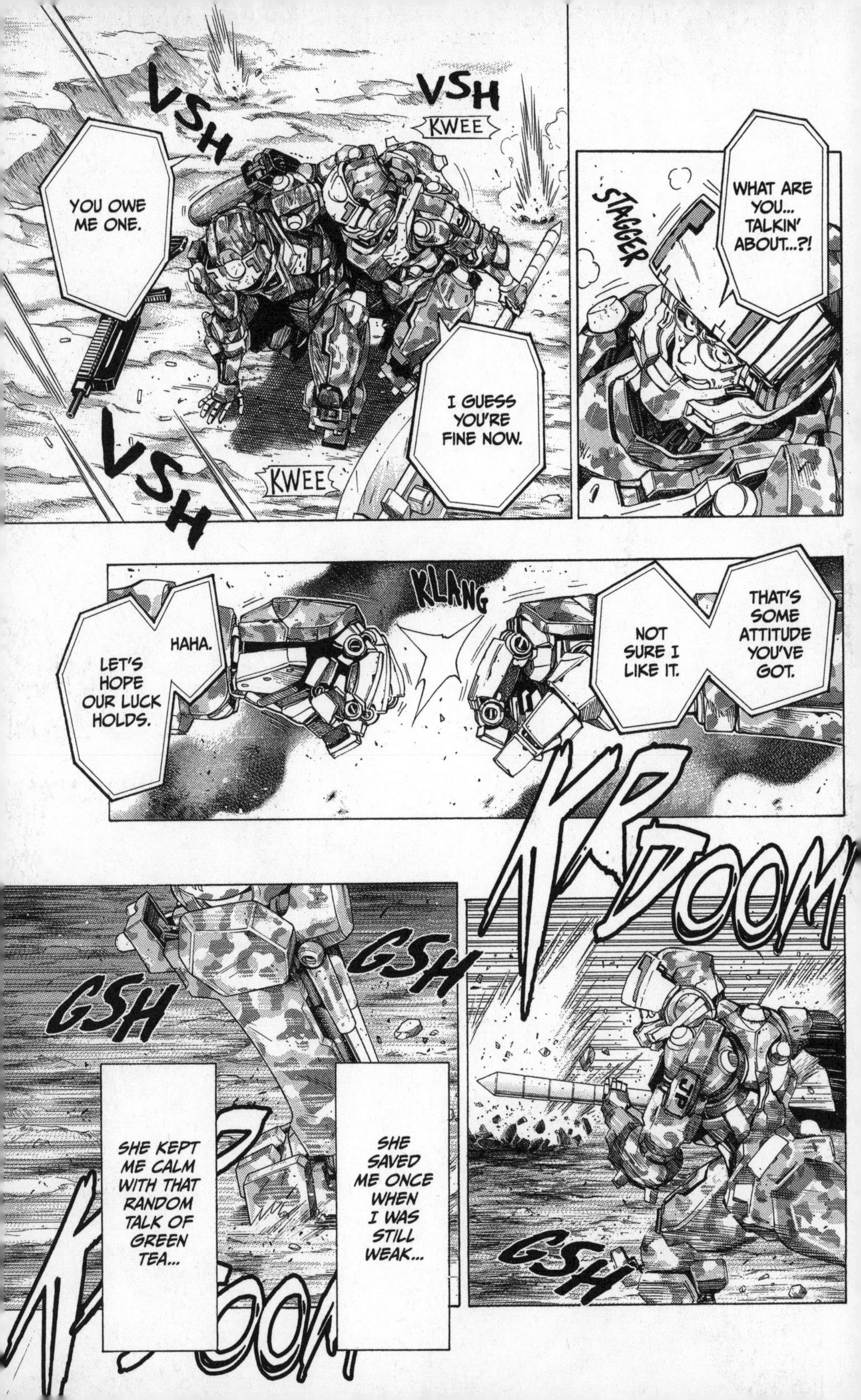
STAGGER
WHAT ARE YOU... TALKIN' ABOUT...?!
VSH
KWEE
VSH
YOU OWE ME ONE.
I GUESS YOU'RE FINE NOW.
VSH
KWEE
THAT'S SOME ATTITUDE YOU'VE GOT.
NOT SURE I LIKE IT.
KLANG
HAHA.
LET'S HOPE OUR LUCK HOLDS.
KRDOOM
GSH
GSH
GSH
SHE SAVED ME ONCE WHEN I WAS STILL WEAK...
SHE KEPT ME CALM WITH THAT RANDOM TALK OF GREEN TEA...

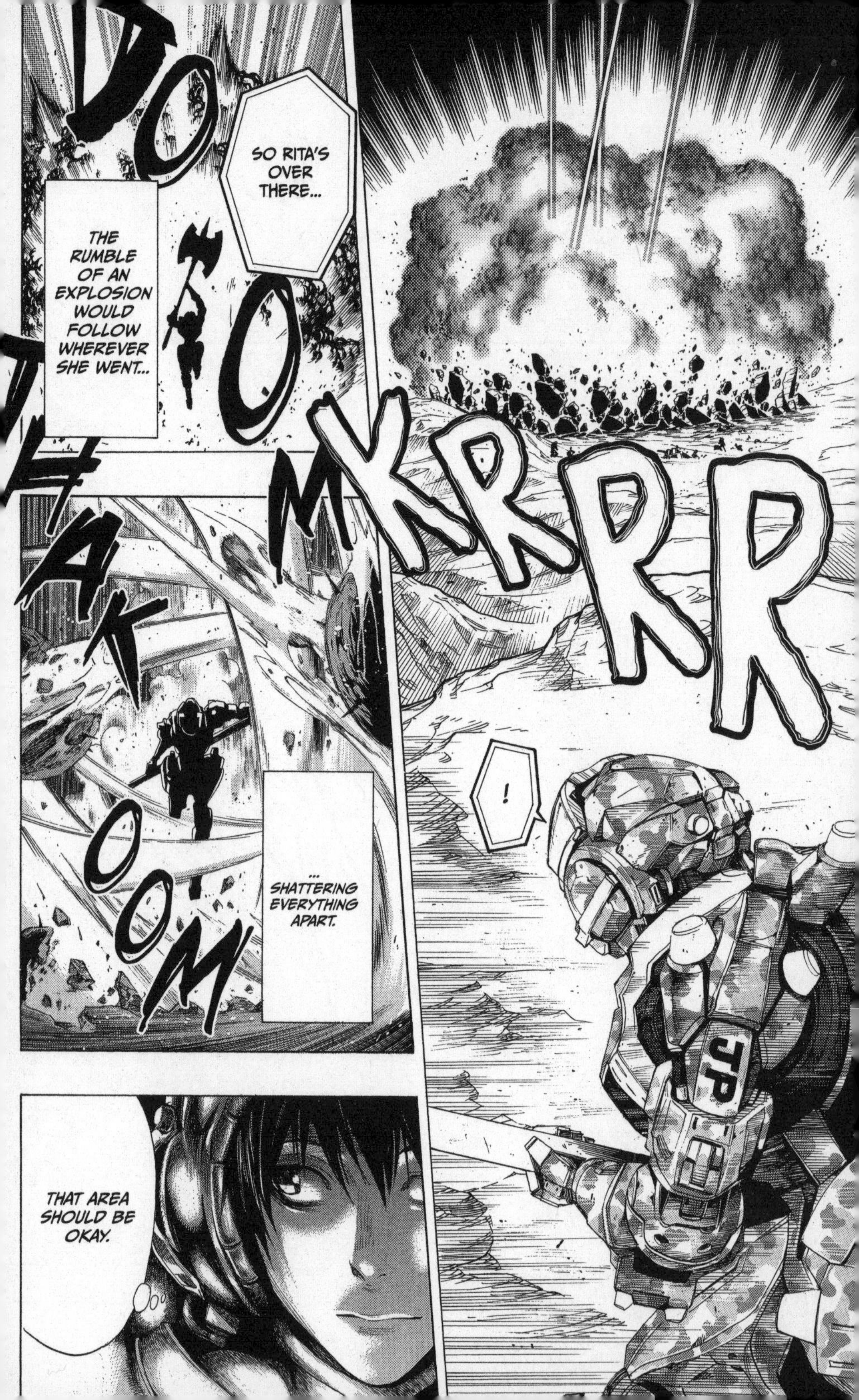
KRRR
!
SO RITA'S OVER THERE...
THE RUMBLE OF AN EXPLOSION WOULD FOLLOW WHEREVER SHE WENT...
DOOOM
...SHATTERING EVERYTHING APART.
THAT AREA SHOULD BE OKAY.

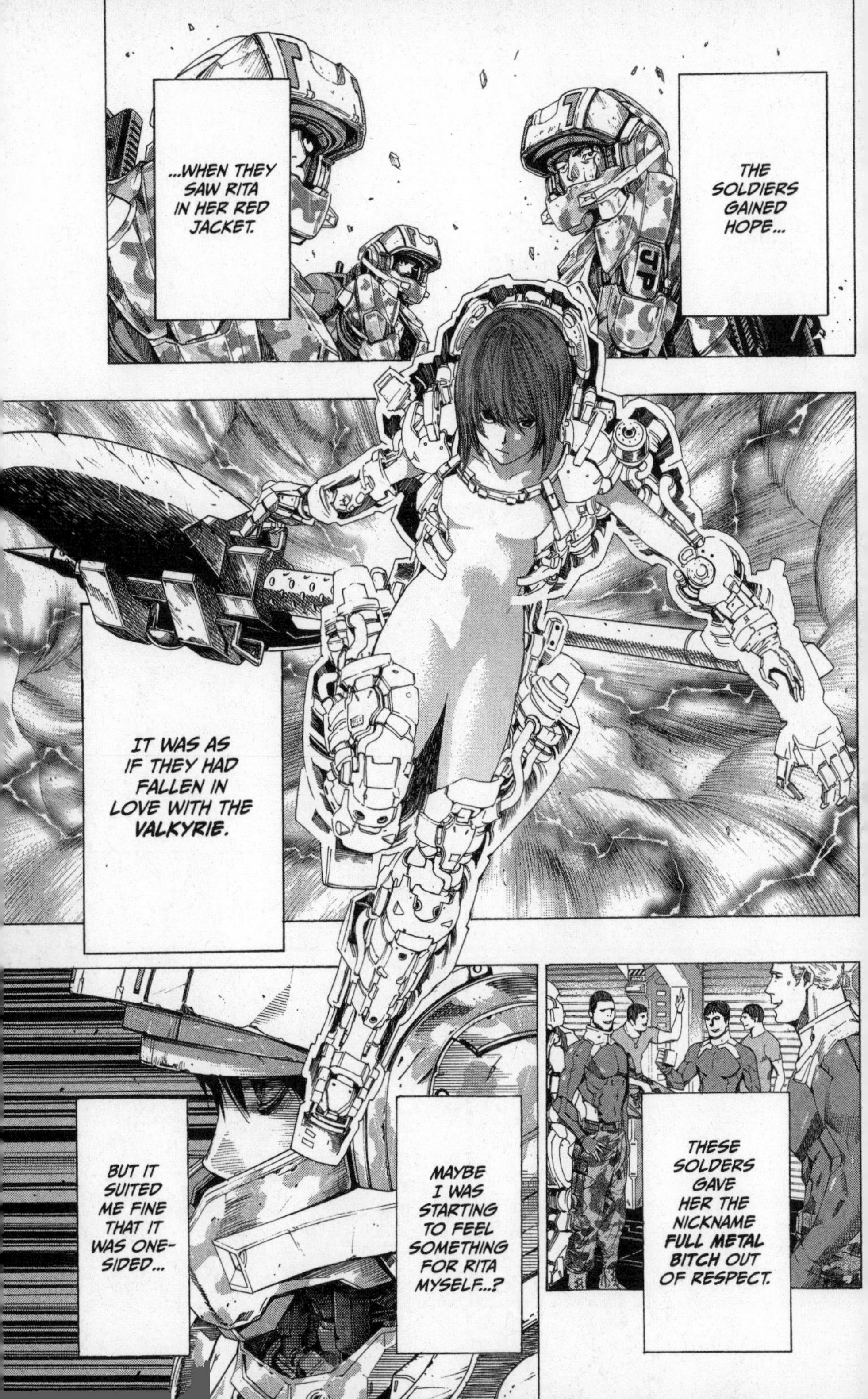
THE SOLDIERS GAINED HOPE...
...WHEN THEY SAW RITA IN HER RED JACKET.
IT WAS AS IF THEY HAD FALLEN IN LOVE WITH THE **VALKYRIE**.
THESE SOLDERS GAVE HER THE NICKNAME **FULL METAL BITCH** OUT OF RESPECT.
MAYBE I WAS STARTING TO FEEL SOMETHING FOR RITA MYSELF...?
BUT IT SUITED ME FINE THAT IT WAS ONE-SIDED...

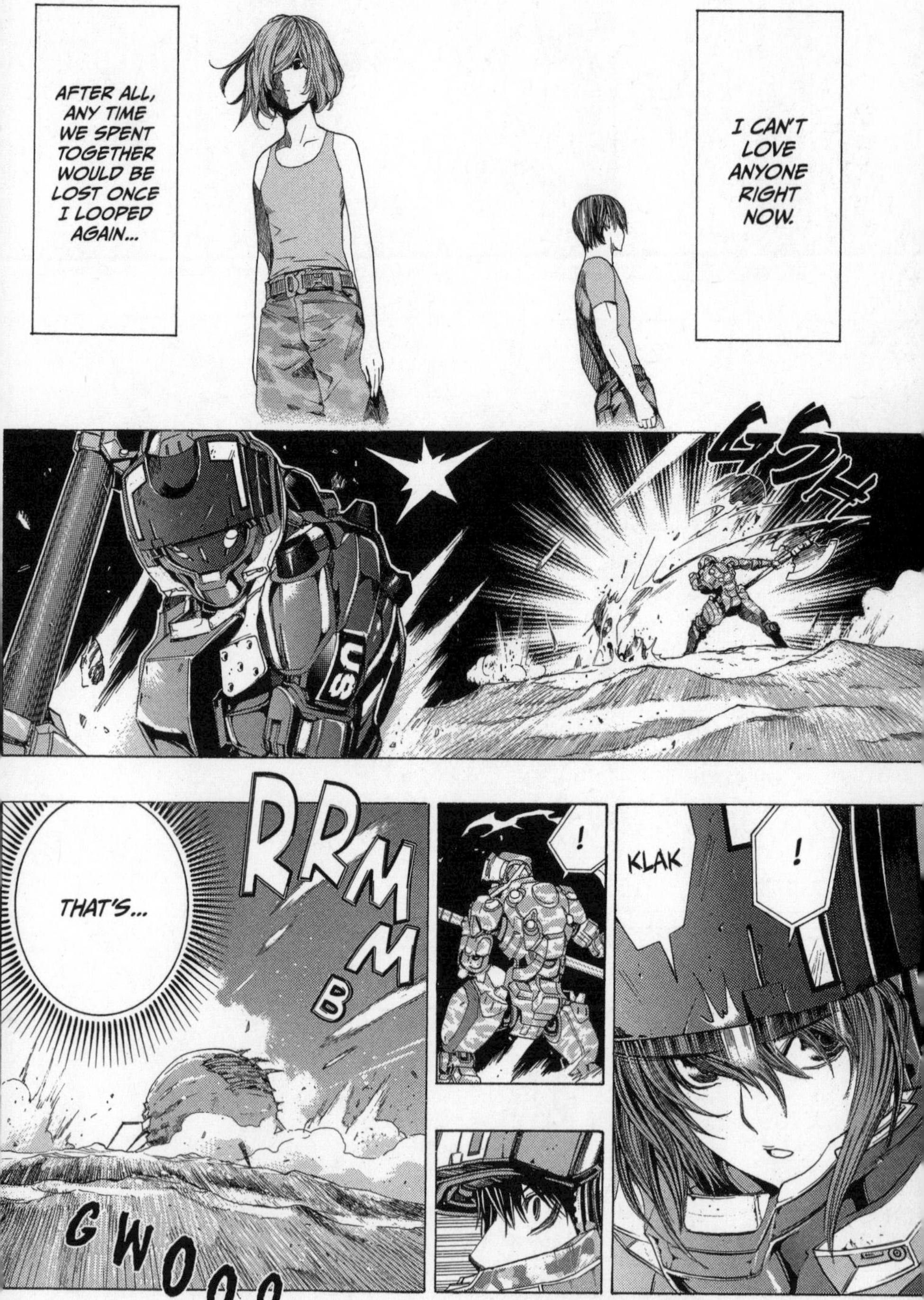
I CAN'T LOVE ANYONE RIGHT NOW.
AFTER ALL, ANY TIME WE SPENT TOGETHER WOULD BE LOST ONCE I LOOPED AGAIN...
GSHK
!
KLAK
!
RRMMB
THAT'S...
GWOOO

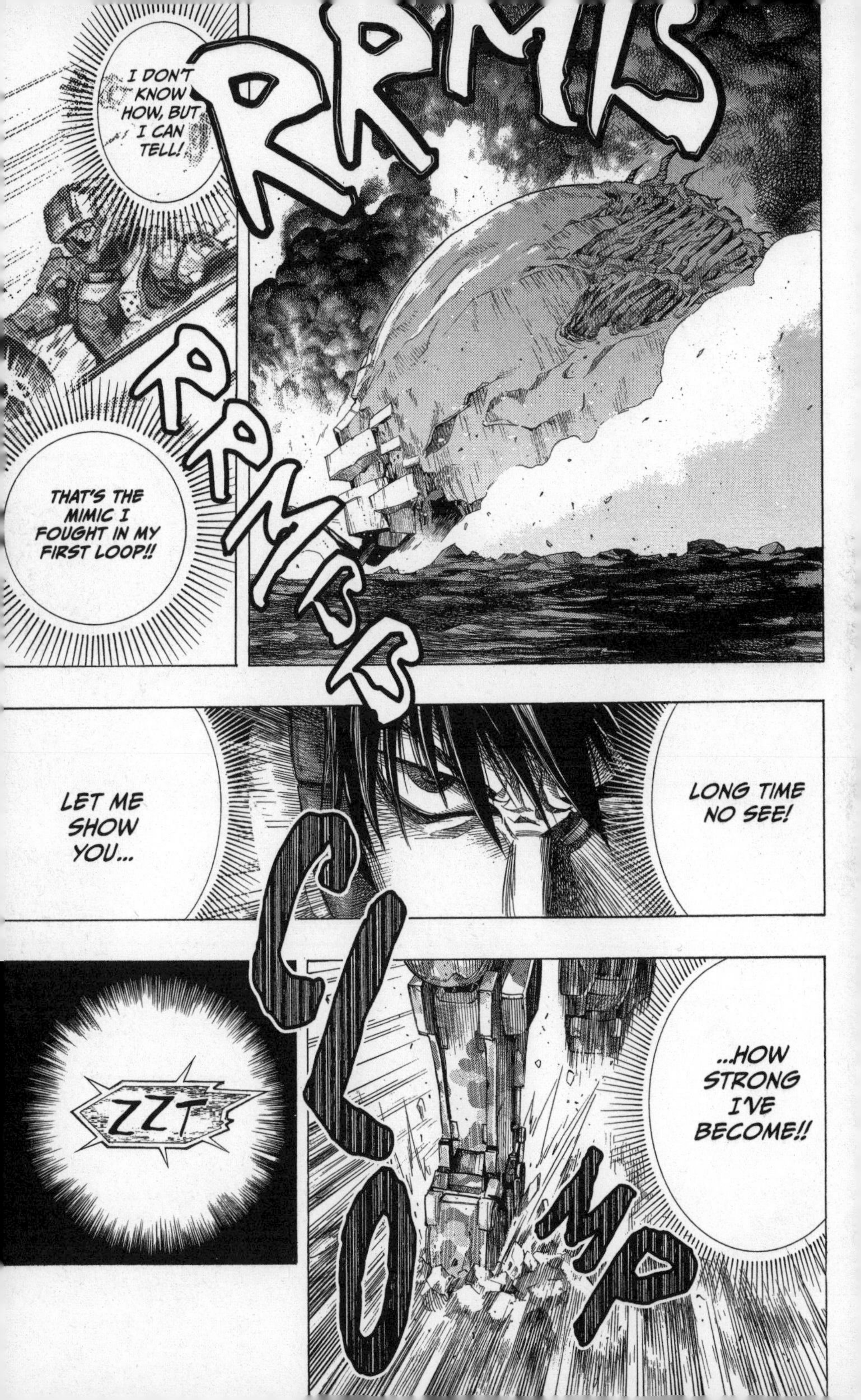
RRMB
RRMBB
I DON'T KNOW HOW, BUT I CAN TELL!
THAT'S THE MIMIC I FOUGHT IN MY FIRST LOOP!!
LONG TIME NO SEE!
LET ME SHOW YOU...
...HOW STRONG I'VE BECOME!!
CLOMP
ZZT

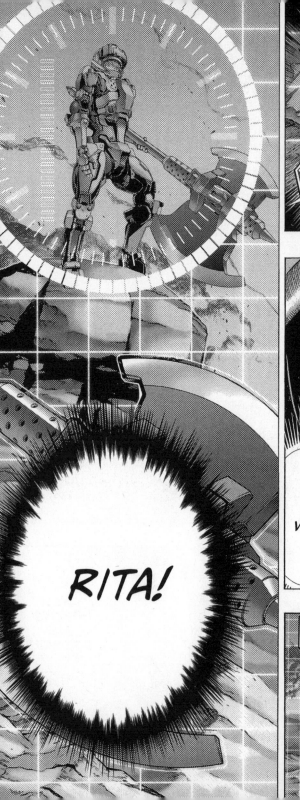

RITA!

Y...
...ERE...

!!

THAT VOICE.

BLIP

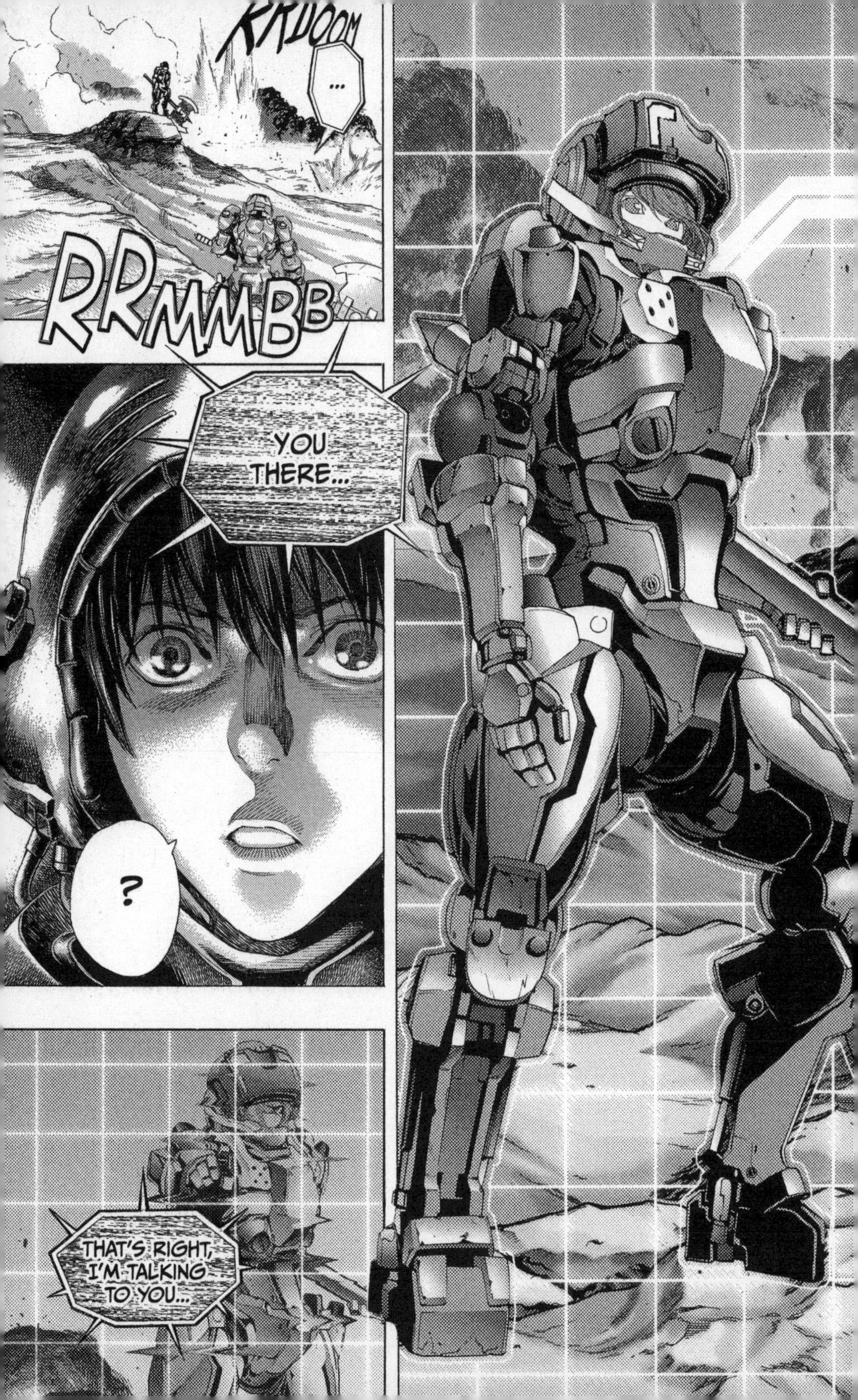
KRDOOM
...
RRMMBB
YOU THERE...
?
THAT'S RIGHT, I'M TALKING TO YOU...

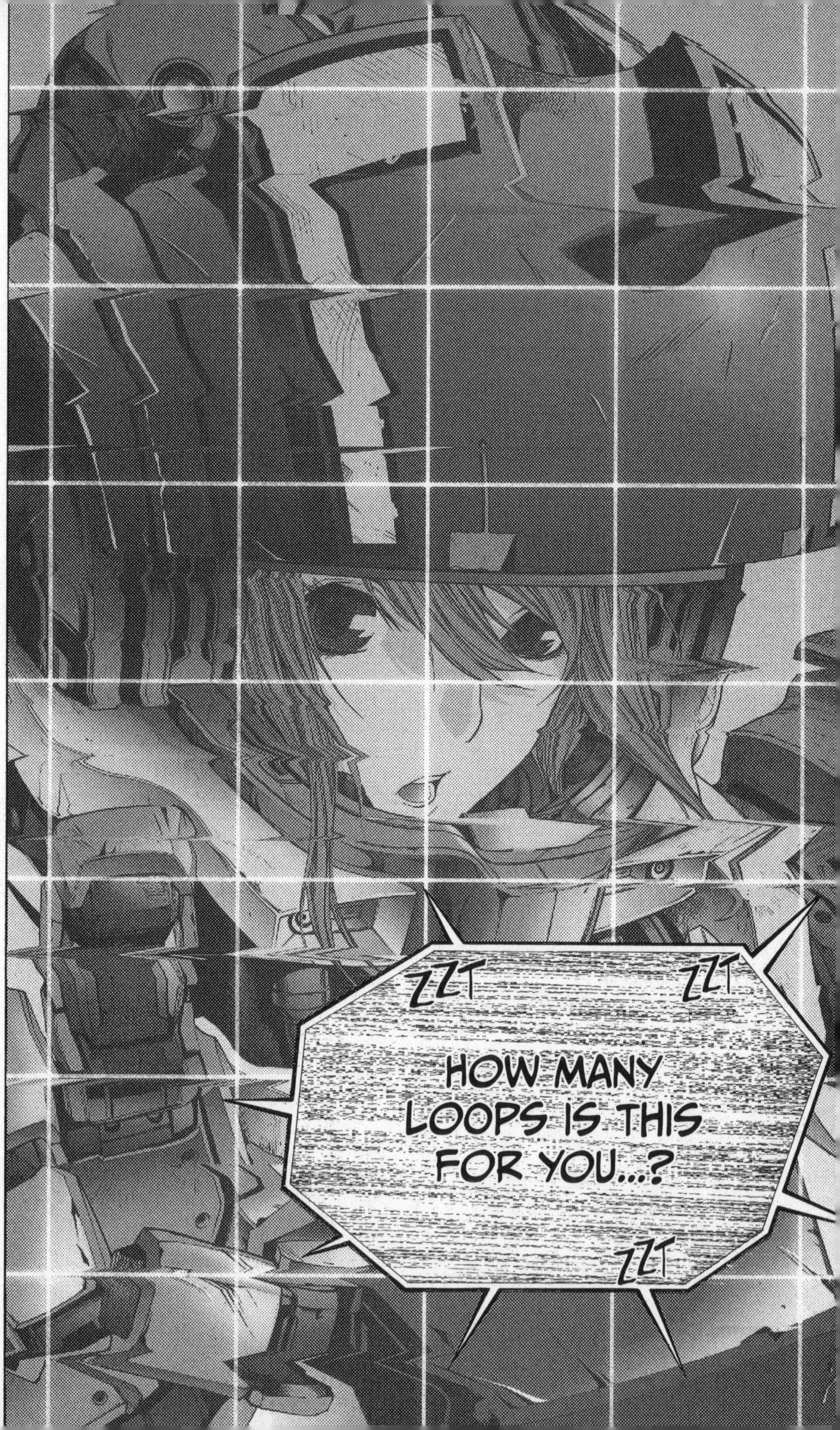
ZZT
ZZT
HOW MANY LOOPS IS THIS FOR YOU...?
ZZT

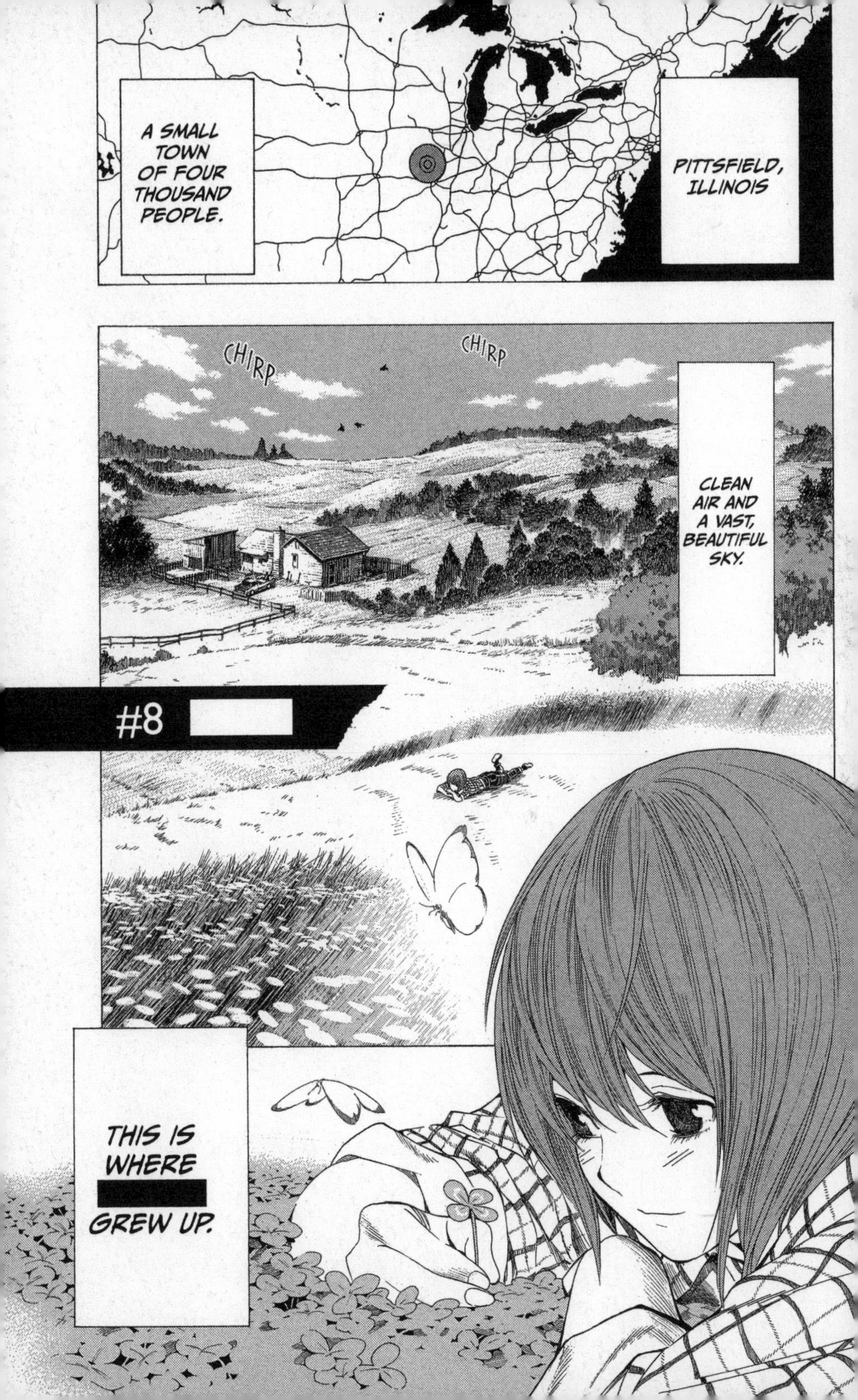
PITTSFIELD, ILLINOIS
A SMALL TOWN OF FOUR THOUSAND PEOPLE.
CHIRP
CHIRP
CLEAN AIR AND A VAST, BEAUTIFUL SKY.
#8
THIS IS WHERE [redacted] GREW UP.

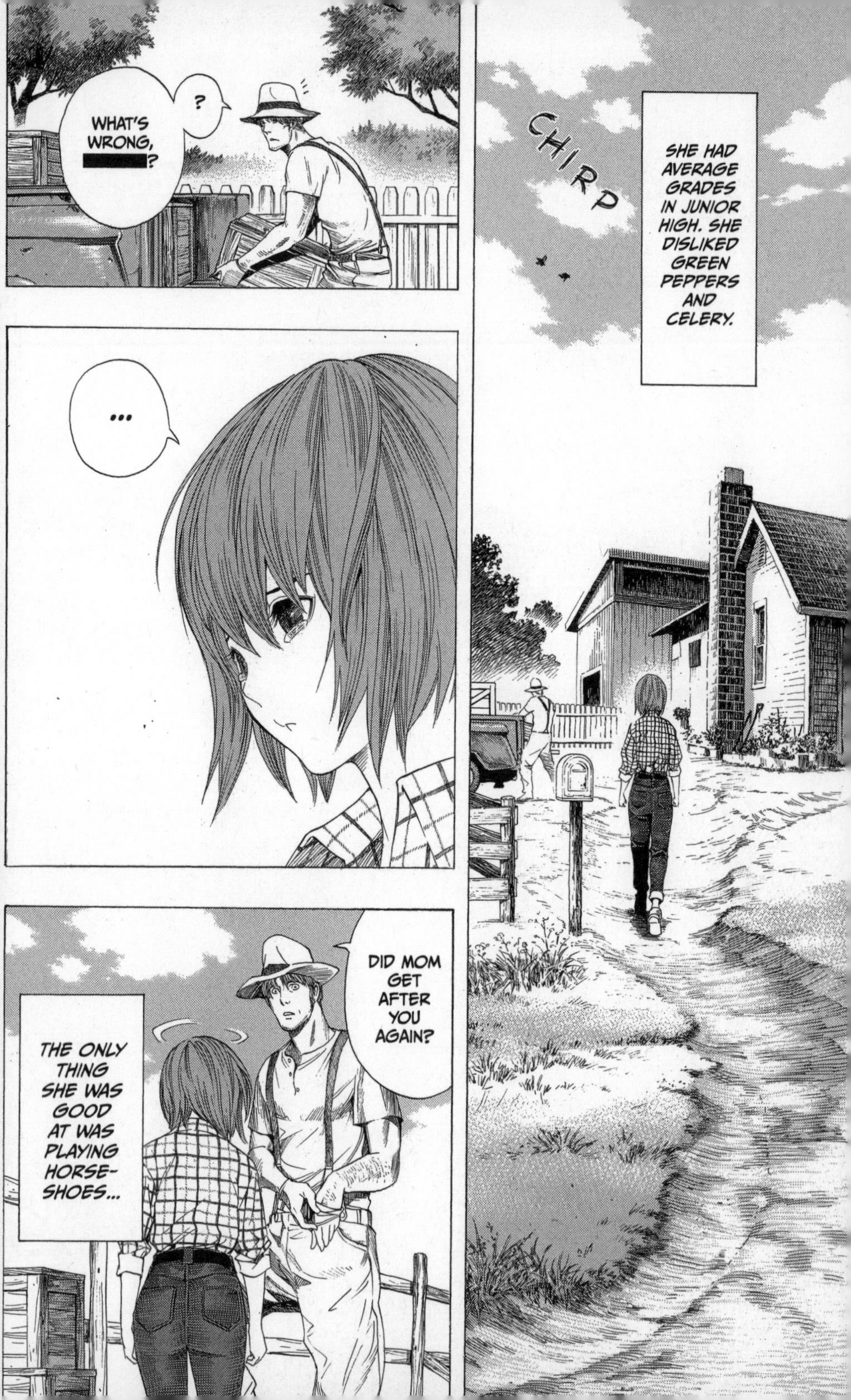
CHIRP
SHE HAD AVERAGE GRADES IN JUNIOR HIGH. SHE DISLIKED GREEN PEPPERS AND CELERY.
?
WHAT'S WRONG, [redacted]?
...
DID MOM GET AFTER YOU AGAIN?
THE ONLY THING SHE WAS GOOD AT WAS PLAYING HORSE-SHOES...

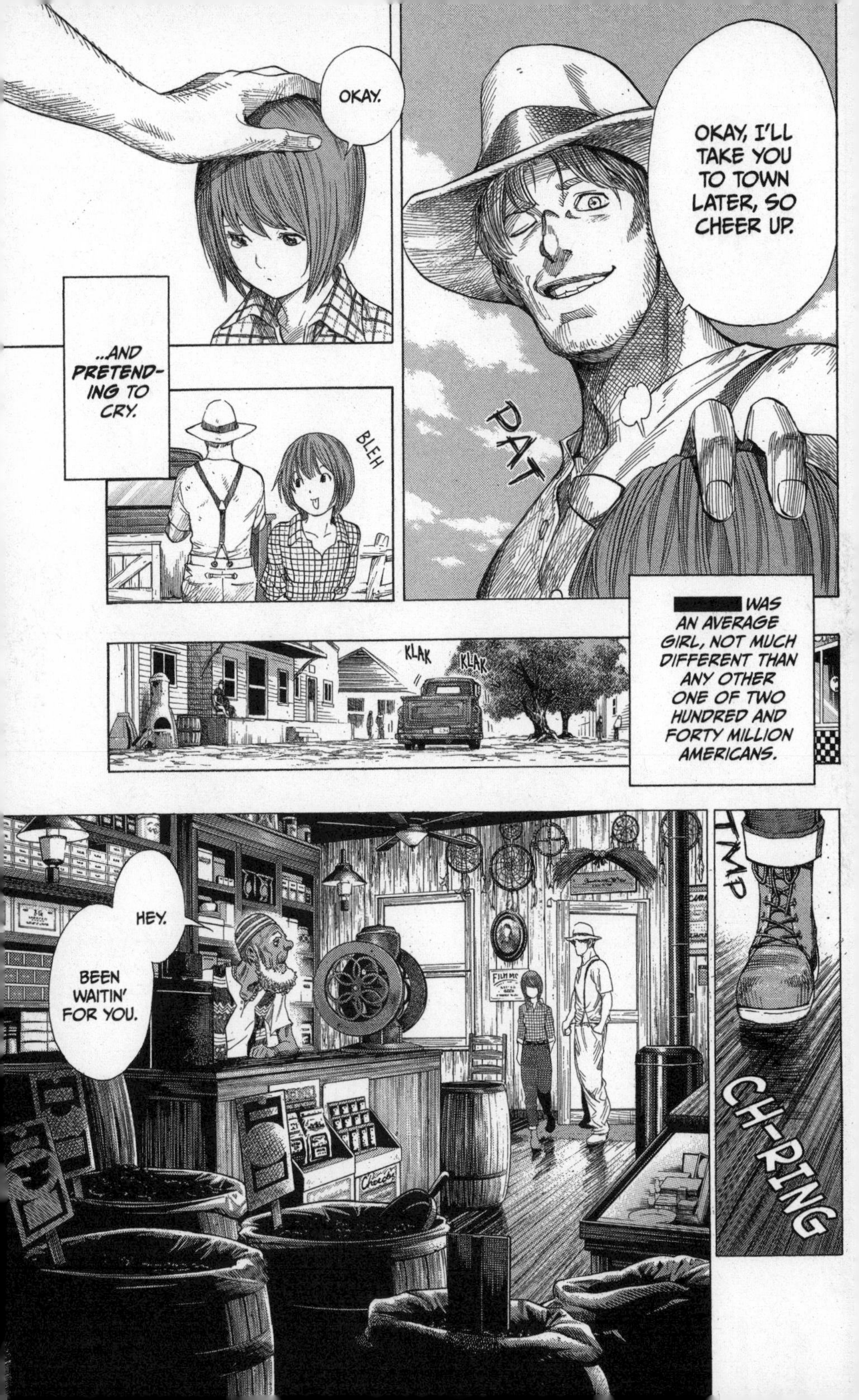
OKAY, I'LL TAKE YOU TO TOWN LATER, SO CHEER UP.
PAT
OKAY.
...AND PRETEND-ING TO CRY.
BLEH
[redacted] WAS AN AVERAGE GIRL, NOT MUCH DIFFERENT THAN ANY OTHER ONE OF TWO HUNDRED AND FORTY MILLION AMERICANS.
KLAK
KLAK
TMP
CH-RING
HEY.
BEEN WAITIN' FOR YOU.

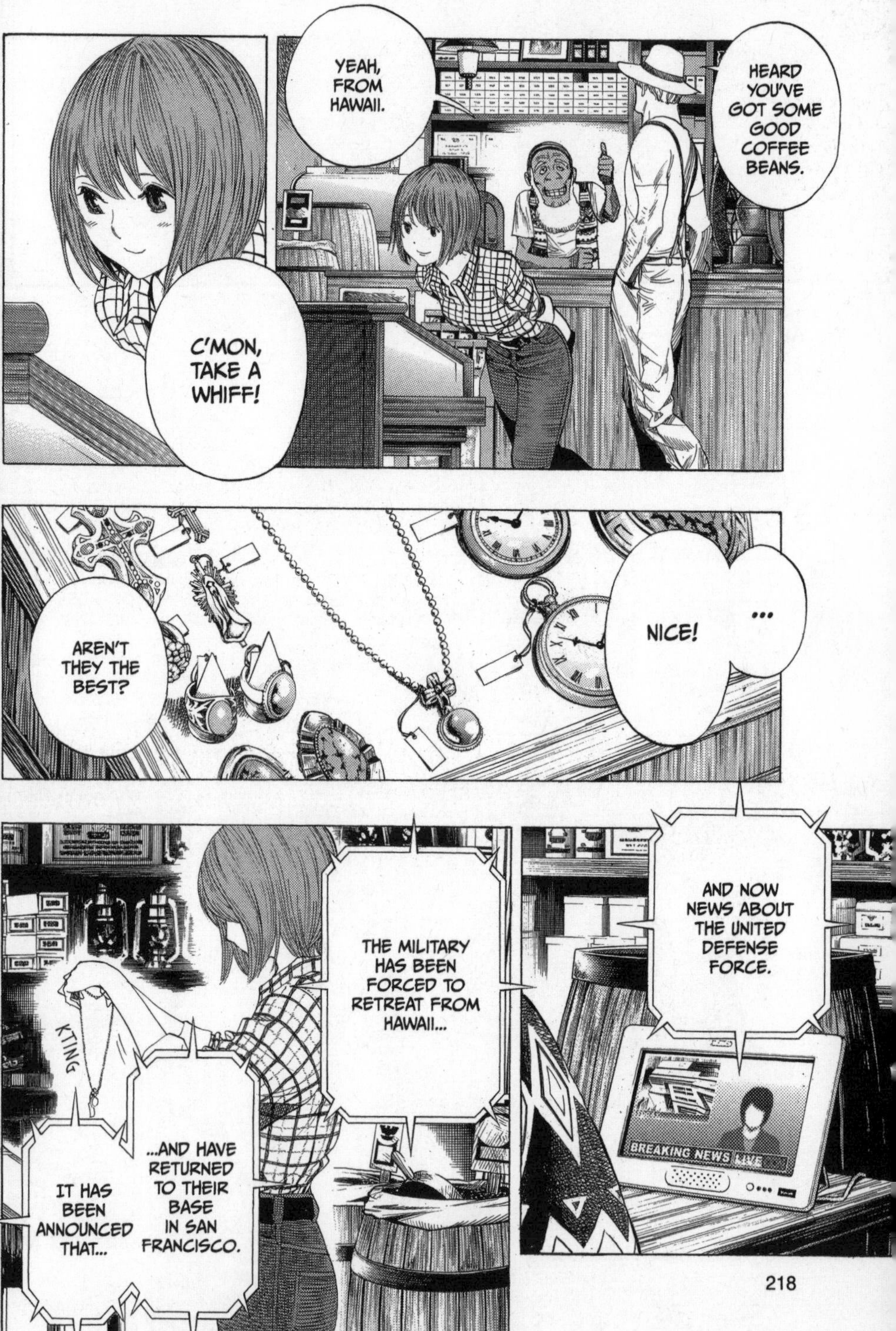
HEARD YOU'VE GOT SOME GOOD COFFEE BEANS.
YEAH, FROM HAWAII.
C'MON, TAKE A WHIFF!
...
NICE!
AREN'T THEY THE BEST?
AND NOW NEWS ABOUT THE UNITED DEFENSE FORCE.
BREAKING NEWS LIVE
THE MILITARY HAS BEEN FORCED TO RETREAT FROM HAWAII...
...AND HAVE RETURNED TO THEIR BASE IN SAN FRANCISCO.
IT HAS BEEN ANNOUNCED THAT...
KTING

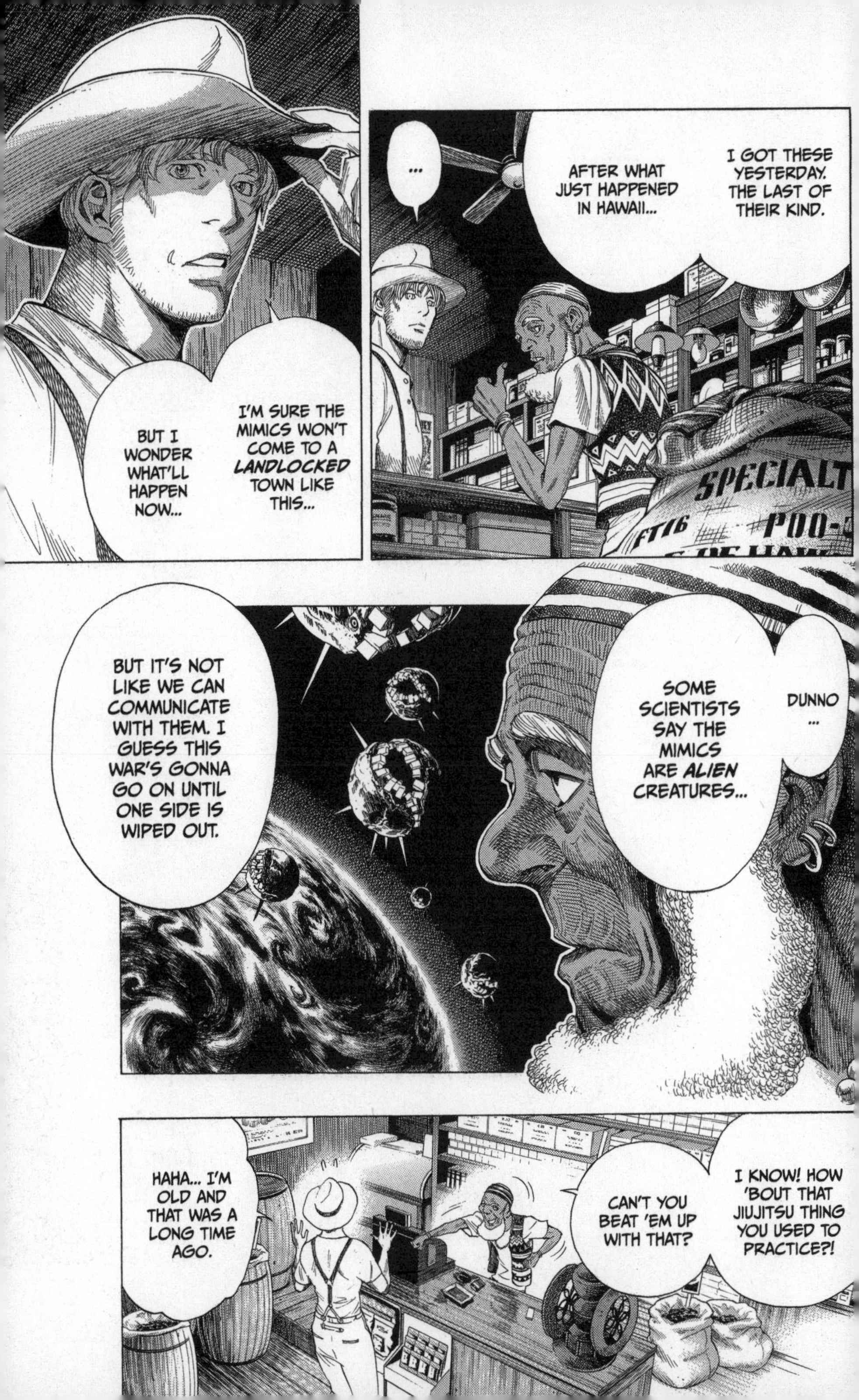
I GOT THESE YESTERDAY. THE LAST OF THEIR KIND.
AFTER WHAT JUST HAPPENED IN HAWAII...
...
I'M SURE THE MIMICS WON'T COME TO A *LANDLOCKED* TOWN LIKE THIS...
BUT I WONDER WHAT'LL HAPPEN NOW...
DUNNO...
SOME SCIENTISTS SAY THE MIMICS ARE *ALIEN* CREATURES...
BUT IT'S NOT LIKE WE CAN COMMUNICATE WITH THEM. I GUESS THIS WAR'S GONNA GO ON UNTIL ONE SIDE IS WIPED OUT.
I KNOW! HOW 'BOUT THAT JIUJITSU THING YOU USED TO PRACTICE?!
CAN'T YOU BEAT 'EM UP WITH THAT?
HAHA... I'M OLD AND THAT WAS A LONG TIME AGO.

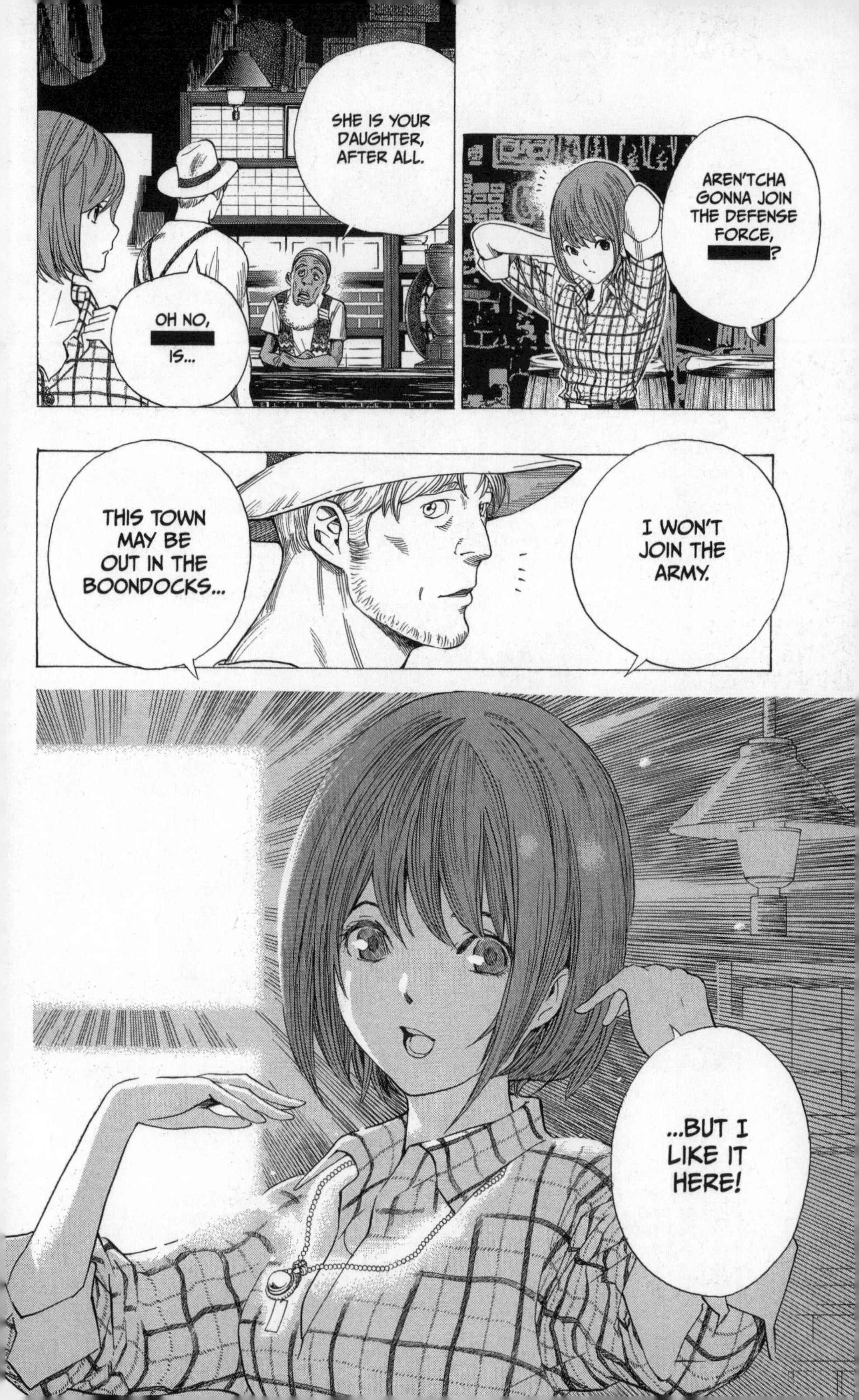
AREN'TCHA GONNA JOIN THE DEFENSE FORCE, [redacted]?
SHE IS YOUR DAUGHTER, AFTER ALL.
OH NO, [redacted] IS...
I WON'T JOIN THE ARMY.
THIS TOWN MAY BE OUT IN THE BOONDOCKS...
...BUT I LIKE IT HERE!

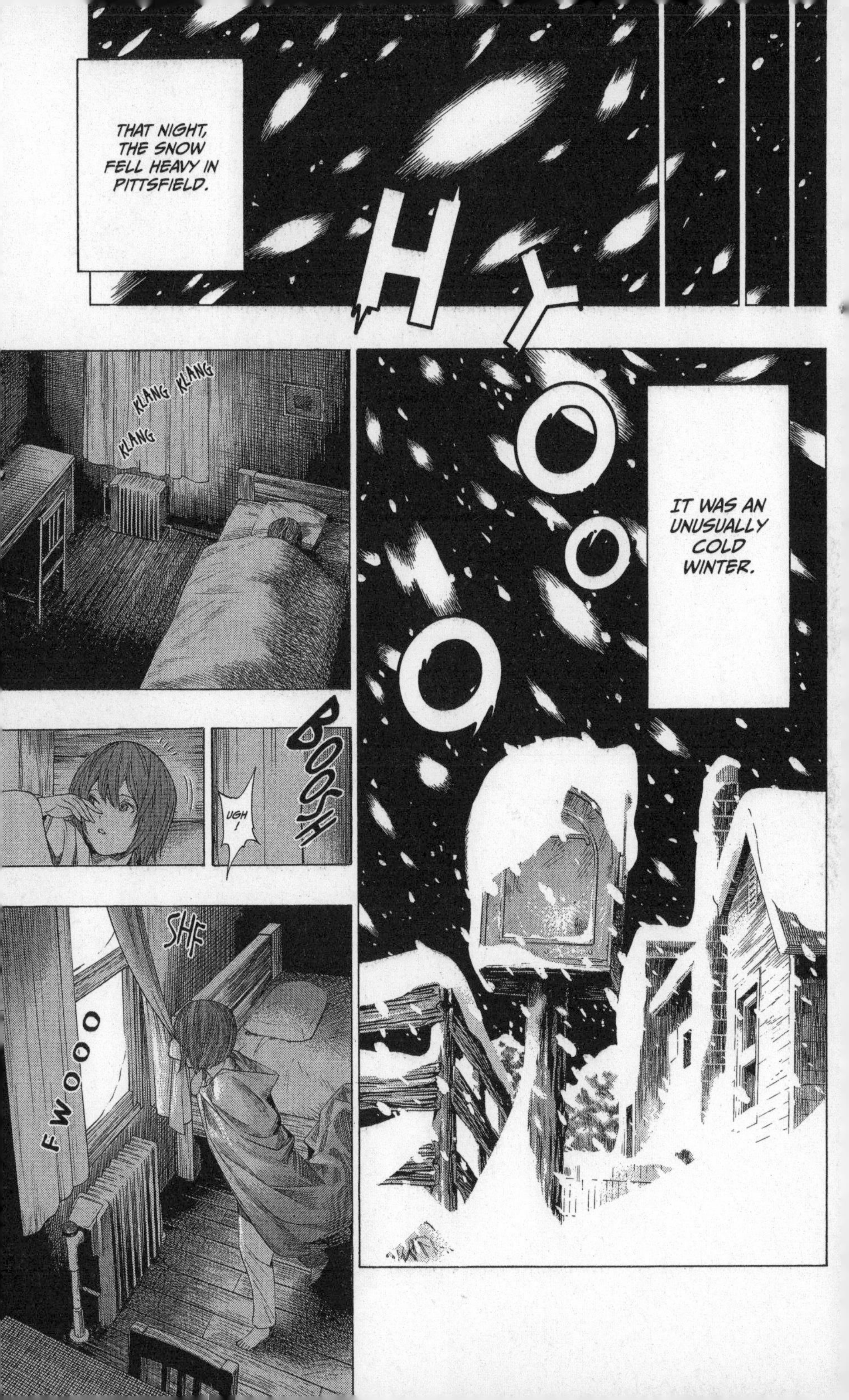
THAT NIGHT, THE SNOW FELL HEAVY IN PITTSFIELD.
HYOOOO
IT WAS AN UNUSUALLY COLD WINTER.
KLANG KLANG
KLANG
BOOSH
UGH!
SHF
FWOOO

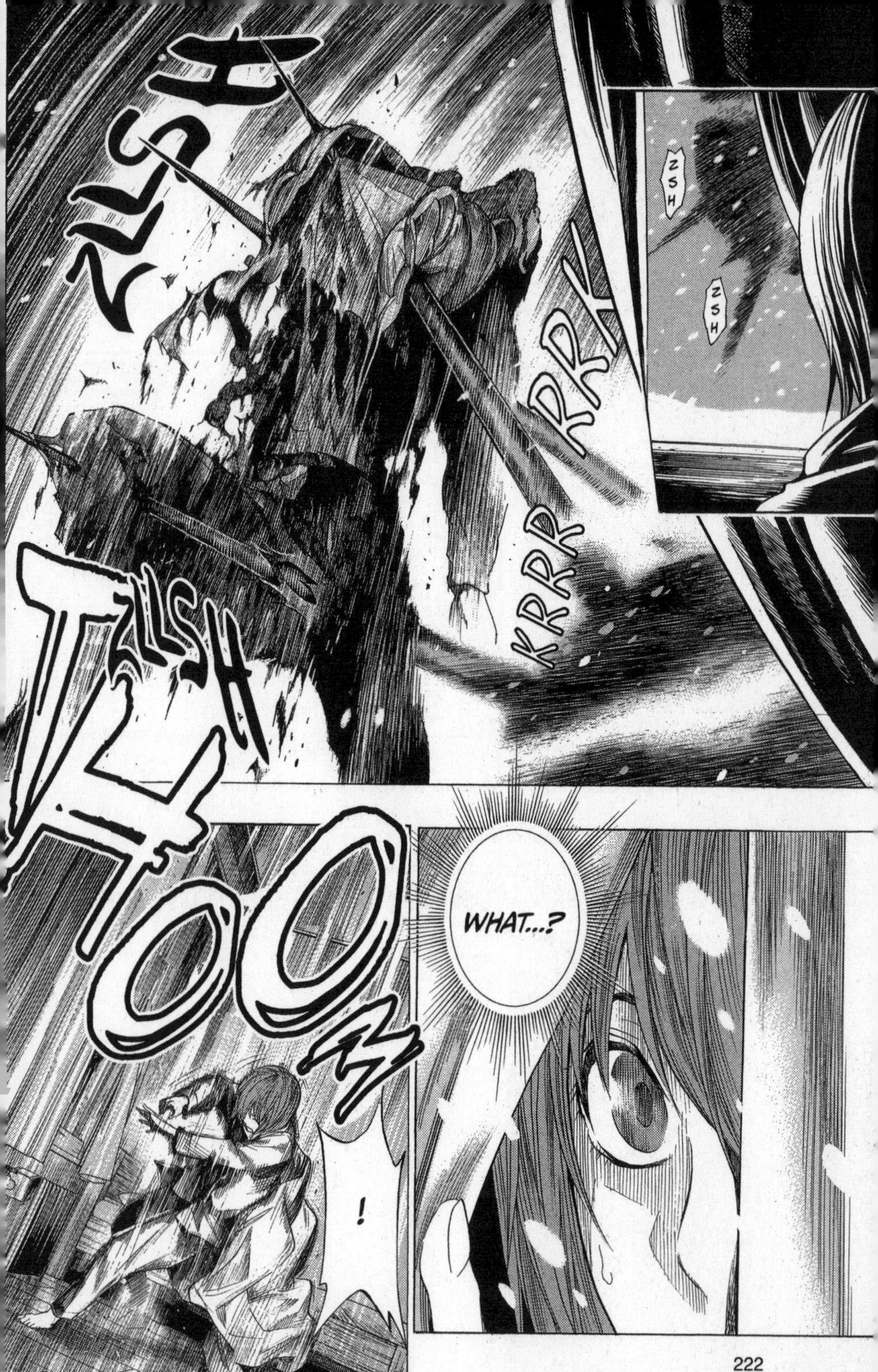
ZSH
ZSH
ZSSH
KRRRK
KRRR
WHAT...?
TZLSH
FOOM
!

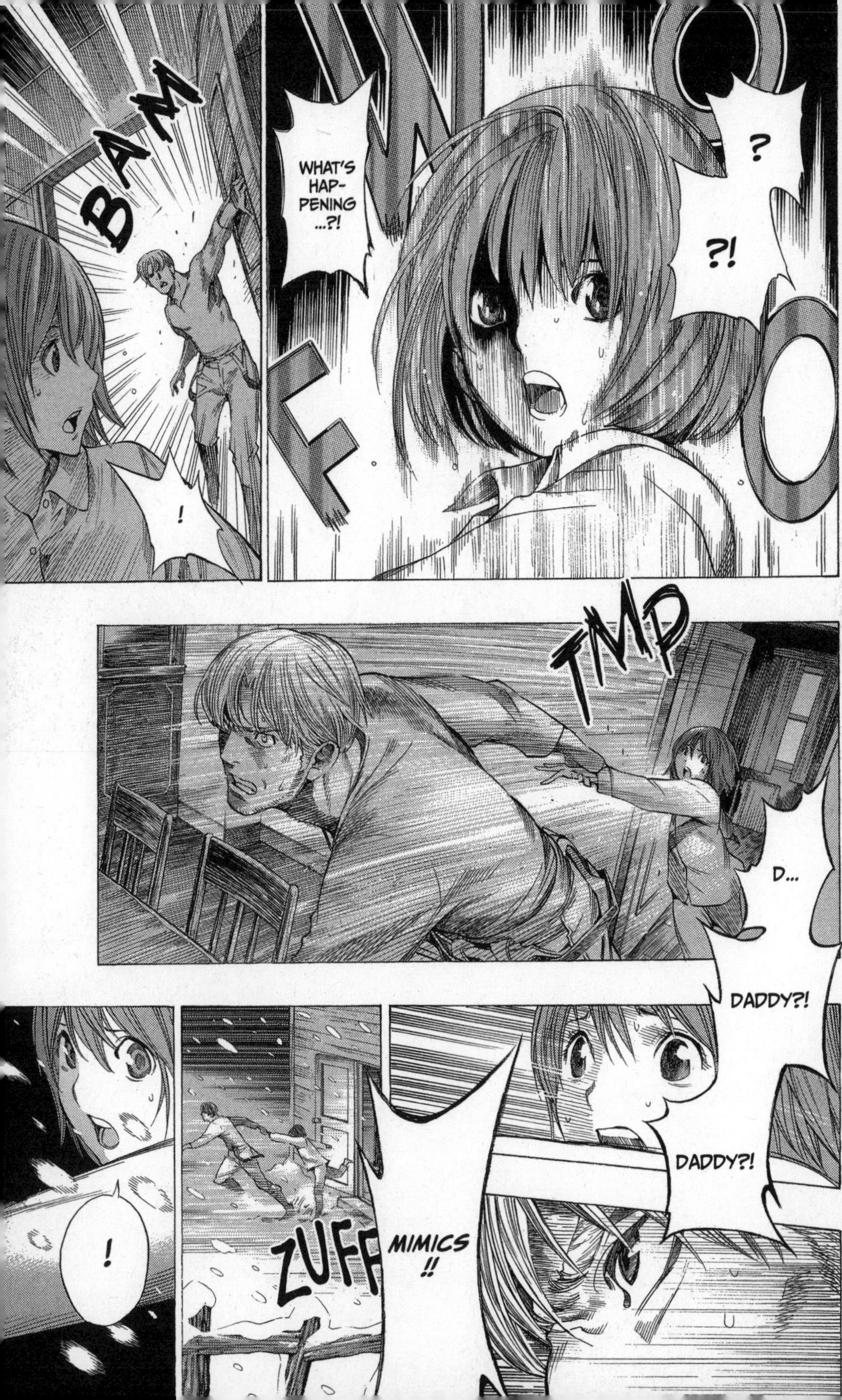
?
?!
WHAT'S HAP-PENING ...?!
BAM
!
TMP
D...
DADDY?!
DADDY?!
MIMICS !!
ZUFF
!

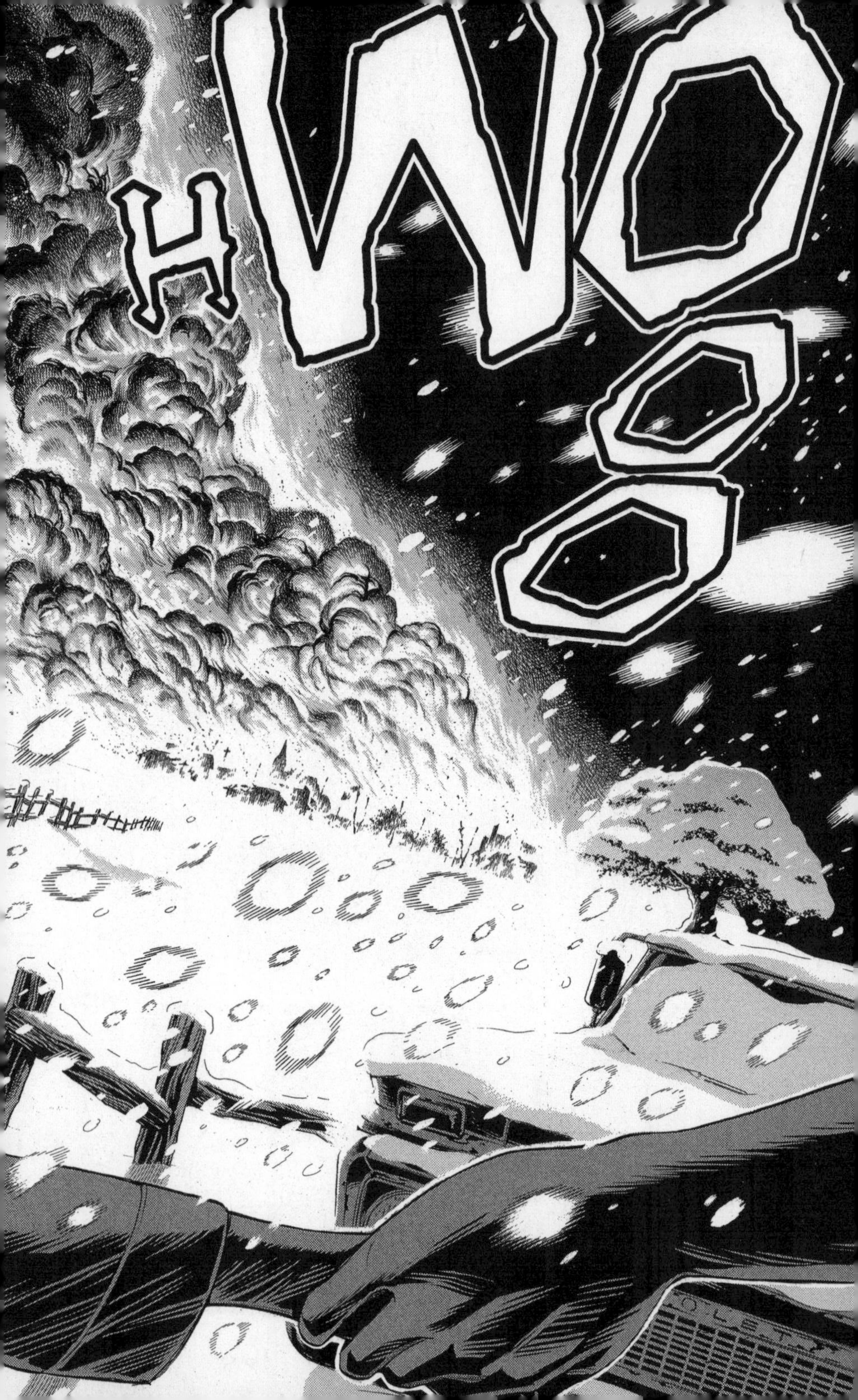
HWOOO

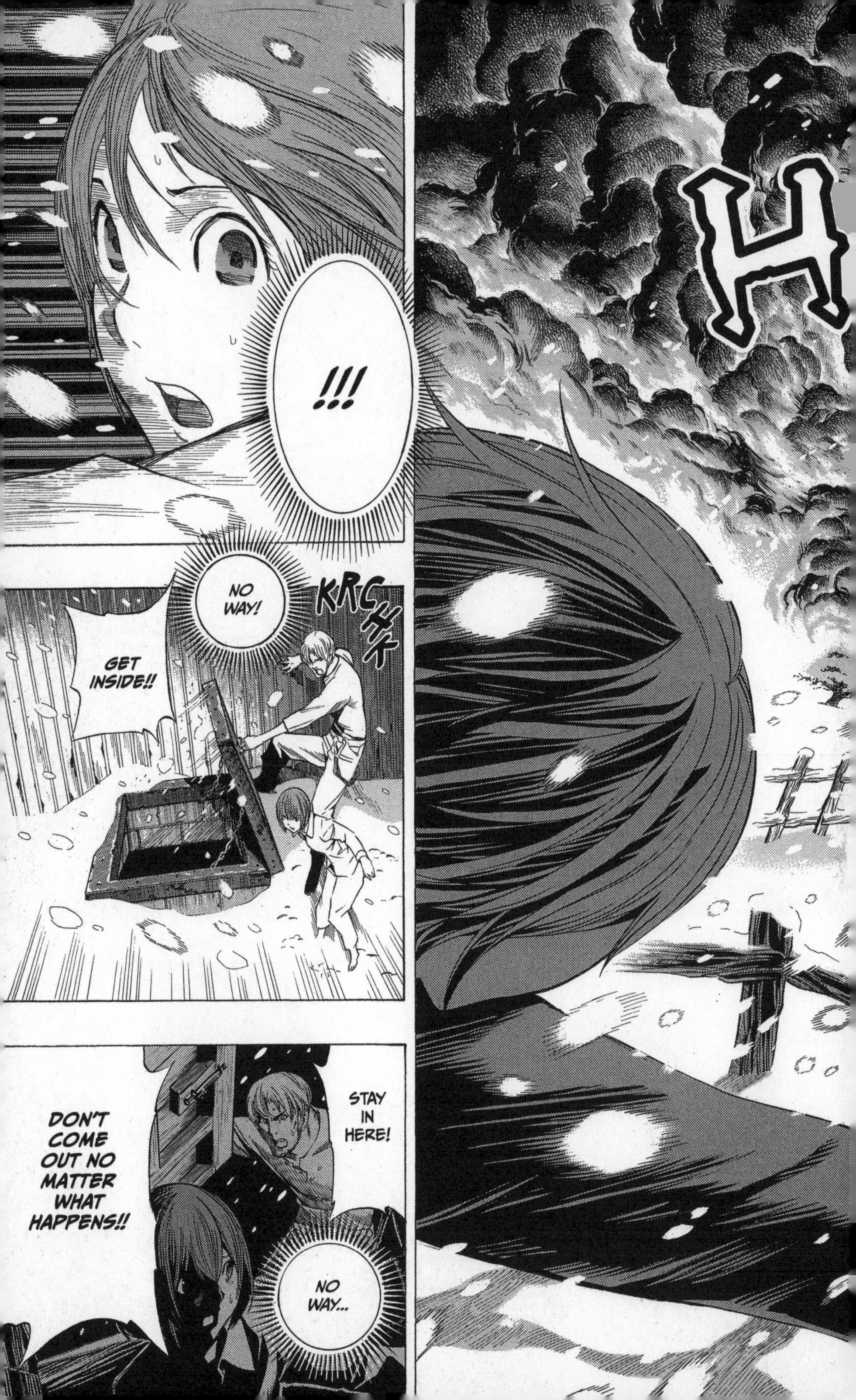
H
!!!
KRCHK
NO WAY!
GET INSIDE!!
STAY IN HERE!
DON'T COME OUT NO MATTER WHAT HAPPENS!!
NO WAY...

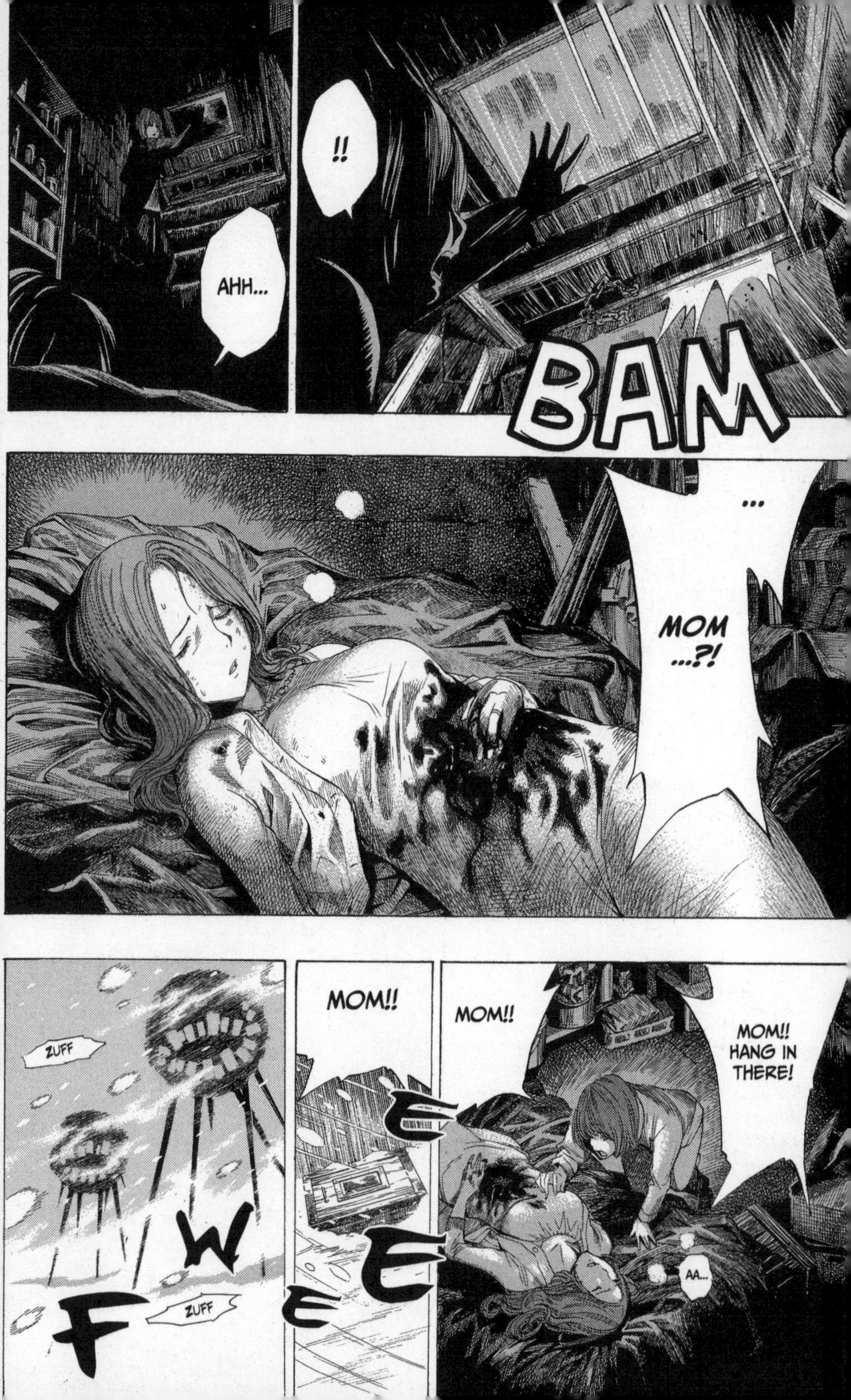

!!
BAM
AHH...
...
MOM ...?!
MOM!! HANG IN THERE!
MOM!!
AA...
MOM!!
ZUFF
FWEEE
ZUFF

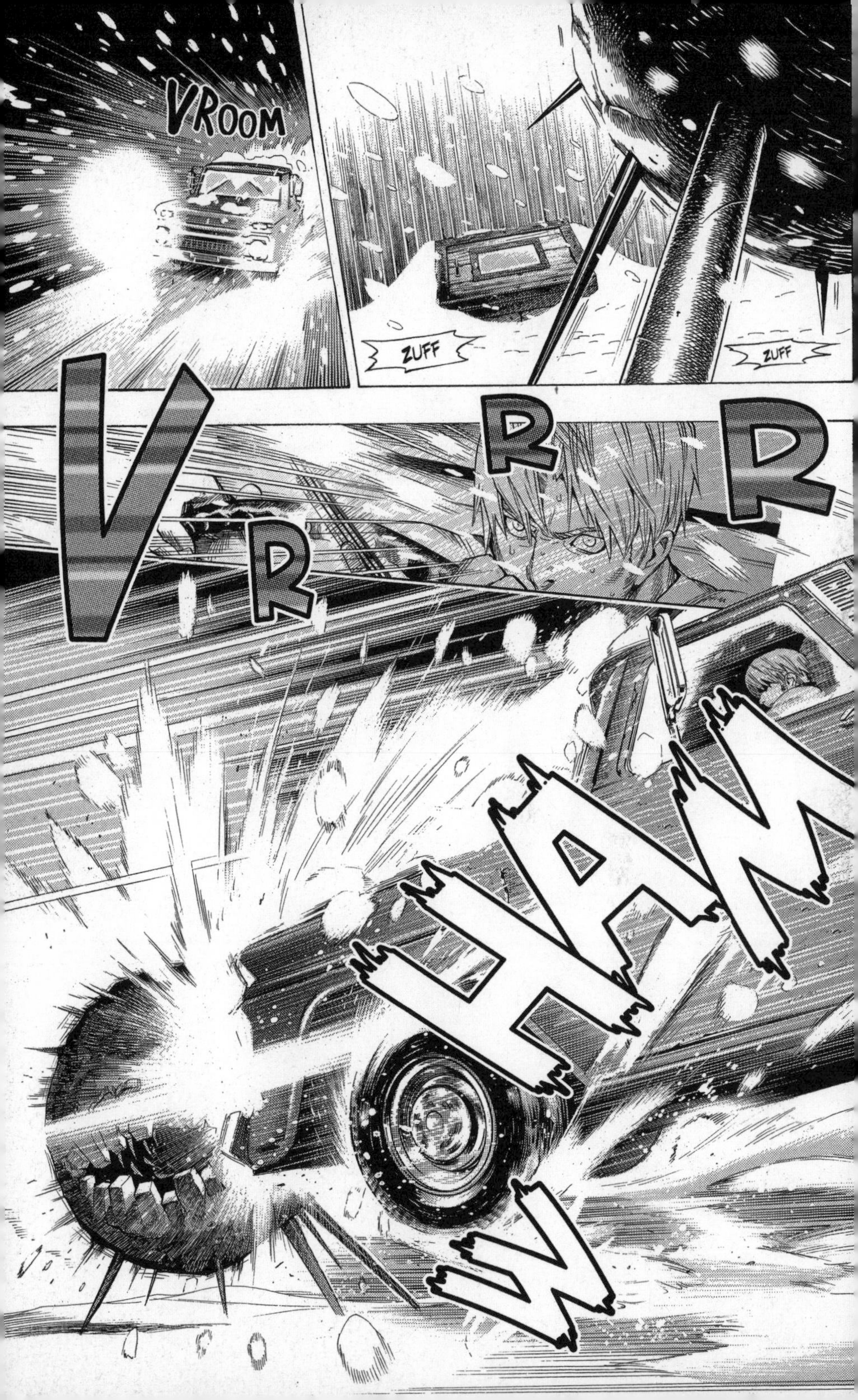
ZUFF
ZUFF
VROOM
VRRR
WHAM

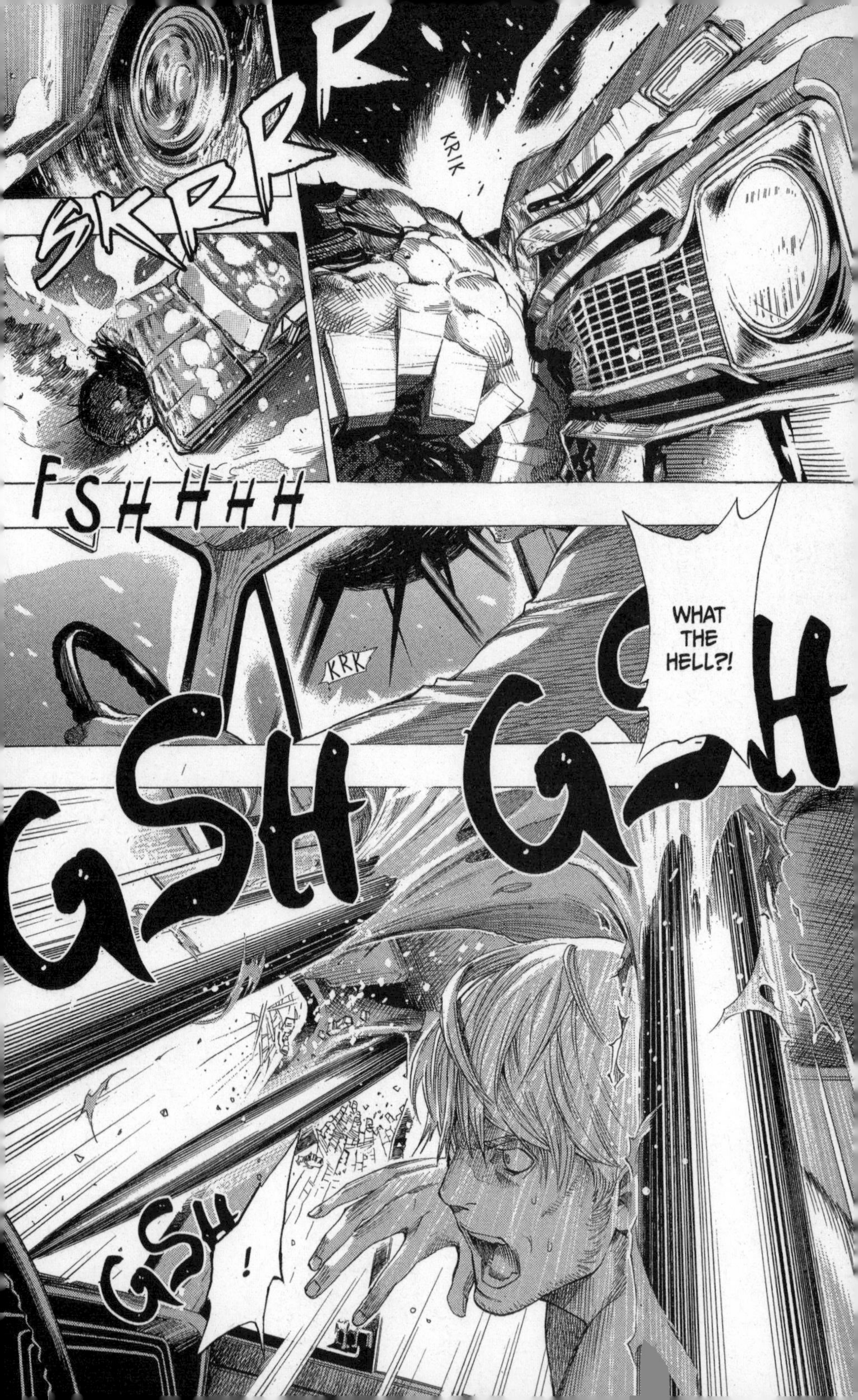
KRIK
SKRRR
FSHHHH
WHAT THE HELL?!
GSH GSH
KRK
GSH
!

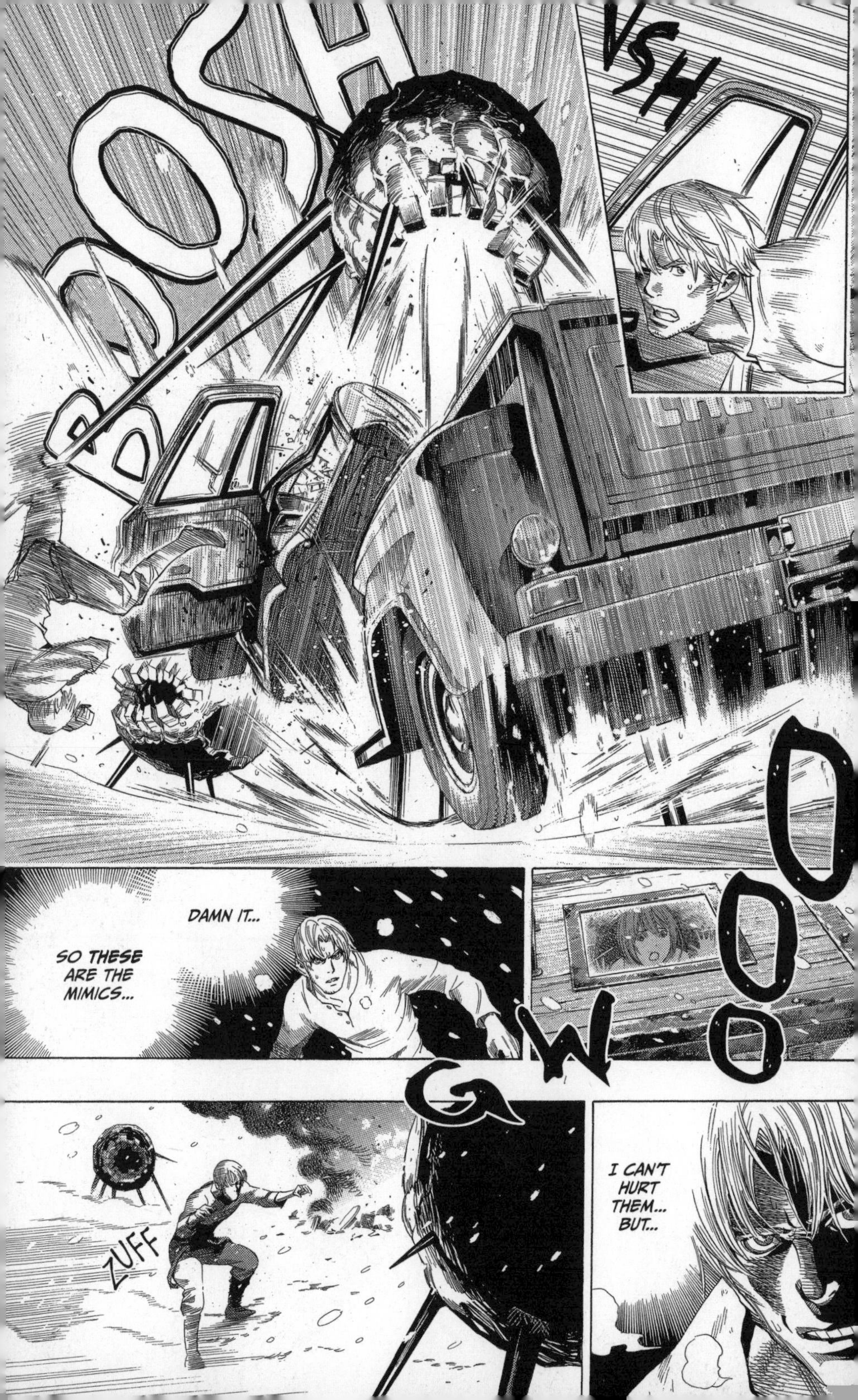
VSH
BOOSH
DAMN IT...
SO THESE ARE THE MIMICS...
GWOOOO
I CAN'T HURT THEM... BUT...
ZUFF

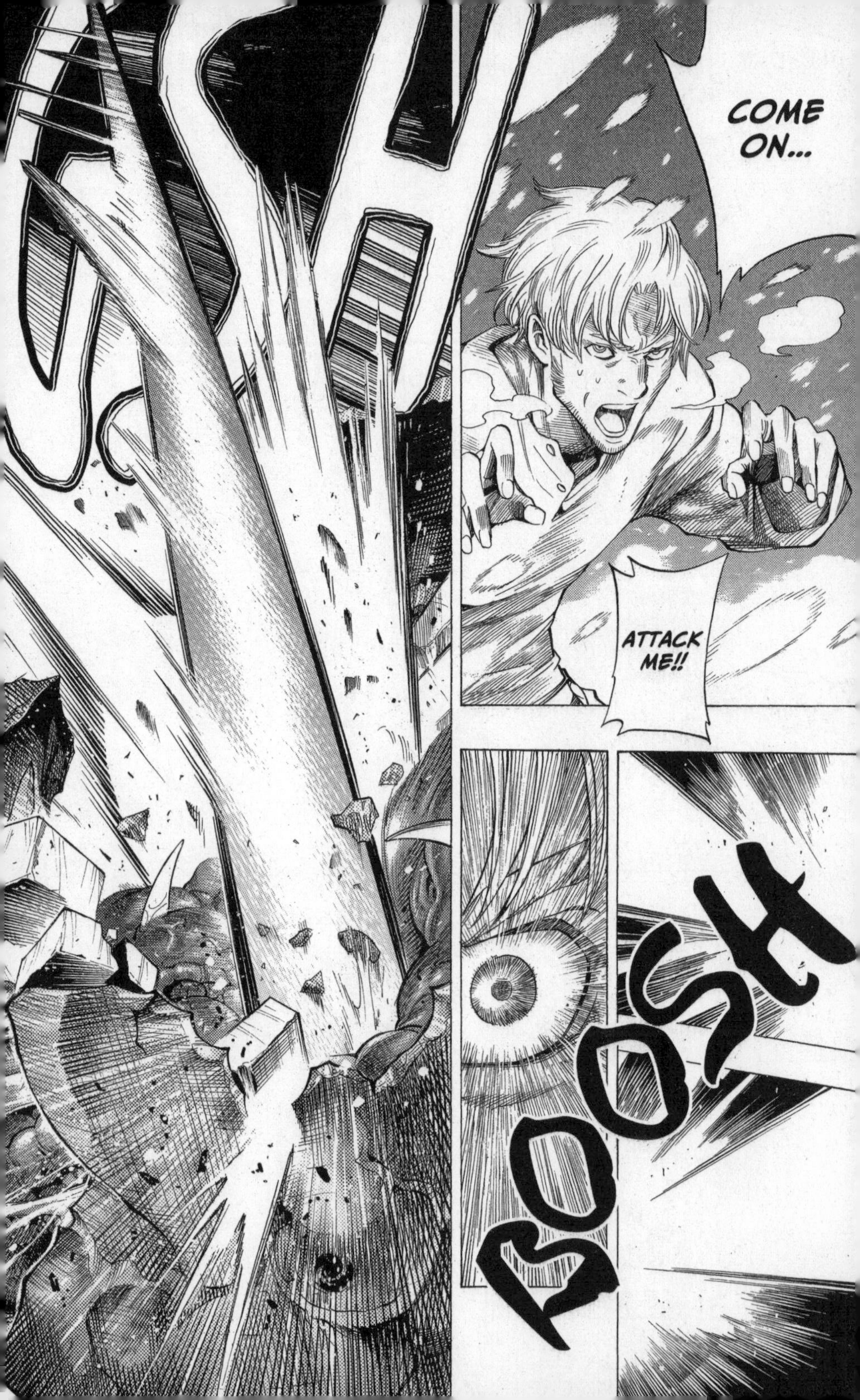
COME ON...
ATTACK ME!!
BOOSH

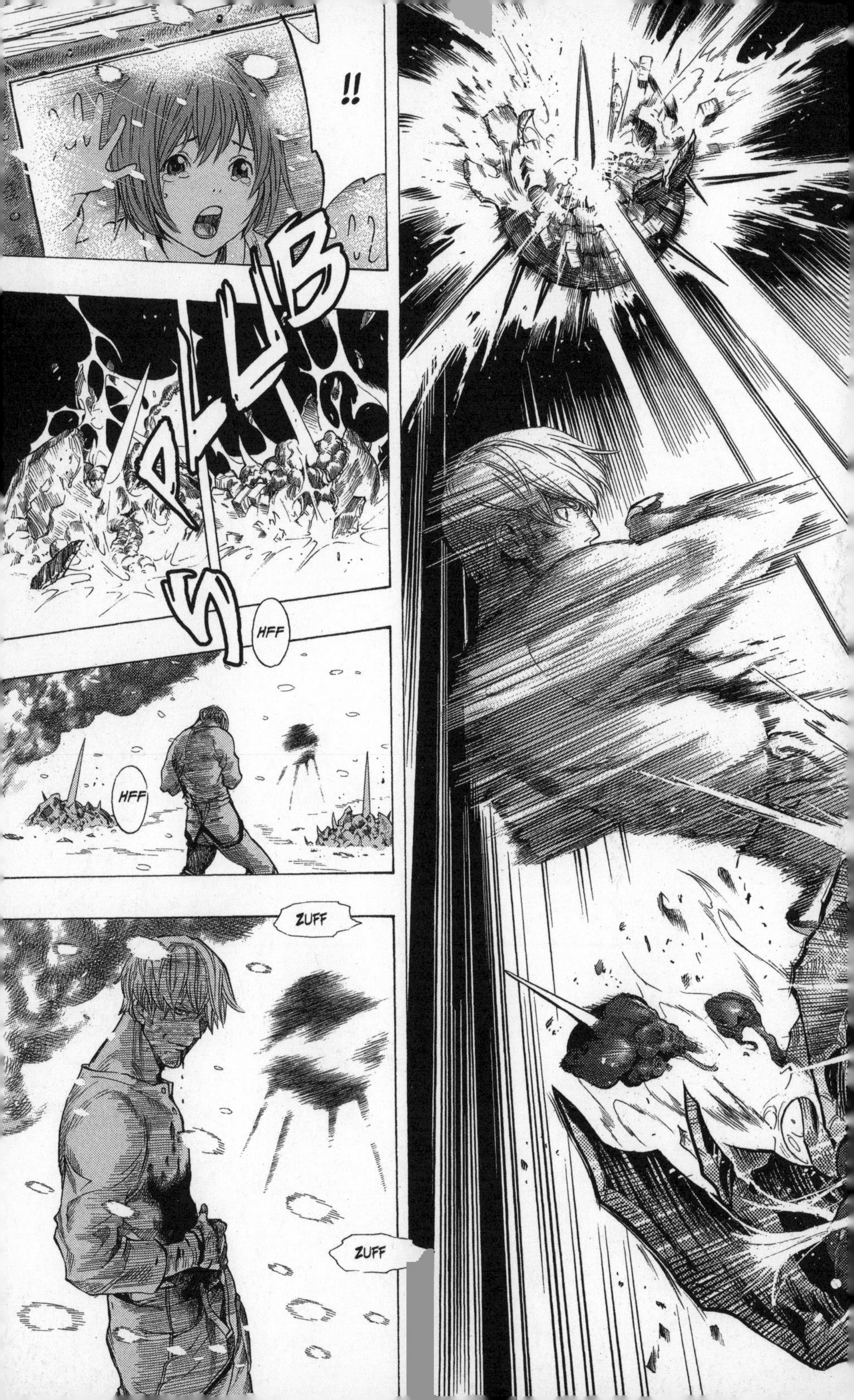
!!
SLUB
HFF
HFF
ZUFF
ZUFF

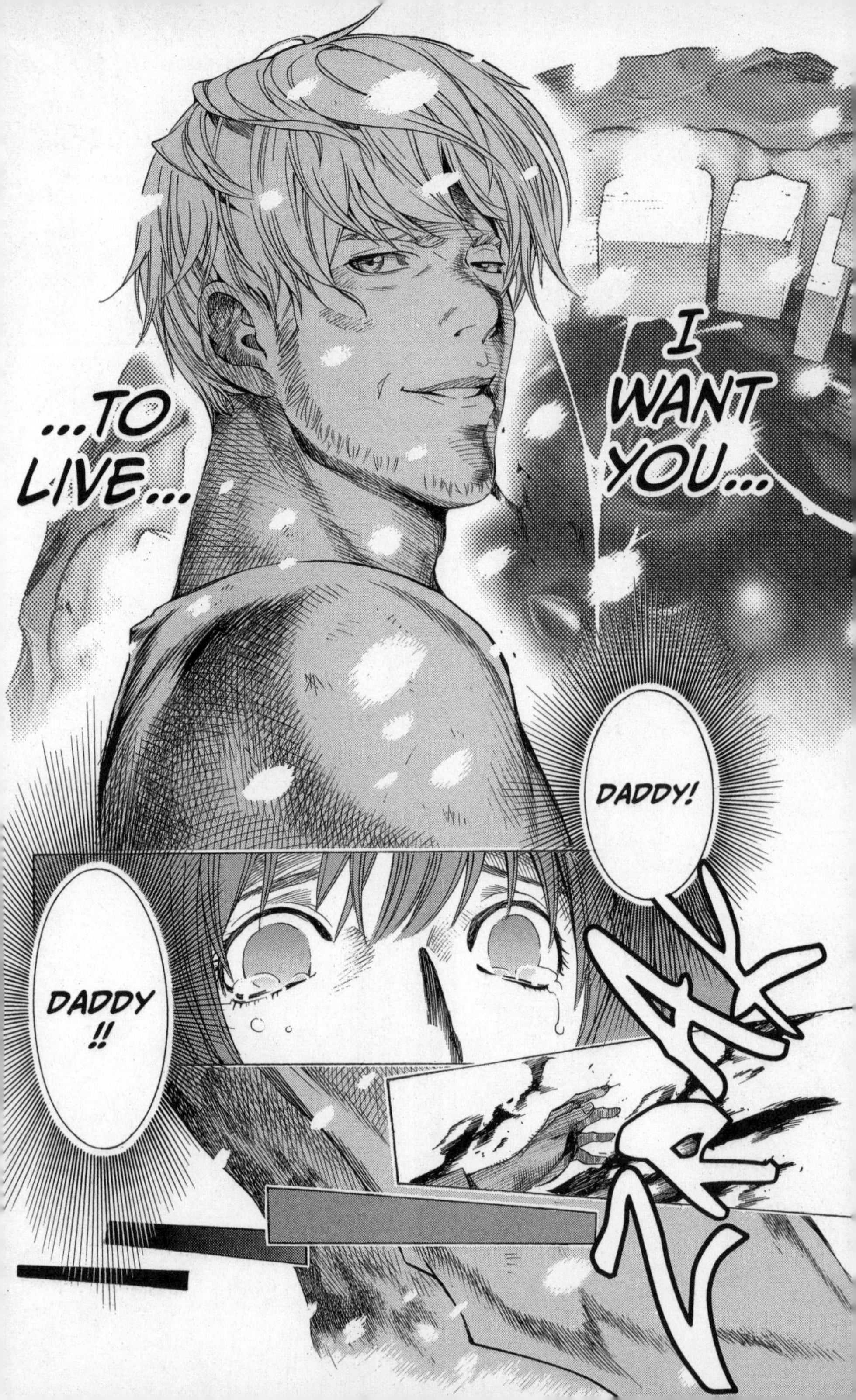
I WANT YOU...
...TO LIVE...
DADDY!
DADDY !!

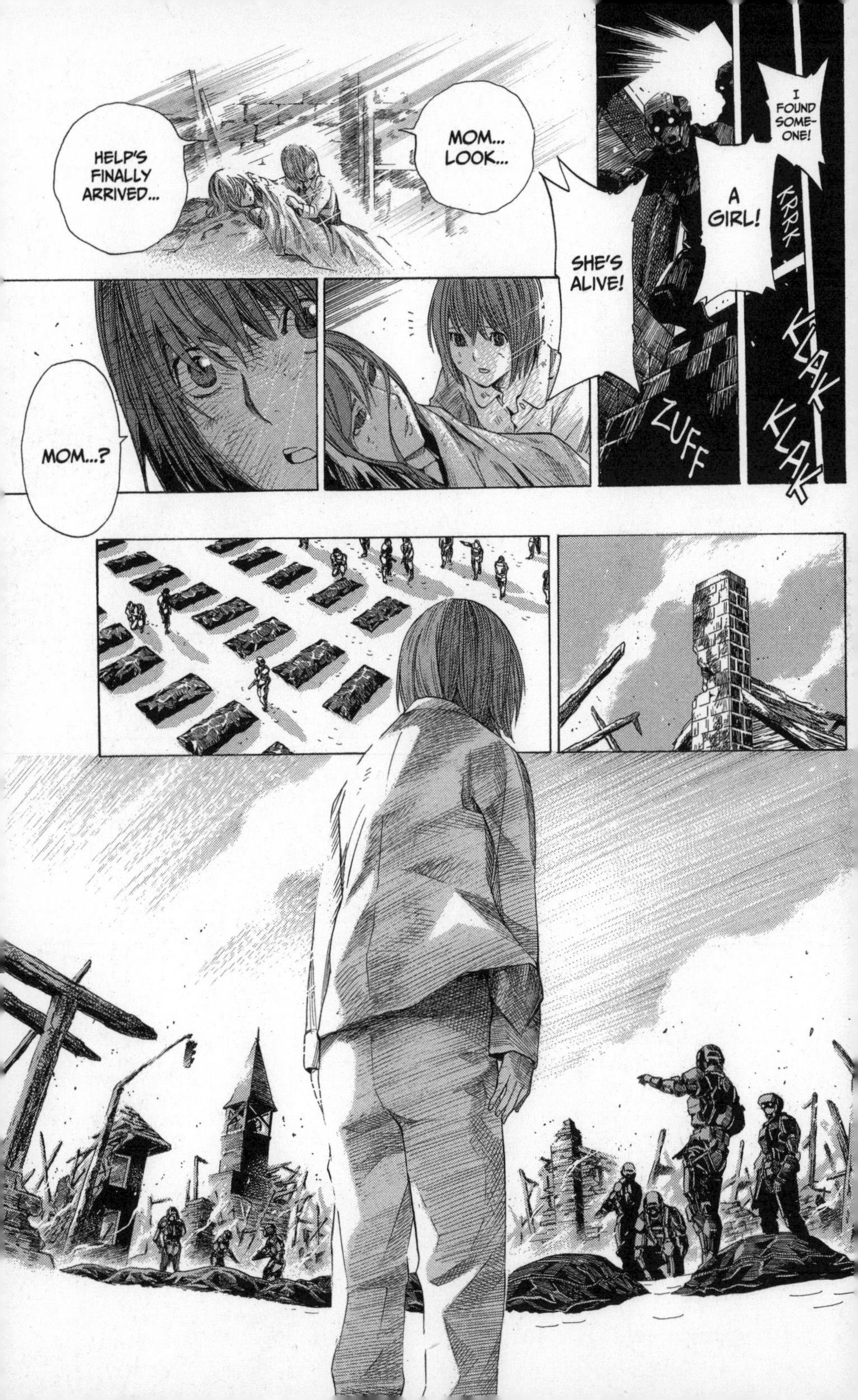
I FOUND SOME-ONE!
A GIRL!
SHE'S ALIVE!
KRRK
KLAK KLAK
ZUFF
MOM... LOOK...
HELP'S FINALLY ARRIVED...
MOM...?

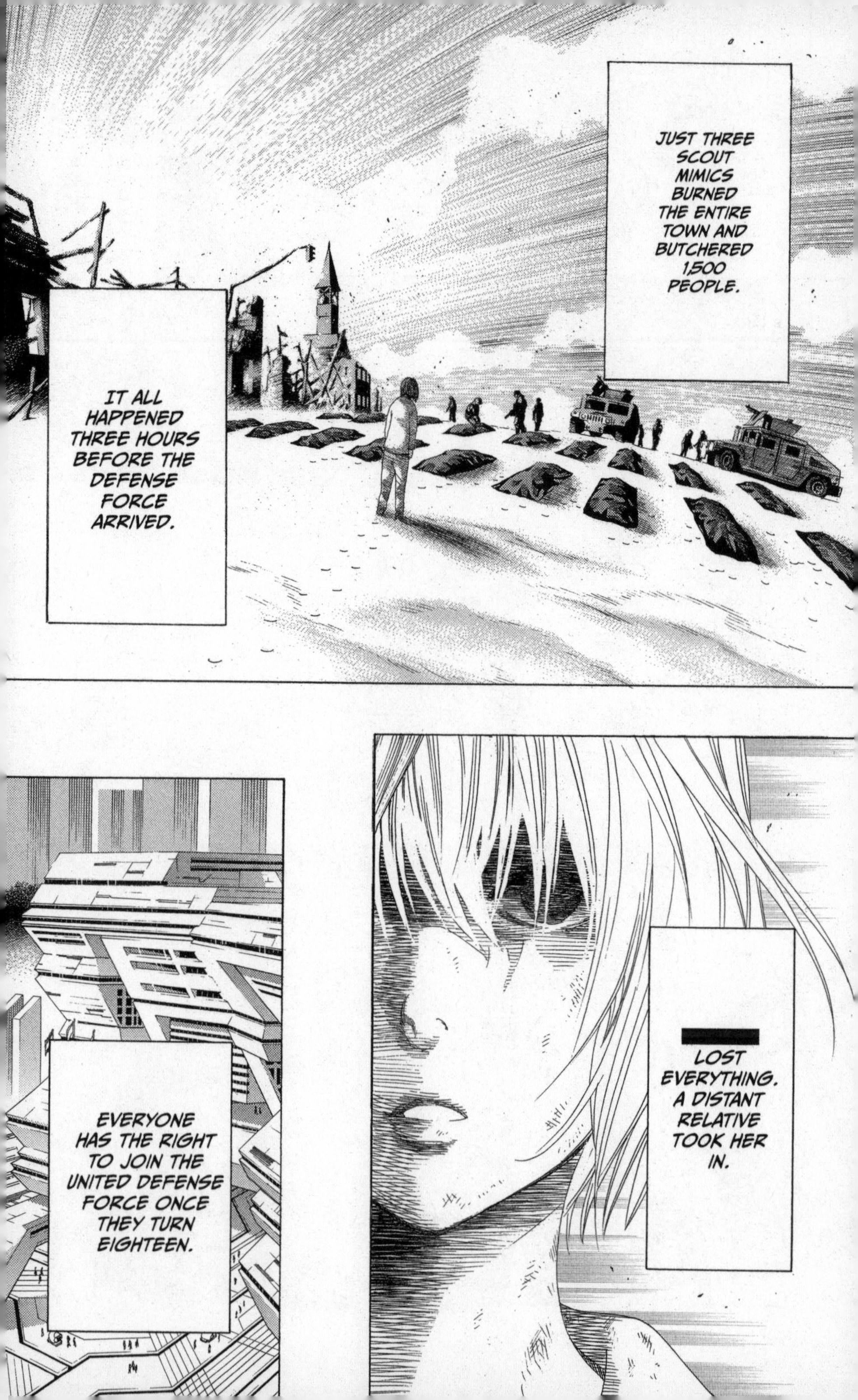
JUST THREE SCOUT MIMICS BURNED THE ENTIRE TOWN AND BUTCHERED 1,500 PEOPLE.
IT ALL HAPPENED THREE HOURS BEFORE THE DEFENSE FORCE ARRIVED.
[redacted] LOST EVERYTHING. A DISTANT RELATIVE TOOK HER IN.
EVERYONE HAS THE RIGHT TO JOIN THE UNITED DEFENSE FORCE ONCE THEY TURN EIGHTEEN.

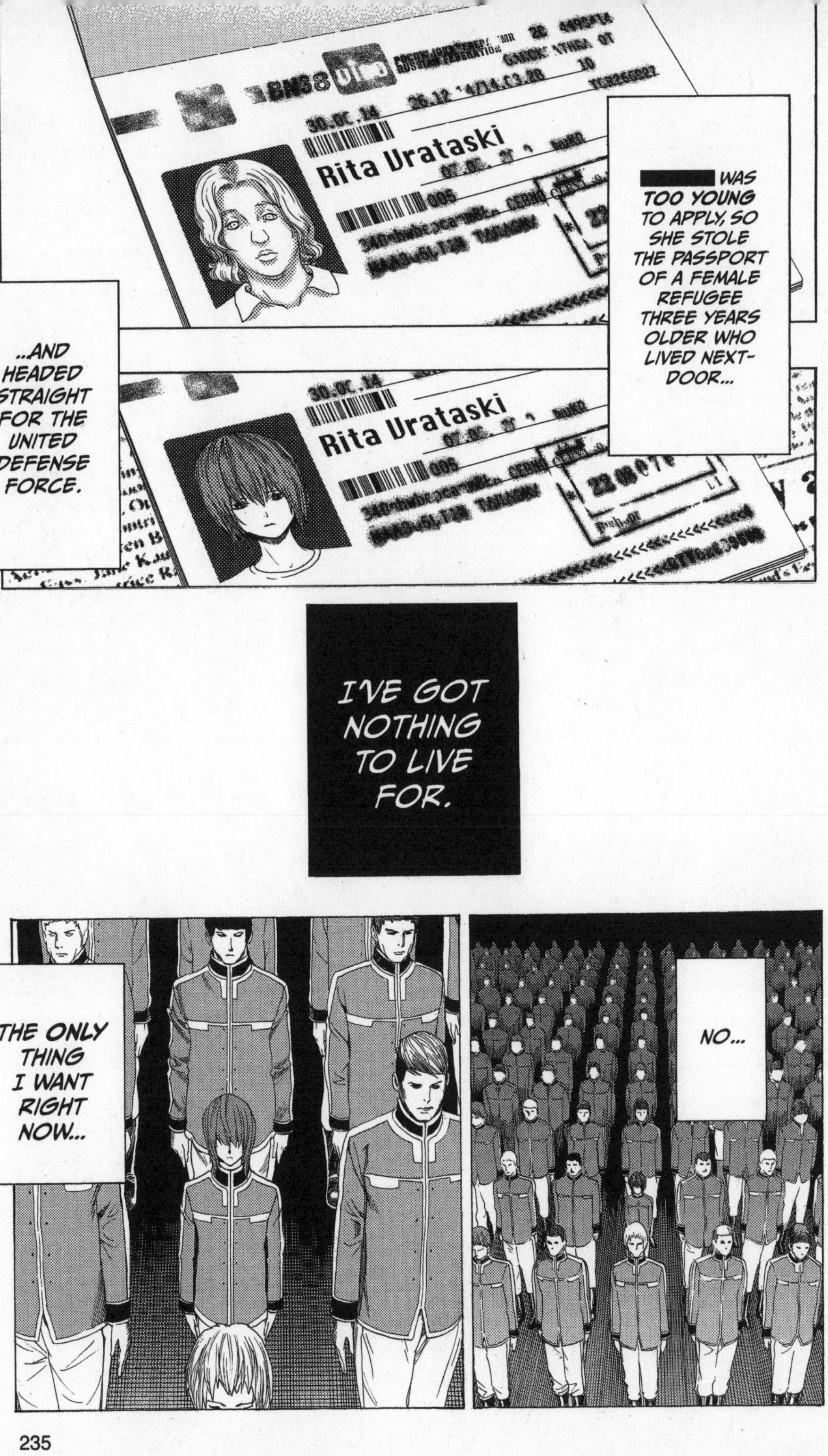
[redacted] WAS TOO YOUNG TO APPLY, SO SHE STOLE THE PASSPORT OF A FEMALE REFUGEE THREE YEARS OLDER WHO LIVED NEXT-DOOR...
Rita Vrataski
Rita Vrataski
...AND HEADED STRAIGHT FOR THE UNITED DEFENSE FORCE.
I'VE GOT NOTHING TO LIVE FOR.
NO...
THE ONLY THING I WANT RIGHT NOW...

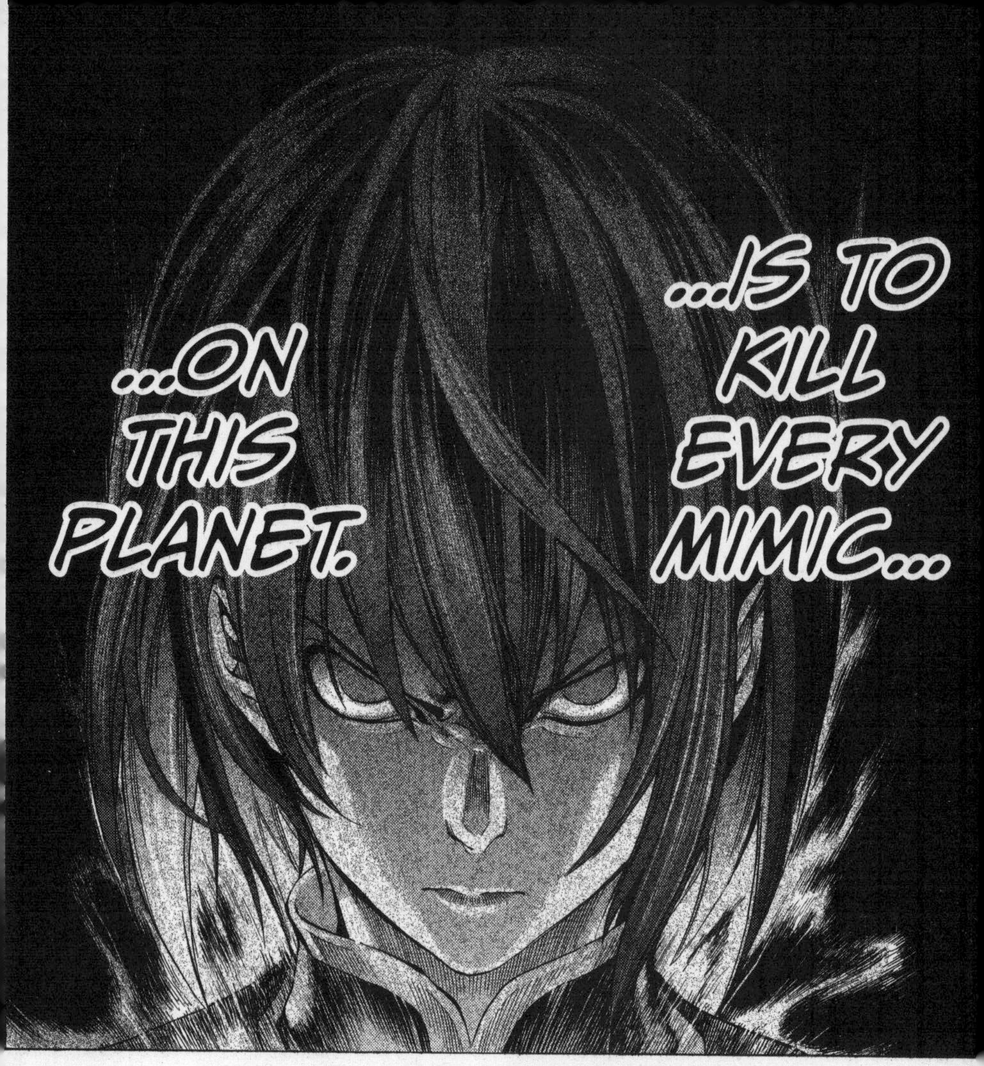
...IS TO KILL EVERY MIMIC...
...ON THIS PLANET.
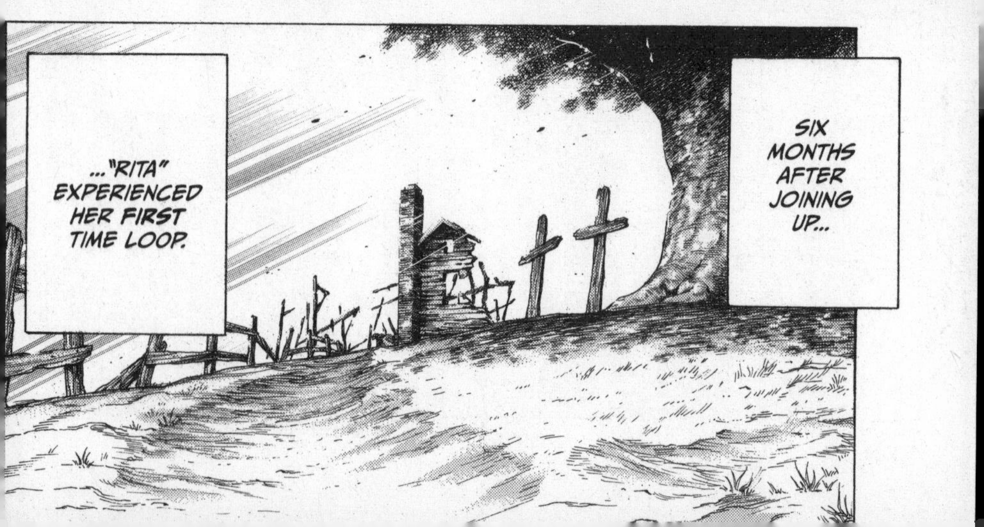
SIX MONTHS AFTER JOINING UP...
..."RITA" EXPERIENCED HER FIRST TIME LOOP.

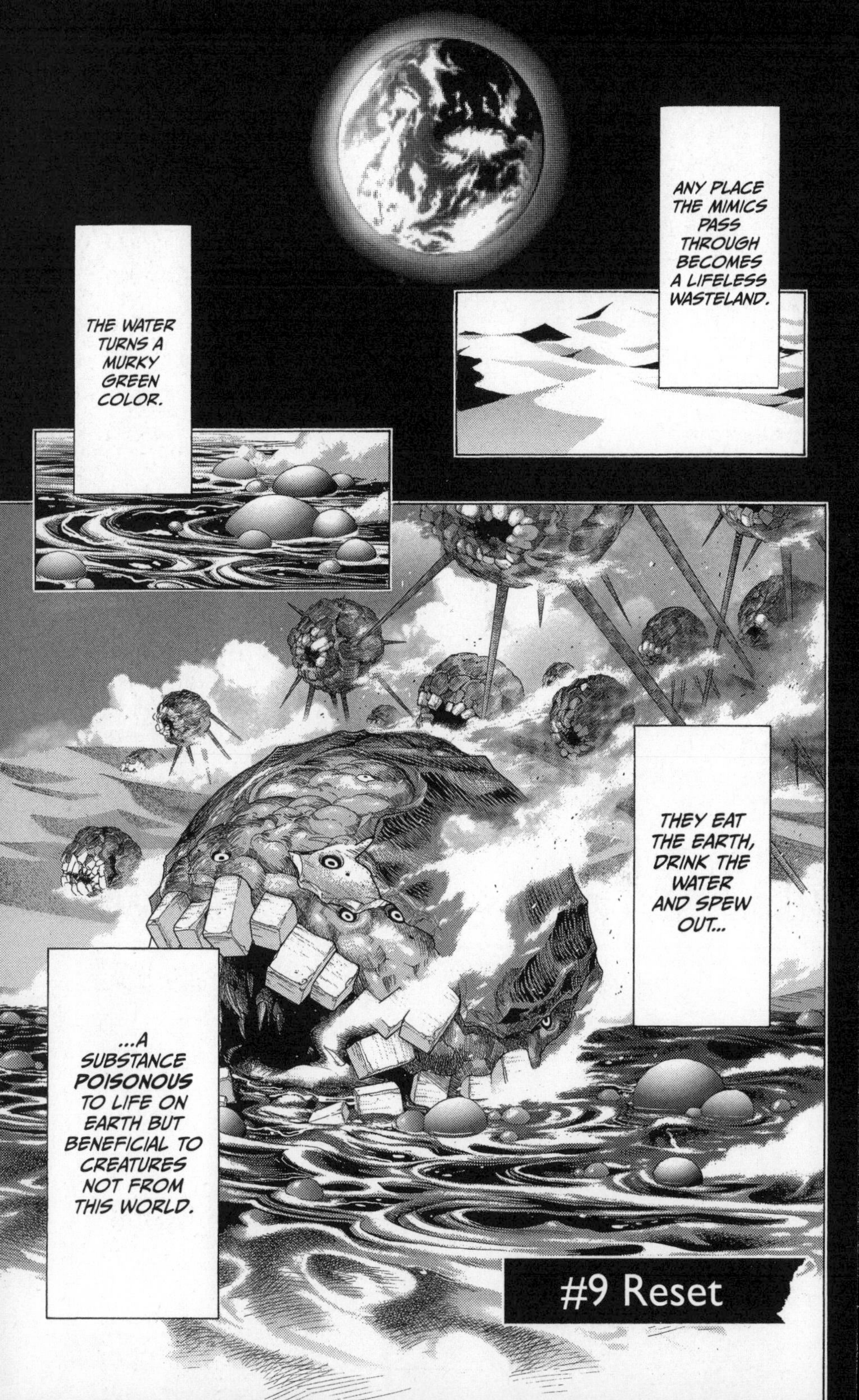
ANY PLACE THE MIMICS PASS THROUGH BECOMES A LIFELESS WASTELAND.
THE WATER TURNS A MURKY GREEN COLOR.
THEY EAT THE EARTH, DRINK THE WATER AND SPEW OUT...
...A SUBSTANCE **POISONOUS** TO LIFE ON EARTH BUT BENEFICIAL TO CREATURES NOT FROM THIS WORLD.
#9 Reset

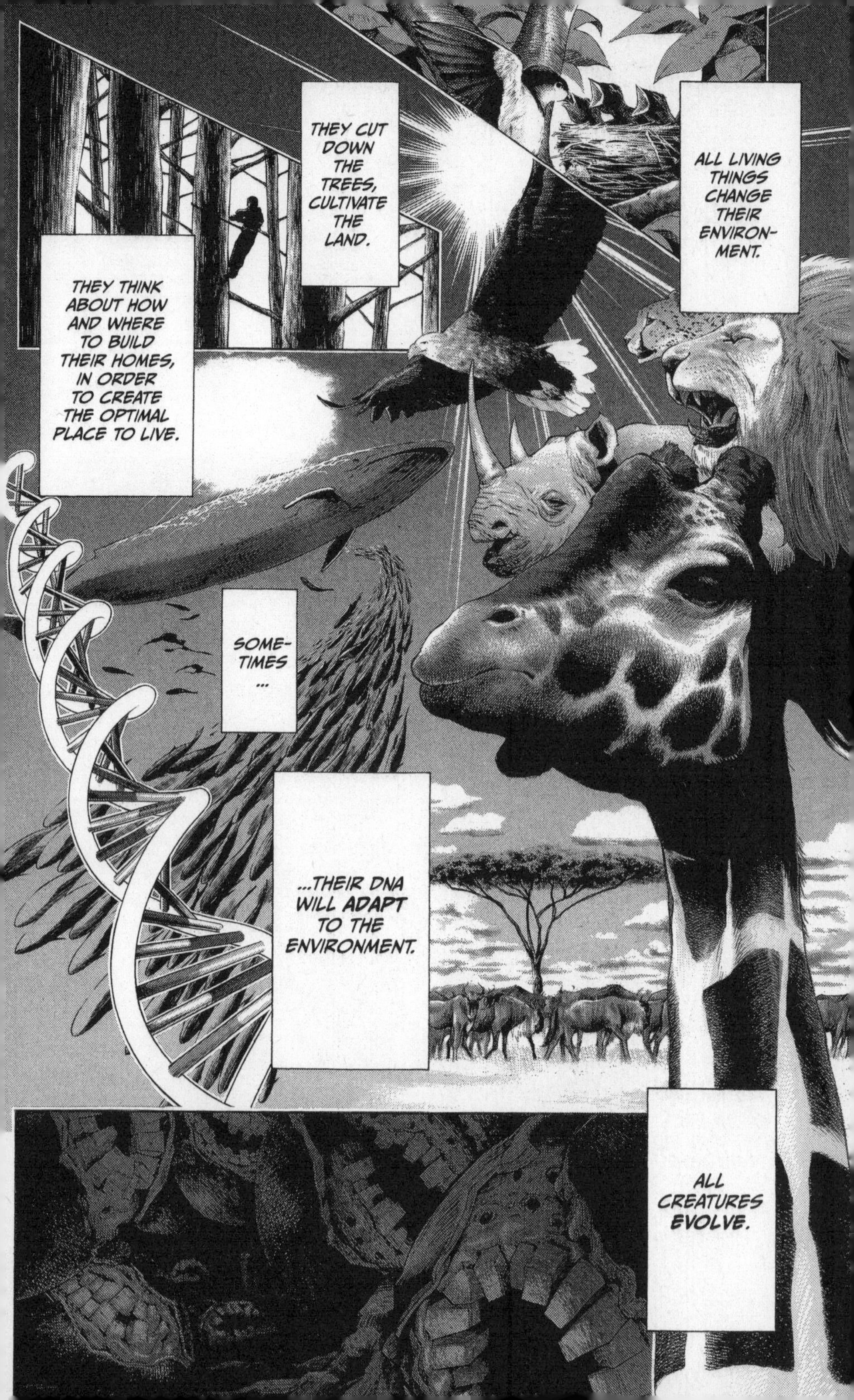
ALL LIVING THINGS CHANGE THEIR ENVIRONMENT.
THEY CUT DOWN THE TREES, CULTIVATE THE LAND.
THEY THINK ABOUT HOW AND WHERE TO BUILD THEIR HOMES, IN ORDER TO CREATE THE OPTIMAL PLACE TO LIVE.
SOMETIMES...
...THEIR DNA WILL ADAPT TO THE ENVIRONMENT.
ALL CREATURES EVOLVE.

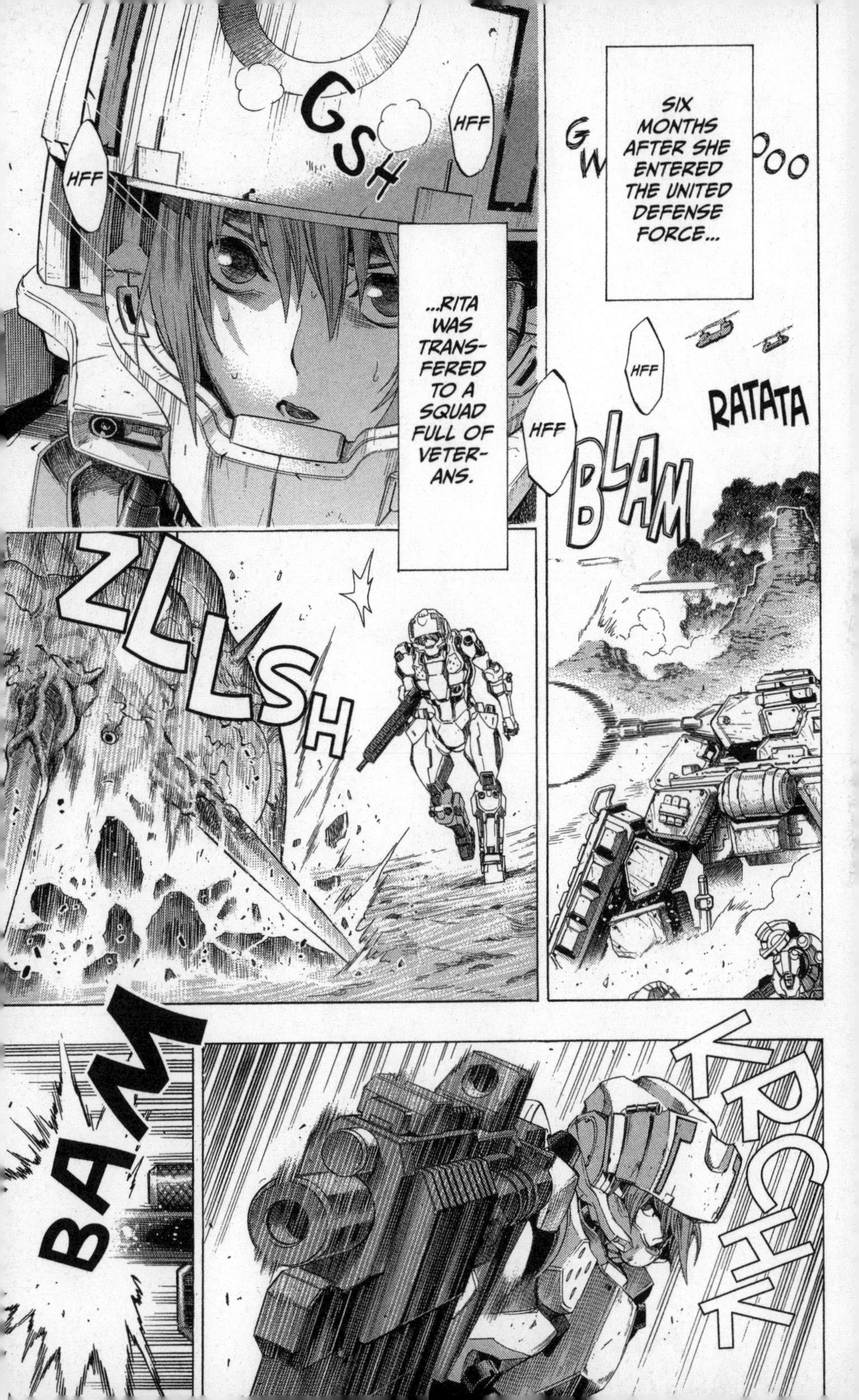
SIX MONTHS AFTER SHE ENTERED THE UNITED DEFENSE FORCE...
GW
OOO
HFF
HFF
RATATA
BLAM
GSH
HFF
HFF
...RITA WAS TRANS-FERED TO A SQUAD FULL OF VETER-ANS.
ZZLLSH
KRCHK
BAM

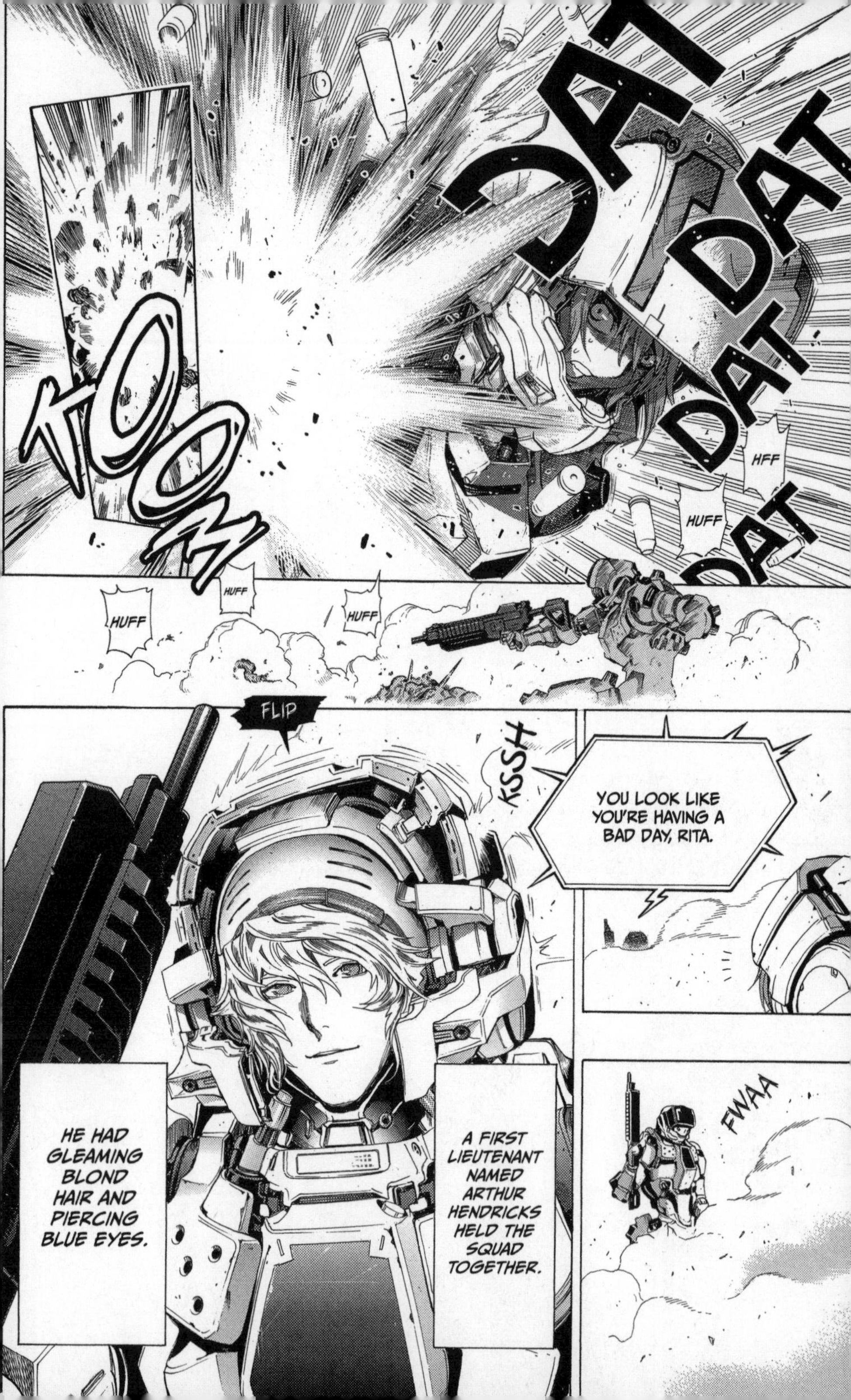
DAT DAT DAT DAT
HFF
HUFF
TOOM
HUFF
HUFF
HUFF
YOU LOOK LIKE YOU'RE HAVING A BAD DAY, RITA.
FWAA
KSSH
FLIP
A FIRST LIEUTENANT NAMED ARTHUR HENDRICKS HELD THE SQUAD TOGETHER.
HE HAD GLEAMING BLOND HAIR AND PIERCING BLUE EYES.

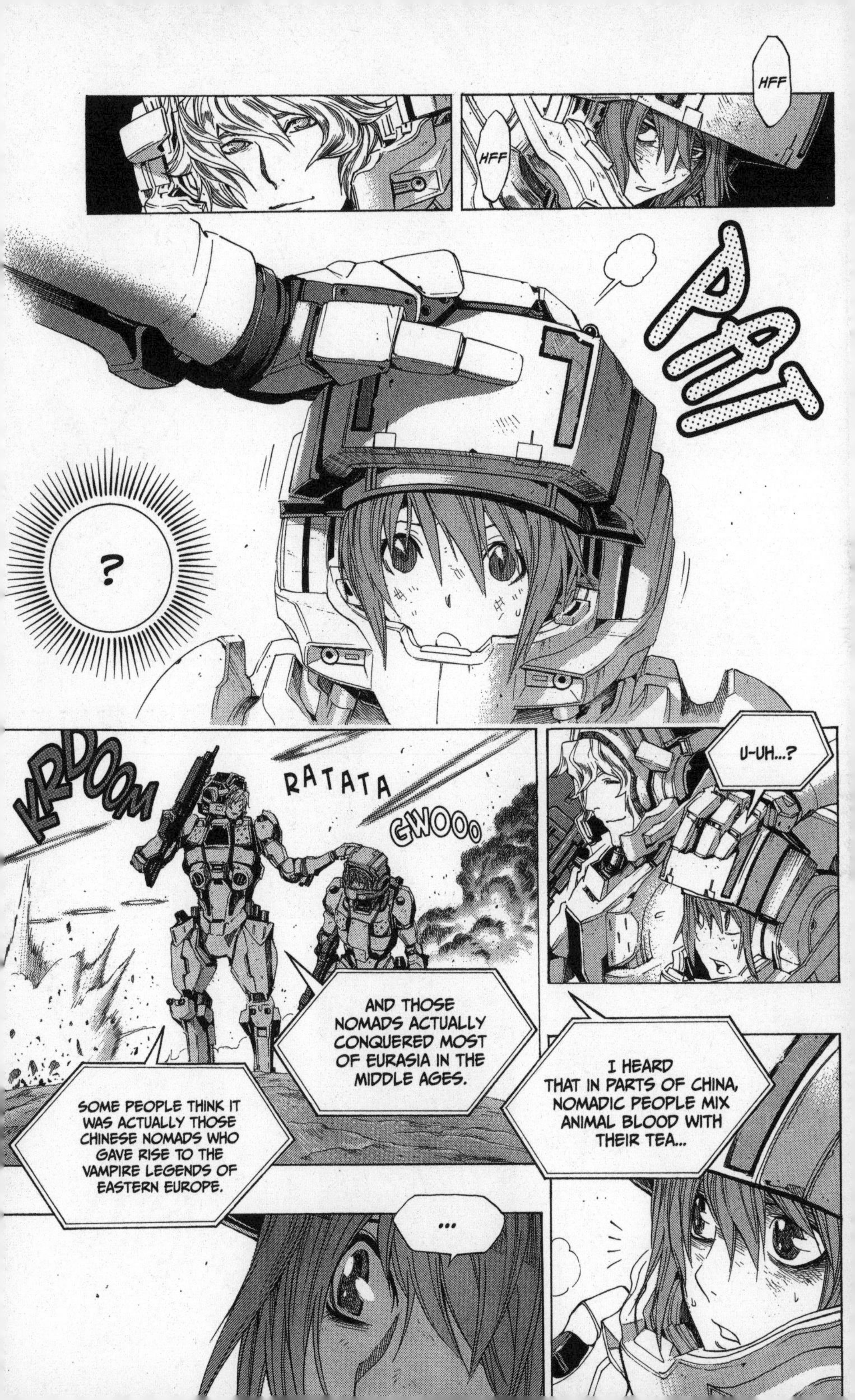
HFF
HFF
PAT
?
U-UH...?
KRDOOM
RATATA
GWOOO
I HEARD THAT IN PARTS OF CHINA, NOMADIC PEOPLE MIX ANIMAL BLOOD WITH THEIR TEA...
AND THOSE NOMADS ACTUALLY CONQUERED MOST OF EURASIA IN THE MIDDLE AGES.
SOME PEOPLE THINK IT WAS ACTUALLY THOSE CHINESE NOMADS WHO GAVE RISE TO THE VAMPIRE LEGENDS OF EASTERN EUROPE.
...

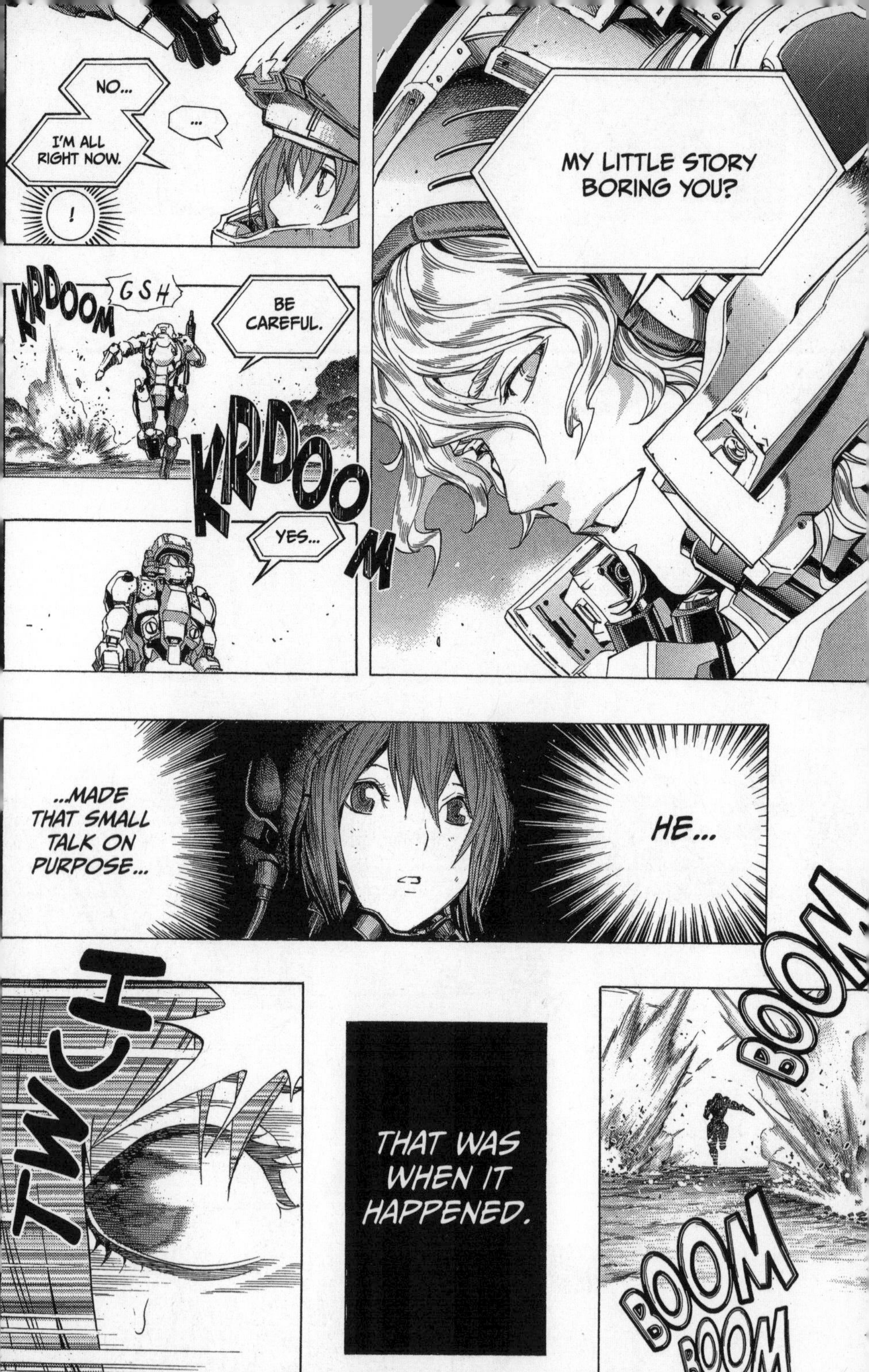
MY LITTLE STORY BORING YOU?
...
NO... I'M ALL RIGHT NOW.
!
GSH
KRDOOM
BE CAREFUL.
KRDOOM
YES...
HE...
...MADE THAT SMALL TALK ON PURPOSE...
BOOM
BOOM
BOOM
THAT WAS WHEN IT HAPPENED.
TWCH

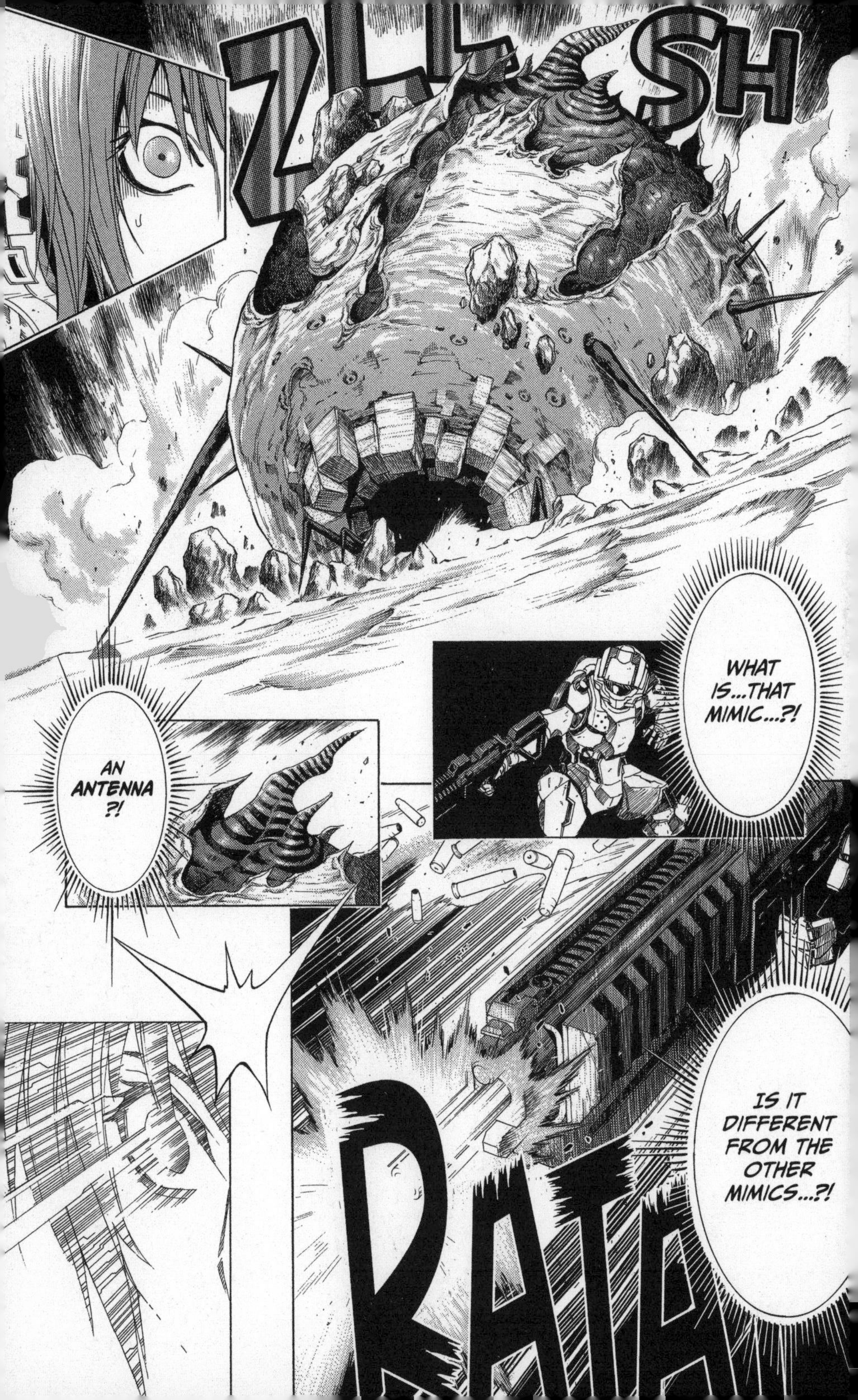
ZLLSH
WHAT IS...THAT MIMIC...?!
AN ANTENNA ?!
IS IT DIFFERENT FROM THE OTHER MIMICS...?!
RATA

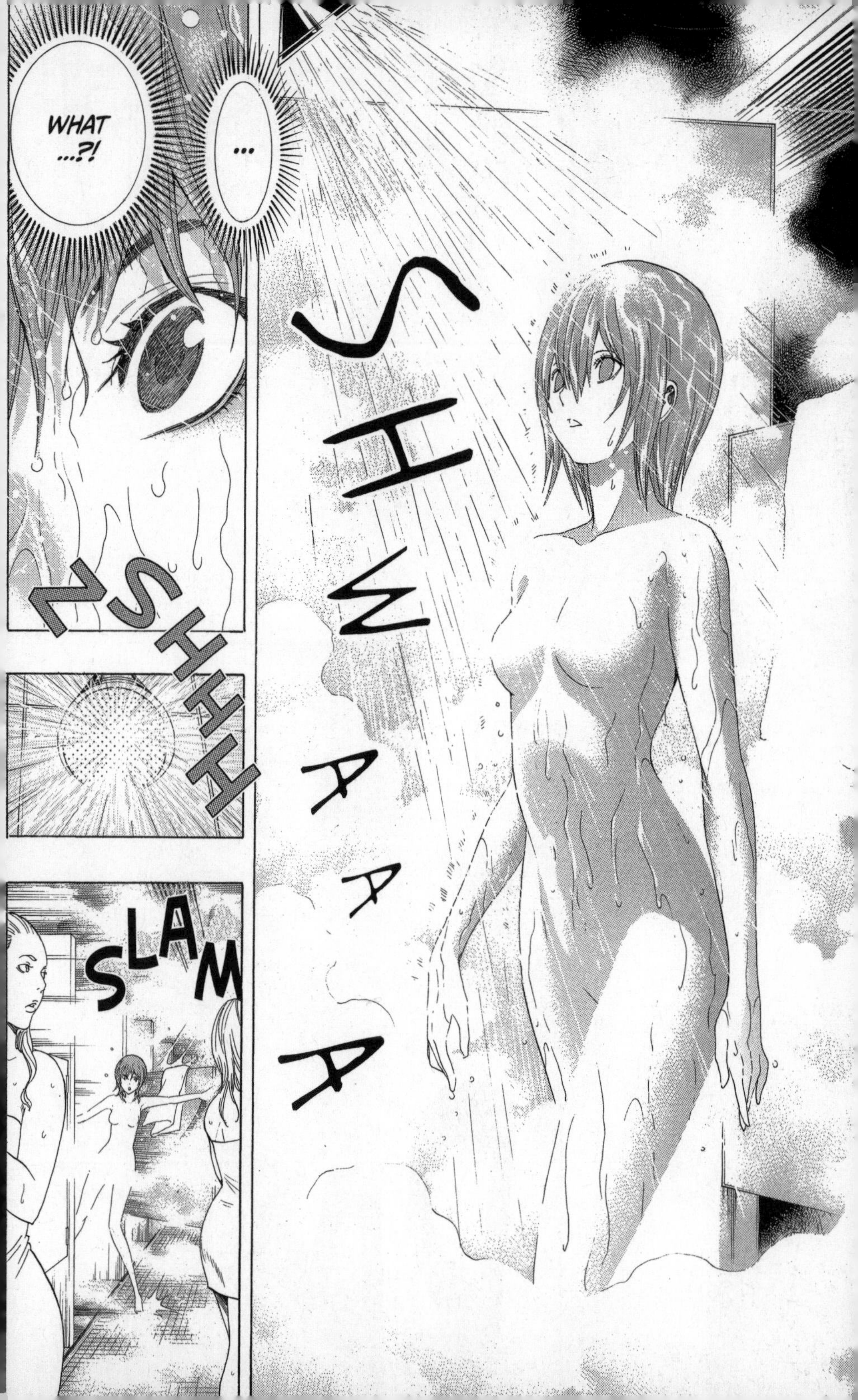
SHWAAAA
...
WHAT ...?!
ZSHHHH
SLAM

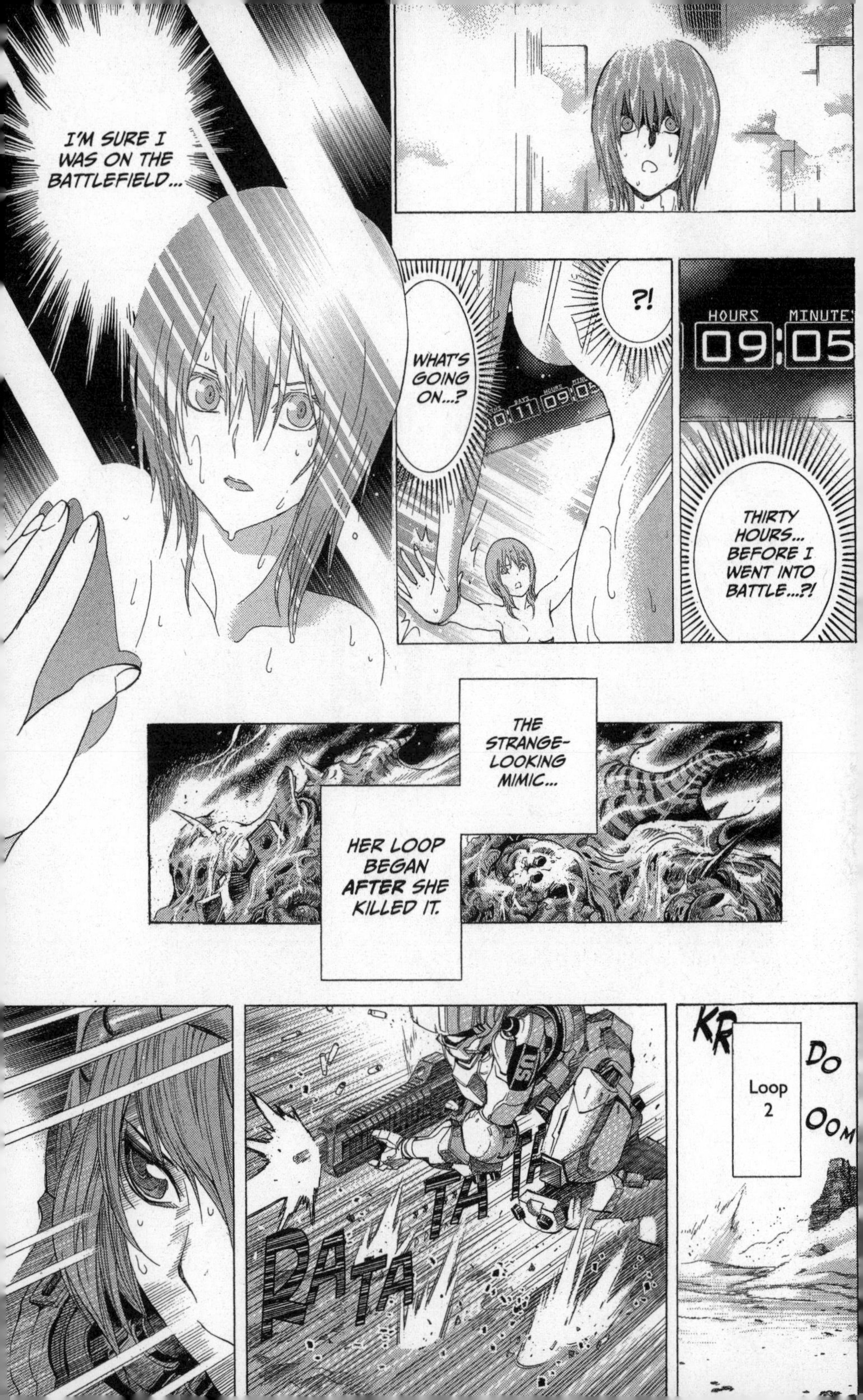
HOURS MINUTE
09:05
THIRTY HOURS... BEFORE I WENT INTO BATTLE...?!
?!
WHAT'S GOING ON...?
I'M SURE I WAS ON THE BATTLEFIELD...
THE STRANGE-LOOKING MIMIC...
HER LOOP BEGAN AFTER SHE KILLED IT.
KR
DOOOM
Loop 2
RATATATA

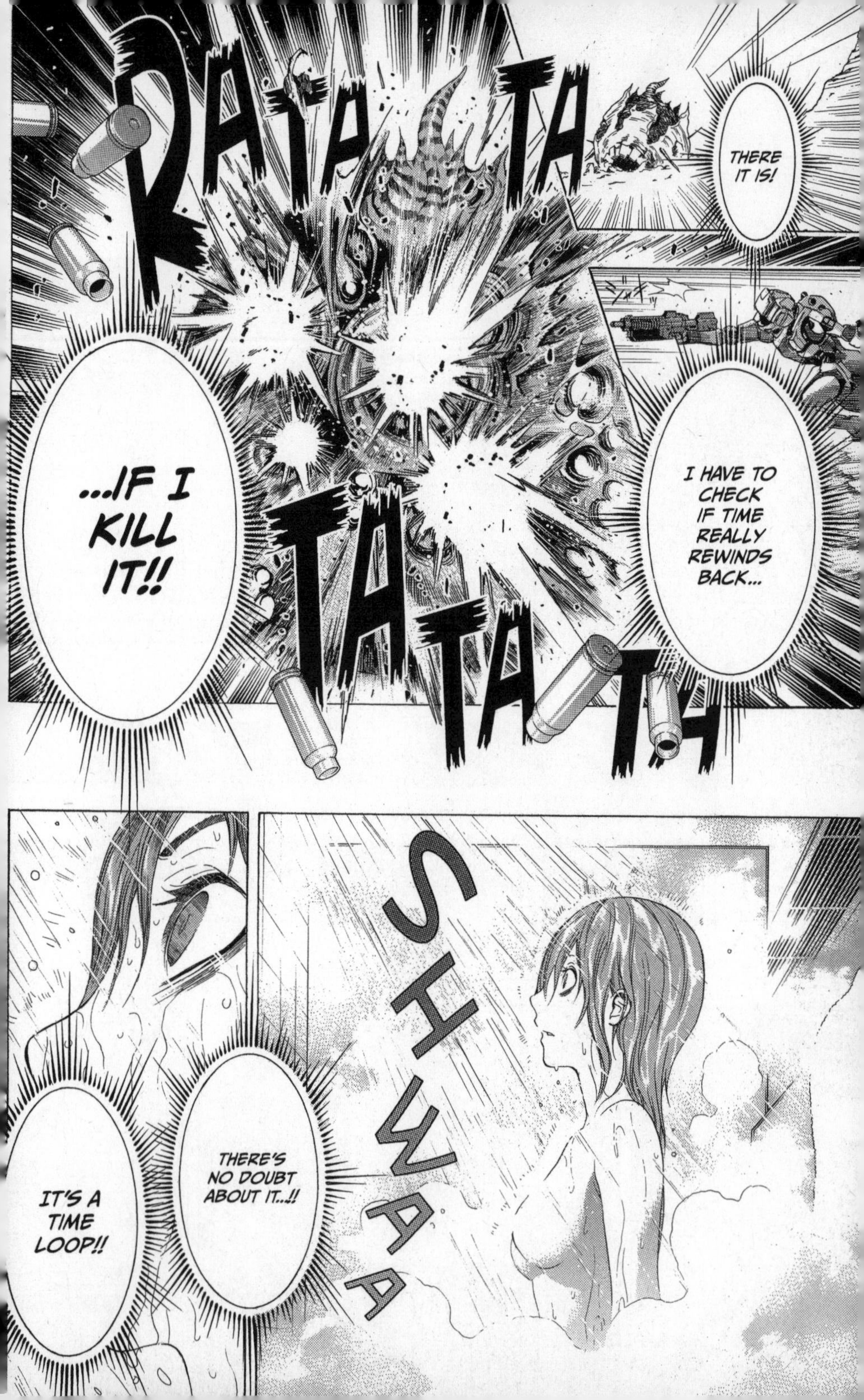
THERE IT IS!
I HAVE TO CHECK IF TIME REALLY REWINDS BACK...
...IF I KILL IT!!
RATATA TA
TA TA TA TA
SHWAA
THERE'S NO DOUBT ABOUT IT..!!
IT'S A TIME LOOP!!

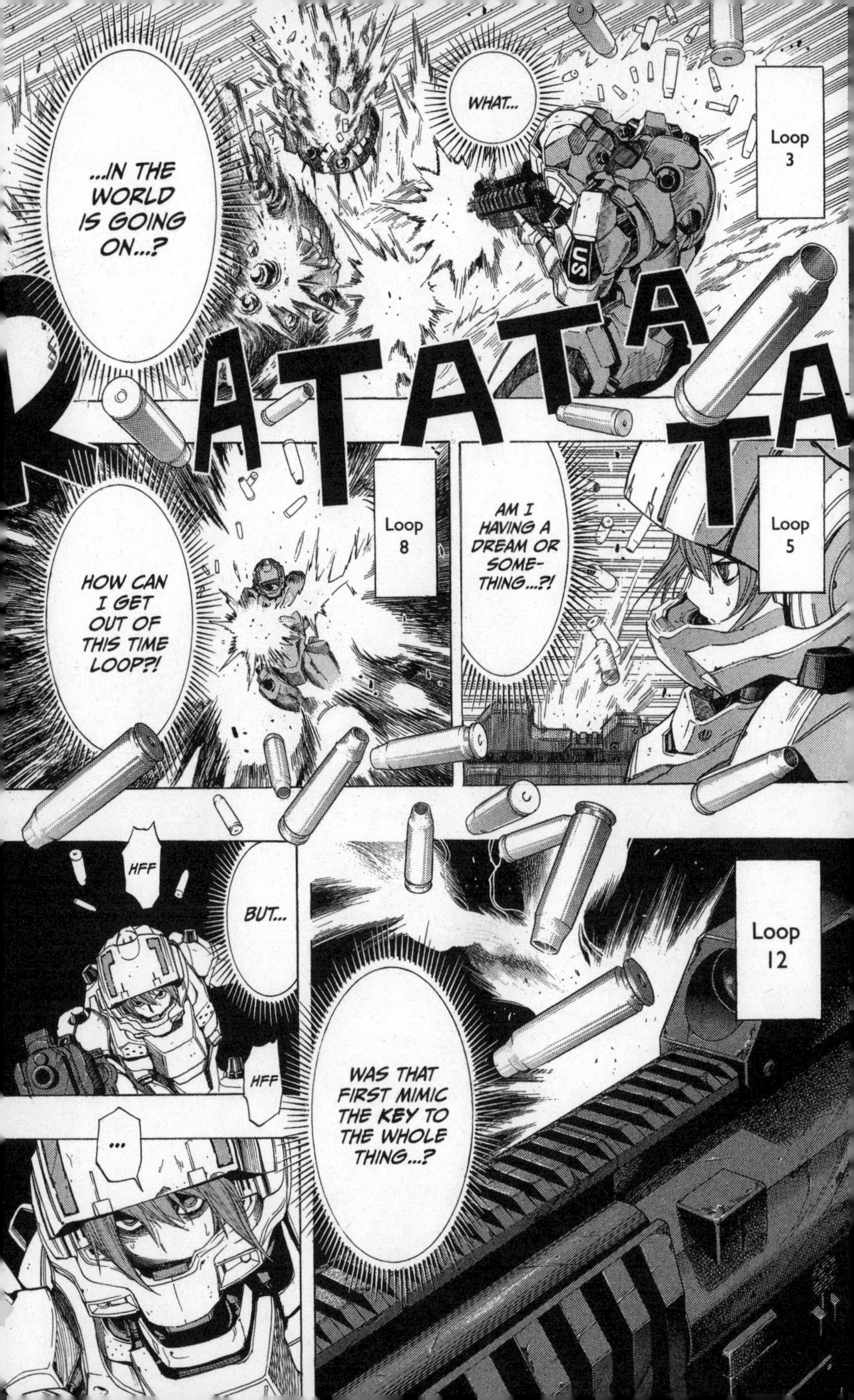
Loop 3
WHAT...
...IN THE WORLD IS GOING ON...?
RATATATA
Loop 5
AM I HAVING A DREAM OR SOME-THING...?!
Loop 8
HOW CAN I GET OUT OF THIS TIME LOOP?!
Loop 12
WAS THAT FIRST MIMIC THE KEY TO THE WHOLE THING...?
BUT...
HFF
HFF
...

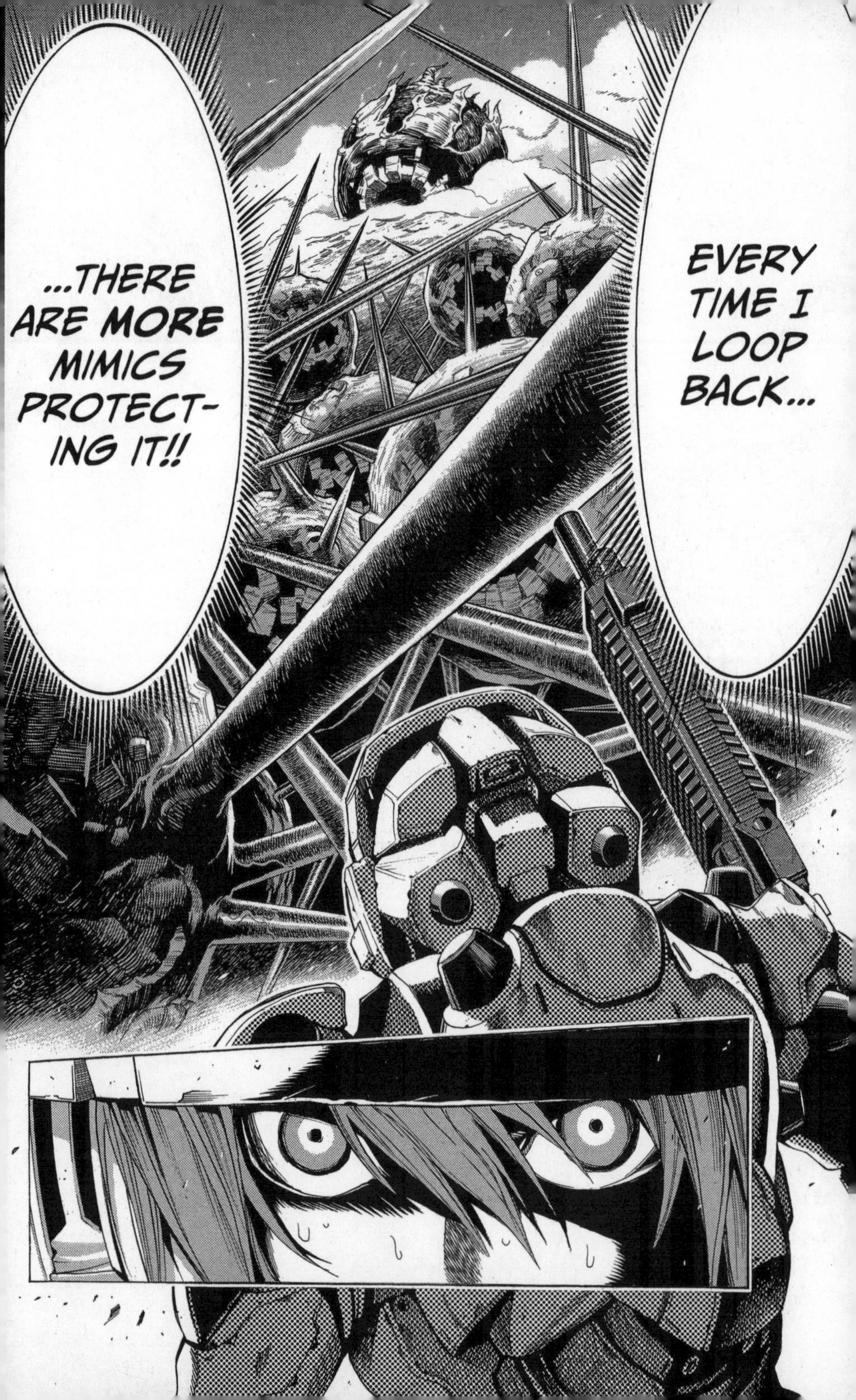
EVERY TIME I LOOP BACK...
...THERE ARE MORE MIMICS PROTECT-ING IT!!

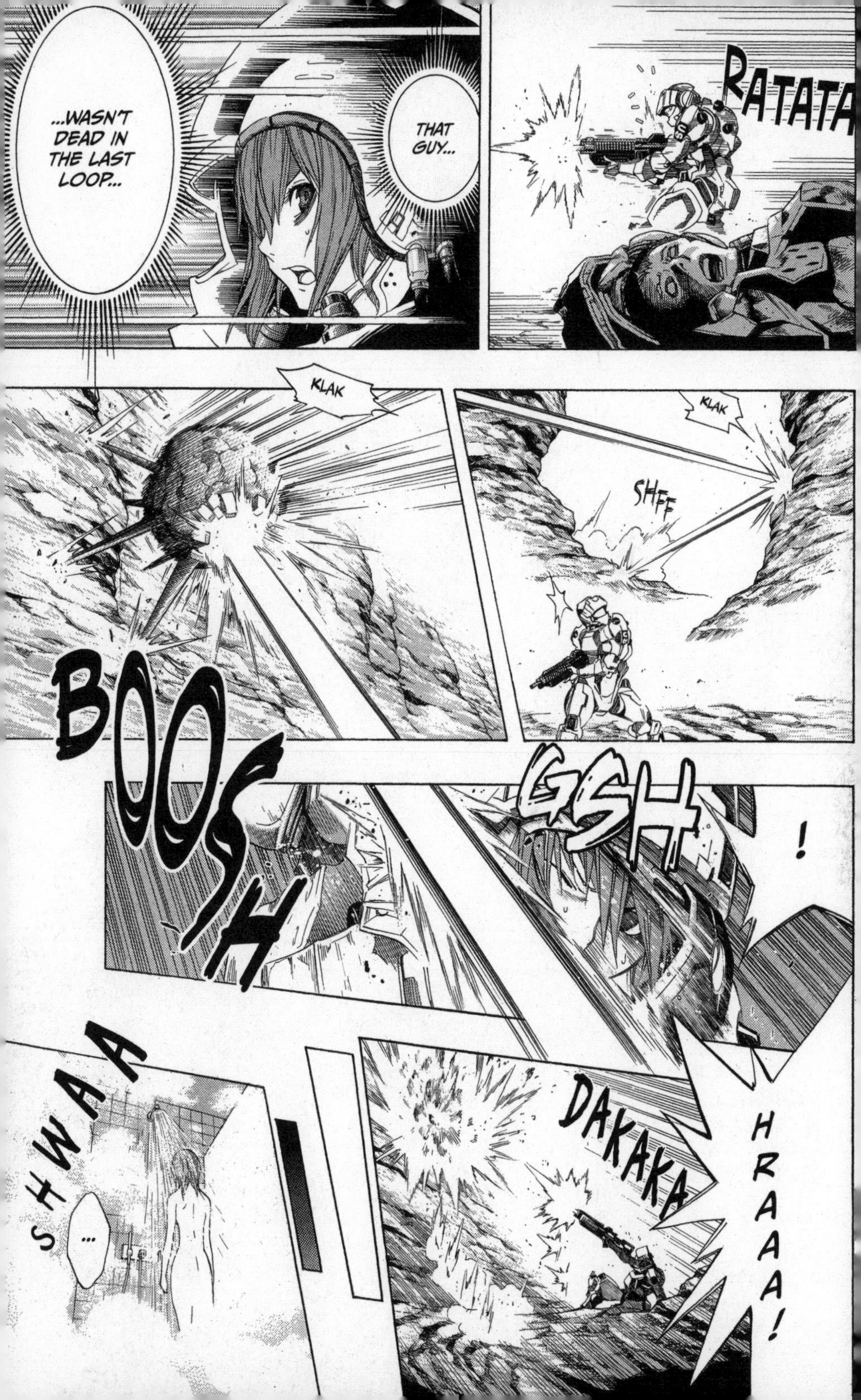
RATATA
THAT GUY...
...WASN'T DEAD IN THE LAST LOOP...
KLAK
SHFF
KLAK
BOOSH
GSH
!
HRAAA!
DAKAKA
SHWAA
...

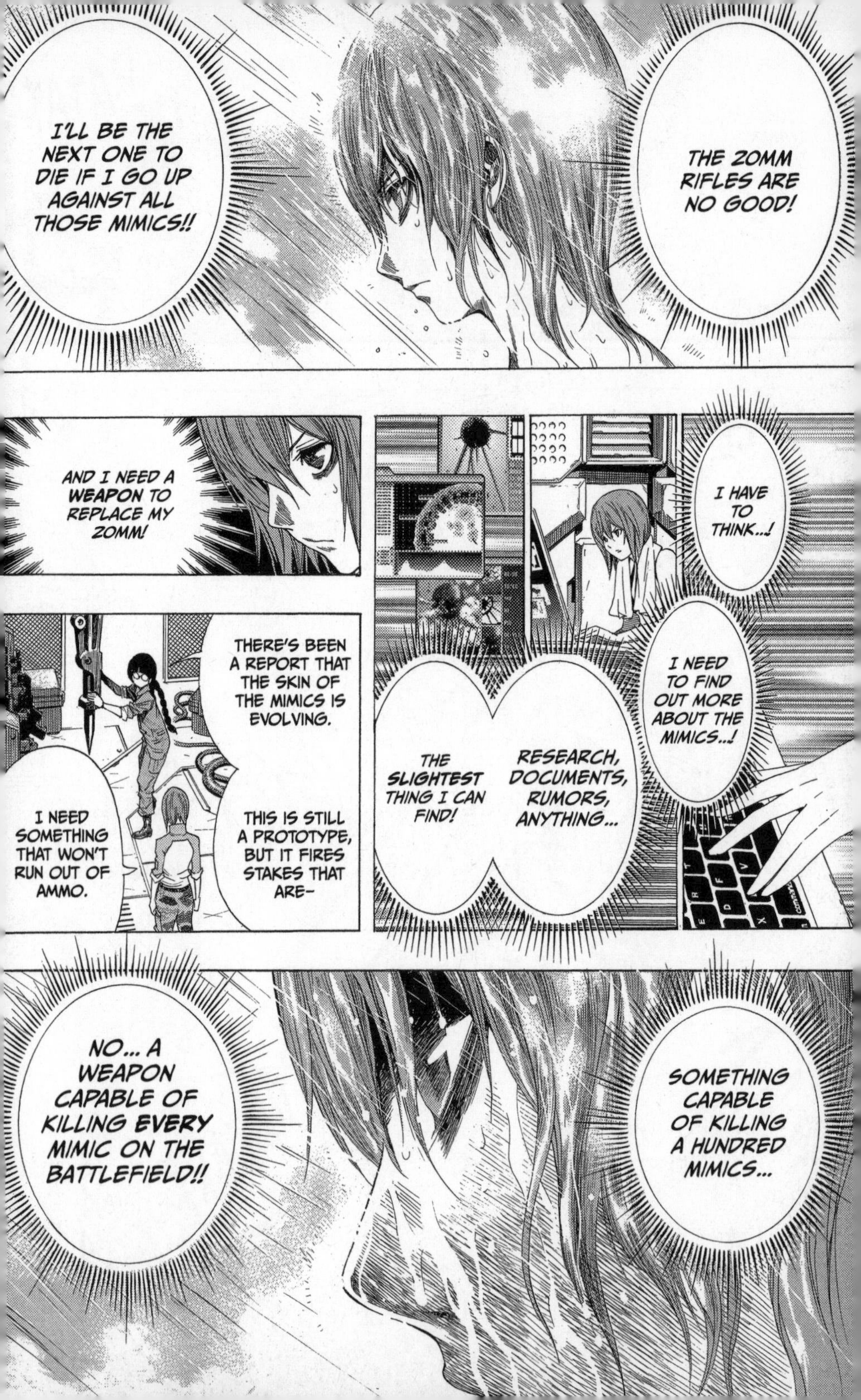
THE ZOMM RIFLES ARE NO GOOD!
I'LL BE THE NEXT ONE TO DIE IF I GO UP AGAINST ALL THOSE MIMICS!!
I HAVE TO THINK...!
I NEED TO FIND OUT MORE ABOUT THE MIMICS...!
RESEARCH, DOCUMENTS, RUMORS, ANYTHING...
THE SLIGHTEST THING I CAN FIND!
AND I NEED A WEAPON TO REPLACE MY ZOMM!
THERE'S BEEN A REPORT THAT THE SKIN OF THE MIMICS IS EVOLVING.
THIS IS STILL A PROTOTYPE, BUT IT FIRES STAKES THAT ARE-
I NEED SOMETHING THAT WON'T RUN OUT OF AMMO.
SOMETHING CAPABLE OF KILLING A HUNDRED MIMICS...
NO... A WEAPON CAPABLE OF KILLING EVERY MIMIC ON THE BATTLEFIELD!!

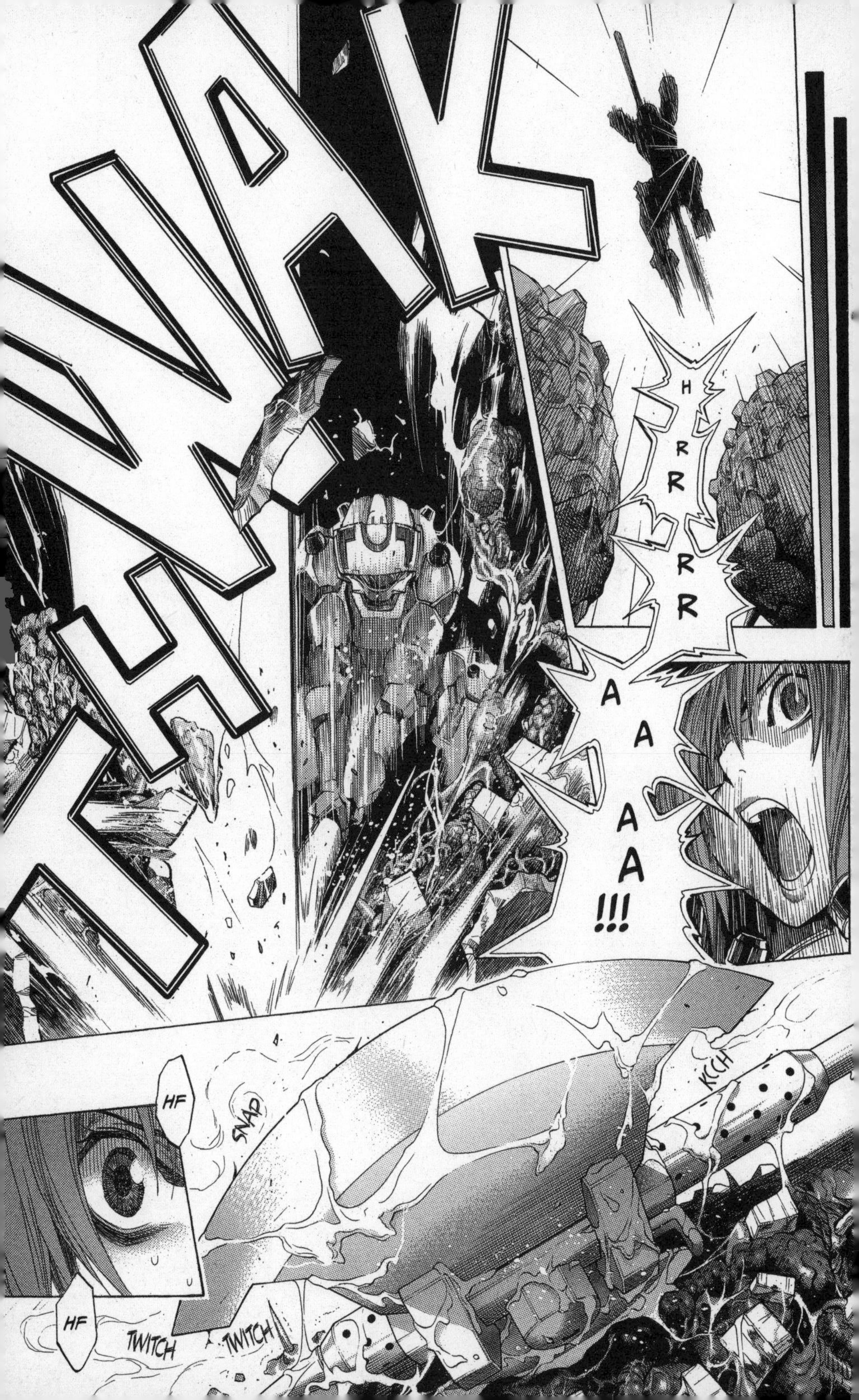
HRRRRR
THWAK
AAAA!!!
KCCH
HF
SNAP
HF
TWITCH
TWITCH

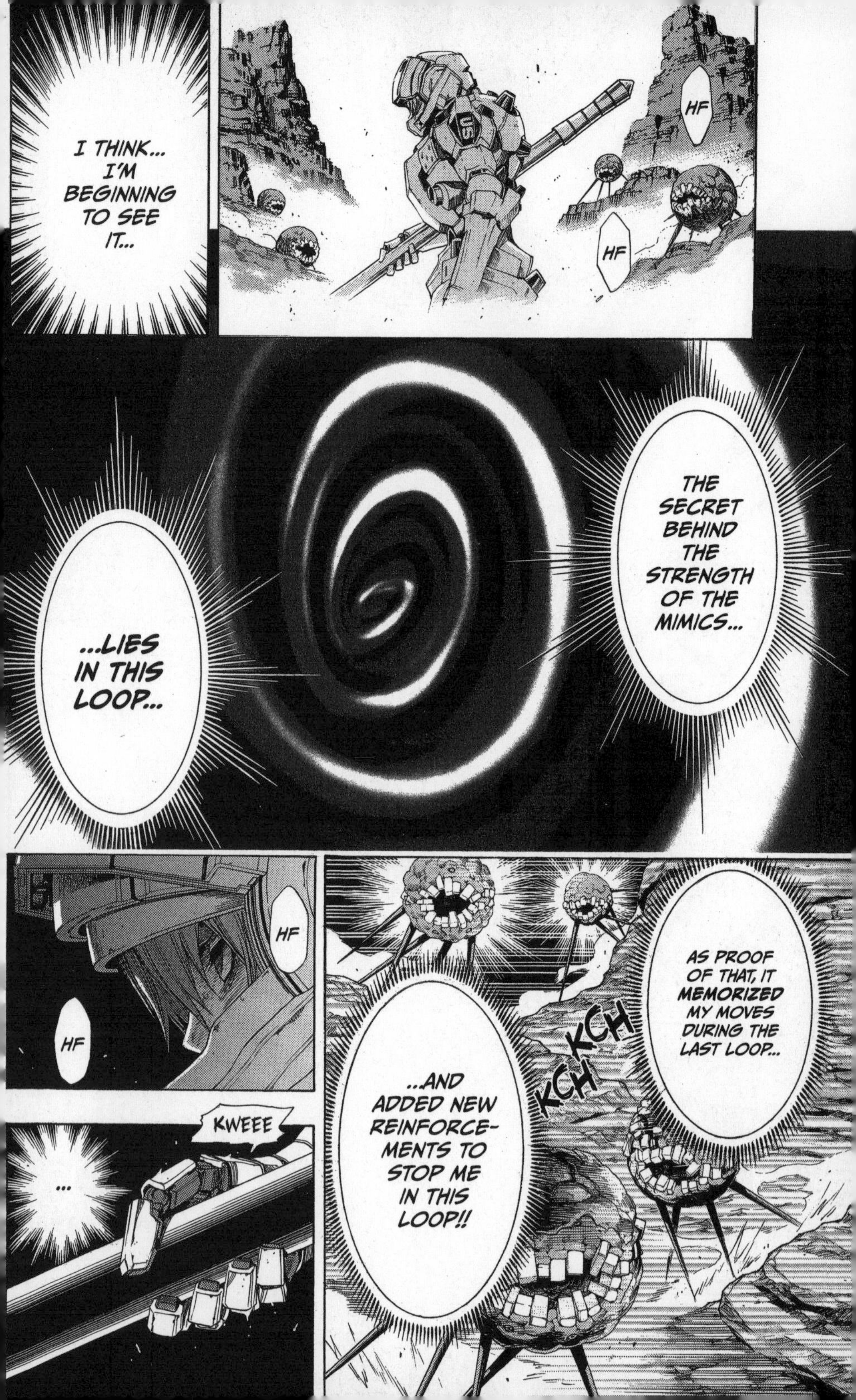
HF
HF
I THINK... I'M BEGINNING TO SEE IT...
THE SECRET BEHIND THE STRENGTH OF THE MIMICS...
...LIES IN THIS LOOP...
AS PROOF OF THAT, IT MEMORIZED MY MOVES DURING THE LAST LOOP...
KCH KCH
...AND ADDED NEW REINFORCE-MENTS TO STOP ME IN THIS LOOP!!
HF
HF
KWEEE
...

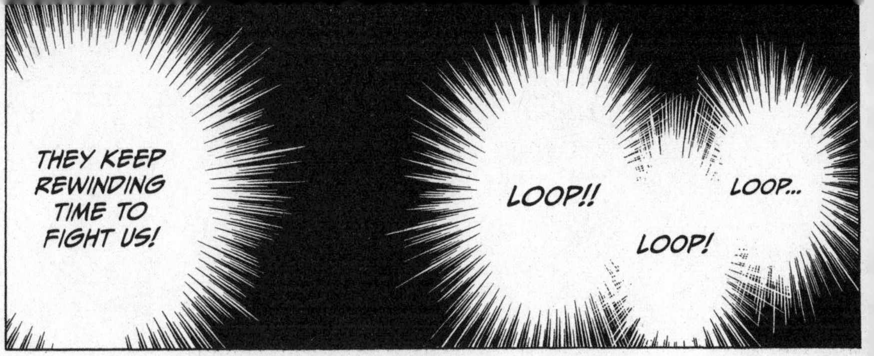
LOOP...
LOOP!!
LOOP!
THEY KEEP REWINDING TIME TO FIGHT US!
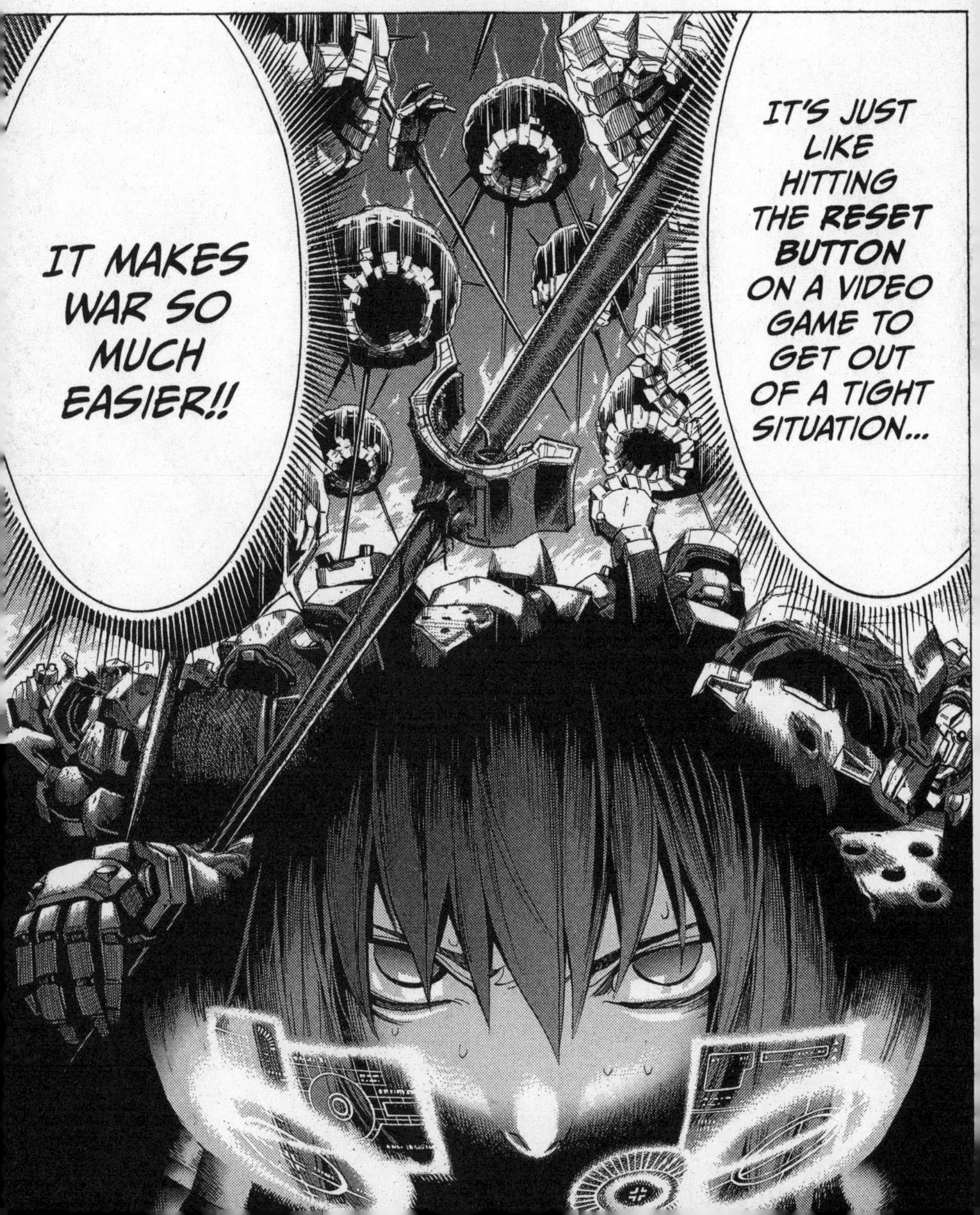
IT'S JUST LIKE HITTING THE **RESET BUTTON** ON A VIDEO GAME TO GET OUT OF A TIGHT SITUATION...
IT MAKES WAR SO MUCH EASIER!!

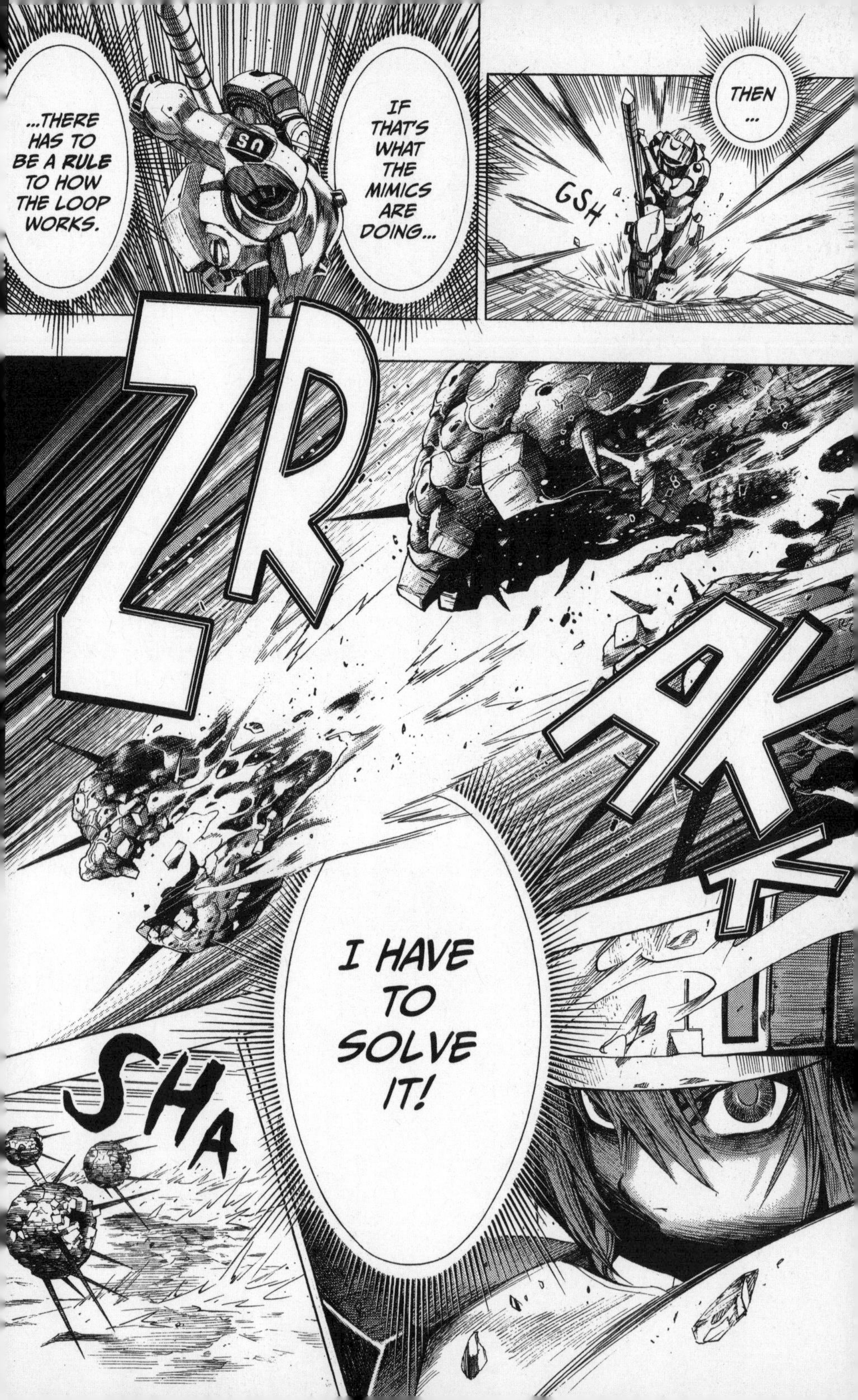
THEN ...
GSH
IF THAT'S WHAT THE MIMICS ARE DOING...
...THERE HAS TO BE A RULE TO HOW THE LOOP WORKS.
ZRAK
I HAVE TO SOLVE IT!
SHA

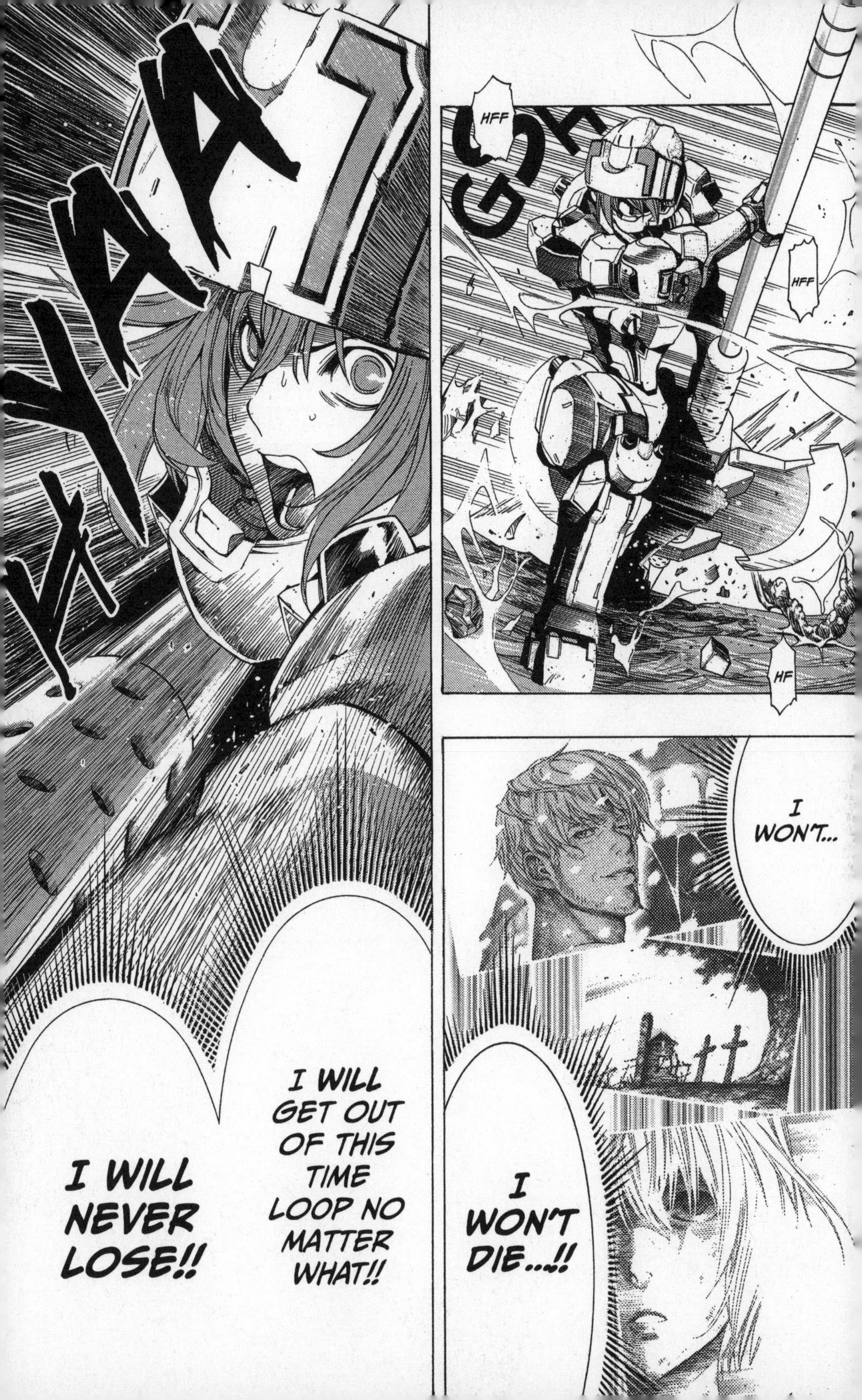
HFF
GOK
HFF
HF
I WON'T...
I WON'T DIE...!!
KYAA
I WILL GET OUT OF THIS TIME LOOP NO MATTER WHAT!!
I WILL NEVER LOSE!!

What if someone who had the
potential to discover a formula to
unlock the mysteries
of the universe wanted to
become a pulp fiction writer?
What if someone who had the
potential to create unparalleled
gastronomic delicacies had his
heart set on civil engineering?
There is what we desire to do,
and what we are able to do.
When those two things don't
coincide, which path should we
pursue to find happiness?

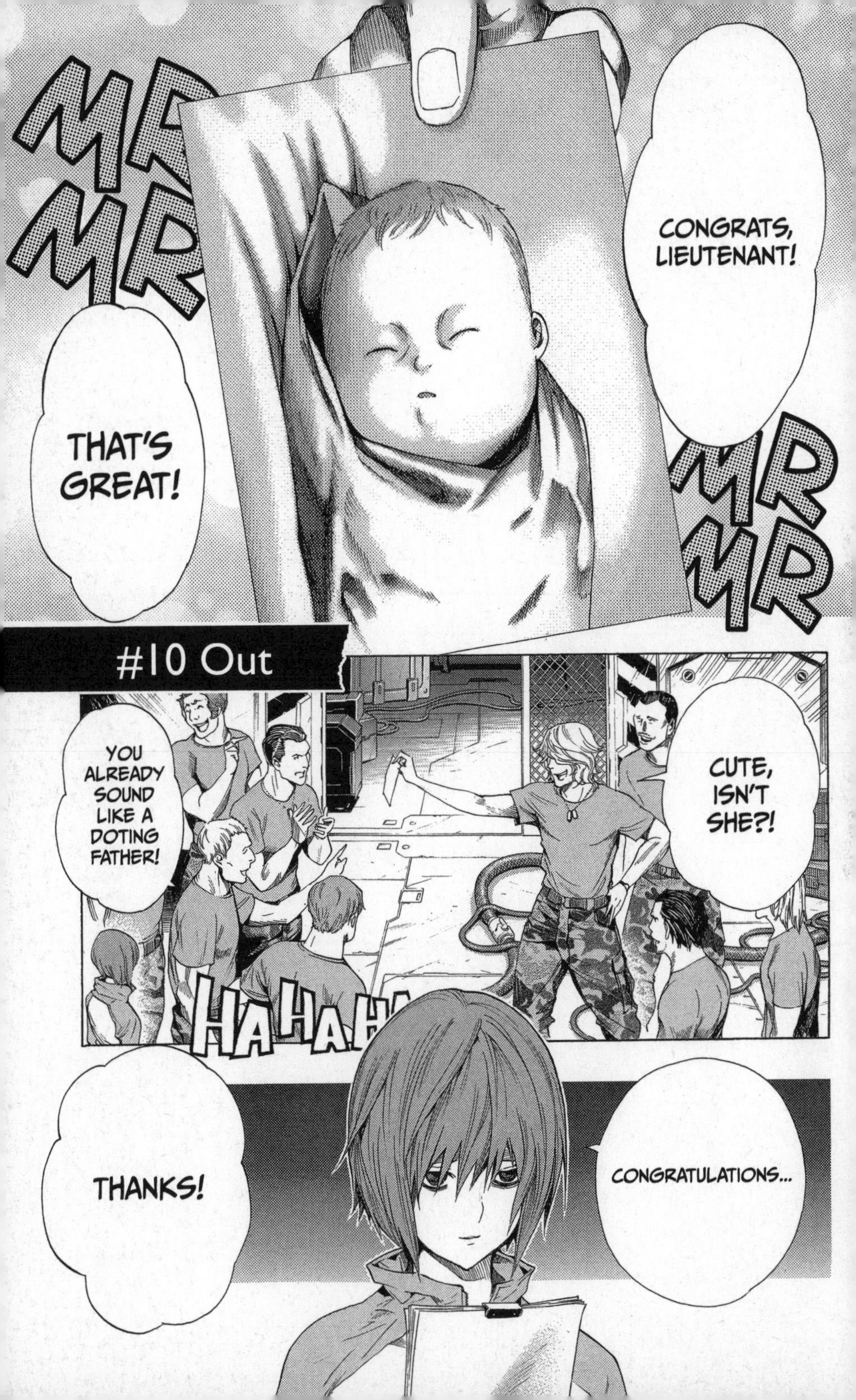
CONGRATS, LIEUTENANT!
MR MR
MR MR
THAT'S GREAT!
#10 Out
CUTE, ISN'T SHE?!
YOU ALREADY SOUND LIKE A DOTING FATHER!
HAHAH
CONGRATULATIONS...
THANKS!

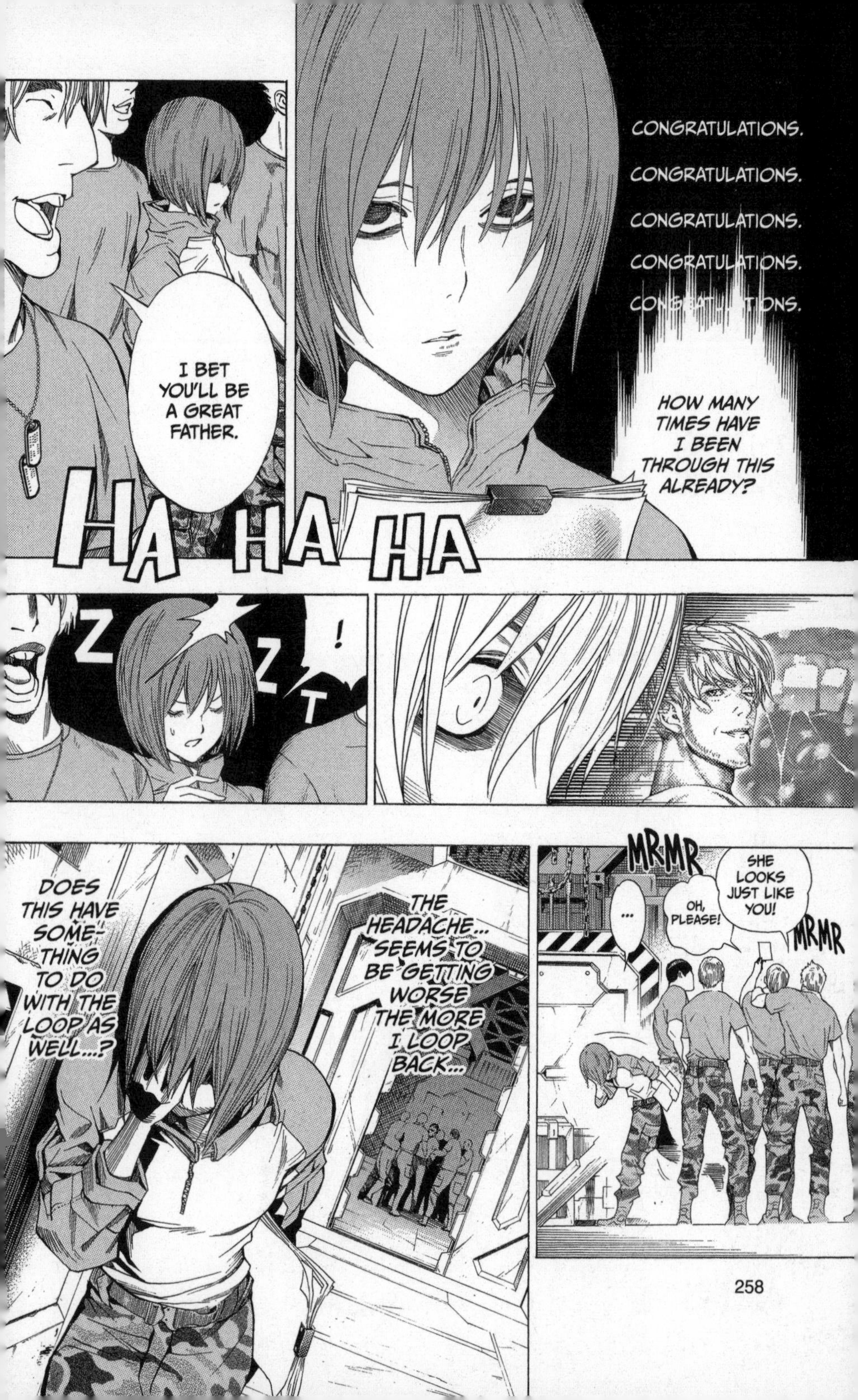
CONGRATULATIONS.
CONGRATULATIONS.
CONGRATULATIONS.
CONGRATULATIONS.
CONGRATULATIONS.
HOW MANY TIMES HAVE I BEEN THROUGH THIS ALREADY?
I BET YOU'LL BE A GREAT FATHER.
HA HA HA
ZZT
!
SHE LOOKS JUST LIKE YOU!
OH, PLEASE!
MRMR
...
MRMR
THE HEADACHE... SEEMS TO BE GETTING WORSE THE MORE I LOOP BACK...
DOES THIS HAVE SOME-THING TO DO WITH THE LOOP AS WELL...?

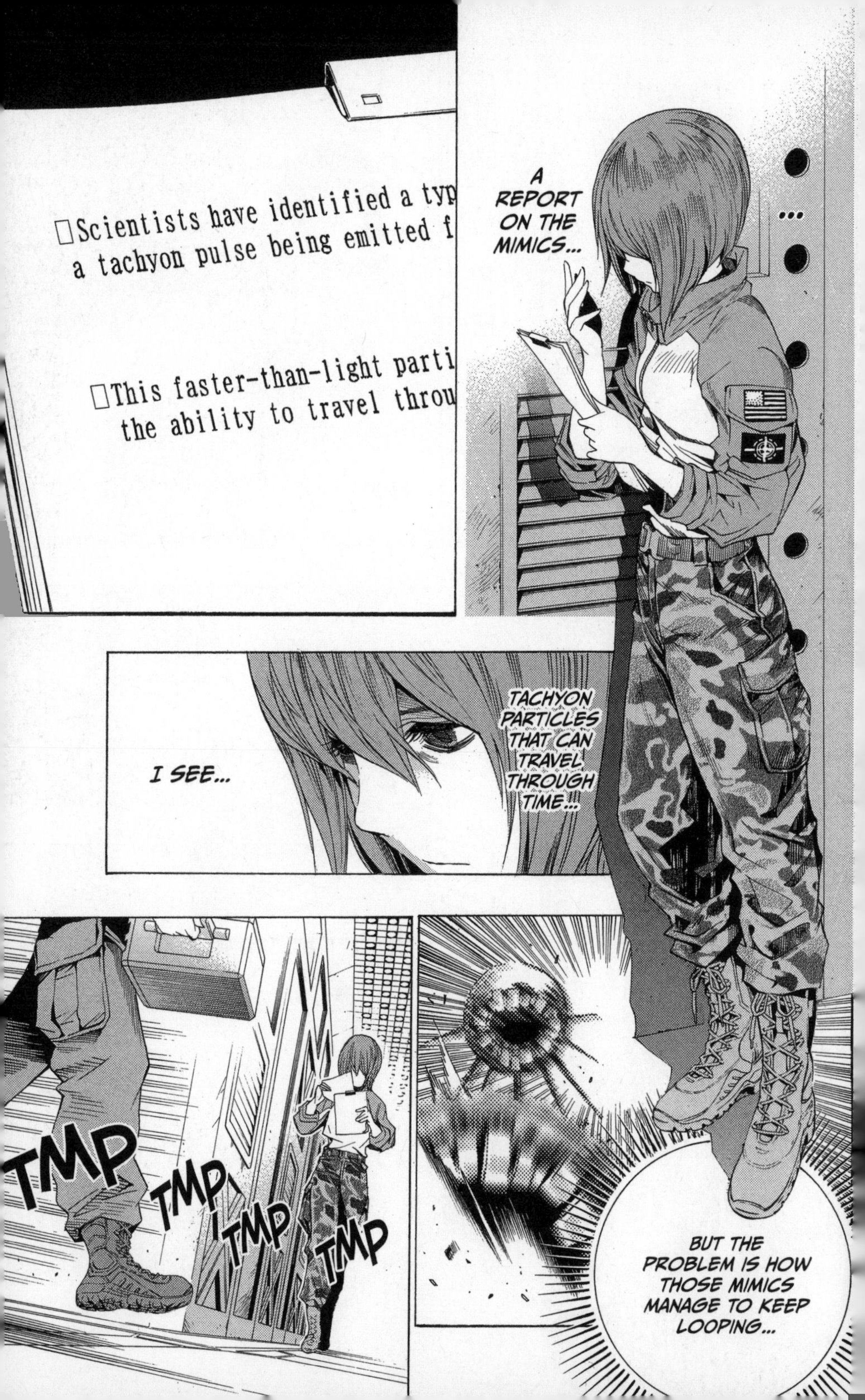

A REPORT ON THE MIMICS...
...
□Scientists have identified a typ
a tachyon pulse being emitted f
□This faster-than-light parti
the ability to travel throu
TACHYON PARTICLES THAT CAN TRAVEL THROUGH TIME...!!
I SEE...
BUT THE PROBLEM IS HOW THOSE MIMICS MANAGE TO KEEP LOOPING...
TMP
TMP
TMP
TMP

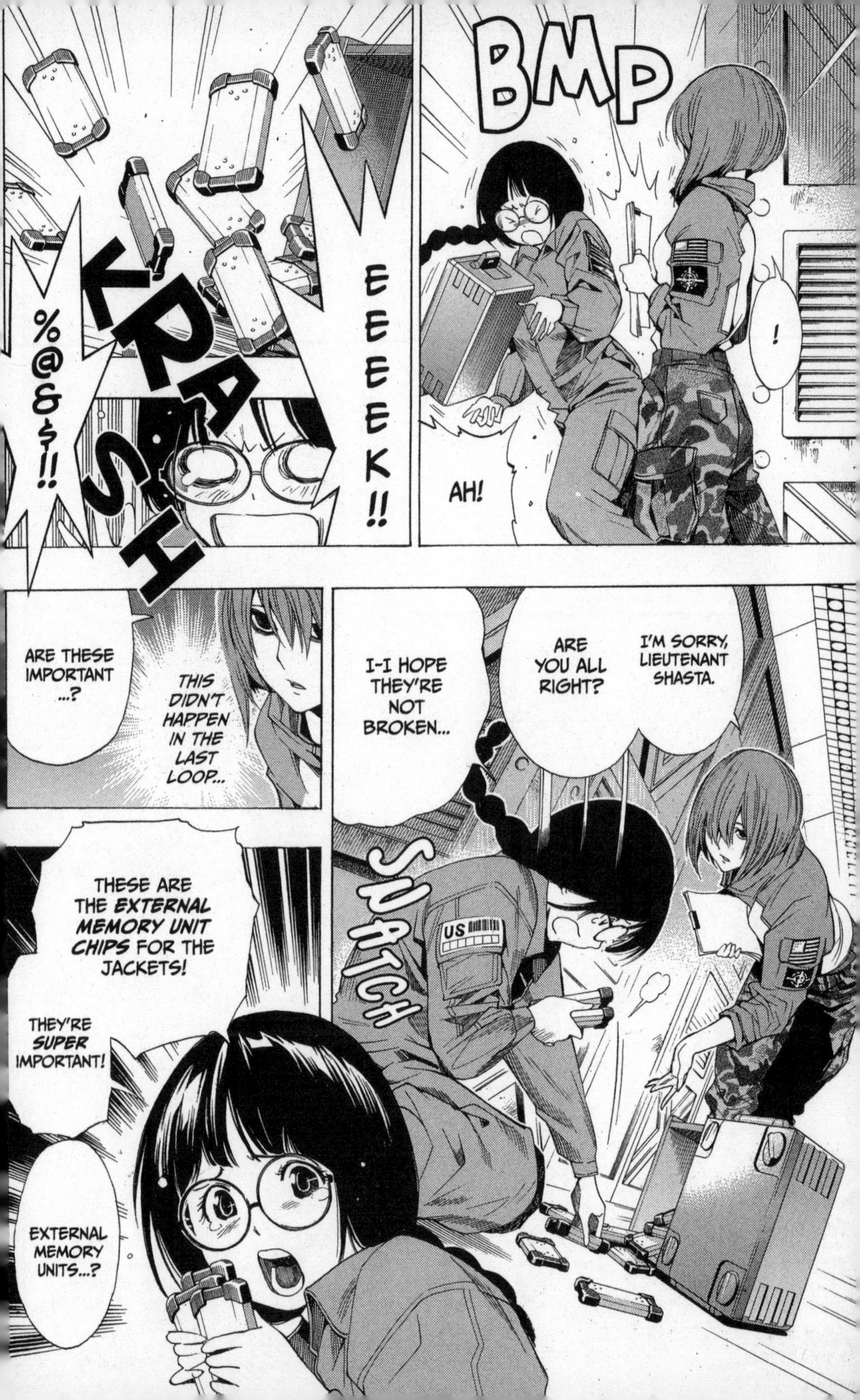

BMP
!
AH!
EEEEK!!
KRASH
%@&$!!
I'M SORRY, LIEUTENANT SHASTA.
ARE YOU ALL RIGHT?
I-I HOPE THEY'RE NOT BROKEN...
SNATCH
ARE THESE IMPORTANT ...?
THIS DIDN'T HAPPEN IN THE LAST LOOP...
THESE ARE THE *EXTERNAL MEMORY UNIT CHIPS* FOR THE JACKETS!
THEY'RE *SUPER* IMPORTANT!
EXTERNAL MEMORY UNITS...?

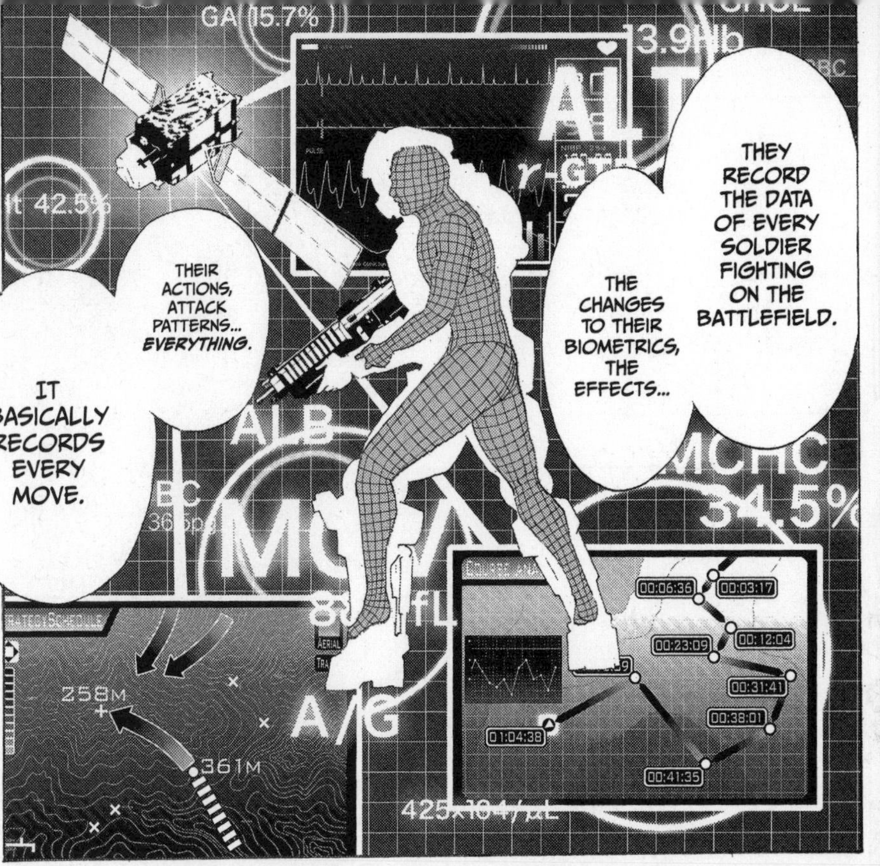
THEY RECORD THE DATA OF EVERY SOLDIER FIGHTING ON THE BATTLEFIELD.
THE CHANGES TO THEIR BIOMETRICS, THE EFFECTS...
THEIR ACTIONS, ATTACK PATTERNS... *EVERYTHING.*
IT BASICALLY RECORDS EVERY MOVE.

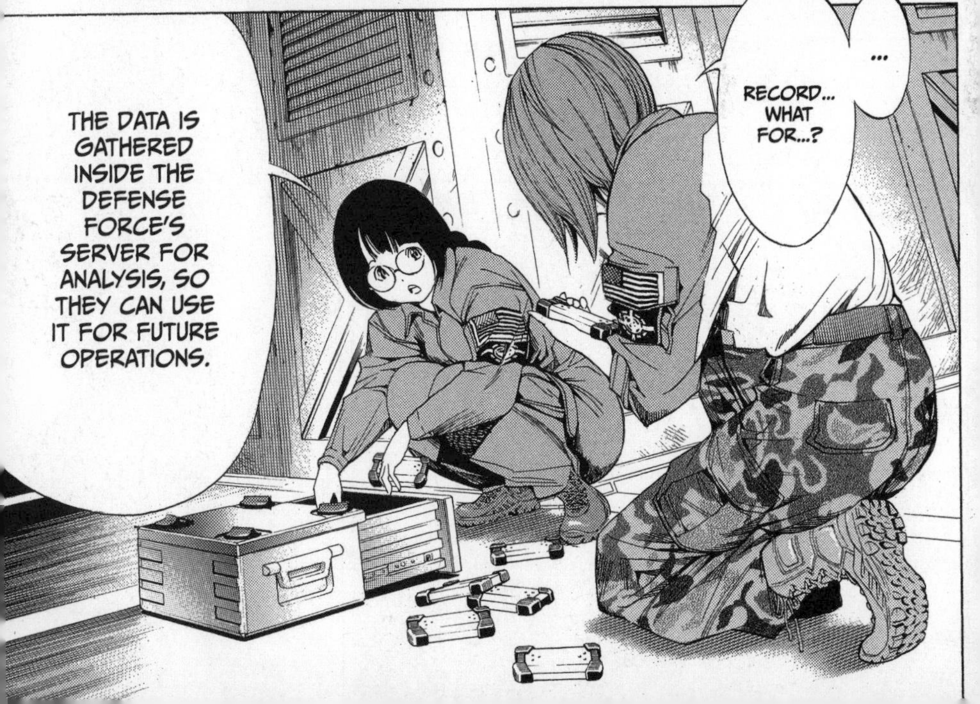
...
RECORD... WHAT FOR...?
THE DATA IS GATHERED INSIDE THE DEFENSE FORCE'S SERVER FOR ANALYSIS, SO THEY CAN USE IT FOR FUTURE OPERATIONS.

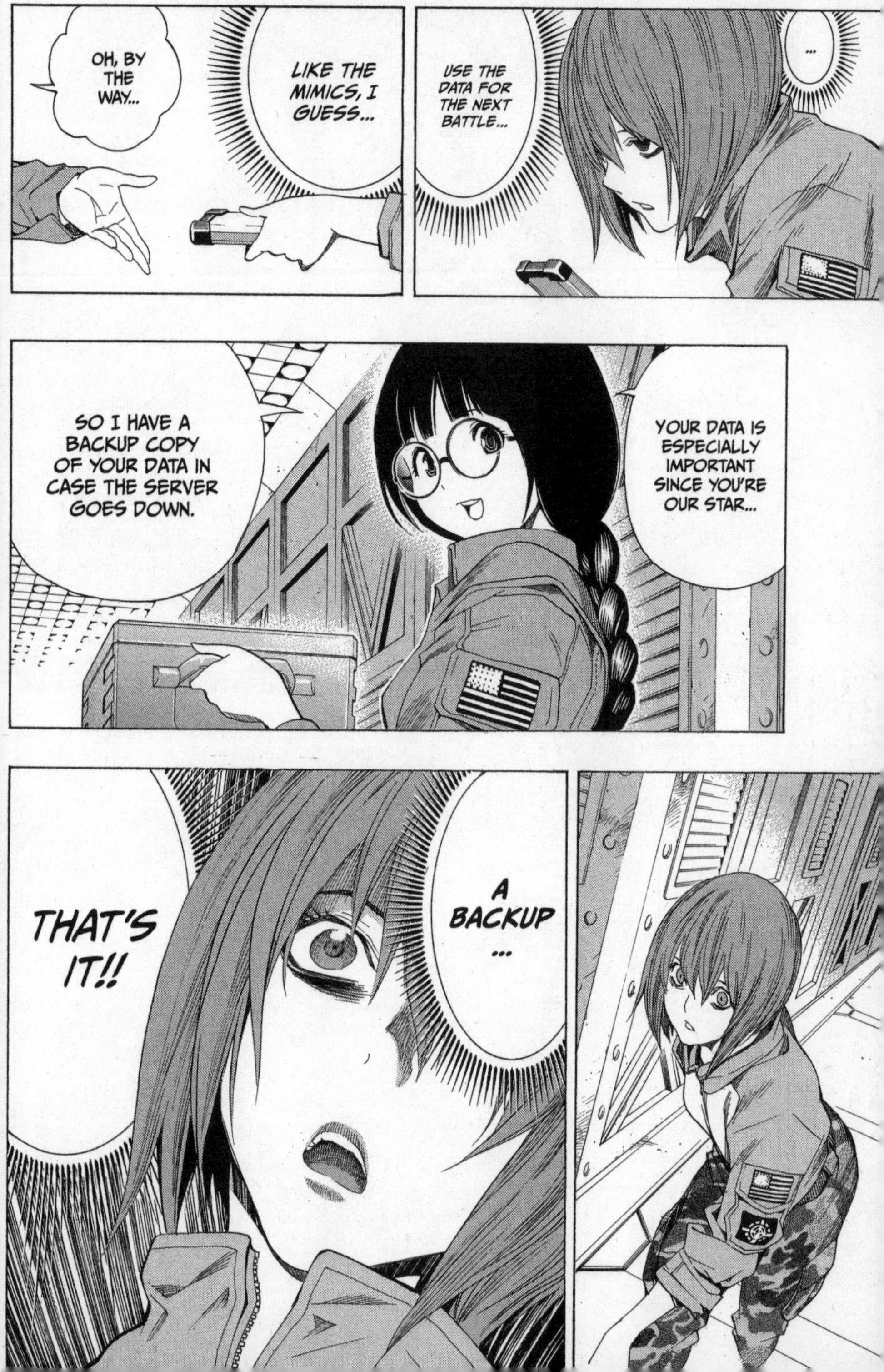
...
USE THE DATA FOR THE NEXT BATTLE...
LIKE THE MIMICS, I GUESS...
OH, BY THE WAY...
YOUR DATA IS ESPECIALLY IMPORTANT SINCE YOU'RE OUR STAR...
SO I HAVE A BACKUP COPY OF YOUR DATA IN CASE THE SERVER GOES DOWN.
A BACKUP ...
THAT'S IT!!

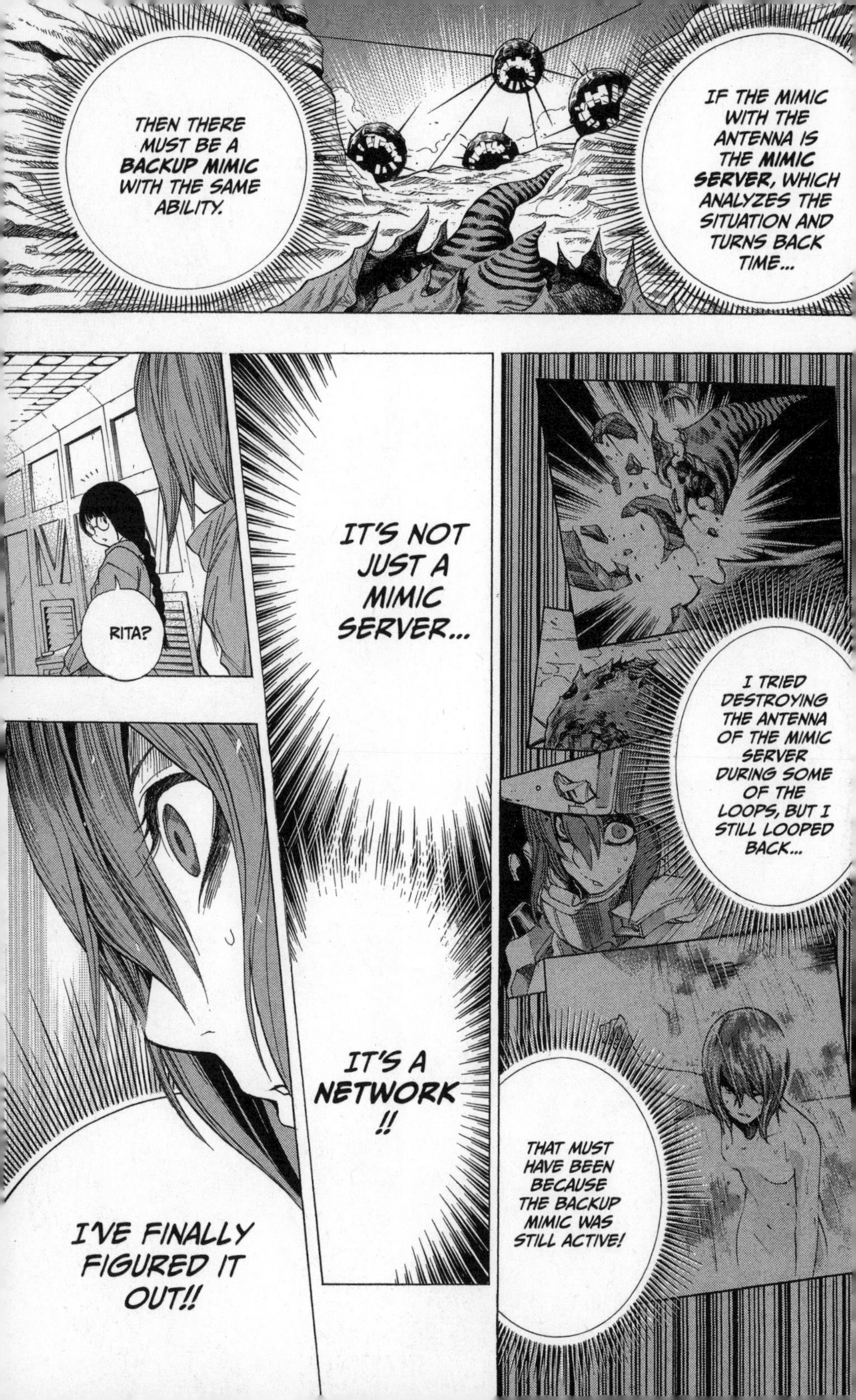
IF THE MIMIC WITH THE ANTENNA IS THE MIMIC SERVER, WHICH ANALYZES THE SITUATION AND TURNS BACK TIME...
THEN THERE MUST BE A BACKUP MIMIC WITH THE SAME ABILITY.
I TRIED DESTROYING THE ANTENNA OF THE MIMIC SERVER DURING SOME OF THE LOOPS, BUT I STILL LOOPED BACK...
THAT MUST HAVE BEEN BECAUSE THE BACKUP MIMIC WAS STILL ACTIVE!
IT'S NOT JUST A MIMIC SERVER...
IT'S A NETWORK!!
RITA?
I'VE FINALLY FIGURED IT OUT!!

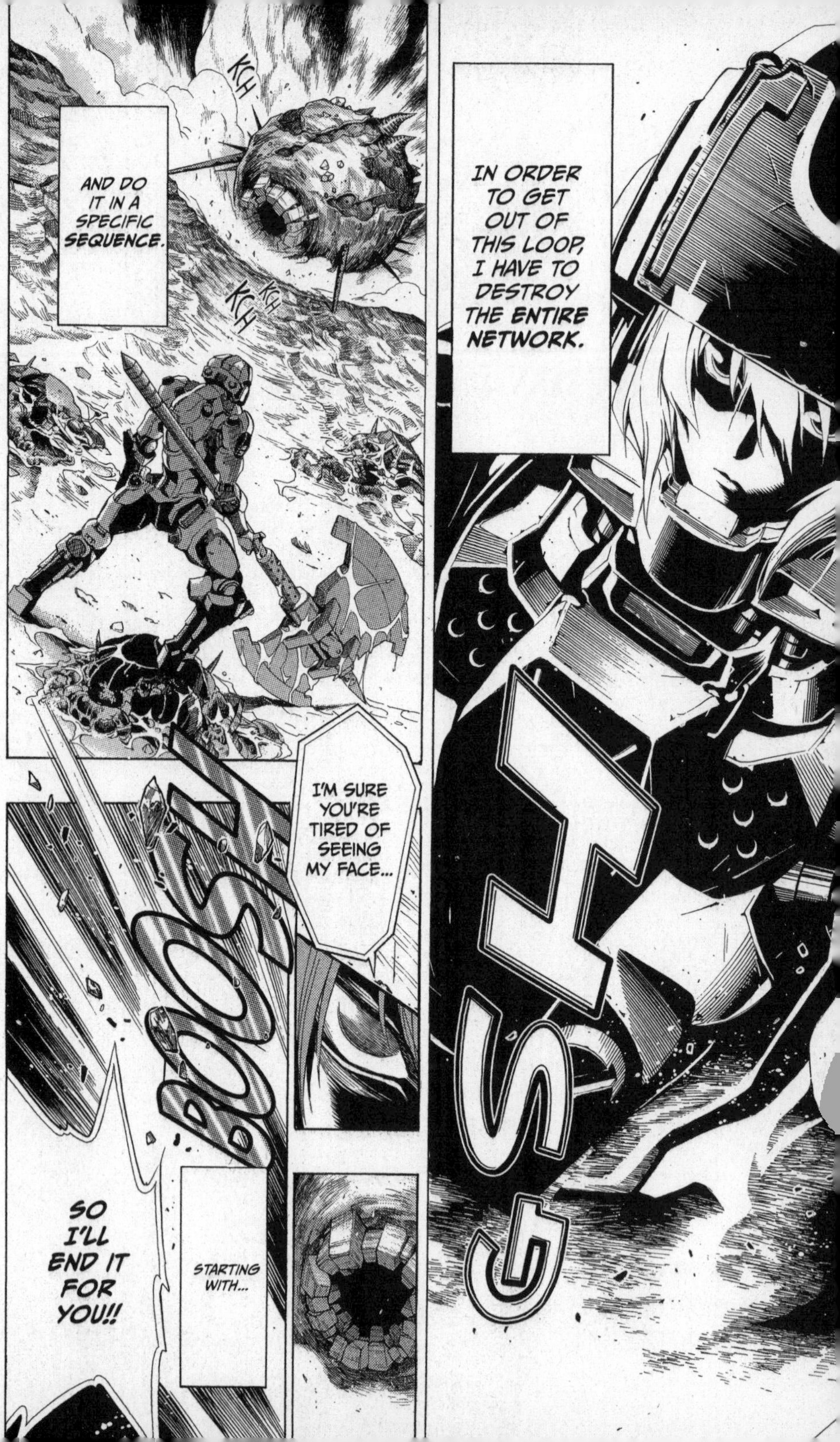
IN ORDER TO GET OUT OF THIS LOOP, I HAVE TO DESTROY THE ENTIRE NETWORK.
KCH
AND DO IT IN A SPECIFIC SEQUENCE.
KCH
KCH
I'M SURE YOU'RE TIRED OF SEEING MY FACE...
STARTING WITH...
SO I'LL END IT FOR YOU!!

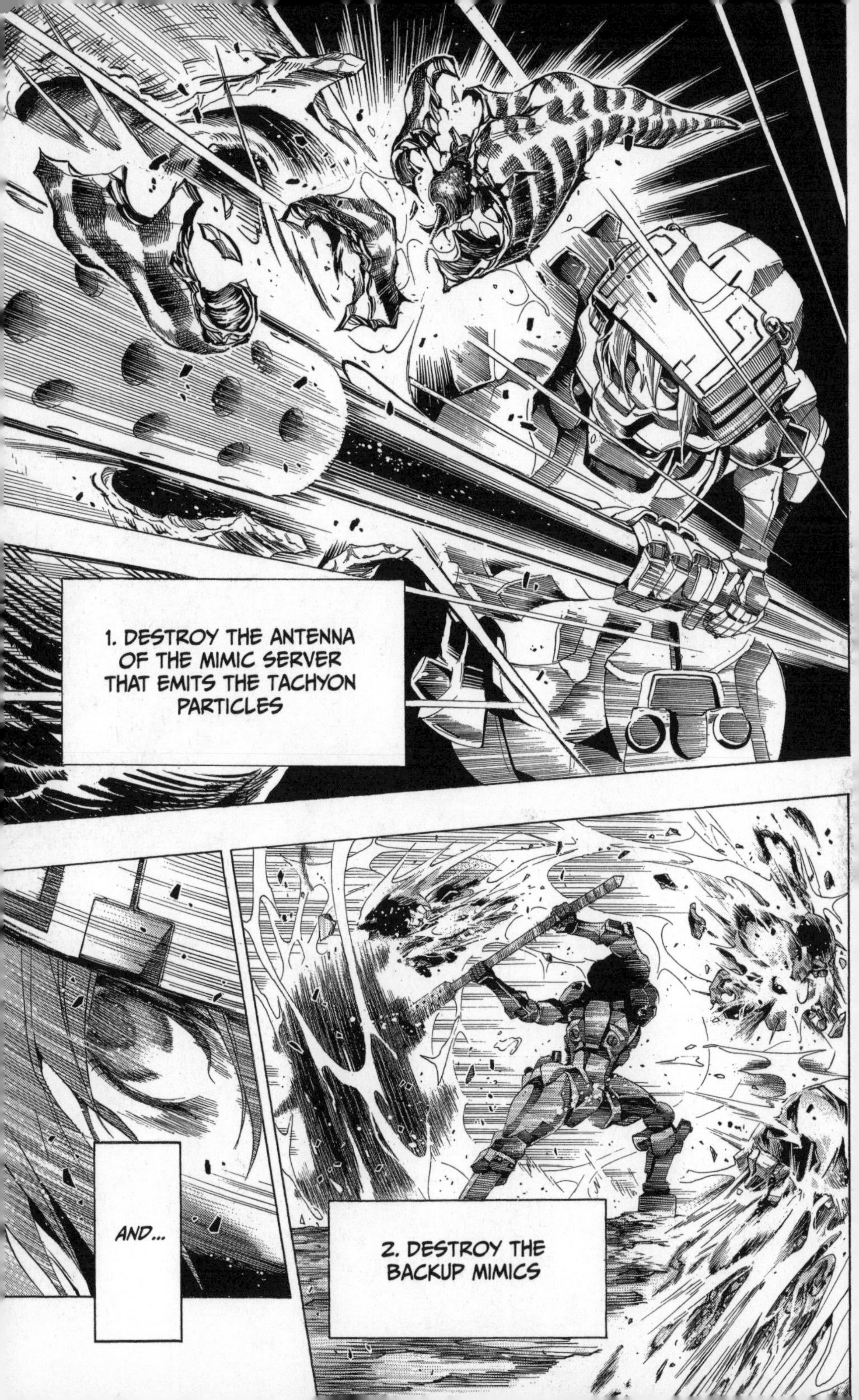
1. DESTROY THE ANTENNA OF THE MIMIC SERVER THAT EMITS THE TACHYON PARTICLES
2. DESTROY THE BACKUP MIMICS
AND...

3. DESTROY THE MIMIC SERVER

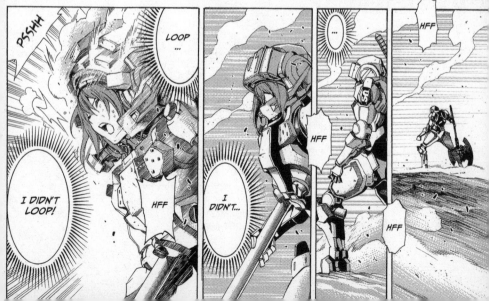

PSSHH

LOOP...

I DIDN'T LOOP!

HFF

...

HFF

I DIDN'T...

HFF

HFF

HFF

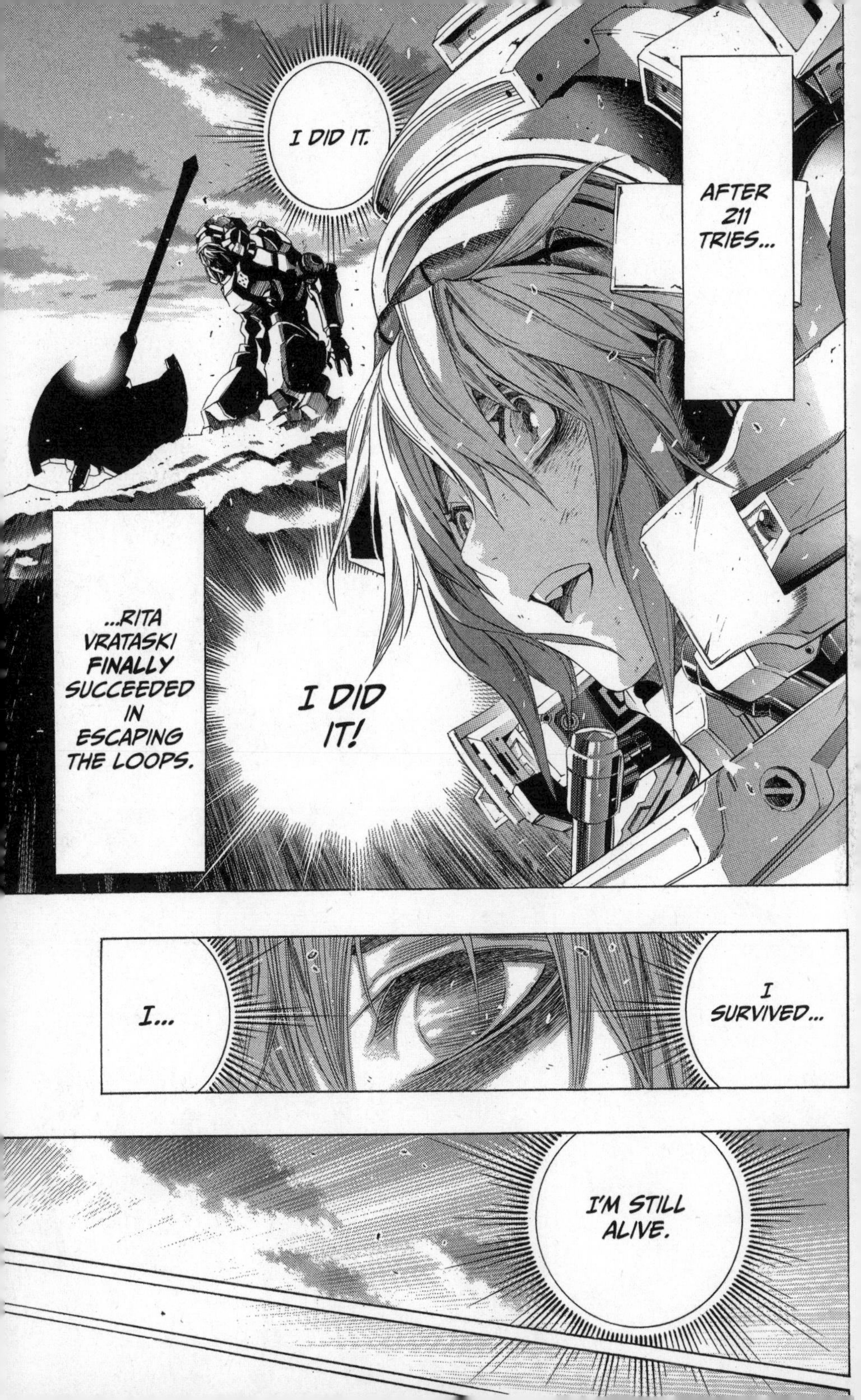
AFTER 211 TRIES...
I DID IT.
...RITA VRATASKI FINALLY SUCCEEDED IN ESCAPING THE LOOPS.
I DID IT!
I SURVIVED...
I...
I'M STILL ALIVE.

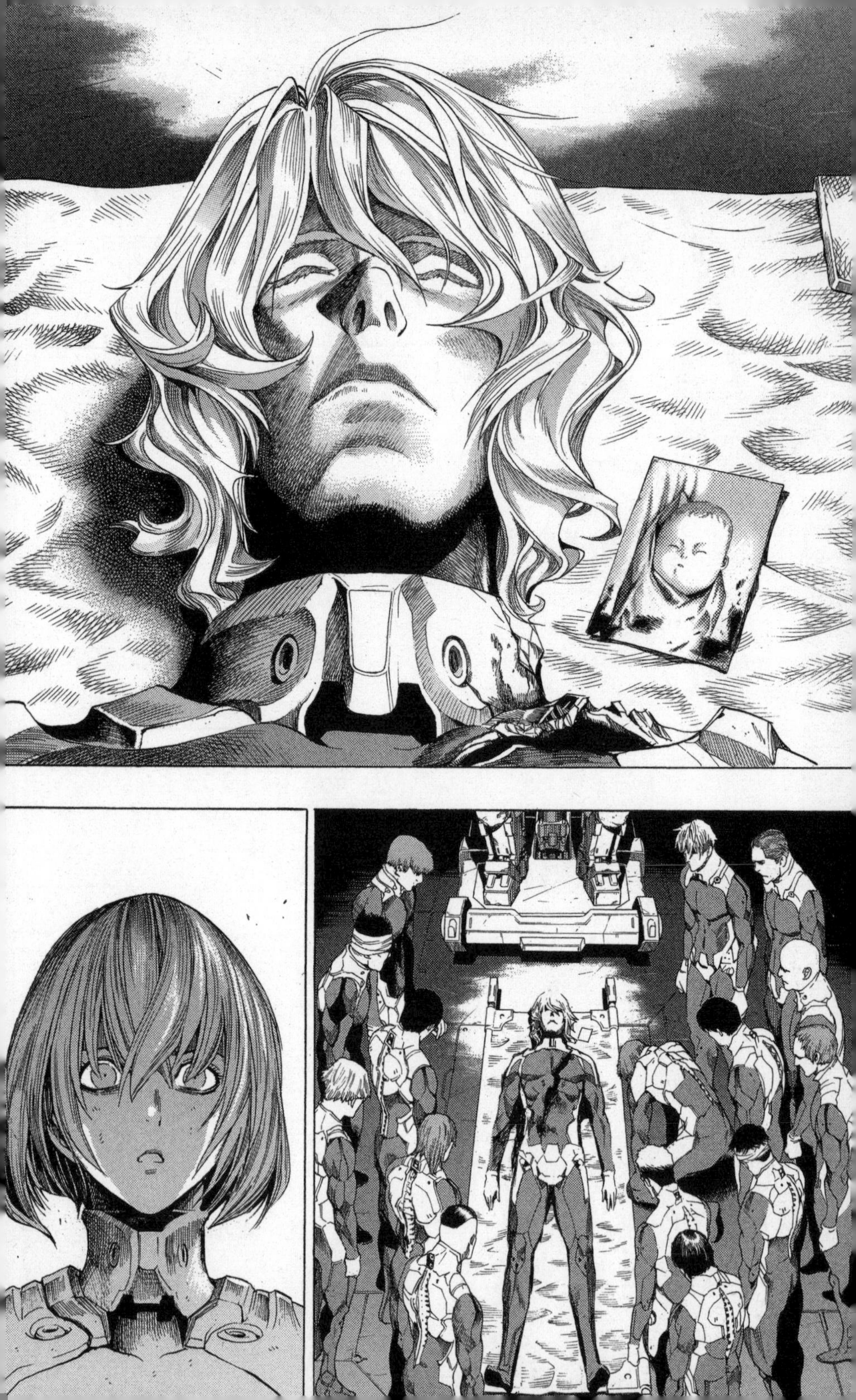

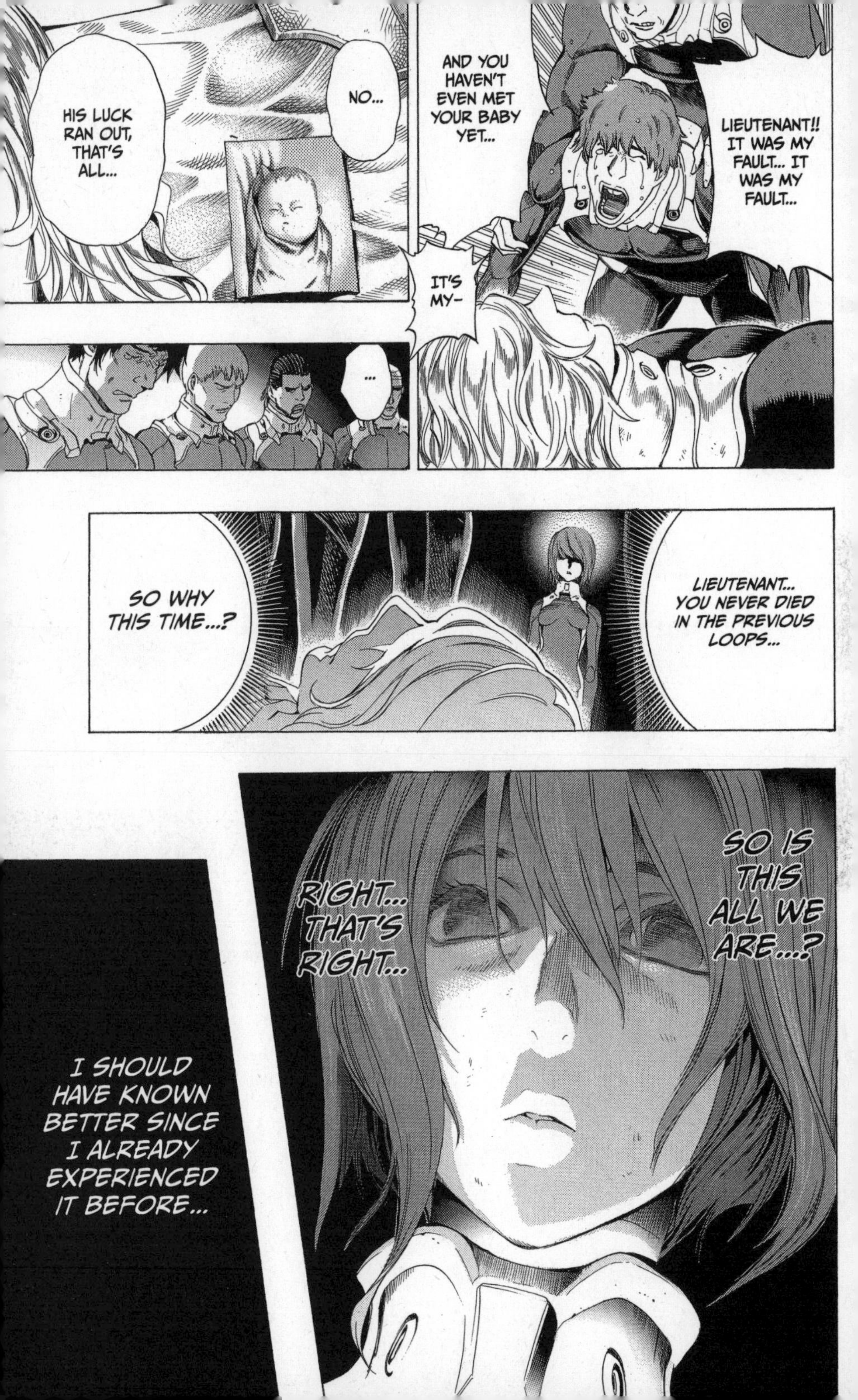
LIEUTENANT!! IT WAS MY FAULT... IT WAS MY FAULT...
AND YOU HAVEN'T EVEN MET YOUR BABY YET...
IT'S MY-
NO...
HIS LUCK RAN OUT, THAT'S ALL...
...
LIEUTENANT... YOU NEVER DIED IN THE PREVIOUS LOOPS...
SO WHY THIS TIME...?
SO IS THIS ALL WE ARE...?
RIGHT... THAT'S RIGHT...
I SHOULD HAVE KNOWN BETTER SINCE I ALREADY EXPERIENCED IT BEFORE...

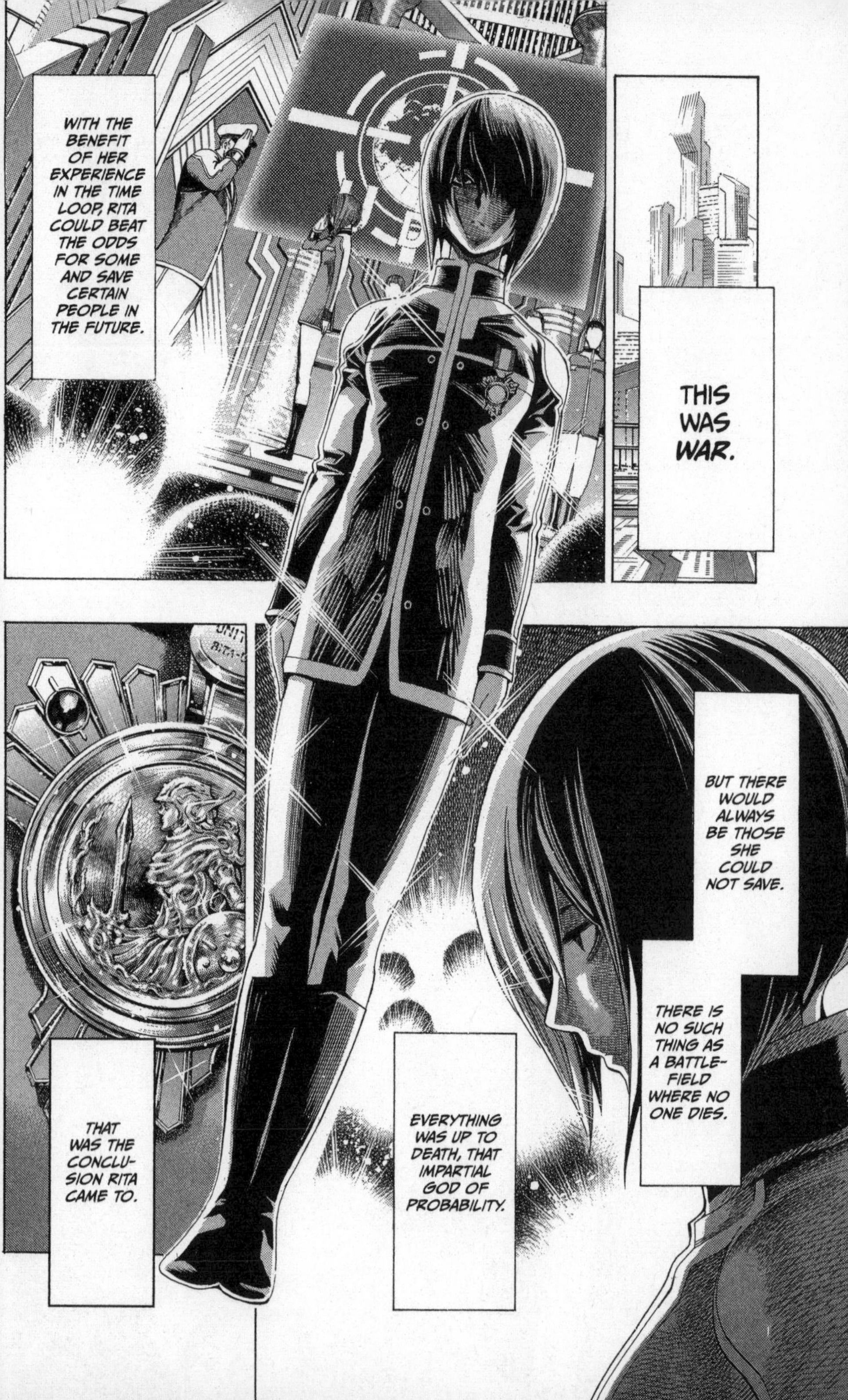
THIS WAS WAR.
WITH THE BENEFIT OF HER EXPERIENCE IN THE TIME LOOP, RITA COULD BEAT THE ODDS FOR SOME AND SAVE CERTAIN PEOPLE IN THE FUTURE.
BUT THERE WOULD ALWAYS BE THOSE SHE COULD NOT SAVE.
THERE IS NO SUCH THING AS A BATTLE-FIELD WHERE NO ONE DIES.
EVERYTHING WAS UP TO DEATH, THAT IMPARTIAL GOD OF PROBABILITY.
THAT WAS THE CONCLU-SION RITA CAME TO.

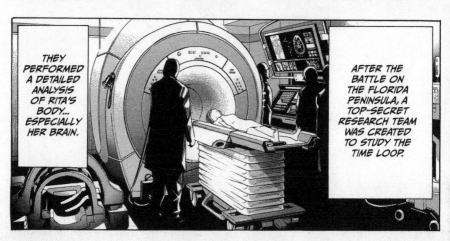

AFTER THE BATTLE ON THE FLORIDA PENINSULA, A TOP-SECRET RESEARCH TEAM WAS CREATED TO STUDY THE TIME LOOP.

THEY PERFORMED A DETAILED ANALYSIS OF RITA'S BODY... ESPECIALLY HER BRAIN.

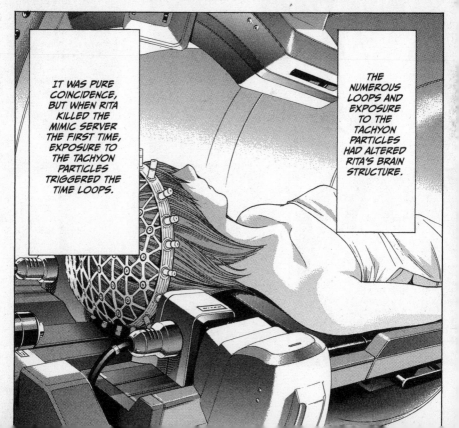

THE NUMEROUS LOOPS AND EXPOSURE TO THE TACHYON PARTICLES HAD ALTERED RITA'S BRAIN STRUCTURE.

IT WAS PURE COINCIDENCE, BUT WHEN RITA KILLED THE MIMIC SERVER THE FIRST TIME, EXPOSURE TO THE TACHYON PARTICLES TRIGGERED THE TIME LOOPS.

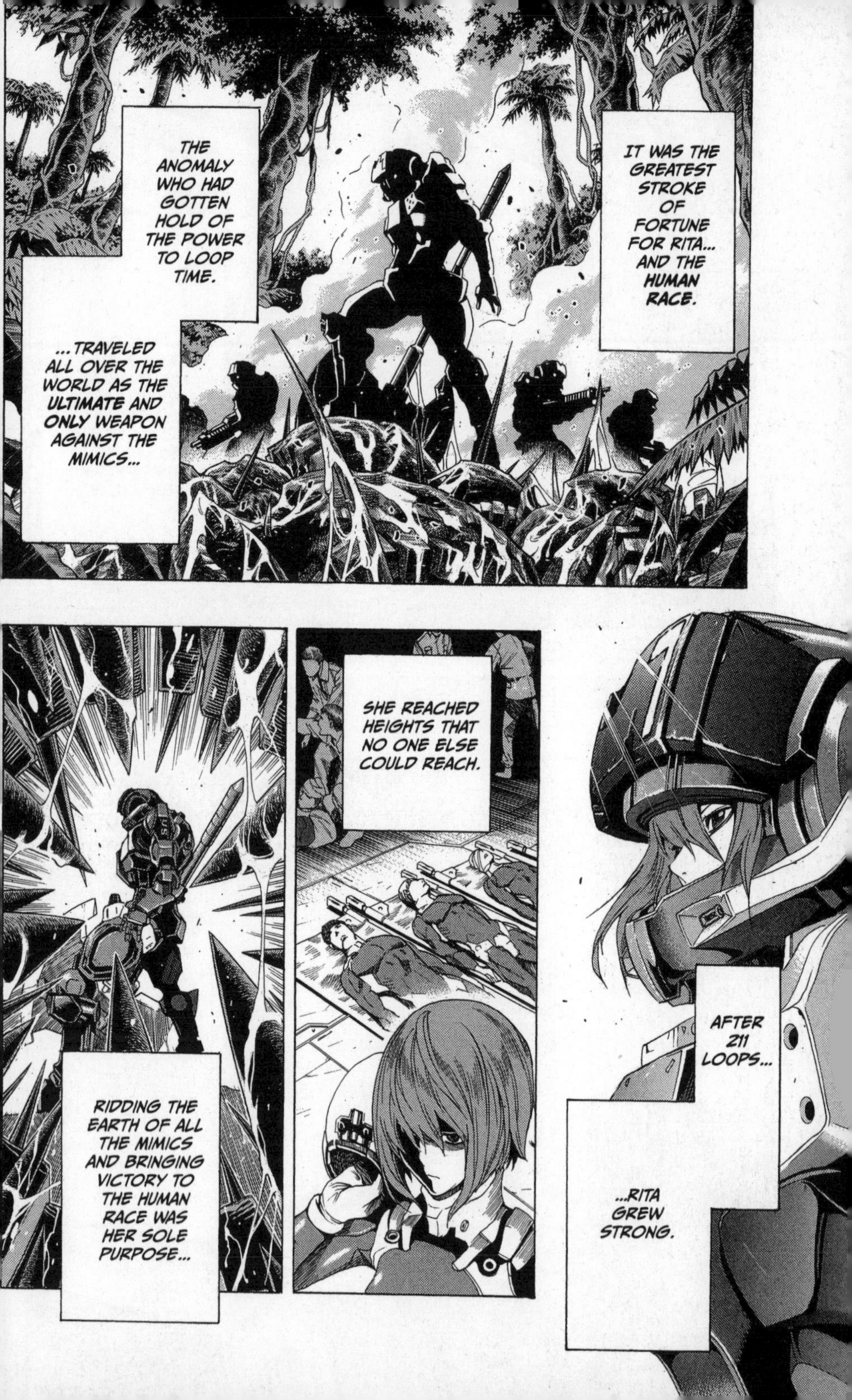
IT WAS THE GREATEST STROKE OF FORTUNE FOR RITA... AND THE HUMAN RACE.
THE ANOMALY WHO HAD GOTTEN HOLD OF THE POWER TO LOOP TIME.
...TRAVELED ALL OVER THE WORLD AS THE ULTIMATE AND ONLY WEAPON AGAINST THE MIMICS...
AFTER 211 LOOPS...
...RITA GREW STRONG.
SHE REACHED HEIGHTS THAT NO ONE ELSE COULD REACH.
RIDDING THE EARTH OF ALL THE MIMICS AND BRINGING VICTORY TO THE HUMAN RACE WAS HER SOLE PURPOSE...

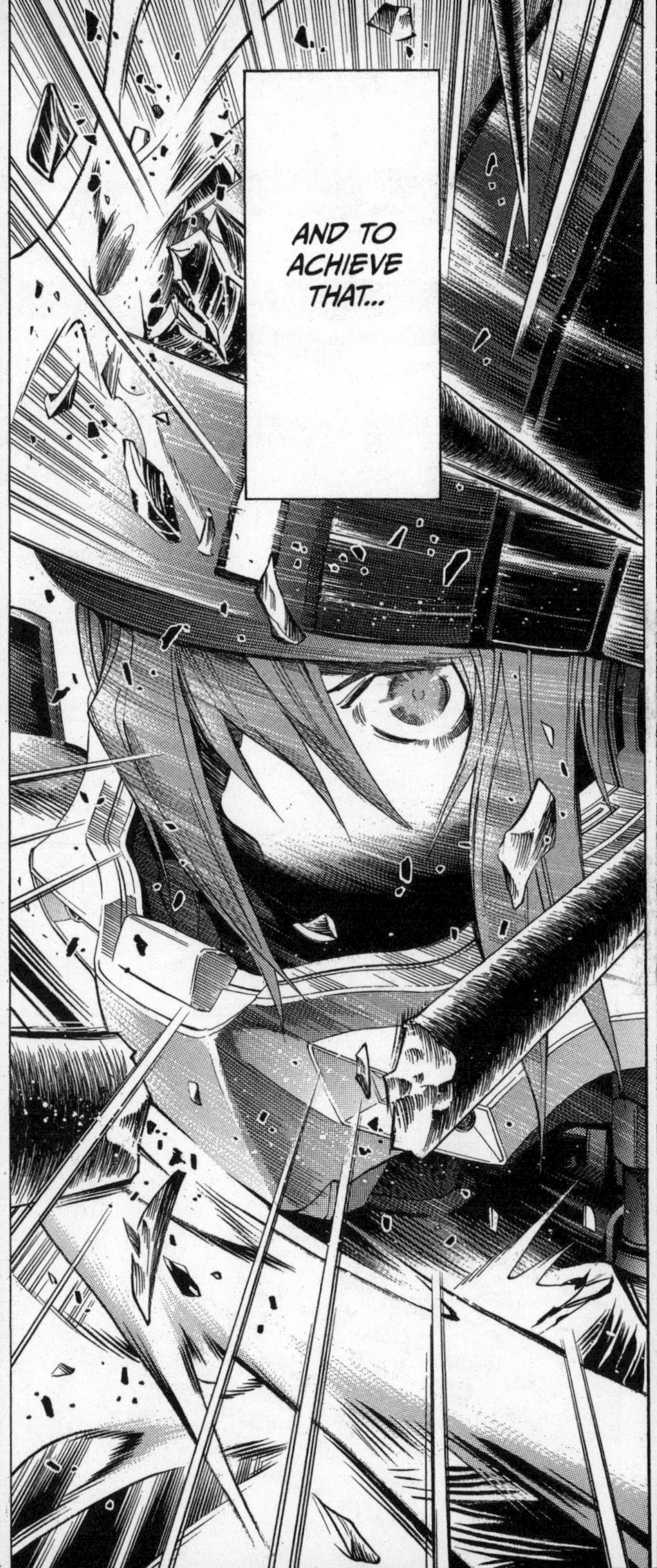
AND TO ACHIEVE THAT...

...THE VALKYRIE CONTINUES TO FIGHT ALONE.

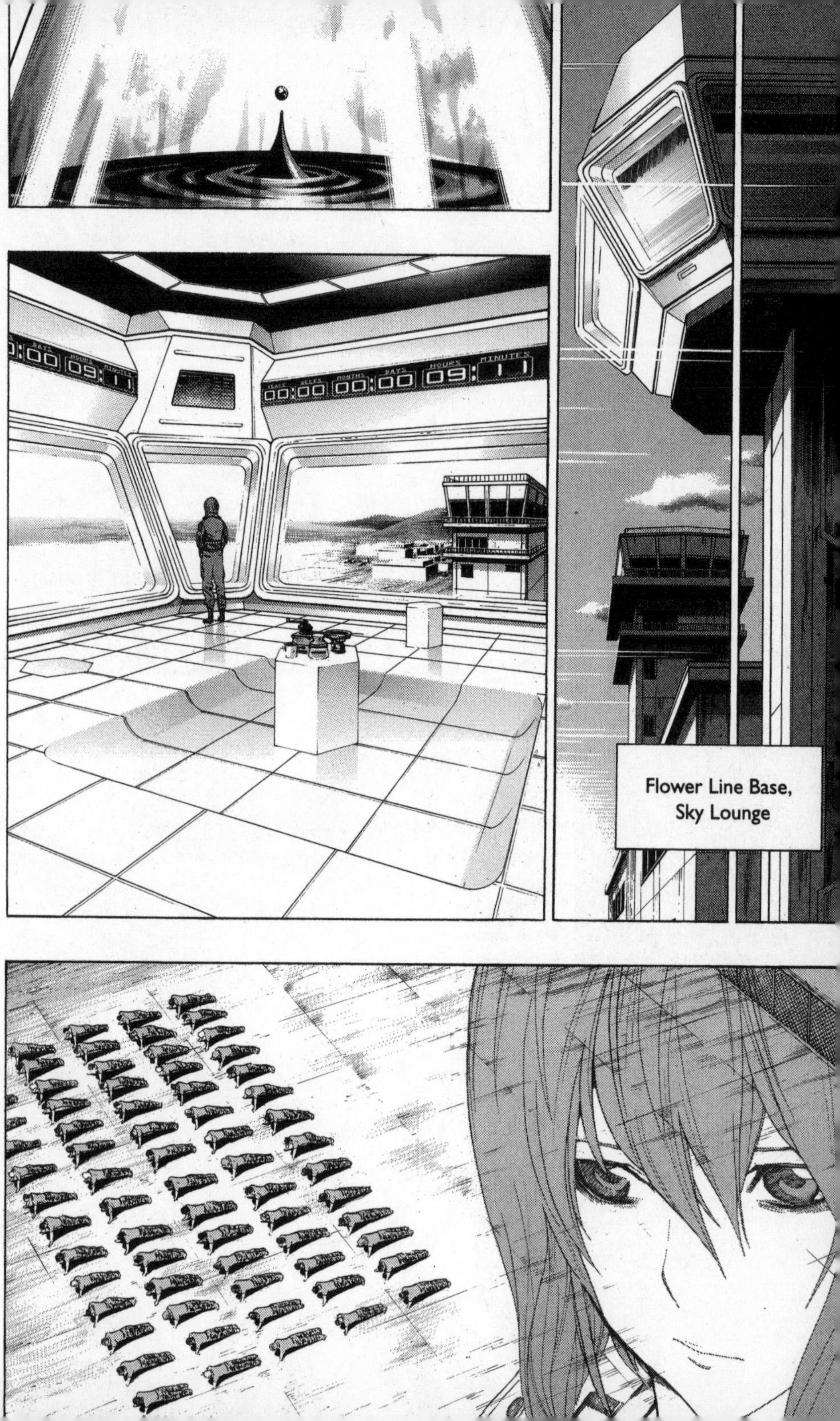
Flower Line Base,
Sky Lounge

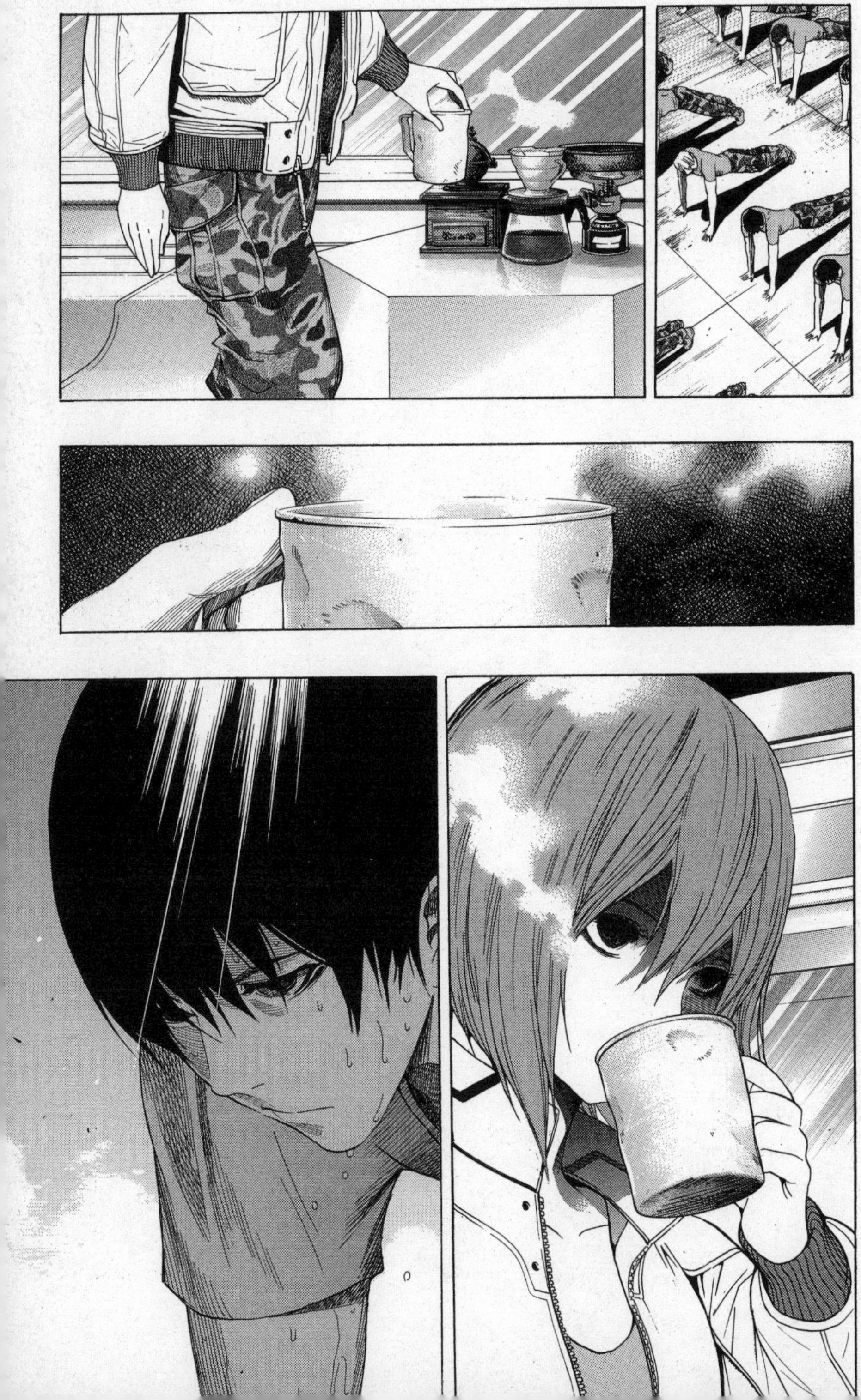

She didn't shed a tear.
Angels don't cry.

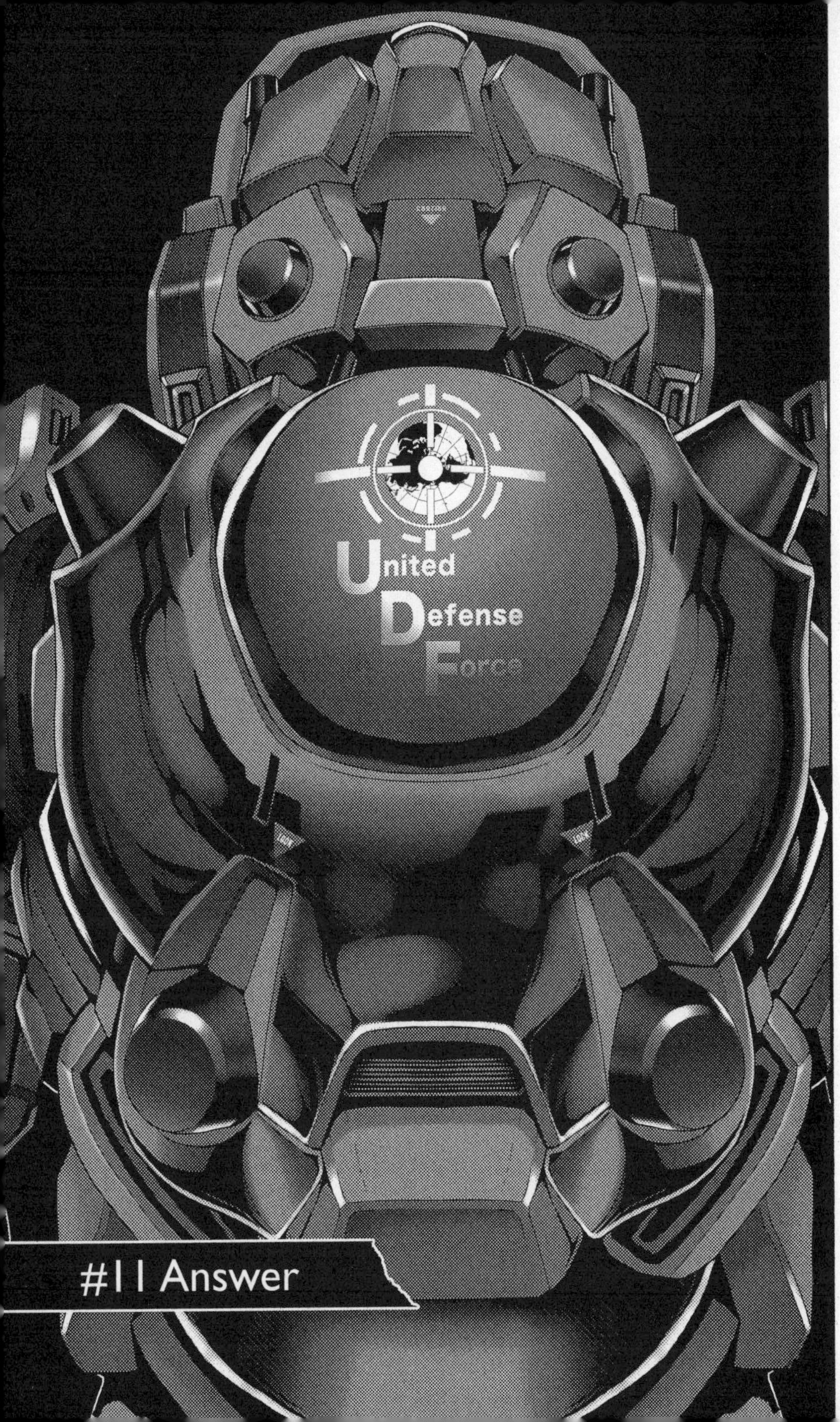
United
Defense
Force

#11 Answer

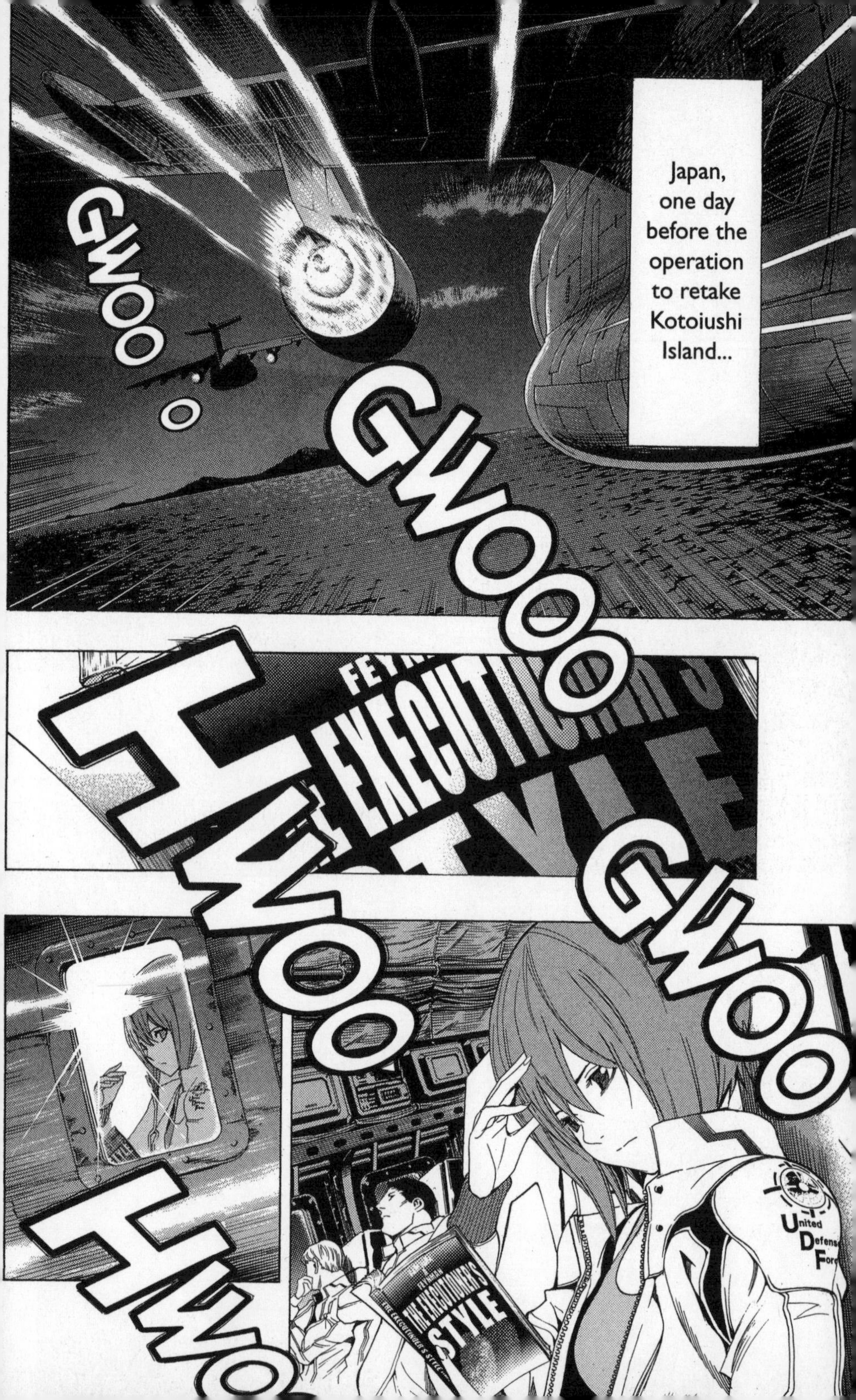

Japan, one day before the operation to retake Kotoiushi Island...
GWOOOOO
GWOOO O
GWOOO
HWOOO
HWO
THE EXECUTIONER'S STYLE

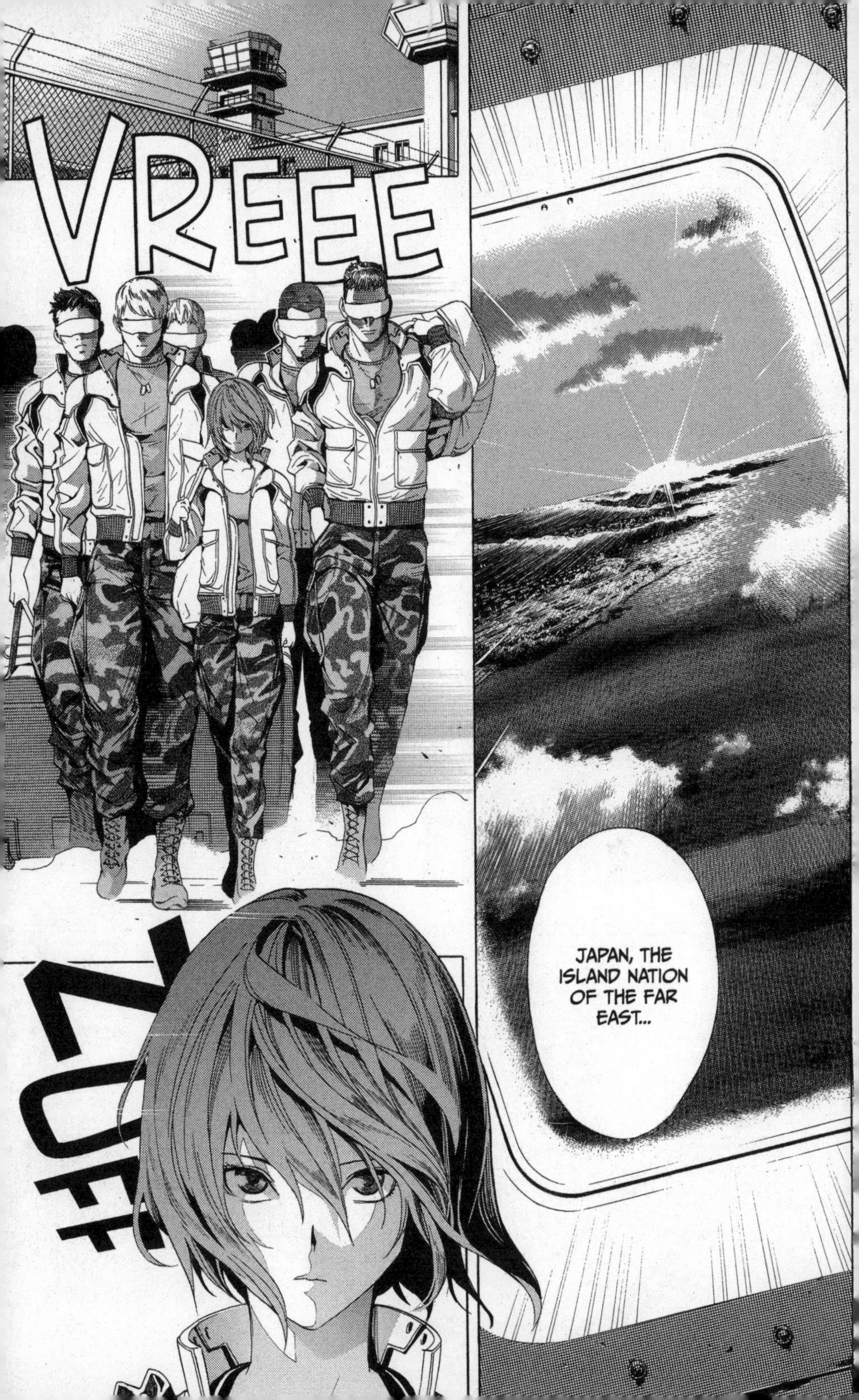
JAPAN, THE ISLAND NATION OF THE FAR EAST...
VREEE
ZUFF

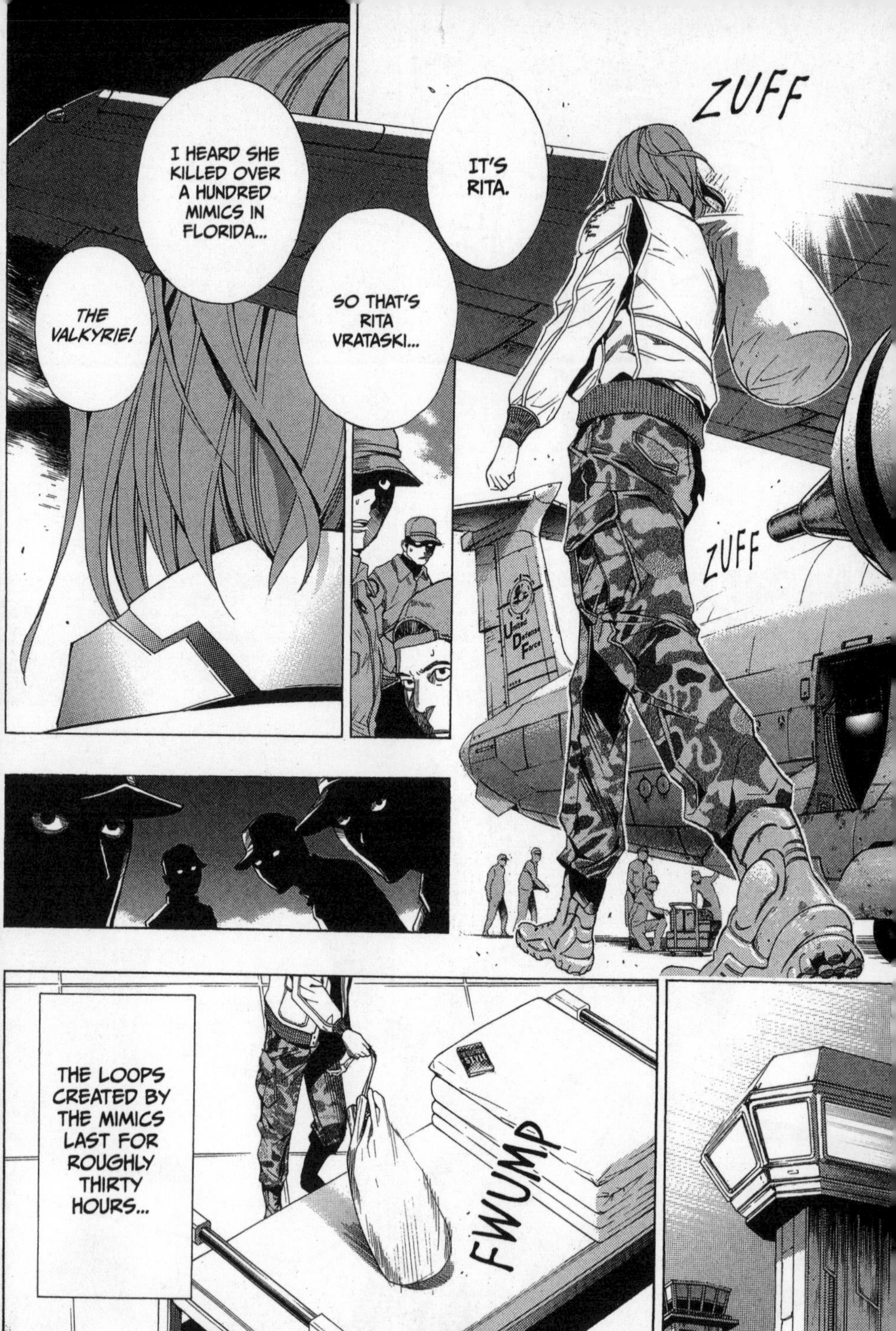
ZUFF
IT'S RITA.
ZUFF
I HEARD SHE KILLED OVER A HUNDRED MIMICS IN FLORIDA...
SO THAT'S RITA VRATASKI...
THE VALKYRIE!
FWUMP
THE LOOPS CREATED BY THE MIMICS LAST FOR ROUGHLY THIRTY HOURS...

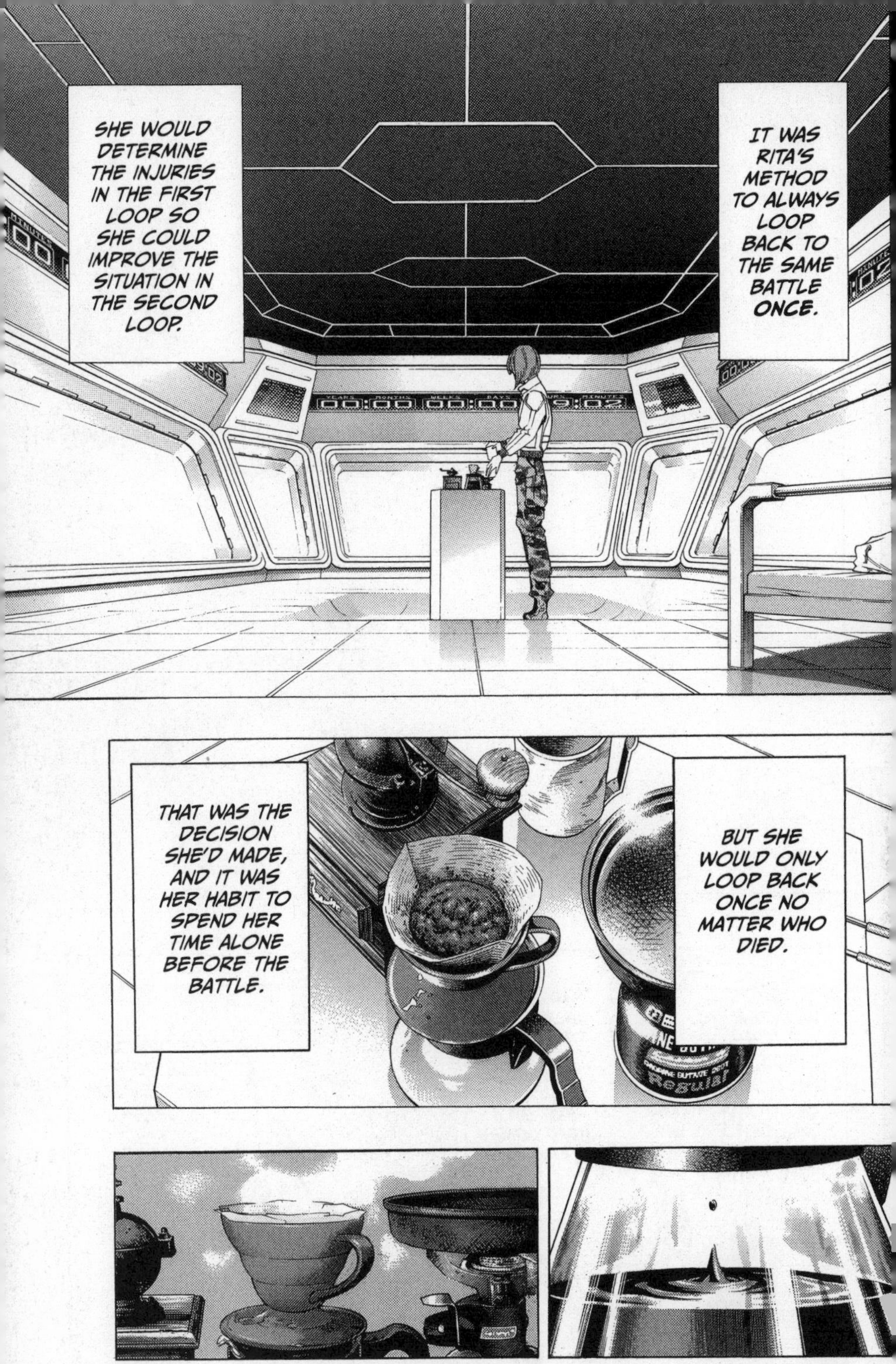
IT WAS RITA'S METHOD TO ALWAYS LOOP BACK TO THE SAME BATTLE ONCE.
SHE WOULD DETERMINE THE INJURIES IN THE FIRST LOOP SO SHE COULD IMPROVE THE SITUATION IN THE SECOND LOOP.
BUT SHE WOULD ONLY LOOP BACK ONCE NO MATTER WHO DIED.
THAT WAS THE DECISION SHE'D MADE, AND IT WAS HER HABIT TO SPEND HER TIME ALONE BEFORE THE BATTLE.

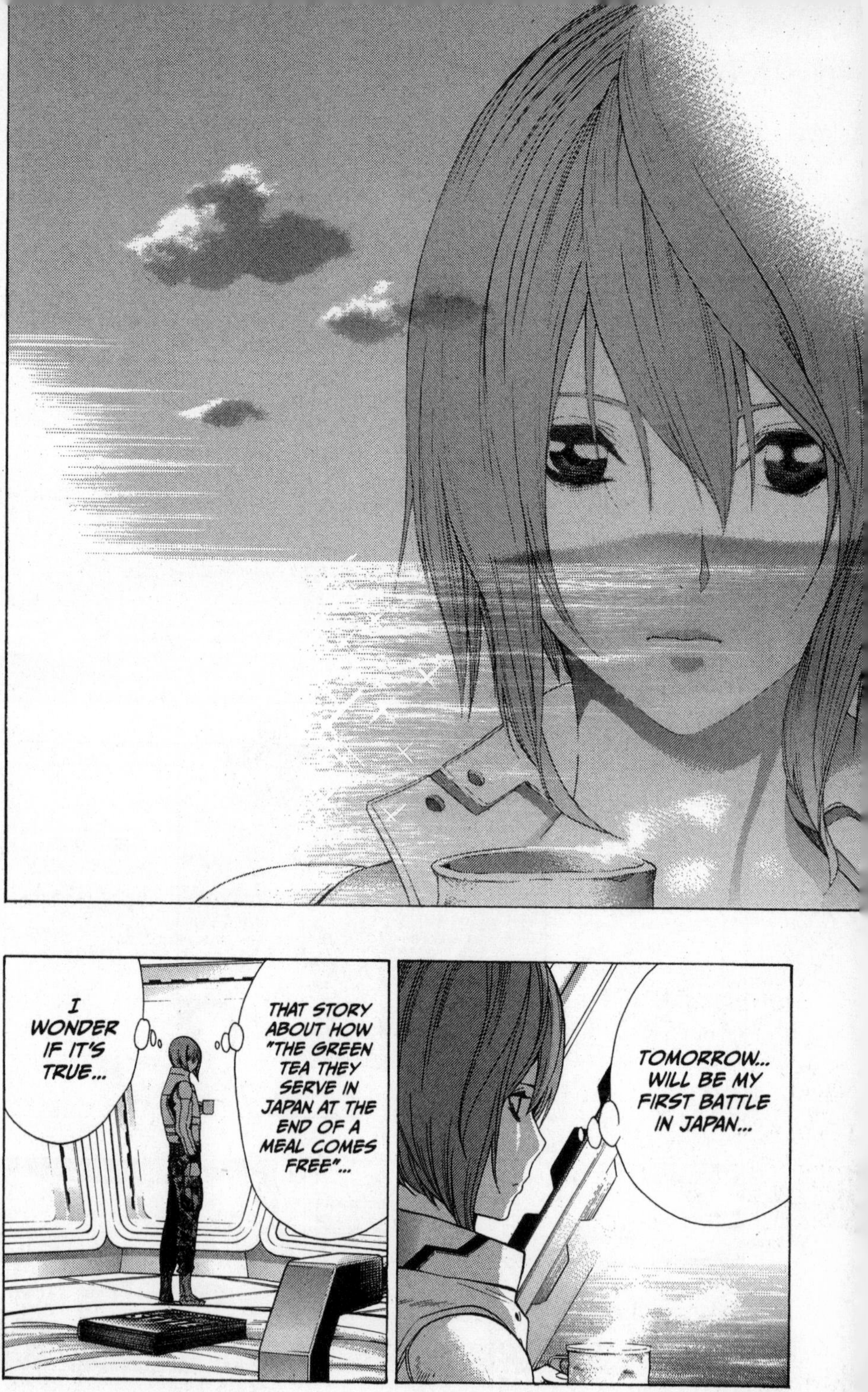
TOMORROW... WILL BE MY FIRST BATTLE IN JAPAN...
THAT STORY ABOUT HOW "THE GREEN TEA THEY SERVE IN JAPAN AT THE END OF A MEAL COMES FREE"...
I WONDER IF IT'S TRUE...

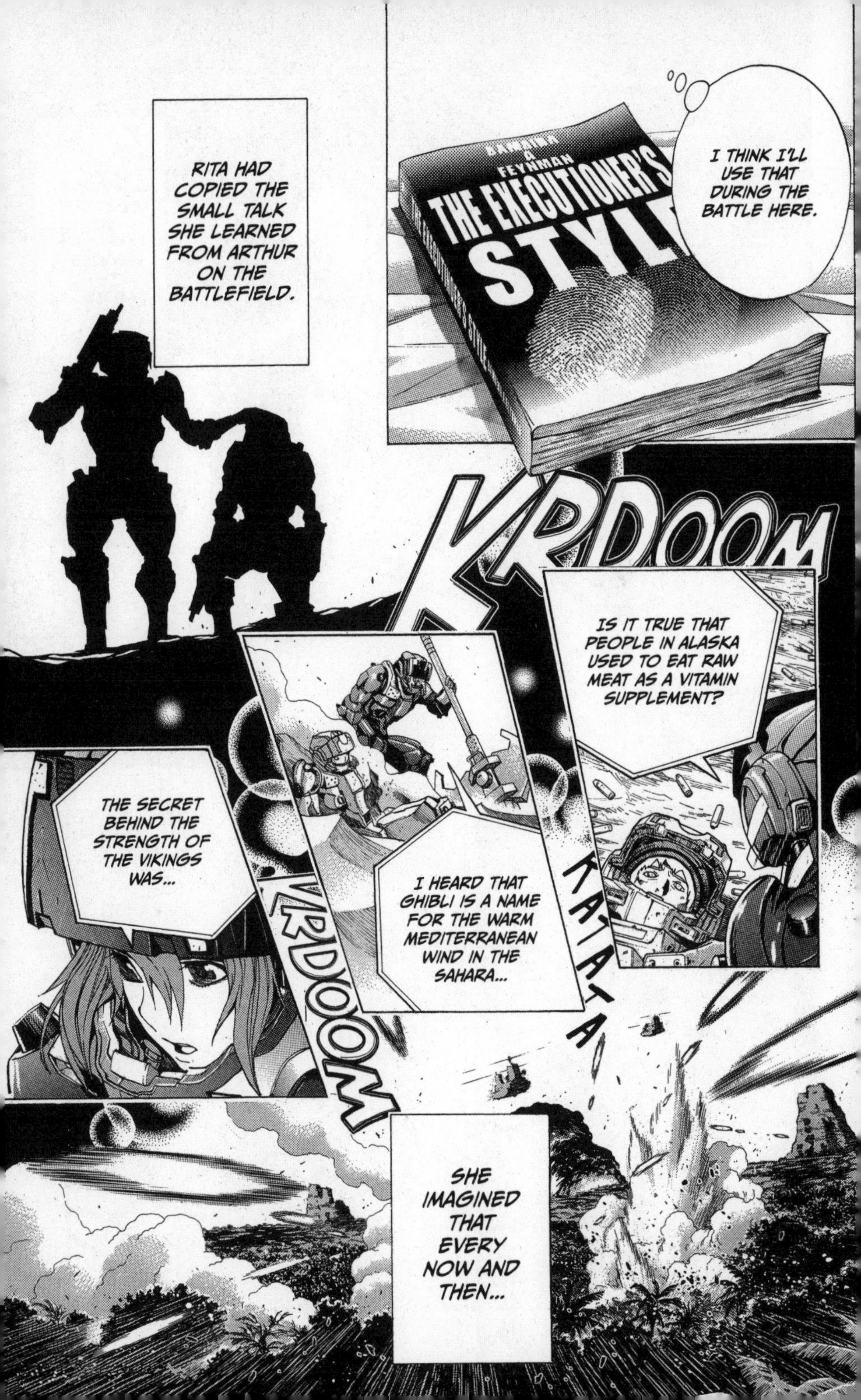
THE EXECUTIONER'S STYLE
I THINK I'LL USE THAT DURING THE BATTLE HERE.
RITA HAD COPIED THE SMALL TALK SHE LEARNED FROM ARTHUR ON THE BATTLEFIELD.
VRDOOM
IS IT TRUE THAT PEOPLE IN ALASKA USED TO EAT RAW MEAT AS A VITAMIN SUPPLEMENT?
KATATATA
I HEARD THAT GHIBLI IS A NAME FOR THE WARM MEDITERRANEAN WIND IN THE SAHARA...
VRDOOOM
THE SECRET BEHIND THE STRENGTH OF THE VIKINGS WAS...
SHE IMAGINED THAT EVERY NOW AND THEN...

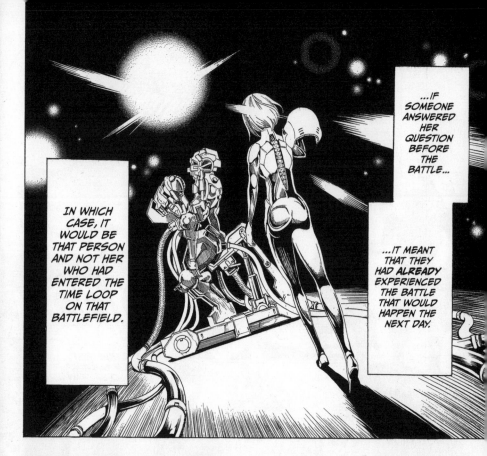

...IF SOMEONE ANSWERED HER QUESTION BEFORE THE BATTLE...
...IT MEANT THAT THEY HAD ALREADY EXPERIENCED THE BATTLE THAT WOULD HAPPEN THE NEXT DAY.
IN WHICH CASE, IT WOULD BE THAT PERSON AND NOT HER WHO HAD ENTERED THE TIME LOOP ON THAT BATTLEFIELD.
BUT THREE YEARS AFTER SHE ESCAPED THE LOOP FOR THE FIRST TIME...
...RITA HAD BEEN ALL AROUND THE WORLD, AND SHE STILL HAD NEVER MET ANYONE LIKE THAT.

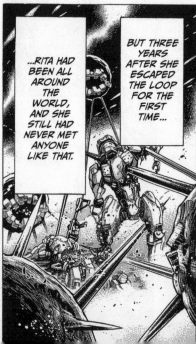

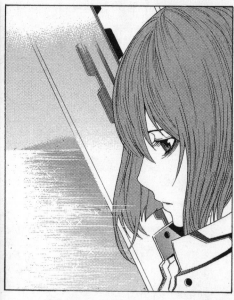

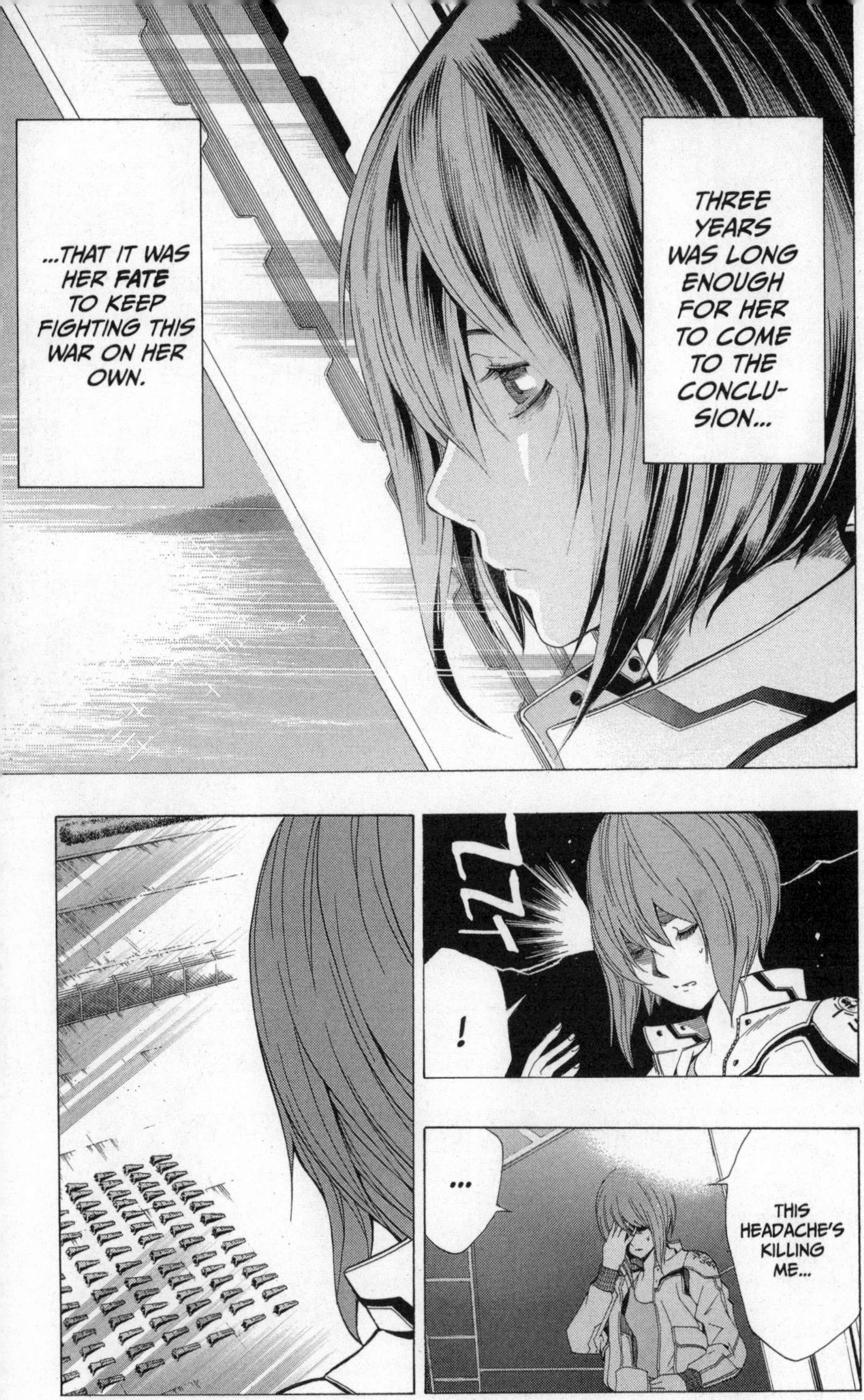
THREE YEARS WAS LONG ENOUGH FOR HER TO COME TO THE CONCLUSION...
...THAT IT WAS HER FATE TO KEEP FIGHTING THIS WAR ON HER OWN.
!
THIS HEADACHE'S KILLING ME...
...

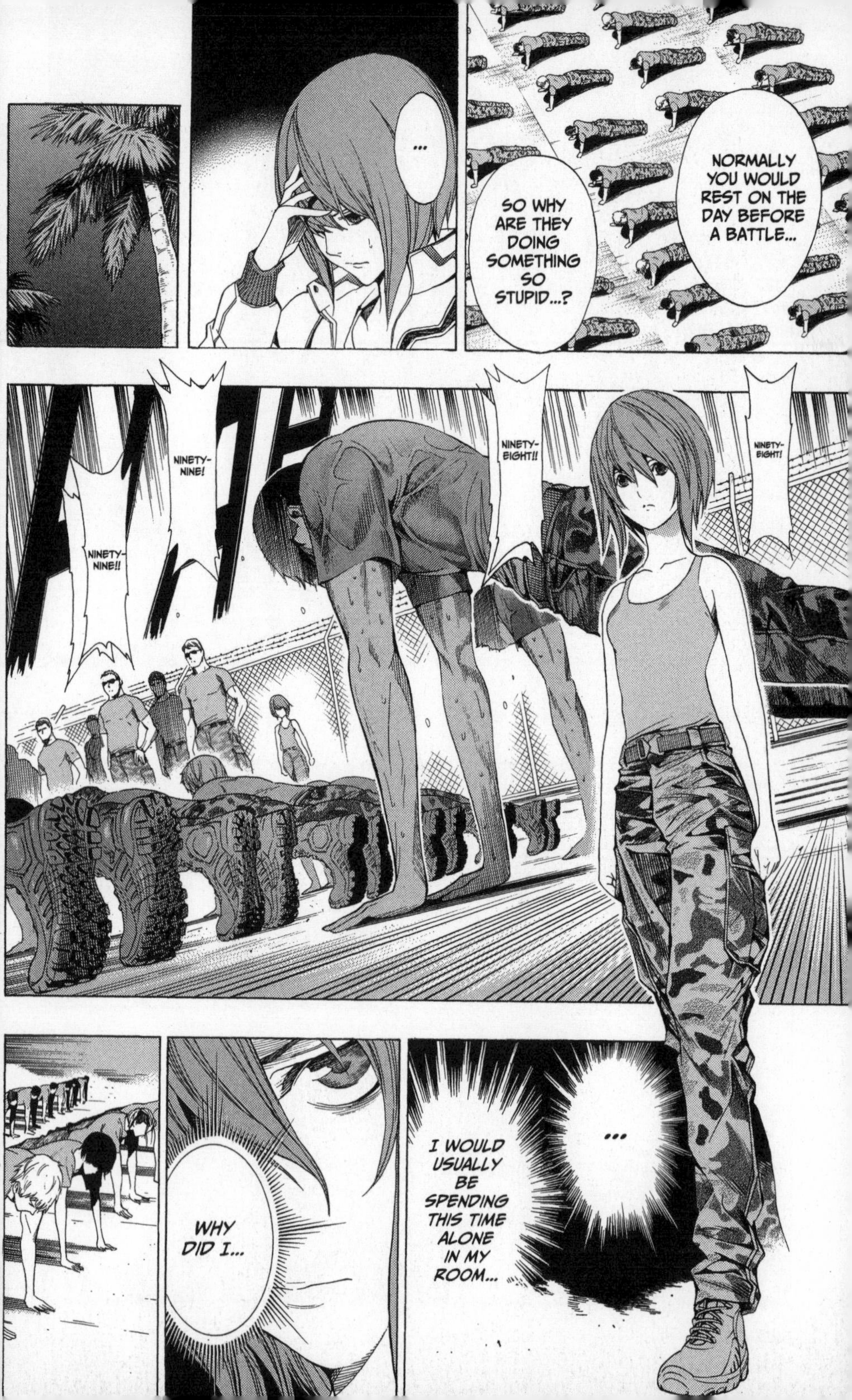
NORMALLY YOU WOULD REST ON THE DAY BEFORE A BATTLE...
SO WHY ARE THEY DOING SOMETHING SO STUPID...?
...
NINETY-EIGHT!
NINETY-EIGHT!!
NINETY-NINE!
NINETY-NINE!!
...
I WOULD USUALLY BE SPENDING THIS TIME ALONE IN MY ROOM...
WHY DID I...

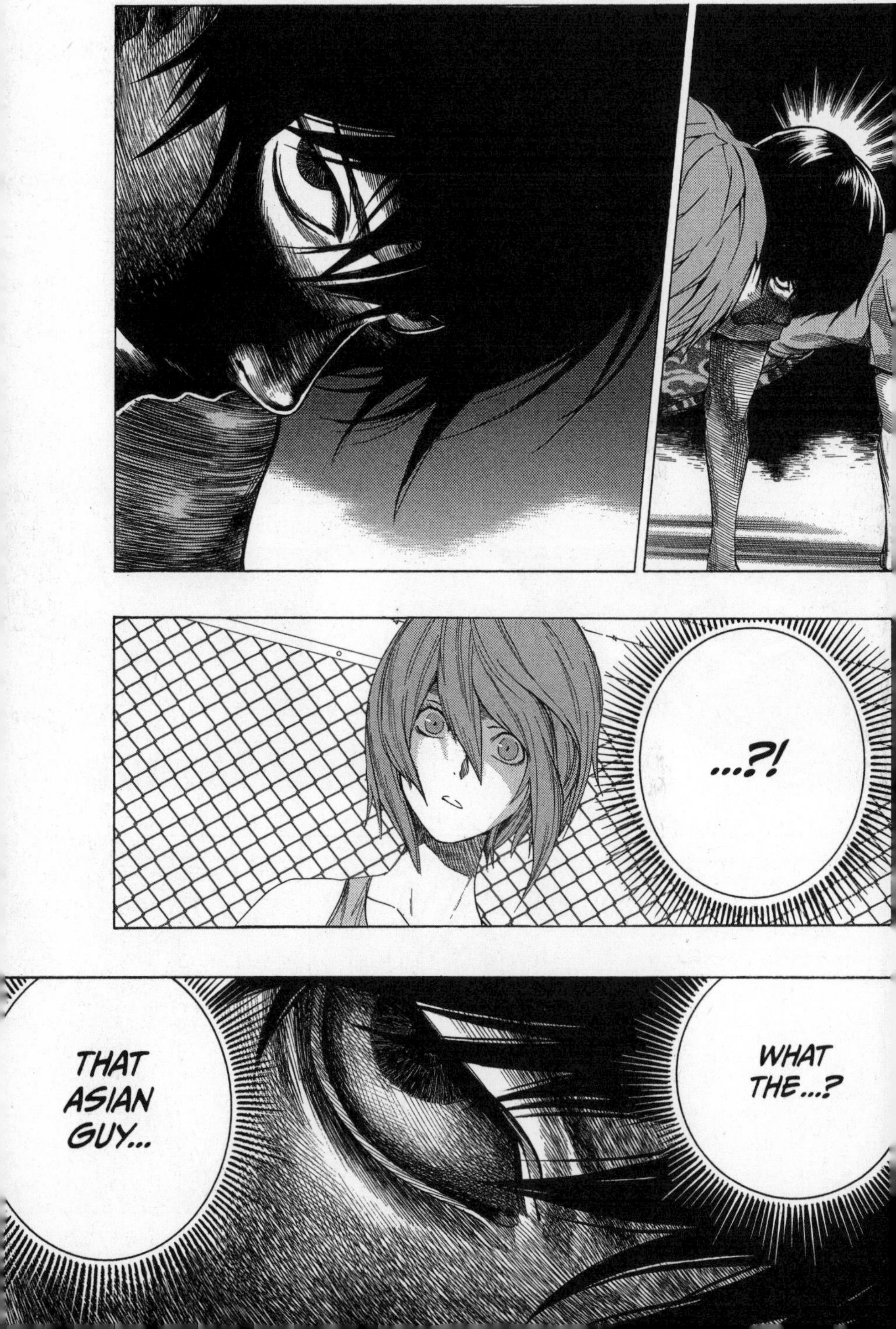
...?!
WHAT THE...?
THAT ASIAN GUY...

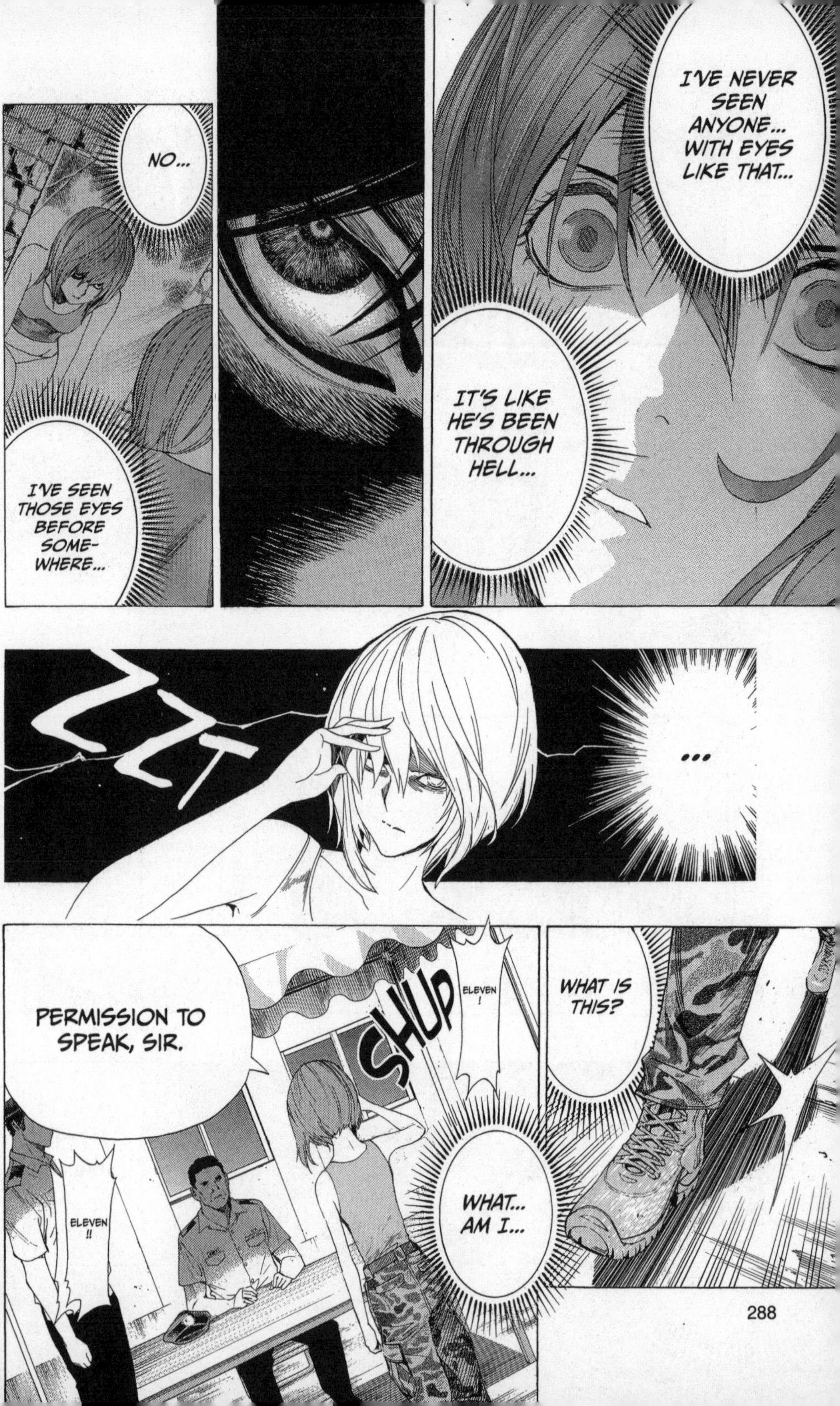
I'VE NEVER SEEN ANYONE... WITH EYES LIKE THAT...
IT'S LIKE HE'S BEEN THROUGH HELL...
NO...
I'VE SEEN THOSE EYES BEFORE SOME-WHERE...
...
WHAT IS THIS?
WHAT... AM I...
ELEVEN!
SHUP
PERMISSION TO SPEAK, SIR.
ELEVEN!!

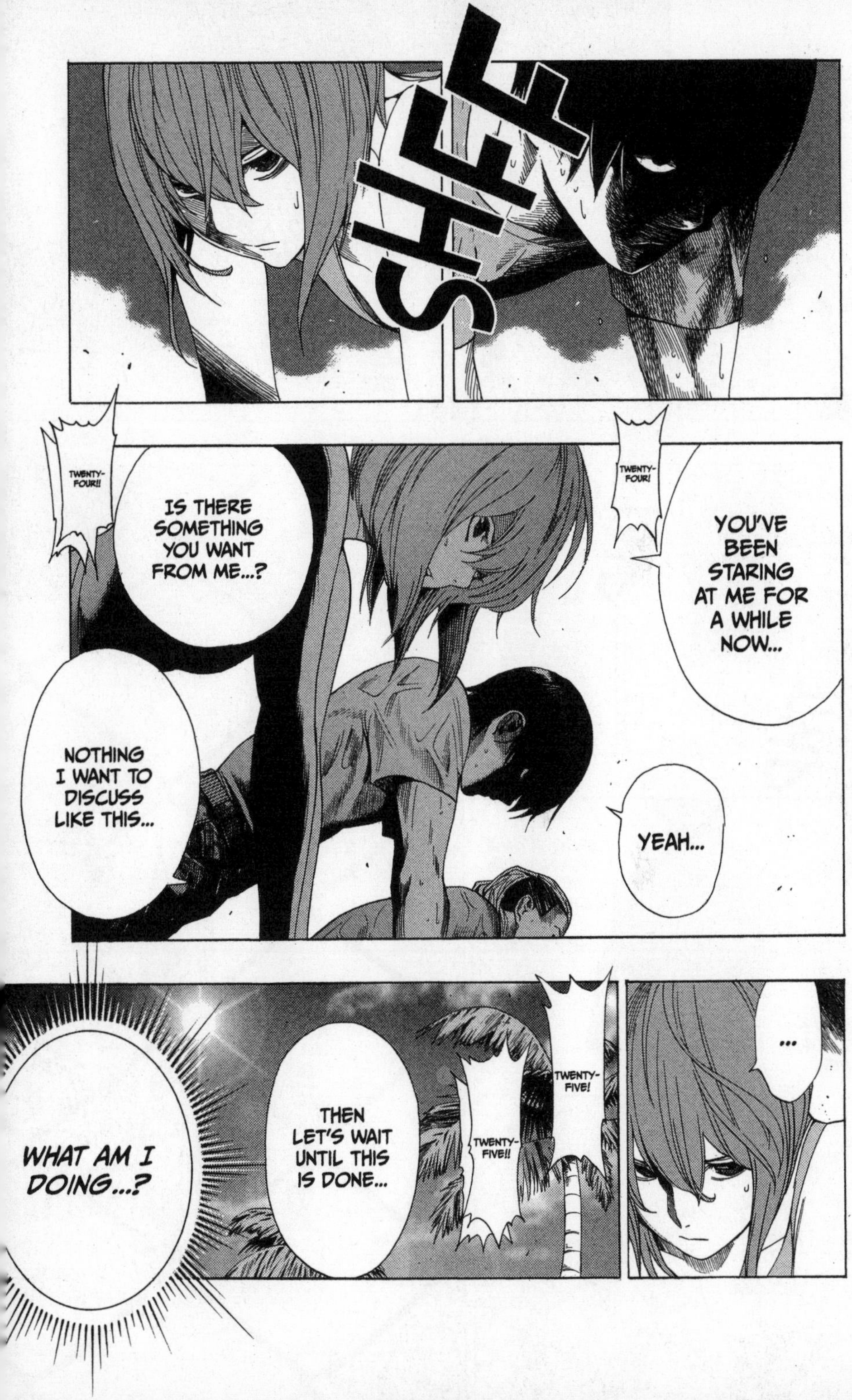
SHFF
TWENTY-FOUR!
YOU'VE BEEN STARING AT ME FOR A WHILE NOW...
TWENTY-FOUR!!
IS THERE SOMETHING YOU WANT FROM ME...?
YEAH...
NOTHING I WANT TO DISCUSS LIKE THIS...
...
TWENTY-FIVE!
TWENTY-FIVE!!
THEN LET'S WAIT UNTIL THIS IS DONE...
WHAT AM I DOING...?

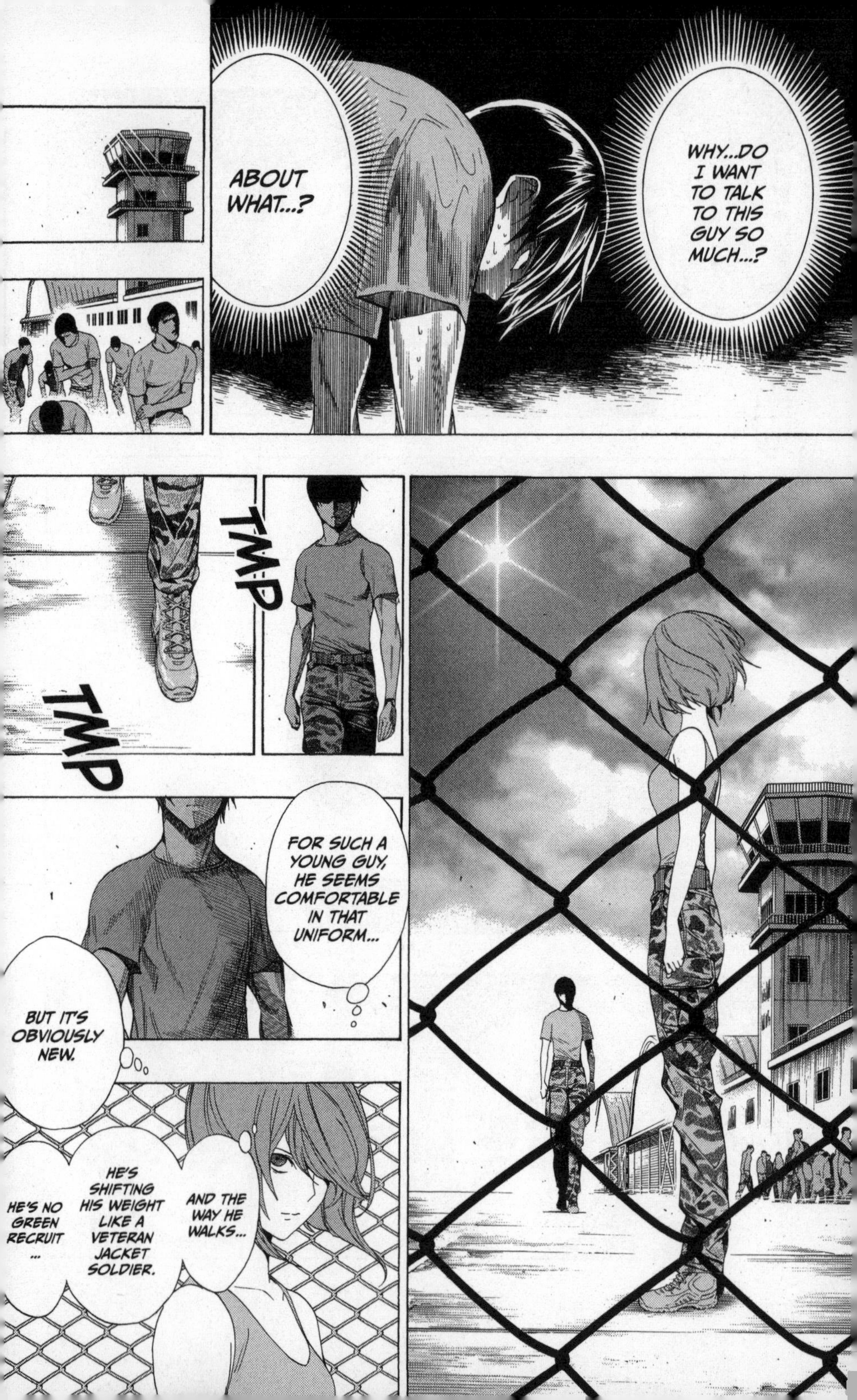
WHY...DO I WANT TO TALK TO THIS GUY SO MUCH...?
ABOUT WHAT...?
TMP
TMP
FOR SUCH A YOUNG GUY, HE SEEMS COMFORTABLE IN THAT UNIFORM...
BUT IT'S OBVIOUSLY NEW.
AND THE WAY HE WALKS...
HE'S SHIFTING HIS WEIGHT LIKE A VETERAN JACKET SOLDIER.
HE'S NO GREEN RECRUIT...

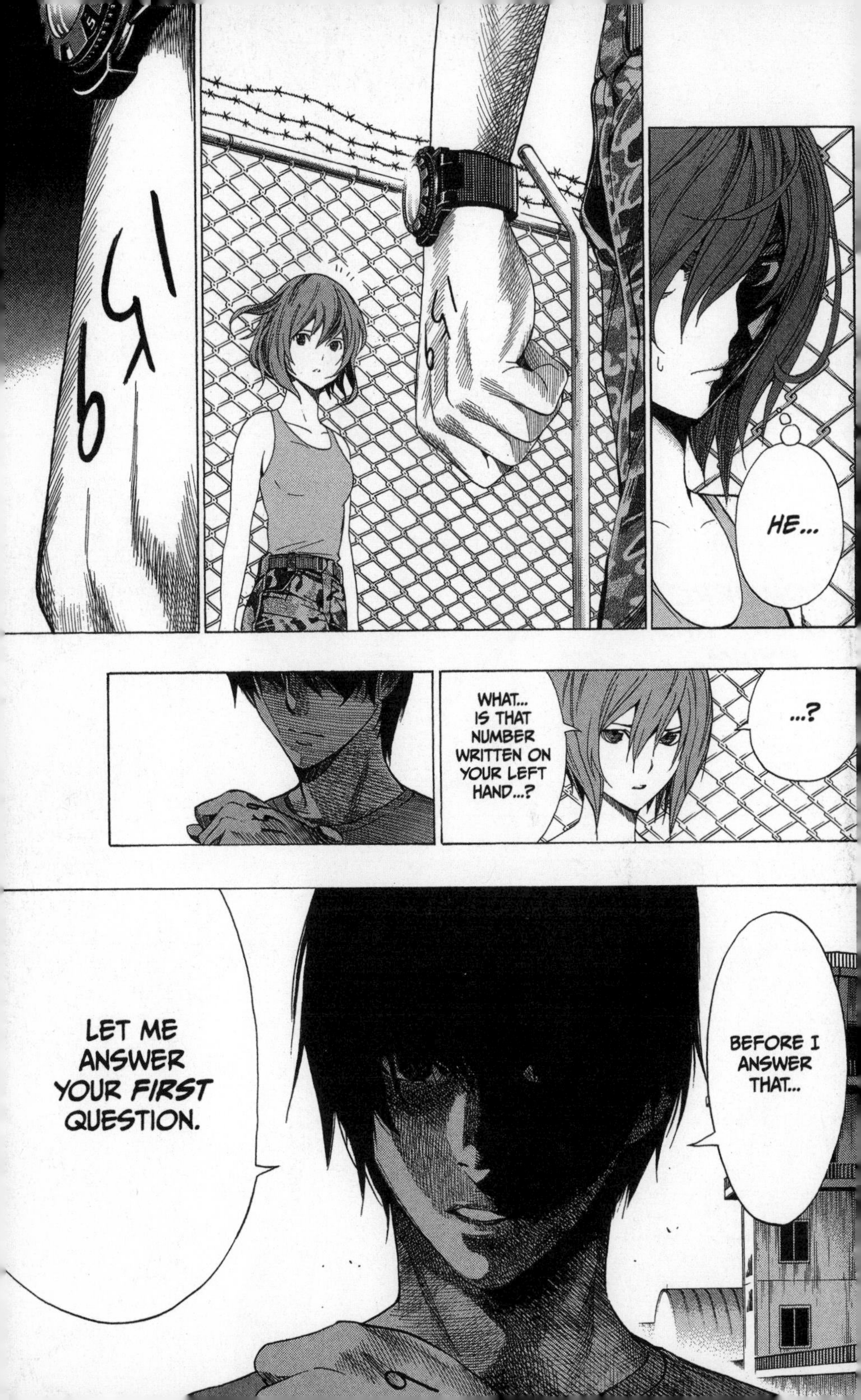

HE...
...?
WHAT... IS THAT NUMBER WRITTEN ON YOUR LEFT HAND...?
BEFORE I ANSWER THAT...
LET ME ANSWER YOUR *FIRST* QUESTION.

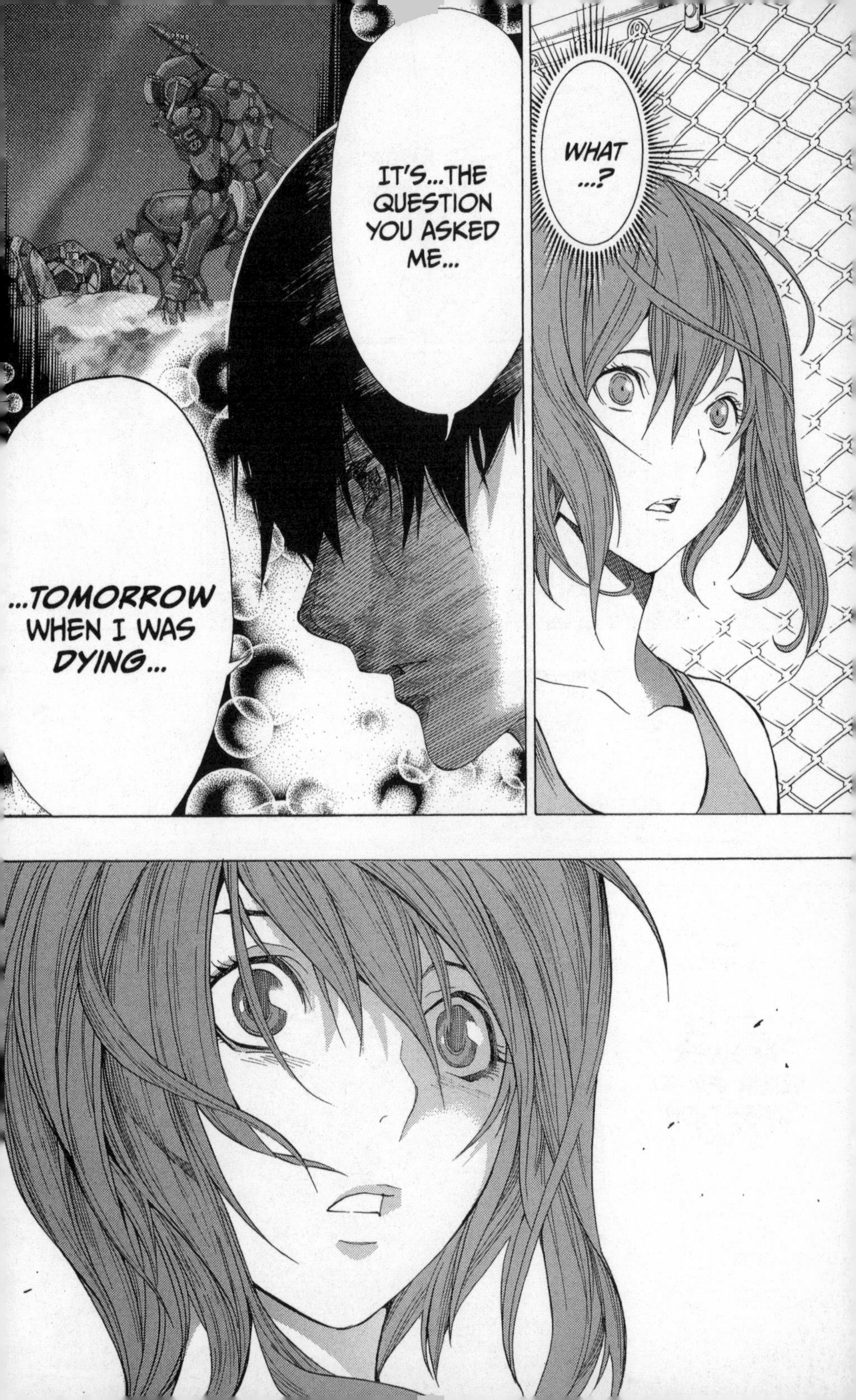
WHAT ...?
IT'S...THE QUESTION YOU ASKED ME...
...TOMORROW WHEN I WAS DYING...

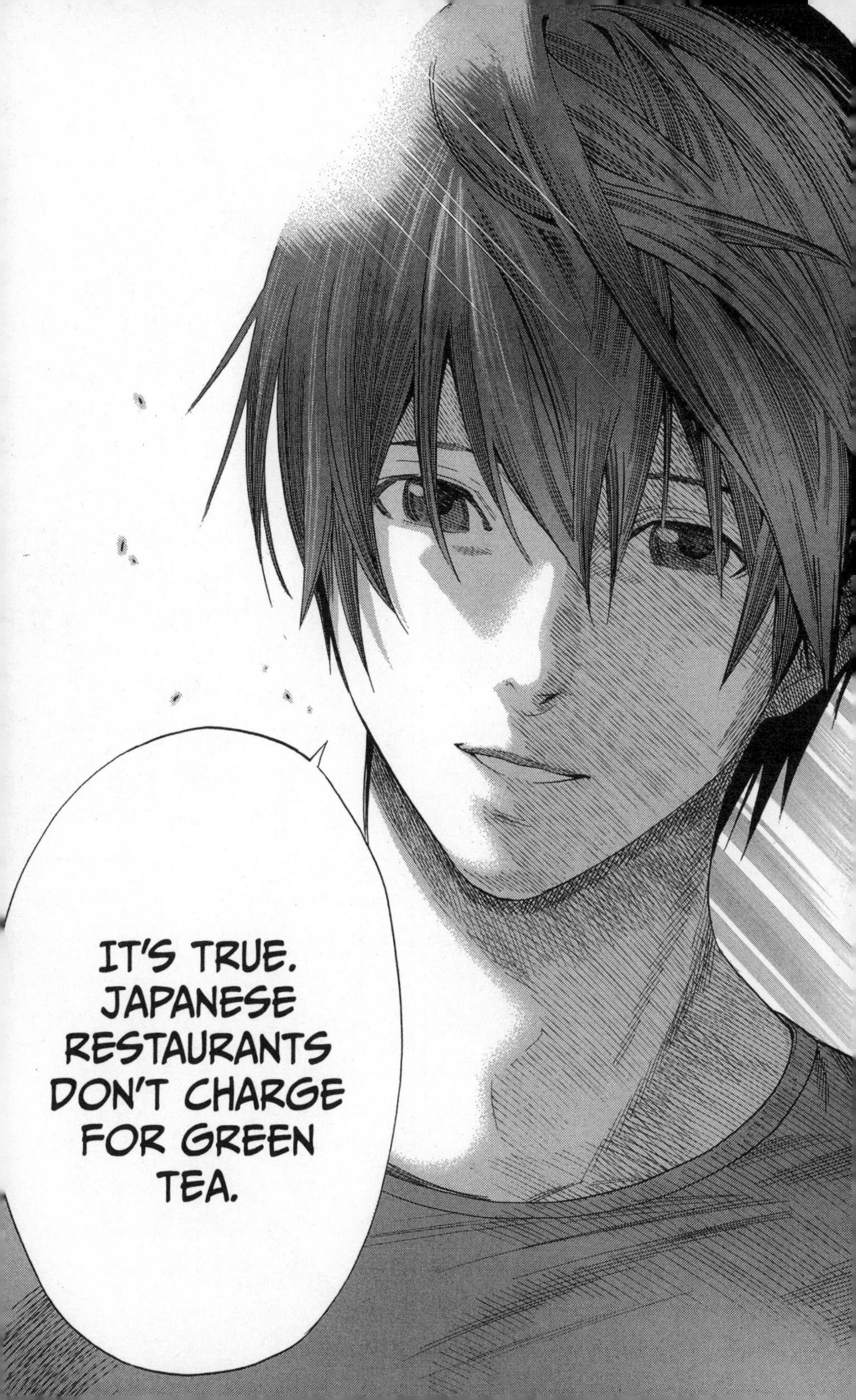
IT'S TRUE. JAPANESE RESTAURANTS DON'T CHARGE FOR GREEN TEA.

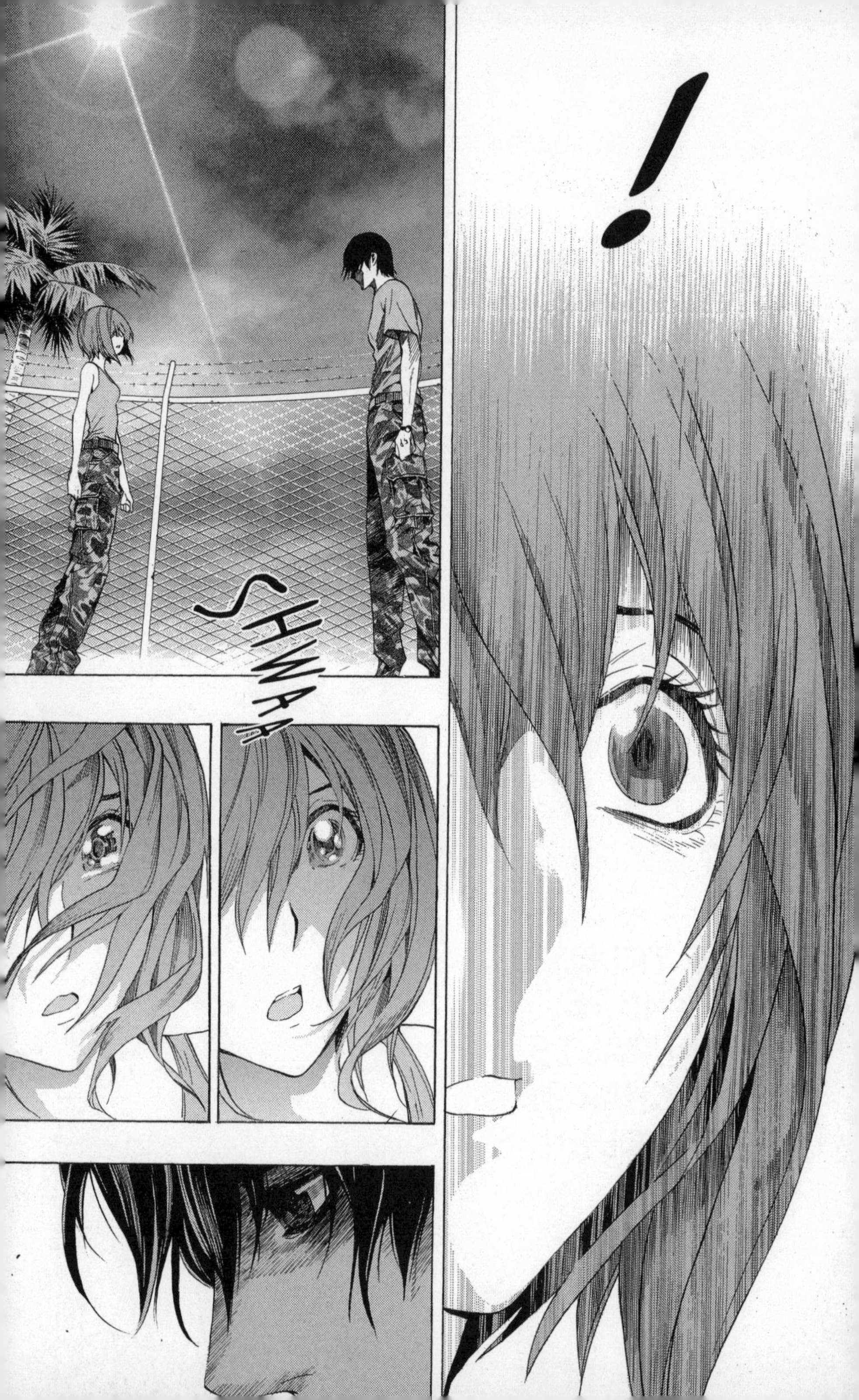
!
SHWAA

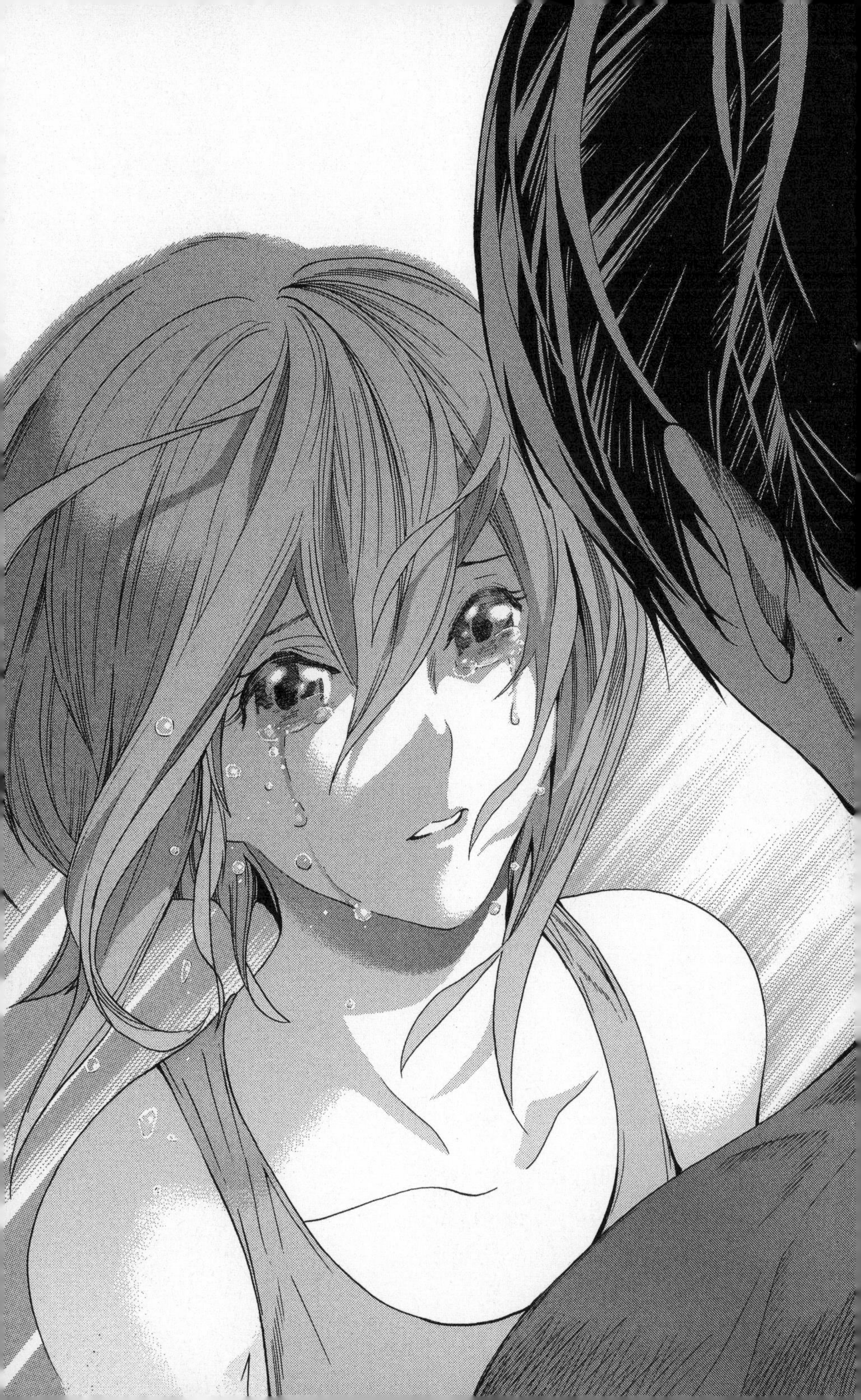

What this nightmarish time
loop from the bowels of Hell
hath joined together, let no
man put asunder.
Only Rita and I understood
each other's solitude, and
we could stand side-by-side,
dicing Mimics into bite-size
chunks until the bitter end.

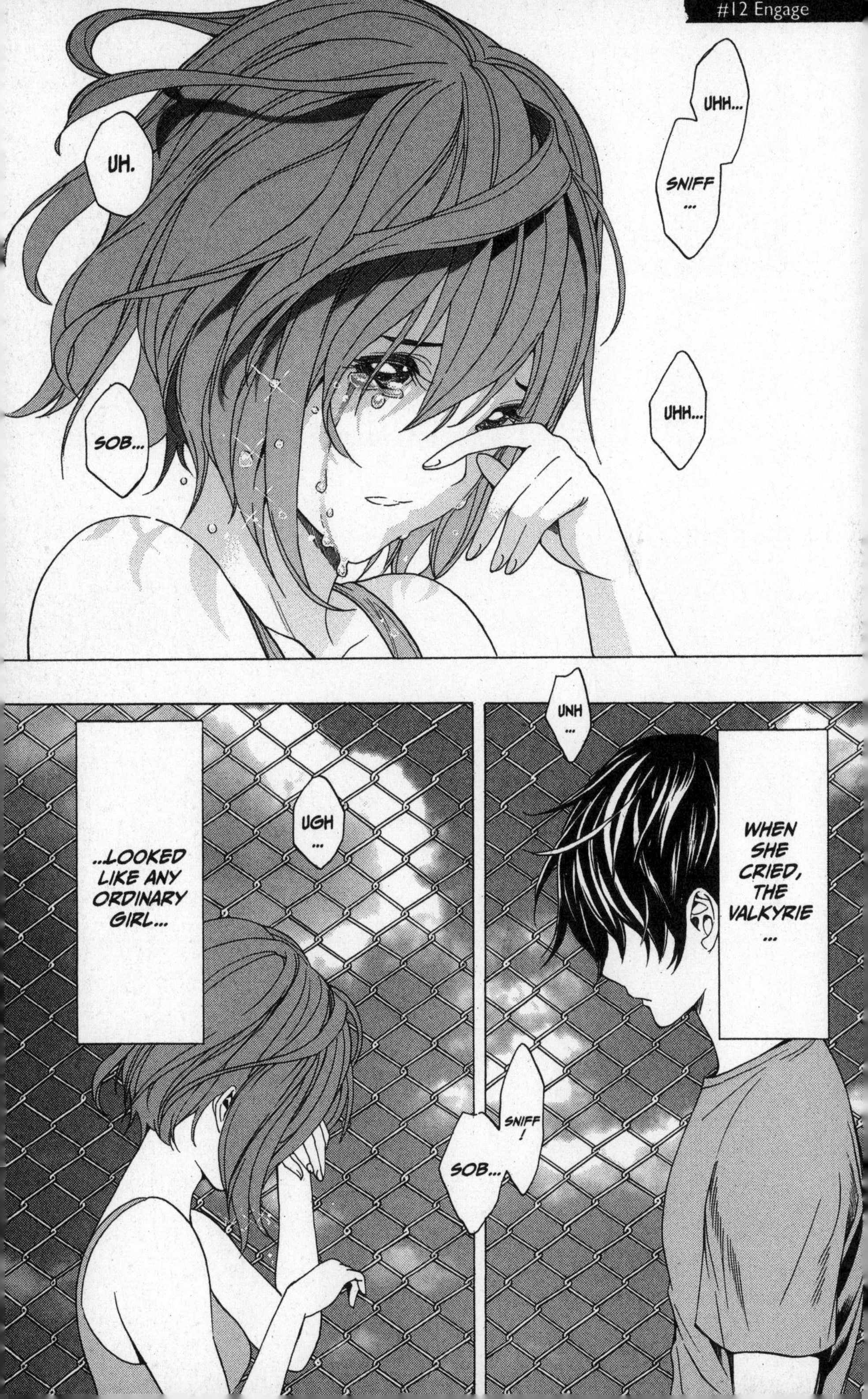
UHH... SNIFF...
UH.
UHH...
SOB...
UNH...
WHEN SHE CRIED, THE VALKYRIE...
SNIFF!
SOB...
UGH...
...LOOKED LIKE ANY ORDINARY GIRL...

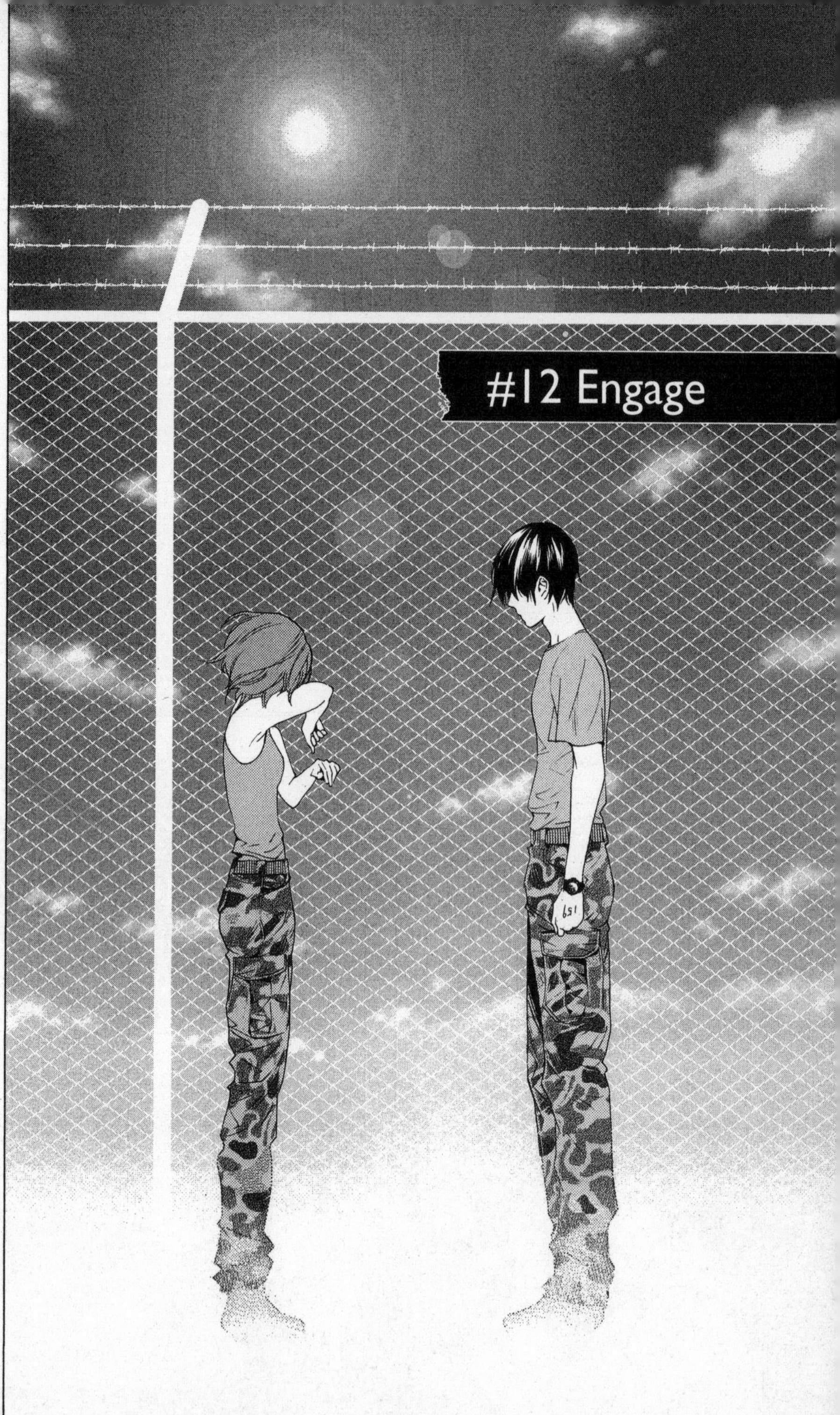
#12 Engage

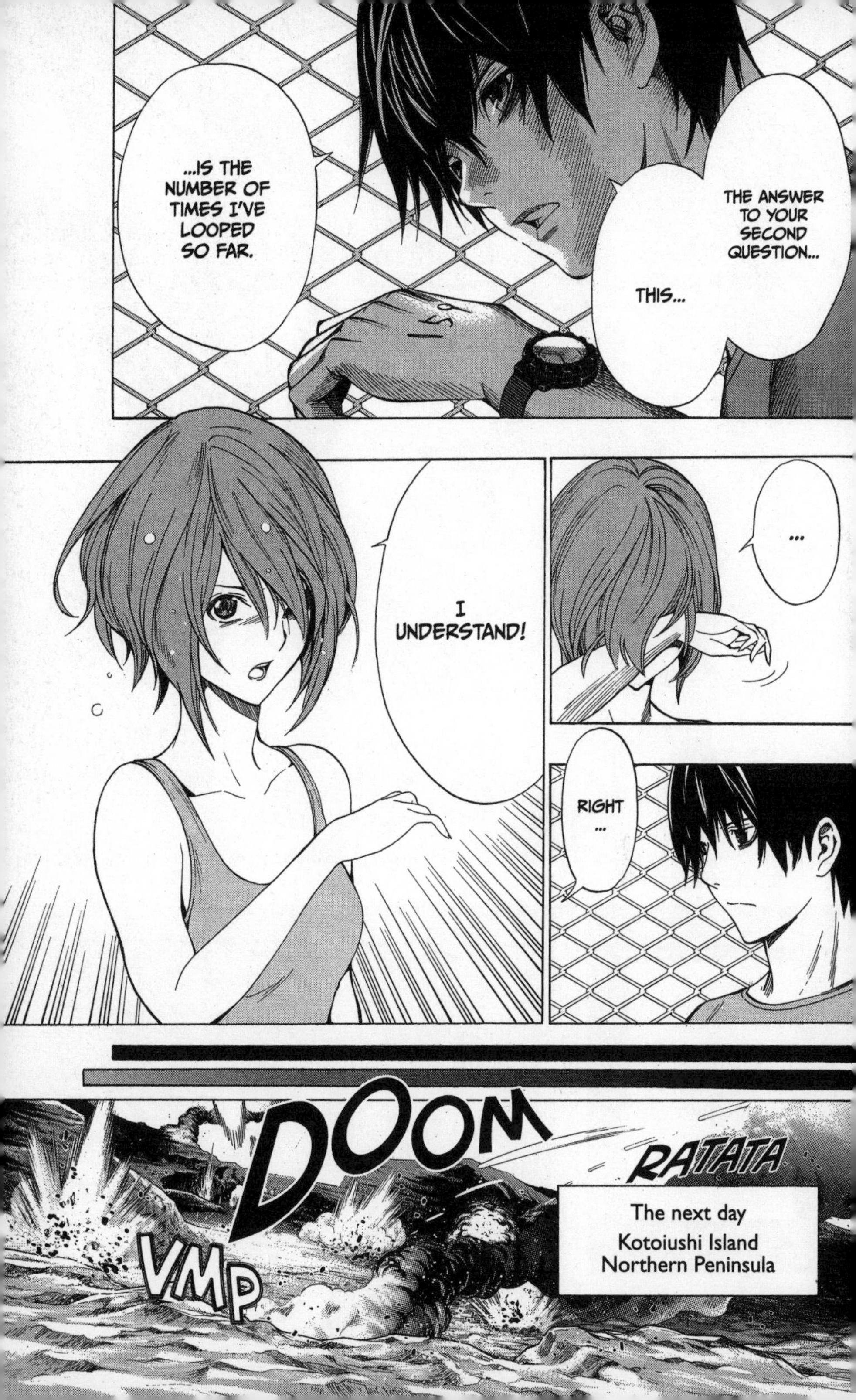
THE ANSWER TO YOUR SECOND QUESTION...
THIS...
...IS THE NUMBER OF TIMES I'VE LOOPED SO FAR.
...
RIGHT ...
I UNDERSTAND!
RATATA
DOOM
The next day Kotoiushi Island Northern Peninsula
VMP

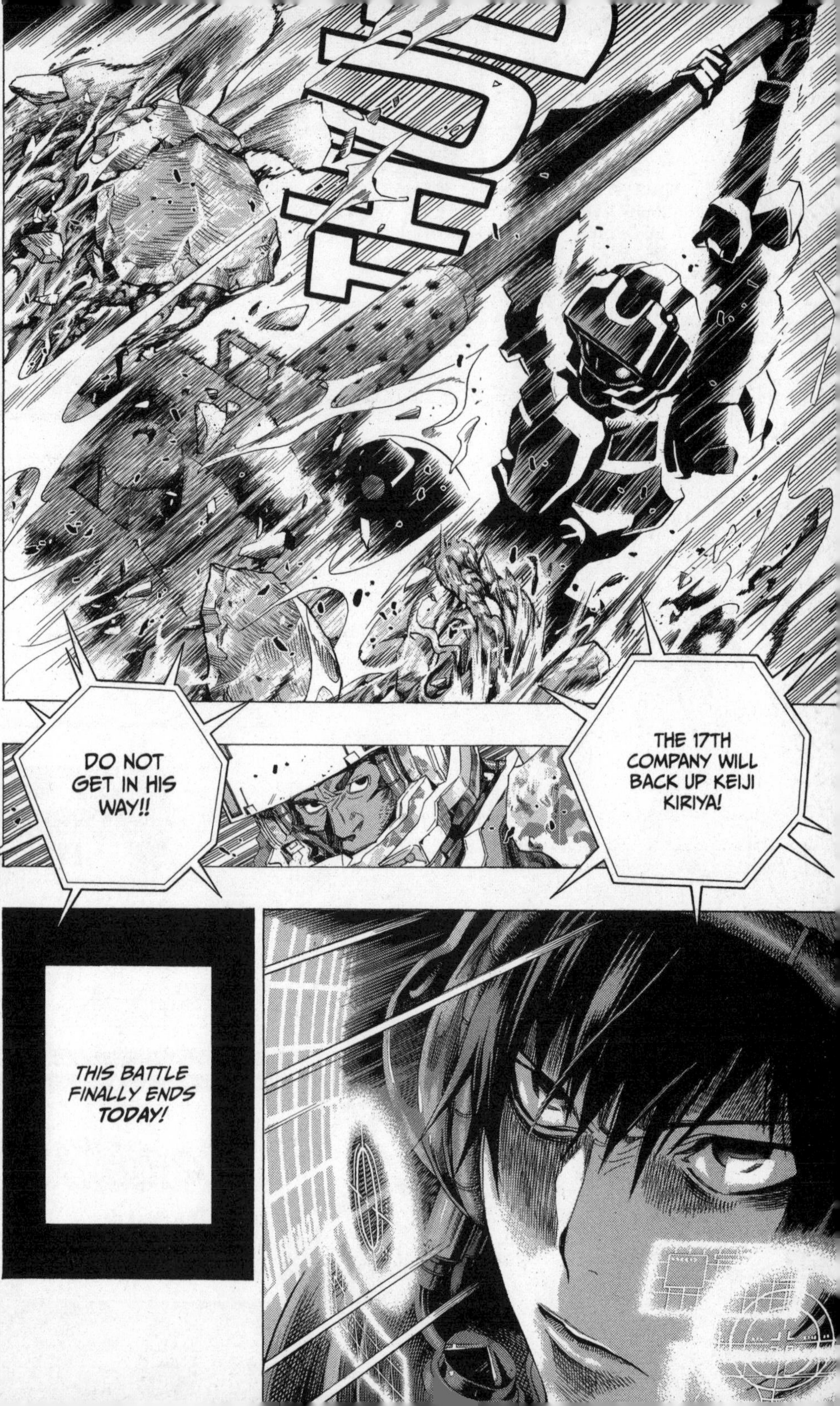
THUD
THE 17TH COMPANY WILL BACK UP KEIJI KIRIYA!
DO NOT GET IN HIS WAY!!
THIS BATTLE FINALLY ENDS TODAY!

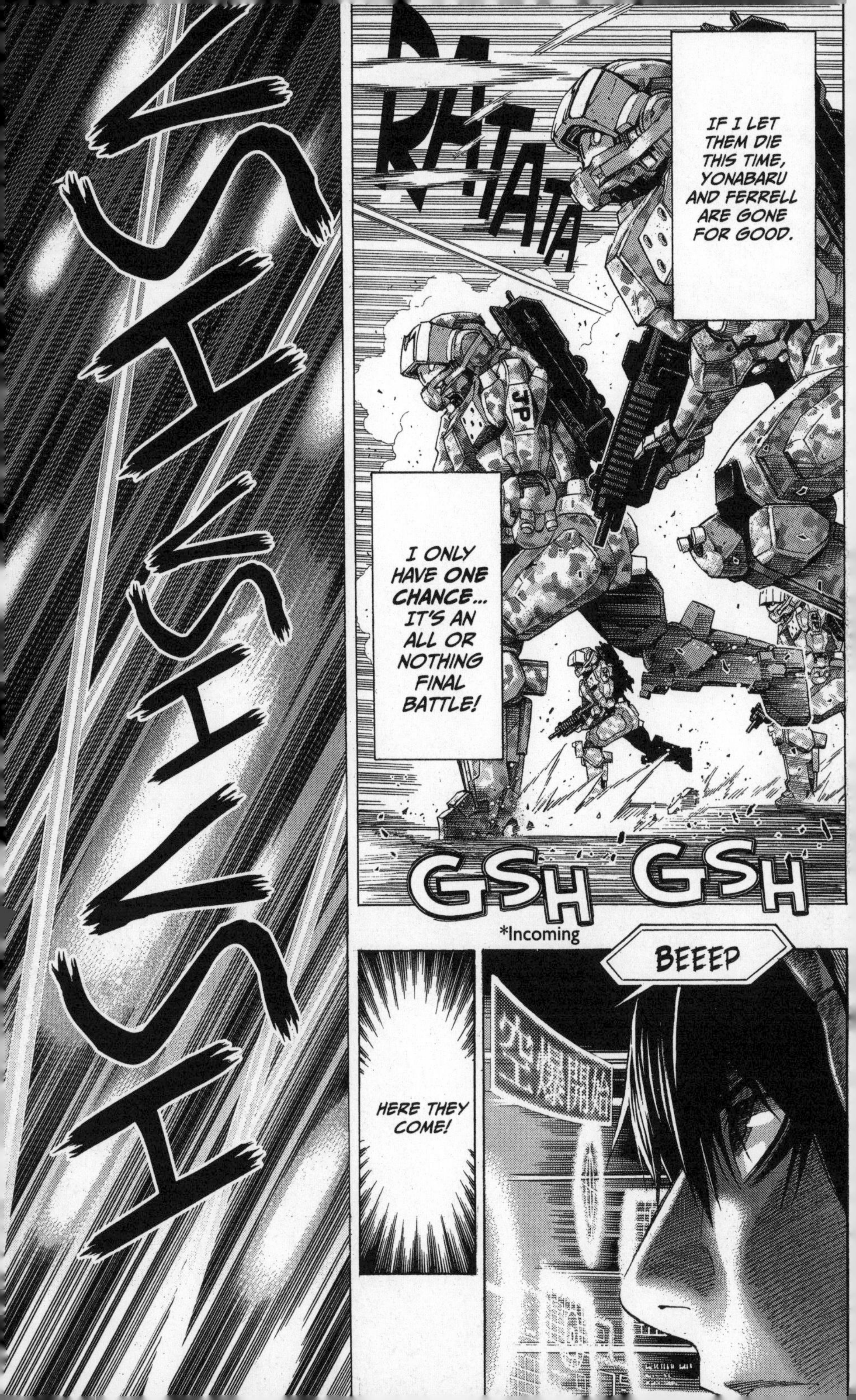
RATATATA
IF I LET THEM DIE THIS TIME, YONABARU AND FERRELL ARE GONE FOR GOOD.
JP
I ONLY HAVE ONE CHANCE... IT'S AN ALL OR NOTHING FINAL BATTLE!
GSH GSH
*Incoming
BEEEP
HERE THEY COME!
SHASHASHA

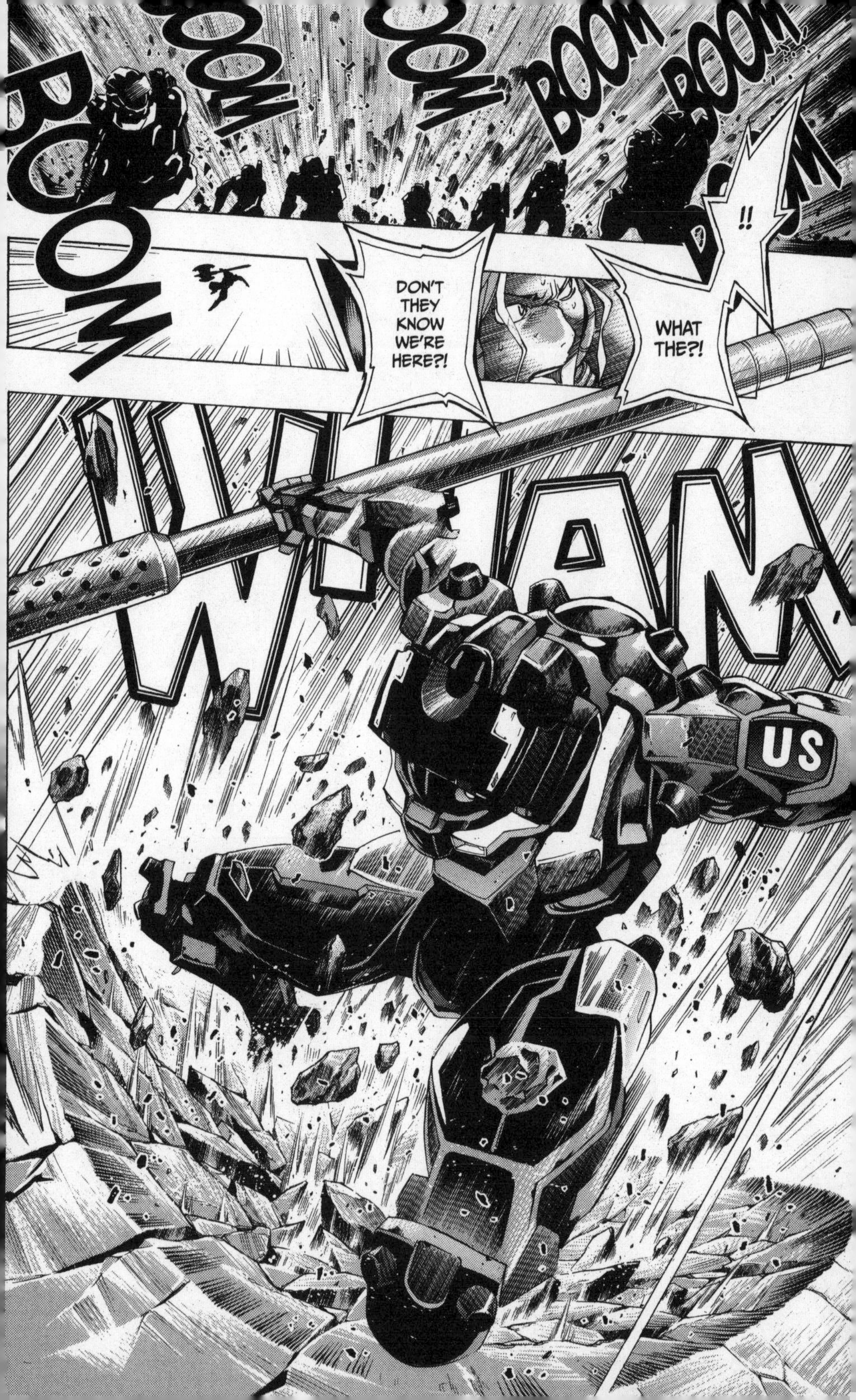
BOOM
BOOM
BOOM
BOOM
!!
WHAT THE?!
DON'T THEY KNOW WE'RE HERE?!
WHAM
US

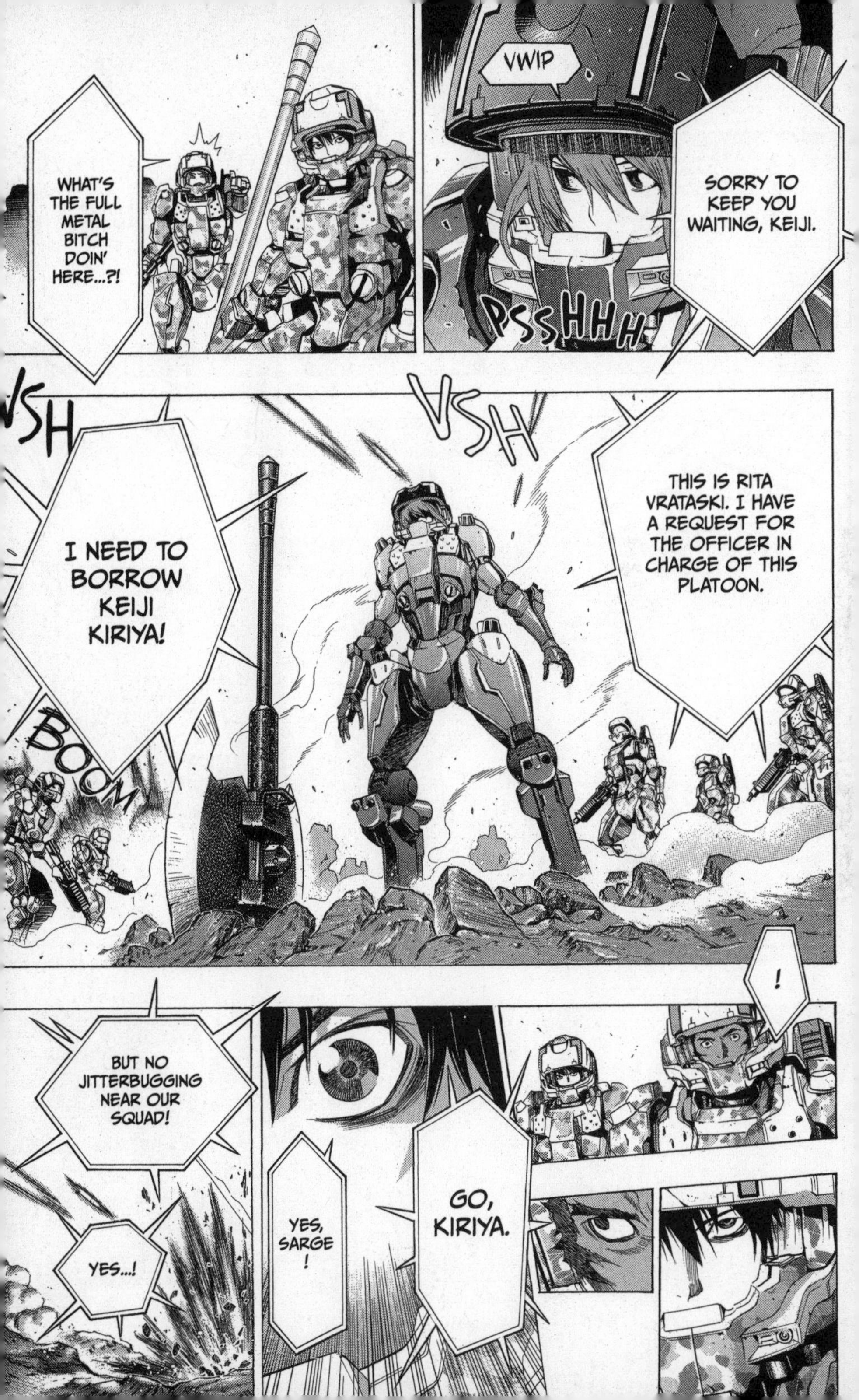
VWIP
SORRY TO KEEP YOU WAITING, KEIJI.
PSSHHH
WHAT'S THE FULL METAL BITCH DOIN' HERE...?!
VSH
VSH
THIS IS RITA VRATASKI. I HAVE A REQUEST FOR THE OFFICER IN CHARGE OF THIS PLATOON.
I NEED TO BORROW KEIJI KIRIYA!
BOOM
!
GO, KIRIYA.
YES, SARGE!
BUT NO JITTERBUGGING NEAR OUR SQUAD!
YES...!

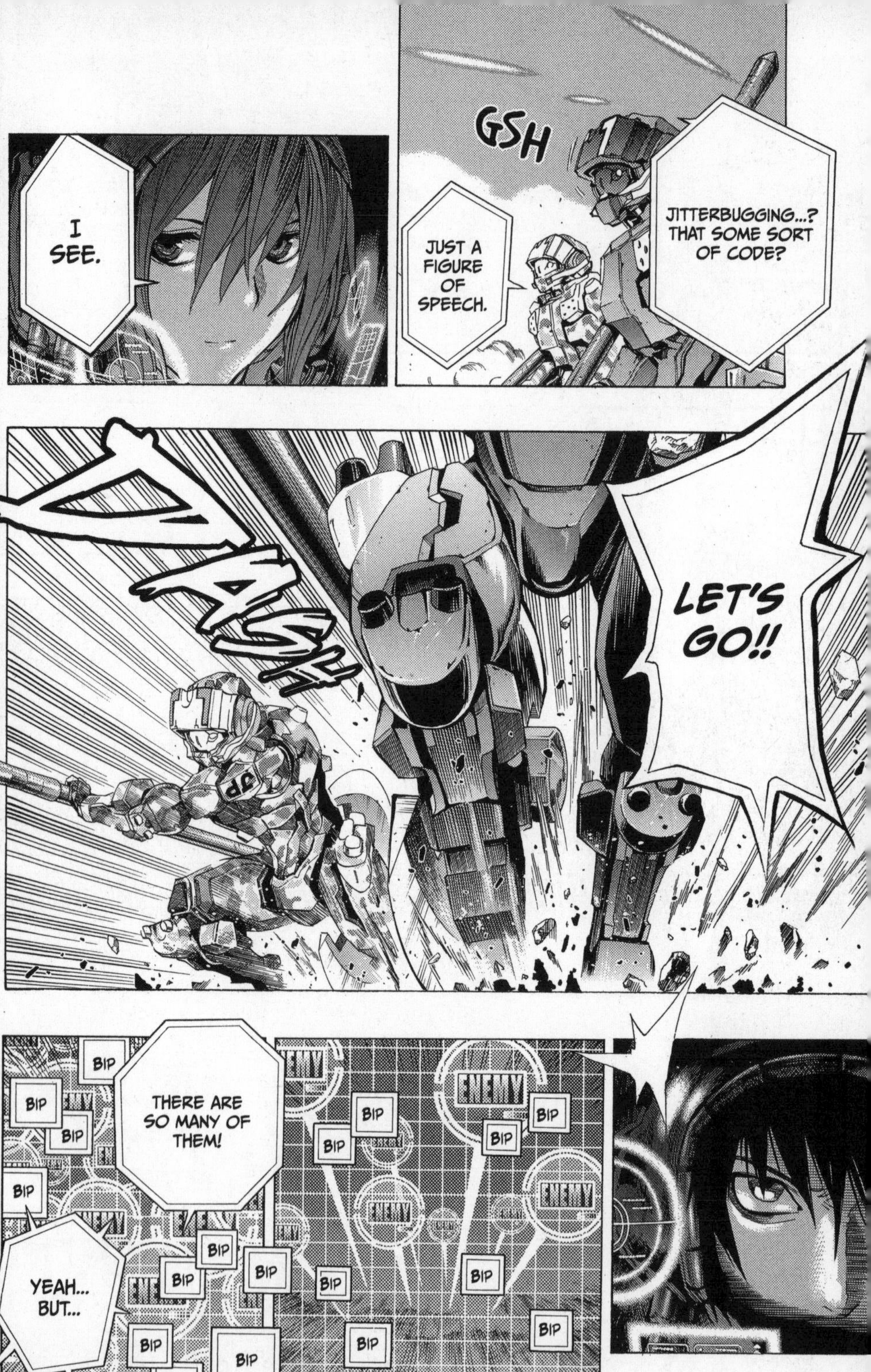
GSH
JITTERBUGGING...? THAT SOME SORT OF CODE?
JUST A FIGURE OF SPEECH.
I SEE.
DASH
LET'S GO!!
ENEMY
BIP
THERE ARE SO MANY OF THEM!
YEAH... BUT...

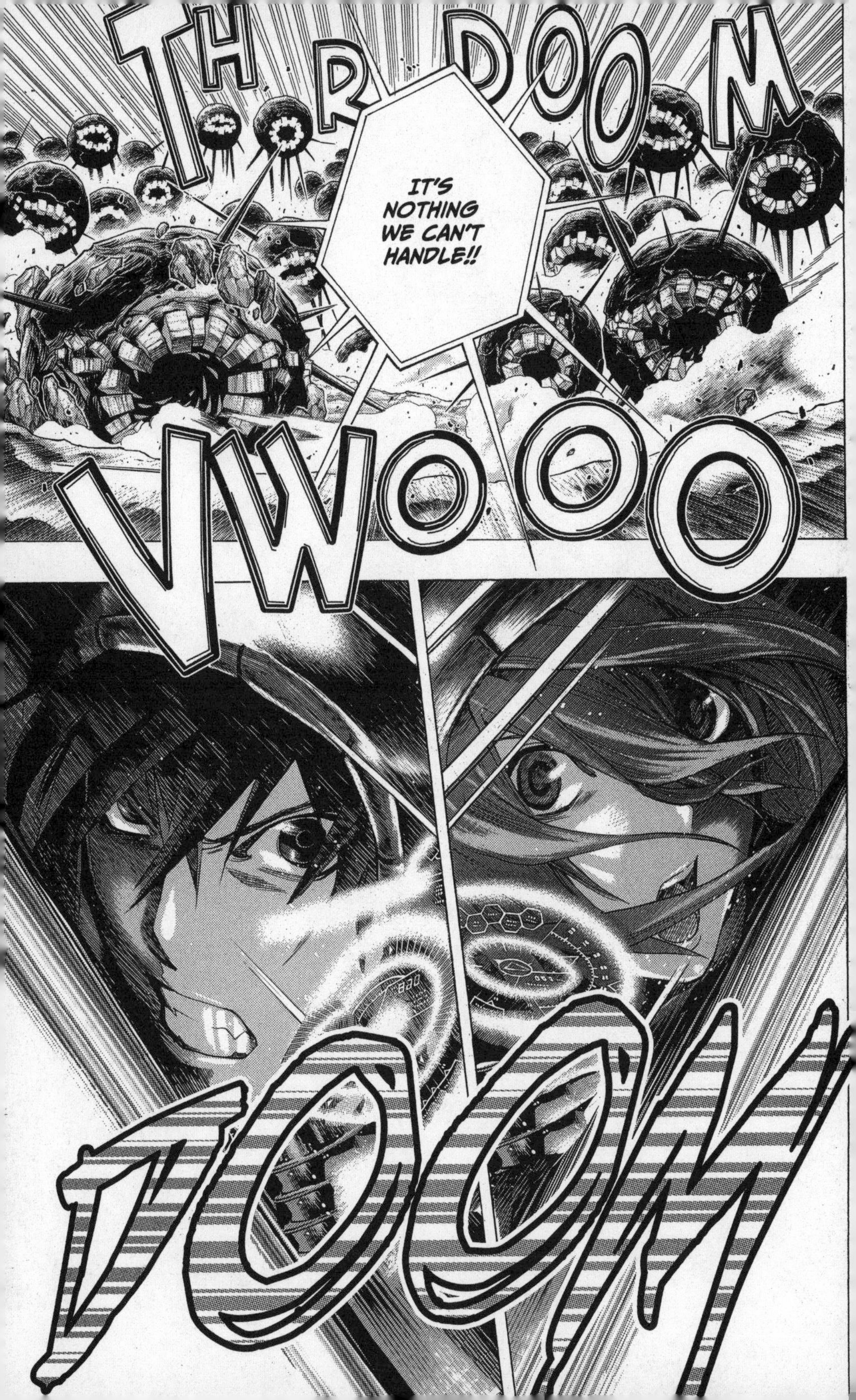
THROOM
IT'S NOTHING WE CAN'T HANDLE!!
VWOOO
VOOM

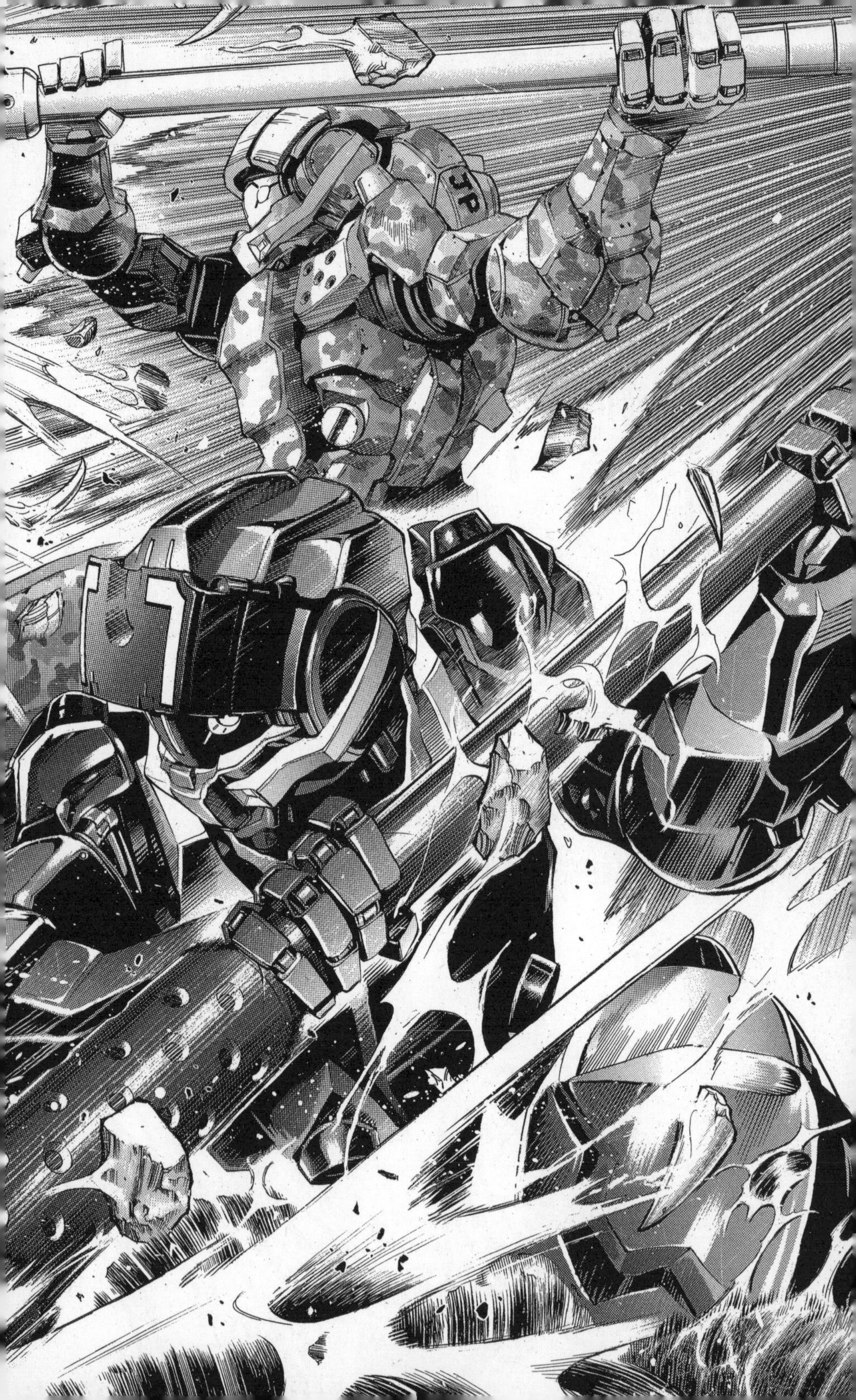
JP

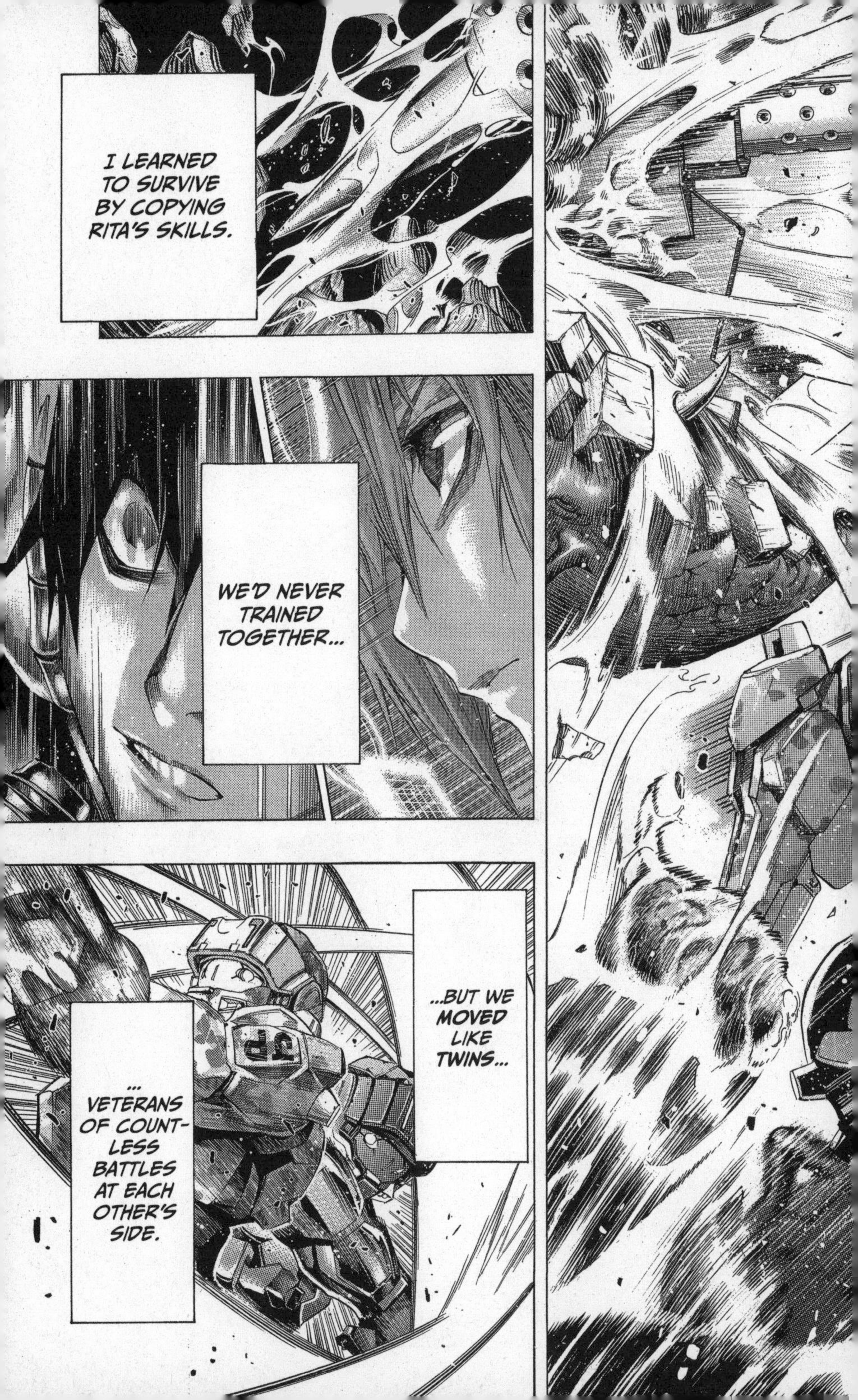
I LEARNED TO SURVIVE BY COPYING RITA'S SKILLS.
WE'D NEVER TRAINED TOGETHER...
...BUT WE MOVED LIKE TWINS...
... VETERANS OF COUNT-LESS BATTLES AT EACH OTHER'S SIDE.

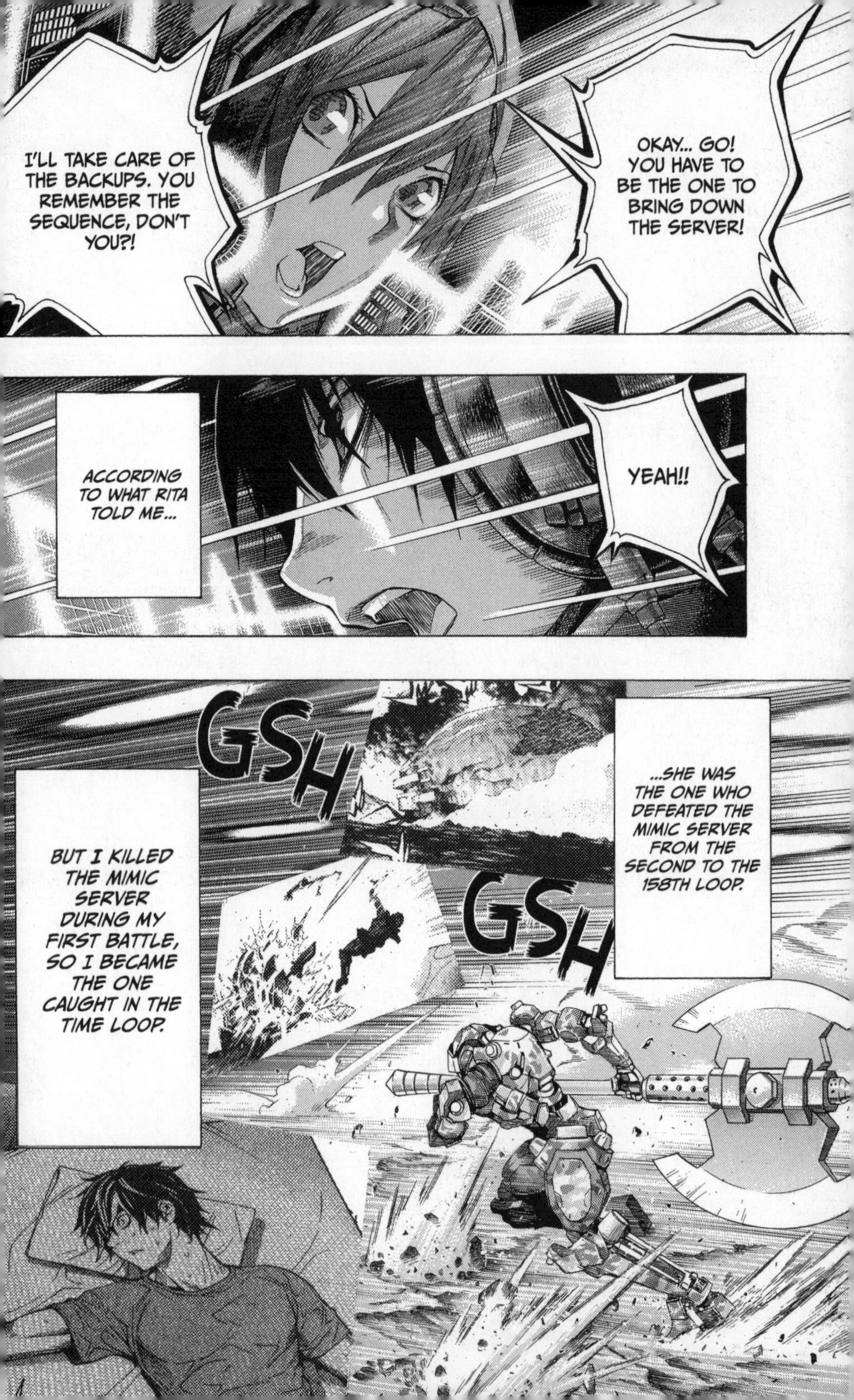
OKAY... GO! YOU HAVE TO BE THE ONE TO BRING DOWN THE SERVER!
I'LL TAKE CARE OF THE BACKUPS. YOU REMEMBER THE SEQUENCE, DON'T YOU?!
YEAH!!
ACCORDING TO WHAT RITA TOLD ME...
...SHE WAS THE ONE WHO DEFEATED THE MIMIC SERVER FROM THE SECOND TO THE 158TH LOOP.
GSH
GSH
BUT I KILLED THE MIMIC SERVER DURING MY FIRST BATTLE, SO I BECAME THE ONE CAUGHT IN THE TIME LOOP.

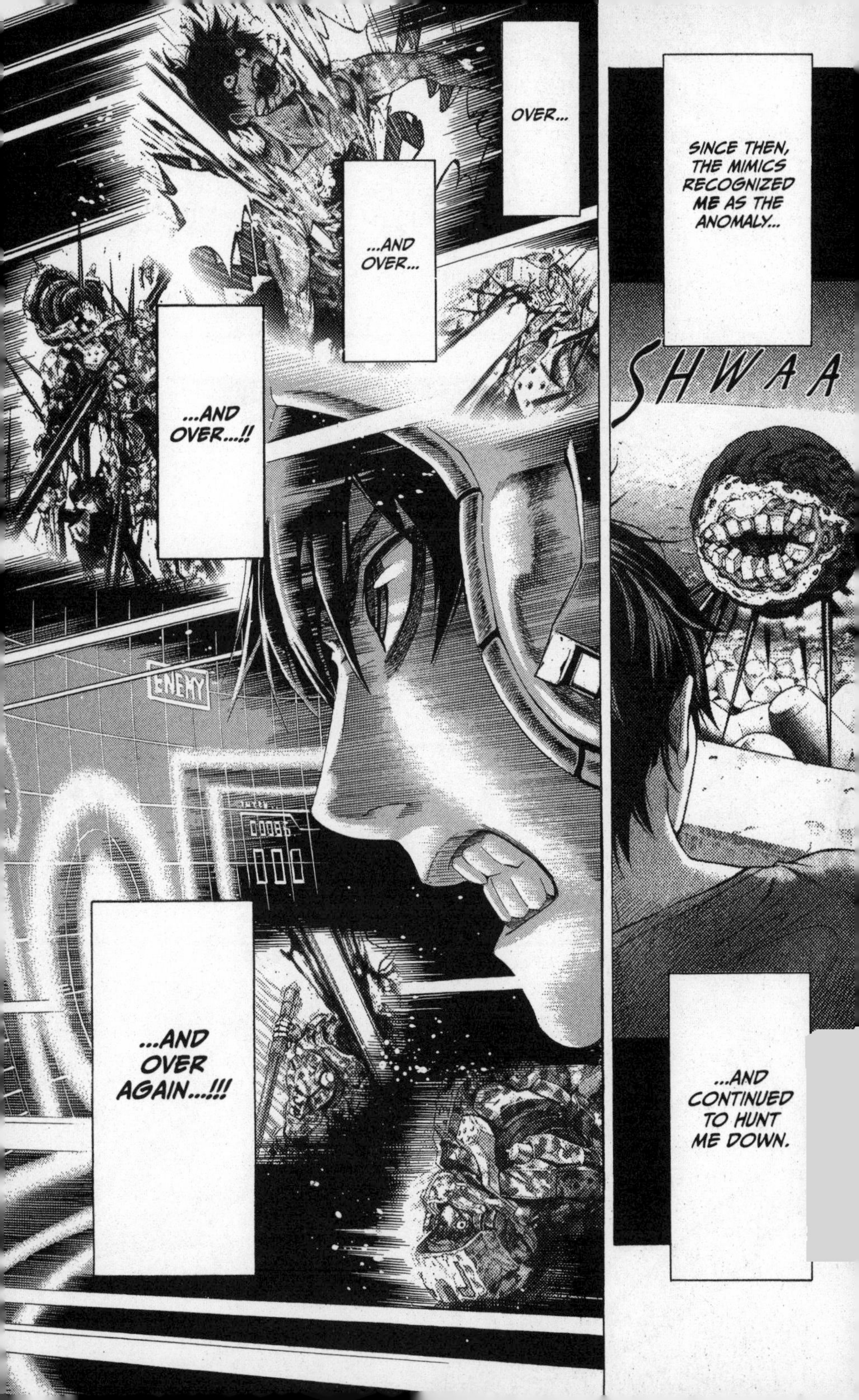
SINCE THEN, THE MIMICS RECOGNIZED ME AS THE ANOMALY...
SHWAA
...AND CONTINUED TO HUNT ME DOWN.
OVER...
...AND OVER...
...AND OVER...!!
ENEMY
...AND OVER AGAIN...!!!

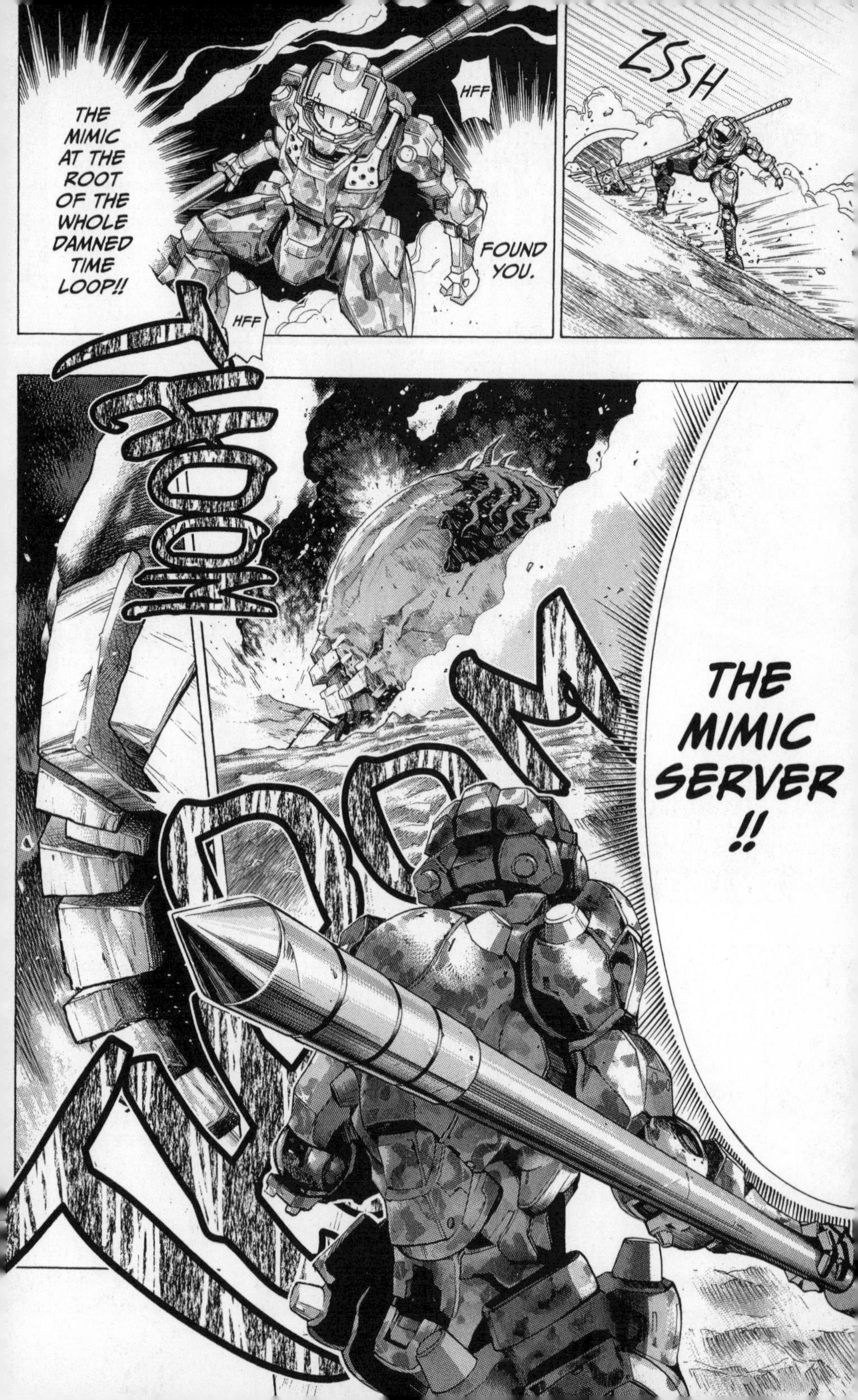
ZSSH
HFF
FOUND YOU.
THE MIMIC AT THE ROOT OF THE WHOLE DAMNED TIME LOOP!!
HFF
THOOM
THE MIMIC SERVER!!

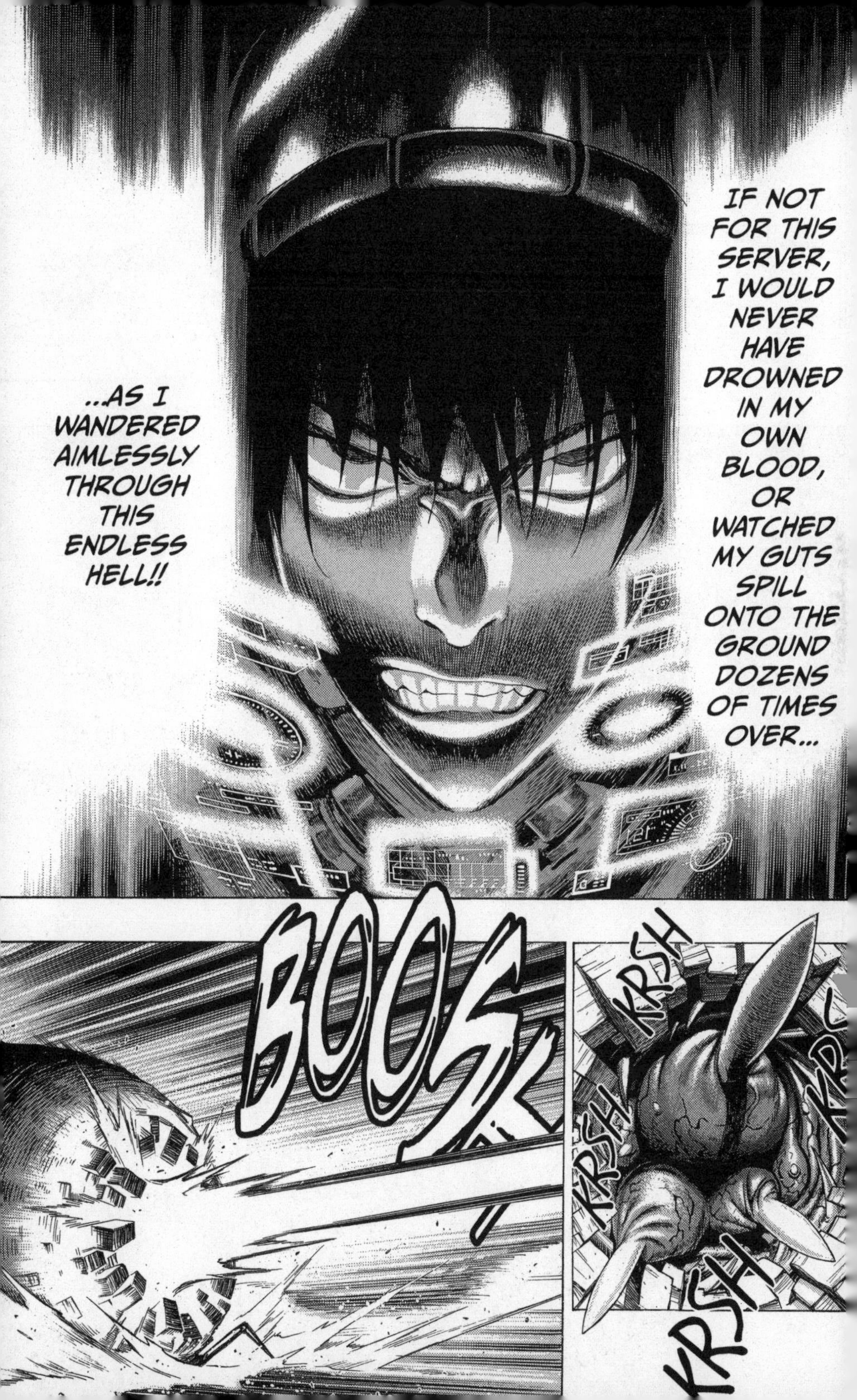
IF NOT FOR THIS SERVER, I WOULD NEVER HAVE DROWNED IN MY OWN BLOOD, OR WATCHED MY GUTS SPILL ONTO THE GROUND DOZENS OF TIMES OVER...
...AS I WANDERED AIMLESSLY THROUGH THIS ENDLESS HELL!!
KRSH
KRSH
KRSH
BOOS

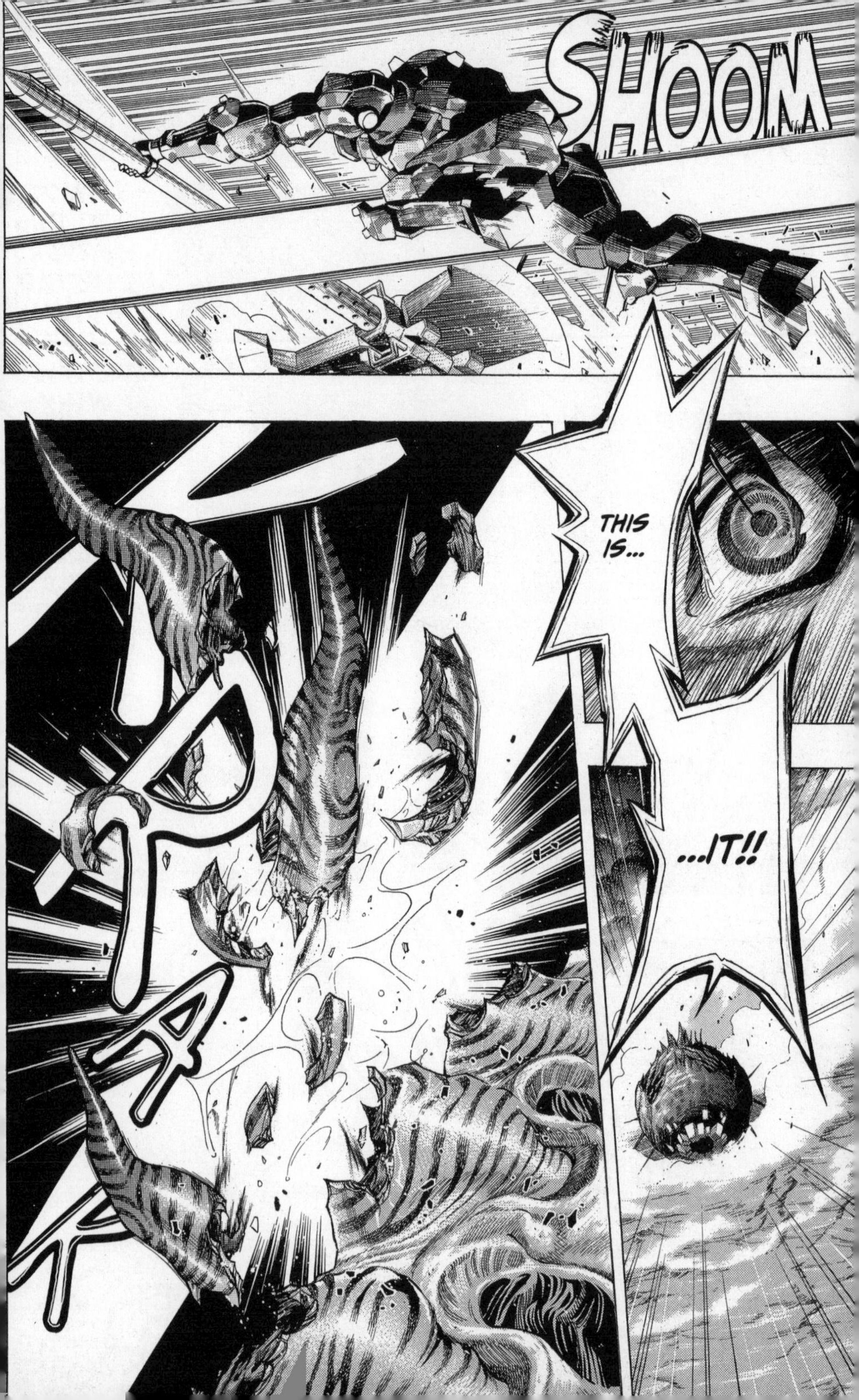
SHOOM
THIS IS...
...IT!!

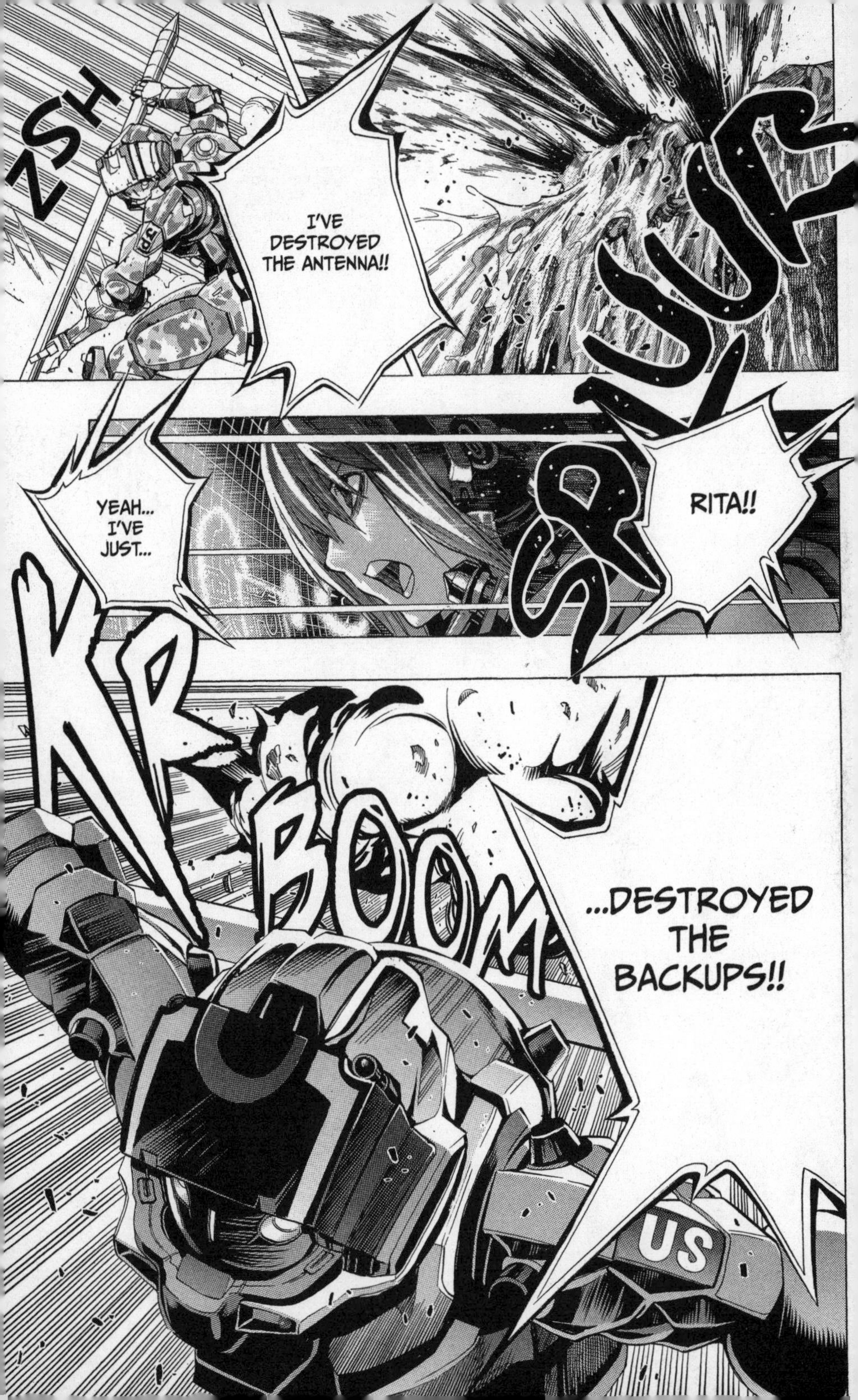
I'VE DESTROYED THE ANTENNA!!
ZSH
JP
RITA!!
YEAH... I'VE JUST...
BOOM
...DESTROYED THE BACKUPS!!
US

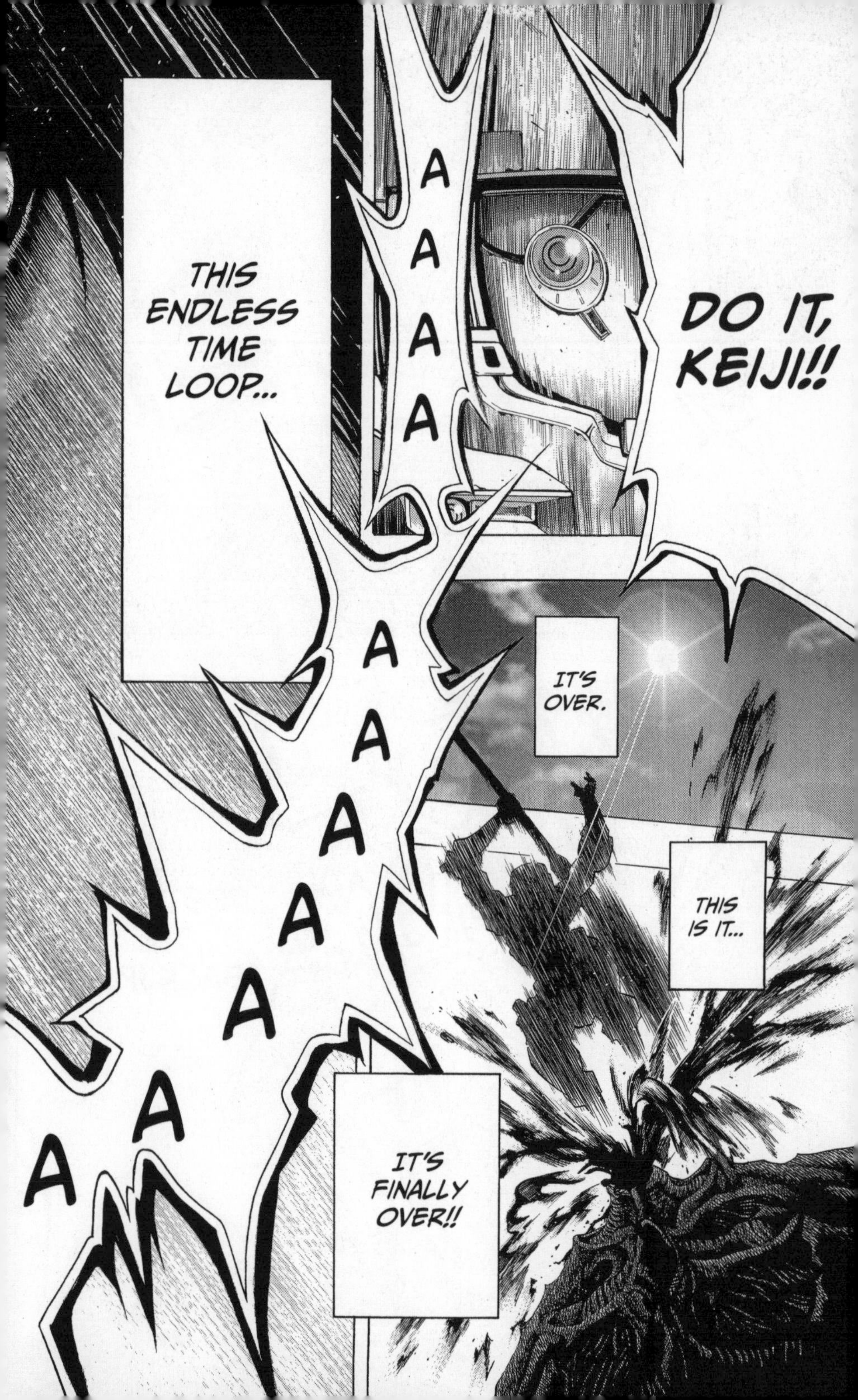
DO IT, KEIJI!!
AAAAAAAAAAA
THIS ENDLESS TIME LOOP...
IT'S OVER.
THIS IS IT...
IT'S FINALLY OVER!!

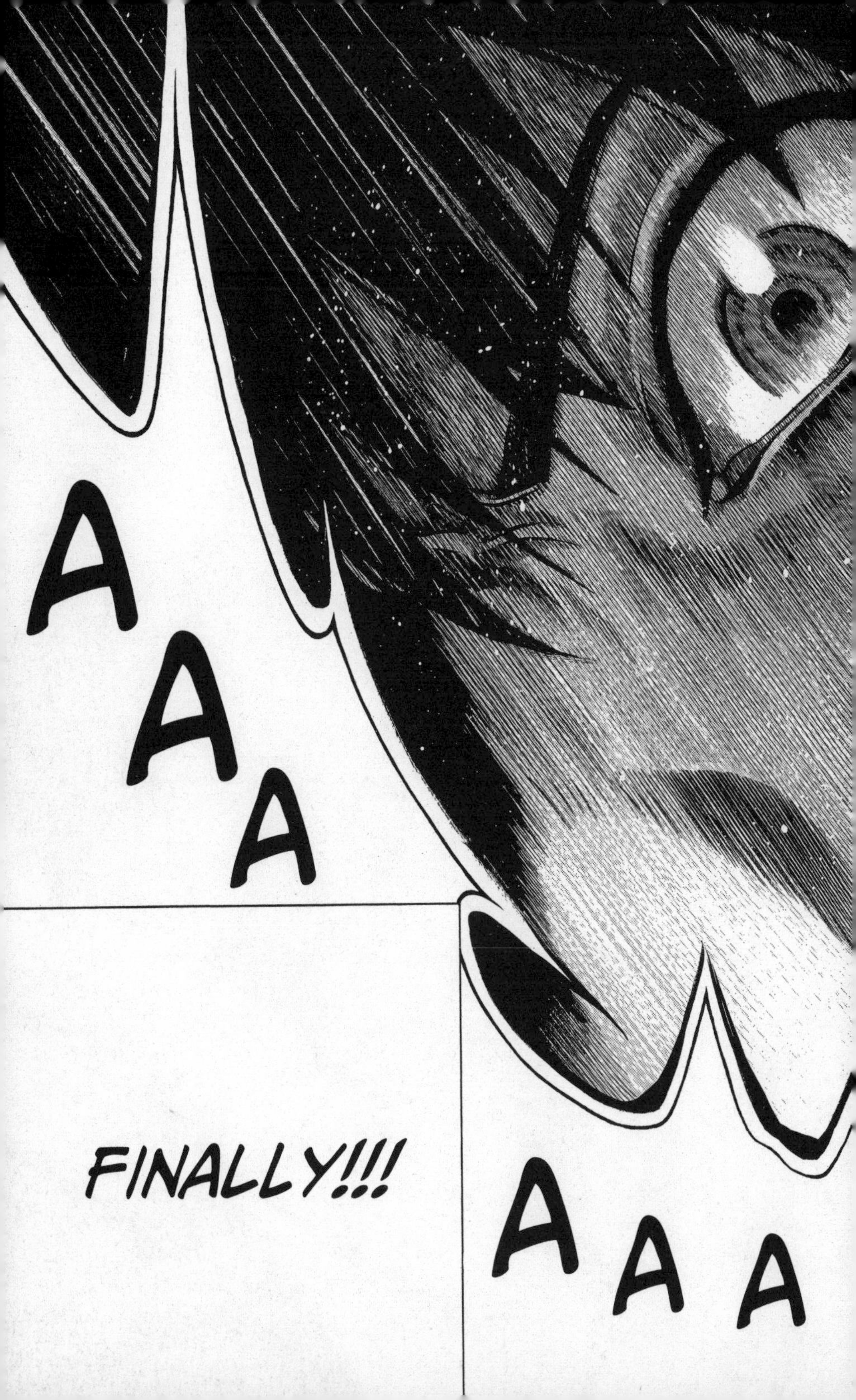
AAA
AAA
FINALLY!!!

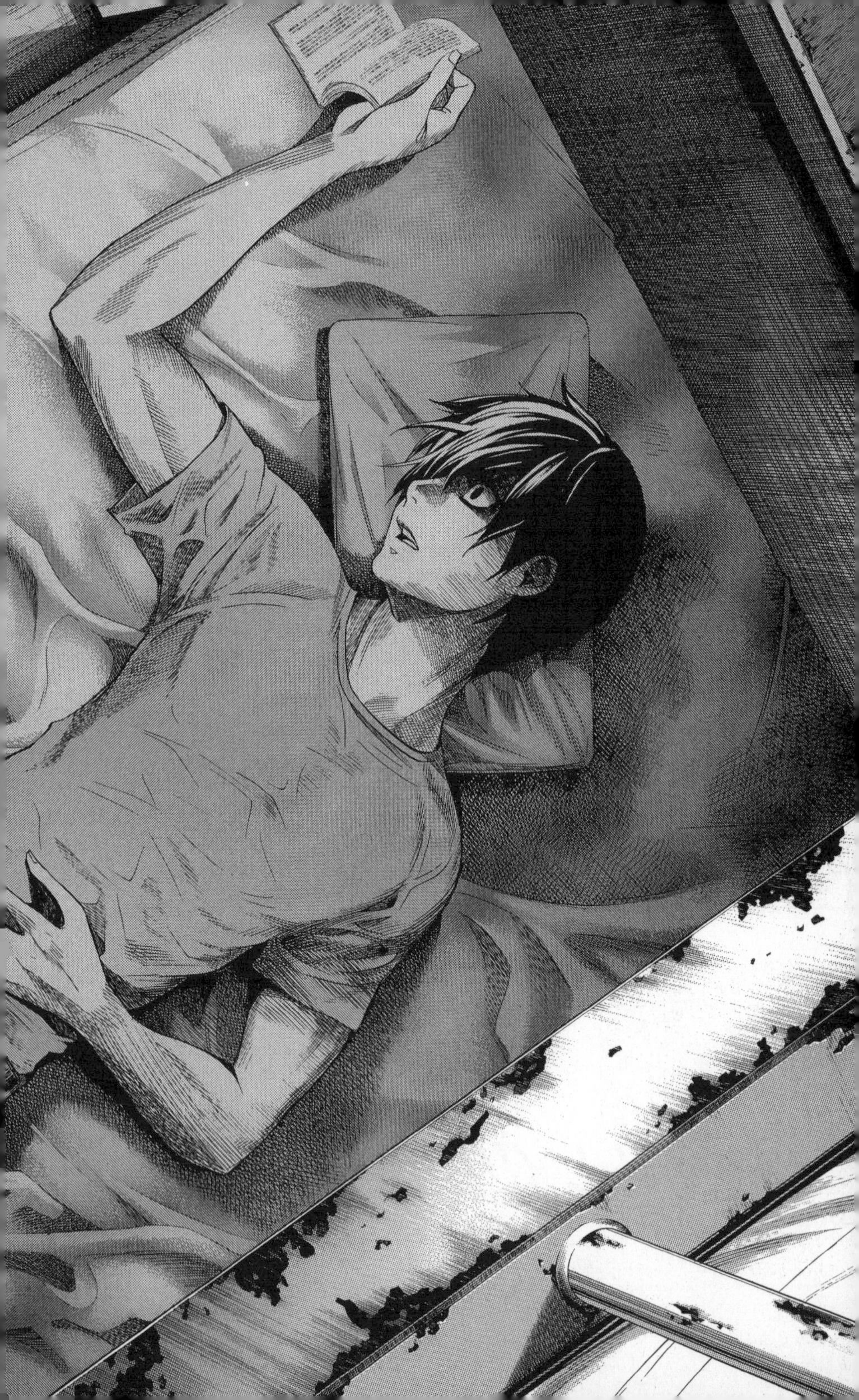

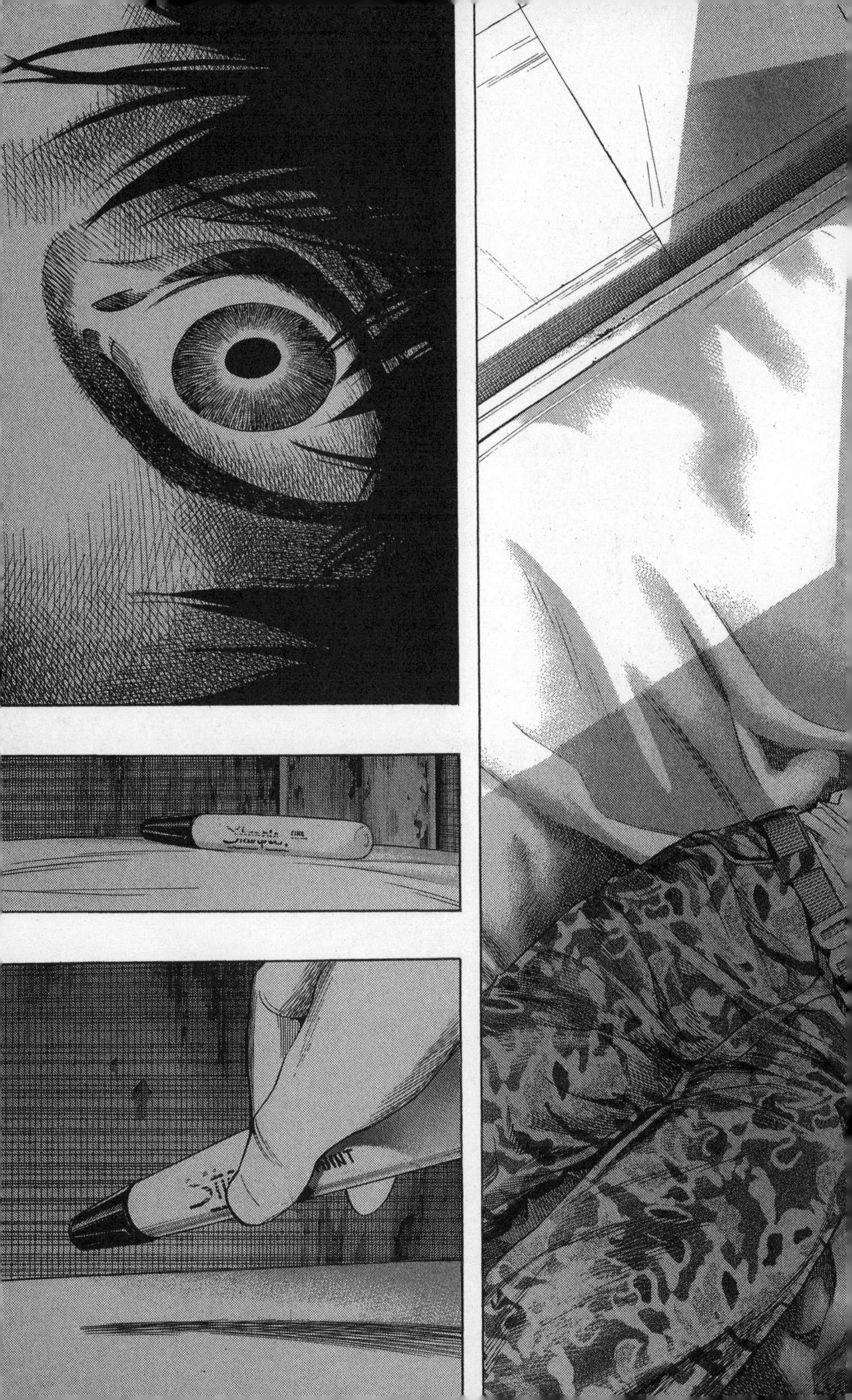

...
DID I FAIL...?!
...
WHY?!
DAMN IT!!

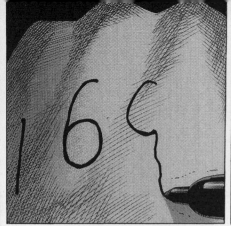

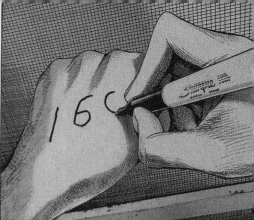

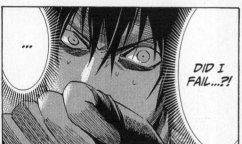

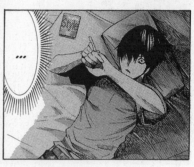

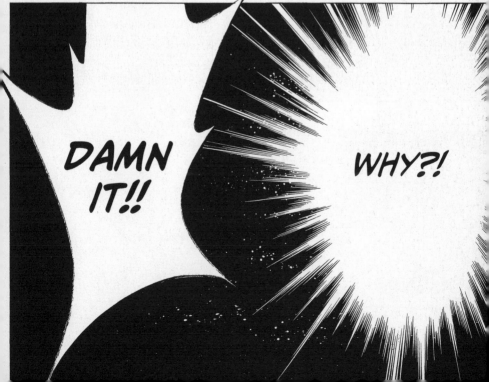

The sky over the No. 1 Training
Field was as clear the 160th
time as it had been the first.
The ten o'clock sun beat down
on us without pity.
PT had just ended, and the
shadows pooled at our feet
were speckled with darker
spots of sweat.

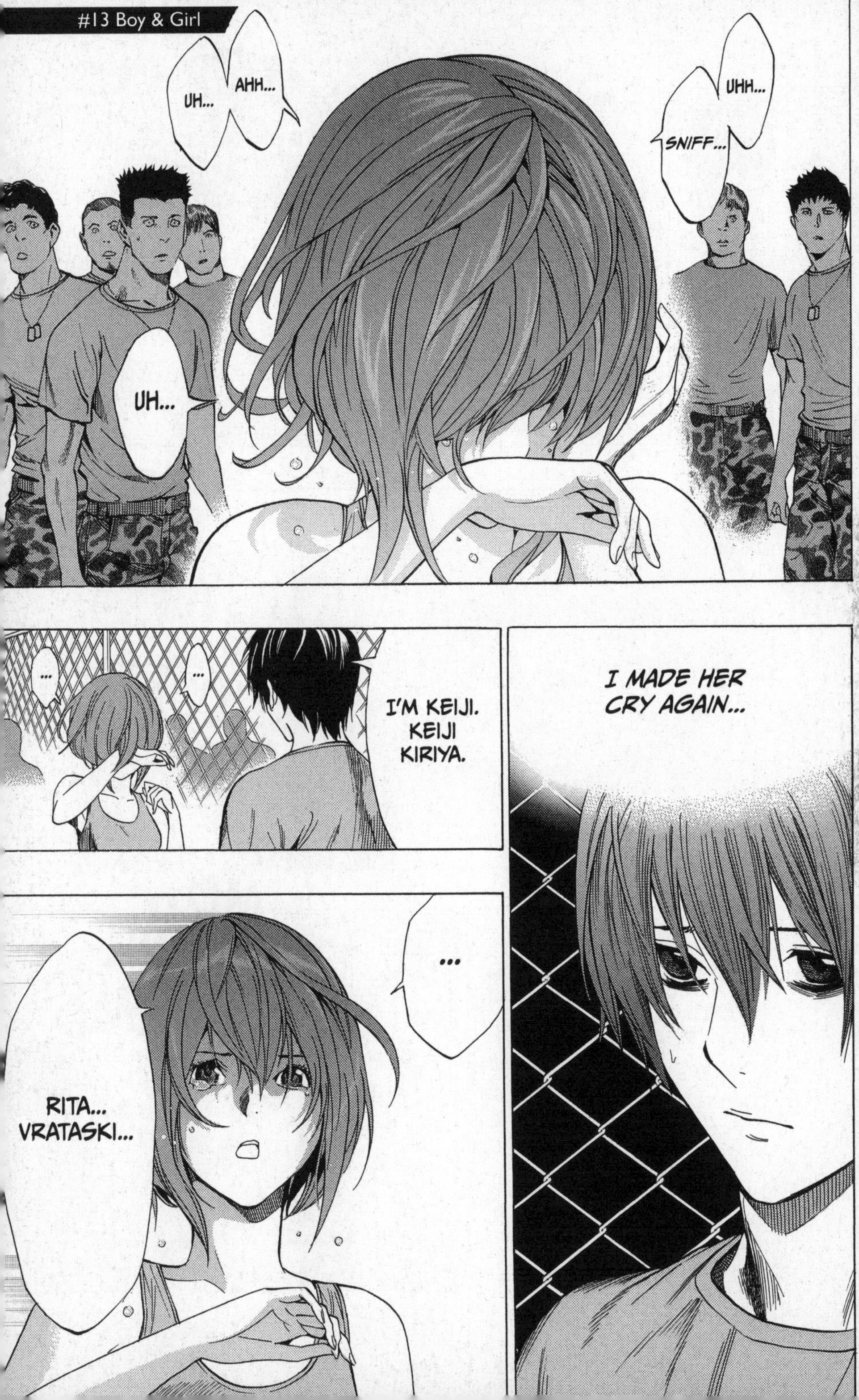
UHH...
SNIFF...
AHH...
UH...
UH...
I MADE HER CRY AGAIN...
I'M KEIJI. KEIJI KIRIYA.
...
...
...
RITA... VRATASKI...

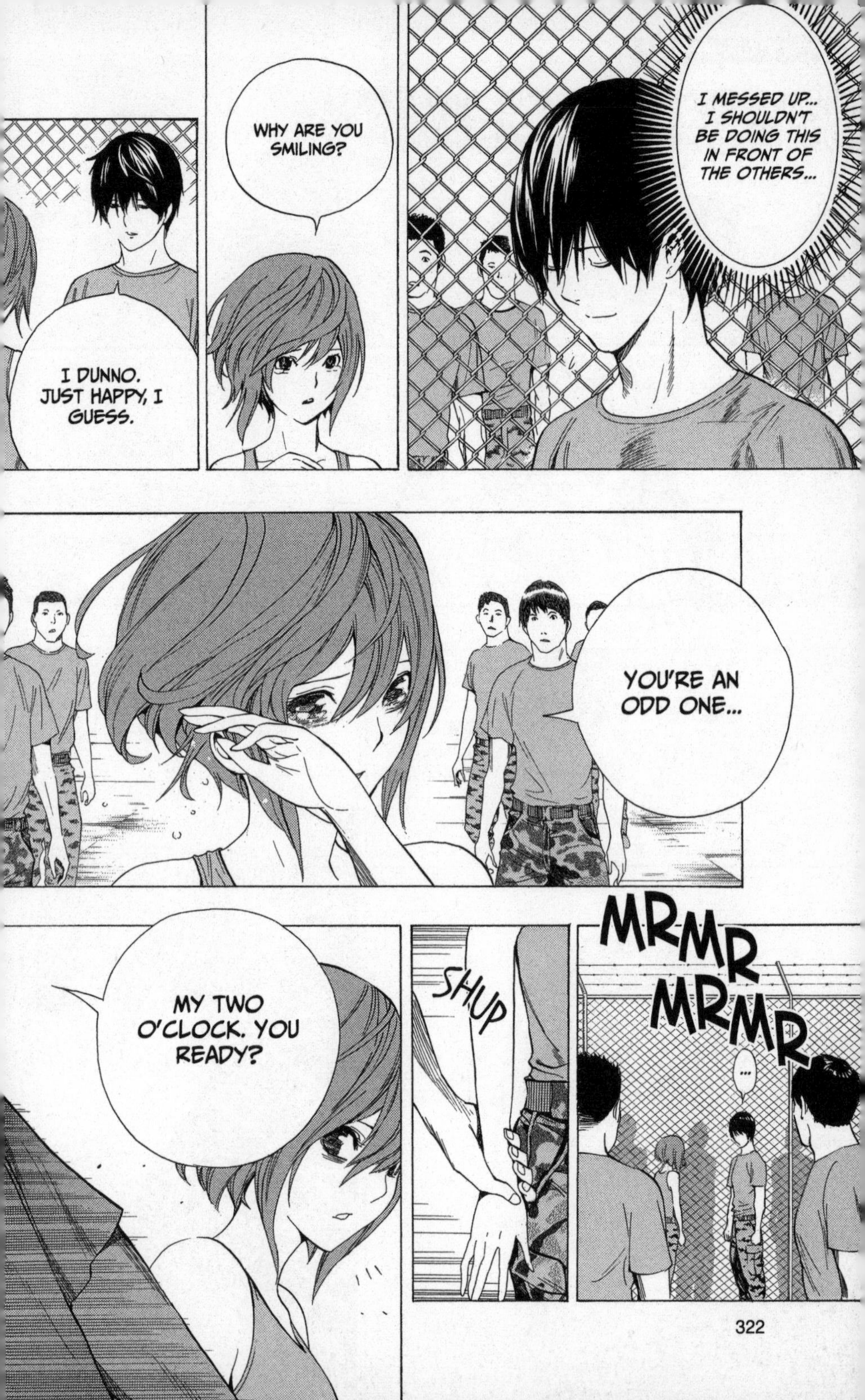
I MESSED UP... I SHOULDN'T BE DOING THIS IN FRONT OF THE OTHERS...
WHY ARE YOU SMILING?
I DUNNO. JUST HAPPY, I GUESS.
YOU'RE AN ODD ONE...
MRMR MRMR
...
SHUP
MY TWO O'CLOCK. YOU READY?

#13 Boy & Girl

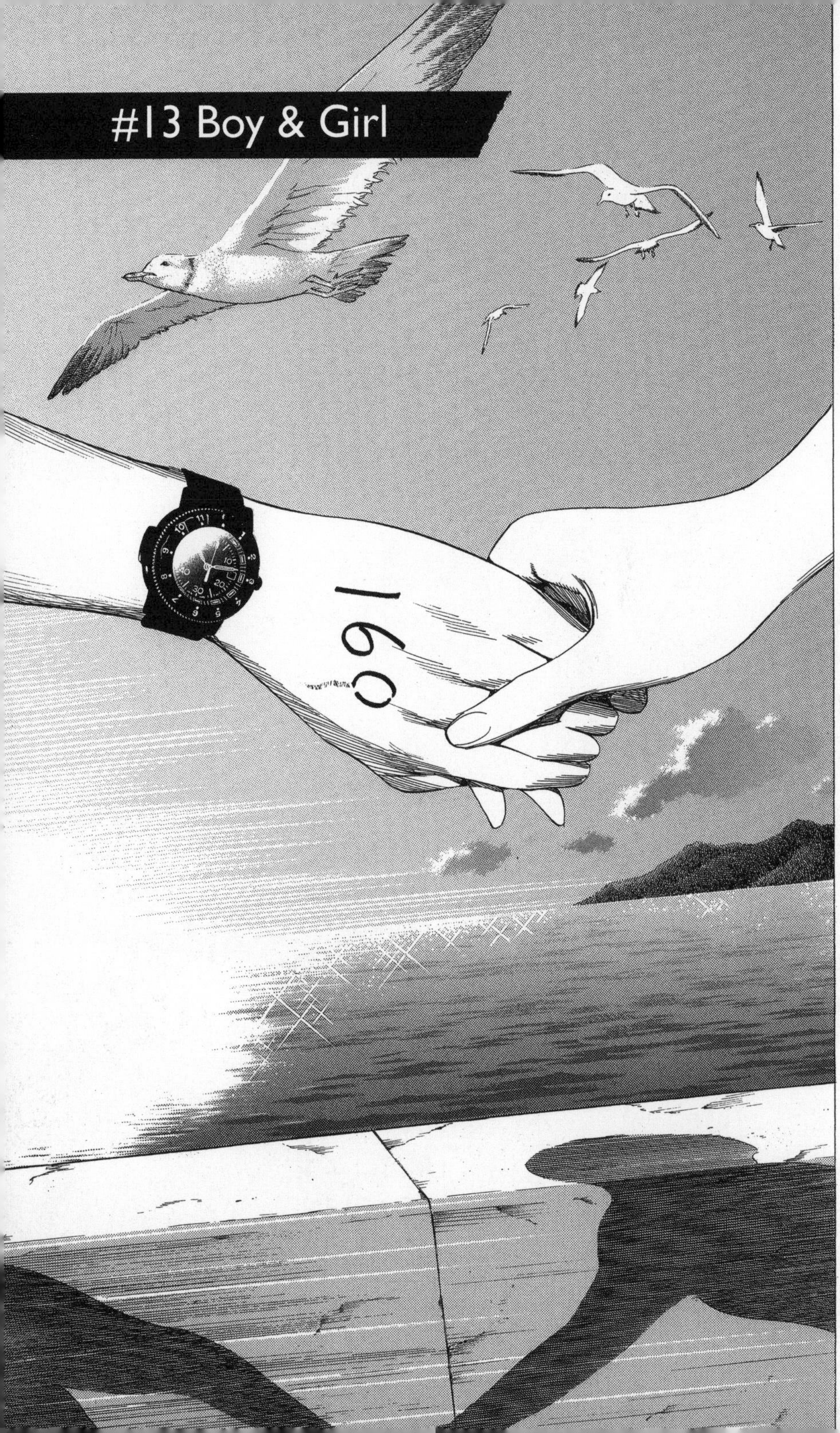
160

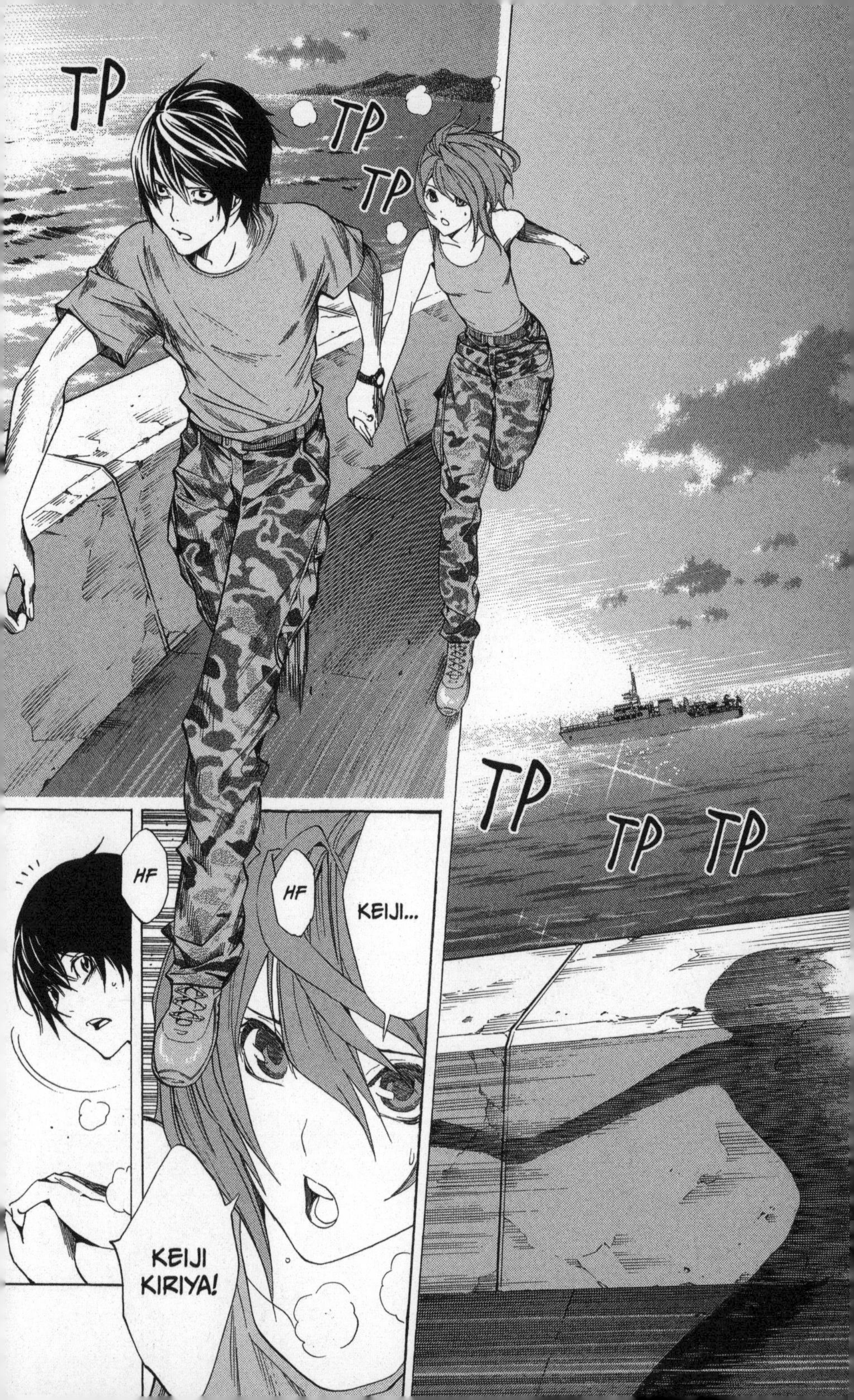
TP
TP TP
TP
TP
TP
TP
HF
KEIJI...
KEIJI KIRIYA!
HF

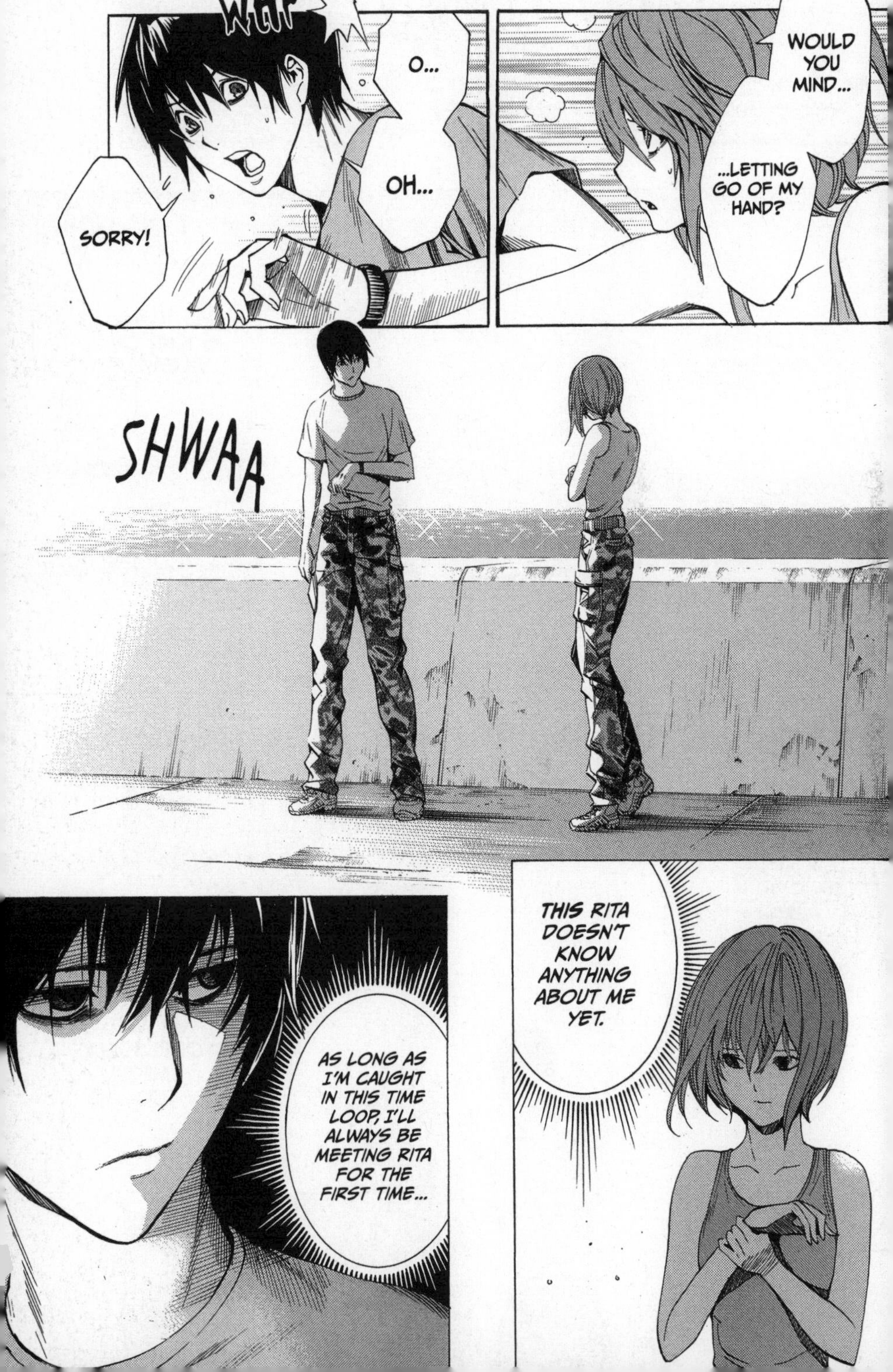
WOULD YOU MIND...
...LETTING GO OF MY HAND?
WHP
O...
OH...
SORRY!
SHWAA
THIS RITA DOESN'T KNOW ANYTHING ABOUT ME YET.
AS LONG AS I'M CAUGHT IN THIS TIME LOOP, I'LL ALWAYS BE MEETING RITA FOR THE FIRST TIME...

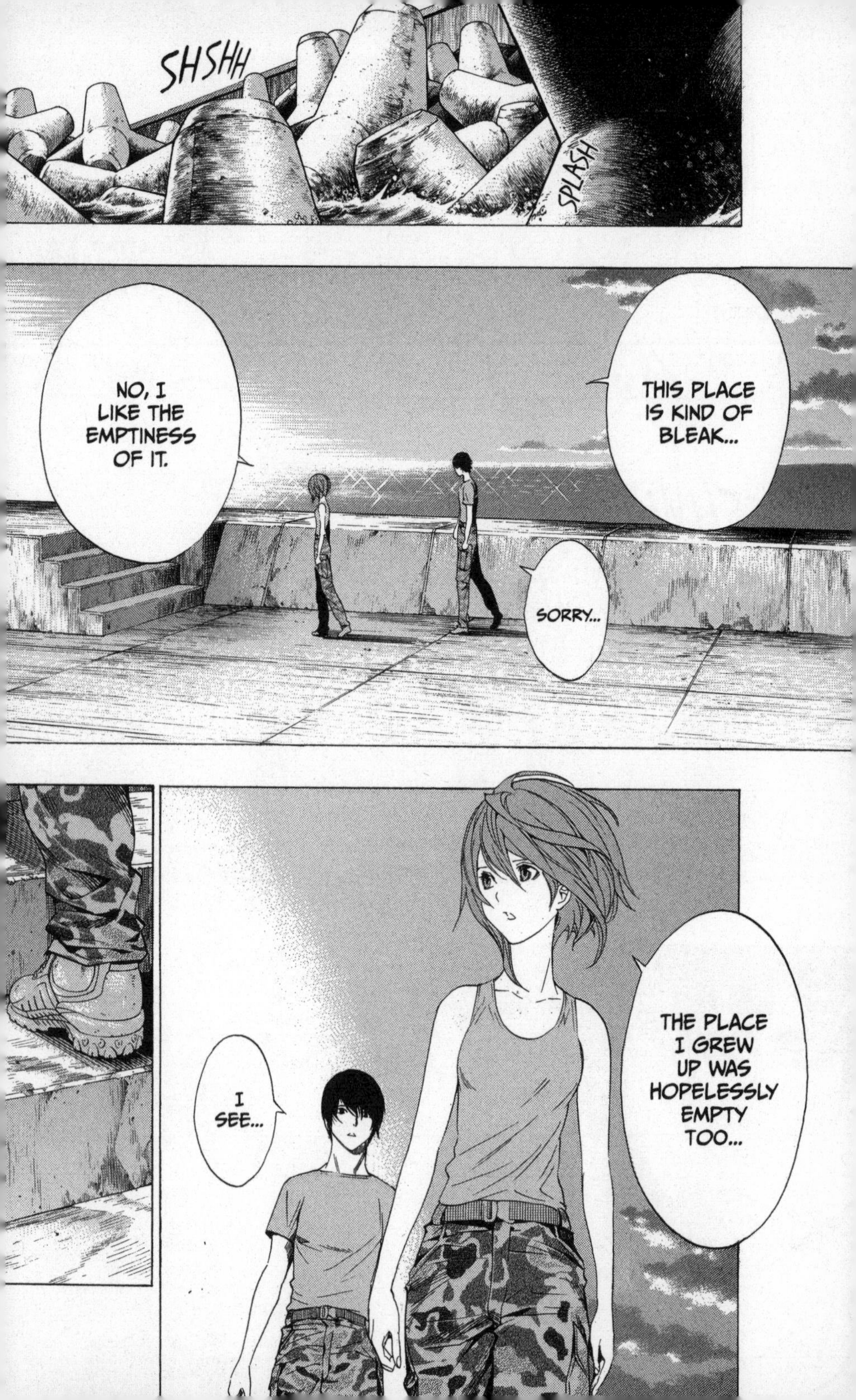
SPLASH
SHSHH
THIS PLACE IS KIND OF BLEAK...
SORRY...
NO, I LIKE THE EMPTINESS OF IT.
THE PLACE I GREW UP WAS HOPELESSLY EMPTY TOO...
I SEE...

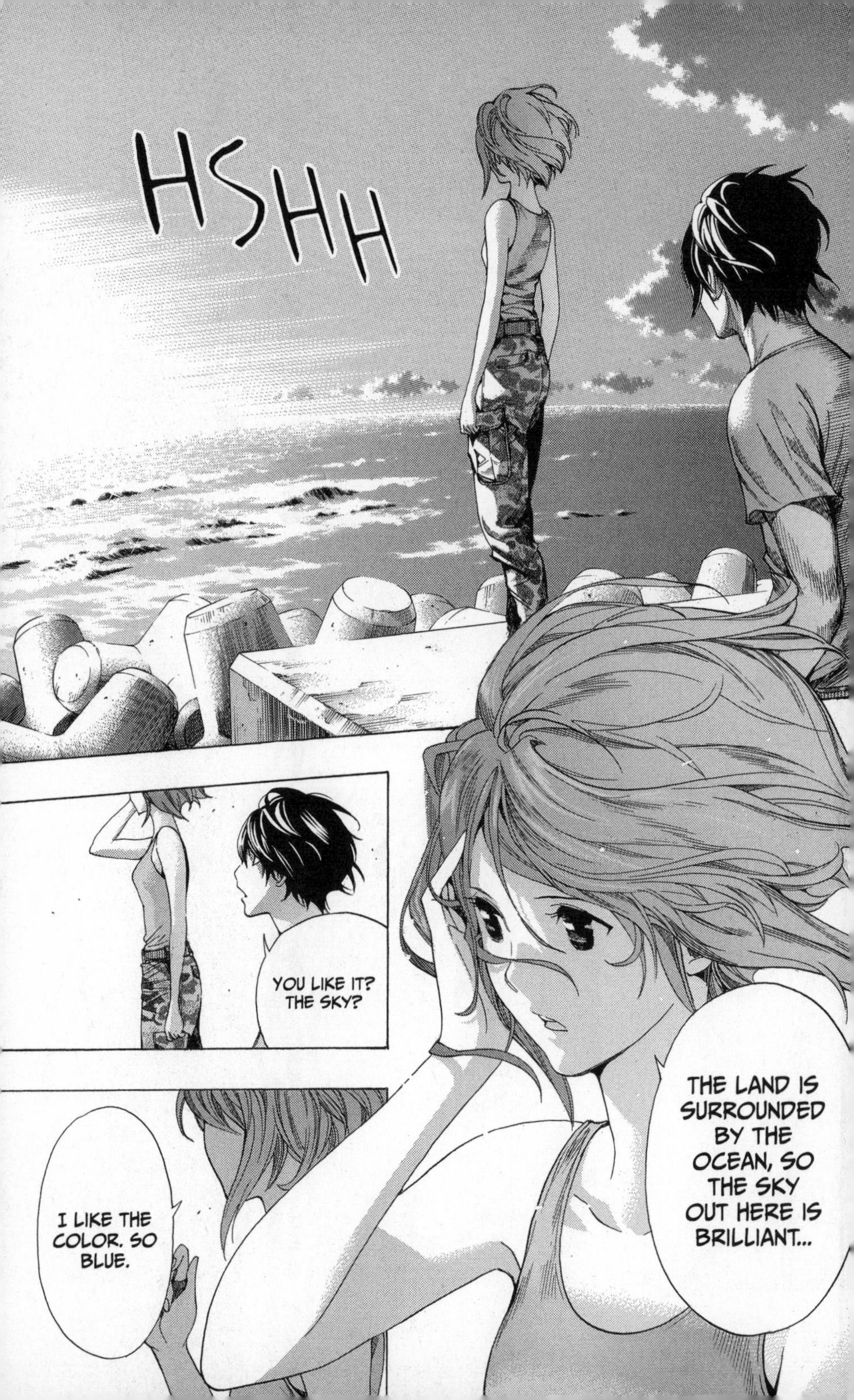
HSHH
THE LAND IS SURROUNDED BY THE OCEAN, SO THE SKY OUT HERE IS BRILLIANT...
YOU LIKE IT? THE SKY?
I LIKE THE COLOR. SO BLUE.

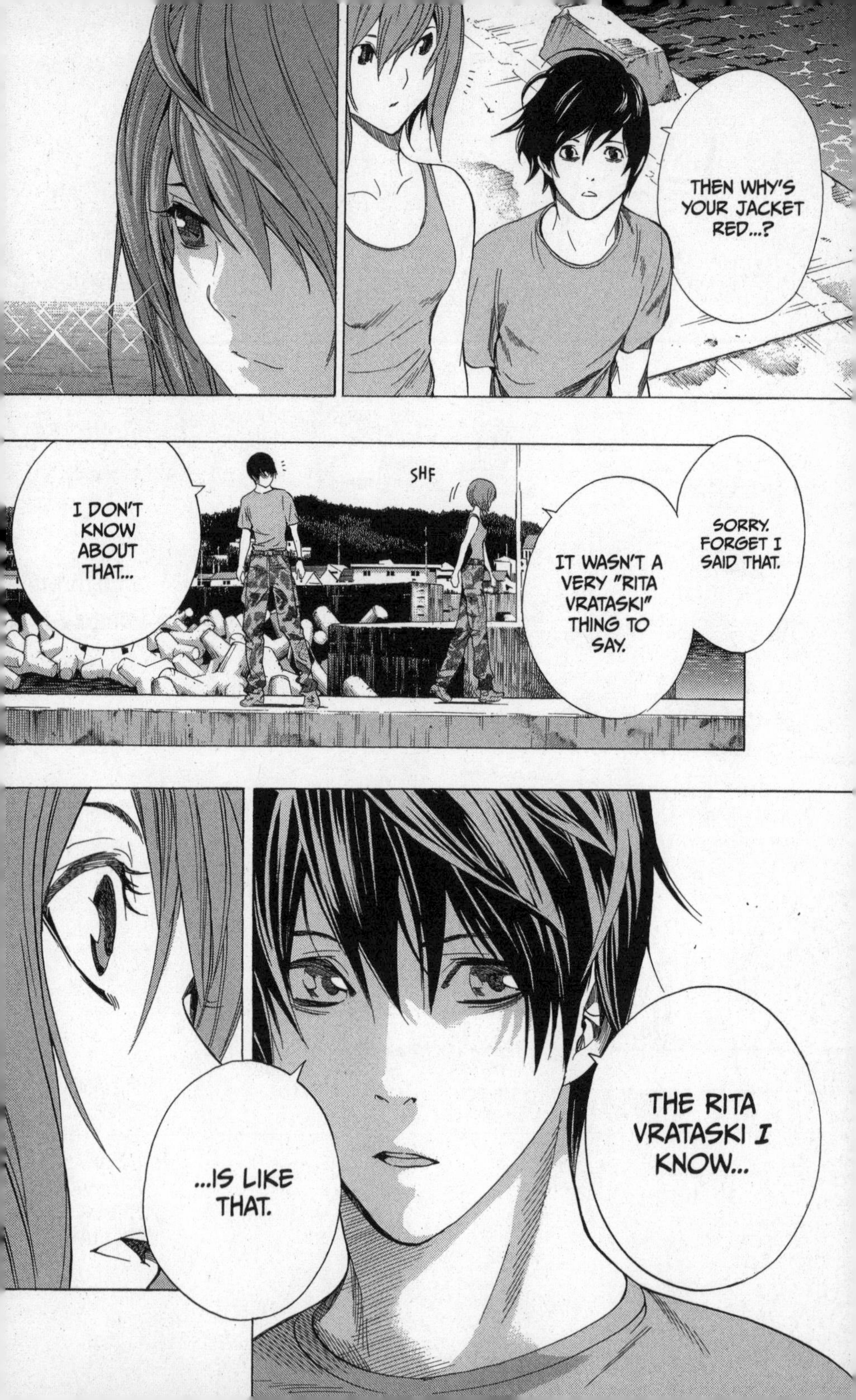
THEN WHY'S YOUR JACKET RED...?
SORRY. FORGET I SAID THAT.
IT WASN'T A VERY "RITA VRATASKI" THING TO SAY.
SHF
I DON'T KNOW ABOUT THAT...
THE RITA VRATASKI I KNOW...
...IS LIKE THAT.

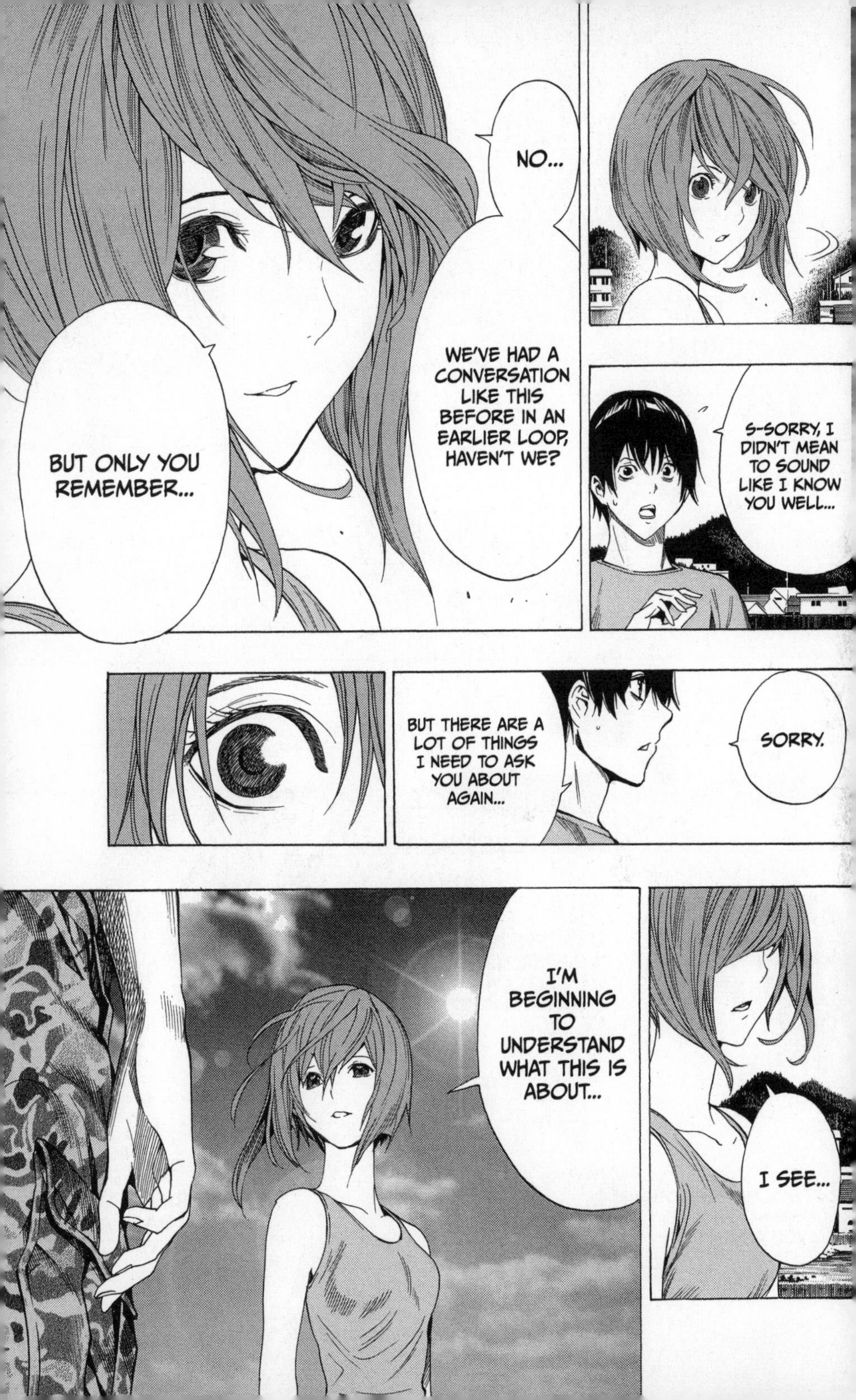
S-SORRY, I DIDN'T MEAN TO SOUND LIKE I KNOW YOU WELL...
NO...
WE'VE HAD A CONVERSATION LIKE THIS BEFORE IN AN EARLIER LOOP, HAVEN'T WE?
BUT ONLY YOU REMEMBER...
SORRY.
BUT THERE ARE A LOT OF THINGS I NEED TO ASK YOU ABOUT AGAIN...
I SEE...
I'M BEGINNING TO UNDERSTAND WHAT THIS IS ABOUT...

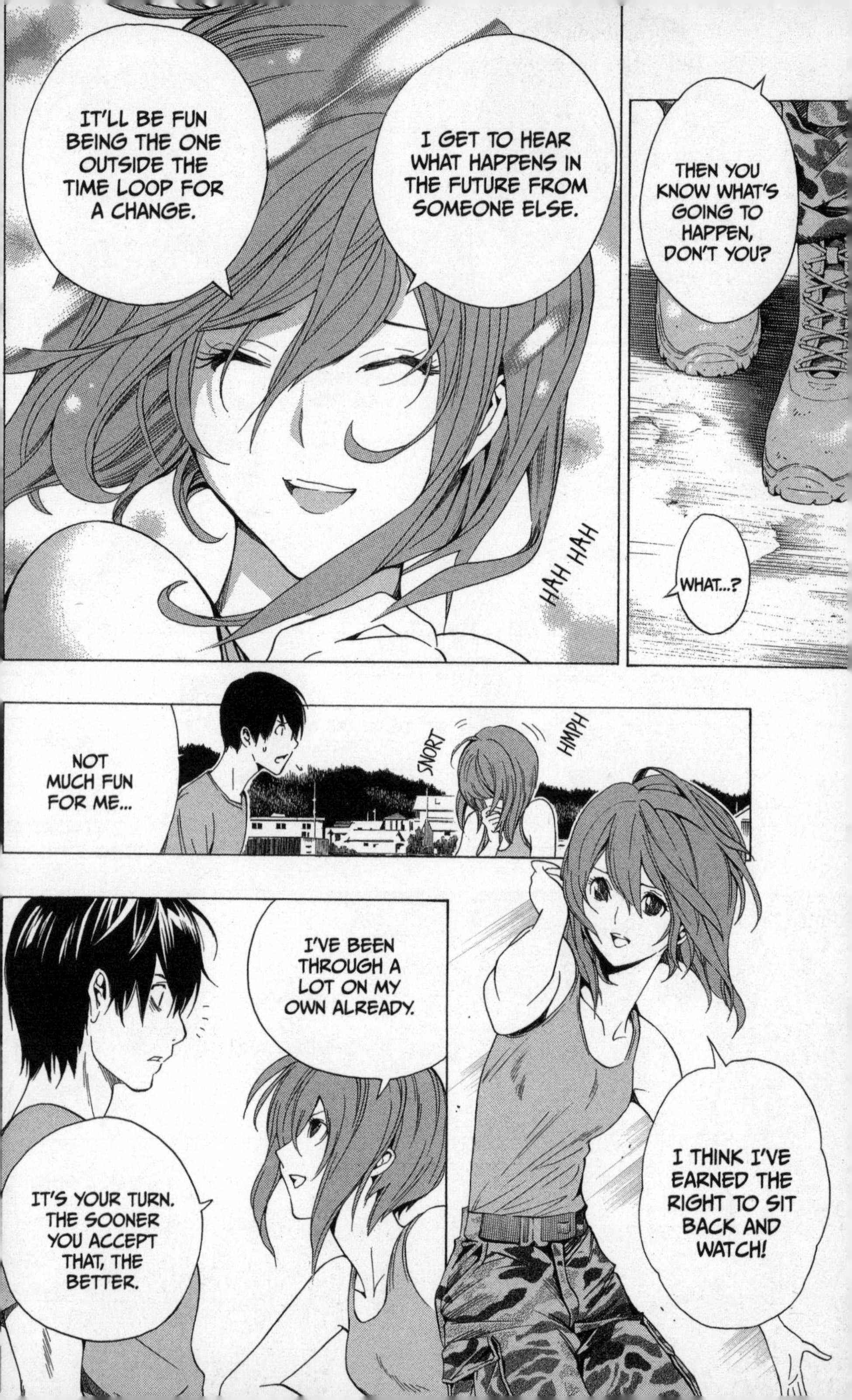
THEN YOU KNOW WHAT'S GOING TO HAPPEN, DON'T YOU?
WHAT...?
I GET TO HEAR WHAT HAPPENS IN THE FUTURE FROM SOMEONE ELSE.
IT'LL BE FUN BEING THE ONE OUTSIDE THE TIME LOOP FOR A CHANGE.
HAH HAH
HMPH
SNORT
NOT MUCH FUN FOR ME...
I'VE BEEN THROUGH A LOT ON MY OWN ALREADY.
I THINK I'VE EARNED THE RIGHT TO SIT BACK AND WATCH!
IT'S YOUR TURN. THE SOONER YOU ACCEPT THAT, THE BETTER.

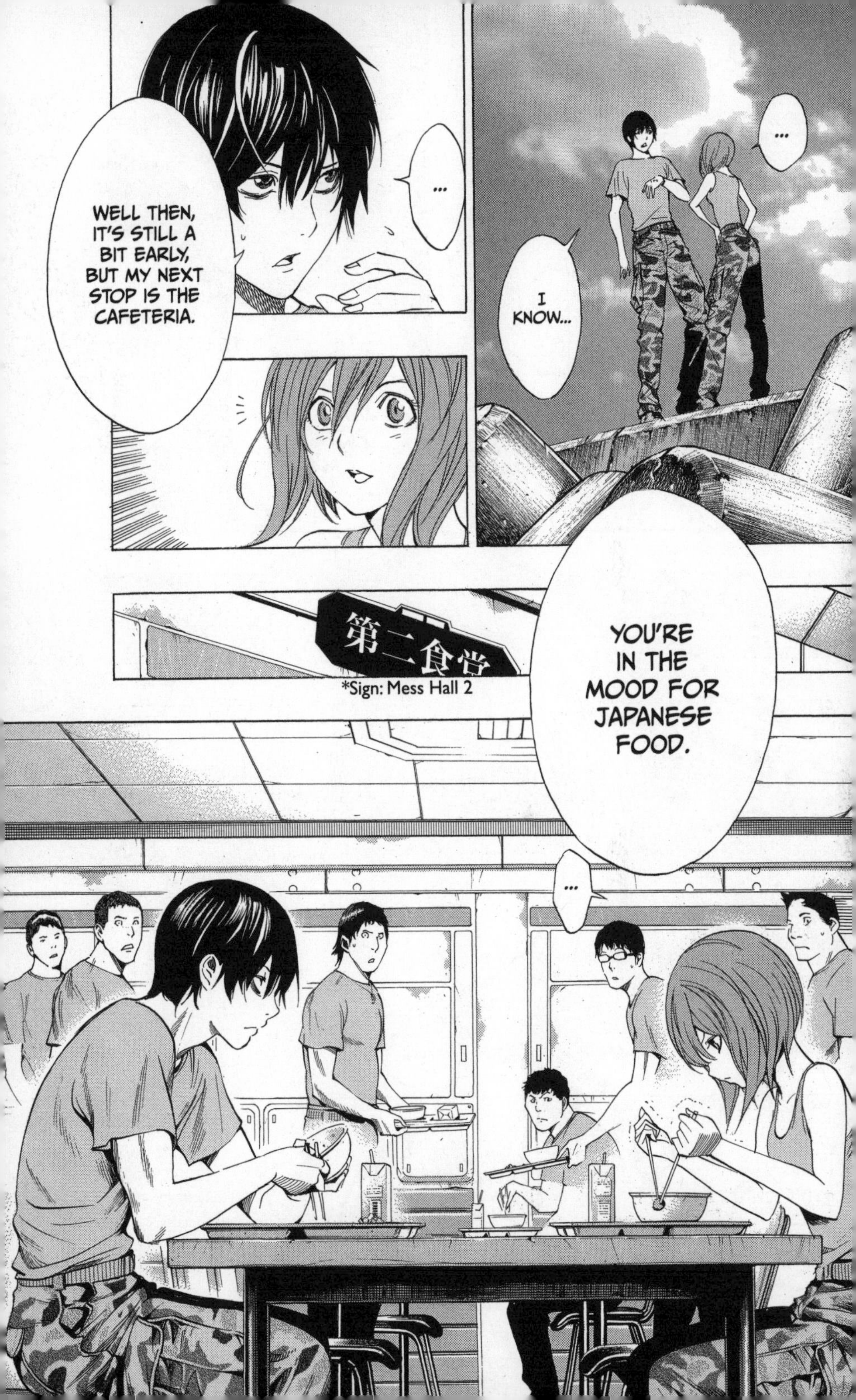
...
I KNOW...
...
WELL THEN, IT'S STILL A BIT EARLY, BUT MY NEXT STOP IS THE CAFETERIA.
第二食堂
*Sign: Mess Hall 2
YOU'RE IN THE MOOD FOR JAPANESE FOOD.
...

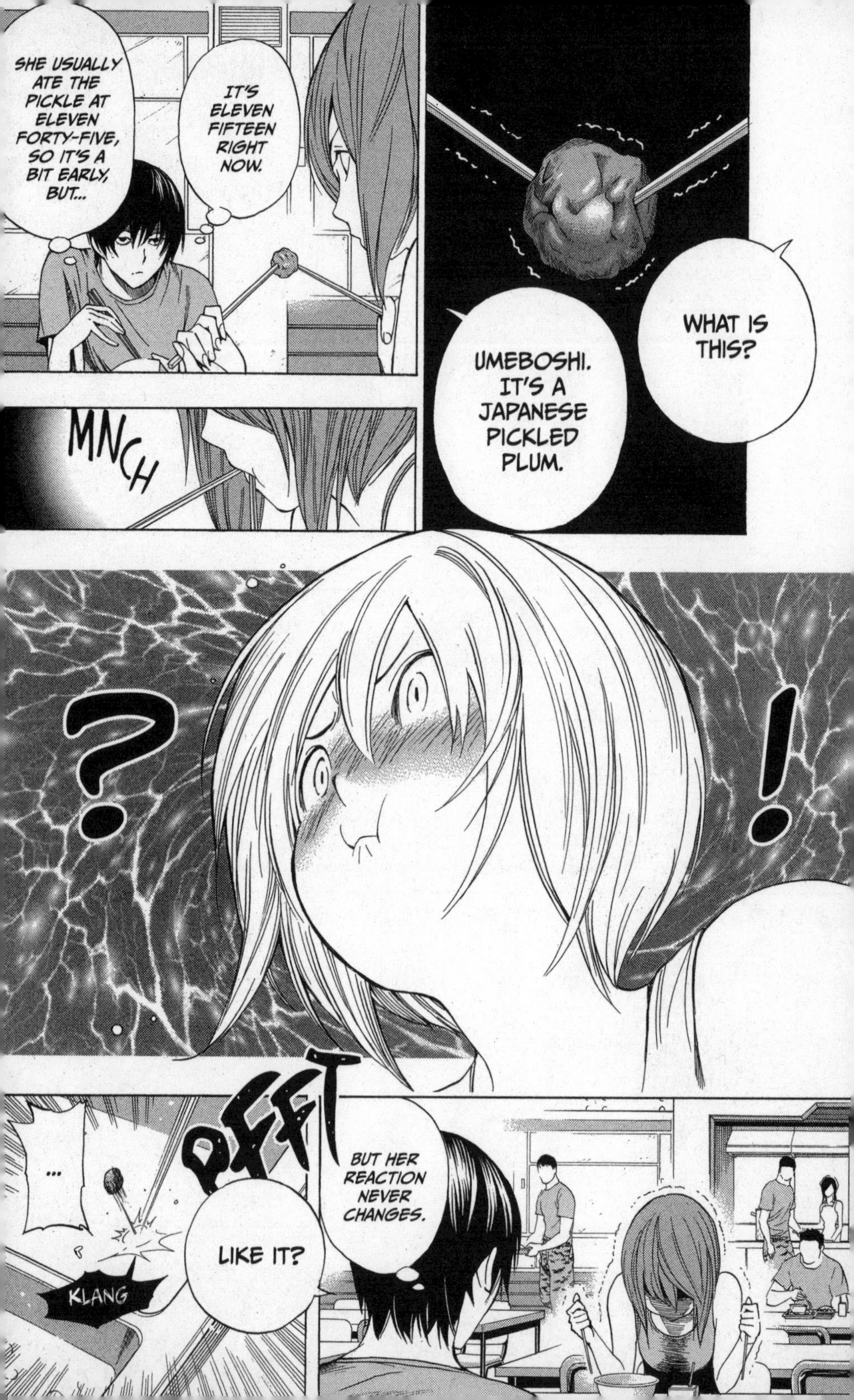
WHAT IS THIS?
UMEBOSHI. IT'S A JAPANESE PICKLED PLUM.
IT'S ELEVEN FIFTEEN RIGHT NOW.
SHE USUALLY ATE THE PICKLE AT ELEVEN FORTY-FIVE, SO IT'S A BIT EARLY, BUT...
MNCH
!
?
BUT HER REACTION NEVER CHANGES.
LIKE IT?
PFFT
...
KLANG

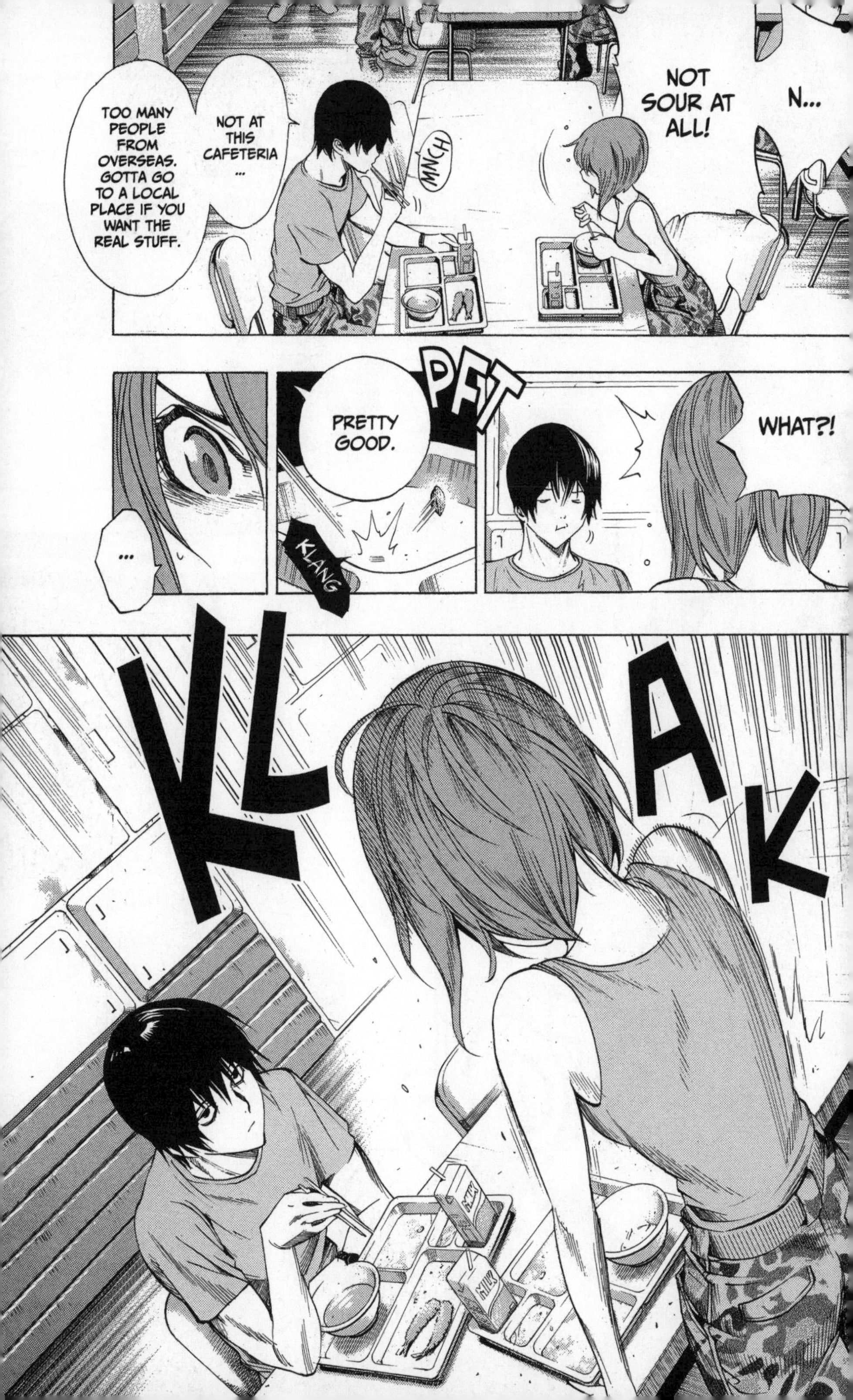
N...
NOT SOUR AT ALL!
MNCH
NOT AT THIS CAFETERIA ...
TOO MANY PEOPLE FROM OVERSEAS. GOTTA GO TO A LOCAL PLACE IF YOU WANT THE REAL STUFF.
WHAT?!
PFFT
PRETTY GOOD.
KLANG
...
KLAK

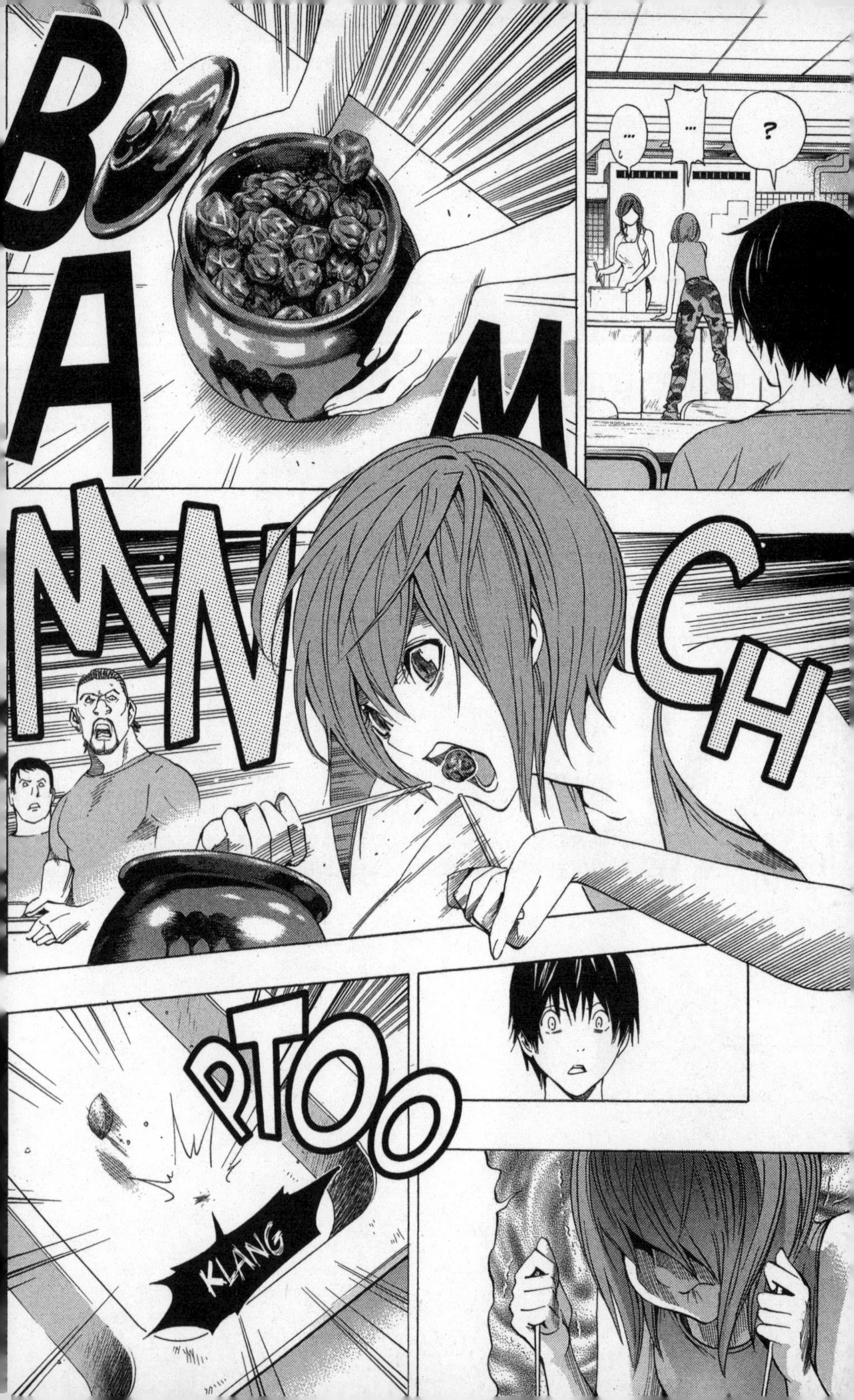
?
...
...
BAM
MMNCH
PTOO
KLANG

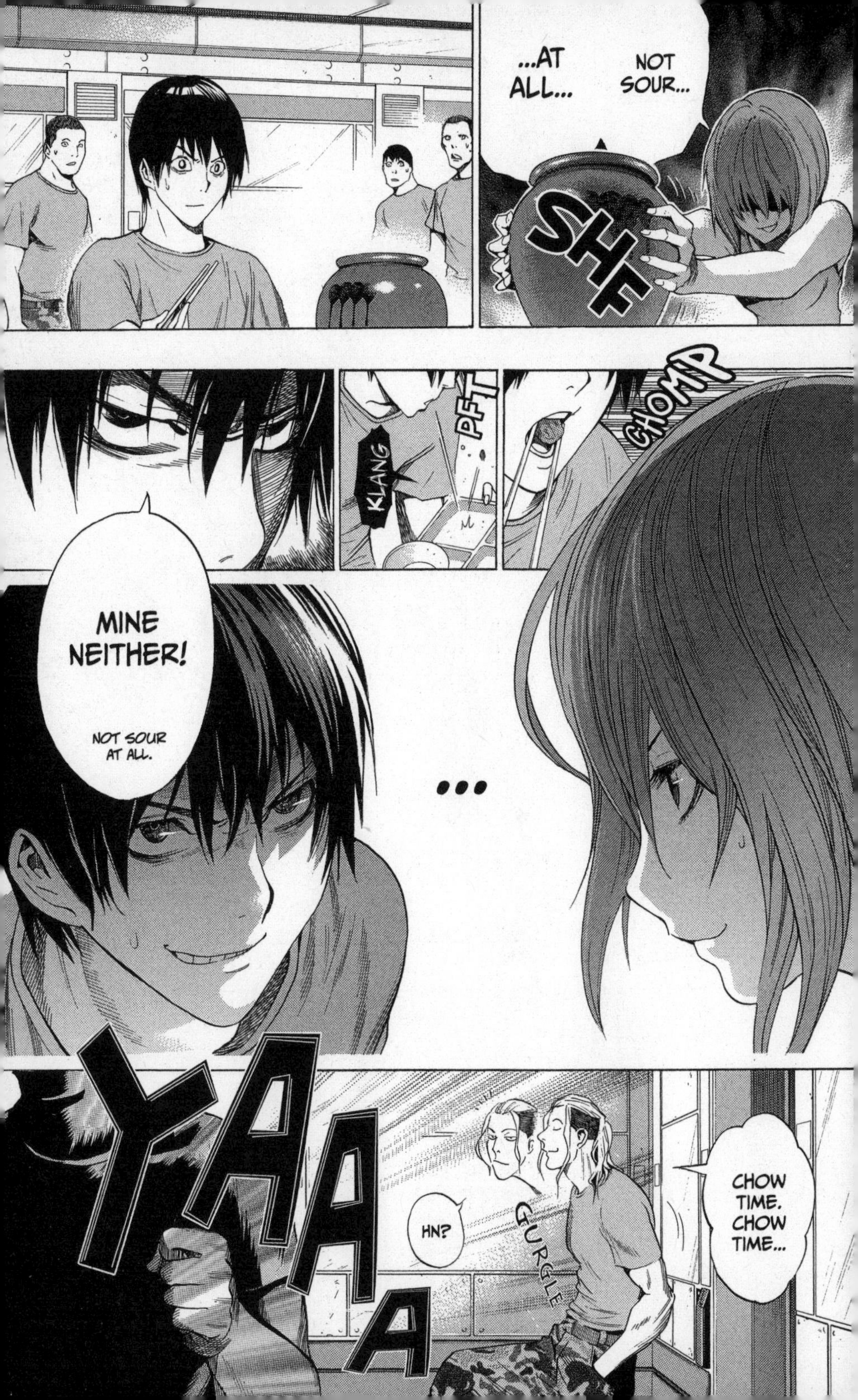
NOT SOUR...
...AT ALL...
SHF
CHOMP
PFT
KLANG
...
MINE NEITHER!
NOT SOUR AT ALL.
CHOW TIME. CHOW TIME...
GURGLE
HN?
YAAAA

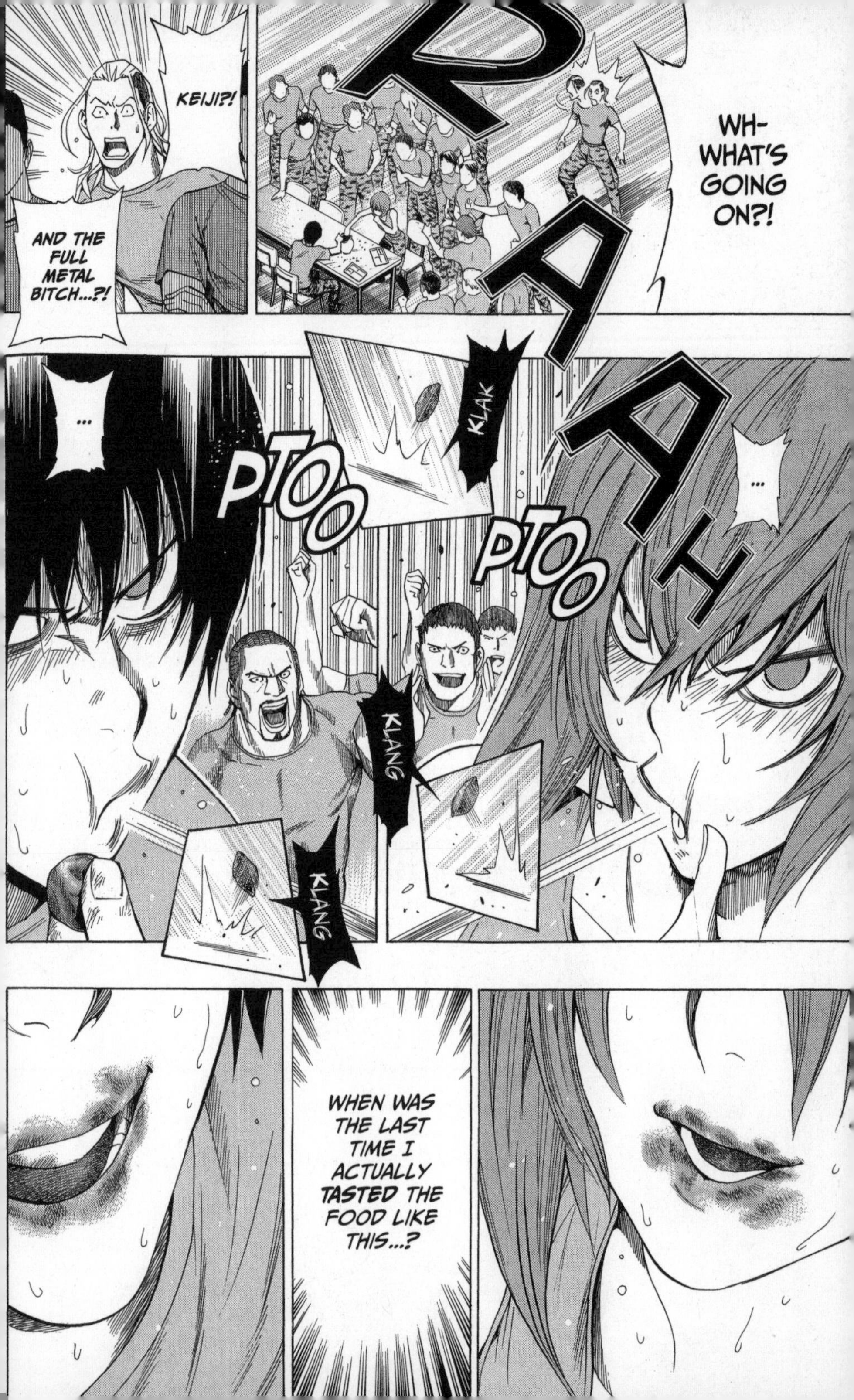
WH- WHAT'S GOING ON?!
RAAH
KEIJI?!
AND THE FULL METAL BITCH...?!
...
PTOO
KLANG
...
KLANG
...
PTOO
KLAK
WHEN WAS THE LAST TIME I ACTUALLY TASTED THE FOOD LIKE THIS...?

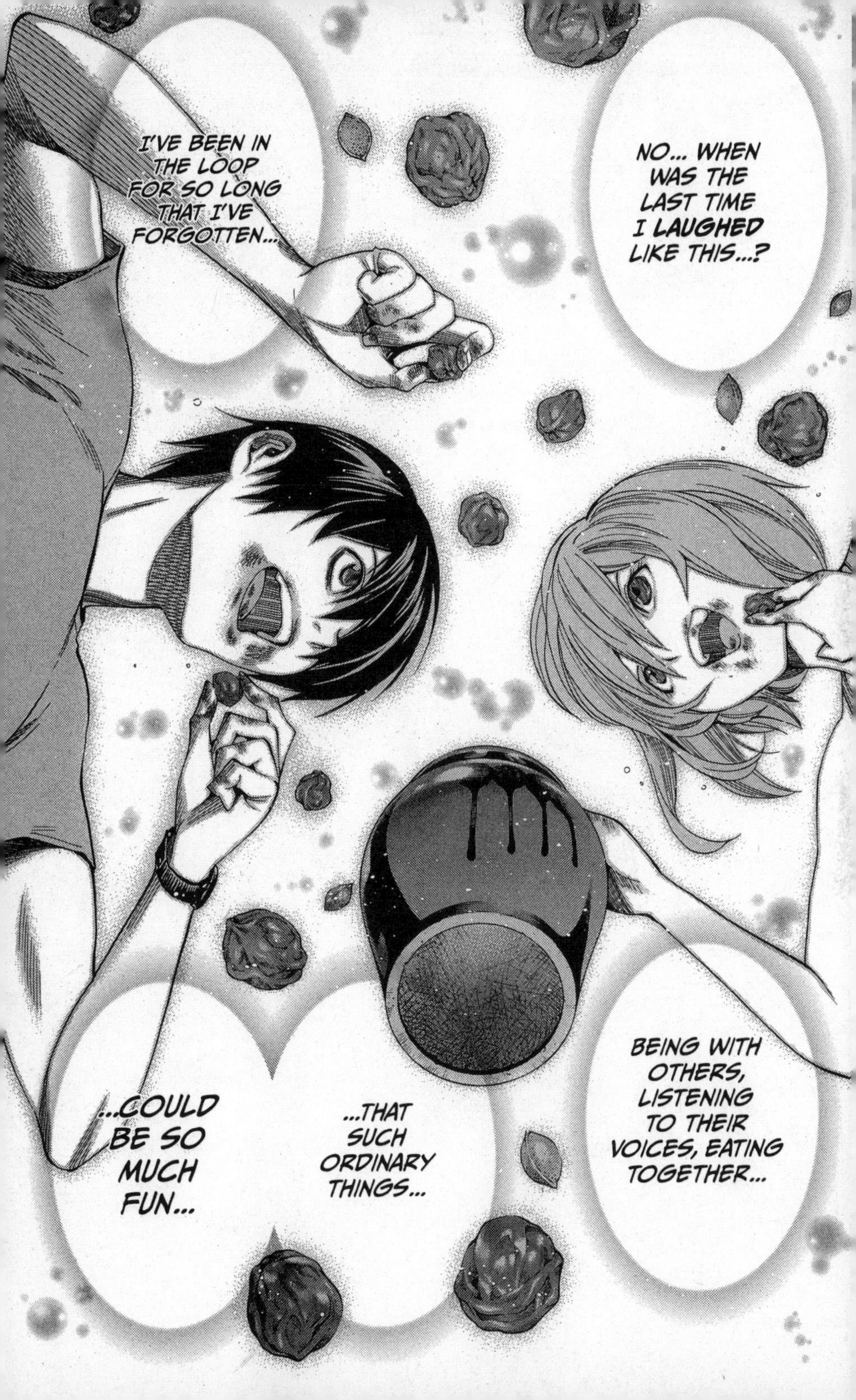
NO... WHEN WAS THE LAST TIME I LAUGHED LIKE THIS...?
I'VE BEEN IN THE LOOP FOR SO LONG THAT I'VE FORGOTTEN...
BEING WITH OTHERS, LISTENING TO THEIR VOICES, EATING TOGETHER...
...THAT SUCH ORDINARY THINGS...
...COULD BE SO MUCH FUN...

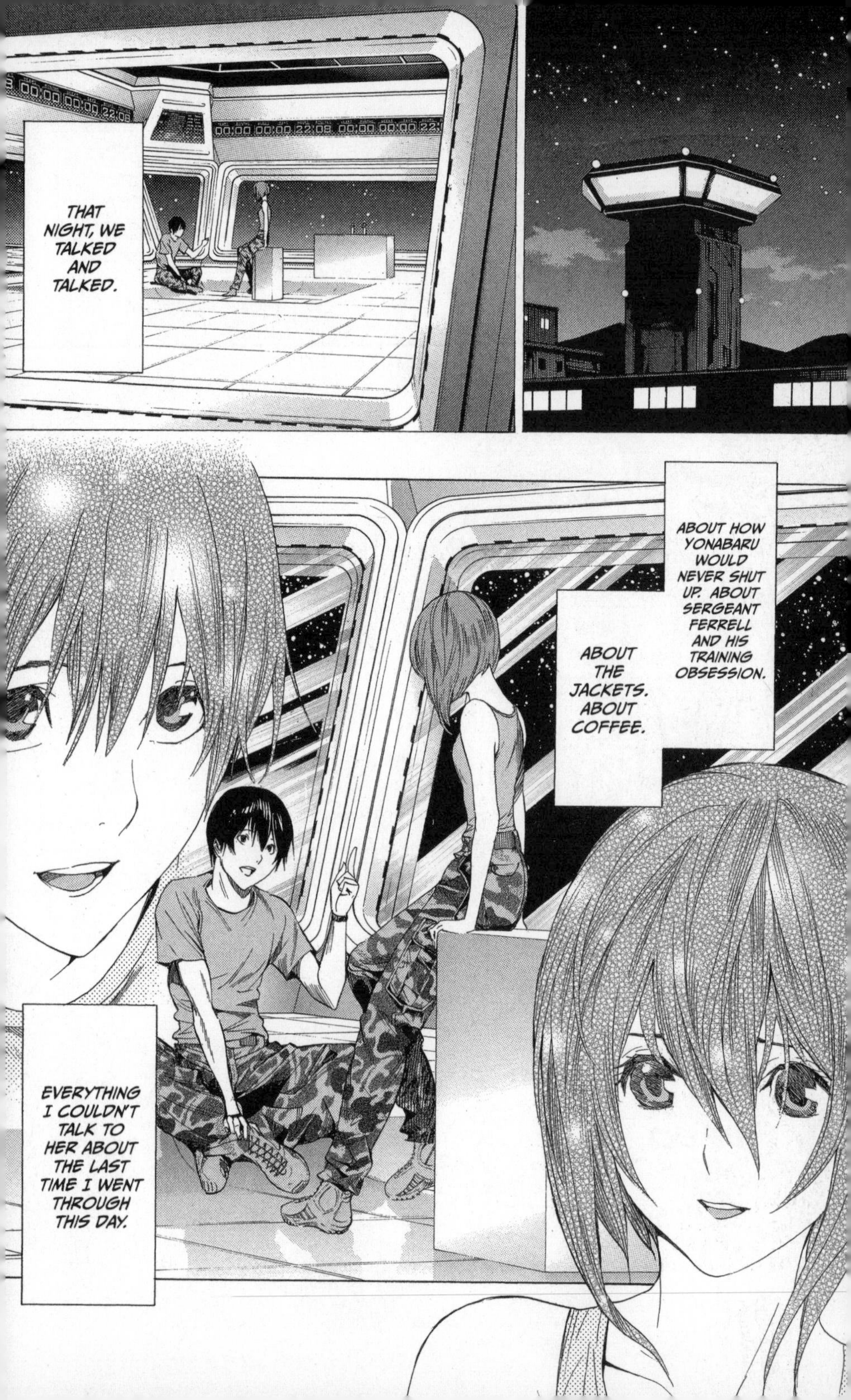
THAT NIGHT, WE TALKED AND TALKED.
ABOUT HOW YONABARU WOULD NEVER SHUT UP. ABOUT SERGEANT FERRELL AND HIS TRAINING OBSESSION.
ABOUT THE JACKETS. ABOUT COFFEE.
EVERYTHING I COULDN'T TALK TO HER ABOUT THE LAST TIME I WENT THROUGH THIS DAY.

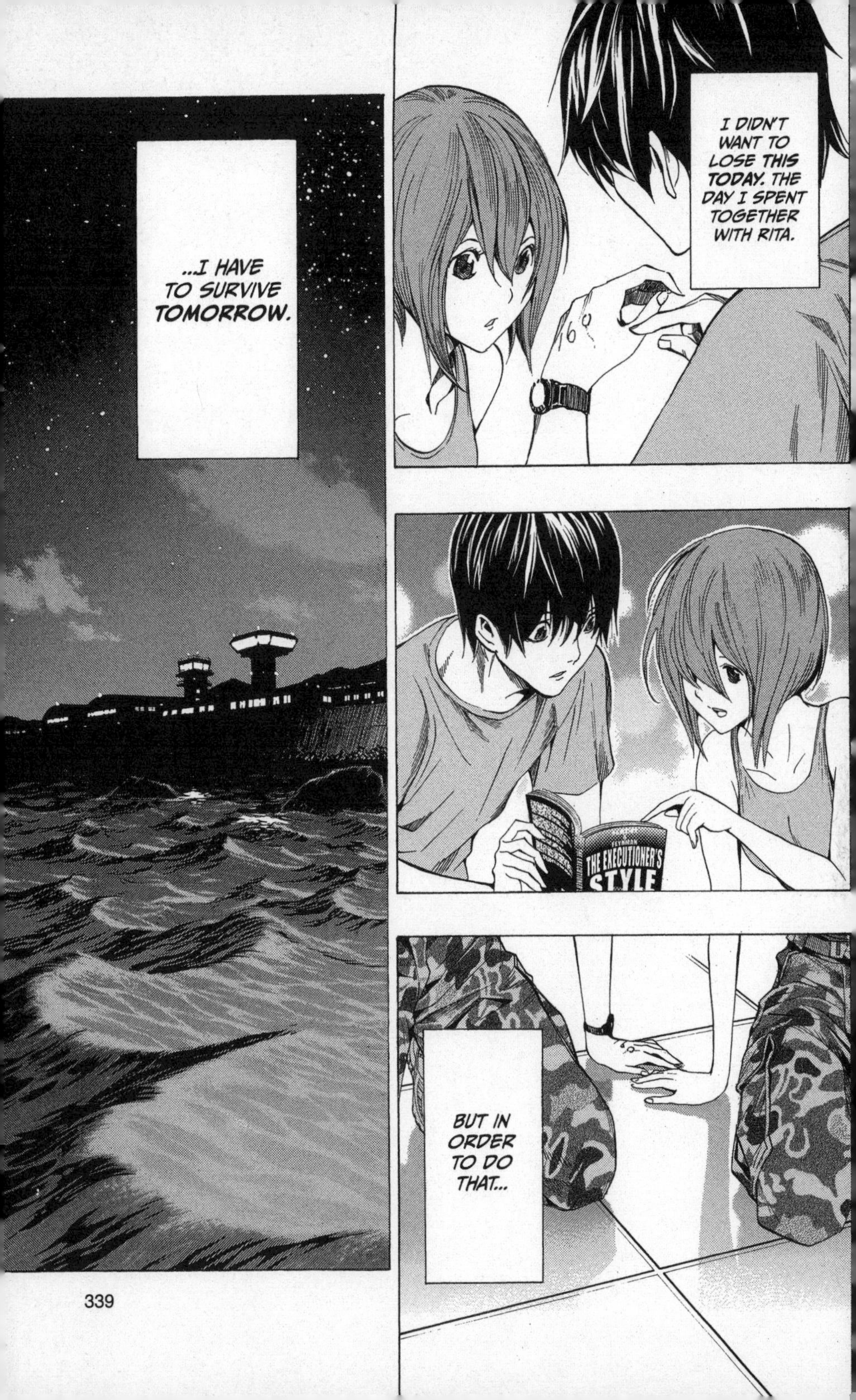
I DIDN'T WANT TO LOSE THIS TODAY. THE DAY I SPENT TOGETHER WITH RITA.
THE EXECUTIONER'S STYLE
BUT IN ORDER TO DO THAT...
...I HAVE TO SURVIVE TOMORROW.

The armored infantry was
Santa Claus, and battle
was our Christmas.
What else for the elves to
do on Christmas Eve but
to let their hair down and
drink a little eggnog.

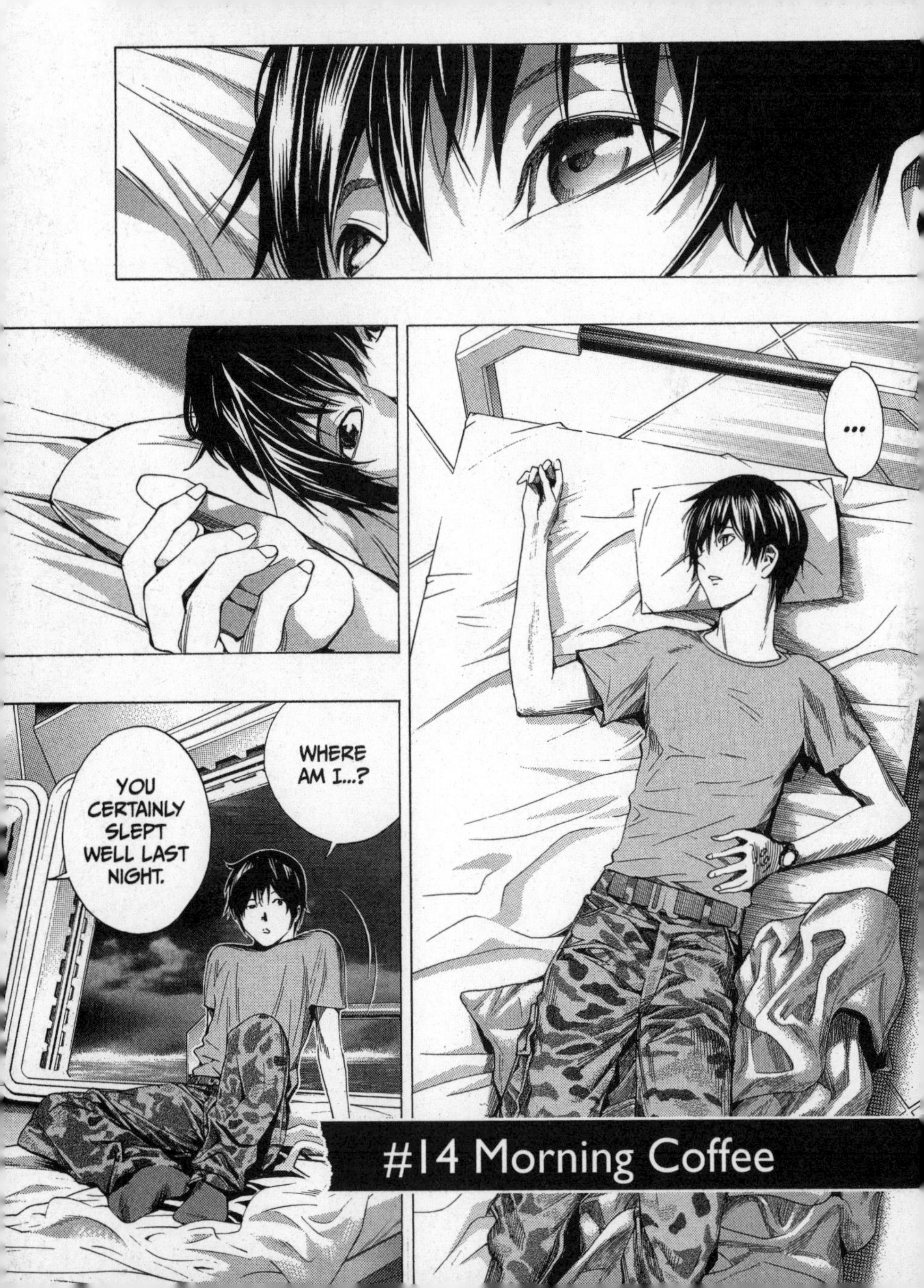
...
WHERE AM I...?
YOU CERTAINLY SLEPT WELL LAST NIGHT.

#14 Morning Coffee

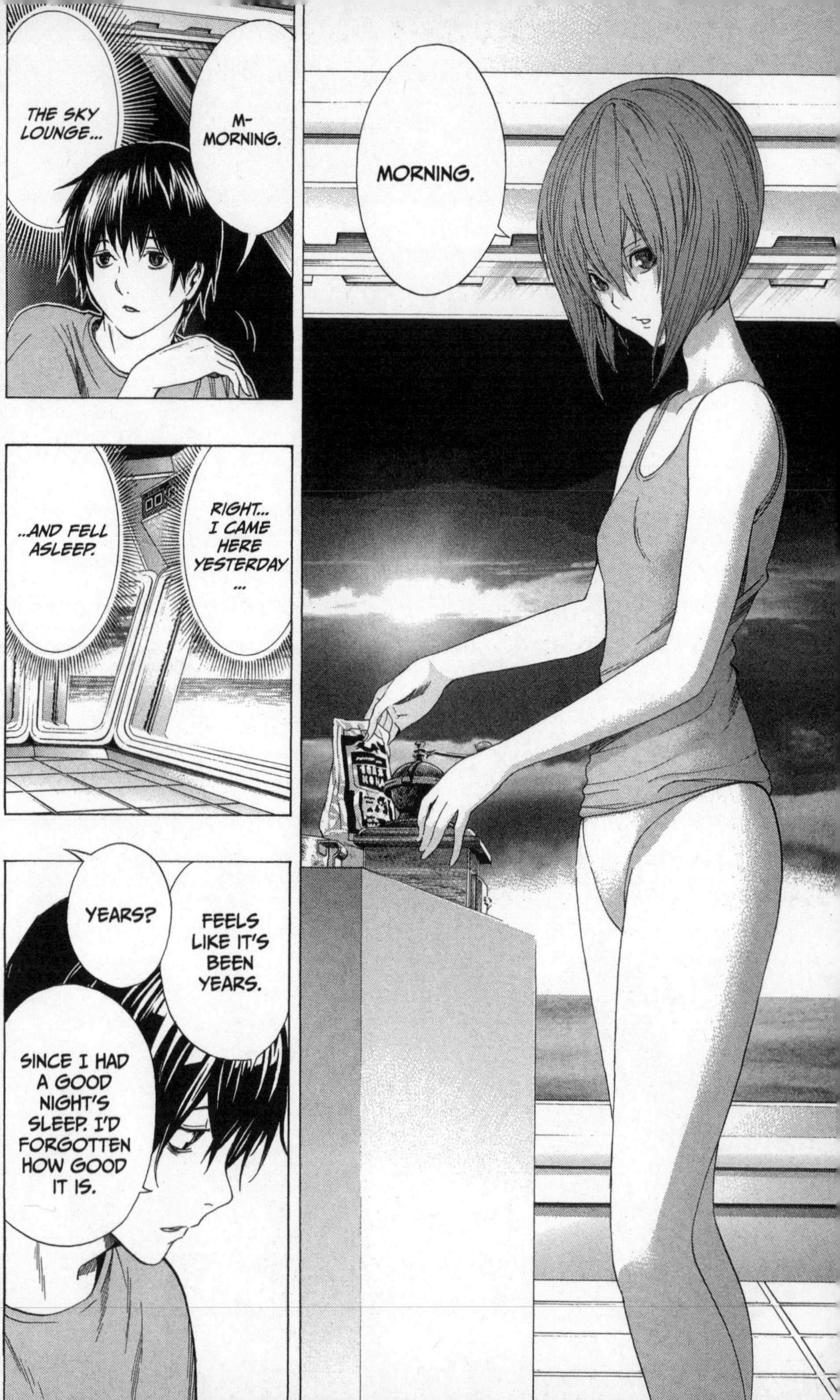
MORNING.
M-MORNING.
THE SKY LOUNGE...
RIGHT... I CAME HERE YESTERDAY ...
...AND FELL ASLEEP.
FEELS LIKE IT'S BEEN YEARS.
YEARS?
SINCE I HAD A GOOD NIGHT'S SLEEP. I'D FORGOTTEN HOW GOOD IT IS.

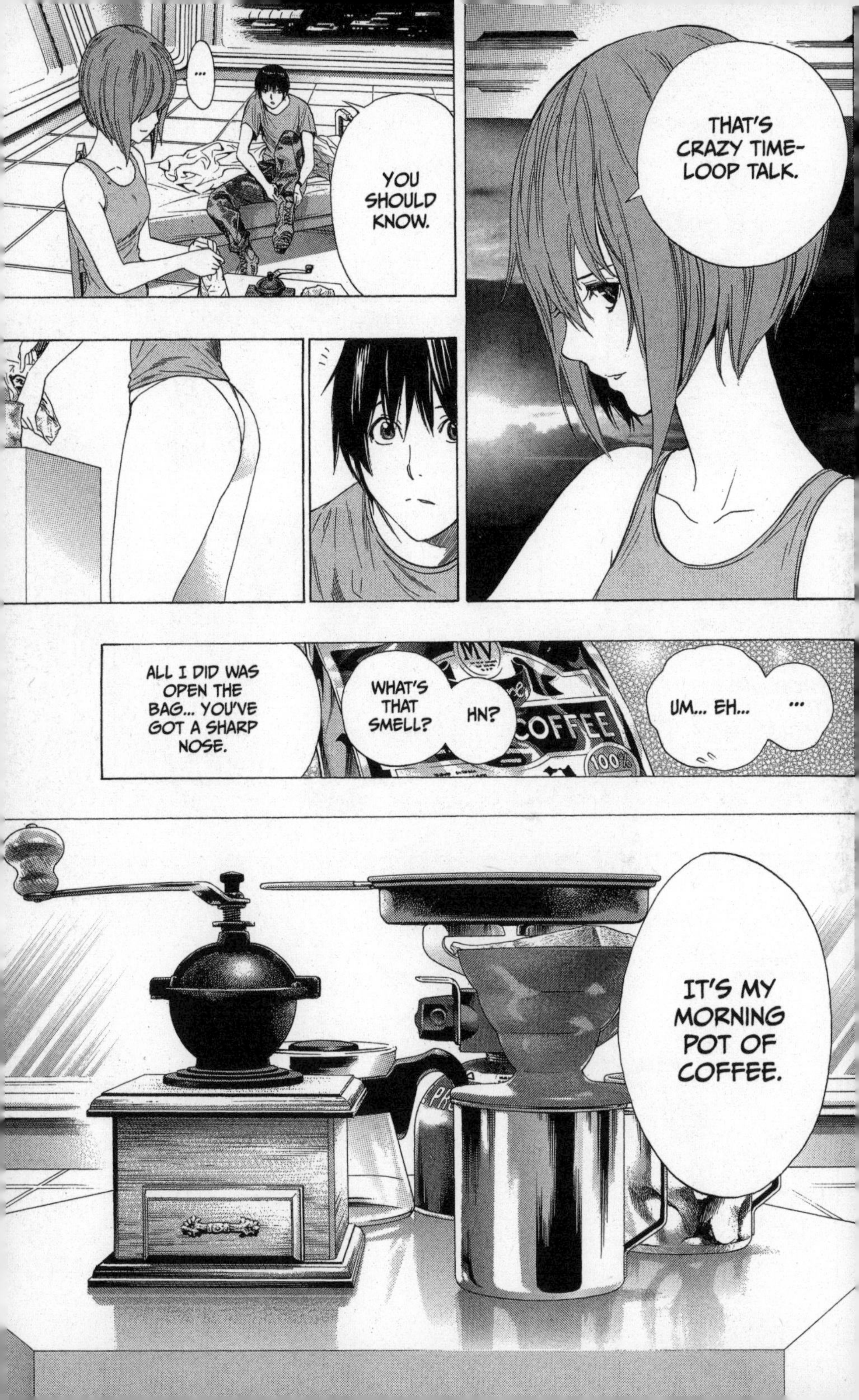
THAT'S CRAZY TIME-LOOP TALK.
YOU SHOULD KNOW.
...
...
UM... EH...
COFFEE
100%
HN?
WHAT'S THAT SMELL?
ALL I DID WAS OPEN THE BAG... YOU'VE GOT A SHARP NOSE.
IT'S MY MORNING POT OF COFFEE.

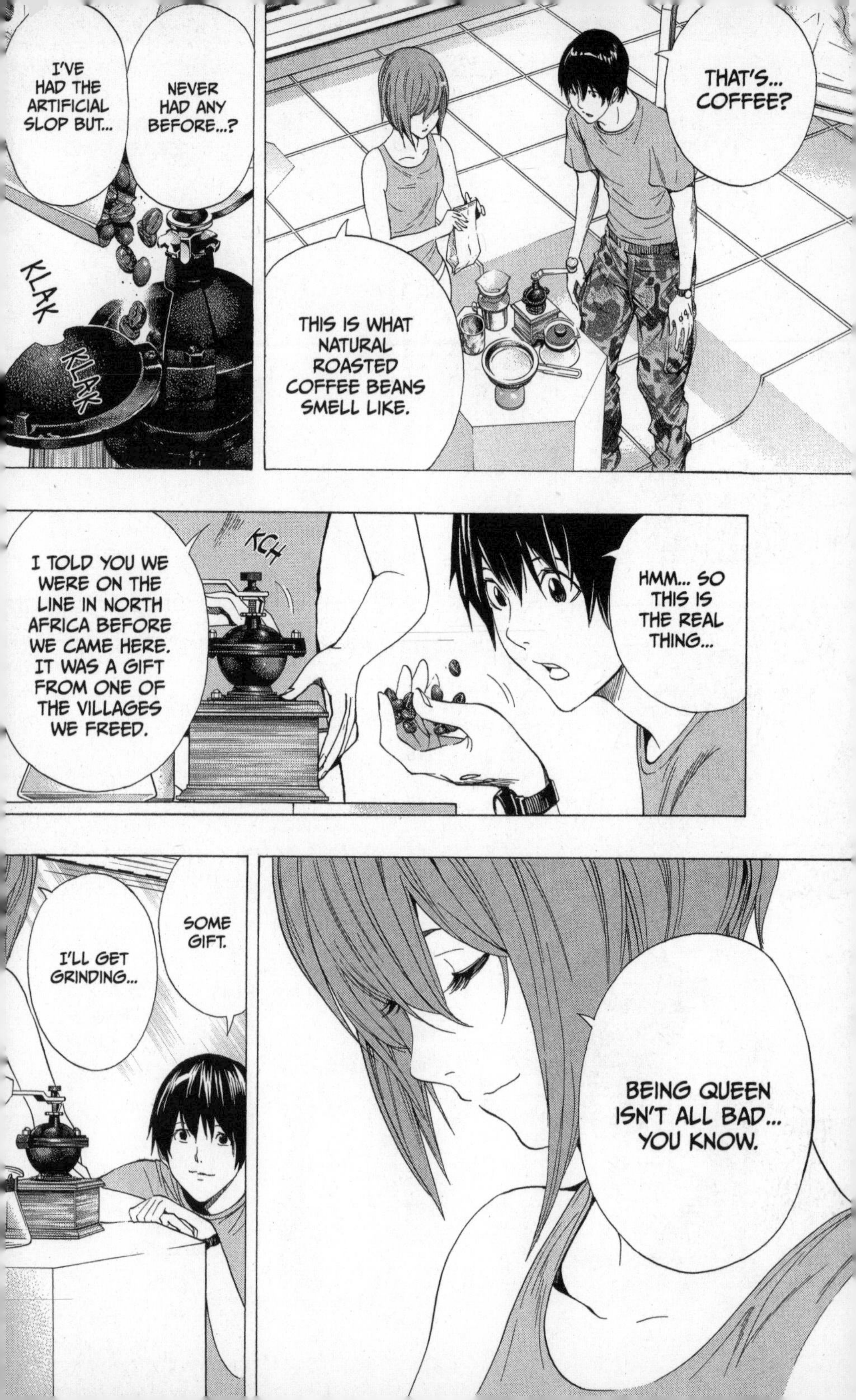
THAT'S... COFFEE?
THIS IS WHAT NATURAL ROASTED COFFEE BEANS SMELL LIKE.
NEVER HAD ANY BEFORE...?
I'VE HAD THE ARTIFICIAL SLOP BUT...
KLAK
KLAK
HMM... SO THIS IS THE REAL THING...
KCH
I TOLD YOU WE WERE ON THE LINE IN NORTH AFRICA BEFORE WE CAME HERE. IT WAS A GIFT FROM ONE OF THE VILLAGES WE FREED.
BEING QUEEN ISN'T ALL BAD... YOU KNOW.
SOME GIFT.
I'LL GET GRINDING...

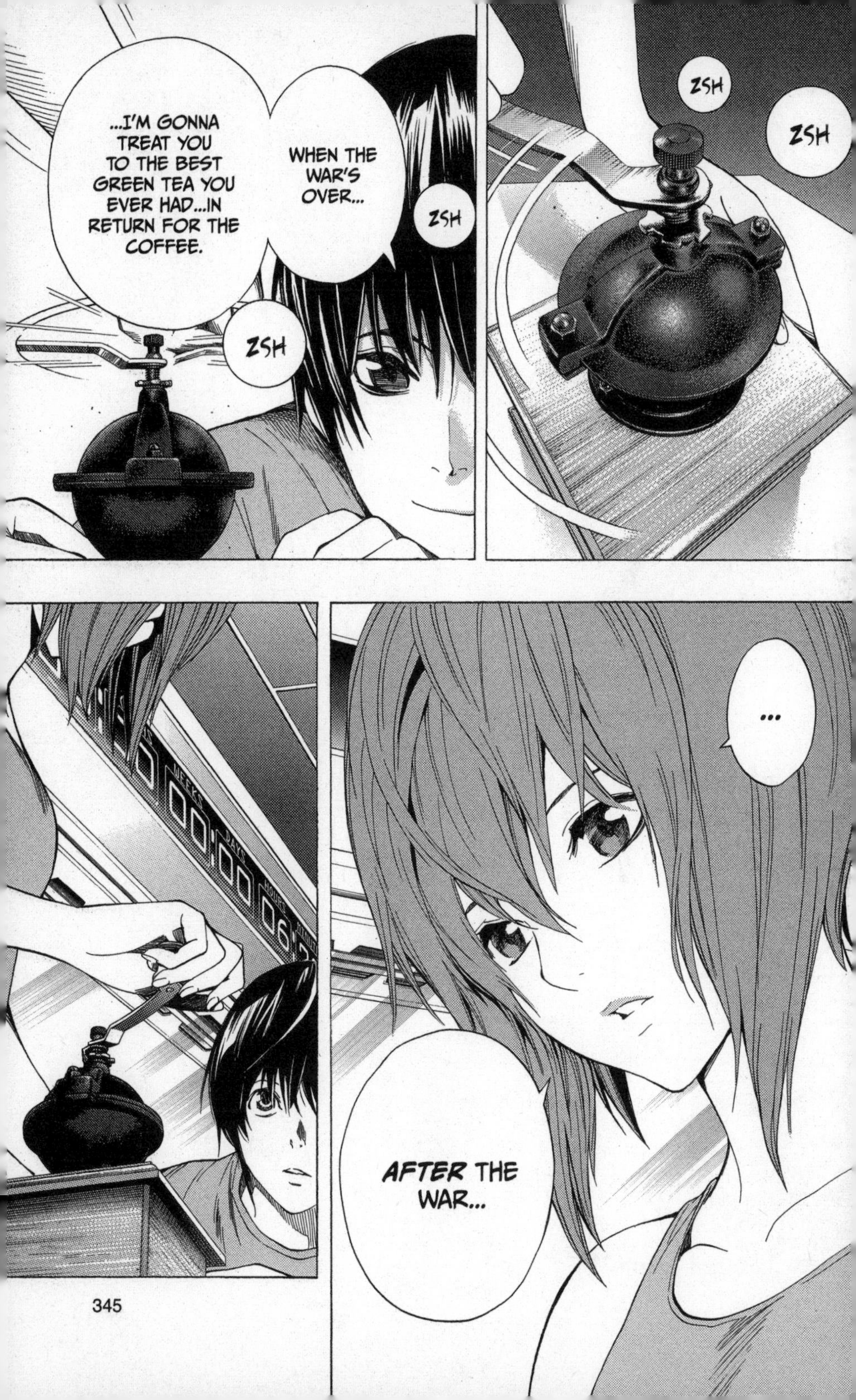
ZSH
ZSH
WHEN THE WAR'S OVER...
...I'M GONNA TREAT YOU TO THE BEST GREEN TEA YOU EVER HAD...IN RETURN FOR THE COFFEE.
ZSH
ZSH
...
AFTER THE WAR...

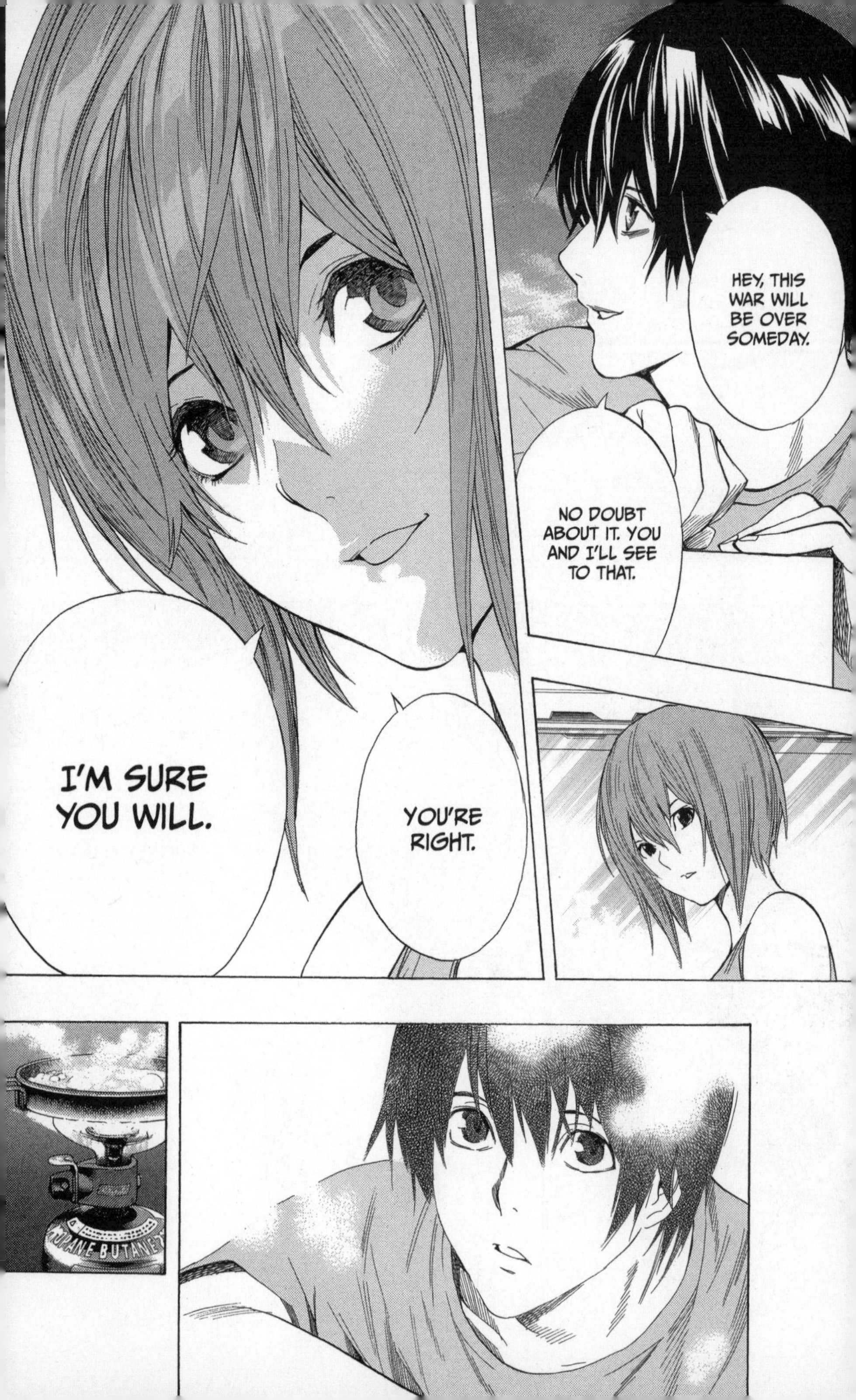
HEY, THIS WAR WILL BE OVER SOMEDAY.
NO DOUBT ABOUT IT. YOU AND I'LL SEE TO THAT.
YOU'RE RIGHT.
I'M SURE YOU WILL.

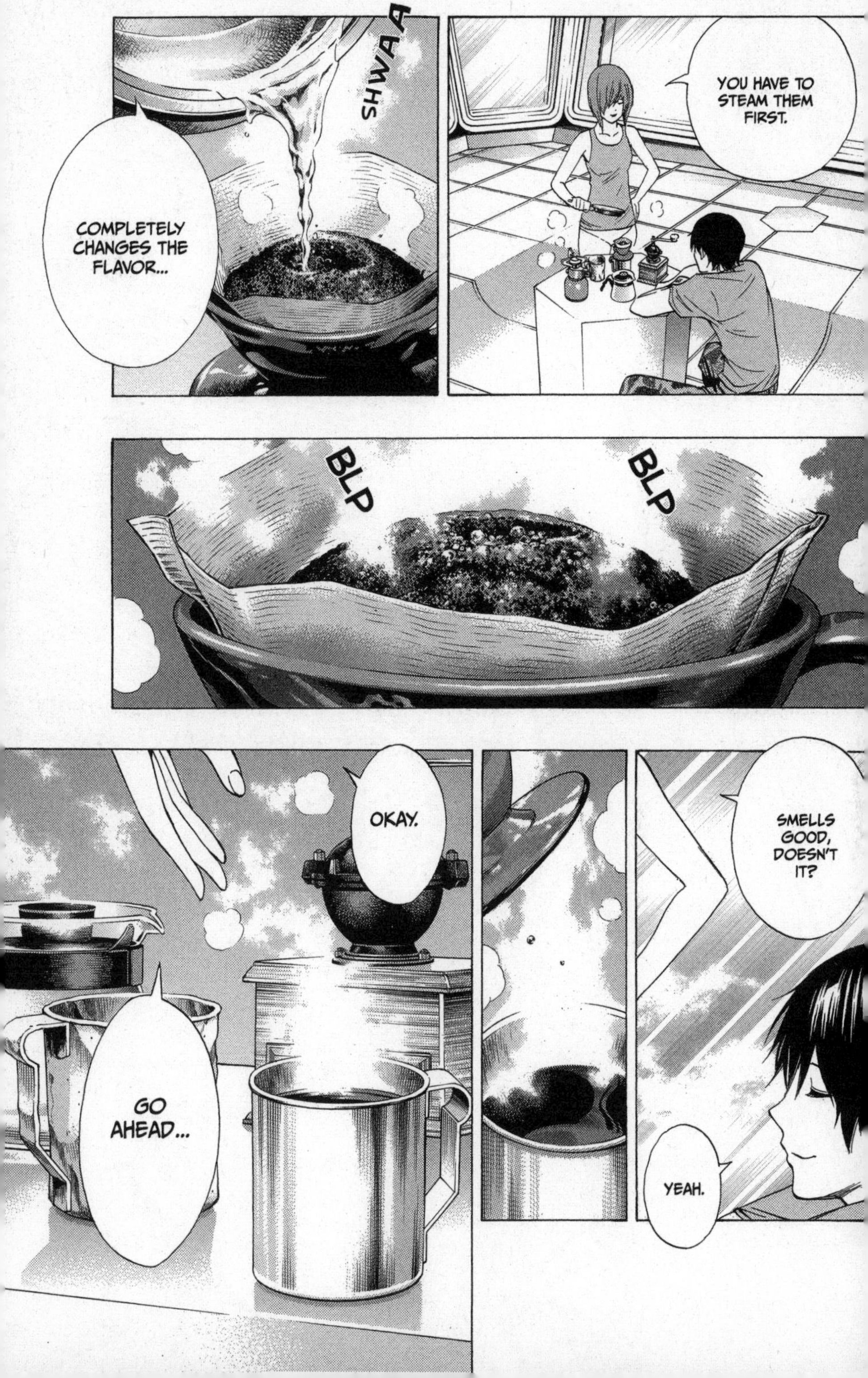
YOU HAVE TO STEAM THEM FIRST.
SHWAA
COMPLETELY CHANGES THE FLAVOR...
BLP
BLP
SMELLS GOOD, DOESN'T IT?
YEAH.
OKAY.
GO AHEAD...

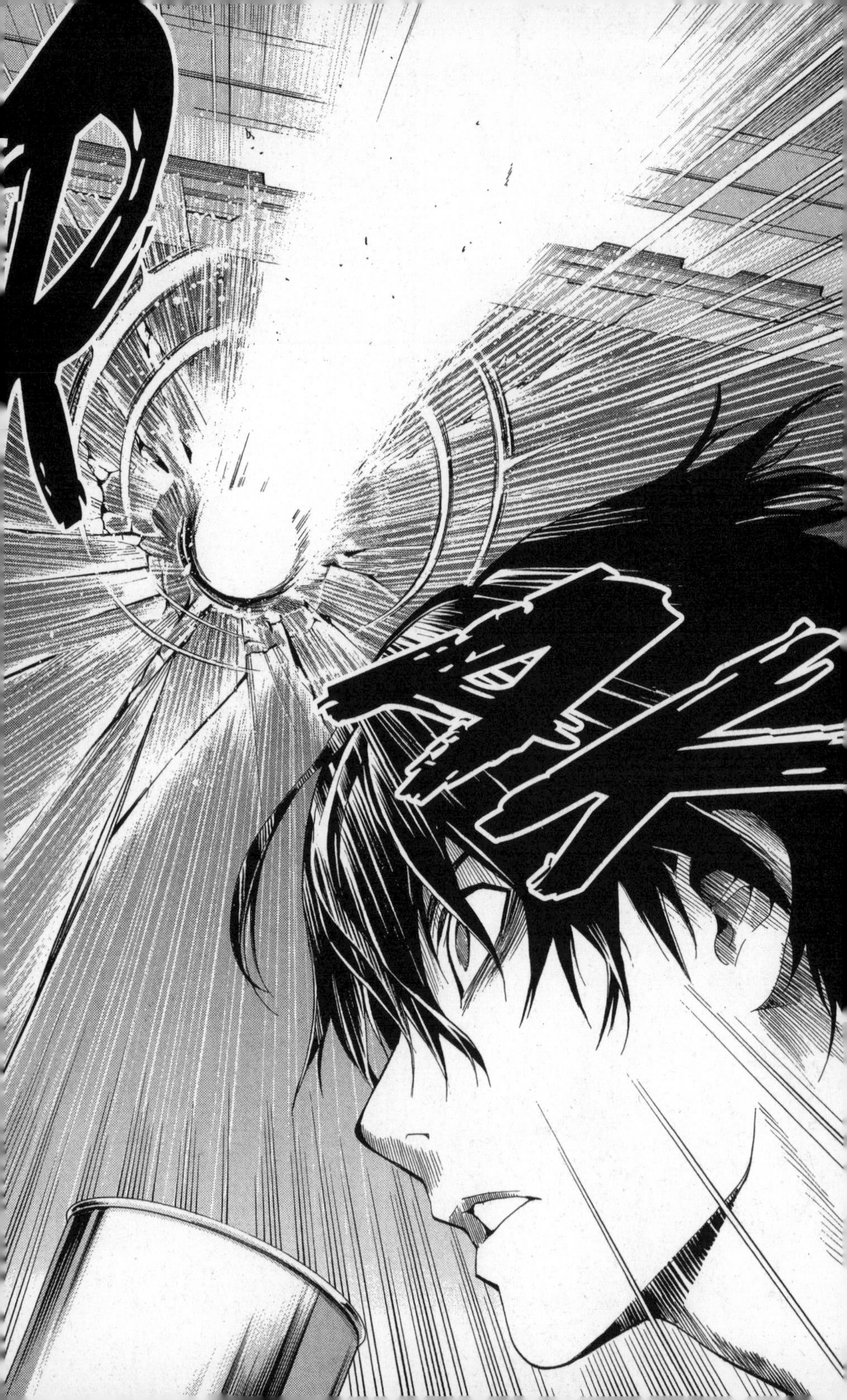

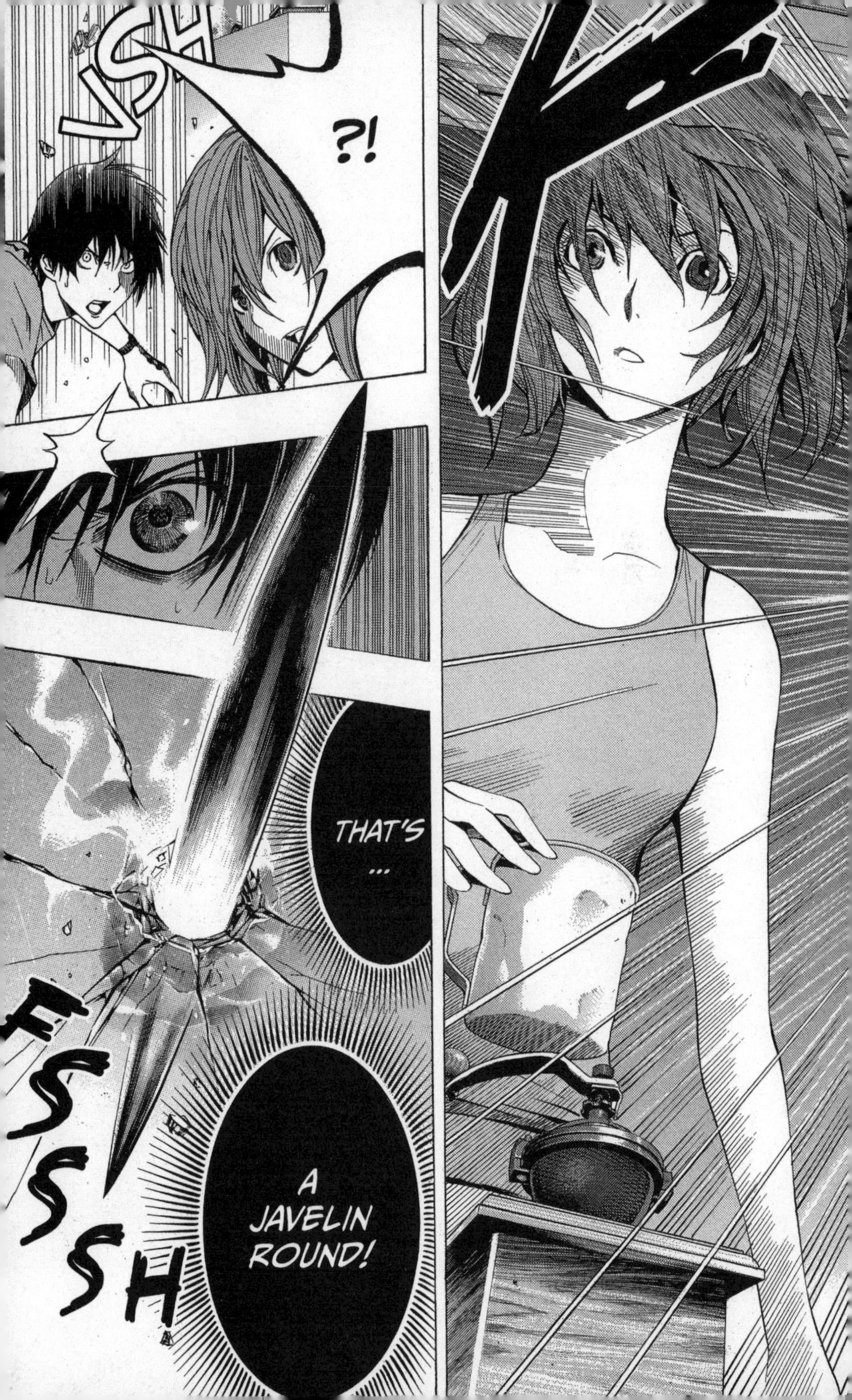
VSH
?!
THAT'S ...
A JAVELIN ROUND!
FSSSH

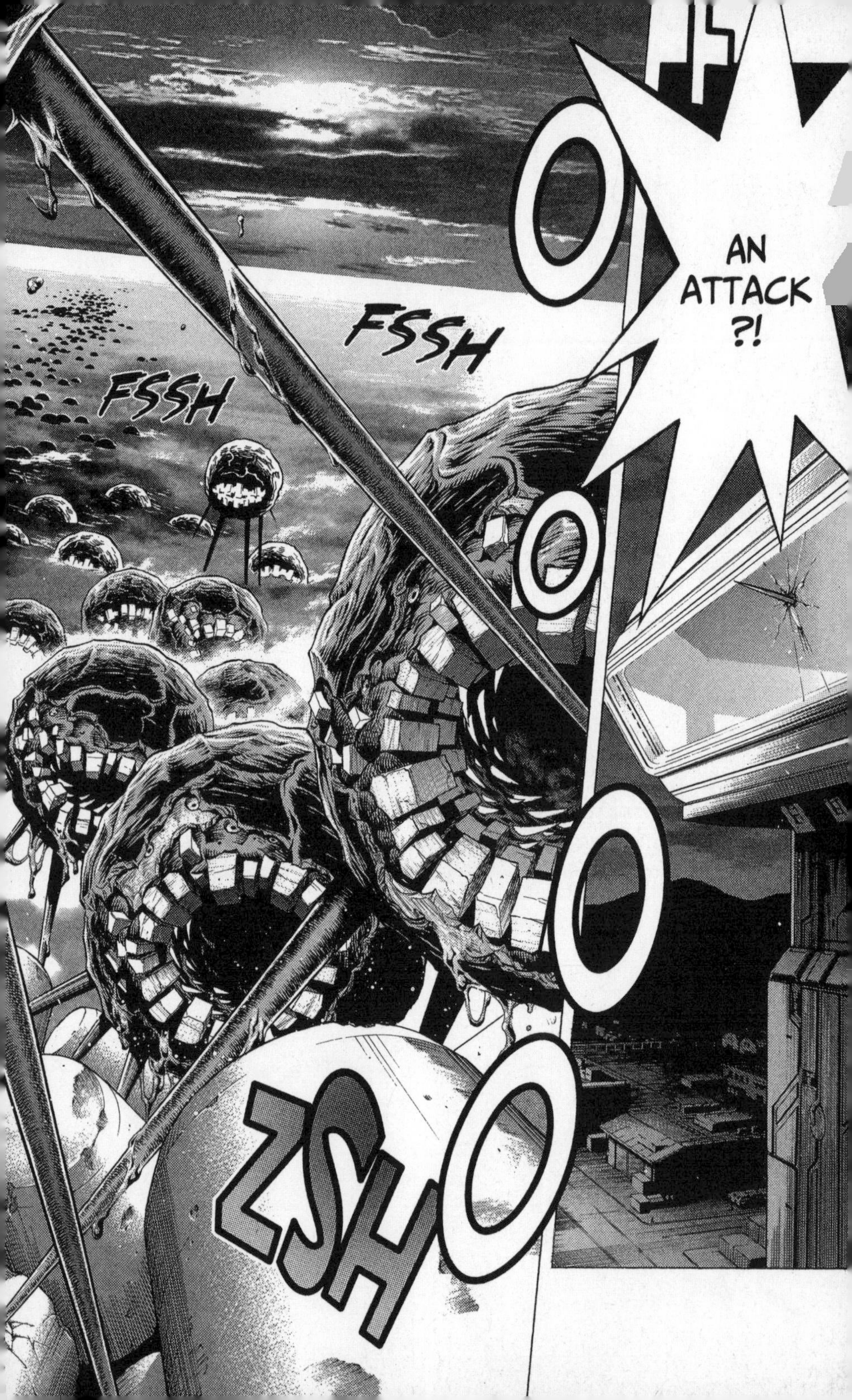
AN ATTACK ?!
FSSH
FSSH
ZSHOOOOO

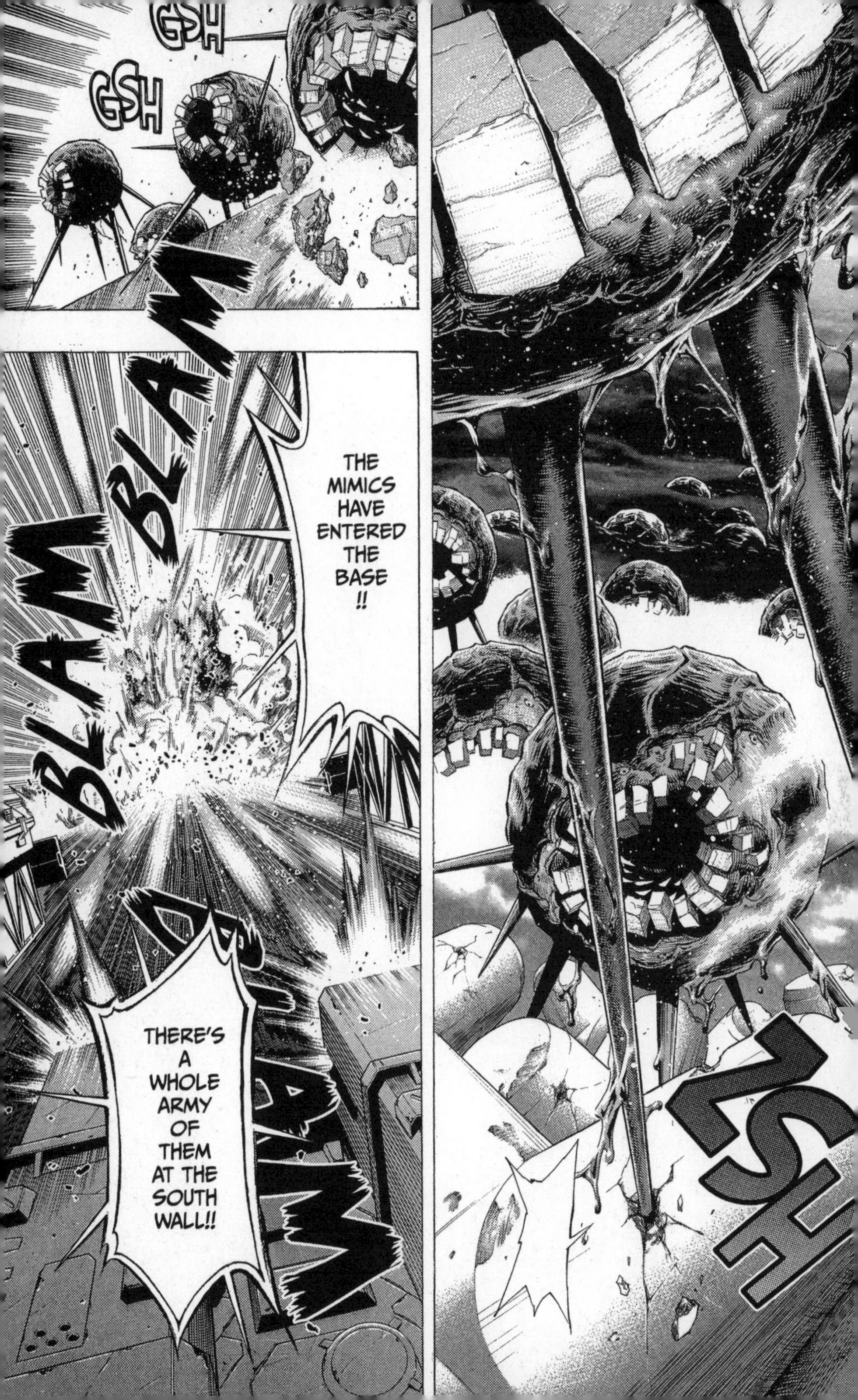
ZSH
GSH
GSH
BLAM
BLAM
BLAM
THE MIMICS HAVE ENTERED THE BASE!!
THERE'S A WHOLE ARMY OF THEM AT THE SOUTH WALL!!

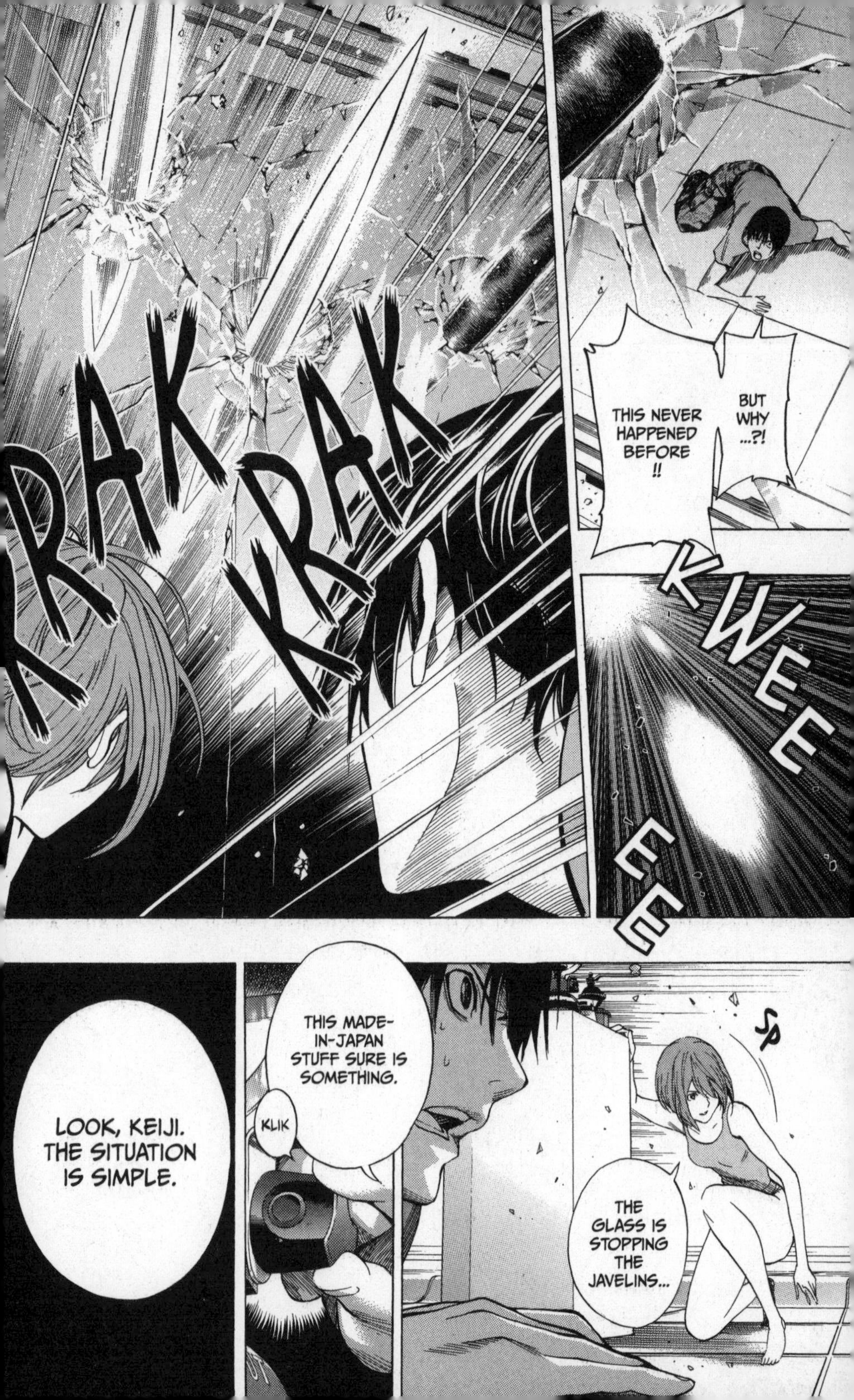

BUT WHY ...?!
THIS NEVER HAPPENED BEFORE !!
KWEEEE
KRAK
RAK
SP
THE GLASS IS STOPPING THE JAVELINS...
THIS MADE-IN-JAPAN STUFF SURE IS SOMETHING.
KLIK
LOOK, KEIJI. THE SITUATION IS SIMPLE.

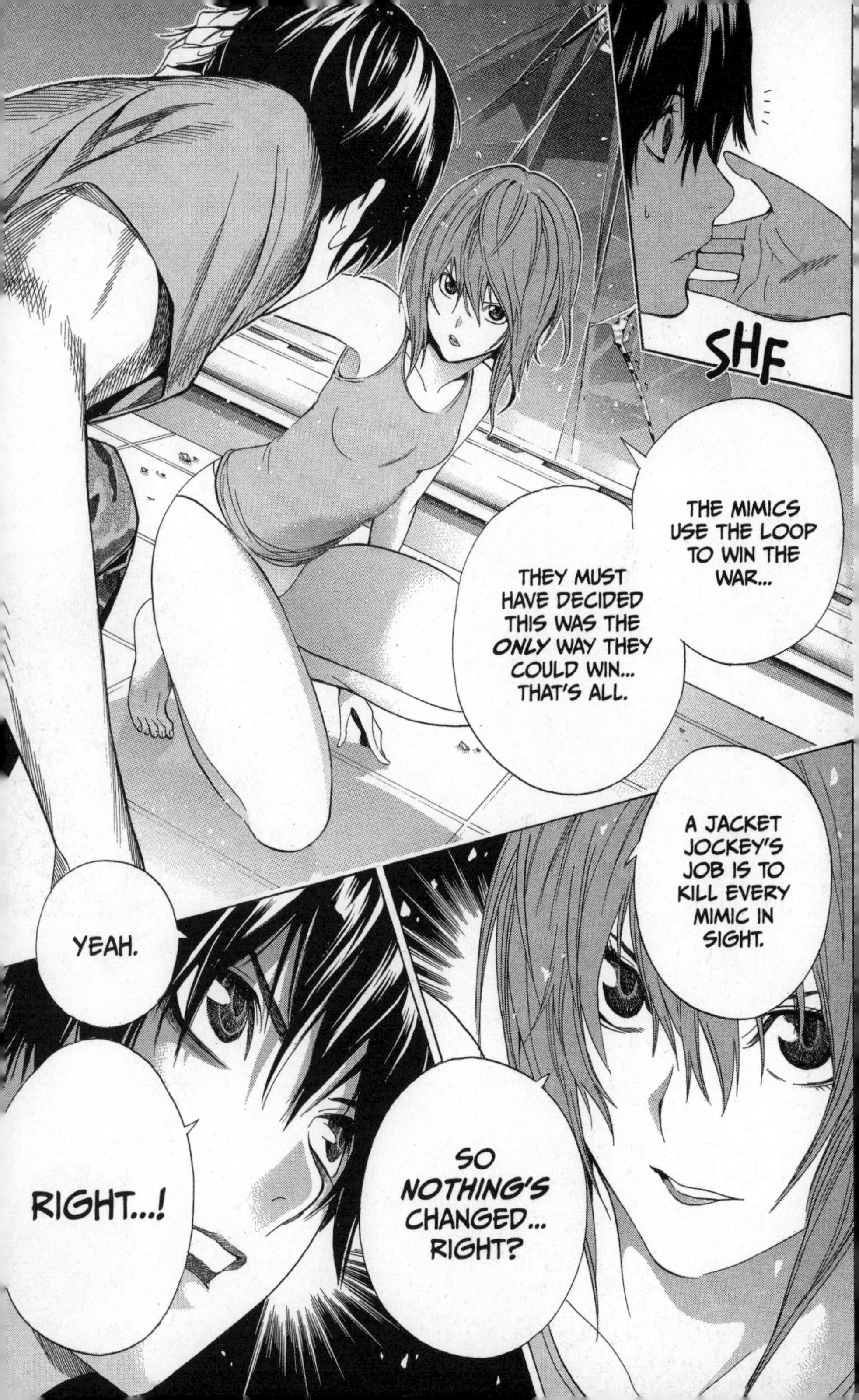
SHF
THE MIMICS USE THE LOOP TO WIN THE WAR...
THEY MUST HAVE DECIDED THIS WAS THE *ONLY* WAY THEY COULD WIN... THAT'S ALL.
A JACKET JOCKEY'S JOB IS TO KILL EVERY MIMIC IN SIGHT.
SO *NOTHING'S* CHANGED... RIGHT?
YEAH.
RIGHT...!

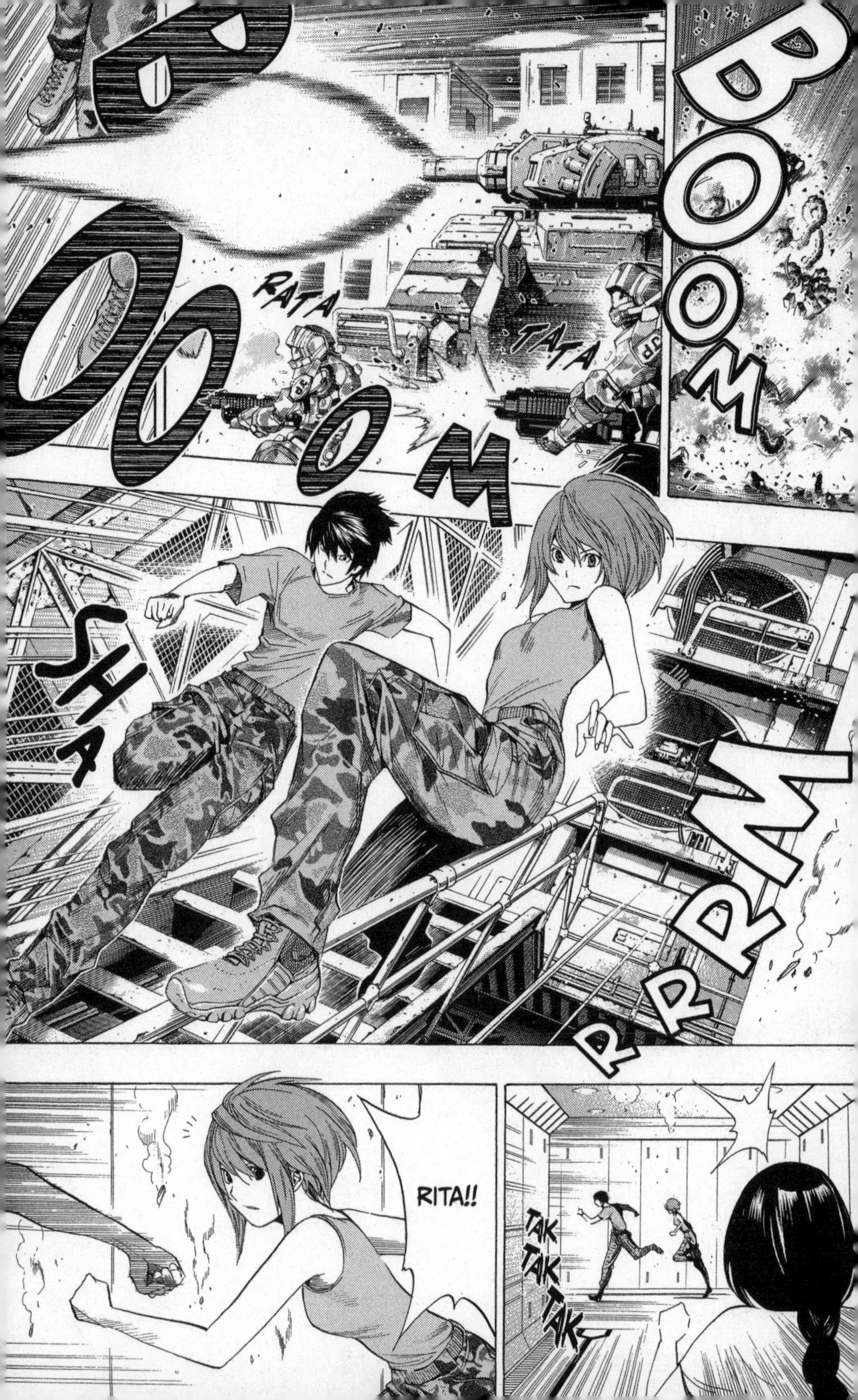
BOOOM
DOOOOM
RATA
TATA
RRRM
SHA
TAK TAK TAK
RITA!!

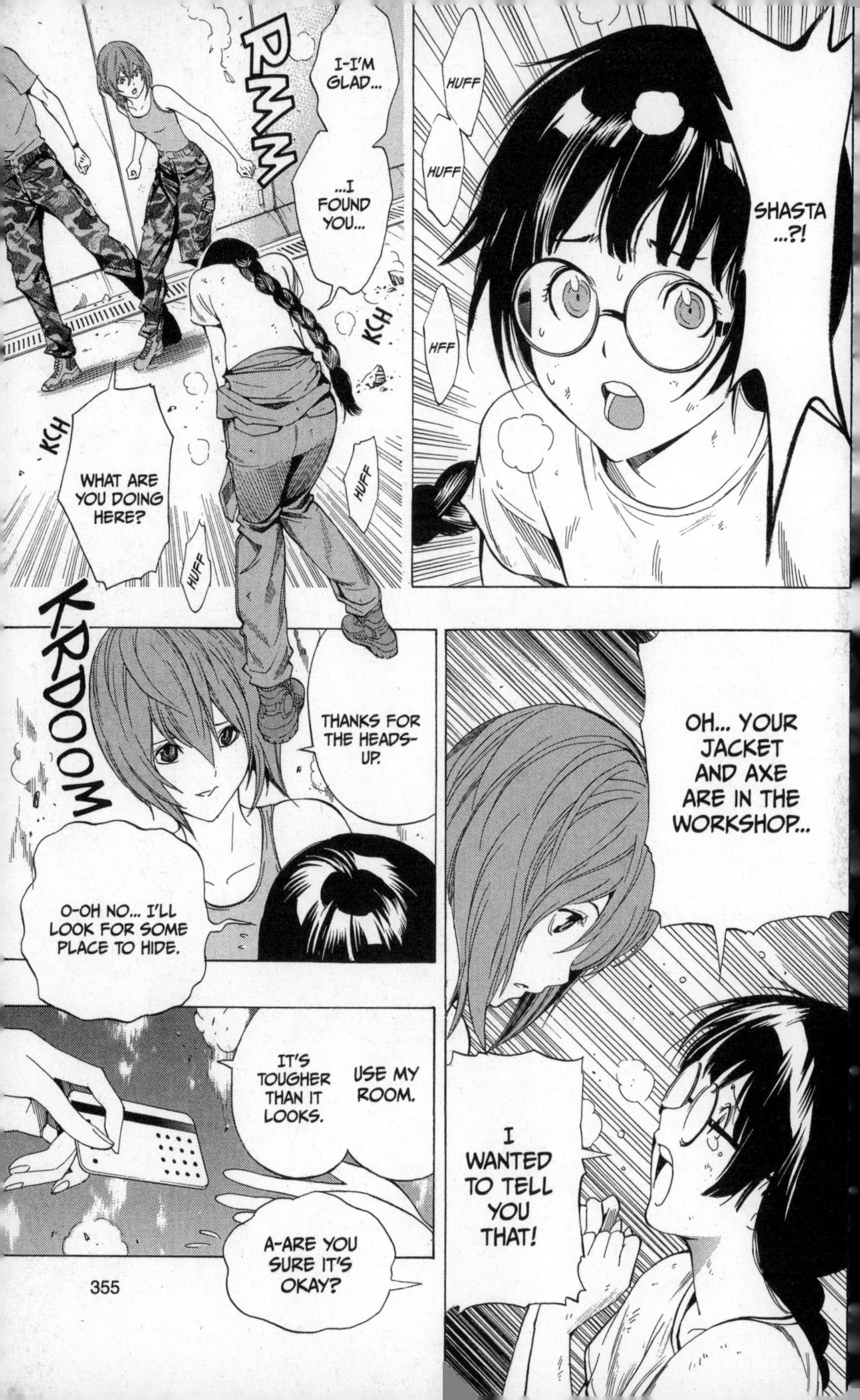
SHASTA ...?!
HUFF
HUFF
HFF
I-I'M GLAD...
RMM
...I FOUND YOU...
KCH
WHAT ARE YOU DOING HERE?
KCH
HUFF
HUFF
OH... YOUR JACKET AND AXE ARE IN THE WORKSHOP...
I WANTED TO TELL YOU THAT!
THANKS FOR THE HEADS-UP.
KRDOOM
O-OH NO... I'LL LOOK FOR SOME PLACE TO HIDE.
USE MY ROOM.
IT'S TOUGHER THAN IT LOOKS.
A-ARE YOU SURE IT'S OKAY?

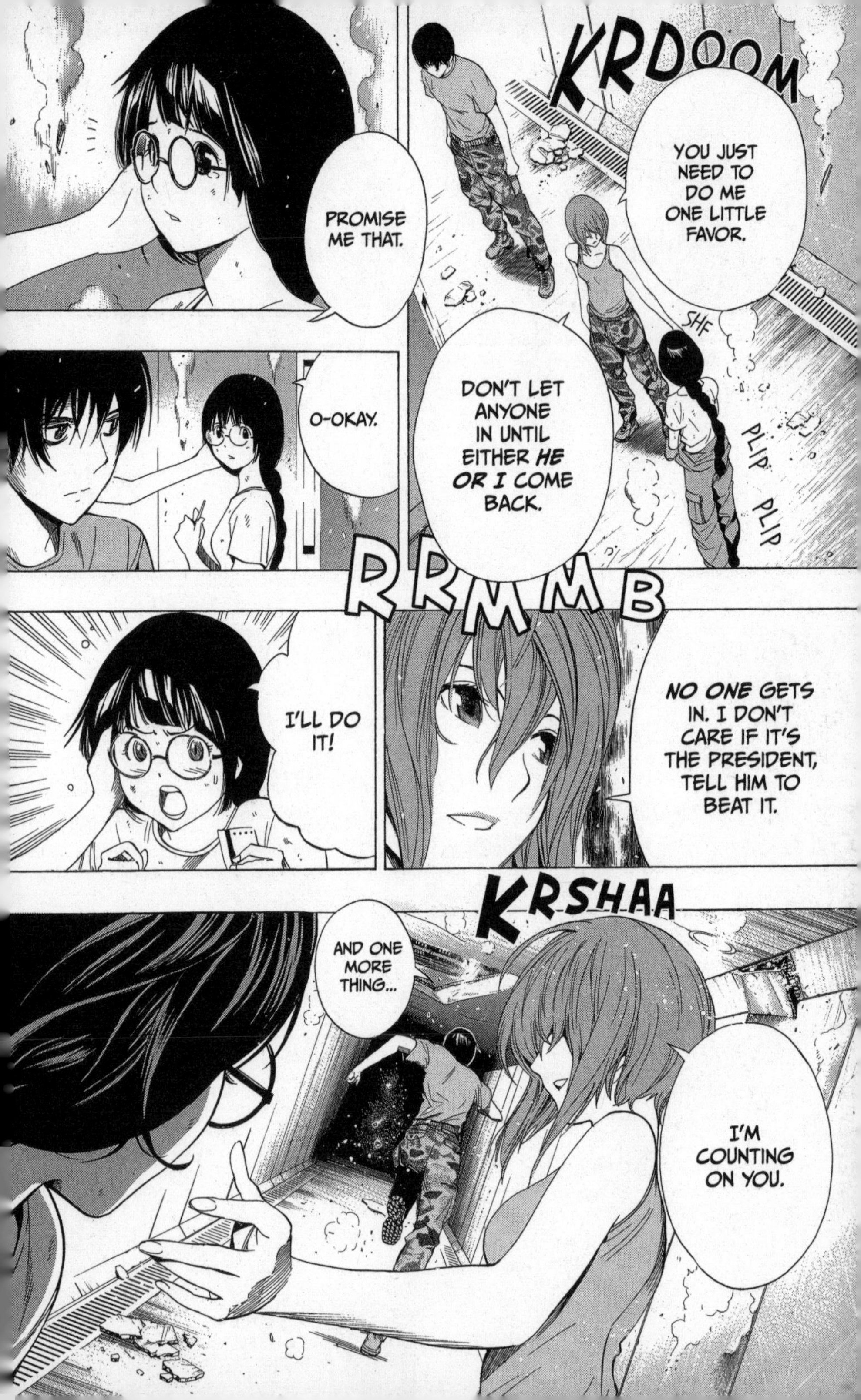
KRDOOM
YOU JUST NEED TO DO ME ONE LITTLE FAVOR.
SHF
DON'T LET ANYONE IN UNTIL EITHER *HE OR I* COME BACK.
PLIP
PLIP
PROMISE ME THAT.
O-OKAY.
RRMMB
NO ONE GETS IN. I DON'T CARE IF IT'S THE PRESIDENT, TELL HIM TO BEAT IT.
I'LL DO IT!
KRSHAA
AND ONE MORE THING...
I'M COUNTING ON YOU.

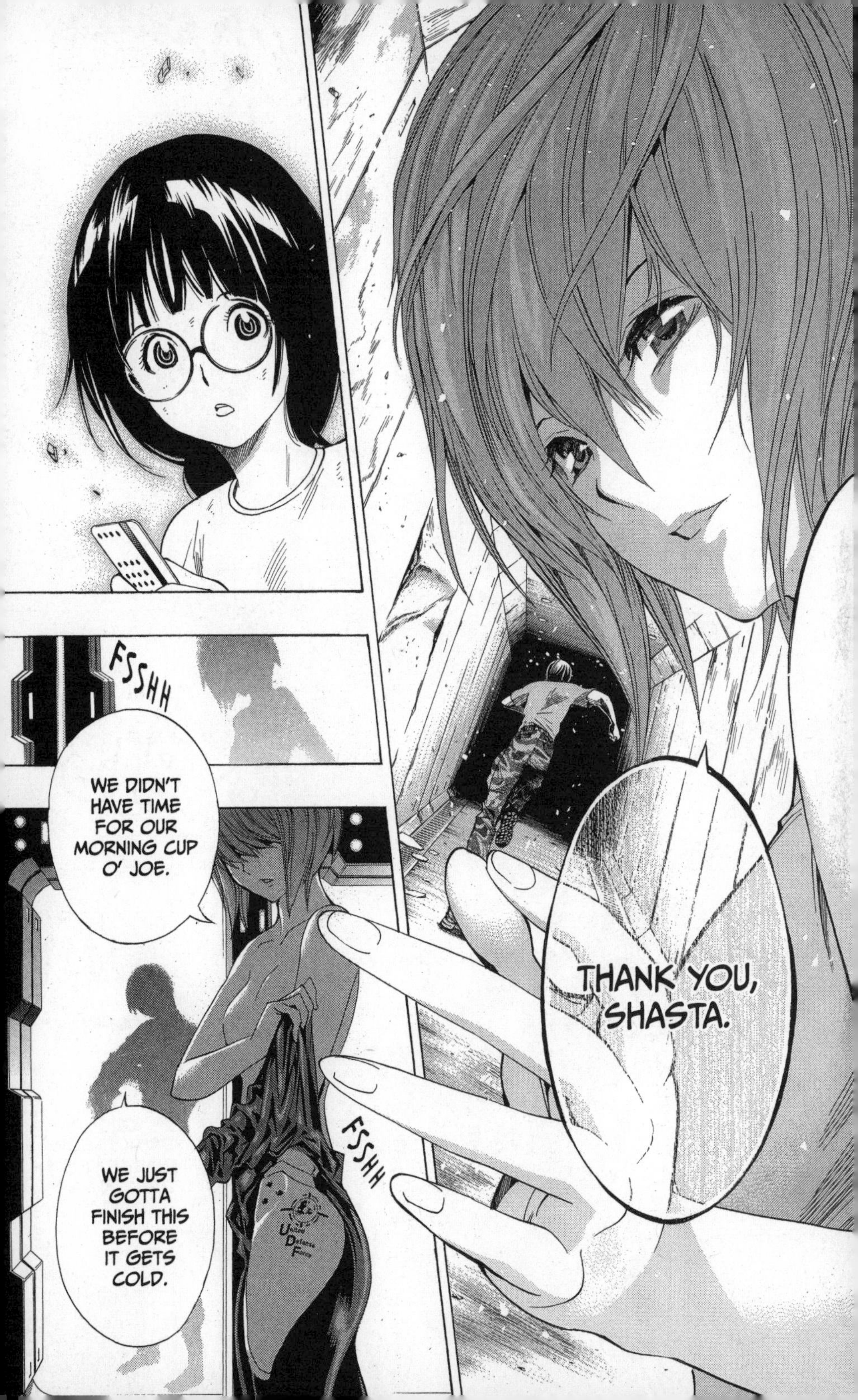
THANK YOU, SHASTA.
FSSHH
WE DIDN'T HAVE TIME FOR OUR MORNING CUP O' JOE.
FSSHH
WE JUST GOTTA FINISH THIS BEFORE IT GETS COLD.
United Defense Force

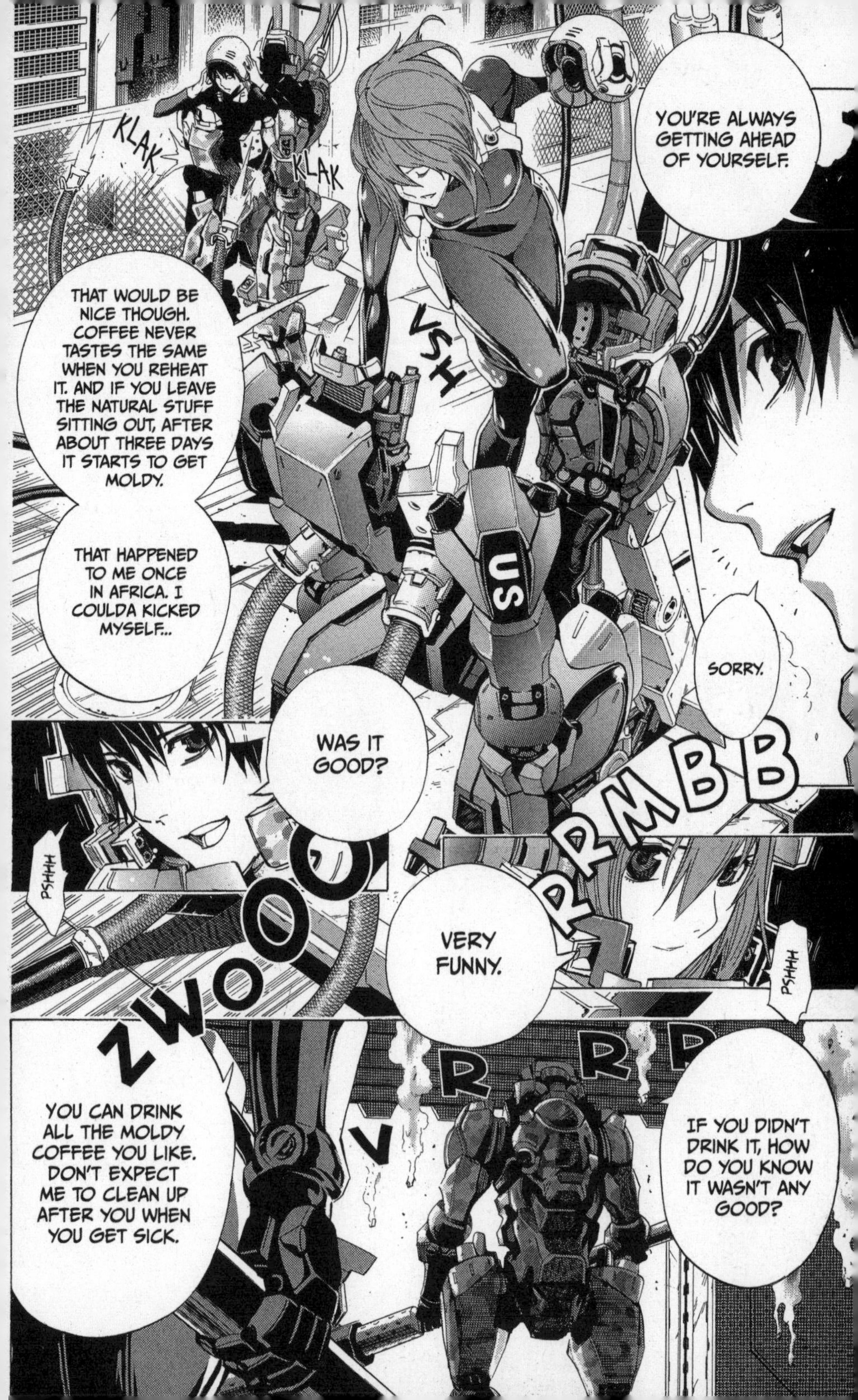
YOU'RE ALWAYS GETTING AHEAD OF YOURSELF.
SORRY.
VSH
KLAK
KLAK
THAT WOULD BE NICE THOUGH. COFFEE NEVER TASTES THE SAME WHEN YOU REHEAT IT. AND IF YOU LEAVE THE NATURAL STUFF SITTING OUT, AFTER ABOUT THREE DAYS IT STARTS TO GET MOLDY.
THAT HAPPENED TO ME ONCE IN AFRICA. I COULDA KICKED MYSELF...
PRMBB
PSHHH
WAS IT GOOD?
VERY FUNNY.
PSHHH
ZWOOOO
VRRRP
IF YOU DIDN'T DRINK IT, HOW DO YOU KNOW IT WASN'T ANY GOOD?
YOU CAN DRINK ALL THE MOLDY COFFEE YOU LIKE. DON'T EXPECT ME TO CLEAN UP AFTER YOU WHEN YOU GET SICK.

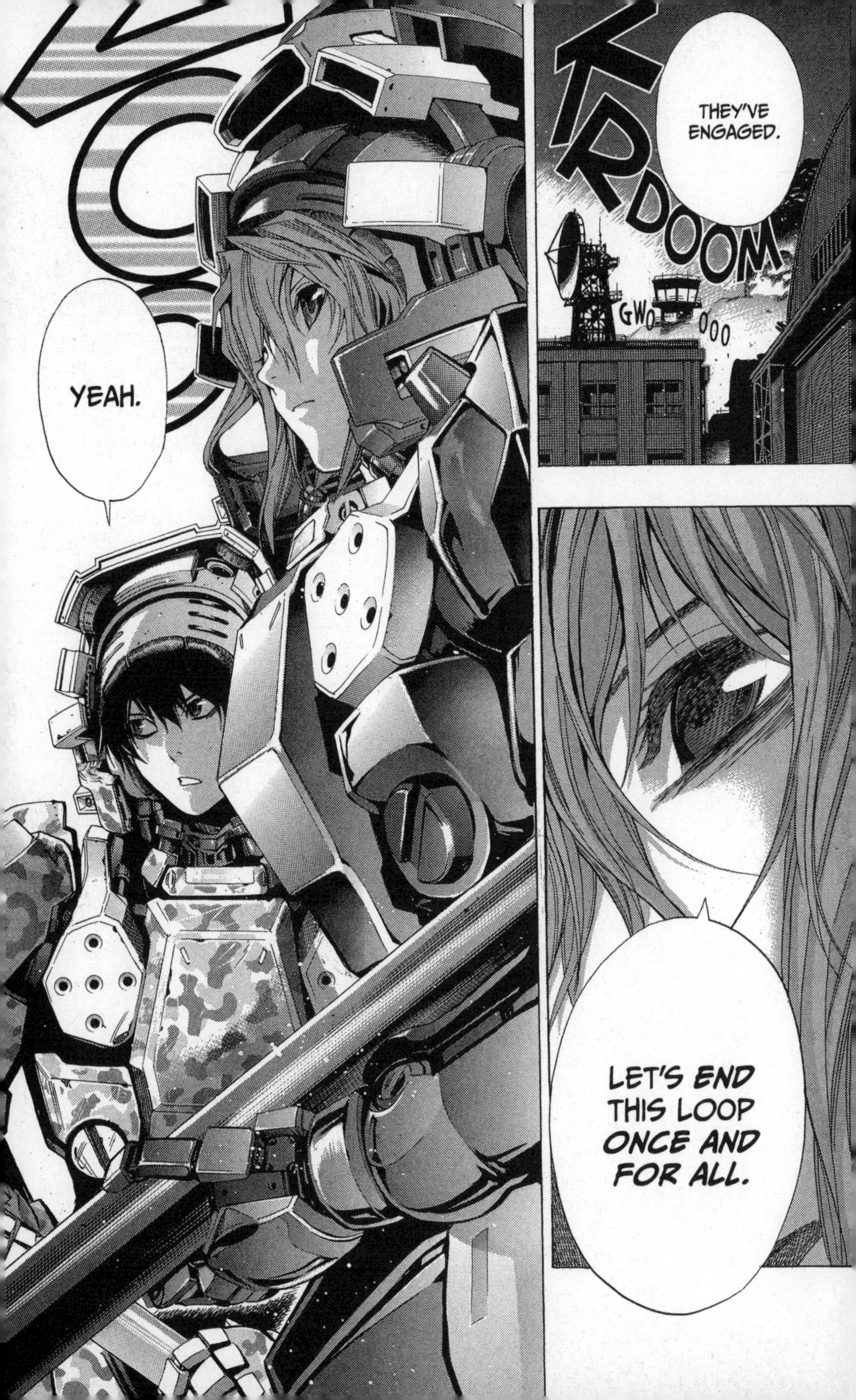
THEY'VE ENGAGED.
TRDOOM
GWOOOO
LET'S END THIS LOOP ONCE AND FOR ALL.
YEAH.

Missiles that dug under and shattered bedrock, cluster bombs that fragmented into a thousand bomblets, vaporized fuel-air bombs that incinerated everything near them. All of mankind's tools of technological destruction were useless on their own. Defeating the Mimics was like defusing a bomb; you had to disarm each piece in the proper order or it would blow up in your face.

#15 Killing Machine

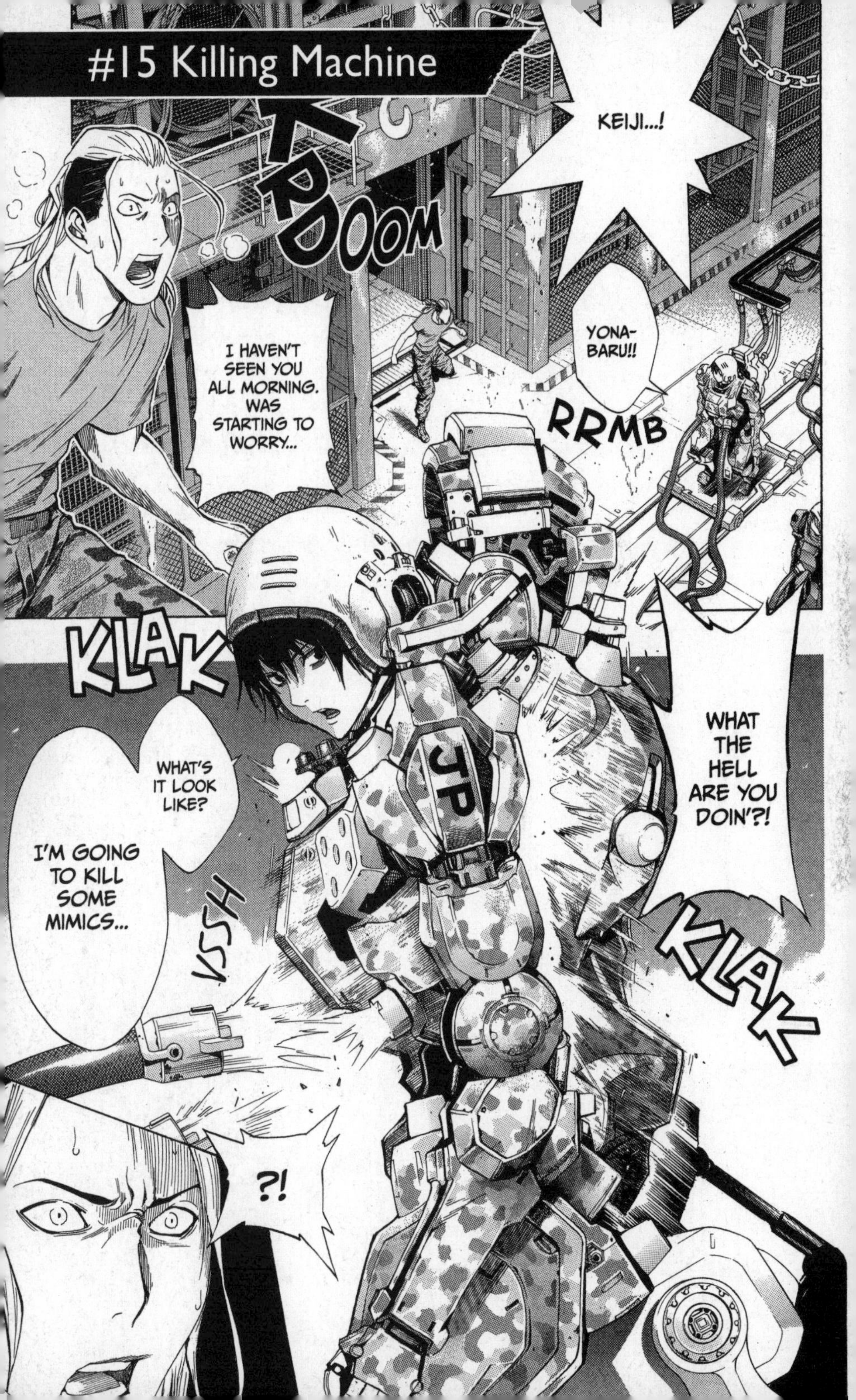
KEIJI...!
KRDOOM
YONA-BARU!!
RRMB
I HAVEN'T SEEN YOU ALL MORNING. WAS STARTING TO WORRY...
WHAT THE HELL ARE YOU DOIN'?!
KLAK
KLAK
WHAT'S IT LOOK LIKE?
I'M GOING TO KILL SOME MIMICS...
VSSH
?!

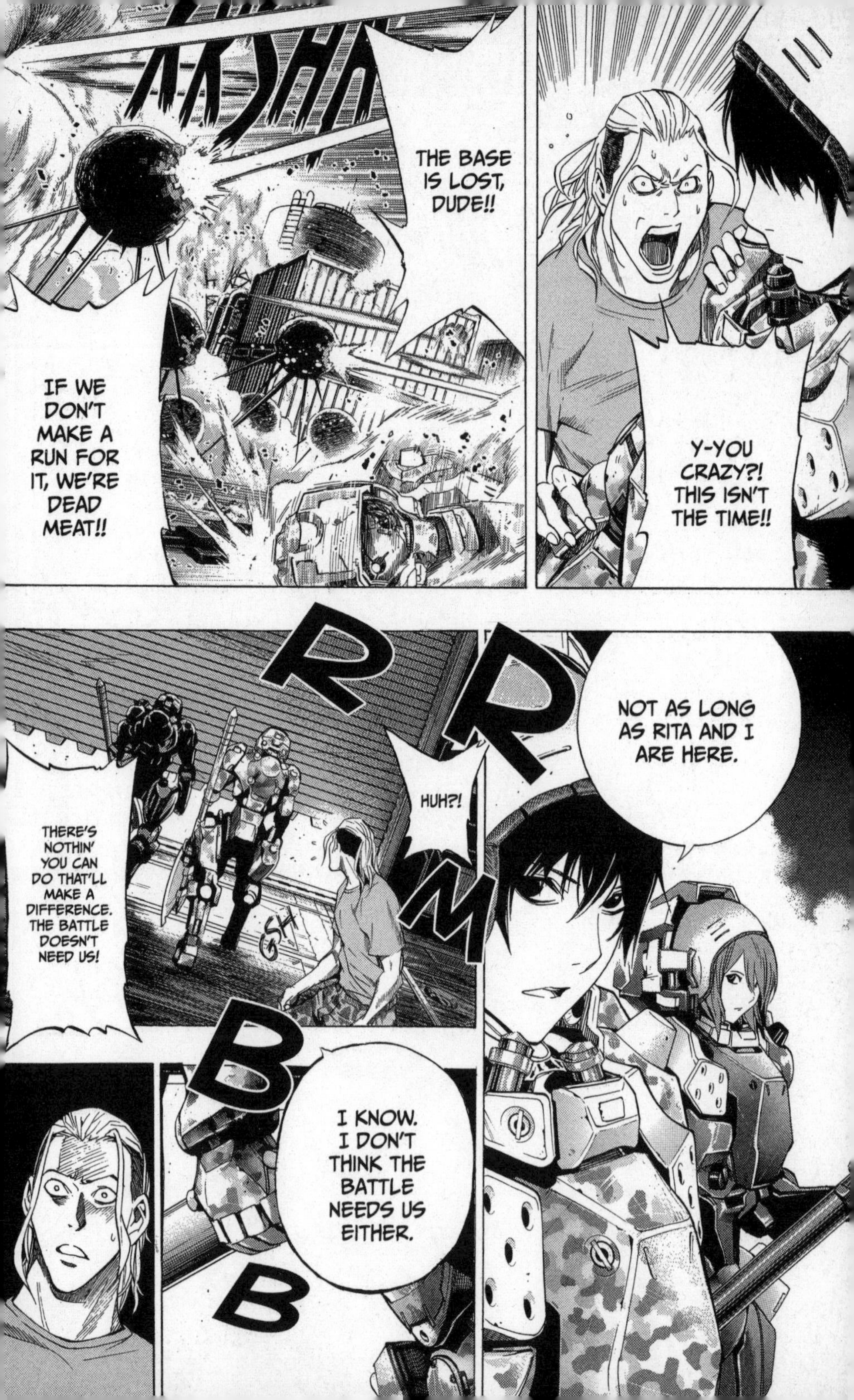
Y-YOU CRAZY?! THIS ISN'T THE TIME!!
THE BASE IS LOST, DUDE!!
IF WE DON'T MAKE A RUN FOR IT, WE'RE DEAD MEAT!!
NOT AS LONG AS RITA AND I ARE HERE.
HUH?!
RRMBB
THERE'S NOTHIN' YOU CAN DO THAT'LL MAKE A DIFFERENCE. THE BATTLE DOESN'T NEED US!
I KNOW. I DON'T THINK THE BATTLE NEEDS US EITHER.

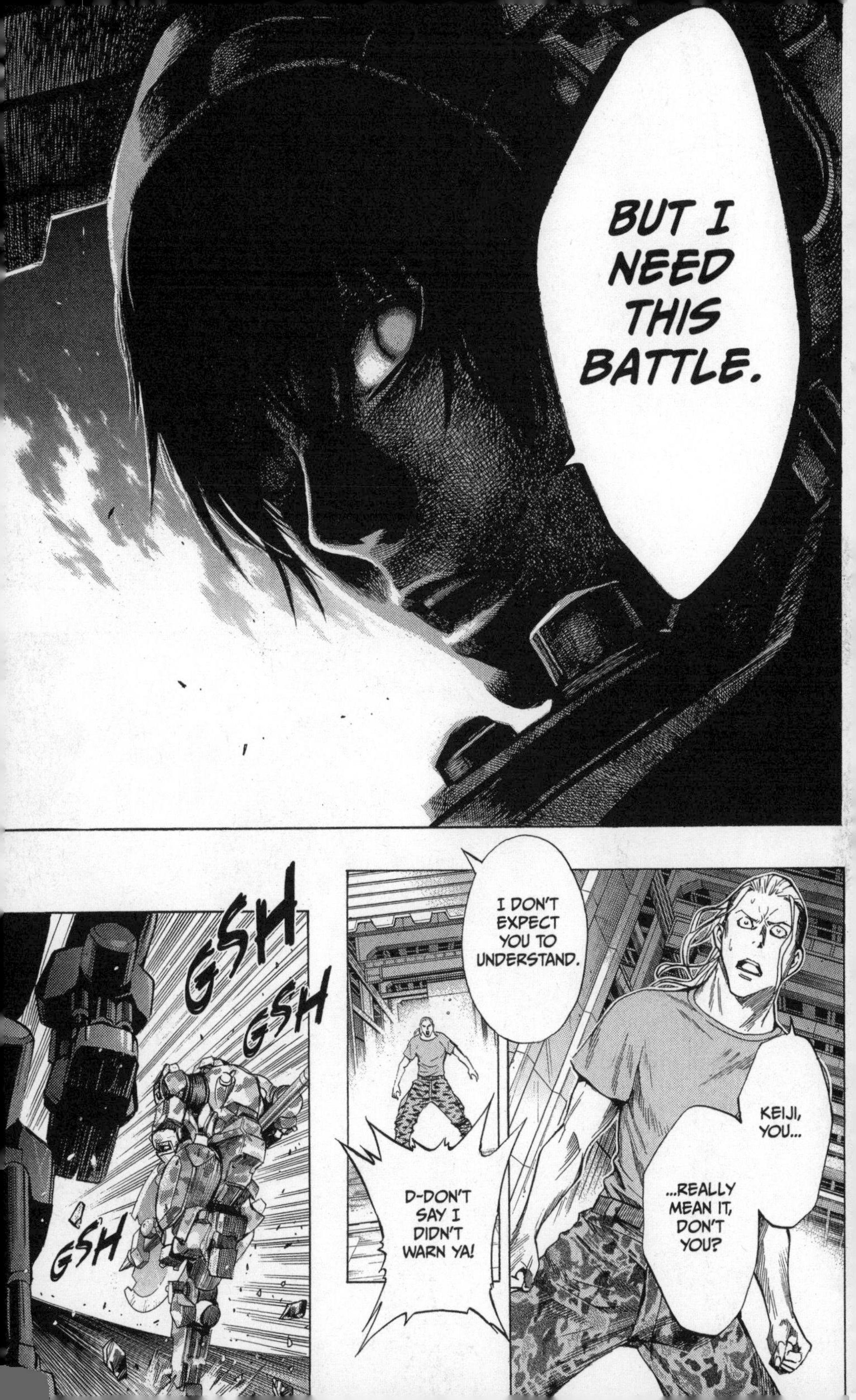
BUT I NEED THIS BATTLE.
I DON'T EXPECT YOU TO UNDERSTAND.
KEIJI, YOU...
...REALLY MEAN IT, DON'T YOU?
D-DON'T SAY I DIDN'T WARN YA!
GSH
GSH
GSH

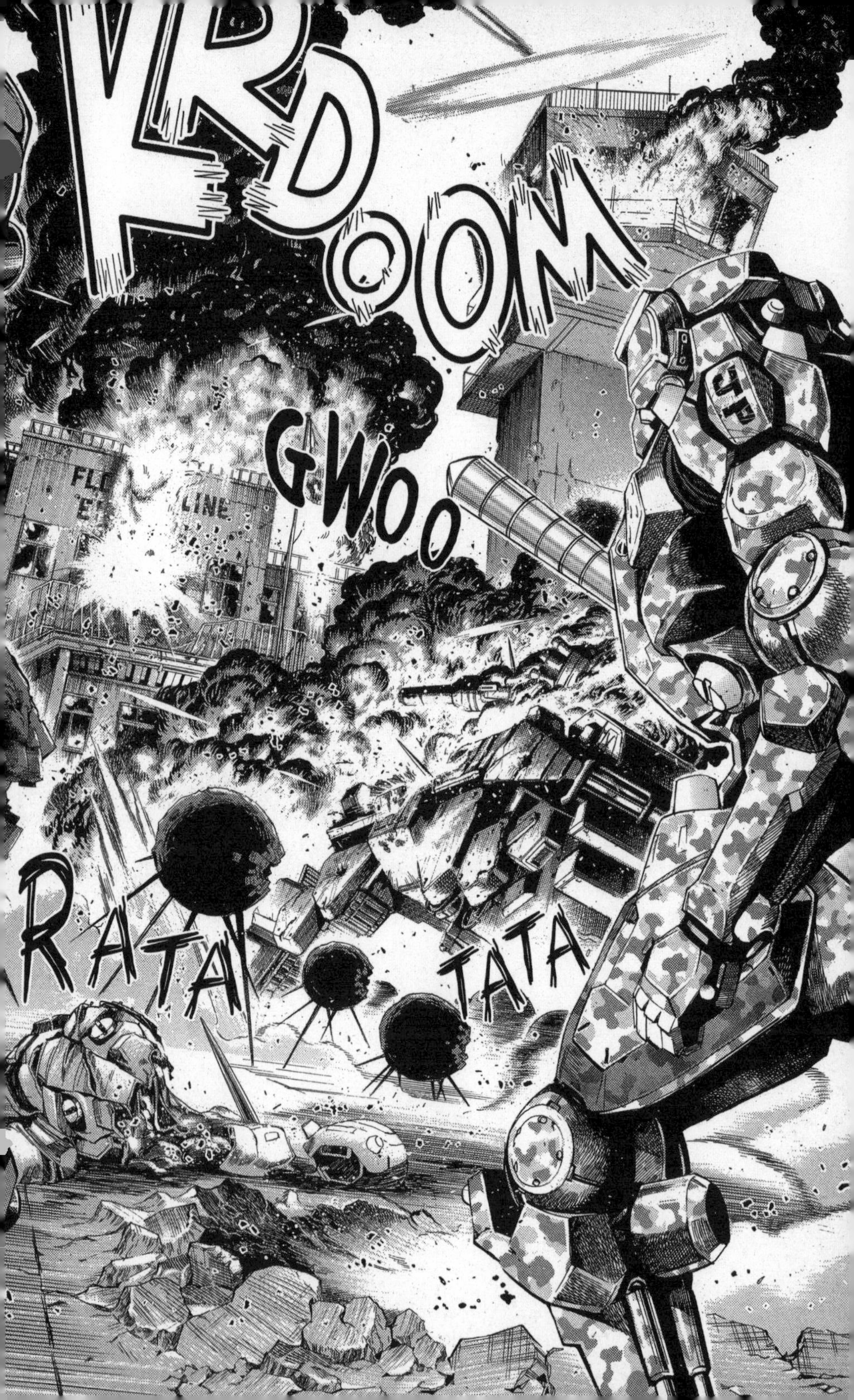
GWOOO
RATA
TATA

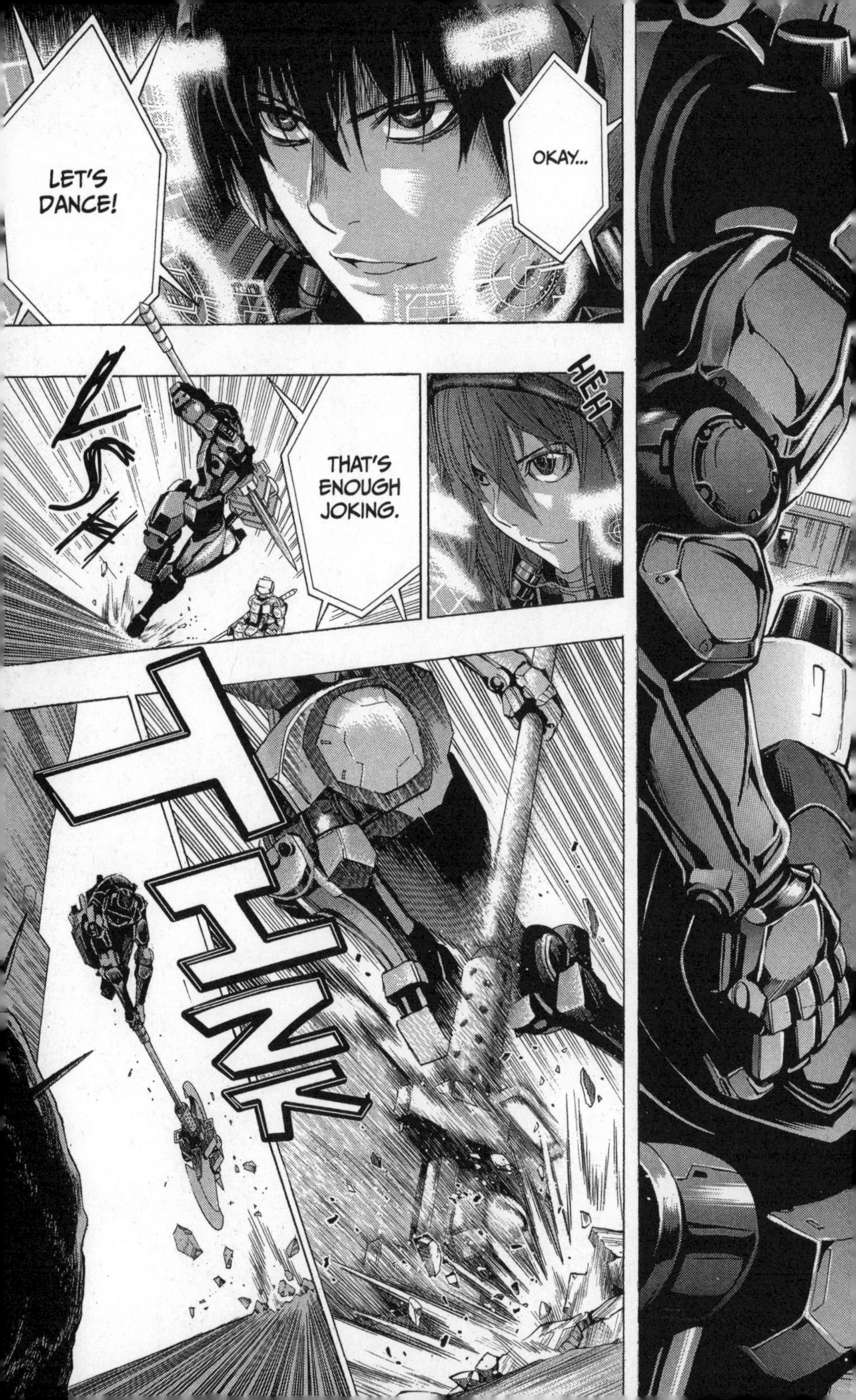
OKAY...
LET'S DANCE!
HEH
THAT'S ENOUGH JOKING.
THUNK

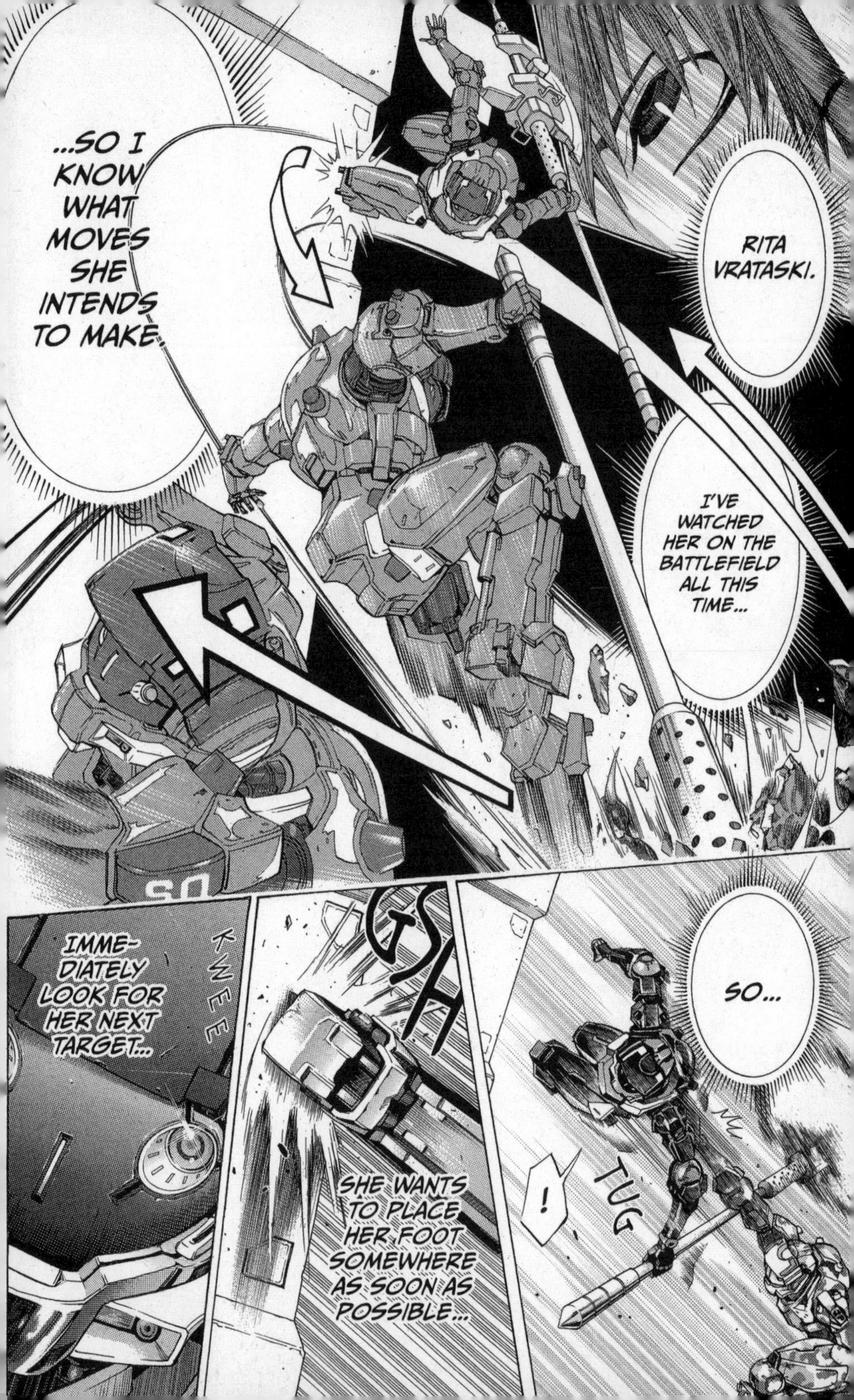

RITA VRATASKI.
I'VE WATCHED HER ON THE BATTLEFIELD ALL THIS TIME...
...SO I KNOW WHAT MOVES SHE INTENDS TO MAKE.
SO...
!
TUG
GSH
SHE WANTS TO PLACE HER FOOT SOMEWHERE AS SOON AS POSSIBLE...
KWEE
IMME-DIATELY LOOK FOR HER NEXT TARGET...

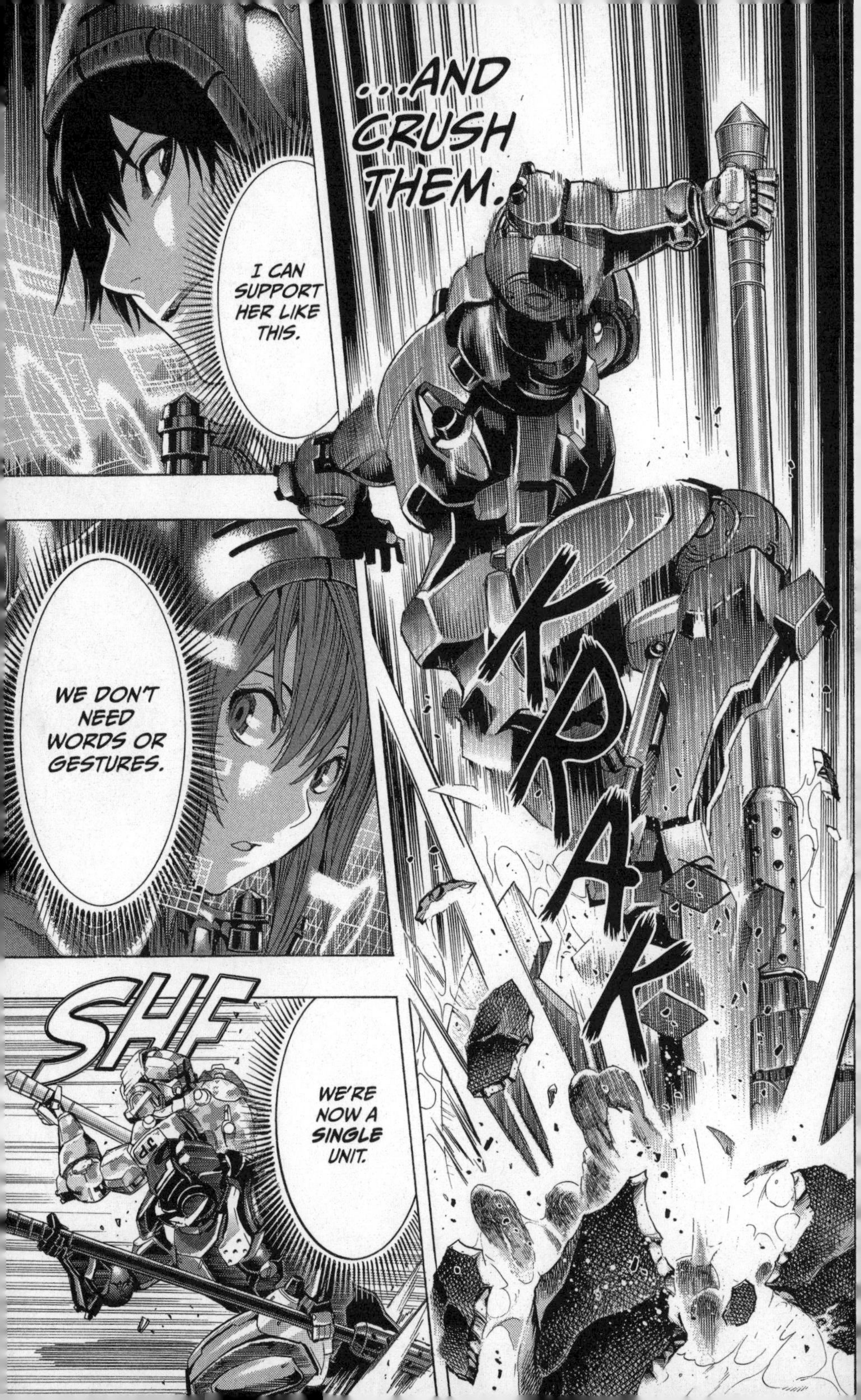

...AND CRUSH THEM.
KRAK
I CAN SUPPORT HER LIKE THIS.
WE DON'T NEED WORDS OR GESTURES.
WE'RE NOW A SINGLE UNIT.
SHF

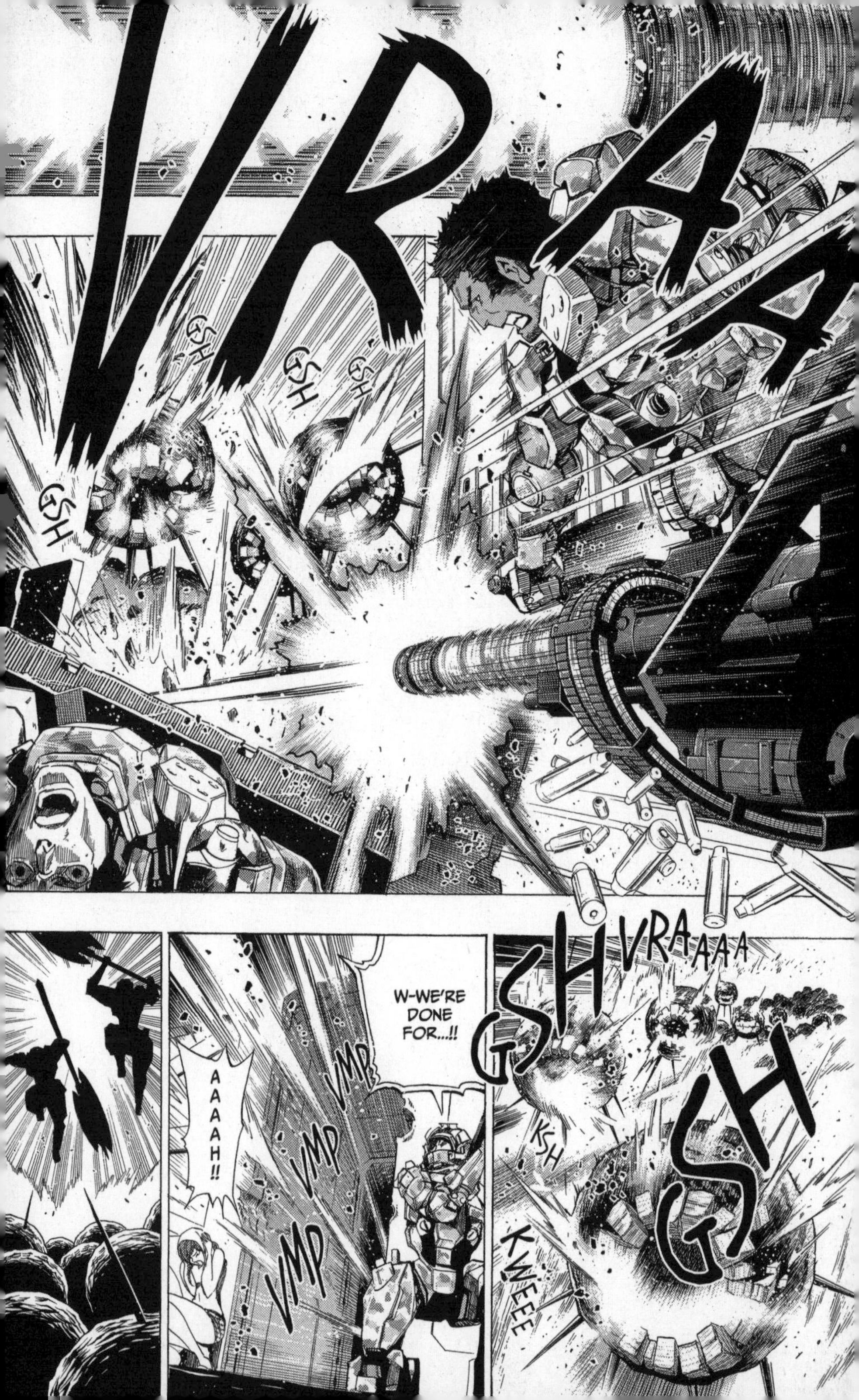
VRAA
GSH
GSH
GSH
GSH
GSH
VRAAAA
GSH
KSH
KWEEE
W-WE'RE DONE FOR...!!
AAAAAH!!
VMP
VMP
VMP
VMP

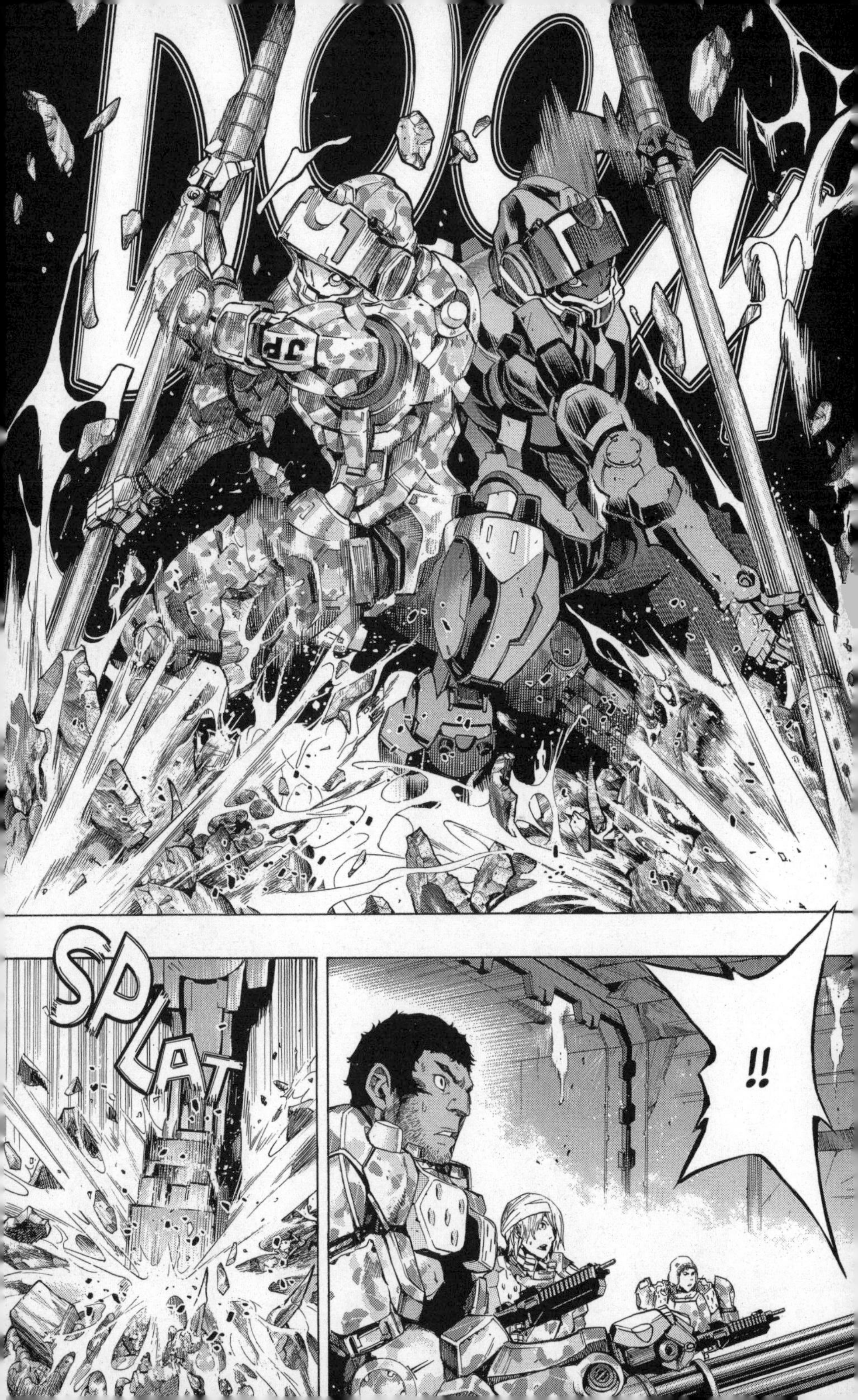
DOOOM
JP
!!
SPLAT

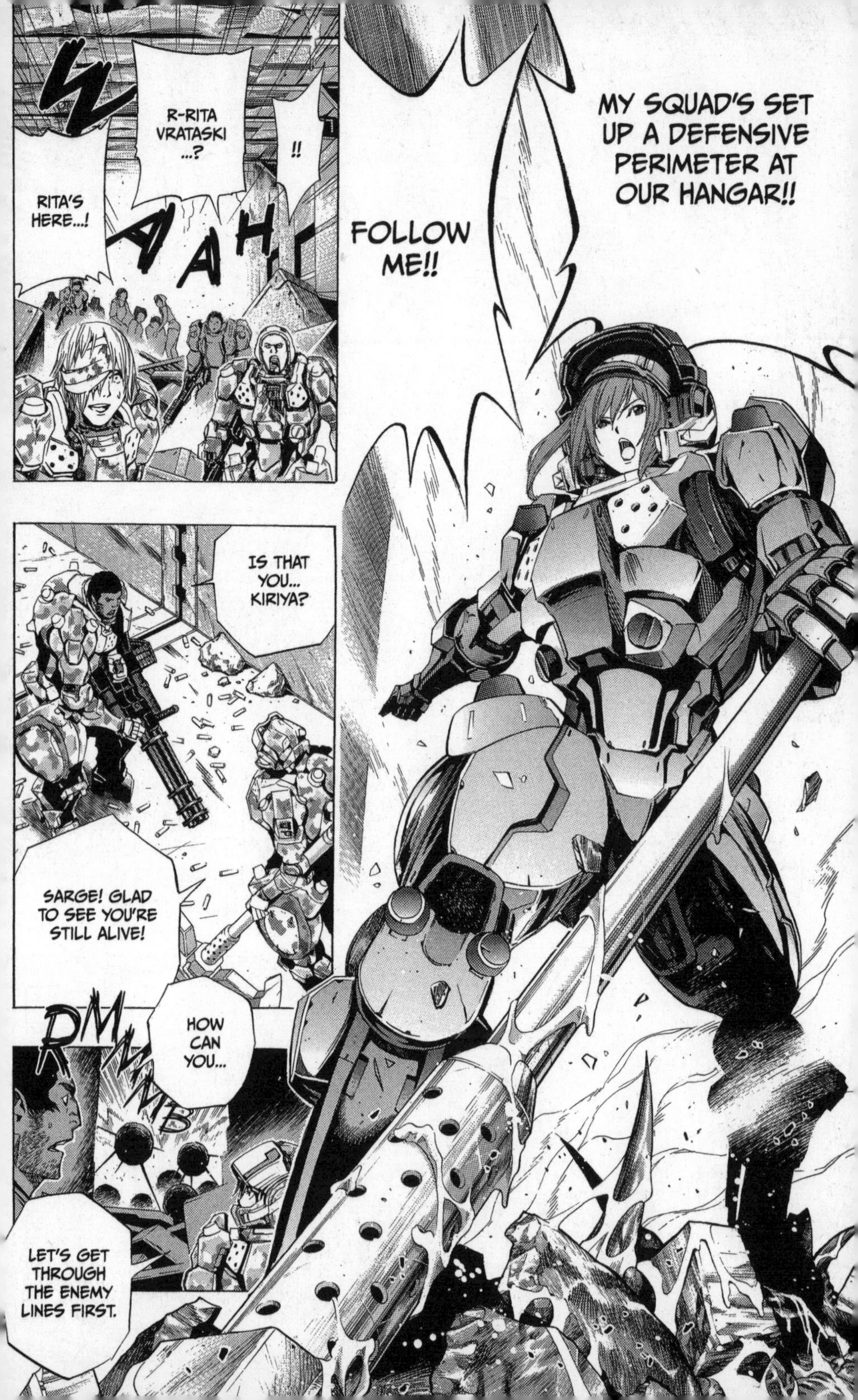
MY SQUAD'S SET UP A DEFENSIVE PERIMETER AT OUR HANGAR!!
FOLLOW ME!!
R-RITA VRATASKI ...?
!!
RITA'S HERE...!
AAAH
IS THAT YOU... KIRIYA?
SARGE! GLAD TO SEE YOU'RE STILL ALIVE!
HOW CAN YOU...
LET'S GET THROUGH THE ENEMY LINES FIRST.

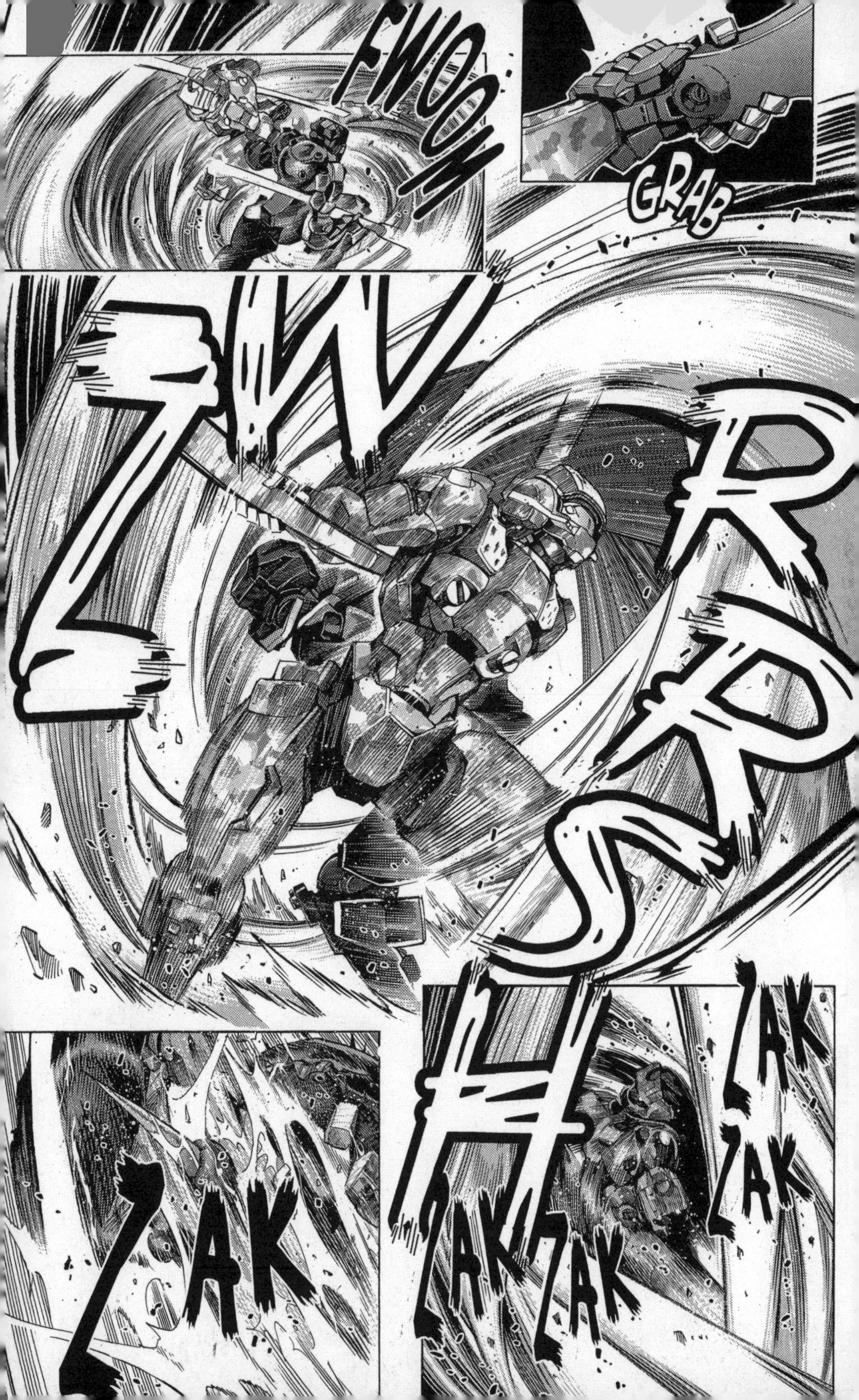
GRAB
FWOOM!!
ZWRRSH
ZAK
ZAK
ZAK
ZAK
ZAK
ZAK

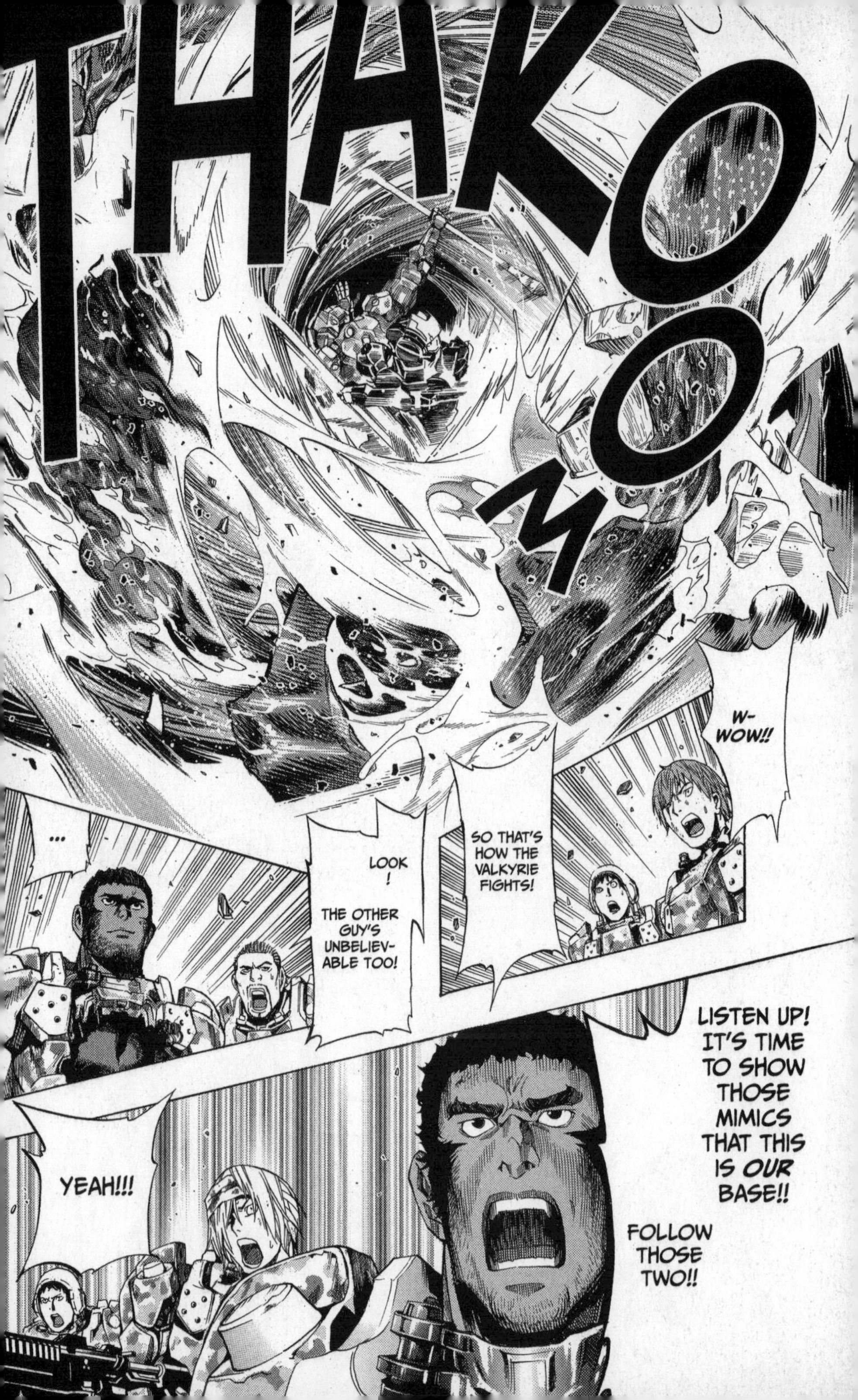
THAKOOOM
W-WOW!!
SO THAT'S HOW THE VALKYRIE FIGHTS!
LOOK! THE OTHER GUY'S UNBELIEVABLE TOO!
...
LISTEN UP! IT'S TIME TO SHOW THOSE MIMICS THAT THIS IS *OUR* BASE!!
FOLLOW THOSE TWO!!
YEAH!!!

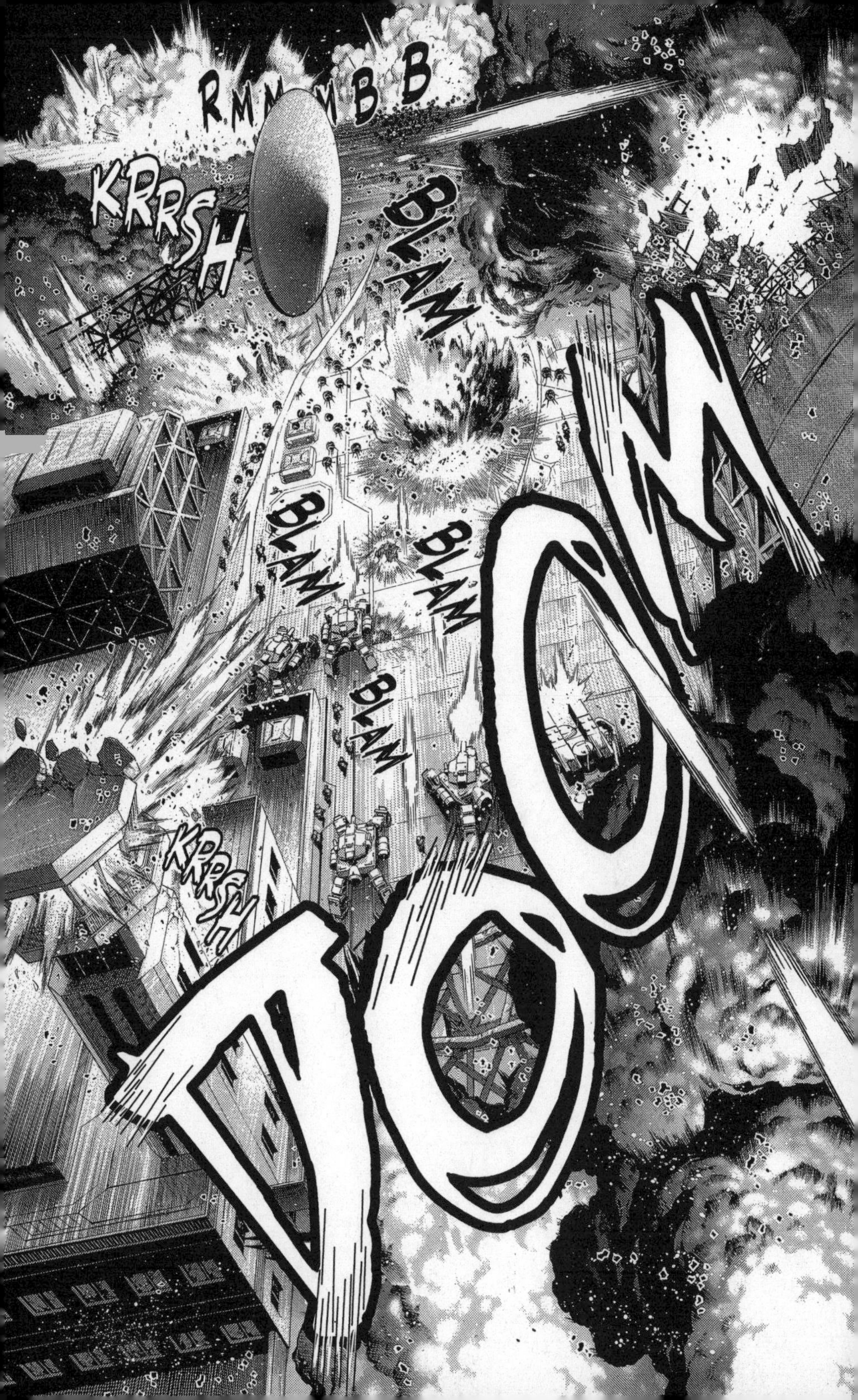
RMMMBB
BLAM
KRRSH
BLAM
BLAM BLAM
BLAM BLAM
DOOM
KRRSH

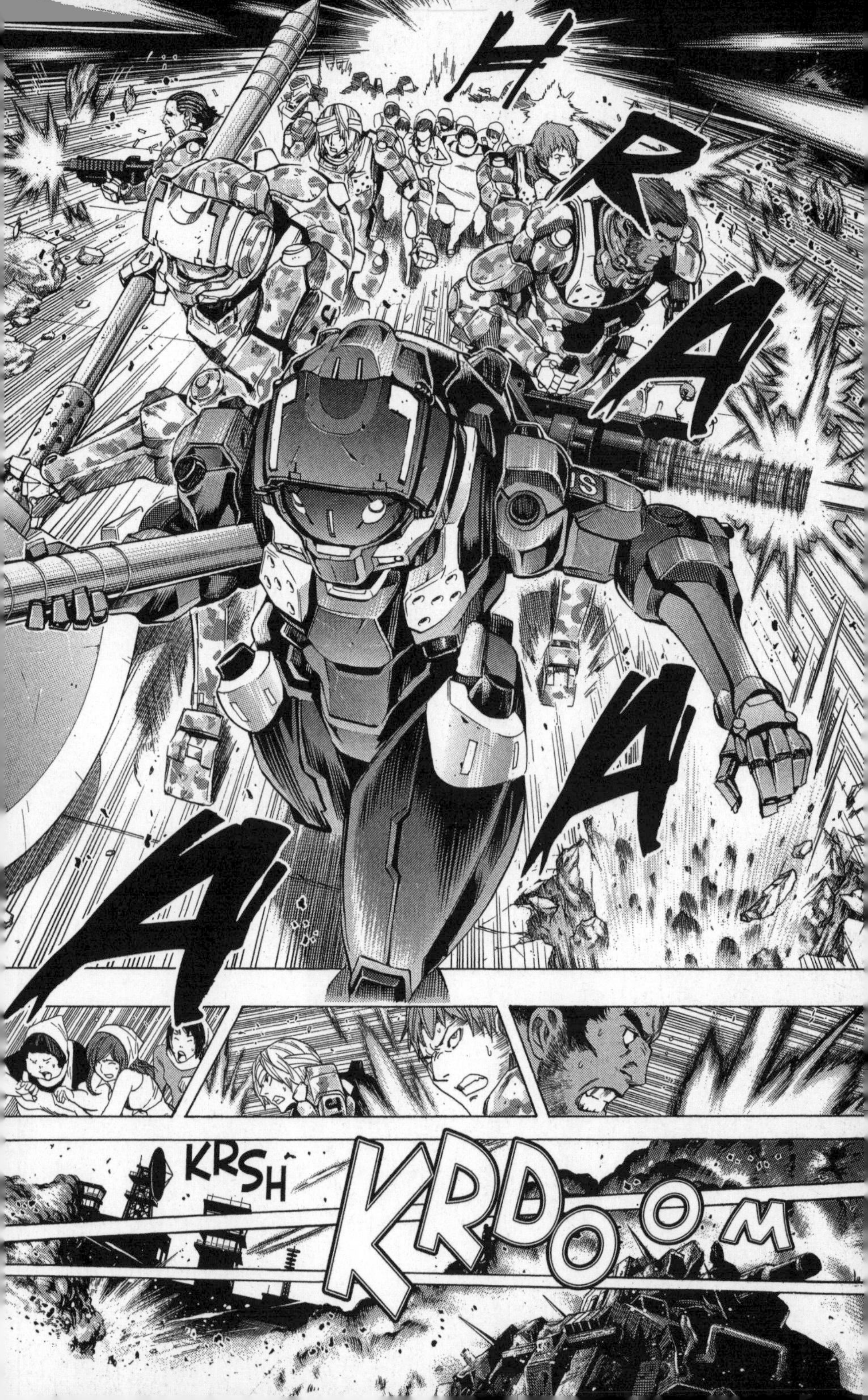
HRAAAA
KRDOOOM
KRSH

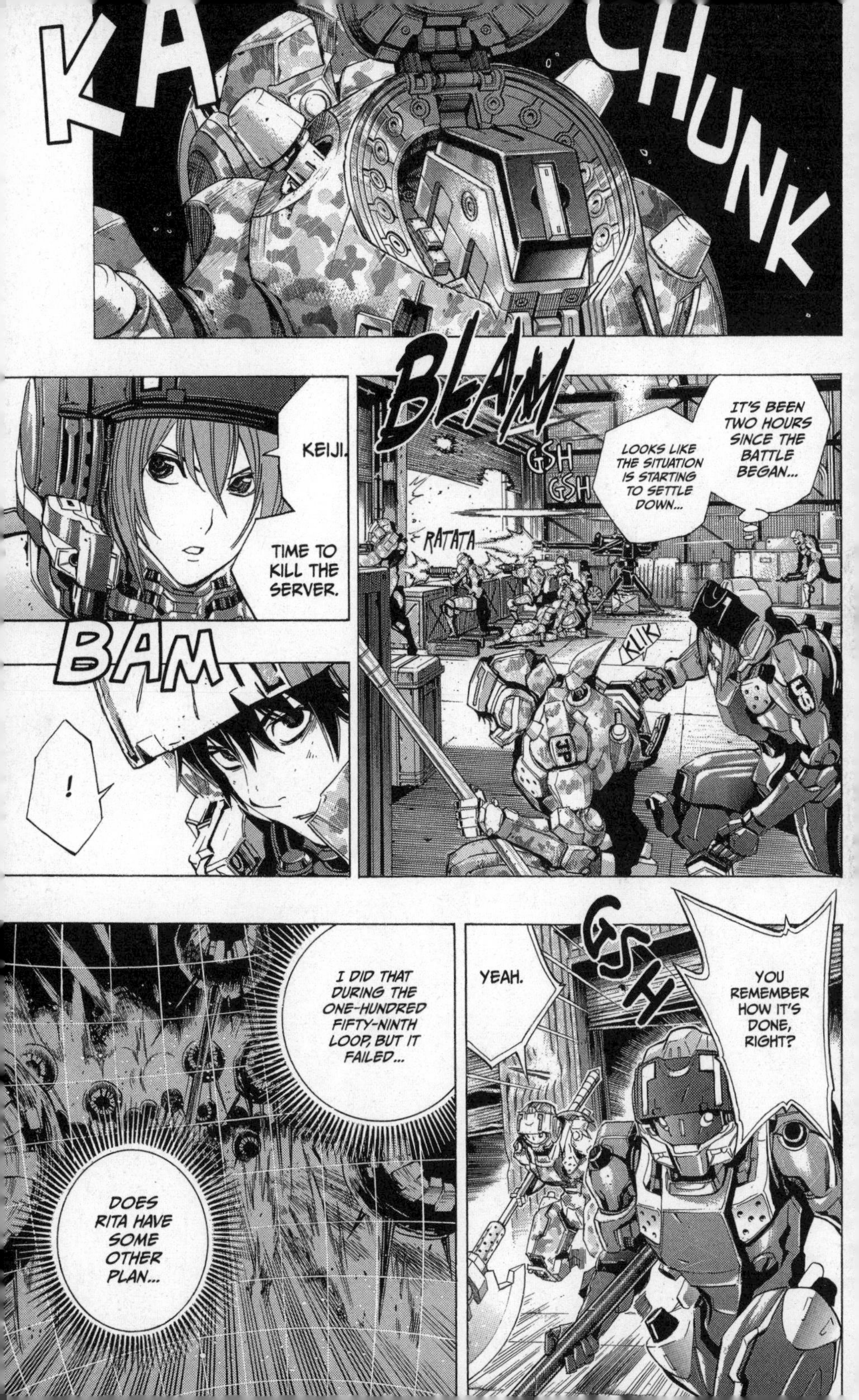
KA
CHUNK
BLAM
IT'S BEEN TWO HOURS SINCE THE BATTLE BEGAN...
LOOKS LIKE THE SITUATION IS STARTING TO SETTLE DOWN...
GSH
GSH
RATATA
KLIK
KEIJI.
TIME TO KILL THE SERVER.
BAM
!
GSH
YOU REMEMBER HOW IT'S DONE, RIGHT?
YEAH.
I DID THAT DURING THE ONE-HUNDRED FIFTY-NINTH LOOP, BUT IT FAILED...
DOES RITA HAVE SOME OTHER PLAN...

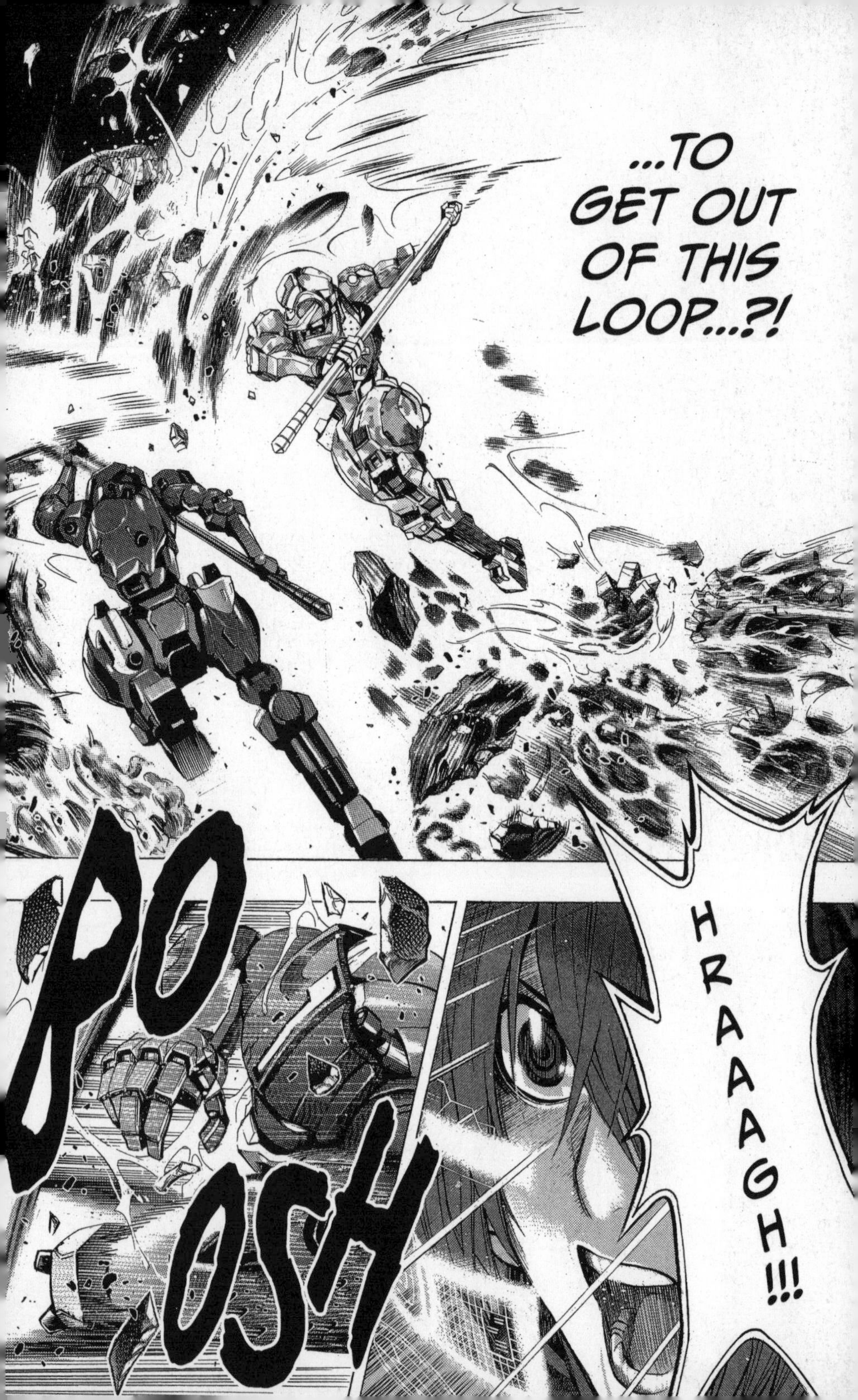
...TO GET OUT OF THIS LOOP...?!
HRAAAGH!!!
BOOSH

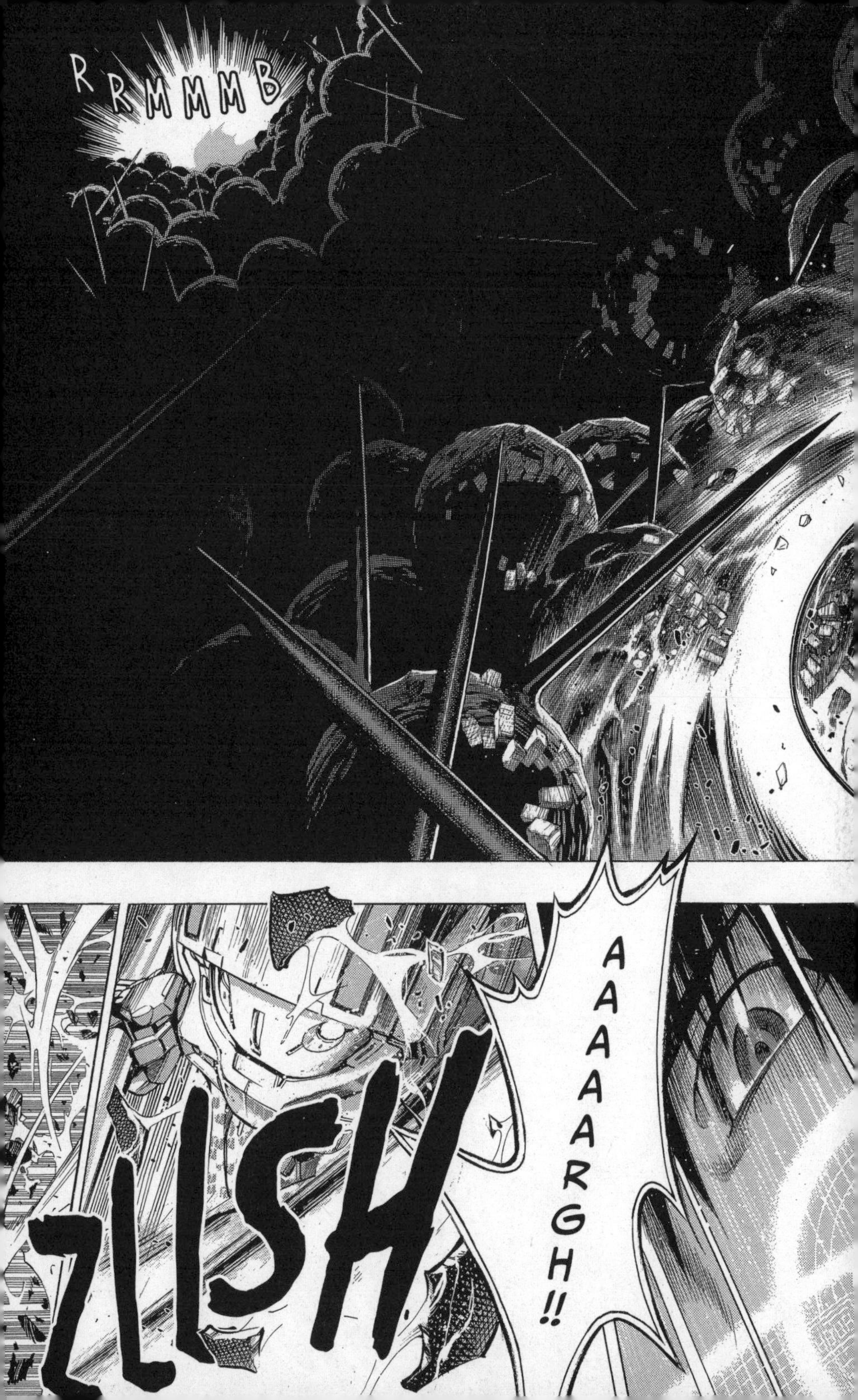
RRMMMB
AAAAARGH!!
ZLISH

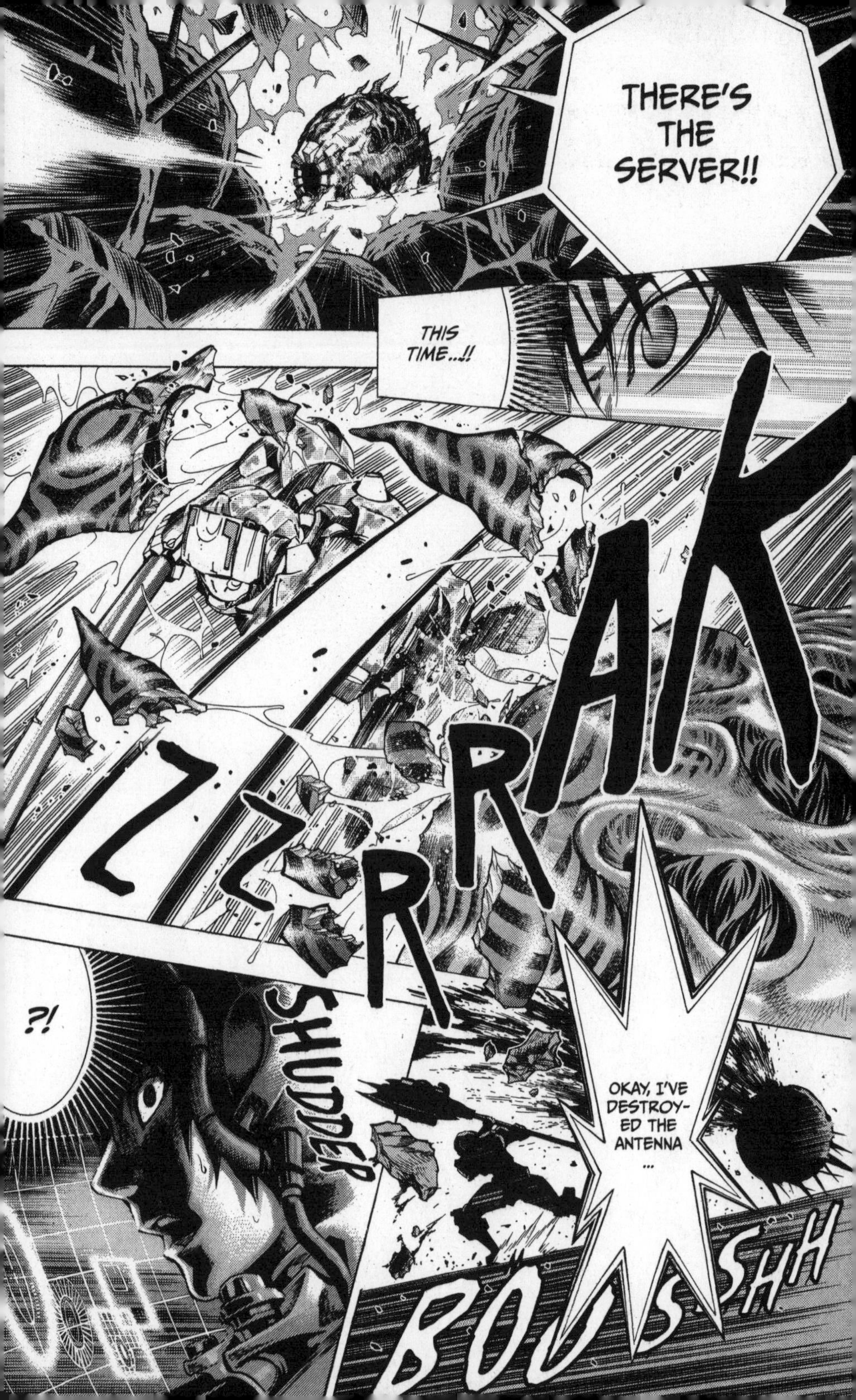
THERE'S THE SERVER!!
THIS TIME...!!
ZZRRAK
OKAY, I'VE DESTROY-ED THE ANTENNA ...
BOOSSHH
?!
SHUDDER

#16 All You Need Is Kill

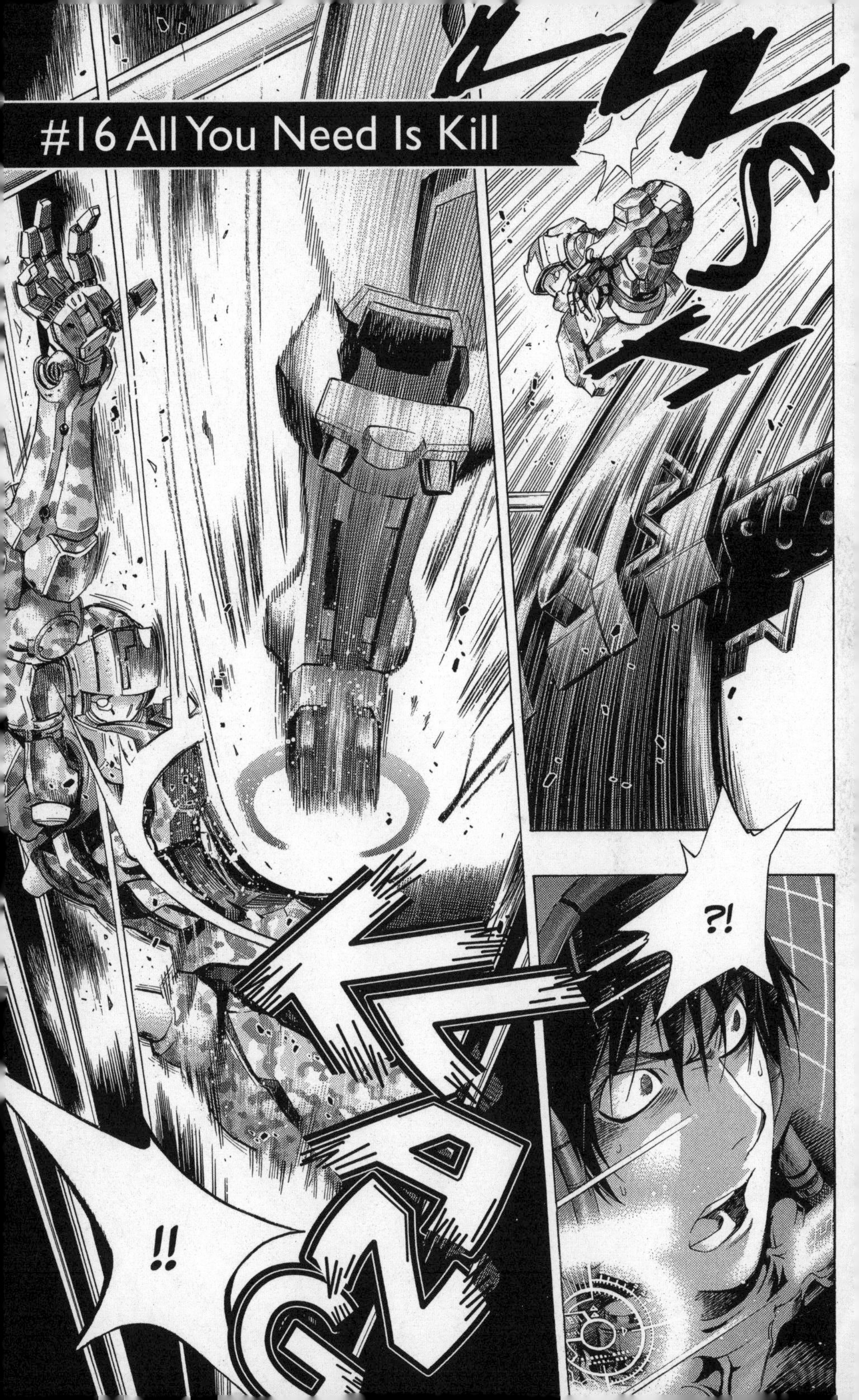
?!
!!

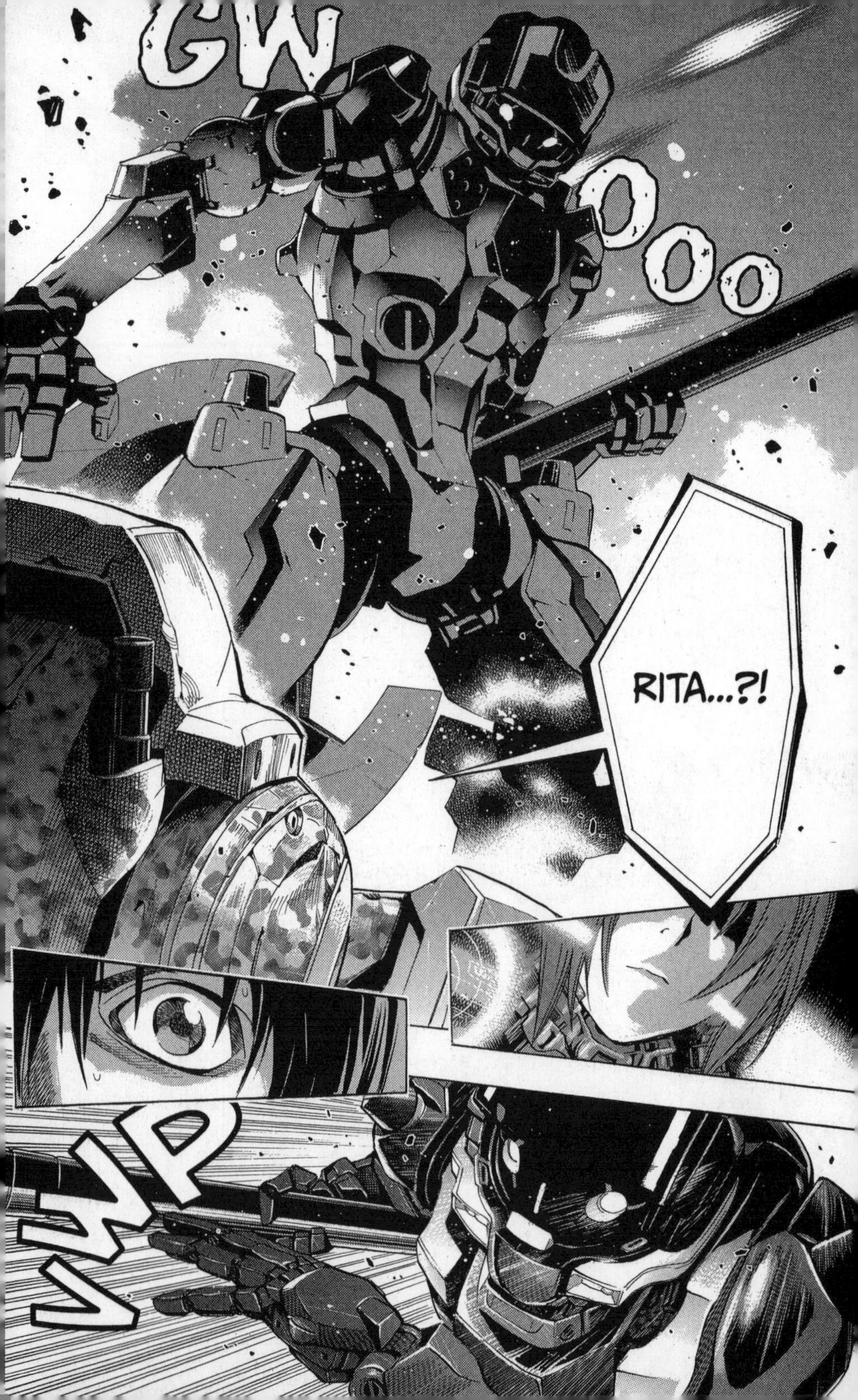
GWOOOO
RITA...?!
VWP

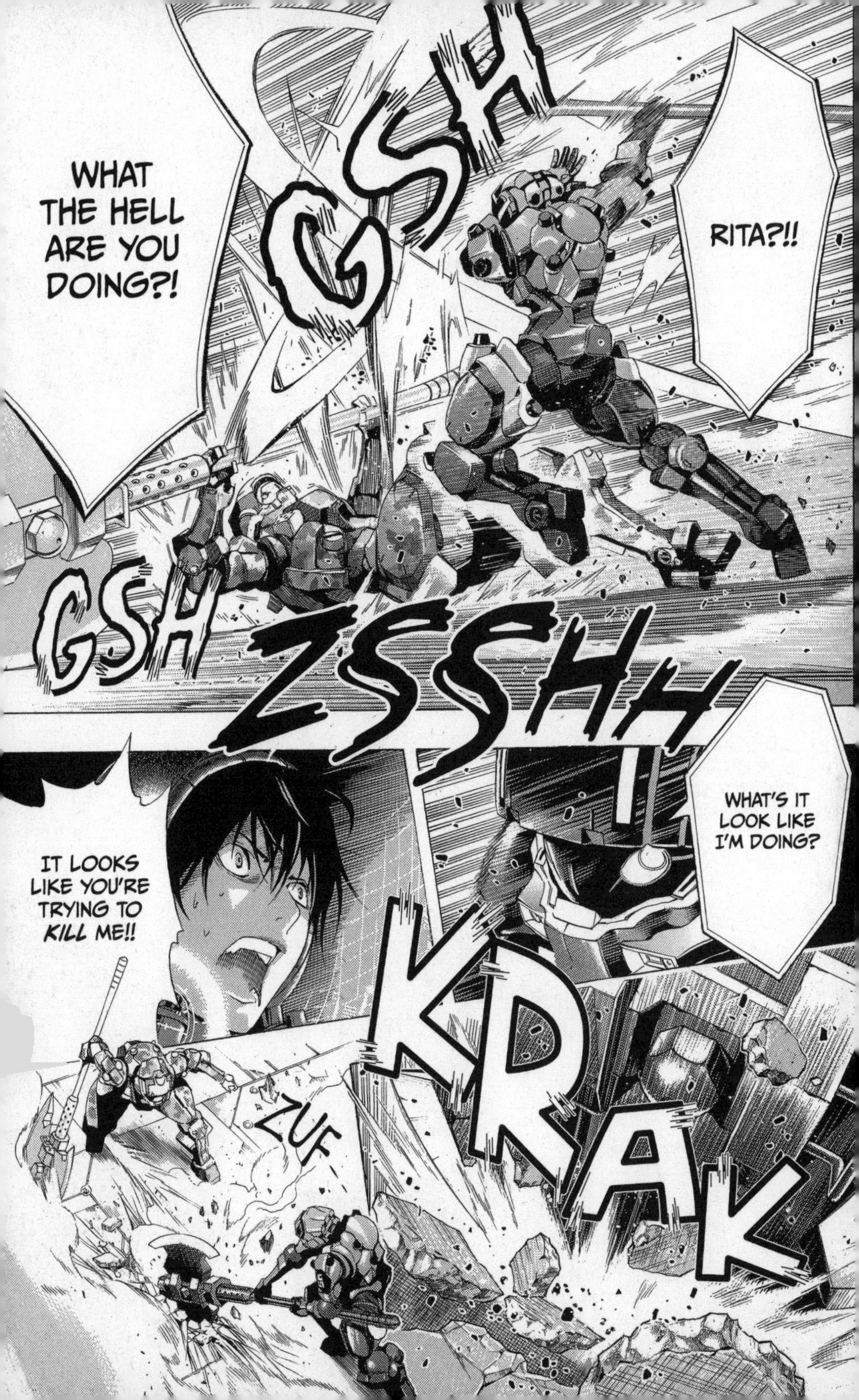
RITA?!!
GSH
WHAT THE HELL ARE YOU DOING?!
GSH
ZSSHH
WHAT'S IT LOOK LIKE I'M DOING?
IT LOOKS LIKE YOU'RE TRYING TO *KILL* ME!!
KRAK
ZUF

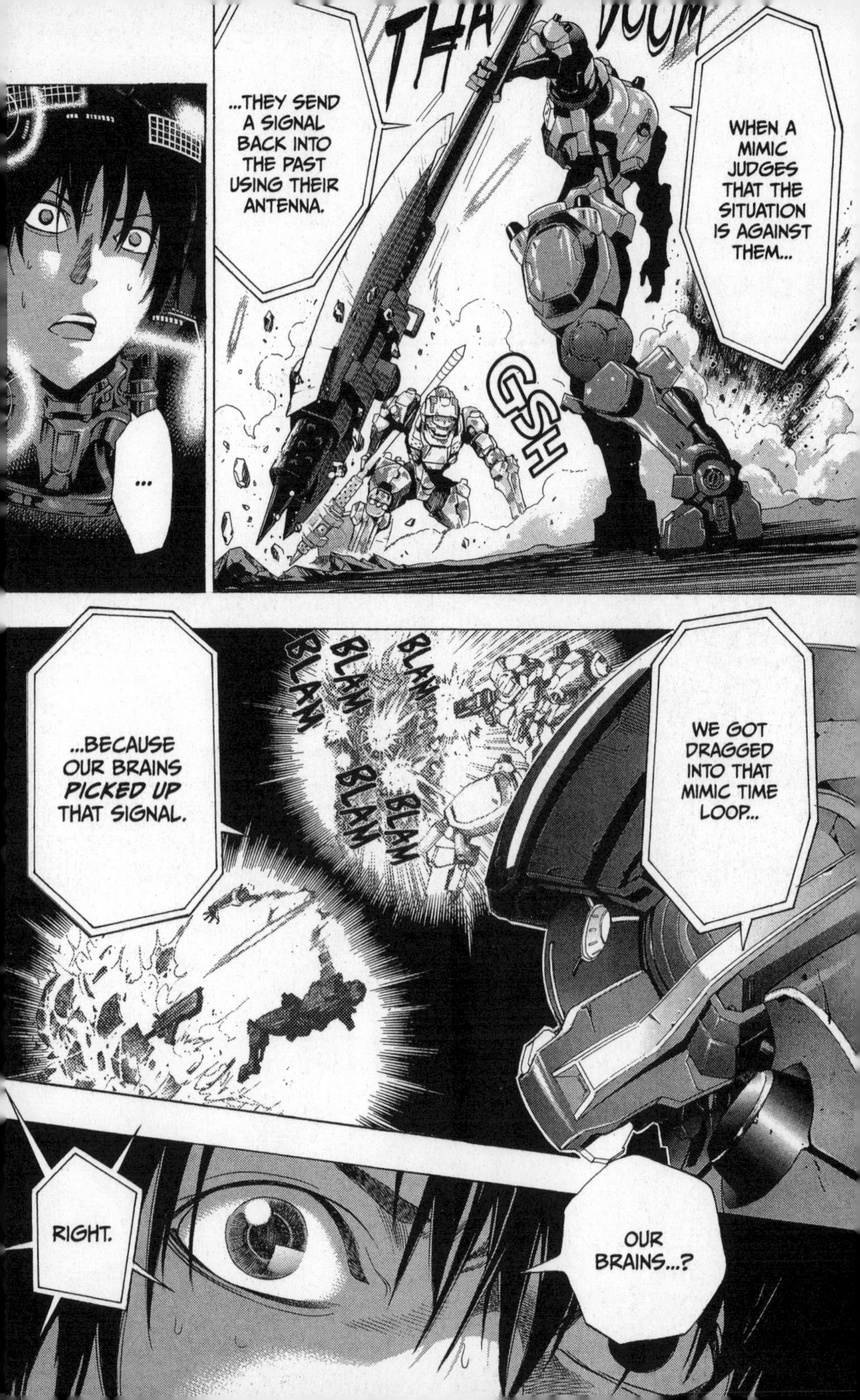
THA
VOOM
WHEN A MIMIC JUDGES THAT THE SITUATION IS AGAINST THEM...
...THEY SEND A SIGNAL BACK INTO THE PAST USING THEIR ANTENNA.
GSH
...
WE GOT DRAGGED INTO THAT MIMIC TIME LOOP...
BLAM BLAM BLAM
BLAM BLAM
...BECAUSE OUR BRAINS *PICKED UP* THAT SIGNAL.
OUR BRAINS...?
RIGHT.

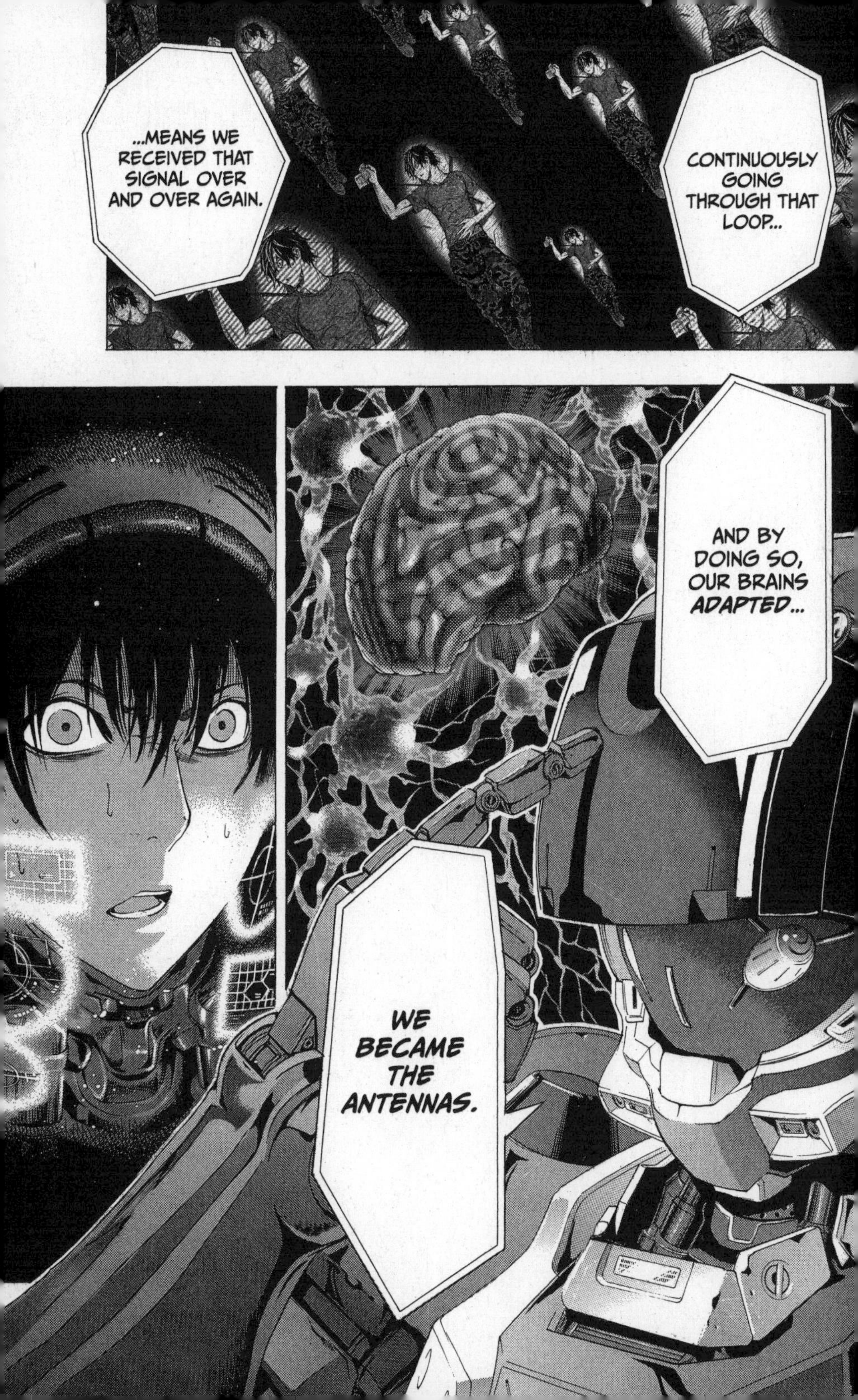
CONTINUOUSLY GOING THROUGH THAT LOOP...
...MEANS WE RECEIVED THAT SIGNAL OVER AND OVER AGAIN.
AND BY DOING SO, OUR BRAINS ADAPTED...
WE BECAME THE ANTENNAS.

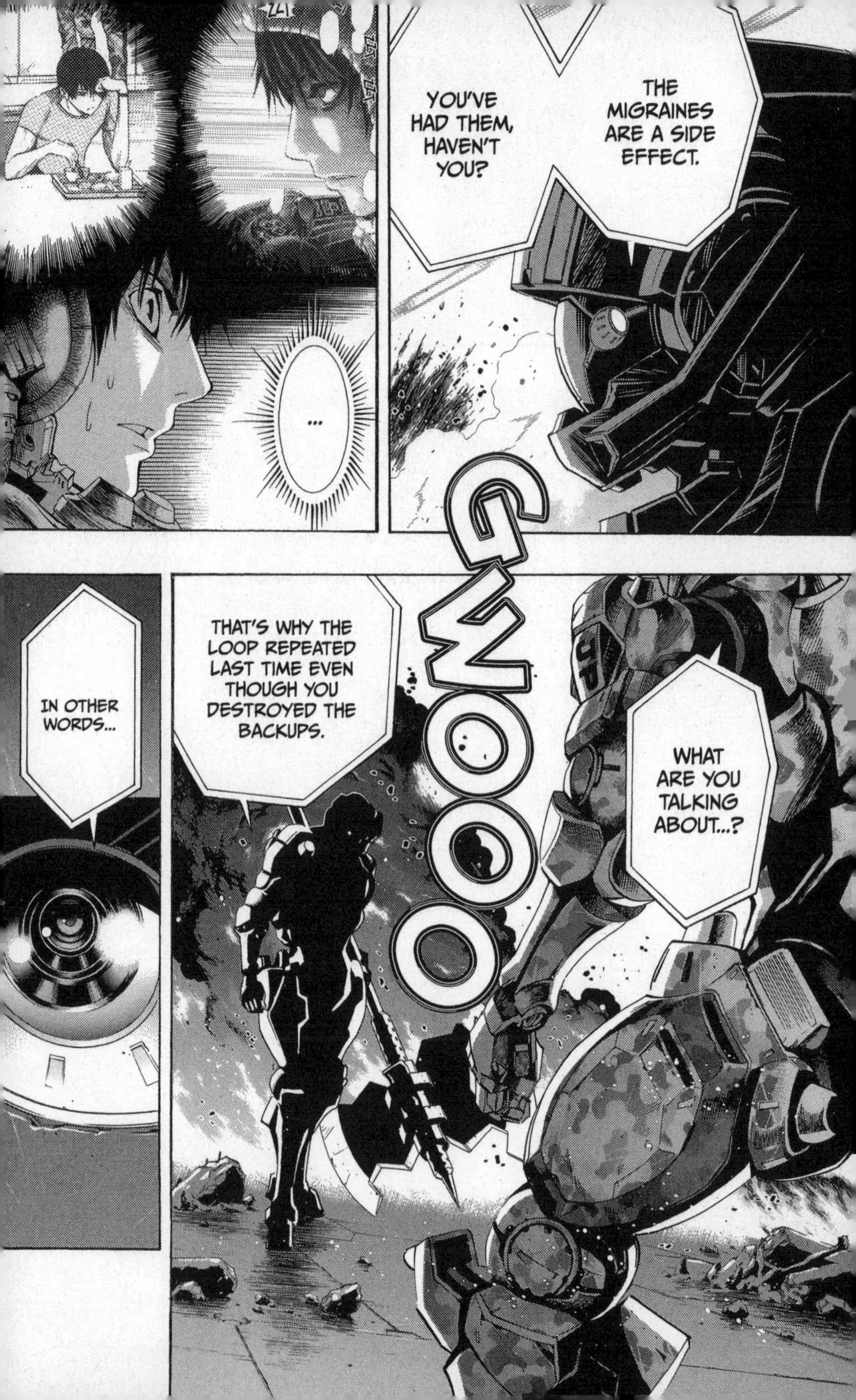
THE MIGRAINES ARE A SIDE EFFECT.
YOU'VE HAD THEM, HAVEN'T YOU?
...
GWOOOO
WHAT ARE YOU TALKING ABOUT...?
THAT'S WHY THE LOOP REPEATED LAST TIME EVEN THOUGH YOU DESTROYED THE BACKUPS.
IN OTHER WORDS...

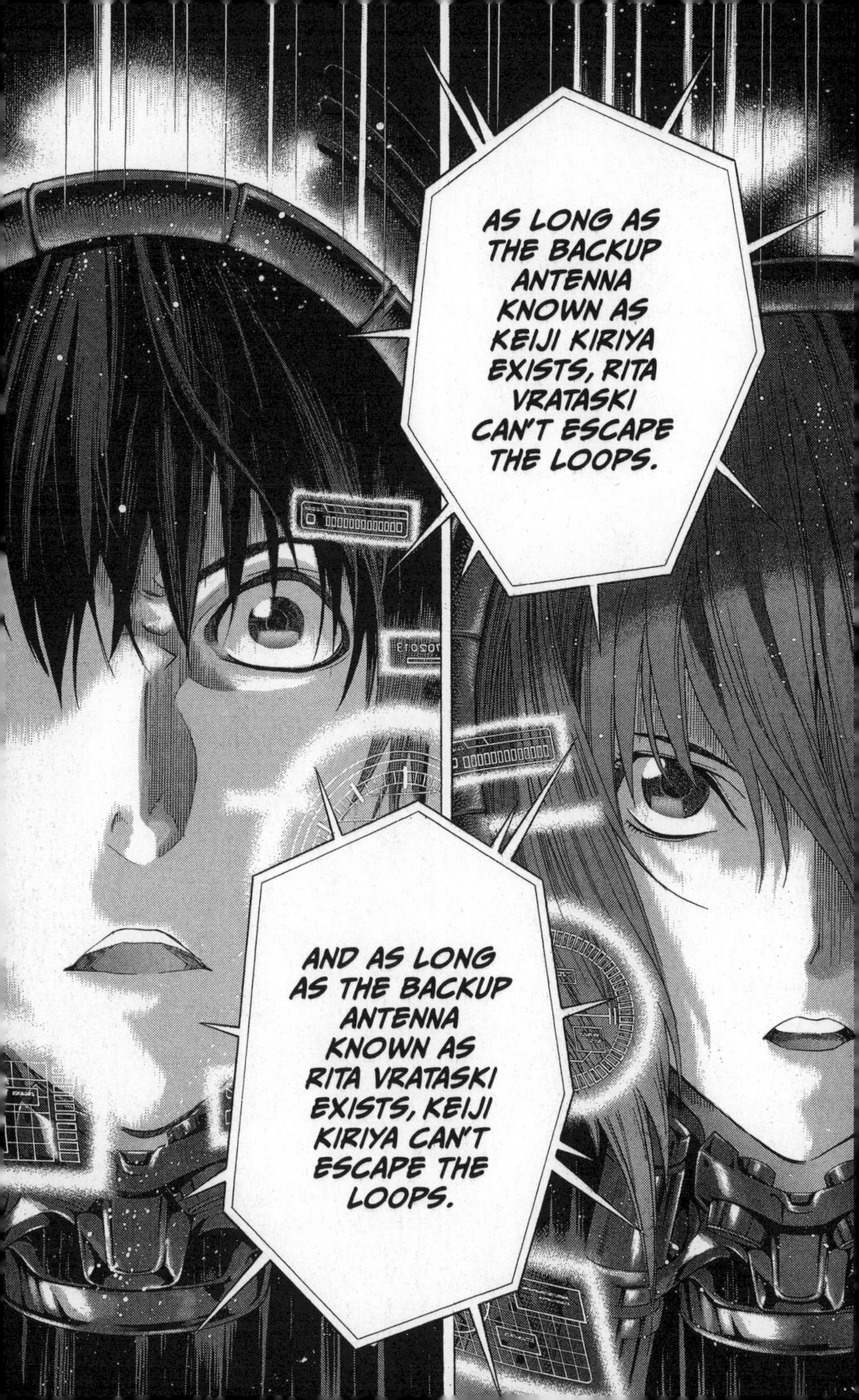
AS LONG AS THE BACKUP ANTENNA KNOWN AS KEIJI KIRIYA EXISTS, RITA VRATASKI CAN'T ESCAPE THE LOOPS.
AND AS LONG AS THE BACKUP ANTENNA KNOWN AS RITA VRATASKI EXISTS, KEIJI KIRIYA CAN'T ESCAPE THE LOOPS.

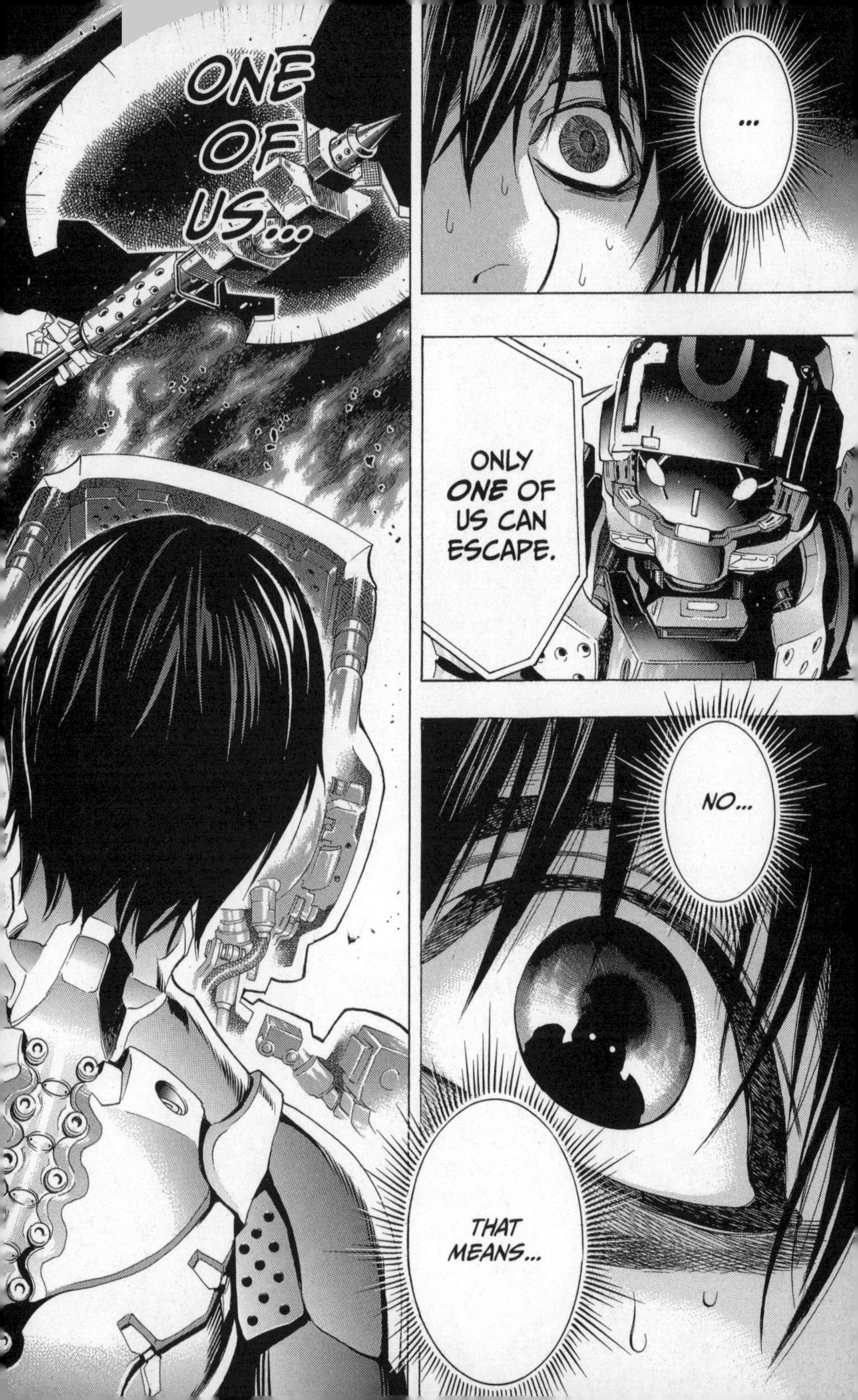
...
ONLY ONE OF US CAN ESCAPE.
NO...
THAT MEANS...
ONE OF US...

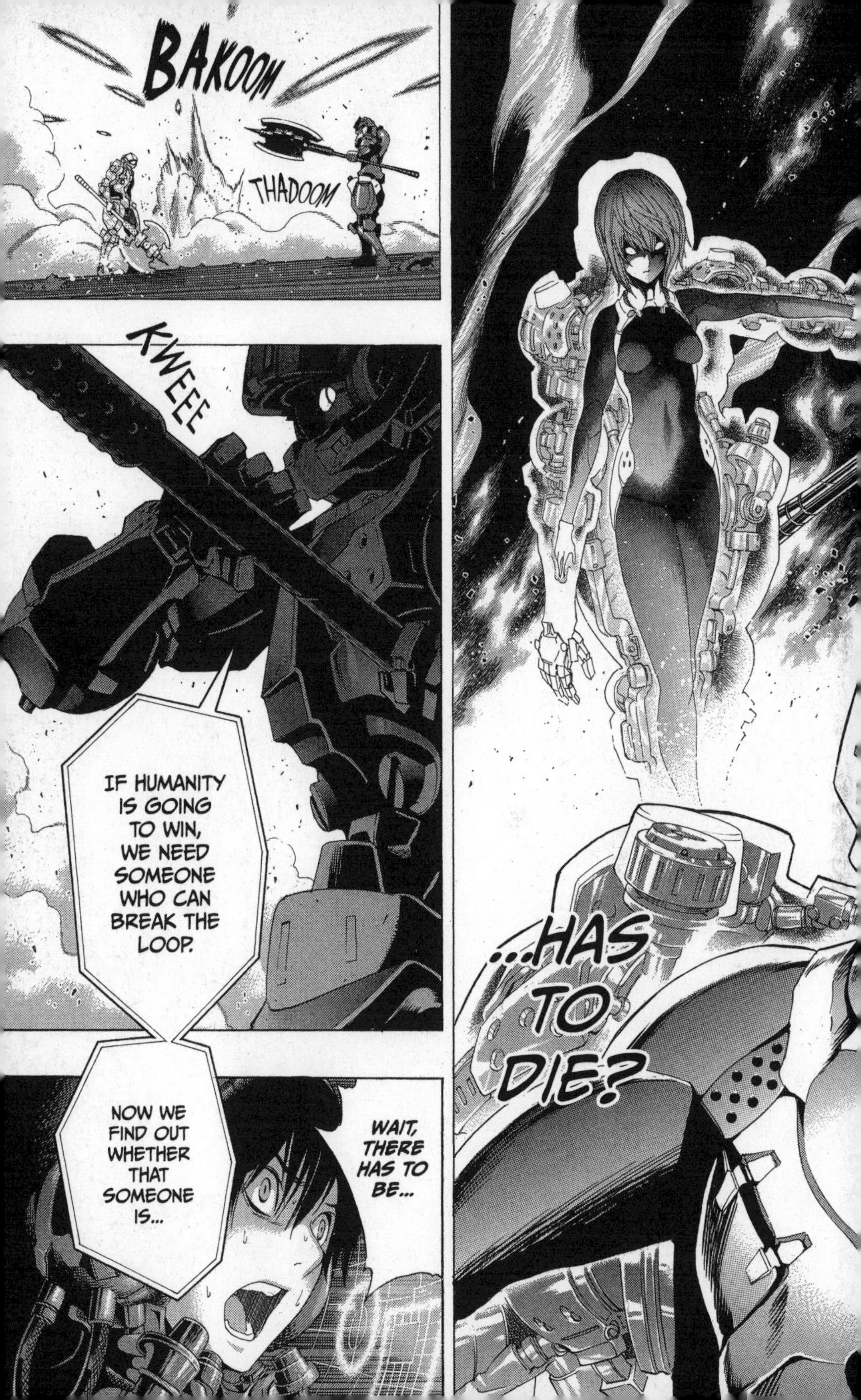
BAKOOM
THADOOM
KWEEE
IF HUMANITY IS GOING TO WIN, WE NEED SOMEONE WHO CAN BREAK THE LOOP.
NOW WE FIND OUT WHETHER THAT SOMEONE IS...
WAIT, THERE HAS TO BE...
...HAS TO DIE?

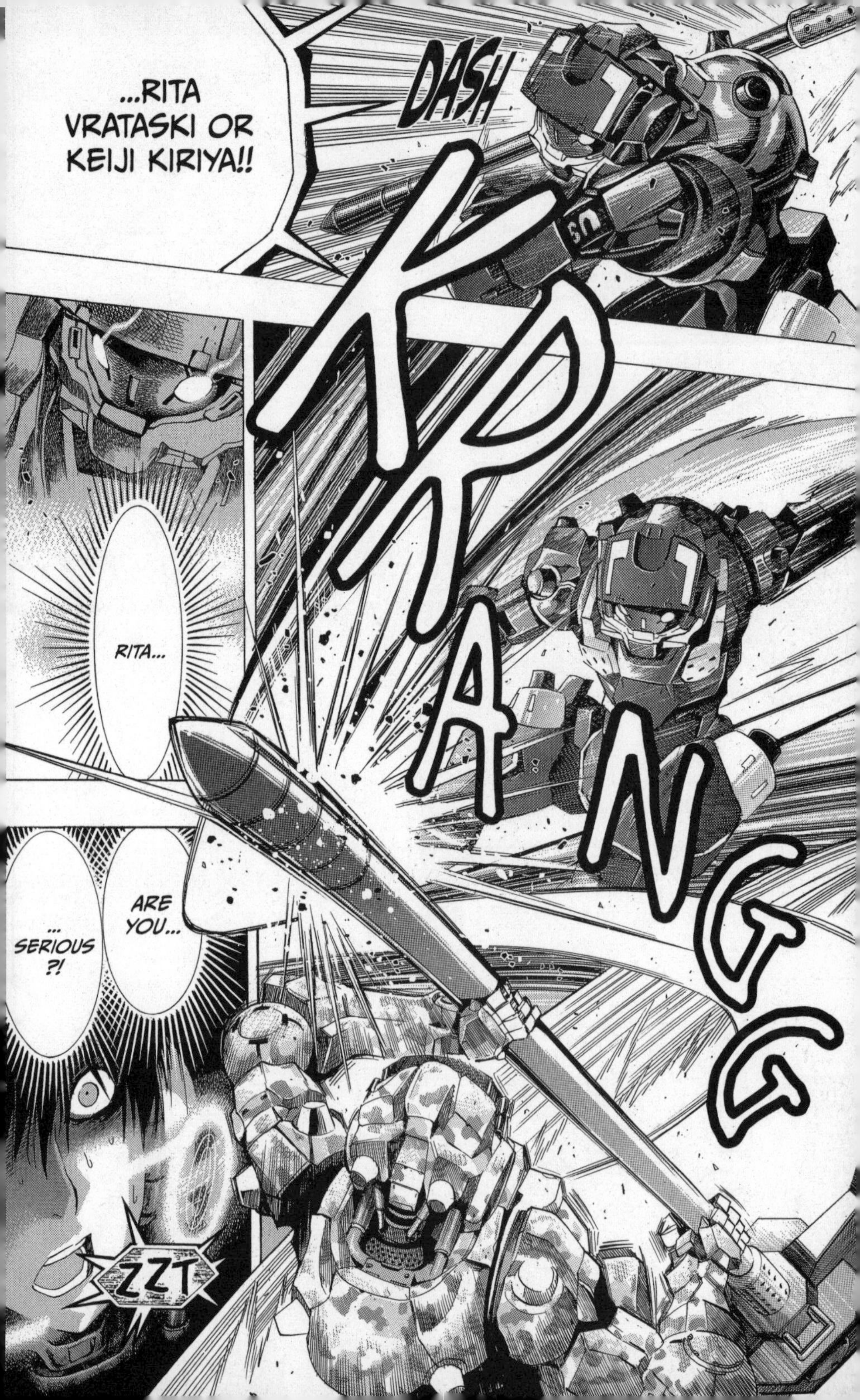
DASH
...RITA VRATASKI OR KEIJI KIRIYA!!
KRAANGG
RITA...
ARE YOU...
...SERIOUS?!
ZZT

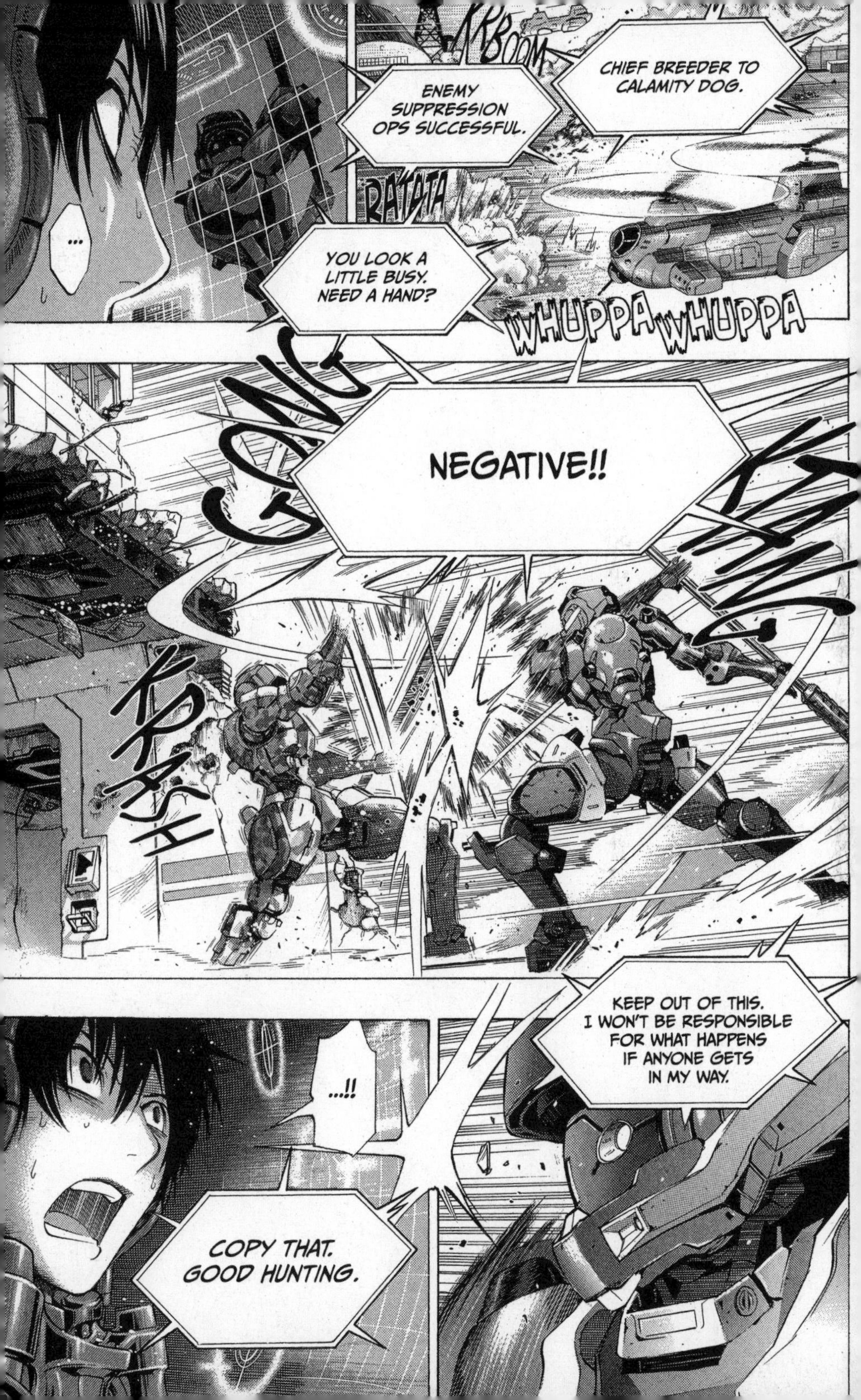
KRBOOM
CHIEF BREEDER TO CALAMITY DOG.
ENEMY SUPPRESSION OPS SUCCESSFUL.
RATATA
YOU LOOK A LITTLE BUSY. NEED A HAND?
WHUPPA WHUPPA
...
NEGATIVE!!
GONG
KRASH
KEEP OUT OF THIS. I WON'T BE RESPONSIBLE FOR WHAT HAPPENS IF ANYONE GETS IN MY WAY.
...!!
COPY THAT. GOOD HUNTING.

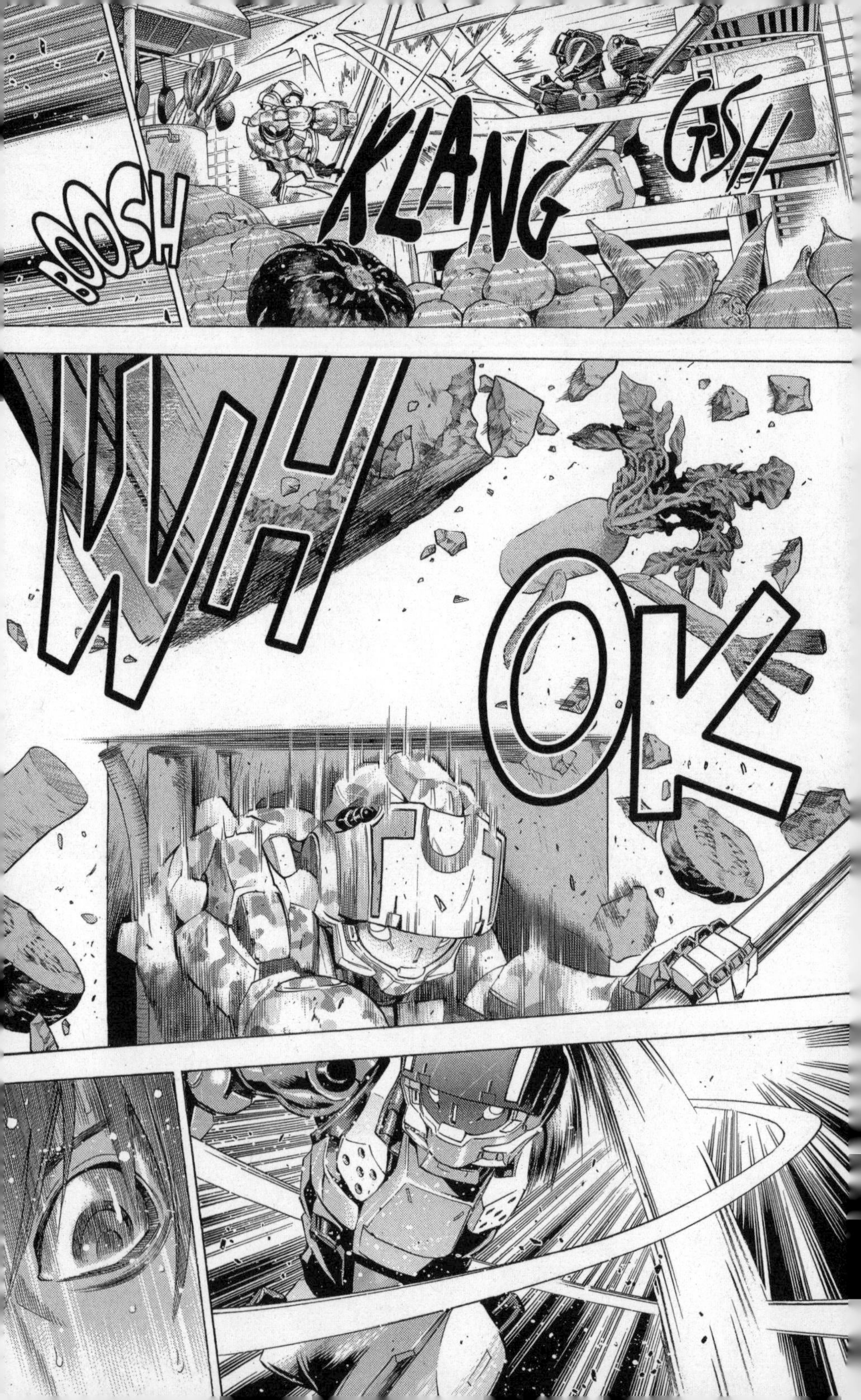
GSH
KLANG
WOOSH
WHOOK

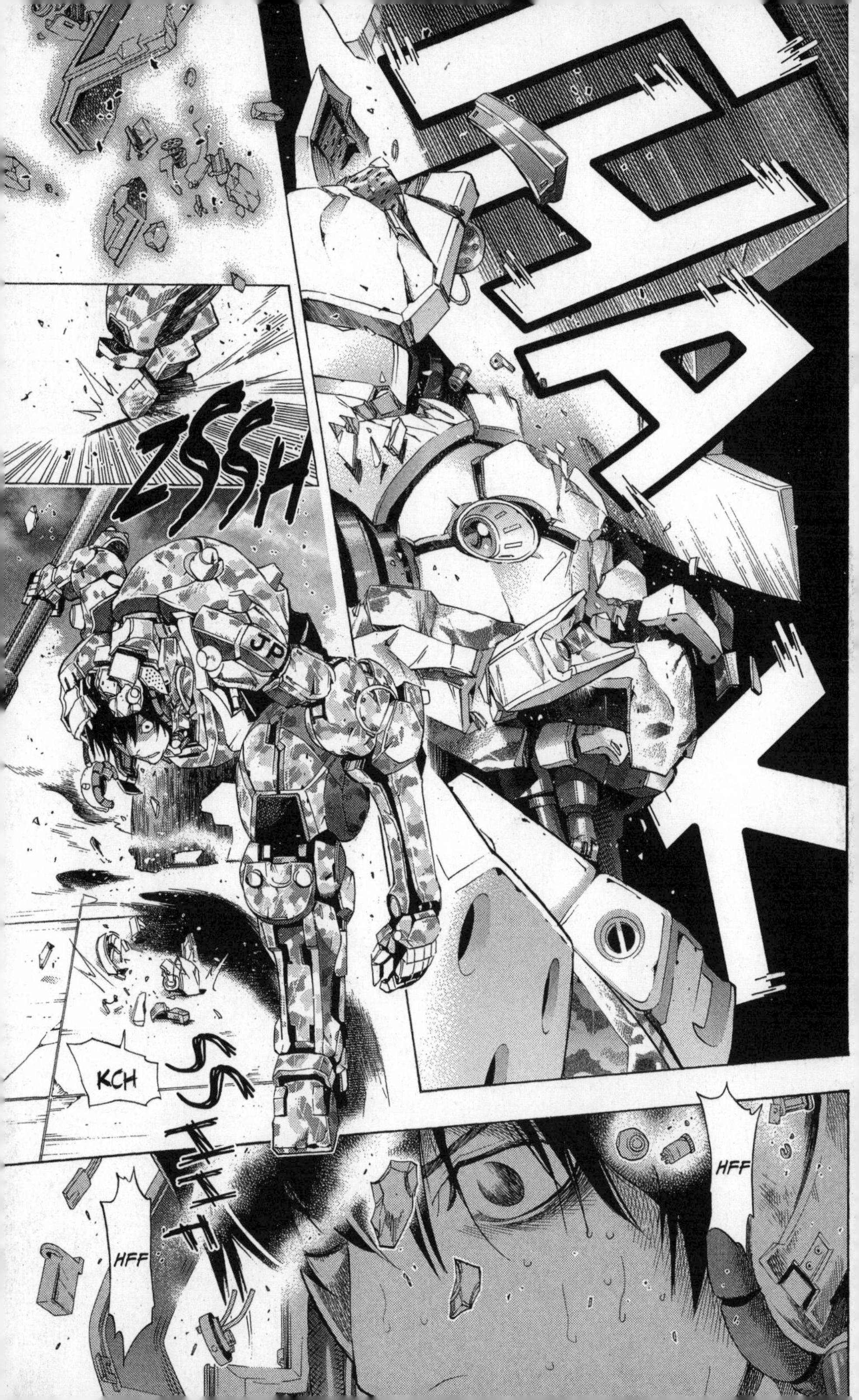
ZSSH
KCH
HFF
HFF

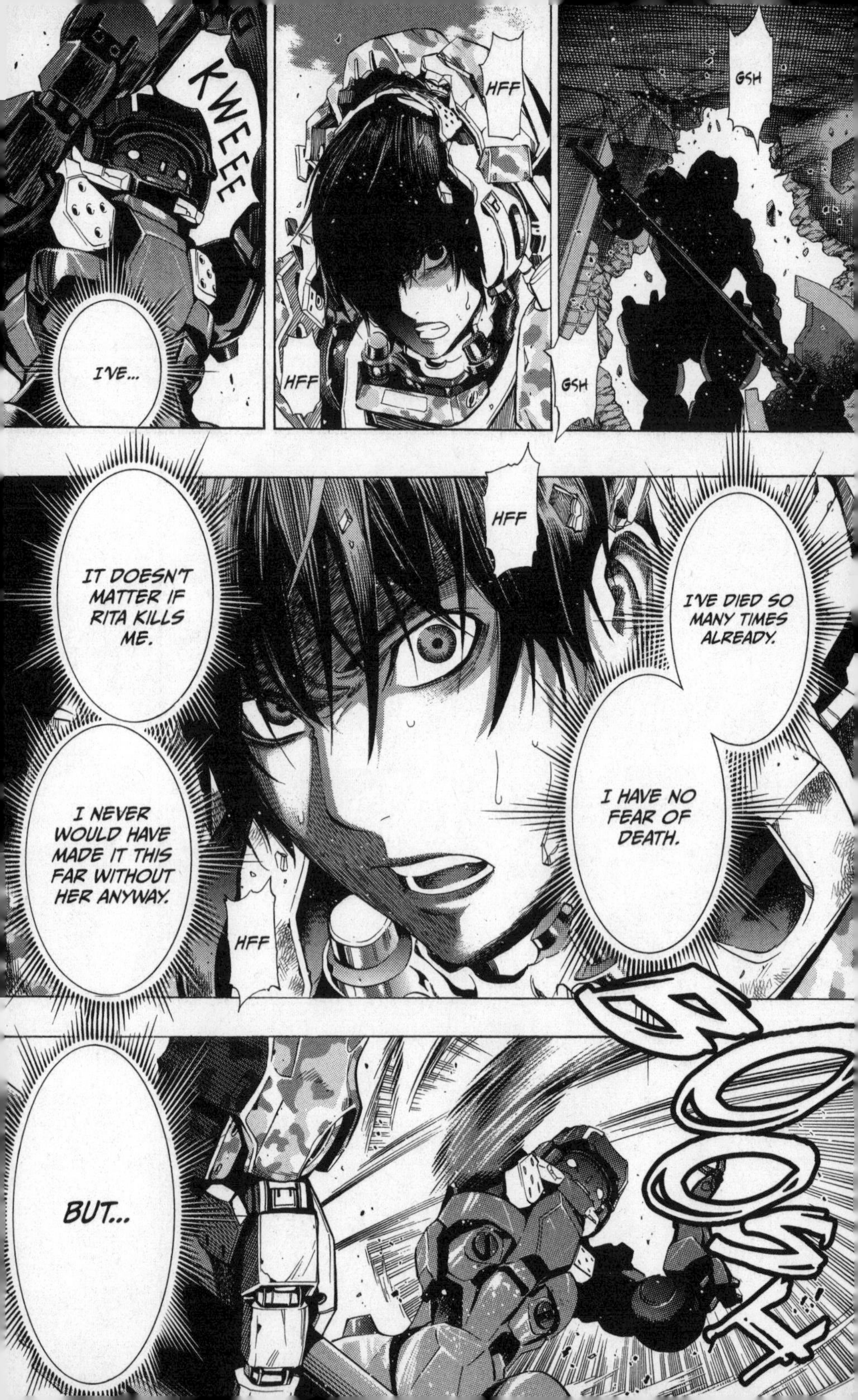
GSH
GSH
HFF
HFF
KWEEE
I'VE...
HFF
I'VE DIED SO MANY TIMES ALREADY.
I HAVE NO FEAR OF DEATH.
IT DOESN'T MATTER IF RITA KILLS ME.
I NEVER WOULD HAVE MADE IT THIS FAR WITHOUT HER ANYWAY.
HFF
BOOSH
BUT...

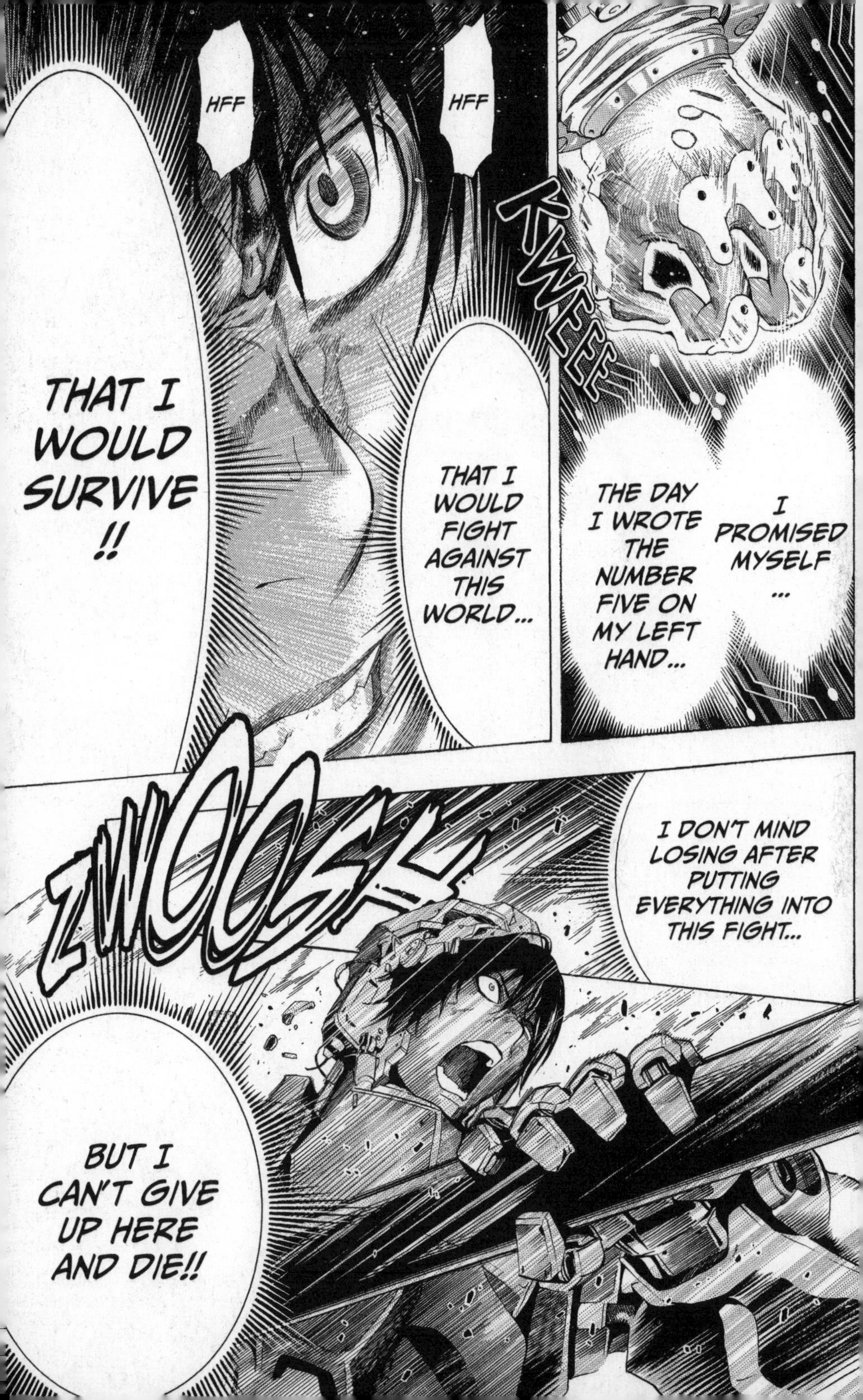
I PROMISED MYSELF...
THE DAY I WROTE THE NUMBER FIVE ON MY LEFT HAND...
KWEEEE
HFF
HFF
THAT I WOULD FIGHT AGAINST THIS WORLD...
THAT I WOULD SURVIVE!!
I DON'T MIND LOSING AFTER PUTTING EVERYTHING INTO THIS FIGHT...
ZWOOSH
BUT I CAN'T GIVE UP HERE AND DIE!!

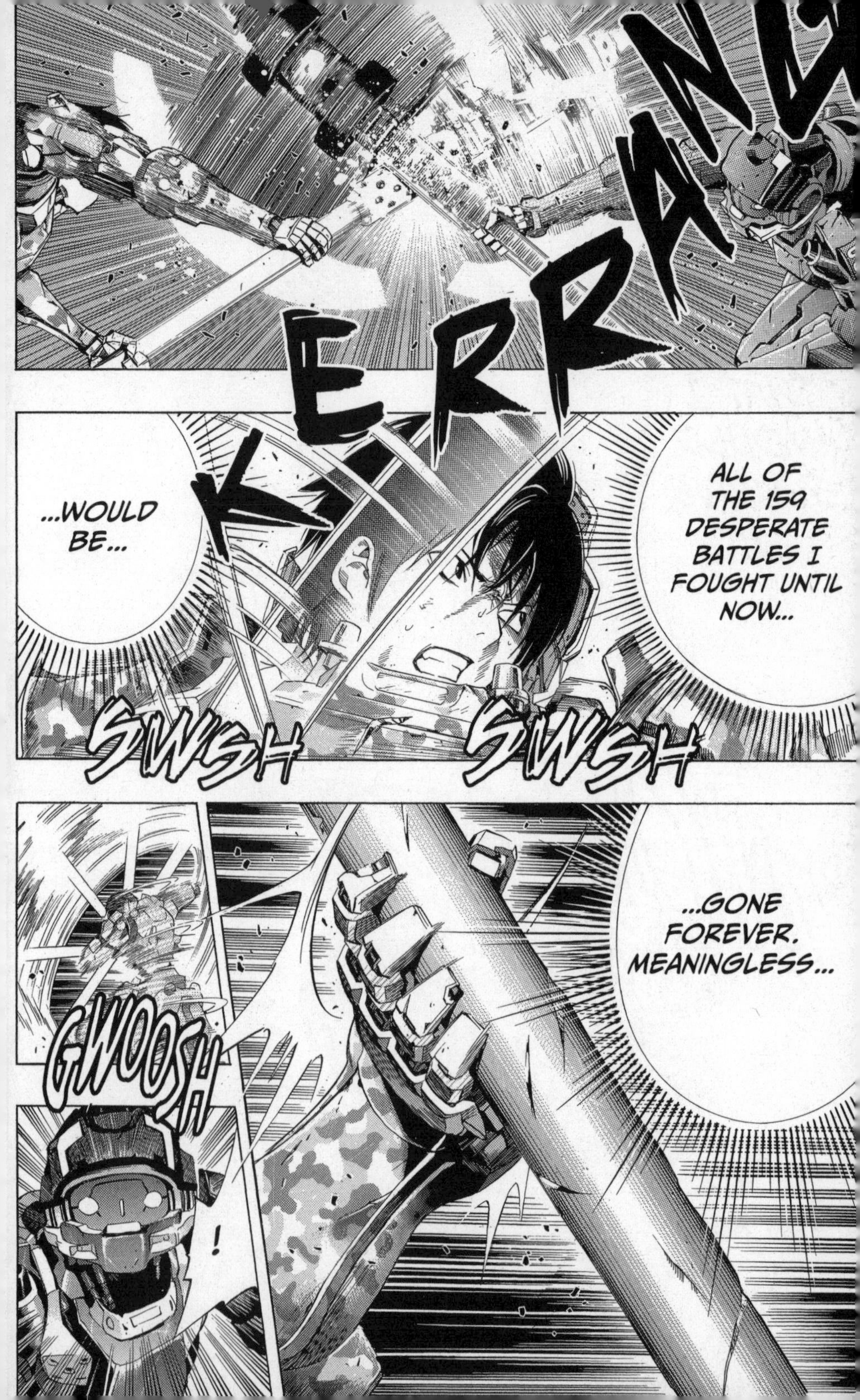
KERRAN
ALL OF THE 159 DESPERATE BATTLES I FOUGHT UNTIL NOW...
...WOULD BE...
SWISH
SWISH
...GONE FOREVER. MEANINGLESS...
GWOOSH
!

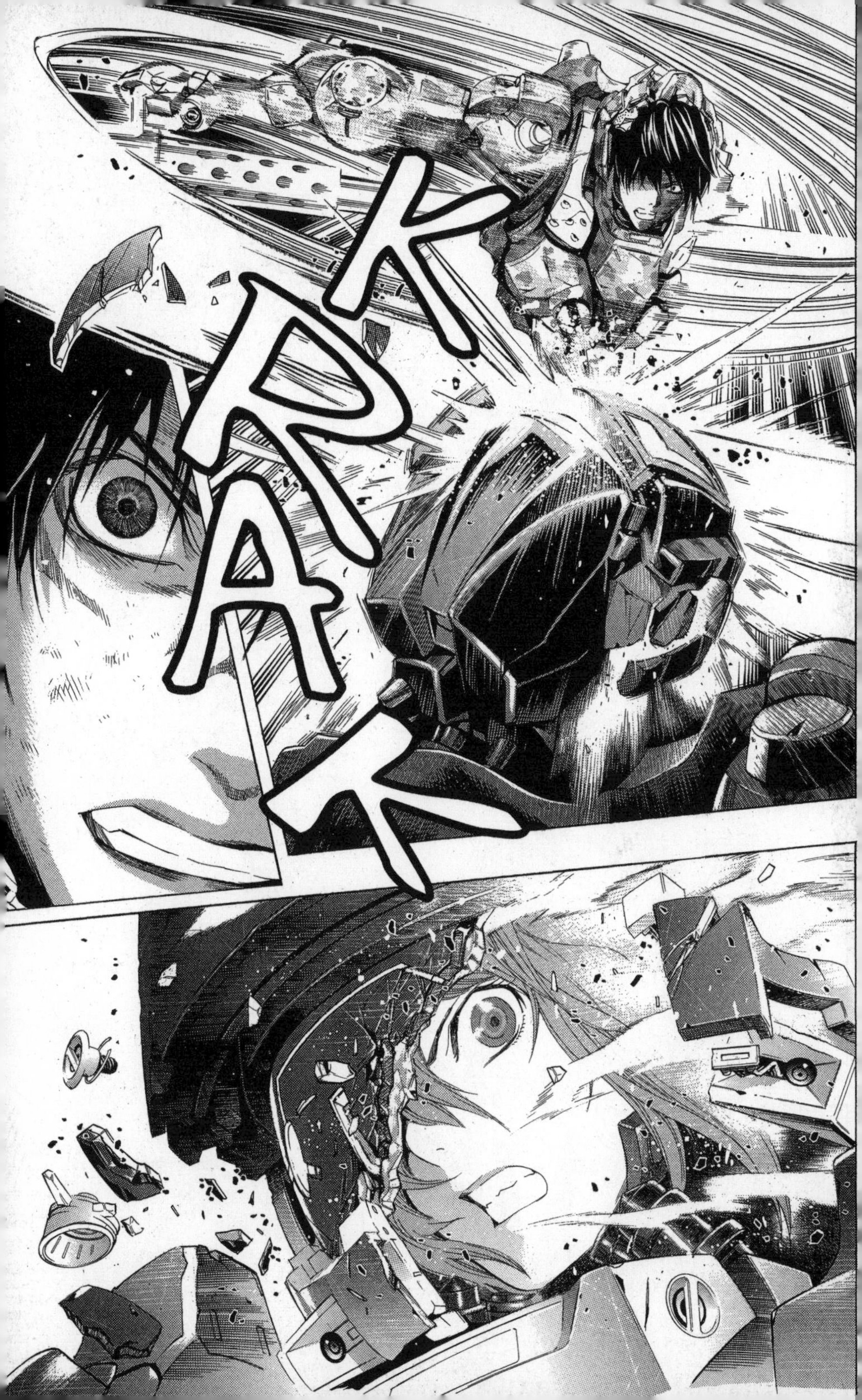
KRAK

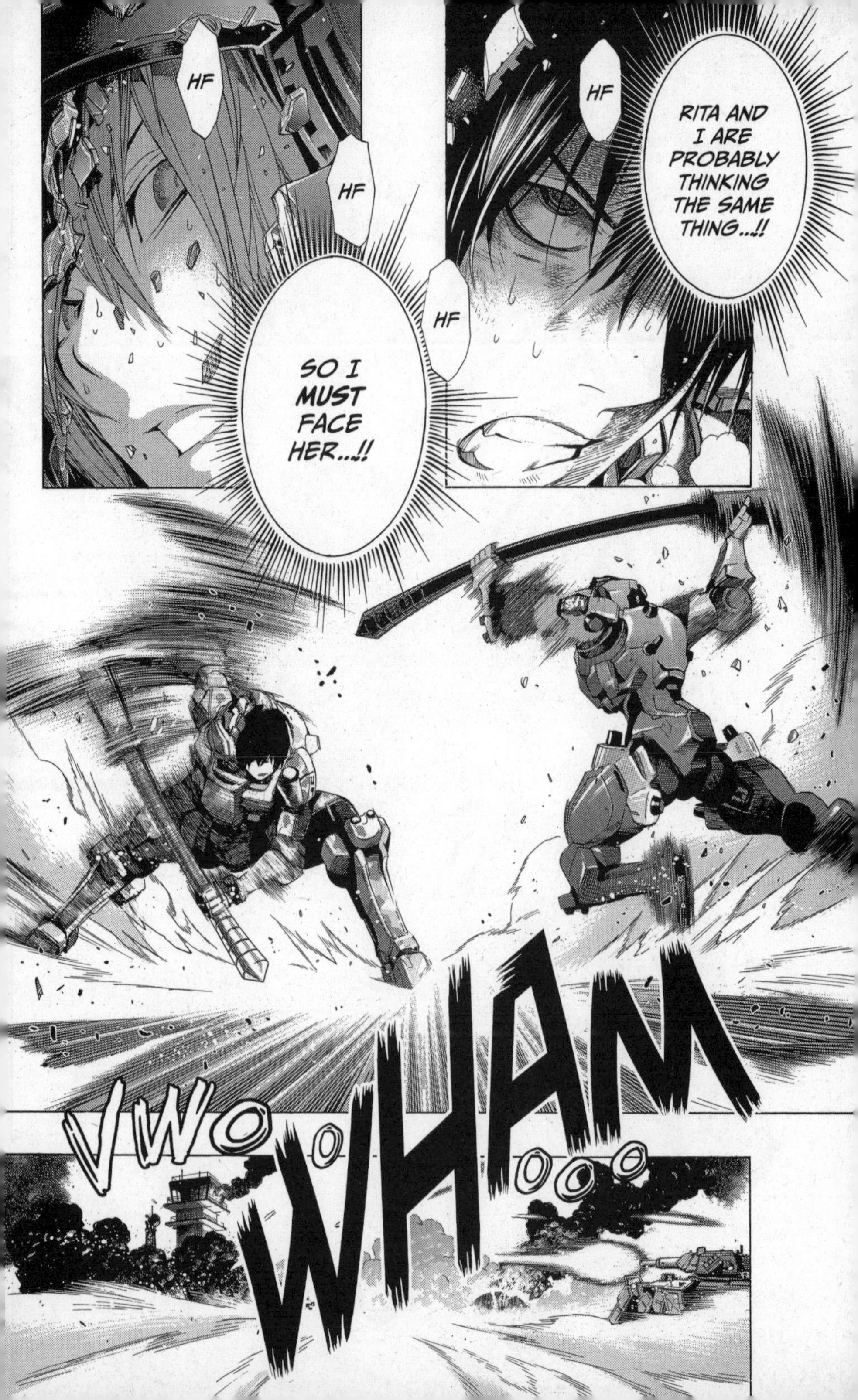
HF
RITA AND I ARE PROBABLY THINKING THE SAME THING...!!
HF
HF
HF
SO I MUST FACE HER...!!
WHAM
VWOOOOOO

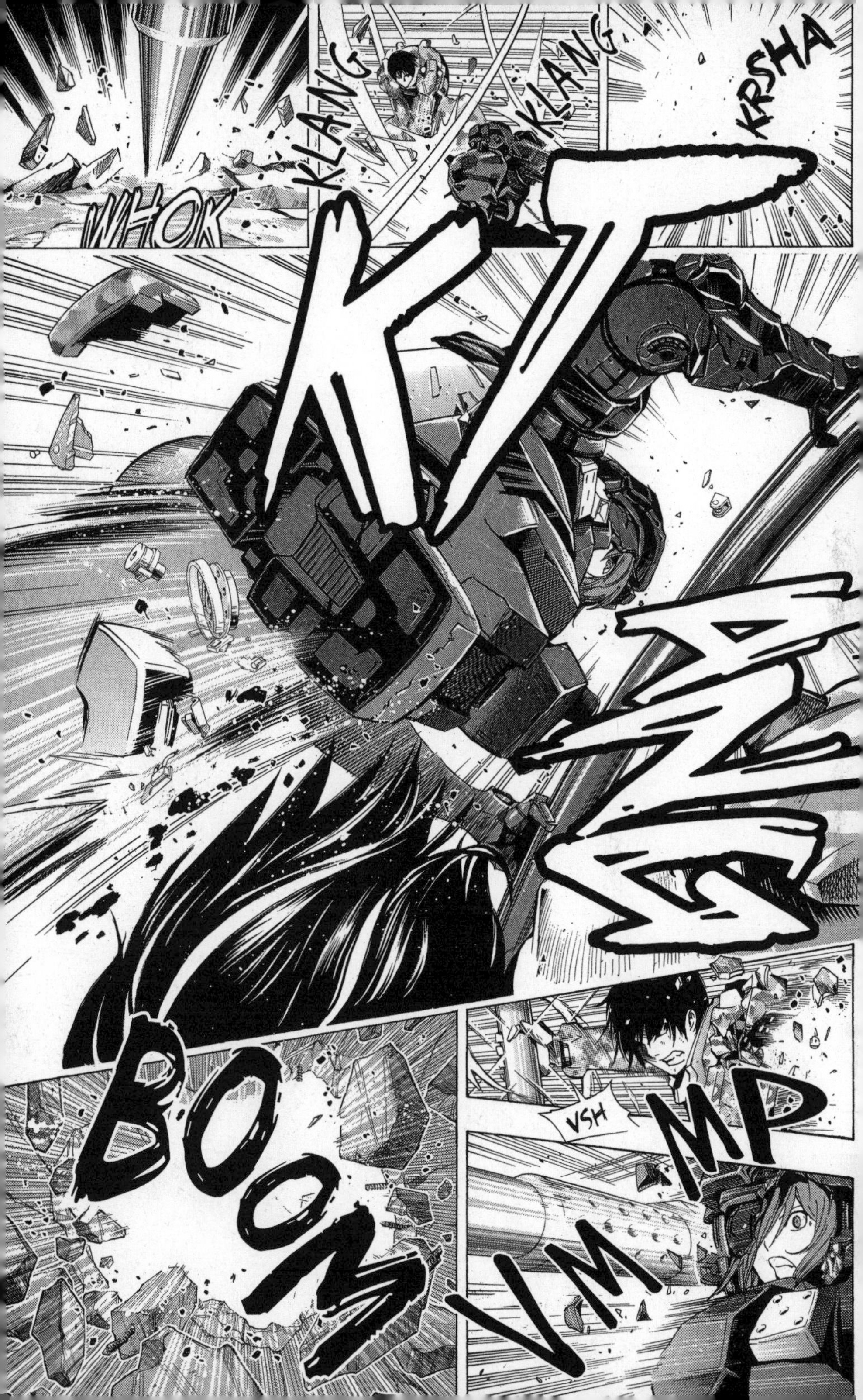
KRSHA
KLANG
KLANG
WHOK
VSH
BOOM

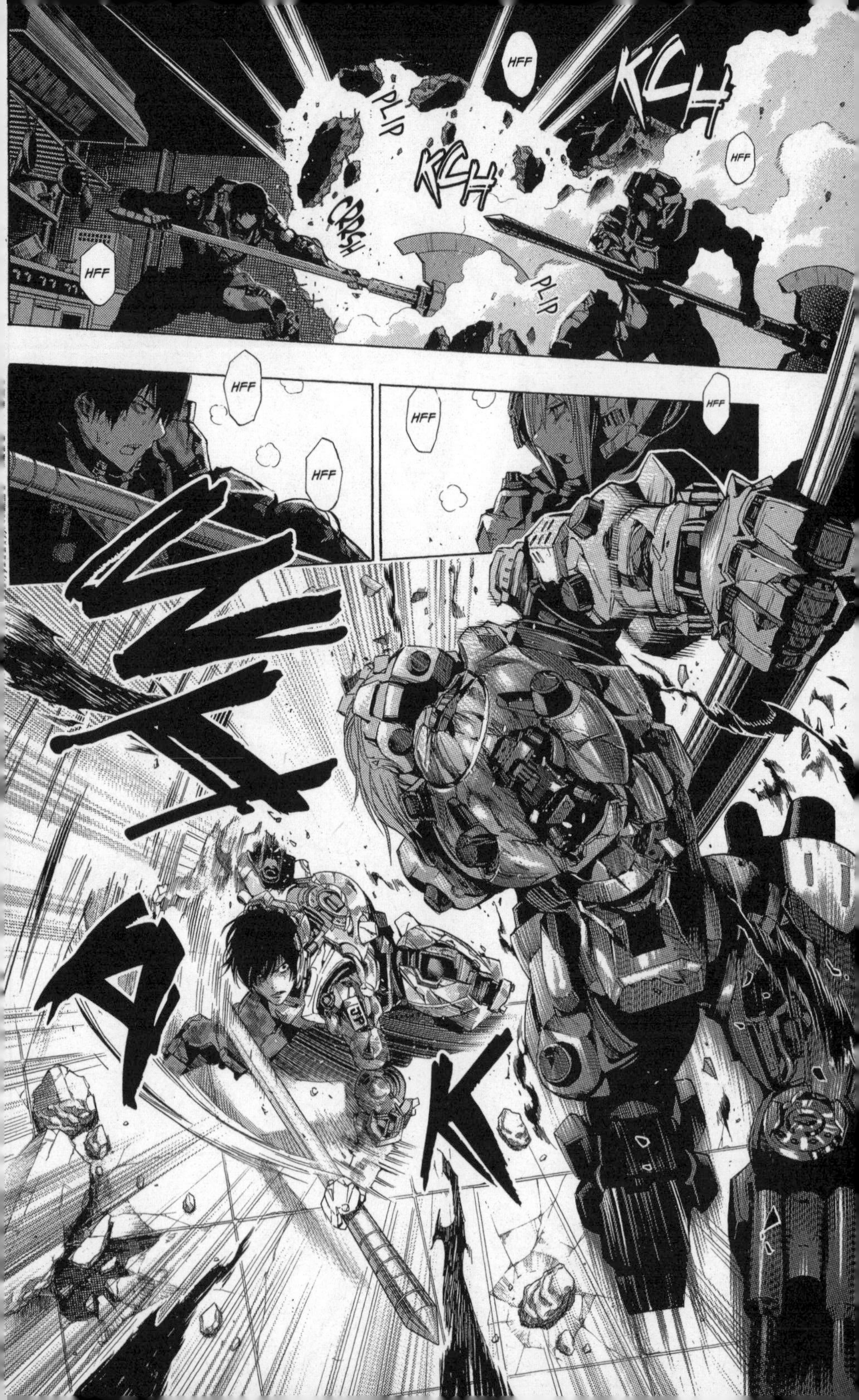
KCH
HFF
HFF
PLIP
KCH
CRRSH
PLIP
HFF
HFF
HFF
HFF
HFF
WHAK

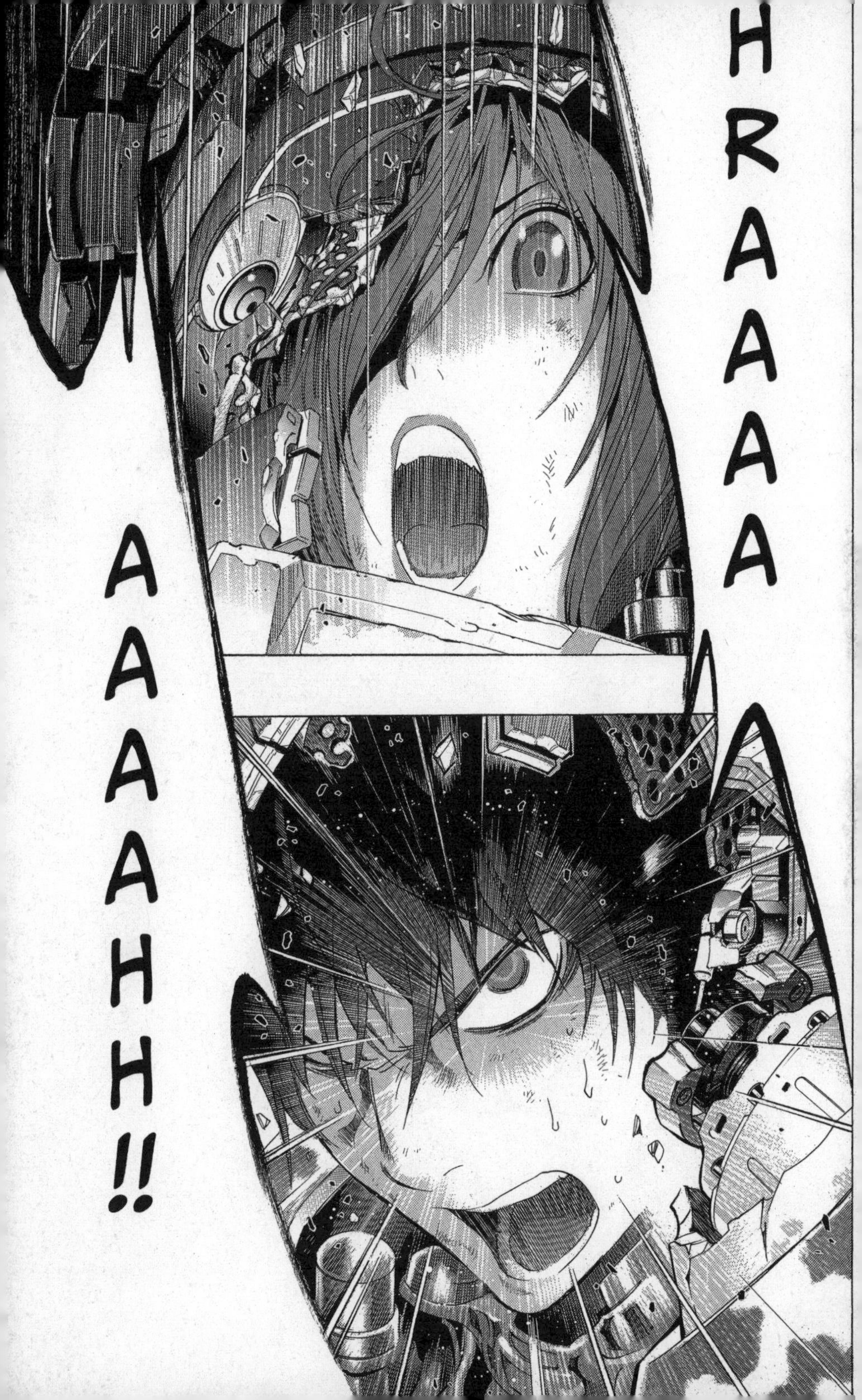
HRAAAAAA
AAAAH!!

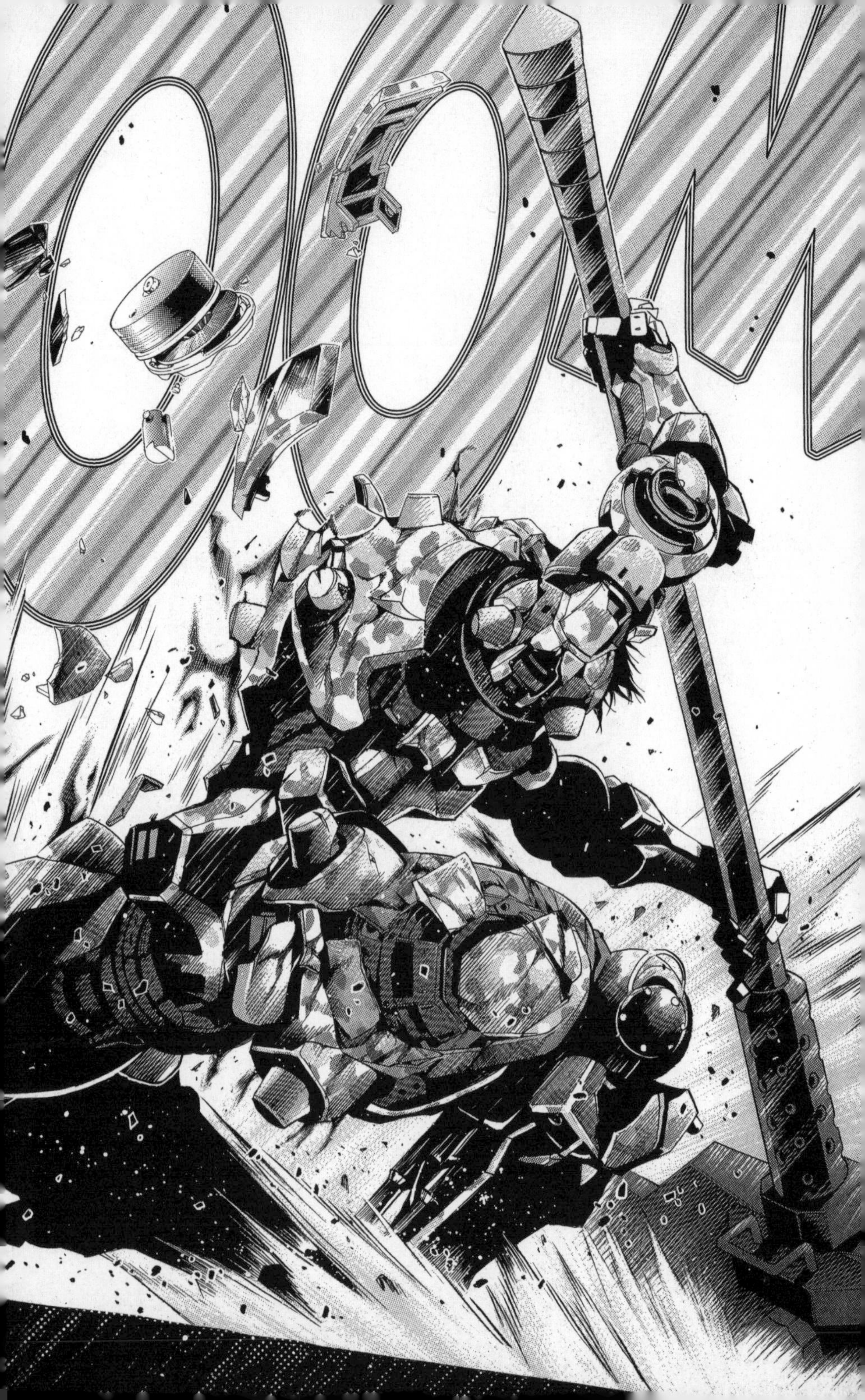

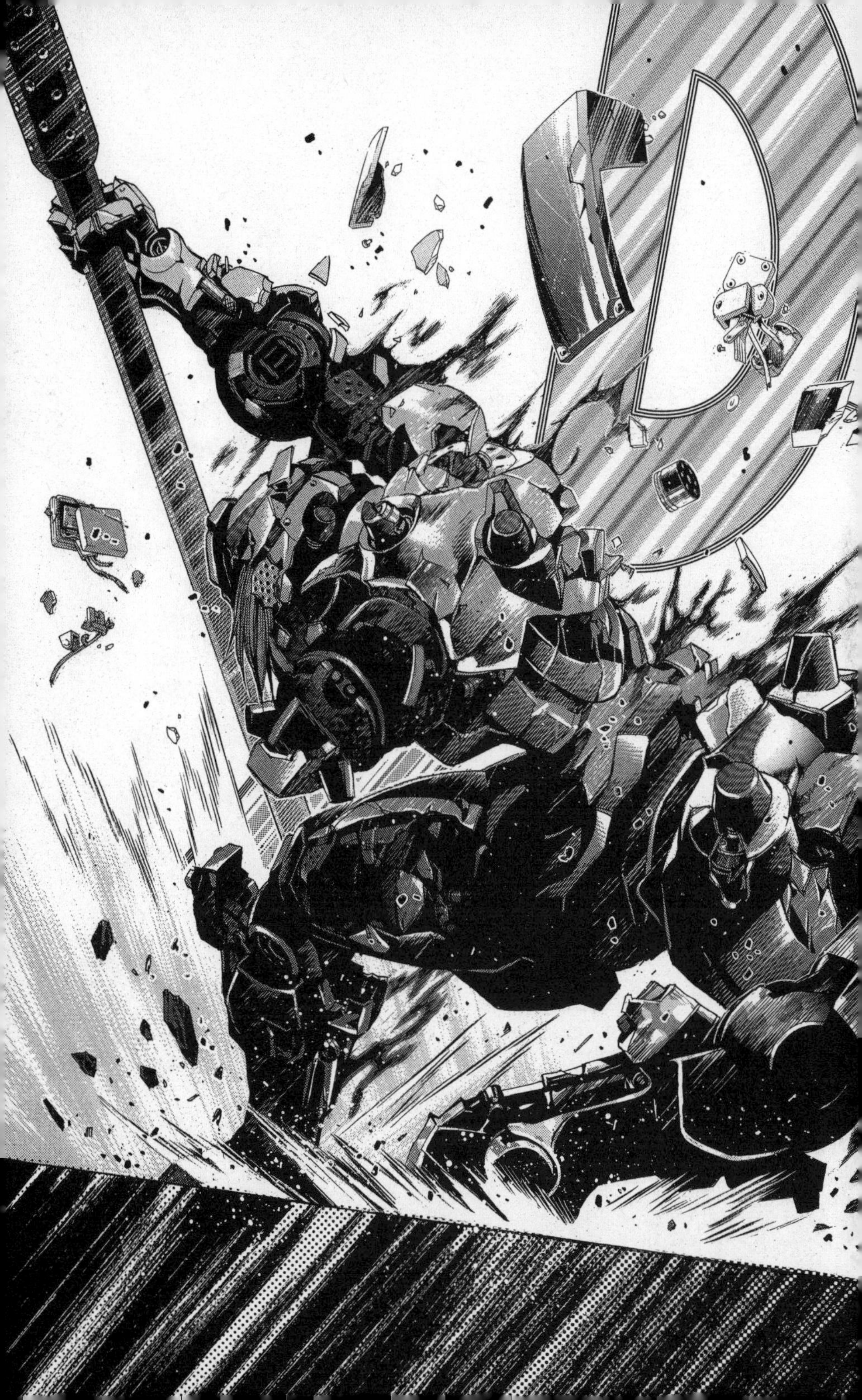

If I lived, she'd die, and I'd never find someone like her again. If she lived, I would have to die. No matter how many ways I ran it through my head, there didn't seem to be another way out. One of us had to die, and Rita didn't want to talk it through. She was going to let our skill decide.

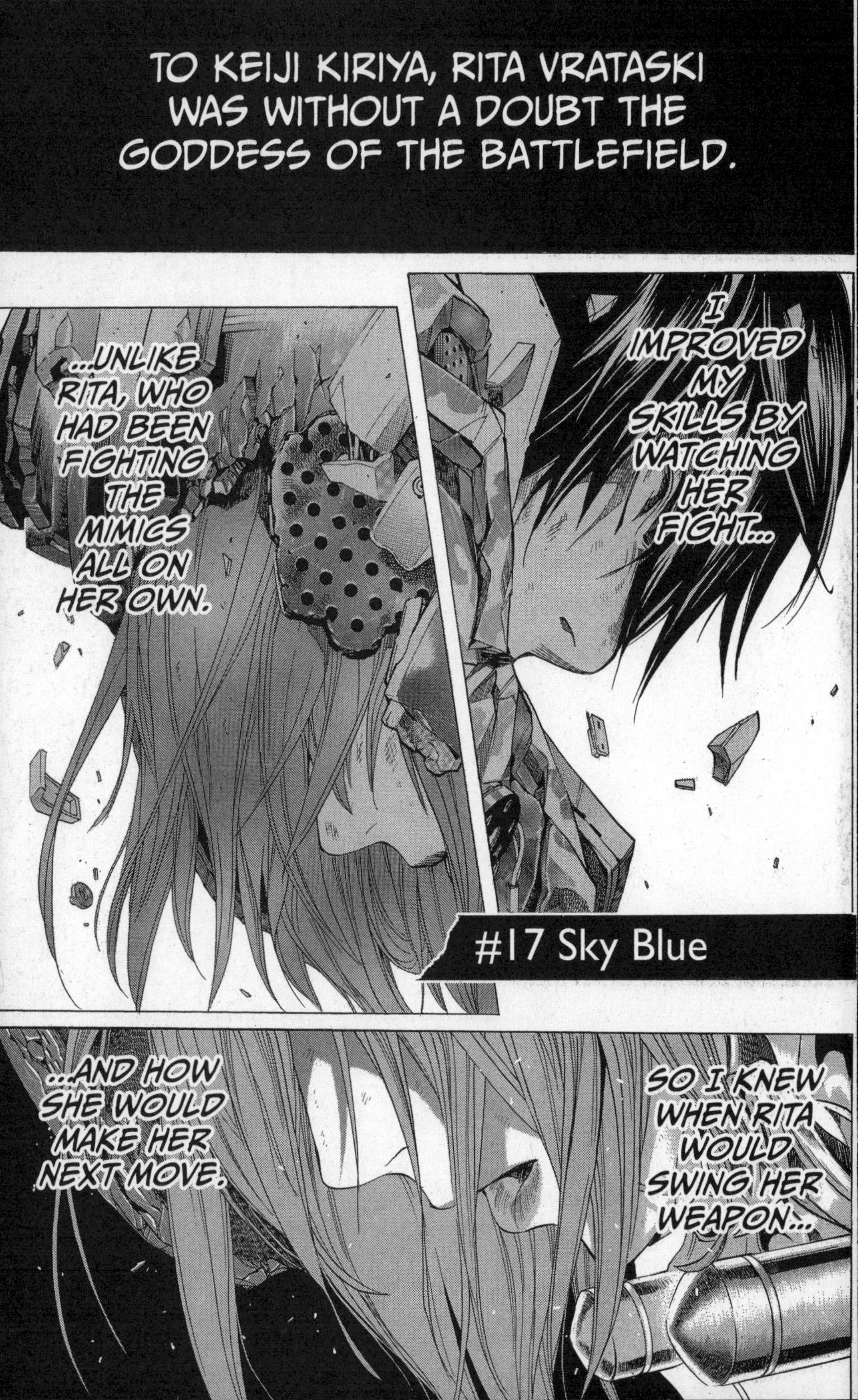
TO KEIJI KIRIYA, RITA VRATASKI WAS WITHOUT A DOUBT THE GODDESS OF THE BATTLEFIELD.
I IMPROVED MY SKILLS BY WATCHING HER FIGHT...
...UNLIKE RITA, WHO HAD BEEN FIGHTING THE MIMICS ALL ON HER OWN.
#17 Sky Blue
SO I KNEW WHEN RITA WOULD SWING HER WEAPON...
...AND HOW SHE WOULD MAKE HER NEXT MOVE.

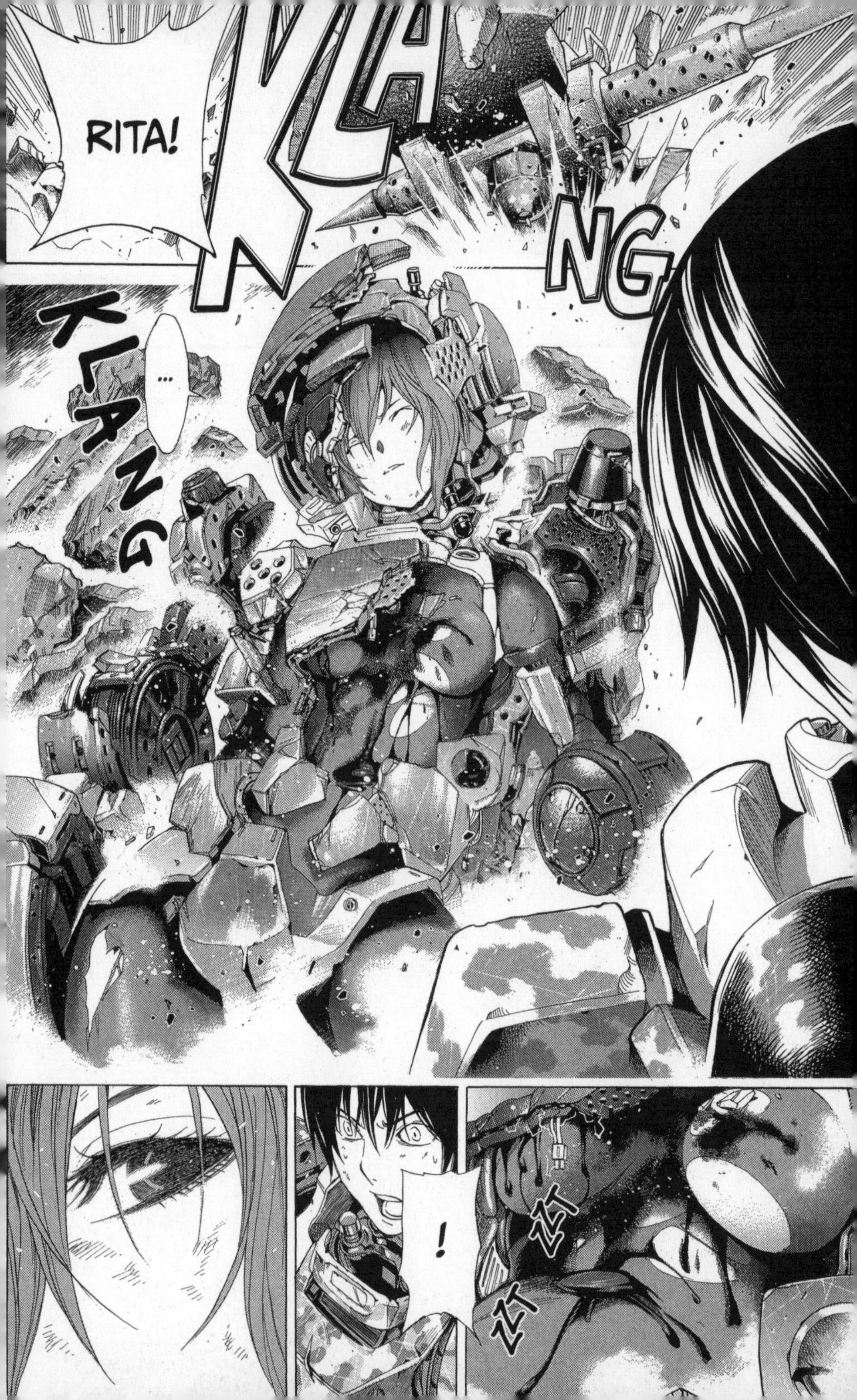
VLANG
RITA!
KLANG
...
ZZT ZZT
ZZT
!

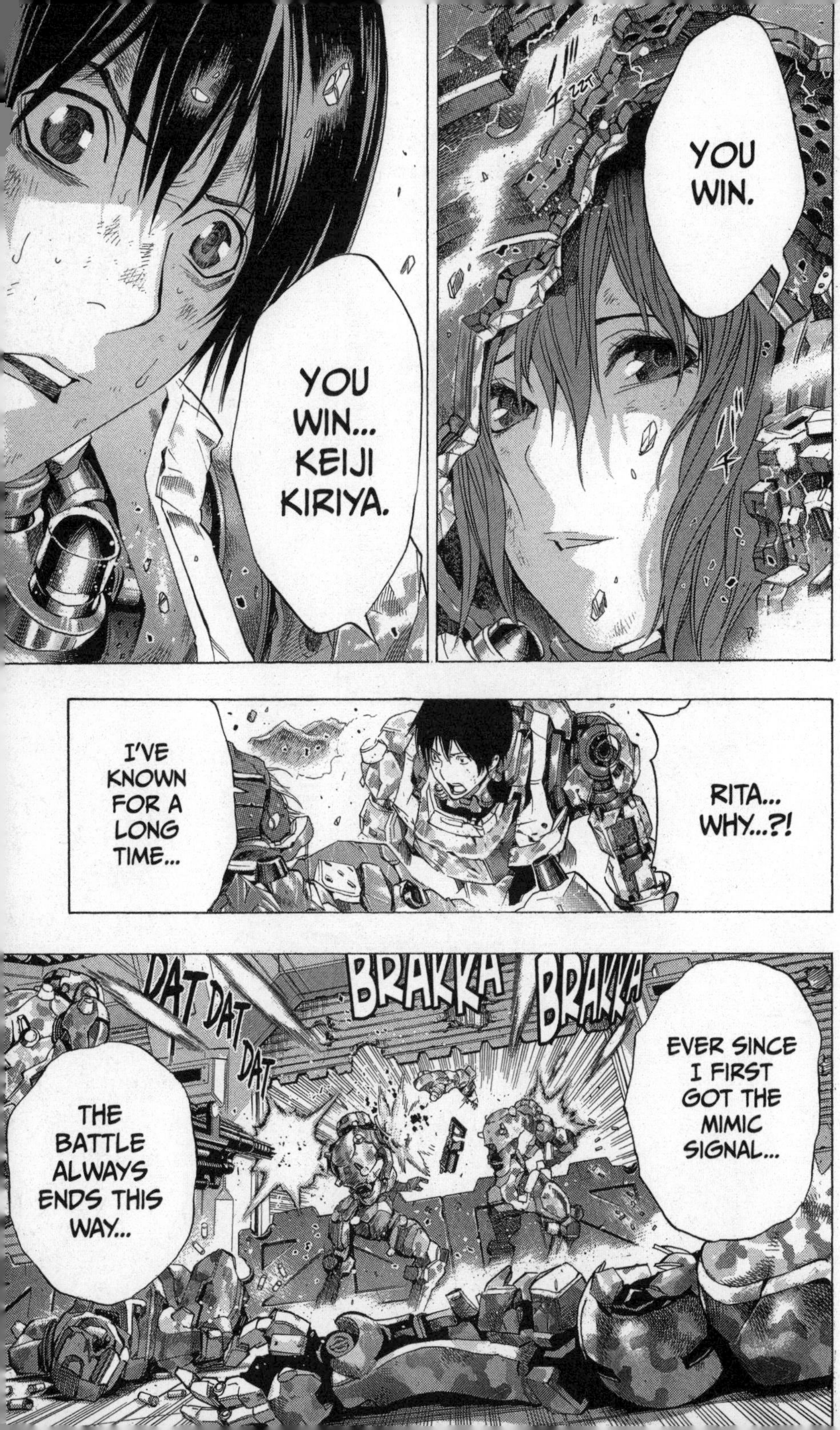
ZZT
YOU WIN.
YOU WIN... KEIJI KIRIYA.
RITA... WHY...?!
I'VE KNOWN FOR A LONG TIME...
BRAKKA
BRAKKA
DAT DAT DAT
EVER SINCE I FIRST GOT THE MIMIC SIGNAL...
THE BATTLE ALWAYS ENDS THIS WAY...

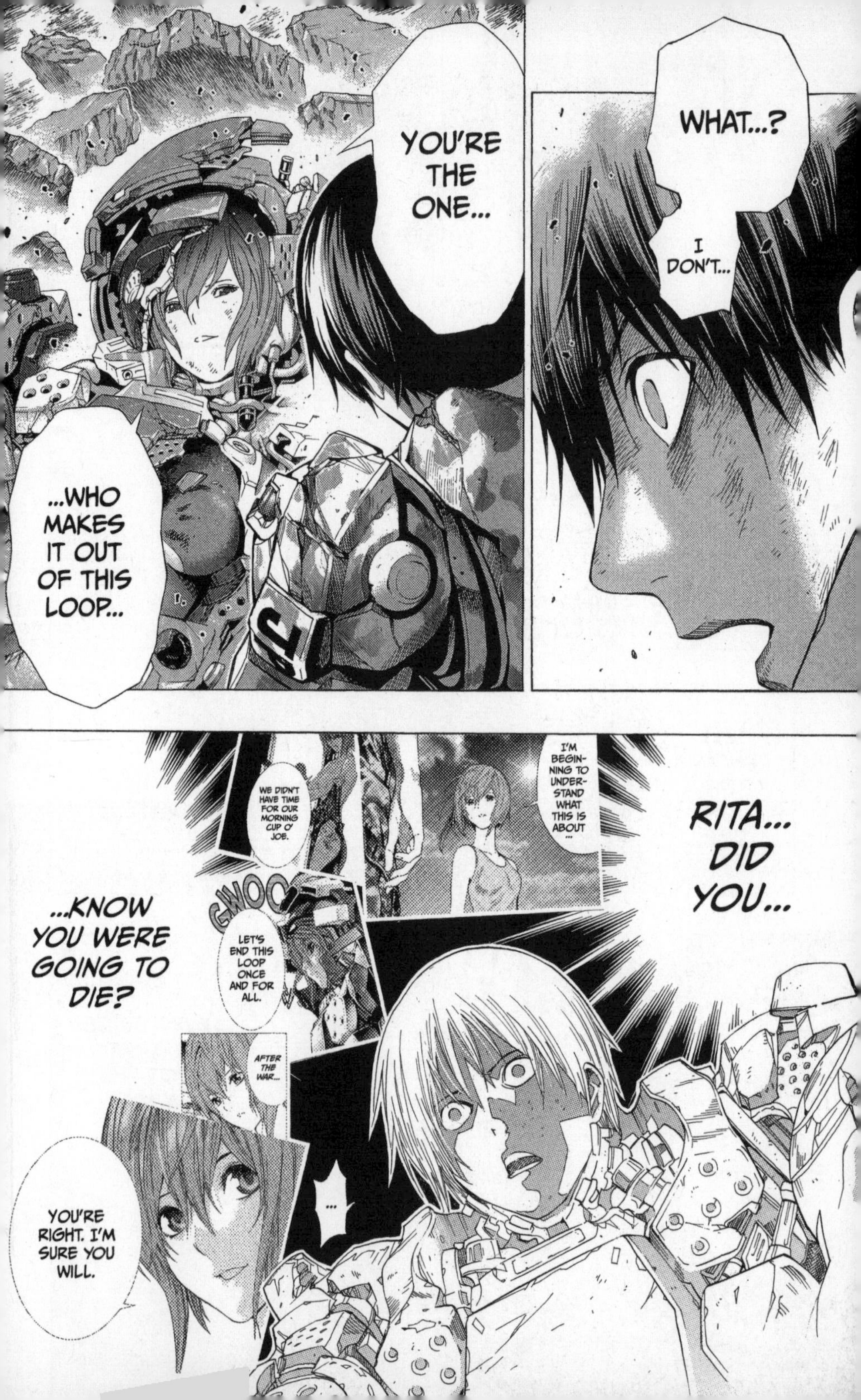
WHAT...?
I DON'T...
YOU'RE THE ONE...
...WHO MAKES IT OUT OF THIS LOOP...
RITA... DID YOU...
I'M BEGINNING TO UNDERSTAND WHAT THIS IS ABOUT...
WE DIDN'T HAVE TIME FOR OUR MORNING CUP O' JOE.
GWOO
LET'S END THIS LOOP ONCE AND FOR ALL.
...KNOW YOU WERE GOING TO DIE?
AFTER THE WAR...
...
YOU'RE RIGHT. I'M SURE YOU WILL.

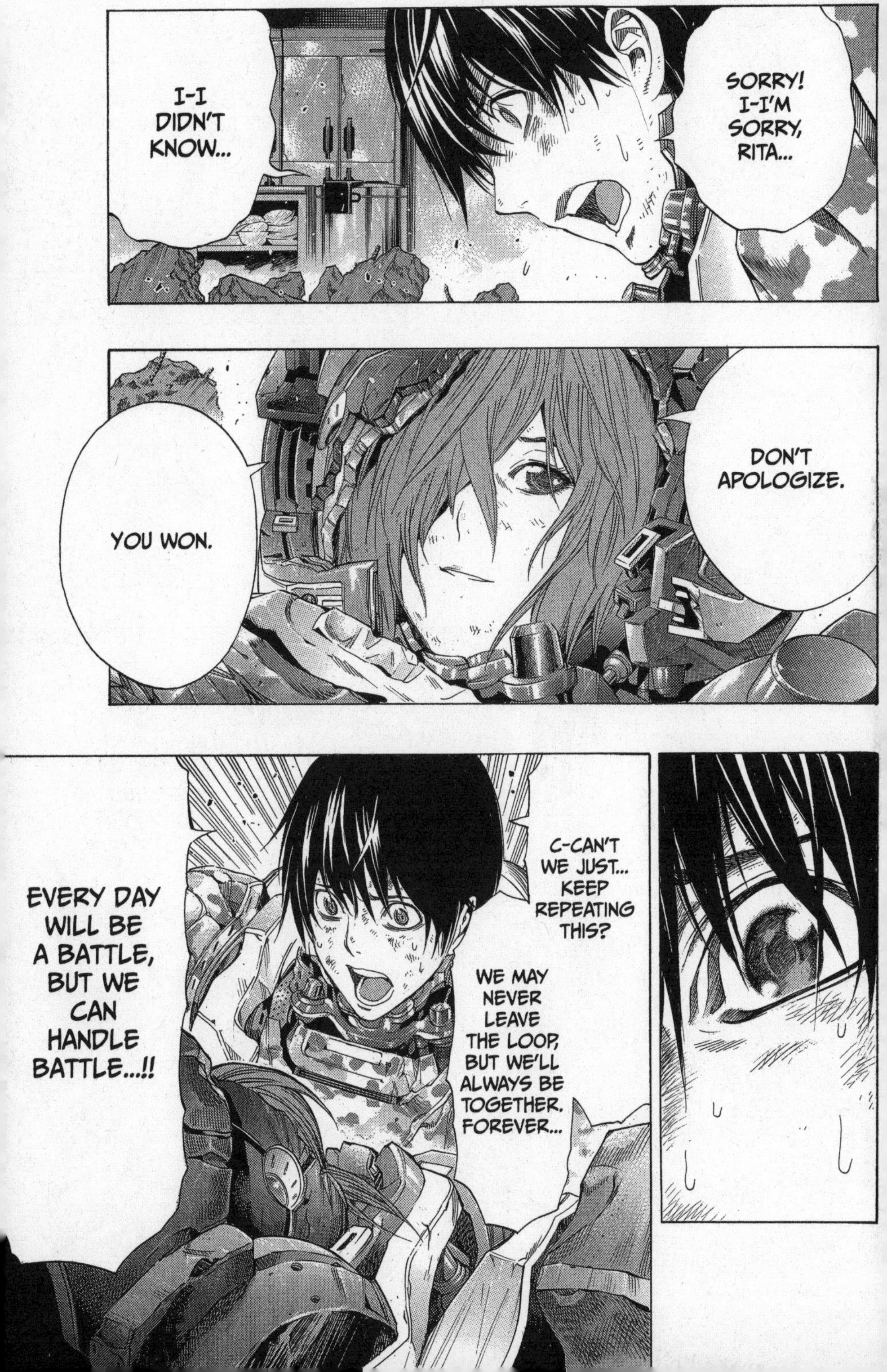
SORRY! I-I'M SORRY, RITA...
I-I DIDN'T KNOW...
DON'T APOLOGIZE.
YOU WON.
C-CAN'T WE JUST... KEEP REPEATING THIS?
WE MAY NEVER LEAVE THE LOOP, BUT WE'LL ALWAYS BE TOGETHER. FOREVER...
EVERY DAY WILL BE A BATTLE, BUT WE CAN HANDLE BATTLE...!!

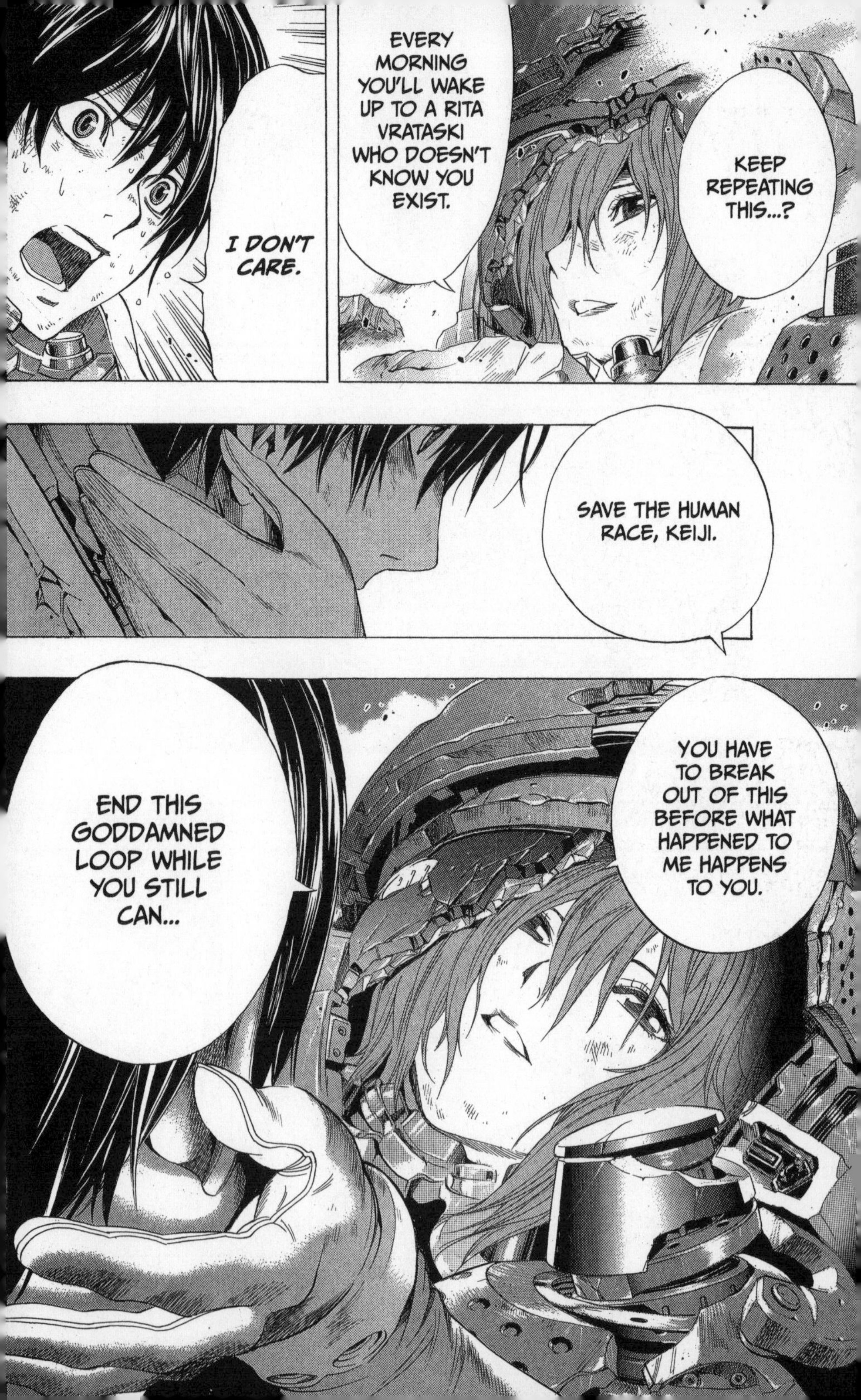
KEEP REPEATING THIS...?
EVERY MORNING YOU'LL WAKE UP TO A RITA VRATASKI WHO DOESN'T KNOW YOU EXIST.
I DON'T CARE.
SAVE THE HUMAN RACE, KEIJI.
YOU HAVE TO BREAK OUT OF THIS BEFORE WHAT HAPPENED TO ME HAPPENS TO YOU.
END THIS GODDAMNED LOOP WHILE YOU STILL CAN...

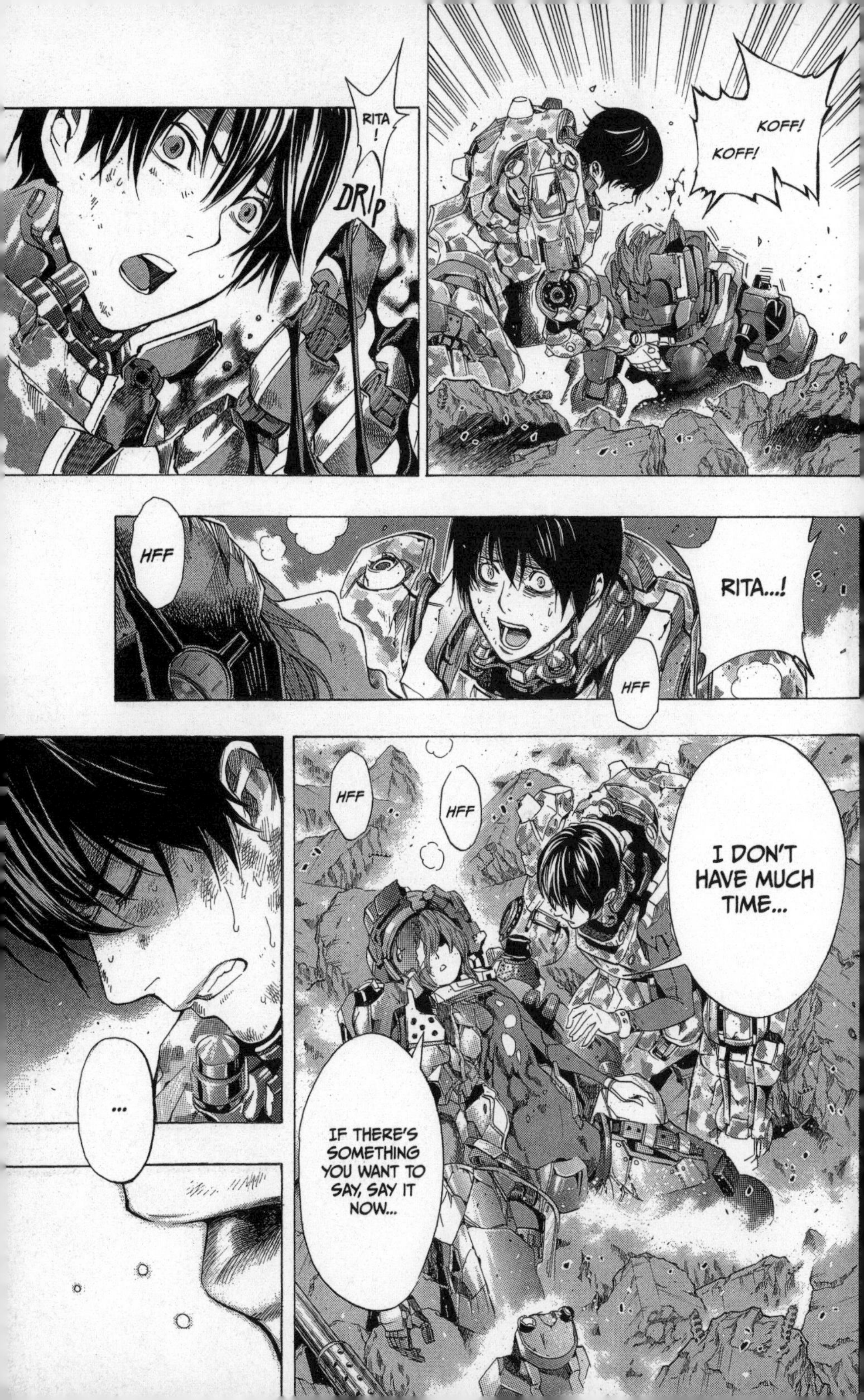
KOFF!
KOFF!
RITA!
DRIP
RITA...!
HFF
HFF
I DON'T HAVE MUCH TIME...
HFF
HFF
IF THERE'S SOMETHING YOU WANT TO SAY, SAY IT NOW...
...

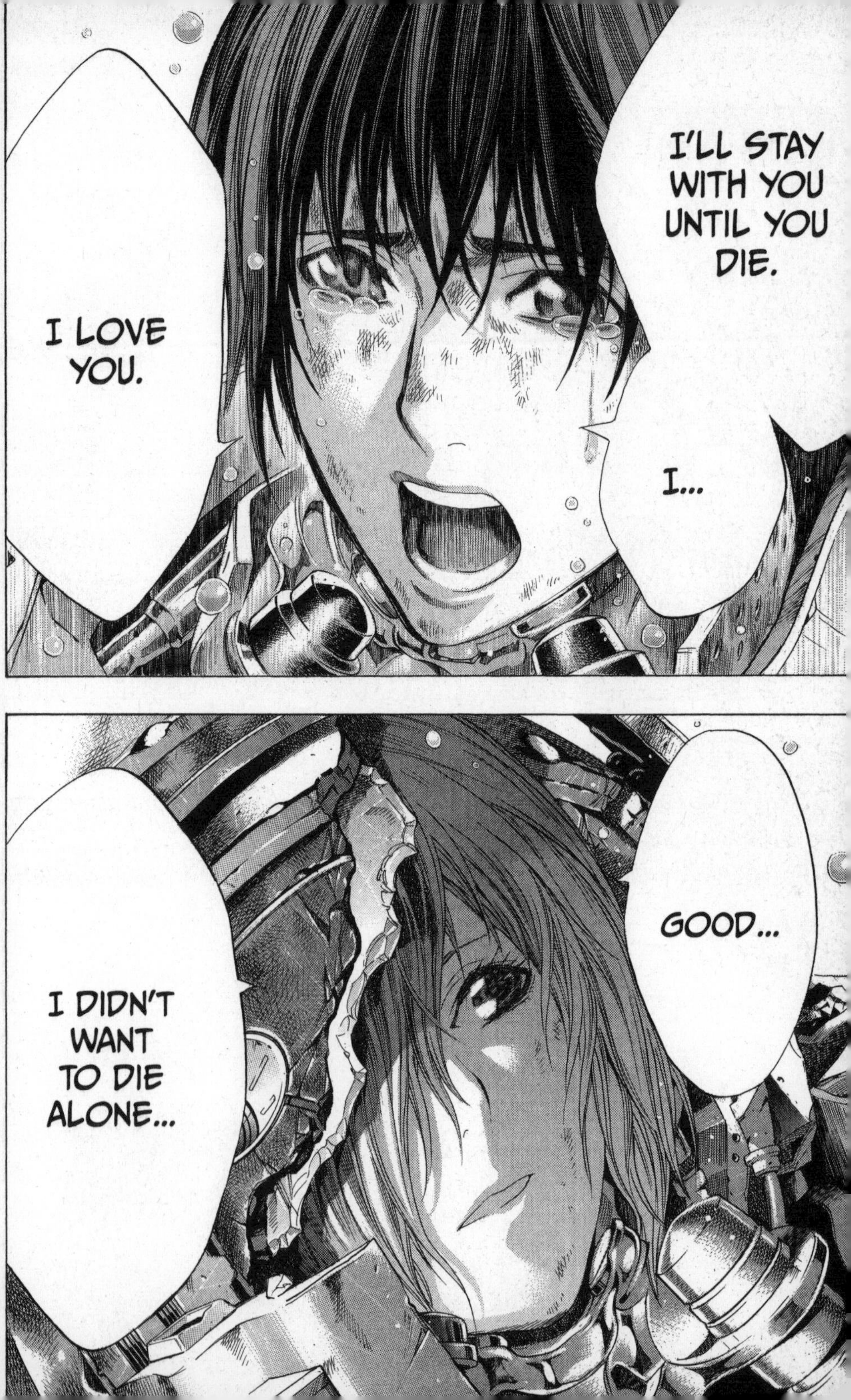
I'LL STAY WITH YOU UNTIL YOU DIE.
I...
I LOVE YOU.
GOOD...
I DIDN'T WANT TO DIE ALONE...

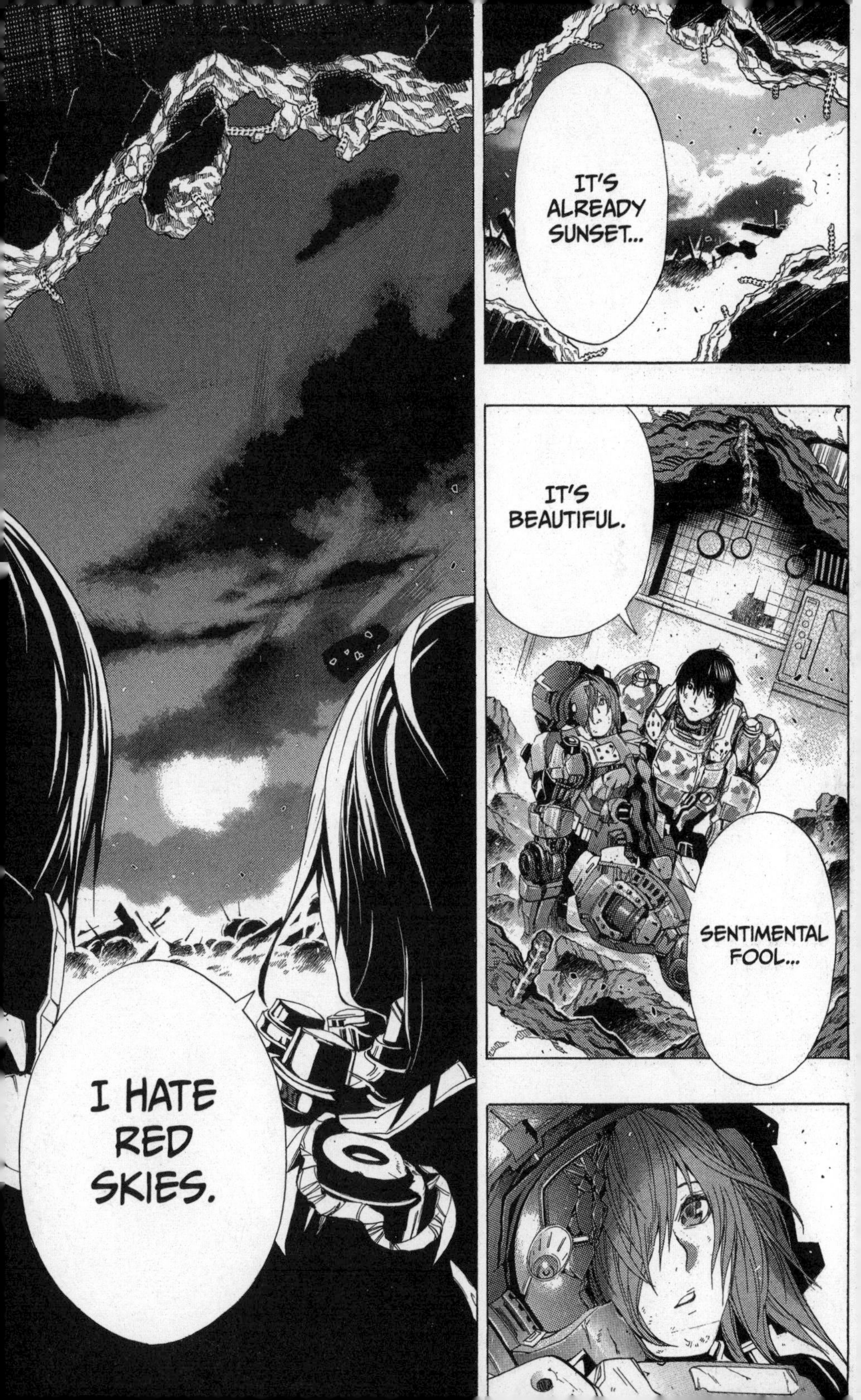
IT'S ALREADY SUNSET...
IT'S BEAUTIFUL.
SENTIMENTAL FOOL...
I HATE RED SKIES.

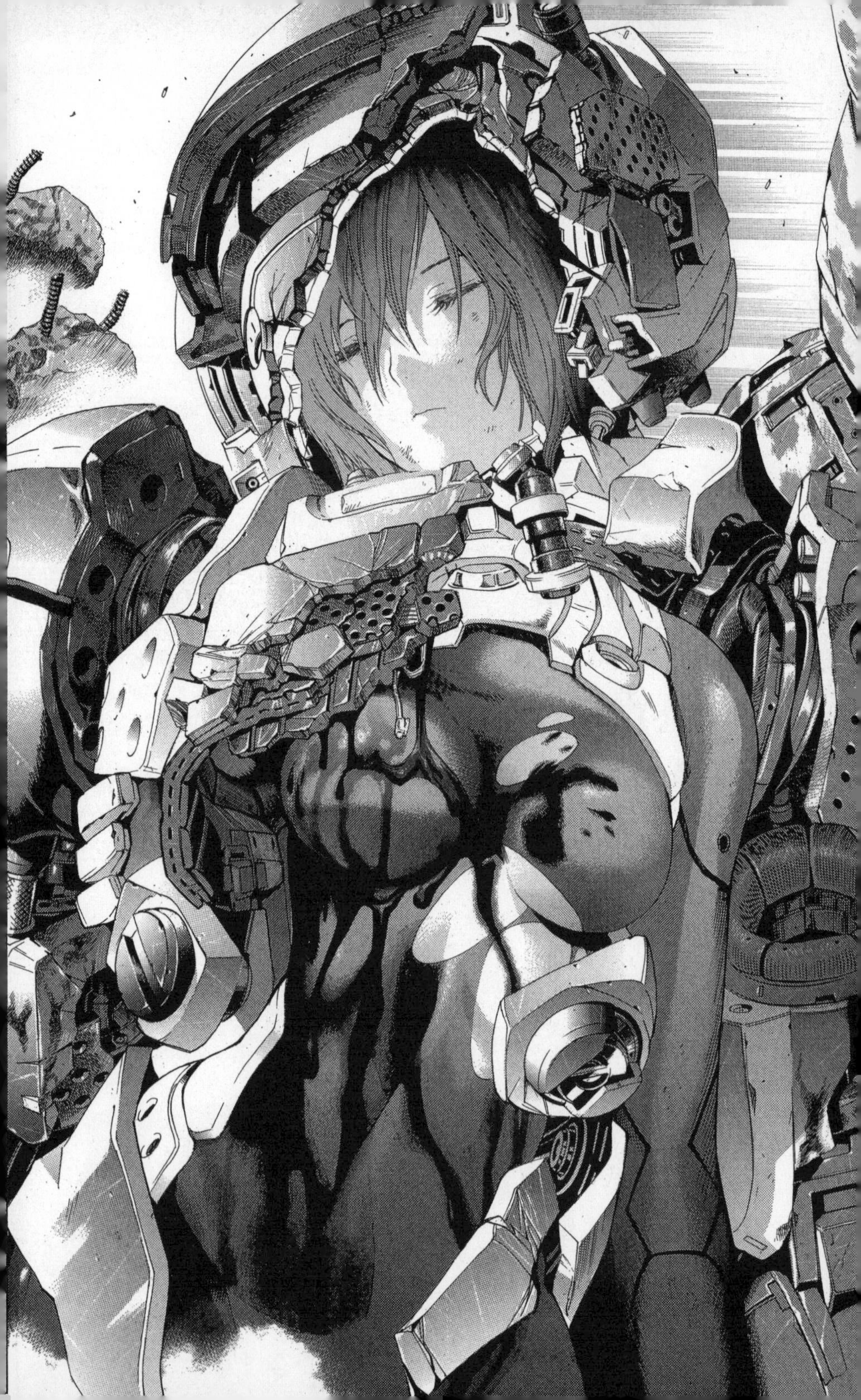

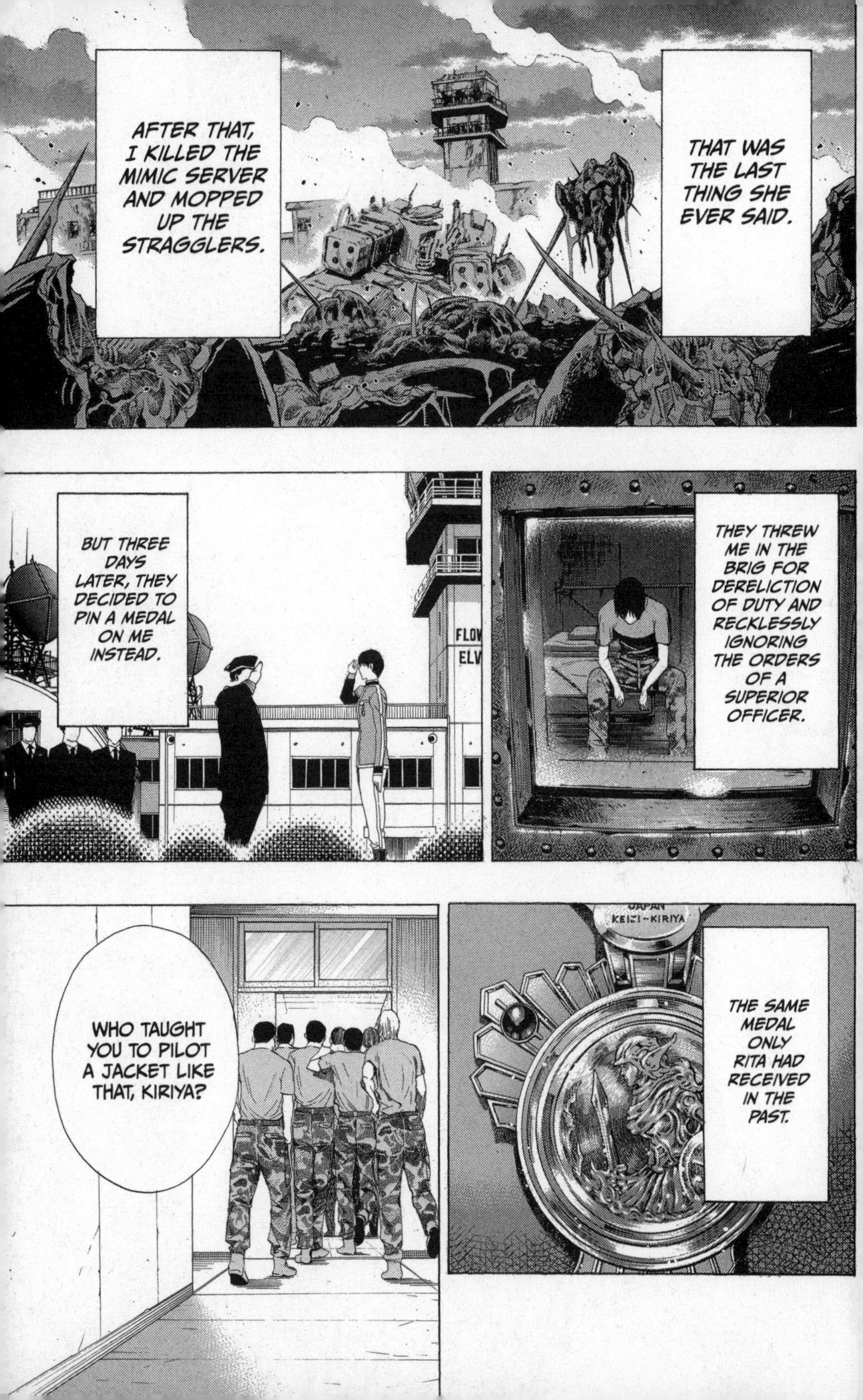
THAT WAS THE LAST THING SHE EVER SAID.
AFTER THAT, I KILLED THE MIMIC SERVER AND MOPPED UP THE STRAGGLERS.
THEY THREW ME IN THE BRIG FOR DERELICTION OF DUTY AND RECKLESSLY IGNORING THE ORDERS OF A SUPERIOR OFFICER.
BUT THREE DAYS LATER, THEY DECIDED TO PIN A MEDAL ON ME INSTEAD.
THE SAME MEDAL ONLY RITA HAD RECEIVED IN THE PAST.
WHO TAUGHT YOU TO PILOT A JACKET LIKE THAT, KIRIYA?

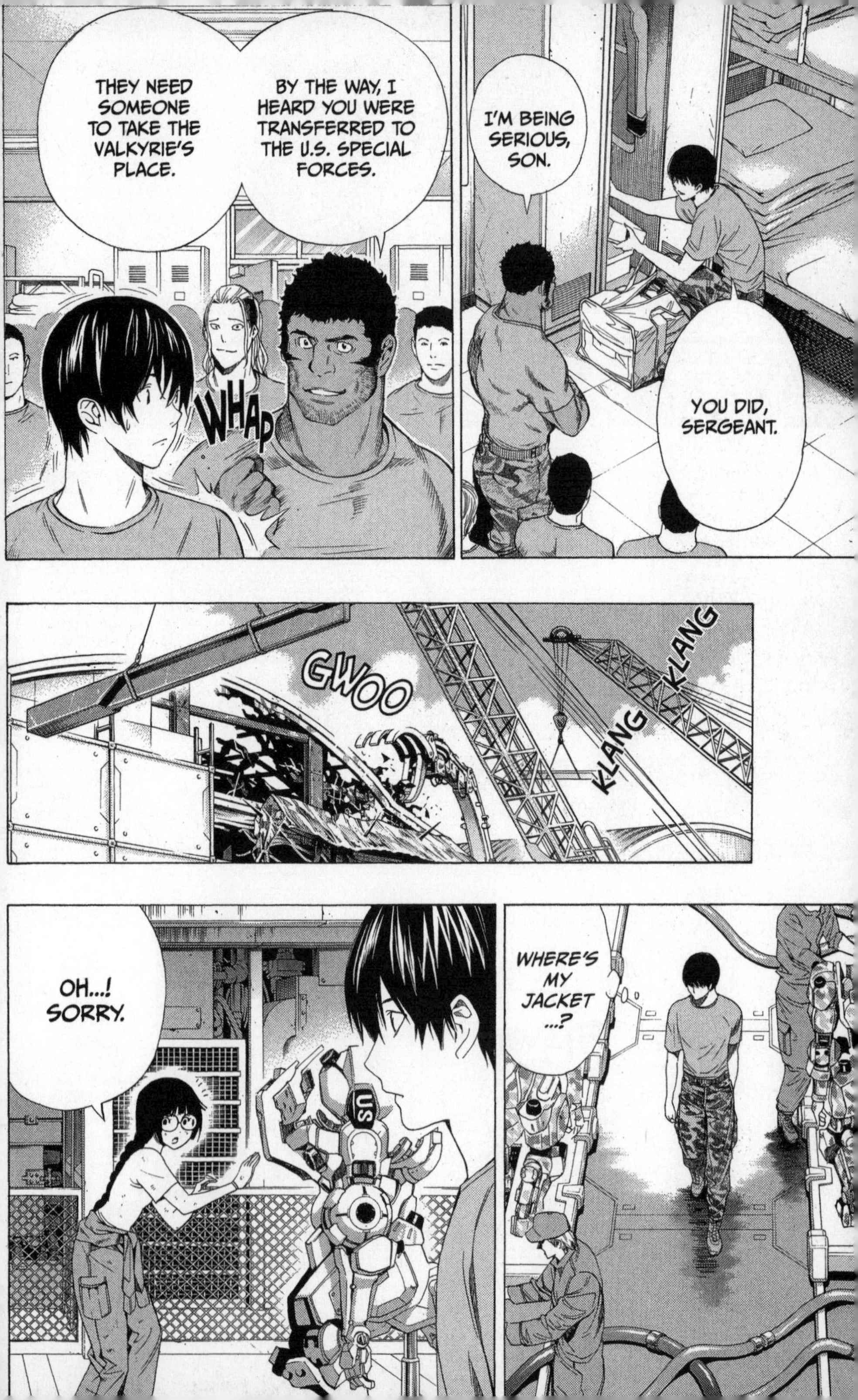
I'M BEING SERIOUS, SON.
YOU DID, SERGEANT.
BY THE WAY, I HEARD YOU WERE TRANSFERRED TO THE U.S. SPECIAL FORCES.
THEY NEED SOMEONE TO TAKE THE VALKYRIE'S PLACE.
WHAP
KLANG KLANG
KLANG
GWOO
WHERE'S MY JACKET ...?
US
OH...! SORRY.

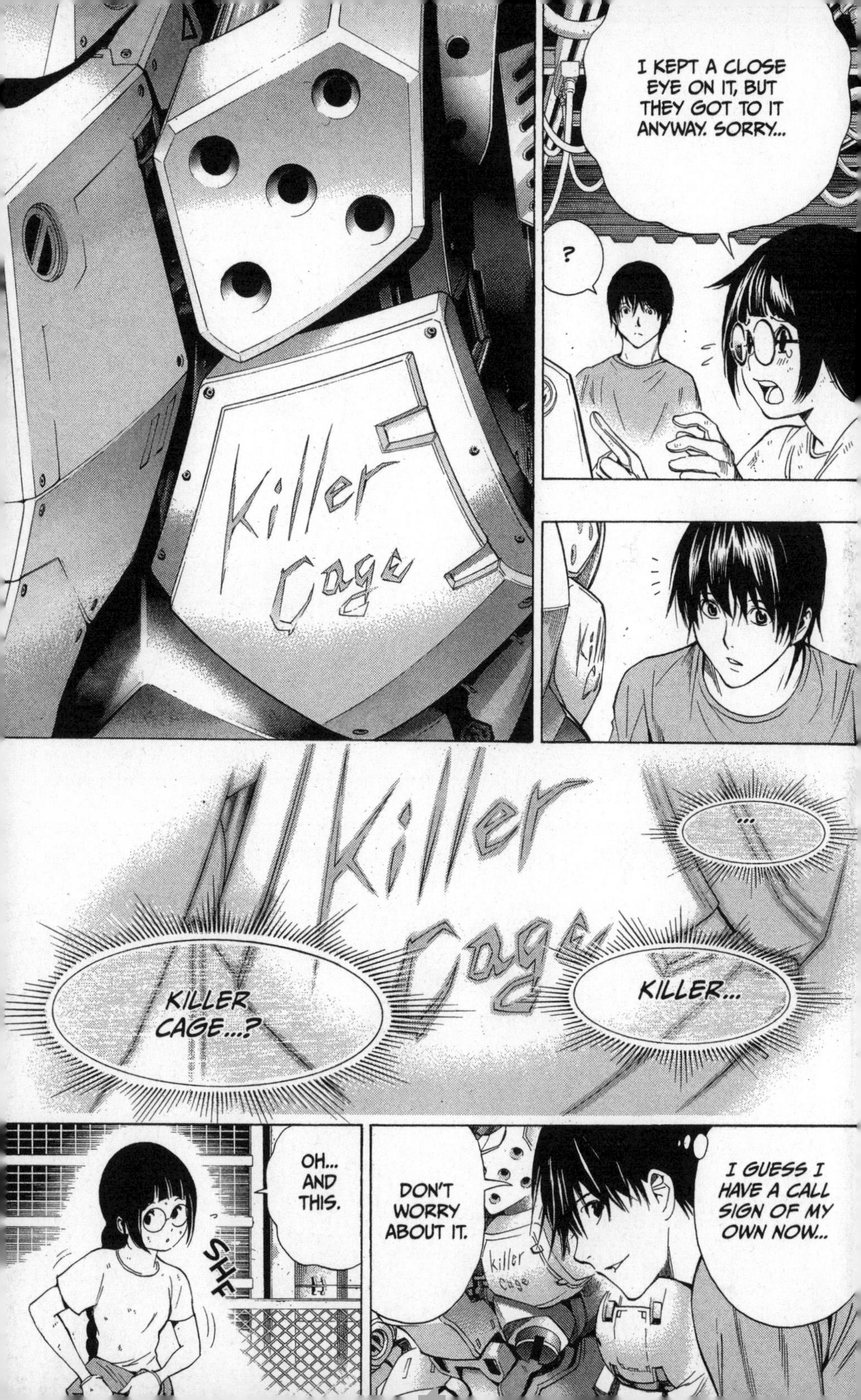
I KEPT A CLOSE EYE ON IT, BUT THEY GOT TO IT ANYWAY. SORRY...
?
killer Cage
...
KILLER...
killer Cage
KILLER CAGE...?
I GUESS I HAVE A CALL SIGN OF MY OWN NOW...
DON'T WORRY ABOUT IT.
killer Cage
OH... AND THIS.
SHF

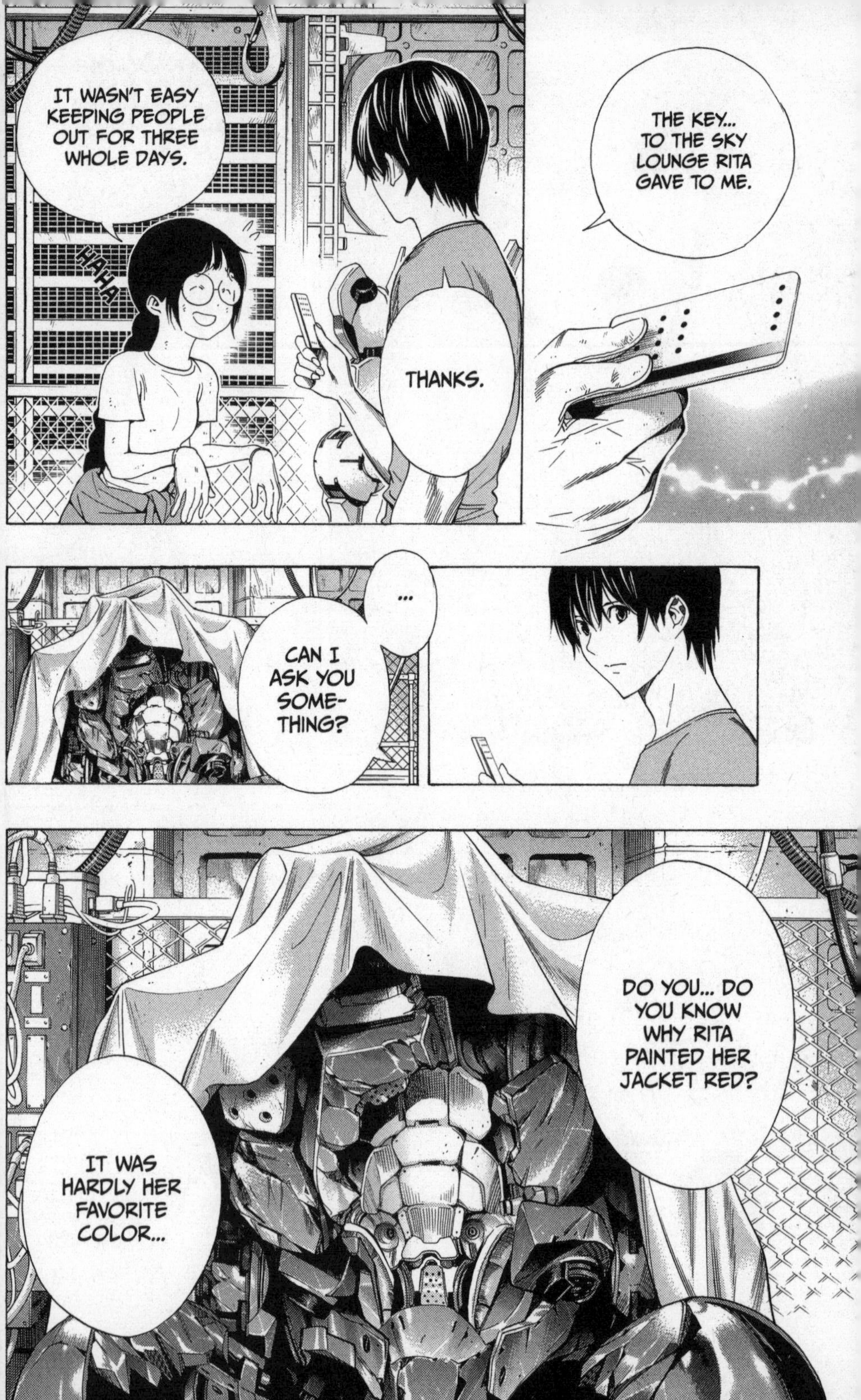
THE KEY... TO THE SKY LOUNGE RITA GAVE TO ME.
IT WASN'T EASY KEEPING PEOPLE OUT FOR THREE WHOLE DAYS.
HAHA
THANKS.
...
CAN I ASK YOU SOME-THING?
DO YOU... DO YOU KNOW WHY RITA PAINTED HER JACKET RED?
IT WAS HARDLY HER FAVORITE COLOR...

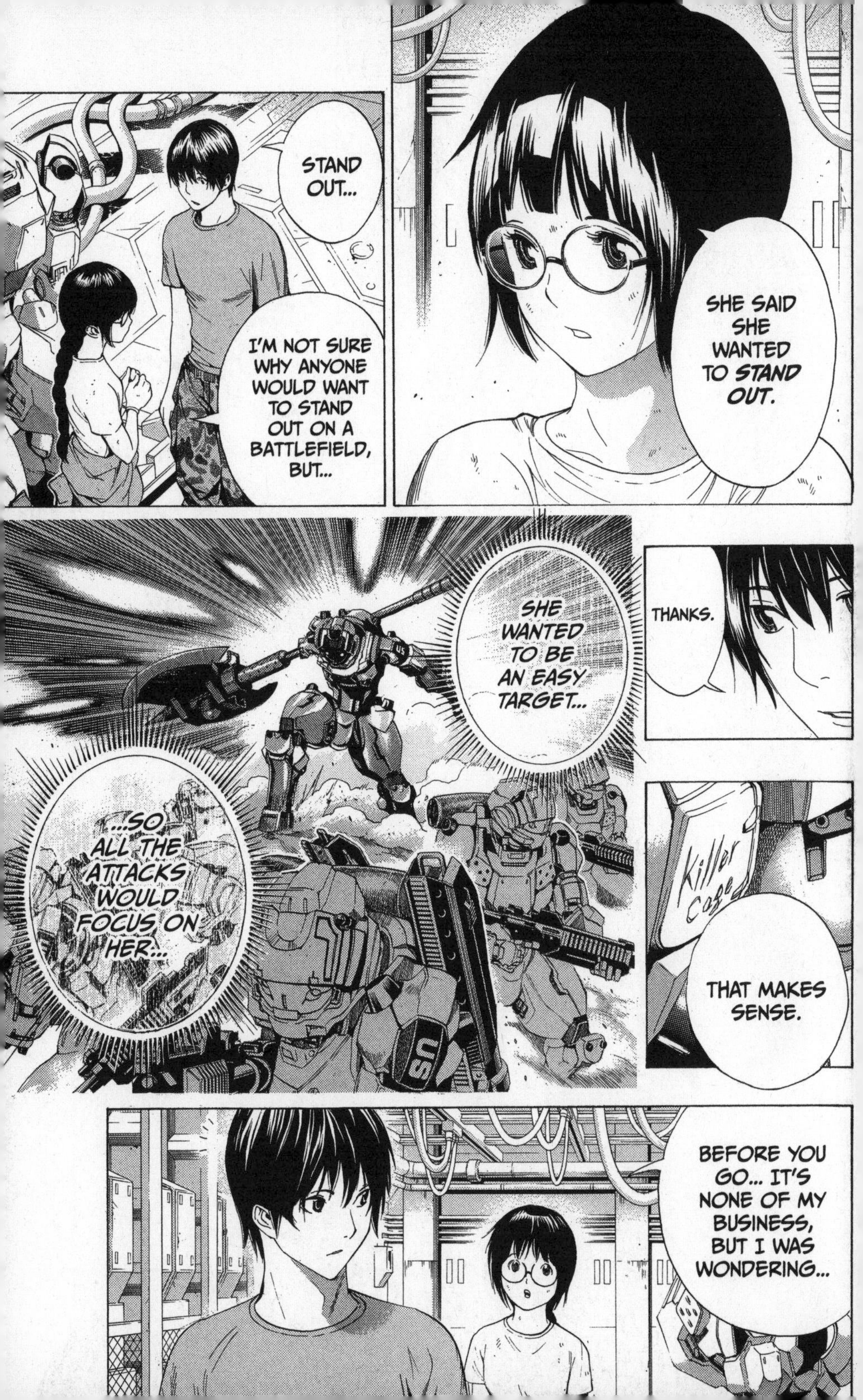
SHE SAID SHE WANTED TO STAND OUT.
STAND OUT...
I'M NOT SURE WHY ANYONE WOULD WANT TO STAND OUT ON A BATTLEFIELD, BUT...
THANKS.
Killer Cage
THAT MAKES SENSE.
SHE WANTED TO BE AN EASY TARGET...
...SO ALL THE ATTACKS WOULD FOCUS ON HER...
BEFORE YOU GO... IT'S NONE OF MY BUSINESS, BUT I WAS WONDERING...

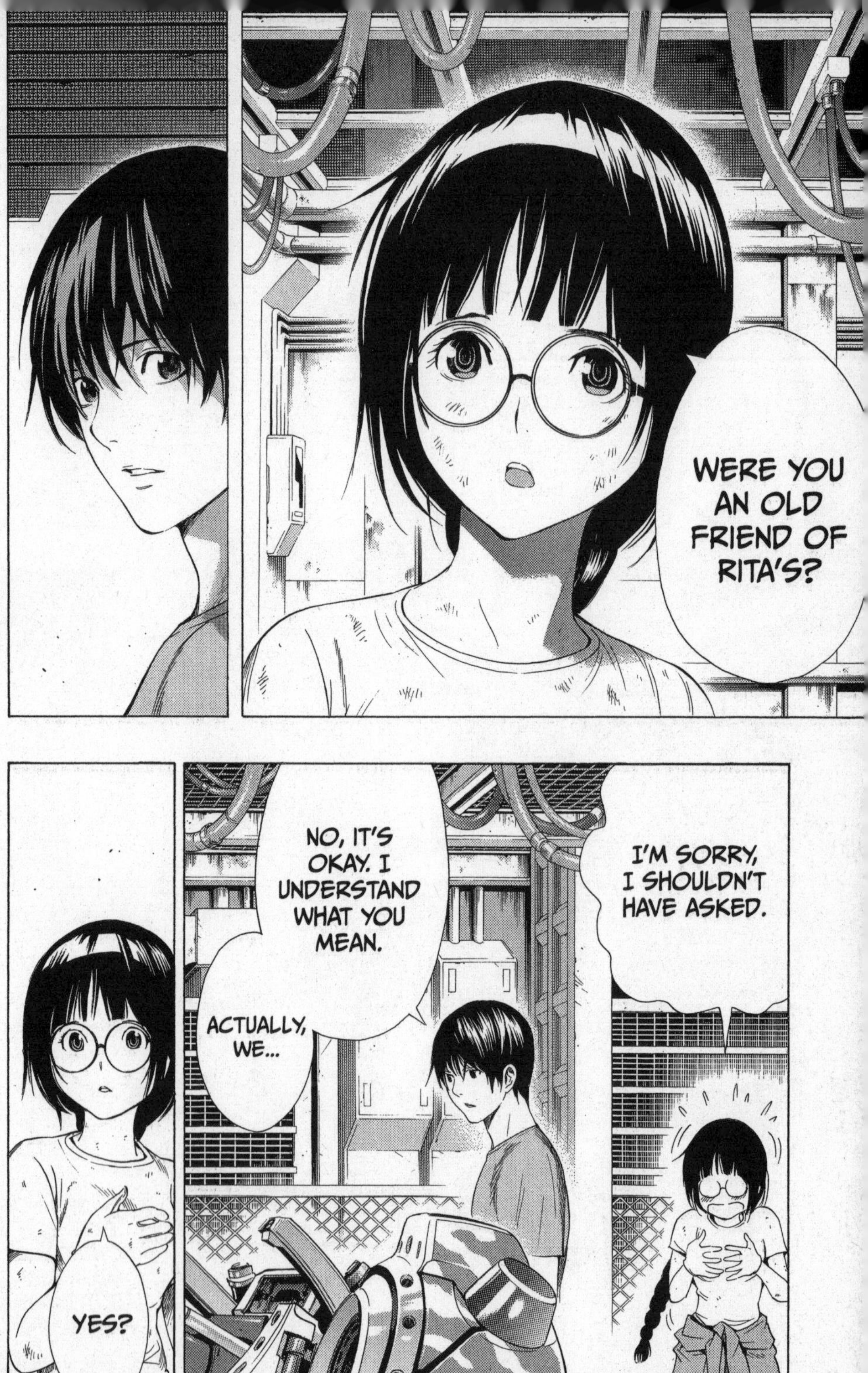
WERE YOU AN OLD FRIEND OF RITA'S?
I'M SORRY, I SHOULDN'T HAVE ASKED.
NO, IT'S OKAY. I UNDERSTAND WHAT YOU MEAN.
ACTUALLY, WE...
YES?

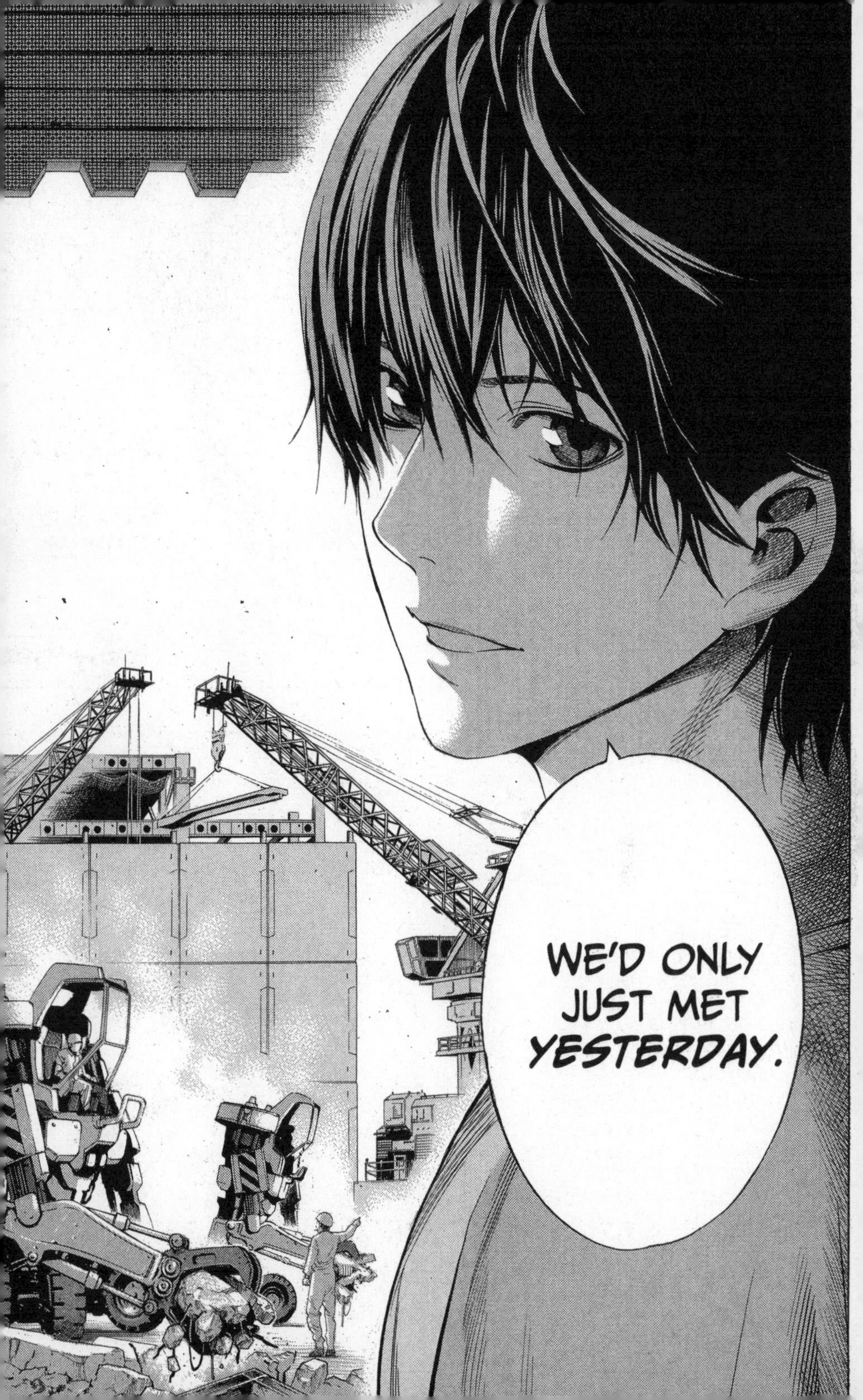
WE'D ONLY JUST MET YESTERDAY.

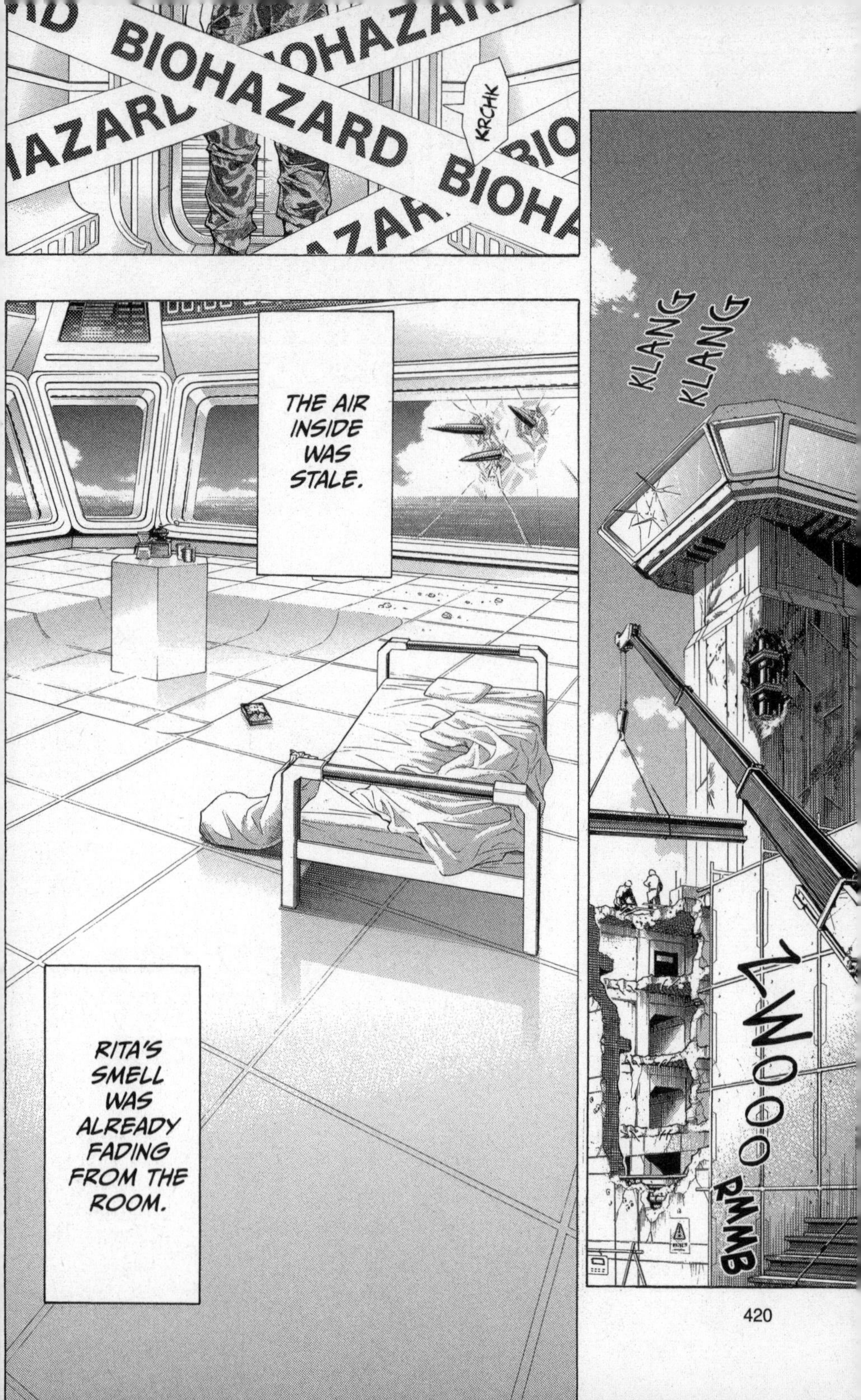
KLANG
KLANG
ZWOOO
RMMB
BIOHAZARD
KRCHK
THE AIR INSIDE WAS STALE.
RITA'S SMELL WAS ALREADY FADING FROM THE ROOM.

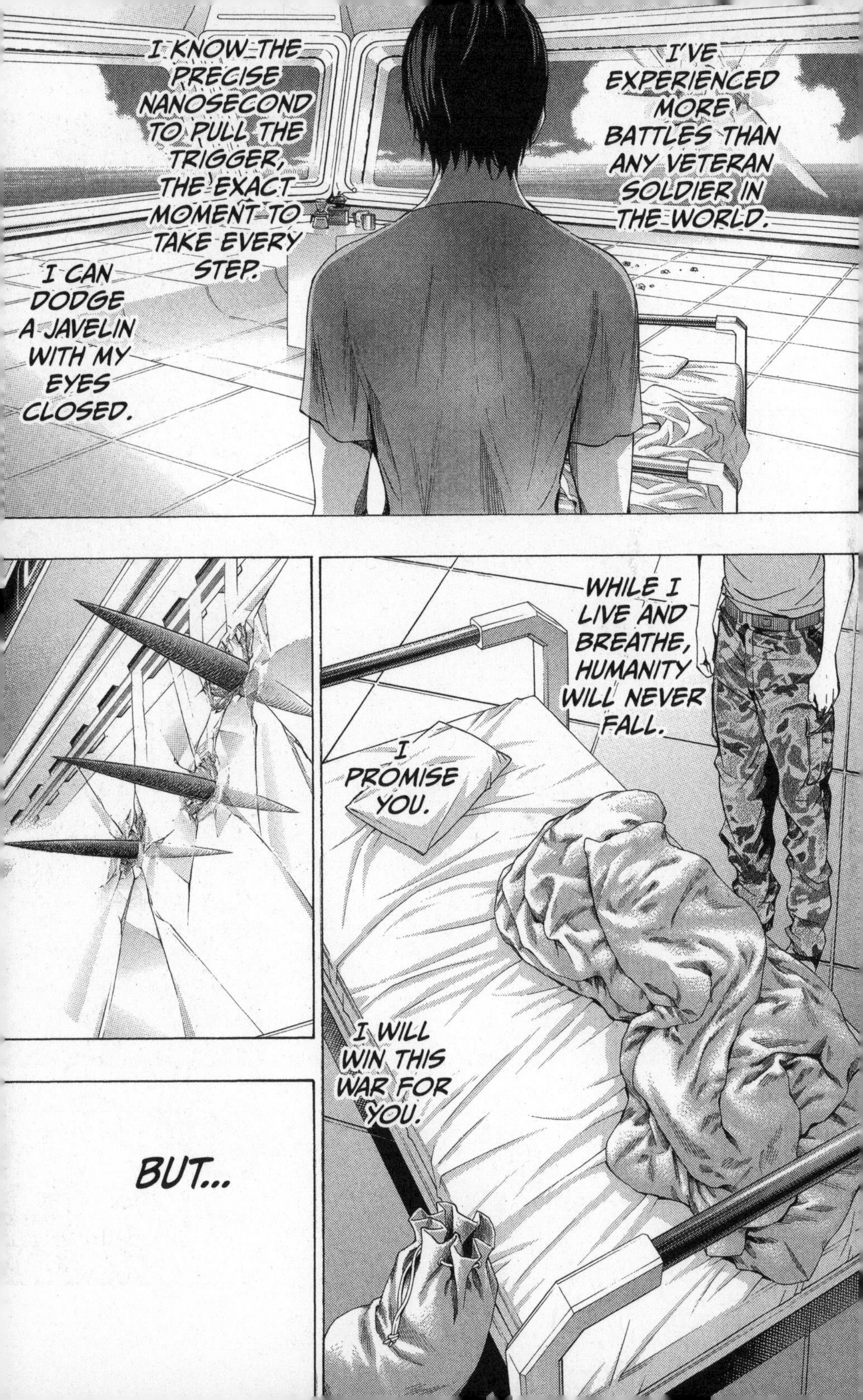
I'VE EXPERIENCED MORE BATTLES THAN ANY VETERAN SOLDIER IN THE WORLD.
I KNOW THE PRECISE NANOSECOND TO PULL THE TRIGGER, THE EXACT MOMENT TO TAKE EVERY STEP.
I CAN DODGE A JAVELIN WITH MY EYES CLOSED.
WHILE I LIVE AND BREATHE, HUMANITY WILL NEVER FALL.
I PROMISE YOU.
I WILL WIN THIS WAR FOR YOU.
BUT...

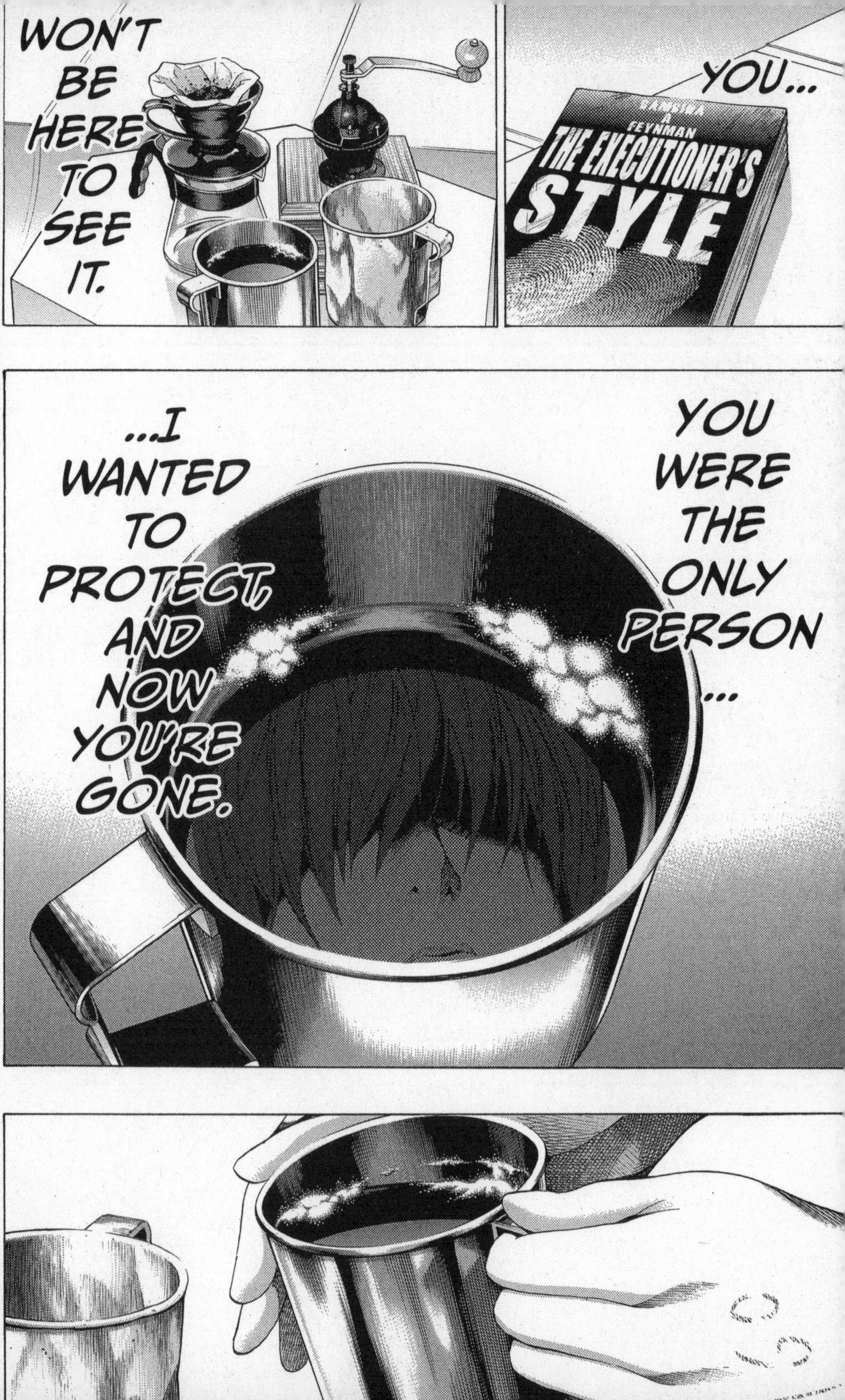
YOU...
FEYNMAN
THE EXECUTIONER'S STYLE
WON'T BE HERE TO SEE IT.
YOU WERE THE ONLY PERSON...
...I WANTED TO PROTECT, AND NOW YOU'RE GONE.

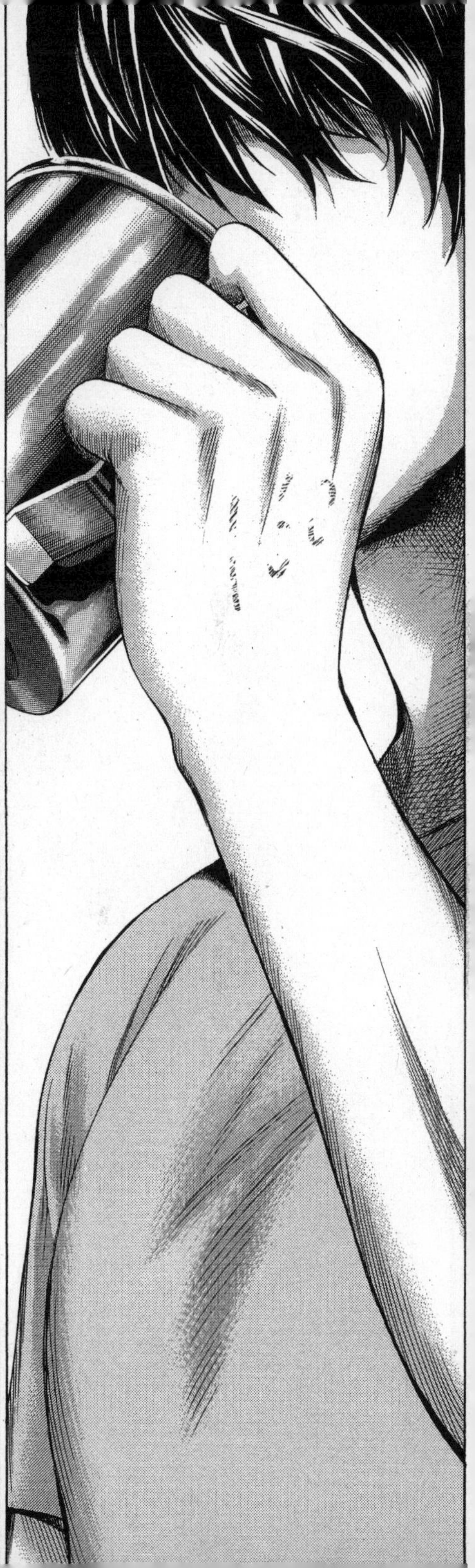

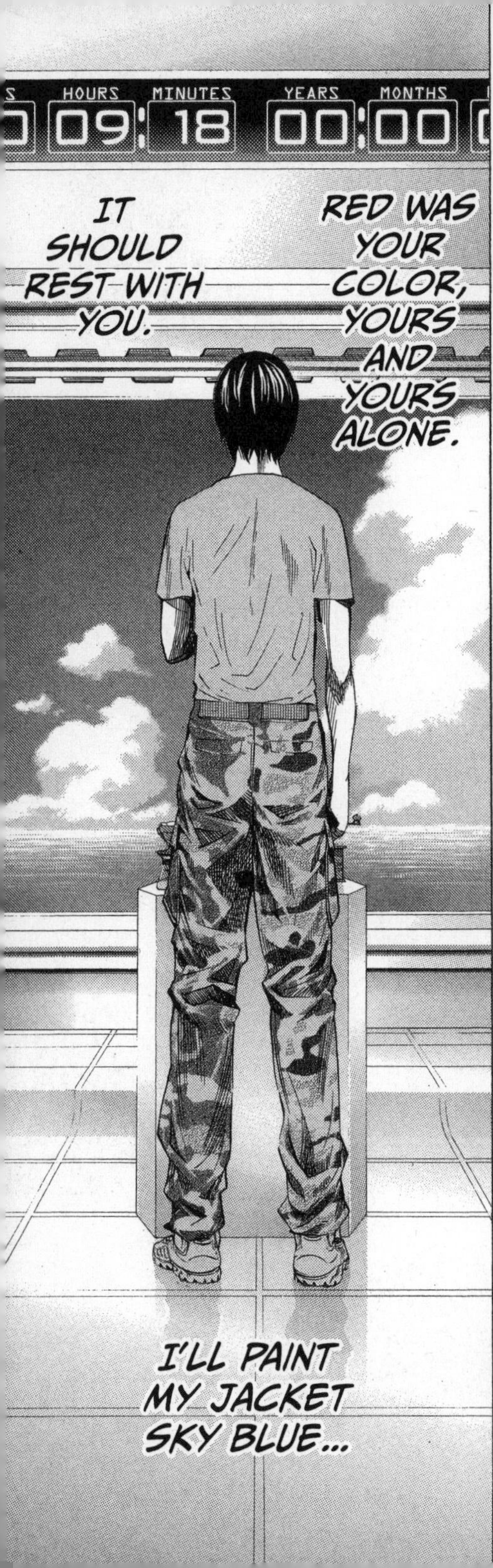
HOURS MINUTES YEARS MONTHS
09: 18 00:00
RED WAS YOUR COLOR, YOURS AND YOURS ALONE.
IT SHOULD REST WITH YOU.
I'LL PAINT MY JACKET SKY BLUE...

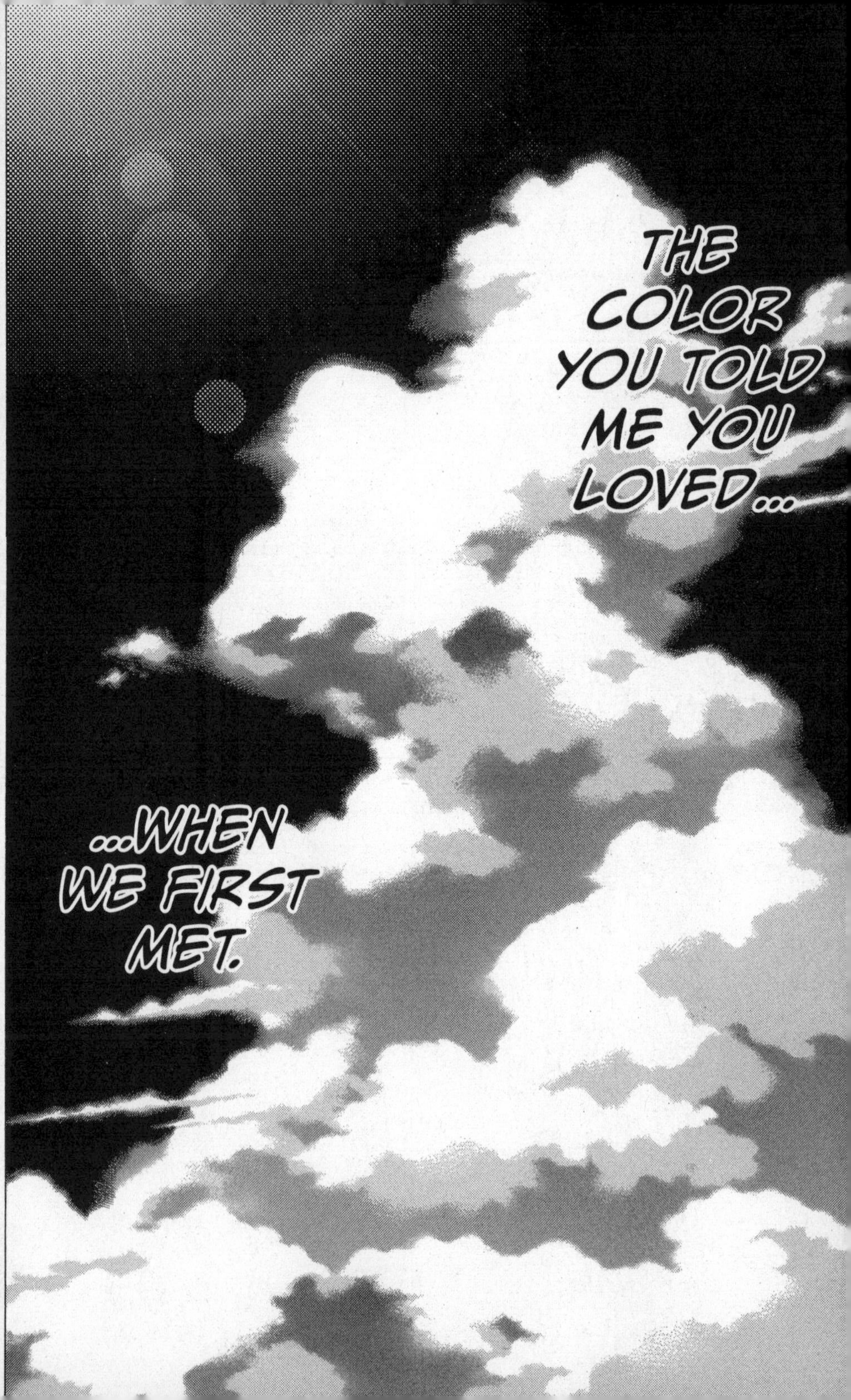
THE COLOR YOU TOLD ME YOU LOVED...
...WHEN WE FIRST MET.

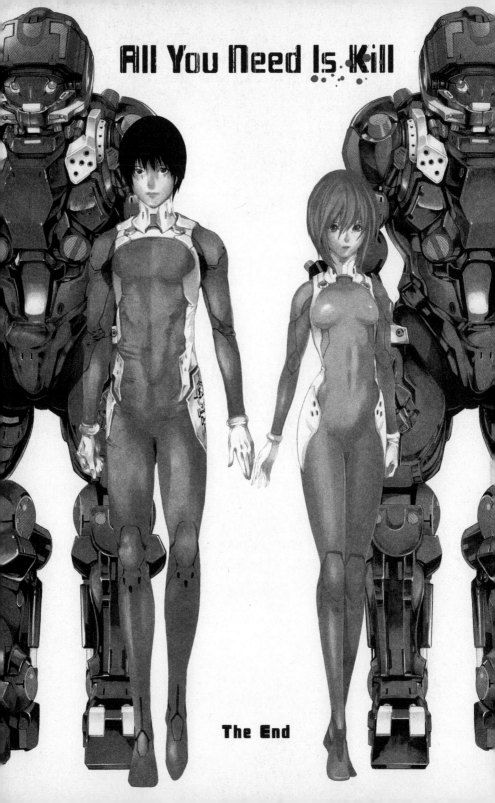

All You Need Is Kill

The End

All You Need Is Kill

Original Story
Hiroshi Sakurazaka

Storyboards
Ryosuke Takeuchi

Original Illustrations
yoshitoshi ABe

Art
Takeshi Obata

Production Staff
**Ryo Ogawa, Motoko Sugawara,
Tatsunosuke Sonoda
Katsuhiko Sato, Tadashi Ashikawa,
Kazushi Hinoki, Akira Obata**

Original Cover Design
Mitsuru Kobayashi
[geni a lòide]

Graphic Novel Editor
Ken Yokoyama
[Gendai Shoin]

Series Editor
Koji Yoshida

Hiroshi Sakurazaka

Hiroshi Sakurazaka was born in Tokyo in 1970. After a career in information technology, he published his first novel, *Modern Magic Made Simple* (*Yoku wakaru gendai mahou*), in 2003 with Super Dash Bunko, a popular young adult light novel imprint. There are now seven volumes in the series, and it was adapted as a manga in 2008 and as a television anime series in 2009. Sakurazaka published *All You Need Is Kill* with Super Dash Bunko in 2004 and with it earned his first Seiun Award nomination for best of the year honors in Japanese science fiction. His 2004 short story "Saitama Chainsaw Massacre" won the 16th *SF Magazine* Reader's Award.

In 2009, *All You Need Is Kill* was the launch title for Haikasoru, a unique imprint dedicated to publishing the most compelling contemporary Japanese science fiction and fantasy for English-speaking audiences. *New York Times* best-selling author John Scalzi declared *All You Need Is Kill* to be a novel that "reads fast, kicks ass, and keeps on coming," and it has proven to be one of Haikasoru's most popular titles. Sakurazaka's other novels include *Characters* (cowritten with Hiroki Azuma) and *Slum Online*, which was published in English by Haikasoru in 2010.

In 2010, Sakurazaka started an experimental digital magazine, *AiR*, with Junji Hotta. He remains one of Japan's most energetic writers of both light novels and adult science fiction.

Ryosuke Takeuchi

Ryosuke Takeuchi's first serialization in *Weekly Shonen Jump* as a writer was *ST&RS* (Stars) with artist Masaru Miyokawa.

yoshitoshi ABe

Illustrator and manga artist, yoshitoshi ABe worked on the character designs for anime series such as *Serial Experiments Lain*, *NieA_7*, *Texhnolyze* and *Haibane Renmei*.

Takeshi Obata

Takeshi Obata was born in 1969 in Niigata, Japan, and is the artist of the wildly popular *Shonen Jump* title *Hikaru no Go*, which won the 2003 Tezuka Osamu Cultural Prize: Shinsei "New Hope" award and the 2000 Shogakukan Manga award. Obata is also the artist of *Arabian Majin Bokentan Lamp Lamp*, *Ayatsuri Sakon*, *Cyborg Jichan G.*, and the smash hit manga *Death Note*. *All You Need Is Kill* is his latest work following the hugely successful series *Bakuman。*.

All You Need Is Kill

ALL YOU NEED IS KILL

SHONEN JUMP ADVANCED Manga Edition

Original Story by Hiroshi Sakurazaka
Storyboards by Ryosuke Takeuchi
Original Illustrations by yoshitoshi ABe

Art by Takeshi Obata

Original cover design by Mitsuru Kobayashi [geni a lòide]

Translation/Tetsuichiro Miyaki
Touch-up Art & Lettering/Evan Waldinger
Cover & Interior Design/Sam Elzway
Shonen Jump Edition Editor/Alexis Kirsch
Editor/Mike Montesa

ALL YOU NEED IS KILL © 2014 by Hiroshi Sakurazaka, Ryosuke Takeuchi,
yoshitoshi ABe, Takeshi Obata/SHUEISHA Inc.
All rights reserved.
First published in Japan in 2014 by SHUEISHA Inc., Tokyo.
English translation rights arranged by SHUEISHA Inc.

Printed in the U.S.A.

Published by VIZ Media, LLC
P.O. Box 77010
San Francisco, CA 94107

10 9 8 7 6 5 4 3 2 1
First printing, November 2014

Hey! You're Reading in the Wrong Direction!

This is the **end** of this graphic novel!

To properly enjoy this VIZ graphic novel, please turn it around and begin reading from **right to left.** Unlike English, Japanese is read right to left, so Japanese comics are read in reverse order from the way English comics are typically read.

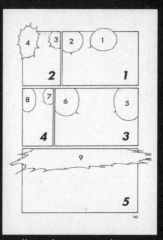

Follow the action this way

This book has been printed in the original Japanese format in order to preserve the orientation of the original artwork. Have fun with it!